AF323663

An Inframarginal Approach to Trade Theory

Increasing Returns and Inframarginal Economics

Series Editors: James Buchanan, Yew-Kwang Ng, (Xiaokai Yang)
Associate Editor: Guang-Zhen Sun

Published
Vol. 1   *An Inframarginal Approach to Trade Theory*
Edited by Xiaokai Yang, Wenli Cheng, Heling Shi &
Christis G. Tombazos

Forthcoming
Vol. 2   *Readings in the Economics of the Division of Labor: The Classical Tradition*
Edited by Guang-Zhen Sun

An Inframarginal Approach to Trade Theory

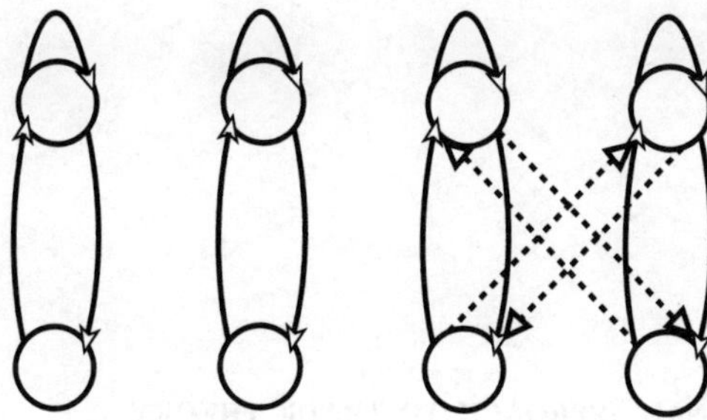

edited by

Xiaokai Yang
Wenli Cheng
Heling Shi
Christis G. Tombazos

Monash University, Australia

World Scientific

NEW JERSEY · LONDON · SINGAPORE · BEIJING · SHANGHAI · HONG KONG · TAIPEI · CHENNAI

Published by

World Scientific Publishing Co. Pte. Ltd.

5 Toh Tuck Link, Singapore 596224

USA office: 27 Warren Street, Suite 401-402, Hackensack, NJ 07601

UK office: 57 Shelton Street, Covent Garden, London WC2H 9HE

British Library Cataloguing-in-Publication Data
A catalogue record for this book is available from the British Library.

AN INFRAMARGINAL APPROACH TO TRADE THEORY

ISBN 981-238-929-6
ISSN 1793-0960

Printed in Singapore by World Scientific Printers (S) Pte Ltd

This book is dedicated to our dear friend and colleague Xiaokai Yang who died earlier this year. Xiaokai was a pioneer in the development of inframarginal analysis and new classical economics and he is one of the co-editors of this project.

It is with great sadness and a heavy heart that the remaining co-editors of this book, Cheng, Shi, and Tombazos, acknowledge this contribution as one of the last joint projects with Xiaokai.

Farewell.

Preface

The inframarginal approach to trade theory has attracted considerable – and rapidly expanding – interest in recent years. Yet, little has been done by way of organizing the accumulated knowledge in a single volume. This book represents a first effort to fill this gap by collecting key articles in this new and important area of research.

As in any collection of reprinted contributions, primary credit for this project goes to the authors of the various chapters. We are also grateful to the original publishers for their permission to reprint articles that appear in this volume.

Unlike the remaining contributions, Chapter 1 is written specifically for this volume. It offers an investigation of the origins of inframarginal analysis in the context of the evolution of economic thought since the publication of Adam Smith's well known 1776 treatise. Reliance of this Chapter on direct quotes from contributions not included in this volume is not so much adopted for stylistic reasons, but as an effort to provide a tangible bridge between the chapters that follow and a body of relevant literature that the usual constraints did not allow inclusion in the volume.

The production of the camera-ready copy of this manuscript was a formidable task, and represents the joint effort of a large number of people. In particular, we thank Cora Ng for outstanding logistical support, and Ye Deng, Tino Filippelli, and Scott Harding for excellent research assistance. We also thank our in-house copy editor Aiko Yoshibayashi for her extraordinary attention to detail, and her hard work in managing almost every aspect of this project.

As well, we gratefully acknowledge the generous financial support of the Department of Economics and the Faculty of Business and Economics of Monash University.

Finally, we thank the Research Centre for Increasing Returns and Economic Organisation of Monash University for providing the hardware and office space without which this project would not have been possible.

Christis G. Tombazos
Managing Editor

Contents

Contents

Part 1

Introduction

CHAPTER 1

DIVISION OF LABOR AND CORNER SOLUTIONS IN POSITIVE TRADE THEORY

Christis G. Tombazos[*]

Monash University

"Even in a world of equals, trade offers mutuality of gain"

James Buchanan[1]

1. Marginalism

Over the last one hundred and thirty years, or so, the notion that optimizing decisions are made "on the margin" has represented the pre-eminent vehicle for research in economics. Currently, the marginalist perspective is viewed by many as a, more or less, comprehensive framework of modern economic analysis, that encapsulates what arguably represent the two most fundamental parameters of economic decision-making: (i) the prevalence of *resource scarcity* – reflected in the, almost ubiquitous, regularity that economic *benefits* are accompanied by economic *costs*; and, *in the context of this nexus,* (ii) the requirement of economic rationality that is specifically characterized across economic agents by the presumption that, at least subconsciously, each subsequent step in any "incremental" *economic* action is undertaken only if it generates additional benefit that is greater than, or, at the very least, equal to, its associated additional cost[a].

---

[*] I thank James Buchanan and Xiaokai Yang for very useful comments and suggestions on earlier drafts of this chapter.

[a] Typically, characterizations of "Marginalism" concentrate on (ii), though, in such cases, (i) is implicit.

3

The greatest asset of the marginalist framework has been its inherent intellectual clarity. For example, few would argue against the notion that, given a strictly quasi-concave utility function and *assuming a non-zero level of consumption*[b] of a particular good, an individual would generally consume that amount that roughly equates her marginal utility with the prevailing price of this commodity[c].

Perhaps an equally important asset of the marginalist school of thought was the notable analytical talent of its early proponents including Augustin Cournot, J.H. von Thunen, H.H. Gossen, W. Stanley Jevons, and Alfred Marshall. The latter, who is perhaps the best known marginalist, was also a trained mathematician who readily translated the main elements of the theory into calculus. Together, these scholars skillfully developed the operational foundations of *Marginalism* – that they subsequently employed both in efforts to provide formal treatment to selected contributions of the classical economists, including Adam Smith and David Ricardo, as well as in their unwavering pursuit of innovation. This latter objective was predominantly focused on the development of an internally consistent and "generally applicable" theory of resource distribution – a contribution that represents the ultimate legacy of the neoclassical thinkers.

The fundamentals of the framework of analysis that resulted from the marginalist revolution may be difficult to characterize comprehensively. Still, even a crude attempt at such a characterization is likely to reflect the notion that, at the very least, this framework exemplified a well articulated process of study of economic behavior; that could be easily accommodated in the context of nineteenth century mathematical formalism; and which had considerable potential for application across the spectrum of economic inquiry. The recipe was irresistible. And

---

[b] The importance of this second assumption has eluded the critical eye of the preponderance of mainstream literature. In general, and particularly in the presence of transaction costs, it is not clear whether a given consumer will consume *some of all goods* that enter her utility function. Corner equilibria are always possible, and acceptance of this premise alters the nature of the ensuing analysis considerably.

[c] In the words of Stanley Jevons (1871)[2] "Our object will always be to maximize the resulting sum in the direction of pleasure, which we may fairly call the positive direction. This object we shall accomplish by accepting everything, and undertaking every action of which the resulting pleasure exceeds the pain which is undergone" (p. 32).

subsequent generations of economists eagerly followed the path outlined by the first marginalists to develop the body of literature known today as *Neoclassical Economics*.

2.   Division of Labor vs. Theory of Distribution

The intuitive appeal of the neoclassical fundamentals, on the one hand, and an associated body of literature that relies on the largely uncontested marginalist orthodoxy and which extends for more than a century, on the other, implicitly define the contemporary preoccupations of the field of economics. It is perhaps for this reason that, as noted by Buchanan and Yoon[3] (p. 512), "Modern economists…do not exhibit the history-of-ideas focus that would lead them to reexamine the late-nineteenth- and early-twentieth-century neoclassical developments in the theory of distribution". Indeed, the majority of economists generally overlook the fact that the notional "switch" from the classical body of thought to the neoclassical, involved a *critically restrictive* reorientation of the early directions of the discipline.

Unlike the Marginalists, who were committed to the development of a theory of distribution, the classical economists, and Adam Smith in particular, focused primarily on matters of economic organization. In this context Adam Smith viewed the benefits of specialization resulting from division of labor central to the task of economic inquiry – a notion exemplified by the introductory sentence of the very first chapter of *The Wealth of Nations*[4] (p. 4):

> The greatest improvement in the productive powers of labour, and the greater part of the skill, dexterity, and judgement with which it is anywhere directed, or applied, seem to have been the effects of the division of labour.

The first three chapters of the celebrated 1776 treatise elaborate on both the causes and the implications of changes in the level of division of labor, and provide insights of considerable intellectual gravity pertaining to the relevance, path, and evolution of economic organization. Along these lines, Adam Smith explained that enhancements in productivity associated with increasing degrees of division of labor, are ultimately only limited by the extent of the market. In this context, Smith's path-breaking work provided a tangible link between economic growth and organization of productive effort: two fundamental dimensions of economic inquiry.

Sadly, neoclassical economists all but ignored Smith's important insights regarding the nature and relevance of economic organization. Perusing the neoclassical manuscripts, one notes that the downgrading of the topic of division of labor was distinctly subtle. Consider for example chapter 22 of Stanley Jevons' *Principles of Economics* entitled "Division of Labour" (p. 98)[5], where he notes:

> We now enter upon **one of the most important topics** in the whole range of economic science. Adam Smith begins the first chapter of his great work by remarking … *on*[d] the division of labour. …**exception may be taken to the logical propriety** of commencing with this subject, **Smith's first three chapters**, all treating of the division of labour, form a **charming introduction** to his treatise[e].

Of course, having the benefit of hindsight, the subtlety of such language does not distract from the fact that the advocates of the neoclassical framework of analysis steered economic inquiry firmly away from questions pertaining to the division of labor and economic organization. Speculation on the relevant motivations is provided by Buchanan and Yoon[3] (p. 512):

> Neoclassical economists may have shied away from follow-on inquiry into Smith's proposition because they thought that acceptance of Smith's relationship would have wreaked havoc on their newly discovered theory of distribution. The advantages of specialization suggest increasing rather than constant or decreasing returns, and the observation that industries did not seem everywhere to become more and more concentrated suggests that abandonment of Smith's theorem was, empirically as well as analytically, less damaging than

---

[d] Italics added for clarity.
[e] Emphasis in the form of bold highlights added.

abandonment of the constant returns postulate so critical to their whole enterprise.

Houthakker[6] (p. 62) adds to the relevant list of hurdles faced by the Marginalists:

> It is in fact from indivisibilities that the division of labor takes its start ... such an analysis involves the use of methods that are rather unlike those by which the classical questions of economics are discussed. These classical questions are treated with the aid of traditional calculus methods (often disguised in literary form) but the latter are not suited to deal with indivisibilities.

a view shared by Yang[7] (p. 8)

> ...the failure of Marshall and other neoclassical economists to formalise *the Smithian framework*[f] *of* economic organisation can be explained by the fact that this would have involved corner solutions and related inframarginal analysis, for which the mathematical techniques were not available until the 1950s.

To summarize: division of labor was viewed by the neoclassical thinkers as leading to firm-specific increasing returns to scale[g] that they considered irreconcilable with (i) their theory of distribution that relied on constant returns; as well as (ii) the empirical observation that industries did not seem to become increasingly concentrated – as would be expected under increasing returns – and, at any rate, division of labor relied on indivisibilities (hence, corner solutions) that were intractable using 19th century (calculus based) mathematics.

---

[f] Italics added for clarity.

[g] In Marshall's words[8], "When the demand for a commodity becomes very large, the process of making it is generally divided among several distinct classes of workers, each with its proper appliances, and each aided by Subsidiary industries; for such a division diminishes the difficulty of making the commodity ... The Law of Division of Labour implies that an increase in the amount of capital and labour which is applied to any process of manufacture is likely to cause a more than proportionate increased return" (p. 57).

It is likely that the empirical observation that industries did not seem to become increasingly concentrated over time lent faith to the marginalists' belief in the general prevalence of constant returns and, therefore, to their theory of resource allocation. Yet, the intellectual integrity of the latter required a formal reconciliation with Smith's proposition (and its presumed *returns to scale* implications). In the spirit of such an effort Marshall[9] advocated an analytical framework in which the production functions of firms within the same industry are interdependent in a manner that facilitates greater scale economies as the network of the division of labor expands. However, in Marshall's model, such scale advantages are realized in the form of "external economies" and may not be exploited by any given firm. In particular, Marshall considered that a sufficiently pronounced skill diversification that facilitates meaningful frameworks of division of labor is more likely in geographically concentrated, or "localized", industries where there is sufficient demand, and many alternative sources of employment, for the various "specialists"[h]. In the context of such a setting, as localization intensifies, skill diversification in the relevant pool of labor expands, within-firm division of labor deepens, and increasing returns to any given firm's variable scale are realized.

Hence, while the *potential* for increasing returns via a greater degree of division of labor exists, it may not be managed *directly* by any given firm and is, at least in general, *not fully realized*[i]. As a result, with the mere invention of "external economies", Marshall evicted the relevance of division of labor from the mainstream field of study of neoclassical economics.

Contemplating this particular facet of the evolution of thought in economics – and particularly the "switch" from the classical to the neoclassical focus – George Stigler[10] notes that the division of labor represents one of Adam Smith's "improper failures" (p.1208) – "a success that Smith should have achieved, but did not" (p.1208).

---

[h] See Marshall[9], p. 267-277.
[i] See Marshall[9], p. 278-290.

The author explains:

> How can it be that the famous opening chapters of his book, and the pin factory he gave immortality, can be considered a failure? Are they not cited as often as any passages in all economics? Indeed, over the generations they are. The failure is different: almost no one used or now uses the theory of division of labor , for the excellent reason that there is scarcely such a theory ... Smith gave the division of labor an immensely convincing presentation – it seems to me as persuasive a case for the power of specialization today as it appeared to Smith. Yet there is no evidence, so far as I know, of any serious advance in the theory of the subject since his time, and specialization is not an integral part of the modern theory of production ... (p. 1208)

In an earlier piece, Houthakker[6] (p. 62) is somewhat more critical of the discipline:

> It is not to the credit of economists that in the 180 years following the publication of the "Wealth of Nations" so little should have been done to clarify that *the division of labor is limited by the extent of the market*[j].

Ironically, it turns out that Marshall's decision to banish Smith's proposition to the intellectual periphery of "external economies" was both unnecessary, as well as misguided given that "...the implications of Smith's principle were not at all those that most neoclassical economists implicitly inferred..." (Buchanan and Yoon[3], p. 517).

As argued by a number of authors, including Young[11]; Houthakker[6]; Rosen[12]; Yang and Borland[13]; and Buchanan and Yoon[3] – to name a few, a broad interpretation of the effects of division of labor extends beyond firm-specific notions of increasing returns to scale. According to such an interpretation, as the economy-wide market expands and as greater degrees of division of labor and specialization are made possible, agents find it profitable to switch from self-production to market production thereby contributing to an environment in which the value of final economy-wide output, relative to the value of required inputs, increases. Rosen[12] refers to this result as "superadditivity", Buchanan and Yoon[3]

---

[j] Italics added for clarity.

favor the term "generalized increasing returns" (GIR), while Yang[7] employs the designation of "economies of specialization" (ES)[k].

There are key differences between economies of specialization and the neoclassical thinkers' definition of (external or internal) increasing returns to scale (IRS)[l]. Economies of specialization are realized in the form of technological advancements that emerge from a greater division of labor *across* the various productive processes that operate in any given economy as the economy-wide market expands. By contrast, IRS reflect "fixed" technology, and are not *directly* linked to the size of the economy-wide market – though they are linked to the market size of the specific output of any given firm[m]. In this context we note that while IRS derive from the production circumstances that link *scale* and *returns*, it is not possible to provide a similarly general characterization of the defining sources of economies of specialization. For example, economies of specialization *may* derive from localized economies of individual productive agents' scale of manual activity. However, even in the absence of such localized economies of activity, economies of specialization may very well derive from exogenous sources of comparative technological advantage across productive agents (or countries) similar to those examined in the Ricardian model of trade (see for example Cheng, Sachs, and Yang[15]). Hence, economies of specialization may therefore be considered to relate more closely to diseconomies of scope than economies of scale.

---

[k] Other characterizations nominated by the same author include "network effects of the division of labor" and "cross-labor-market economies of occupation diversity".

[l] In this chapter I do not investigate recent formalizations of technical economies of scale (TES) such as those outlined in Hart[14]. Still, it is important to note that, unlike the case of IRS, TES may prevail outside the defining parameters of a firm given an absence of asymmetric residual rights to control and returns relevant to a productive capacity characterized by scale economies.

[m] Of course, as the size of the market pertaining to the product of any one industry expands, the size of the economy-wide market also expands. In this context, it is important to note that according to the framework proposed by the neoclassical thinkers, it is enlargement of the former that leads to an expansion of division of labor, not expansion of the latter. It is also important to note that even in the absence of enlargement of any one *established* industry, the economy-wide market may still expand as improvements in transaction efficiency can stimulate specialization and transform home production to market production: a process that would entail the creation of new industries.

Whatever the source giving rise to economies of specialization, such economies prevail at the market- or economy- wide level, while IRS are firm-specific. More importantly, as ES do not require good-specific scale advantages[n], they are perfectly consistent with constant returns to scale within each and every productive process, as well as for the economy at large. That is, given a fixed network of division of labor, successive increases in inputs lead to proportionate increases in outputs in the context of constant returns (Buchanan and Yoon[3]).

3. Inframarginal Economics

Better understanding of the causes and implications of division of labor that has been achieved during the earlier part of the 20th century represents a necessary first step in the reintroduction of division of labor and economic organisation to the mainstream of economic inquiry. This process was however made possible only with the development of appropriate analytical frameworks of non-classical mathematical programming[o] that allow the formalization of corner solutions. The importance of such elements derives from the fact that they represent key dimensions in common patterns of economy-wide networks of production and consumption that characterize the nature and evolution of division of labor, and which typically involve corner equilibria. The combination of the Smithian focus on division of labor and the extent of the market, together with the classical perspective of optimizing agents characterized by dual consumer-producer identities (and who are not artificially required to assume the distinct nature of either a producer or a consumer *ex ante*)[p], in conjunction with economic frameworks that allow

---

[n] Though, it should be noted, existence of such good-specific scale advantages may very well give rise to economies of specialization.

[o] This includes linear and non-linear programming, mixed integer programming, dynamic programming, and control theory.

[p] The importance of the Smithian feature of dual producer-consumer identities cannot be underestimated in the context of models that investigate matters relevant to the division of labor. This feature represents a requirement for well defined labor allocation matrices for productive agents, and in its absence economy-wide as well as intra-firm levels of division of labor assume vacuous dimensions.

the prevalence of corner equilibria is referred to in the literature as *Inframarginal Economics*[7] or *New Classical Economics*[16].

Inframarginal Economics assumes its name from its reliance on *Inframarginal Analysis*: a *methodology* that represents the backbone of any comprehensive study of general equilibrium models that, on the one hand, do not assume an *ex ante* dichotomy between consumers and firms and, on the other, allow not only interior solutions (that may be adequately studied using marginal – calculus based – analysis), but also the possibility of corner solutions.

Generally speaking, inframarginal analysis represents a three-step approach. In the first step, the theorist determines all potential globally optimum networks of division of labor. In the second step, marginal analysis is employed to determine optimum decisions that may prevail in the context of any local equilibrium characterized by any given (potentially globally optimum) structure of a network of division of labor. Finally, the theorist undertakes a demarcation of the parameter space in parameter value subsets within which each local equilibrium represents the global equilibrium. Inframarginal comparative statics are performed by considering discontinuous jumps across the various structures representing alternative patterns of production, consumption, and exchange, that may be initiated as parameters reach certain critical values – or as parameter values shift between parameter value subsets that demarcate the relevant structures.

The first applications of such a methodology can be found in Coase (1946)[17]; Koopman (1957)[18]; and Arrow *et al.* (1958)[19]. The term "inframarginal analysis" was coined by Buchanan and Stubblebine in 1961[20], and a systematic development of the inframarginal approach in conjunction with a consolidated framework of new classical economics has been pioneered by Gary Becker (1982)[21], Sherwin Rosen (1978[12], 1983[12]), Avinash Dixit (1987[22], 1989[23]), and Xiaokai Yang[q], and was further developed by these and other authors – many of whom are represented in this volume – over the course of the last two decades[r].

---

[q] A recent survey of this author's relevant contributions may be found in Yang (2001)[7].
[r] Excellent reviews of this literature may be found in Yang and Y-K Ng (1993)[16] and Yang and S. Ng (1998)[24].

4.   An Inframarginal Approach to Trade Theory

Trade theory represents a field of economics that appears to have benefited disproportionately from the inframarginal revolution. This is largely due to the fact that, perhaps more so than other fields of the discipline, neoclassical trade theory – encompassing new trade theory – is characterized by important weaknesses that derive directly and explicitly from its excessive reliance on classical mathematical programming, which is confined to the limiting parameters of interior solutions, and its resulting neglect of classical insights regarding the relevance of economic organisation. By way of a few key examples, we note that dependence on marginalism and interior solutions:

(a) has hindered the study of key aspects of the *economic process* that leads to the *emergence* of trade;

(b) has undermined efforts to endogenize the degree of market integration (or the degree of globalization) *in conjunction with* the degree of specialization by individual agents;

(c) requires that comparative advantage either derives from exogenously determined characteristics of production frameworks that differ across countries (such as technology in the Ricardian model, and factor endowments in the Heckscher-Ohlin[25]), or is "acquired" (as in the case of new trade theory) in the sense that it derives from the extent to which trade facilitates exploitation of scale economies. Hence, orthodox trade theory does not allow the study of endogenous comparative advantage that, as shown by papers included in this volume, can derive from the potential of trade to facilitate more pronounced cross-country frameworks of division of labor;

(d) has, at least in the case of the Heckscher-Ohlin model of trade – the workhorse of trade theory, promoted an exogenous treatment of cross country patterns of production that has consistently relied on outcomes that prevail within the diversification cone. The predominant force responsible for concentrating research effort on the study of such outcomes is likely to have methodological origins as the study of equilibria that exist outside the cone, represented by *corner solutions* in the optimization framework, extends beyond the reach of the marginal perspective. Focus on outcomes consistent with the diversification cone represents an important limitation of relevant research given that core propositions of the Heckscher-Ohlin, such as factor price equalization, require this assumption in order to hold[s].

The inframarginal approach to trade theory can extend the scope of inquiry of the neoclassical perspective in the important directions outlined above, as well as in a plethora of related areas. For this reason the ensuing field of study has attracted considerable – and rapidly expanding! – interest in recent years. Yet, little has been done by way of organizing the accumulated knowledge in a single volume.

This book fills this gap by collecting a selection of key articles that mark distinct stages in the evolution of research in the area of inframarginal applications to trade theory. In this context, this volume represents an excellent introduction of this novel and exciting field of study to the new researcher, and an invaluable source of reference to those actively involved in inframarginal applications to trade theory.

References

1.   J. M. Buchanan and Y. J. Yoon, *Journal of the History of Economic Thought*, 43 (2000).
2.   W. S. Jevons, *The Theory of Political Economy* (Kelley and Millman, Inc., New York, 1871, 5th reprint edition 1957).
3.   J. M. Buchanan and Y. J. Yoon, *History of Political Economy*, 511 (1999).
4.   A. Smith, *An Inquiry into the Nature and Causes of the Wealth of Nations* (David Campbell Publishers Ltd., London, 1776, reprint edition 1991).
5.   W. S. Jevons, *The Principles of Economics* (Augustus M. Kelley, New York, 1905, reprint edition 1965).
6.   H. S. Houthakker, *Kyklos*, 181 (1956).
7.   X. Yang, *Economics: New Classical Versus Neoclassical Frameworks* (Blackwell Publishers, Malden and Oxford, 2001).
8.   A. Marshall and M. P. Marshall, *The Economics of Industry* (Thoemmes Press, Bristol, 1879, reprint edition 1994).

---

[s] For a relevant discussion beyond what is contained in chapters that appear in this volume see Tombazos, Yang, and Zhang (2003)[26].

9. A. Marshall, *Principles of Economics* (Macmillan, London, 1890, reprint edition 1961).

10. G. J. Stigler, *Journal of Political Economy*, 1199 (1976).

11. A. Young, *Economic Journal*, 527 (1928).

12. S. Rosen, *Economica*, 235 (1978).

13. X. Yang and J. Borland, *Journal of Political Economy*, 460 (1991).

14. O. Hart, *Firms, Contracts, and Financial Structure* (Clarendon Press, Oxford, 1995).

15. W. L. Cheng, J. Sachs, and X. Yang, *Review of International Economics*, 208 (2000).

16. X. Yang and Y.-K. Ng, *Specialization and Economic Organization: A New Classical Microeconomic Framework* (North-Holland, Amsterdam, London, and Tokyo, 1993).

17. R. Coase, *Economica*, 169 (1946).

18. T. C. Koopman, *Three Essays on the State of Economic Science* (McGraw-Hill, New York, 1957).

19. K. J. Arrow, L. Hurwicz, and H. Uzawa, *Studies in Linear and Non-linear Programming* (Stanford University Press, Stanford, 1958).

20. J. M. Buchanan and W. C. Stubblebine, *Economica*, 371 (1962).

21. G. S. Becker, *A Treatise on the Family* (Harvard University Press, Cambridge, MA, 1982).

22. A. Dixit, *Journal of International Economics*, 201 (1987).

23. A. Dixit, *Quarterly Journal of Economics*, 195 (1989).

24. X. Yang and S. Ng, in *Increasing Returns and Economics Analysis*, edited by K. J. Arrow, Y.-K. Ng and X. Yang (Macmillan, London, 1998).

25. B. Ohlin, *Interregional and International Trade* (Harvard University Press, Cambridge, 1933).

26. C. Tombazos, X. Yang, and D. Zhang, Beyond the Diversification Cone: A Neo-Heckscher-Ohlin Model of Trade with Endogenous Specialization *Department of Economics Discussion Paper - Monash University* Vol. 03. No. 22 (2003).

Part 2

Origins of Inframarginal Applications to Trade Theory

CHAPTER 2

ECONOMICS AND BIOLOGY: SPECIALIZATION AND SPECIATION*

Hendrik S. Houthakker*

Harvard University

It is well known that Charles Darwin's work on evolution, according to his own statement, was partly inspired by Malthus' theory of population. To this extent economics may therefore count itself among the sources of modern biology. Apart from this initial link, however, economics has had less contact with biology than with almost any other major science. With the physical sciences, particularly classical mechanics and thermodynamics, economics at least has some conscious affinity of method, and with the social sciences it shares the subject matter (though little else), but with biology it appears to have nothing in common. It would be presumptuous for an economist to argue that closer relations between economics and biology would benefit the other field. All I want to point out here is that economists may derive some useful insight from observation of the non-human living world. This is particularly true for that much-neglected but centrally important chapter of economics: the division of labor, or specialization as it may be more appropriately called in the present context. Specialization, as we shall see, is closely, connected with what biologists call speciation, or the formation of species.

Adam Smith, in his unsurpassed discussion, declared the division of labor to be peculiar to human societies. He viewed it as the result of a

* Reprinted from *Kyklos*, 9(2), Houthakker, H.S., "Economics and Biology: Specialization and Speciation," 181-89, 1956, with permission from Blackwell.

* I am indebted to my collegues Melvin Reder and Tibor Scitovsky for useful comments.

mysterious "propensity to truck," from which animals are somehow immune. We do not, he observed, see two dogs make a fair and reasonable exchange of one bone for another. Related arguments to this effect are also supported by canine examples. It seems that Smith's interest in the animal world did not go beyond dogs; otherwise he might have thought of ants and bees. Even in his day something like division of labor was known to exist in insect societies, and Linnaeus had already described aphids as ants' cows.

Smith was carefully ambiguous about the question whether the propensity to truck can itself be reduced to more immediately rational considerations, but he did point out the advantages of following that propensity. These advantages are the increase in skill, the saving of time otherwise necessary to switch from one job to another, and the enhanced possibilities of using tools and machinery. Without much explanation he also indicated how far specialization can go in the famous statement that "the division of labor is limited by the extent of the market."

It is not to the credit of economists that in the 180 years following the publication of the *Wealth of Nations* so little should have been done to clarify this statement, the simplicity of which is quite deceptive. Most economists have probably regarded the division of labor, in Schumpeter's words, as an "eternal commonplace," yet there is hardly any part of economics that would not be advanced by a further analysis of specialization and related phenomena. It should be added, however, that such an analysis involves the use of methods that are rather unlike those by which the classical questions of economics are discussed. These classical questions are treated with the aid of traditional calculus methods (often disguised in literary form) but the latter are not suited to deal with indivisibilities.

It is in fact from indivisibilities that the division of labor takes its start, and the basic indivisibility is that of the individual, whether human or animal. This may seem like a play on words, or what is almost the same thing, bad metaphysics, but it is more serious than that. For our purpose we may regard an individual as a coordinated complex of activities. The indivisibility of the individual consists in the fact that, although it may be capable of a great many different activities, it can perform only few activities simultaneously because most activities utilize the same resources and more particularly that coordinating resource which is known as the brain. The larger the number of simultaneous activities, the greater the difficulty of coordinating them and of carrying out each one properly, and the smaller therefore the output from each activity. This applies not only to simultaneous activities, but also to activities that are spread out over time. In the first place some shorter or longer interval is usually needed to switch from one activity to another; in the second place it is usually easier to perform activities that are known from previous experience than to perform them for the first time.

All this, the economist will note at once, can be put in terms of increasing returns. We have increasing returns to the extent that, if several activities are replaced by a single one, there is less need for coordination and switching time and more scope for acquiring experience. The output of the single activity may thus be raised above the combined outputs of the several activities.

If we have two activities, for instance, the simplest shape of the production possibility curve exhibiting these features will be as in Figure 1. If the individual produces only the first commodity he can obtain AP units, and if only the second AQ units, but if he produces both simultaneously he is bounded by the straight line $P'Q'$. The segments PP' or QQ' therefore represent the loss of production due to the need for coordination, etc. If the individual cannot trade with others he will normally be unable to specialize, at least if both commodities are necessary to him. He will then be at a point such as R, where an indifference curve touches the production possibility curve.

As soon as another individual appears on the scene specialization may arise (Figure 2). The individual may then get to a point such as V, whose exact location depends on the respective offer curves (cases of incomplete specialization are also possible). The posttrade point V is better than either of the pretrade points R and U, and both parties therefore gain, but it is possible that only one party gains and the other remains where he was.

The case here described differs from the Ricardian case of constant cost in that there will be a tendency to specialization even if there are no differences in relative efficiency (that is, even if $P'Q'$ and $S'T'$ are parallel). Specialization may even go against the comparative advantage (that is, $P'Q'$ may have a flatter slope than $S'T'$). Under the Ricardian assumptions the benefits of specialization consist wholly in the utilization of comparative advantages, but in the present case, which is essentially that of Adam Smith, the benefit comes mainly from the avoidance of coordination costs (in the widest sense) by the two

                            H. S. Houthakker

individuals. It may be noted that Smith went out of his way to deny the existence of innate differences between individuals: in his theory such differences were unnecessary. Like the Declaration of Independence, which dates from the same year 1776, the *Wealth of Nations* is based on the premise that all men are born equal.

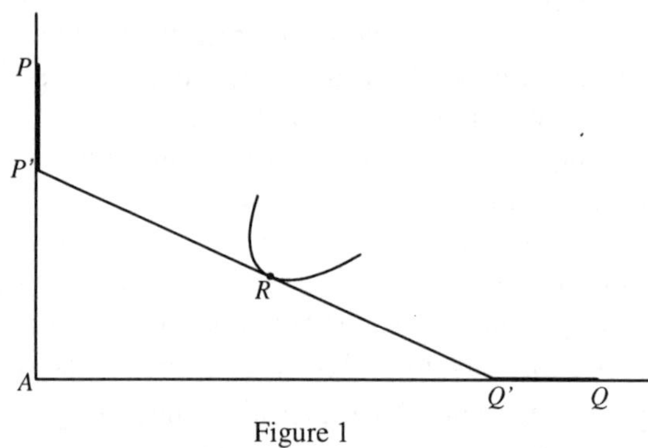

Figure 1

Although specialization will lead to the avoidance of *individual* coordination costs, it may in turn call for coordination *between* the two individuals. The simplest example is transportation cost. These external coordination costs may be heavy enough to outweigh the saving in internal coordination costs. In a box diagram such as Figure 2, transportation costs may be represented by shifting all points referring to the second individual to the left, thus narrowing the area between $P'Q'$ and $S'T'$ within which specialization is advantageous. The division of labor is thus limited by the extent of the market.

Let us consider a slightly different example of specialization, which has attracted the attention of students of spatial competition such as Hotelling[1] and Loesch.[2] Imagine a population which is spread out, not necessarily evenly, along a road and which consumes a single commodity. This good is sold by firms who deliver it at the customer's door. All firms have the same cost function, consisting of a part proportional to their sales, a part proportional to the aggregate distance over which they have to deliver, and a part that is constant. There is free

---

[1] Harold Hotelling, "Stability in Competition," *Economic Journal,* 1929, p. 41.

[2] August Loesch, *Die räumliche Ordnung der Wirtschaft,* Jena 1940 (English translation, *The Economics of Location*, New Haven, Conn., 1954).

entry, so that no firm can make a profit over its total cost. Consumers buy in the cheapest market, but otherwise their demand is inelastic.

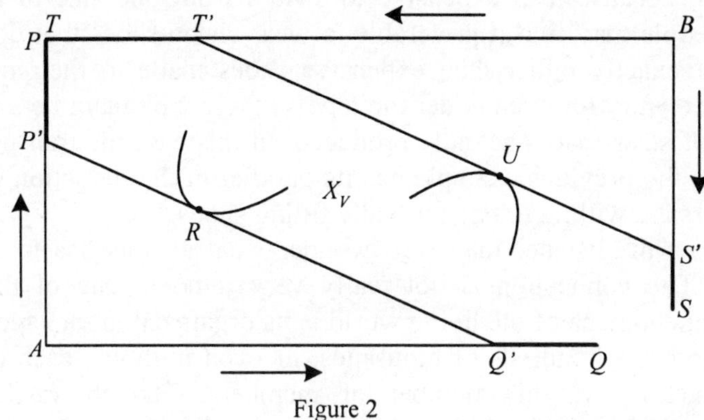

Figure 2

A complete solution of this problem would have to specify the location of each firm and the prices it charges to its various customers. For our purpose we need only mention some general characteristics of the solution. The area served by each firm has to be just large enough to provide a margin of revenue over variable costs equal to the fixed costs. At the boundary between the territories of two firms both must charge the same price, since otherwise customers near the boundary would switch to the cheaper firm. This price at the boundary has to be equal to variable cost (the cost of the commodity plus transportation cost from the firm's location), without any allowance for fixed costs. The latter have to be recouped from the customers inside the territory, and the prices charged to them will be the highest that will prevent new firms from establishing themselves at the boundaries between existing firms. In the case of a uniform distribution of demand, for instance, the price charged will be the same everywhere.

What matters to us at the moment is not the level of prices, but rather the fact that the above conditions determine the *number* of firms, though no explicit general formula for that number has as yet been derived. It is clear, however, that the number of firms depends critically on the ratio between the fixed costs and the transportation costs, or more generally, between the external and the internal coordination costs.

Another example may serve to show that the above case is of wider importance than may appear at first sight. People's feet are of different sizes, and shoes are the more comfortable the more their size corresponds to the size of the foot. On the other hand, the unit cost of a pair of shoes of a given size decreases with the number of pairs of that size that is produced, because it is expensive to switch from one size to another. Hence people may find it preferable to wear cheap shoes that do not fit their feet exactly rather than expensive shoes made to their measure. Under free entry (or even under monopoly) there will again be a definite number of sizes that is actually produced. In this case the transportation cost from the previous example has its parallel in the reduction of price consumers are willing to pay for badly fitting shoes.

By now the listener may well wonder what all this has to do with biology. The connection is not really very remote. One of the most striking phenomena of the living world is its organization into species, of which there are hundreds of thousands, or even millions, each of them with a greatly varying number of members. Though vastly more complicated, this pattern has some analogy to that of the firms along a road, or of the discretely varying shoe sizes. Each species may be compared to one size of shoe, and its members to the shoes produced of that size. The advantages and disadvantages of the biological pattern can therefore not be too dissimilar from those of the economic pattern.

We may, for instance, consider each species as adapted to one particular range of foods (though this is by no means the whole story). The wider the range of foods, the more complicated the anatomical and physiological arrangements necessary to obtain and digest each type of food efficiently; or in the above terminology, the higher the internal coordination cost. On the other hand, a wider range of foods makes possible a larger number of members of the species, because the danger of starvation is smaller. For each species there will consequently be an optimum range and an optimum number of individuals, as there was in the case of shoes. In reality this balance between range and number is only one element, though probably a basic one, in the structure of advantages and disadvantages.

It may of course be asked: advantages and disadvantages to whom? When it comes to the explanation of the characteristics of separate species biologists tend to use the word "advantage" quite freely, and usually in the sense of something which promotes survival. This may easily lead to paradoxical results; thus R. A. Fisher in his *Genetical*

Theory of Natural Selection[3] maintains that evolution leads to an increase in fitness, which he defines as the chance of survival, from which it follows, oddly enough, that a species has the best chance of survival just before it becomes extinct. If we consider not separate species, but the whole animal world, the notion of advantage becomes even more tenuous. Since the purpose of nature is unknown, and it may indeed be meaningless to ask if there is a purpose, teleological explanations may appear to be ruled out. This, it is often held, contributes the dividing line between the social and the biological sciences.

It appears, however, that this view overestimates the purposefulness of human behavior. It is true that the rational man has long been a favorite with economists, but recently his standing has somewhat declined. The development of the theory of choice, for instance, has cast doubt on many of the qualities with which the rational man was traditionally endowed. The realization of the importance of uncertainty has further undermined the concept of rationality, for which no satisfactory definition appropriate to uncertainty has yet been found. Moreover, it is sometimes argued that economic activities are primarily distinguishable by the manner in, rather than by the motive with which they are carried out. Although nature may have no discernible motives, it may nevertheless operate in the same way as if it had a motive.

Since there are therefore no major objections, what is the advantage of extending economic analysis to biological phenomena? There is, I think, one important advantage. In economics we also observe species, such as different commodities, occupations, etc., but the boundaries between them are often vague for lack of a precise criterion of classifycation. Consequently any attempt to count the number of "individuals" in a "species" would meet with considerable conceptual difficulties. In biology, however, there is a more definite criterion, even though it is not absolutely precise. Species are defined by the criterion of interfertility, the ability to produce fertile offspring. The species of biology are therefore much more clearly defined than those of economics, and this is their principal advantage as an object of research.

In this lecture I have indulged in rather wild speculation, but I hope I need not apologize for it. Provided it is administered in small doses and counterbalanced by large quantities of more solid inquiry, speculation is

---

[3] Oxford, 1930.

healthy for any science even though most of its results turn out to be wrong.

Summary

Adam Smith, whose discussion of specialization has not been superseded so far, declared the division of labor to be peculiar to human societies, but this view is disputed here. Specialization is shown to arise from indivisibilities; in the individual the latter appear in the form of internal coordination costs. By specializing the individual can avoid internal coordination costs at the expense of creating external coordination costs (such as transport charges). The optimum amount of specialization therefore. depends on the balance between internal and external coordination costs. This is illustrated by an example from location theory, namely the distribution of sellers along a line when there are fixed costs. Another interpretation of the same model is the distribution of shoe sizes, and this is in turn held to be similar to the organization of living beings into species. If animal species are specialized in different kinds of food, the internal coordination costs consist in the anatomical and physiological arrangements necessary to obtain and utilize each kind of food efficiently. The external coordination costs are reflected in the difficulty of finding suitable foodstuffs and the corresponding danger of starvation. There will consequently be a balance between the range of foods and the number of individuals in a species. These considerations involve the notion of biological advantage, which is held to be inessential. By extending economic analysis to biological data, the study of specialization may be facilitated to the extent that biological species are more precisely defined than economic species.

References

Fisher, Ronald A. *The Genetical Theory of Natural Selection*. Oxford: Clarendon Press, 1930.

Hotelling, Harold. "Stability in Economic Competition." *Economic Journal* 39 (March 1929): 41-57.

Loesch, August. *Die Räumliche Ordnung der Wirtschaft*. Jena, 1940. Trans. The Economics of Location. New Haven: Yale University Press, 1954.

CHAPTER 3

SUBSTITUTION AND DIVISION OF LABOUR[*]

Sherwin Rosen

University of Chicago and NBER

1. Introduction

Recent advances in production theory and in computer technology now make it possible to estimate complex production relationships involving many inputs. Yet the theory remains somewhat cavalier about its primitives, particularly the definition of labour inputs. In what follows, the theory of optimum assignment and comparative advantage is used to analyse the structure of work activities within firms. A job is defined as a collection of production tasks assigned to the worker who holds it, but the packaging of work activities into bundles is itself the endogenous outcome of economic decisions.

How do the requirements of technology and the distribution of worker skills interact to determine which work activities are selected and bundled into observed job assignments and occupations? Furthermore, how are different members of the labour force allocated to them and what are the characteristics of the match between job attributes and worker talents? Section 2 is addressed mainly to the first question and Section 3 mainly to the second. As will be seen, the division of labour corresponding to the optimum assignment determines marginal rates of substitution between certain workers or between certain work activities.

---

[*] Reprinted from *Economica*, 45 (179), Rosen, S., "Substitution and Division of Labor," 235-50, 1978, with permission from Blackwell.

The observable elasticities of substitution so implied are not necessarily inherent in the production technology, but rather are "swept out" of the distribution of skills as optimum work assignments respond to final demand and factor supply conditions. Thus the division of labour in part determines the nature and extent of product and factor substitutions in the economy.

2. Indirect Production Functions

A basic result on the optimum division of labour and derived factor substitution is most easily obtained in the context of a simple engineering production function with fixed coefficients. Capital is ignored without apology, in what follows. The technology is given by

$$x = \min\left(\frac{T_1}{\alpha_1}, \frac{T_2}{\alpha_2}, ..., \frac{T_n}{\alpha_n}\right) \tag{1}$$

where x is output, T_i is a production activity (input) and α_i is the input requirement per unit output. For example (1) might be the engineering production function for the proverbial pin factory. Then (T_i) represents steps in the production process, such as drawing the wire, sharpening the points, and so forth. Each T_i is associated with an independent "task", and a collection of tasks, a partition of (T_i), constitutes a job.

Let there be m types of workers. Workers of type j are described by a skill or capacity vector $(t_{1j}, t_{2j},..., t_{nj})$, $j = 1,...,m$. t_{ij} indicates the maximum amount of task i obtainable from a worker of type j when the task is pursued full-time. Assume that output in each activity is proportional to the time devoted to it, with no interactions if the worker's time is divided among several activities. Then a worker is completely described by the value of (t_j). Comparing workers i and j, worker i will be said to have a comparative advantage in task h relative to task k if $t_{hi}/t_{ki} > t_{hj}/t_{kj}$. Equivalently, worker j has a comparative advantage in task k. Comparative advantage is assumed to exist in all tasks and among all types; i.e.,

$$t_{hi}/t_{ki} \neq t_{hj}/t_{kj} \tag{2}$$

for all pairs (h,k) and (i,j).

The problem is to find the assignment of workers to production activities that maximizes output. The solution consists of two steps. First, calculate all the possible assignments that maximize activity levels attainable from a given labour force. This defines a "task possibility set", as it were. Second, maximize output relative to the efficient set.

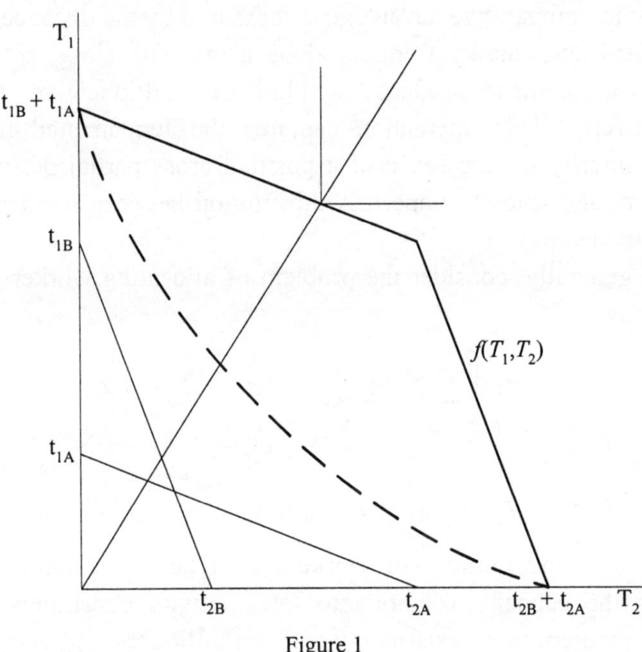

Figure 1

A familiar 2 x 2 example illustrates the method. In Figure 1 there are two activities, T_1 and T_2, and two workers, A and B. The straight lines with intercepts (t_{2A}, t_{1A}) and (T_{2B}, t_{1B}) depict the capacity vectors, and are drawn under the assumption that A has a comparative advantage in T_2 and B in T_1. The efficient assignments or "task possibility frontier" is labelled $f(T_1, T_2)$ and has two facets: B is completely specialized to T_1 and A is engaged in both activities along the upper edge, due to B's comparative advantage in T_1; A and B are completely specialized at the corner; while A is specialized to T_2 and B's time is divided between both activities along the lower edge. All assignments other than

                    S. Rosen

$f(T_1, T_2)$ sacrifice activity levels. The case where A and B act as independent agents of production is of particular interest. Since the engineering technology dictates the use of activities in fixed proportions, the autarky total activity frontier is the sum of A's and B's independent allocations along arbitrary rays through the origin. It is shown by the curve and is inefficient because comparative advantage is not exploited. The gain from forming a production team and dividing up the work according to comparative advantage is measured by the distance between the efficient and autarky frontiers along a ray with slope α_2/α_1. The optimum assignment produces a kind of multiplicative effect or superadditivity. This interaction captures the fundamental notion of complementarity (in the sense of a positive cross partial derivative) in production, and leads to imperfect substitution between worker types A and B in the team.

More generally, consider the problem of allocating workers to tasks to maximize

$$x = \min\left(\sum_j T_{1j}/\alpha_1, \sum_j T_{2j}/\alpha_2, ..., \sum_j T_{nj}/\alpha_n\right) \tag{3}$$

subject to

$$T_{1j}/t_{1j} + T_{2j}/t_{2j} + ... + T_{nj}/t_{nj} \leq N_j, \qquad j = 1, 2, ..., m \tag{4}$$

where N_j is the number of workers of type j available and (4) translates the capacity vectors into total activity constraints. By the envelope theorem there exist non-negative multipliers $(q_1, ..., q_m)$ and a quasi-concave function $x = F(N_1, N_2, ..., N_m)$ such that

$$x = F(N_1, ..., N_m) \equiv \max_{T_{ij}} \left\{ \min\left(\sum_j T_{1j}/\alpha_1, ..., \sum_j T_{nj}/\alpha_n\right) \right.$$

$$\left. + \sum_j q_j \left(N_j - \sum_j T_{ij}/t_{ij}\right) \right\}. \tag{5}$$

The function $F(N)$ is an efficient "indirect" production function of the neoclassical type. Its derivatives when defined satisfy $\partial x/\partial N_i = q_i$ and represent induced marginal products of worker types. It is quasi-concave so the isoquants are convex. The theorem holds for any n and m, not necessarily of the same dimension, but obviously gains considerable interest when the number of activities (n) greatly exceeds the number of types of workers (m), because it provides a natural aggregation into a factor space of much smaller dimension than equation (1). The remainder of this section treats the case $n > m$ in more detail.

The conceptual experiment that maps out the indirect production function involves assigning members of a given workforce to maximize production activities, then varying the numbers of workers of each type and efficiently reassigning them along the way to maintain a fixed level of output. The first part of this general class of allocation problems has been studied by McKenzie (1954), Jones (1961) and Whitin (1953) to analyse world production in international trade. For the problem at hand, the set of efficient assignments for a given labour force is found by solving an artificial maximum problem (cf. Dorfman, Samuelson and Solow, 1958). Define a set of shadow prices for production activities (p_i), which in context are conveniently thought of as piece rates; and maximize the value of production activities subject to the capacities of each type of worker. That is, maximize

$$V = \sum \sum p_i T_{ij} \tag{6}$$

Subject to

$$\sum_i T_{ij}/t_{ij} \le N_j \quad j = 1,...,m . \tag{7}$$

The dual problem requires choosing shadow prices on worker types (w_j) such that

$$V = \min_{w_j} \sum w_j N_j \tag{8}$$

subject to

$$w_j/t_{ij} \ge p_i , \quad i = 1,...,n \text{ and } j = 1,...,m \tag{9}$$

where w_j has the natural interpretation of the wage rate of worker type j_i. Expression (6) maximizes the value of work effort, while (8) minimizes the cost of labour.

Solution algorithms for (6) and (8) are well known. However, it is instructive to consider in detail the one case where an analytic solution is available, for it reveals the internal structure of (5) and the nature of derived factor substitution most clearly. In particular, great simplification is achieved when $m = 2$ because production tasks can be naturally ordered by comparative advantage. Let $j = A, B$ and $i = 1, 2, ..., n$ with $n > 2$. Then activities can be ordered on the index i such that

$$t_{1A}/t_{1B} > t_{2A}/t_{2B} > ... > t_{nA}/t_{nB} \qquad (10)$$

with strict inequalities following from assumption (2). When $m = 2$, the two constraints of (7) imply that two of the constraints in (9) must be binding at the minimum labour cost assignment. Therefore there are n^2 possible assignments. n of the basic solutions assign members of A and B to the same activity:

$$w_A = t_{iA} p_i \quad \text{and} \quad w_B = t_{iB}\, p_i \qquad (11)$$

with inequality for the rest. (11) applies when p_i is very large relative to the other shadow prices. In addition there are $(n-1)$ basic solutions involving noncongruent activities T_i and T_j. Here elementary manipulation of (9) and (10) show that assignments follow comparative advantage, with

$$w_A = t_{iA} p_i \text{ and } w_B = t_{jB}\, p_j \quad \text{for } i < j \qquad (12)$$

and inequality for the rest. (11) and (12) together correspond to all the specialization points of the efficient frontier illustrated by Figure 1, and all other points in the efficient set are linear combinations of them.

It is now possible to derive the unit isoquant of (5). Actually, it is slightly more convenient to derive its dual, the factor price frontier. One more constraint is necessary however, because (6) and (7) do not incorporate the restriction that all activities must be operated at non-zero levels to produce positive output. The constraint is obtained from the fact that the firm produces only if there is non-negative profit, or if

$$p_1 T_1 + p_2 T_2 + ... + p_n T_n \leq px$$

where p is the price of output and $T_k = \sum T_{kj}$. Normalize p at unity, divide through by x and substitute the input-output coefficients from (1) to obtain the restriction

$$p_1 \alpha_1 + p_2 \alpha_2 + ... + p_n \alpha_n \leq 1. \qquad (13)$$

Suppose sufficient numbers of workers of each type are available to produce a unit of output. Then the efficient programme partitions (i) in such a way that members of group A are assigned to activities $(1,2,...,k)$ and members of group B are assigned to $(k+1,k+2,...,n)$ and also possibly to k, for some $k \geq 0$. Members of both groups will be found to have a comparative advantage in all tasks to which they are optimally assigned relative to all those on which they are optimally not assigned. A simple example illustrates the argument. Assume that B's are non-optimally assigned to $1, j, j+1,...,n$, with $j > 2$. Now consider reassigning a full-time equivalent B from 1 to j along with a sufficient amount of A's time from j to 1 to maintain activity level 1. The amount of A required for this manoeuvre is t_{1B}/t_{1A}, since that is the rate of substitution between A and B on the first activity. The change in activity level j is therefore $t_{jB} - (t_{1B}/t_{1A})t_{jA} = t_{jA}\{(t_{jB}/t_{jA}) - (t_{1B}/t_{1A})\}$, which is strictly positive from the ordering in (10). Thus if unit output was produced before the reassignment, some workers were redundant, and so it goes.

Alternatively, (8) and (9) determine shadow wage rates w_A and w_B for given factor supplies N_A and N_B. The marginal cost to the firm of producing activity level j with an A is w_A/t_{jA} and is w_B/t_{jB} if it is produced with a B. A or B are optimally assigned to j according to the cost-minimization criteria $w_A/t_{jA} \lessgtr w_B/t_{jB}$ or $w_A/w_B \lessgtr t_{jA}/t_{jB}$. Therefore, the A's are assigned to all activities for which their comparative advantage exceeds the relative shadow price of workers and similarly for the B's. However, there may be one activity for which the comparative advantage ratio just equals the shadow price ratio, in which case A and B are both assigned to that activity (this corresponds to a solution on a facet rather than a corner of the task possibility frontier). In any case, they can share no more than one task for a solution to (8), and equalities (11), (12) and the requirement that $x > 0$ imply

$$w_A = t_{1A}p_1 = ... = t_{kA}p_k, \qquad w_A \geq t_{k+1A}p_{k+1} \text{ and } w_A > t_{lA}p_l$$
$$\text{for } l > k+1$$
$$w_B = t_{k+1B}p_{k+1} = ... = t_{nB}p_n, \quad w_B \geq t_{kB}p_k \qquad \text{and } w_B > t_{lA}p_l$$
$$\text{for } l < k. \tag{14}$$

Substituting the equalities of (14) into (13) yields

 S. Rosen

$$w_A\left(\frac{\alpha_1}{t_{1A}}+\ldots+\frac{\alpha_k}{t_{kA}}\right)+W_B\left(\frac{\alpha_{k+1}}{t_{k+1B}}+\ldots+\frac{\alpha_n}{t_{nB}}\right)\leq 1 \qquad (15)$$

for all values of k.

Inequalities (15) establish the factor price possibility set and its extreme points define the factor price frontier, $g(w_A, w_B) = 0$. An example in which $n = 5$ is shown in Figure 2.

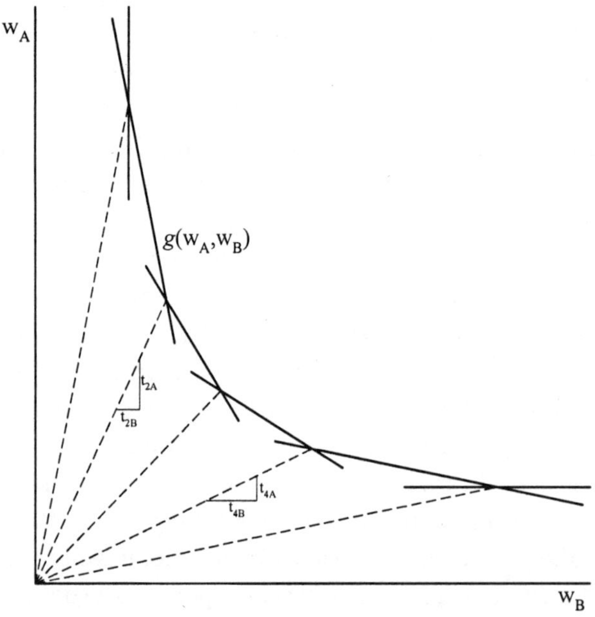

Figure 2

Since flats of the factor price frontier correspond to corners of the unit isoquant and vice versa, the unit isoquant is a piecewise linear function consisting of n-connected line segments, as shown in Figure 3. Successive pairwise comparisons of the equalities in (15) reveals that the corners of $g(w_A, w_B)$ lie along the ordered rays (from highest to lowest) $w_A/w_B = t_{kA}/t_{kB}$, $k = 1,\ldots,n$, which in turn are equal to marginal rates of substitution along linear segments of the unit isoquant. The isoquant always cuts both axes. For example, the A's must be assigned to all work activities if no B's are present. When a few B's become available it pays to specialize them in task T_n, for they have the greatest comparative advantage there. Type A workers may still be engaged in all tasks, but as more B's are added they ultimately can replace all of the A's time on task n. At the specialization point corresponding to the first corner of the isoquant, the A's are found on tasks $T_1, ..., T_{n-1}$ and the B's only on task T_n. The addition of still more B's allows their encroachment into task T_{n-1}, for which they have the next largest comparative advantage and for which the A's have the next smallest comparative disadvantage. In that segment the A's and B's have task T_{n-1} in common, until again the B's are sufficiently numerous to replace all of the A's time allocated to T_{n-1}. At that point the A's occupy $T_1, ..., T_{n-2}$ and B's occupy T_n, T_{n-1}, and so forth. The commonality of the task in each segment determines the marginal rate of substitution between N_A and N_B there.

The derivation of the factor price frontier shows that the indirect production function is supported by a price system. But it is supported by a competitive labour market as well. For example, a worker of type j chooses T_{iA} in the market to maximize income w_j with

$$w_j = p_1 T_{1j} + p_2 T_{2j} + ... + p_n T_{nj} \tag{16}$$

and is constrained by capacities

$$T_{1j}/t_{1j} + T_{2j}/t_{2j} + ... + T_{nj}/t_{nj} \leq 1 \tag{17}$$

and has exactly the same solution as (6) and (7): the market solution is efficient. Further, market arbitrage must make wage and piece rate payments equivalent in this problem. The market solution also satisfies (14), and the market piece rates are determined by the gradient of the efficient task possibility frontier. Therefore, variations in factor supplies N_A and N_B set relative market wage rates w_A/w_B equal to the marginal rate of substitution, and variations in factor supplies trace out the indirect production function.

In summary, the partition of (T_j) into "territories" and the bundling of tasks into job packages is responsive to *per capita* worker endowments and to total factor supplies. The boundary of the partition occurs at a marginal task common to both types of workers, and relative efficiencies on that task fix the marginal rate of substitution between worker types

                    S. Rosen

there. Moreover, observed substitution around a corner is determined by a measure of "distance" between skill endowments, e.g. in Figure 3 by the ratio $(t_{k+1A}/t_{kA}) \div (t_{k+1B}/t_{kB})$ Substitution of one kind of worker for another is more difficult the more dissimilar they are.

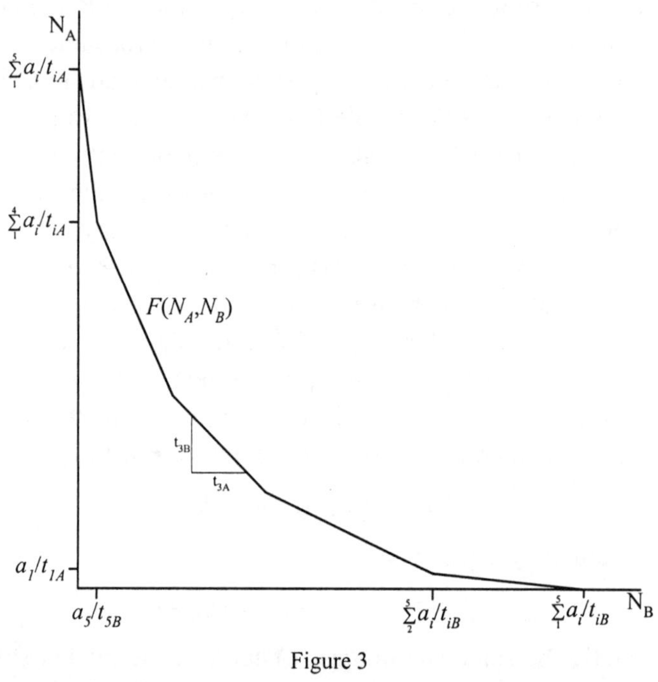

Figure 3

This last point warrants elaboration. As an approximation, imagine a continuum of tasks on an index s defined over $[0, 1]$ (this concept has been employed in trade theory by Dornbusch, Fischer and Samuelson, 1977). Workers' skill endowments and input requirements are described by continuous (assumed twice differentiable) functions $t_j(s)$ and $\alpha(s)$. Define $r(s) = t_A(s)/t_B(s)$ and choose s such that $r'(s) < 0$. The efficient assignment is readily extended to a continuum: there is a marginal task ρ that divides the spectrum s such that it is optimal to assign $0 < s < \rho$ to the A's and $\rho < s < 1$ to the B's. Consequently the unit isoquant is defined parametrically by

$$(N_A/x) = \int_0^\rho \{\alpha(s)/t_A(s)\}\, ds = \theta(\rho)$$

$$(N_B/x) = \int_\rho^1 \{\alpha(s)/t_B(s)\}\, ds = \phi(\rho) \tag{18}$$

where t_j/α measures worker skills in "efficiency units" and its inverse is the worker demand per unit of output. The marginal rate of substitution at ρ is

$$d(N_A/x)/d(N_B/x) = \theta'(\rho)/\phi'(\rho) = -t_B(\rho)/t_A(\rho) = -1/r(\rho)$$

and the elasticity of substitution $\sigma(\rho)$ at ρ is

$$\sigma(\rho) \equiv \frac{d\ln(N_A/x)/(N_B/x)}{d\ln(-r)}$$

$$= \left(\frac{\alpha/t_A}{N_A} + \frac{\alpha/t_B}{N_B} \right) \Big/ \left(t'_A/t_A - t'_B/t_B \right) \tag{19}$$

where all arguments of (19) are evaluated at ρ, and the expressions $(\alpha/t_j)/N_j$ are ratios of marginal to total demand for labour of type j at ρ. Substitution is inversely related to the gradient $-d\ln\{t_A(\rho)/t_B(\rho)\}/d\rho$, from (19). Apart from scale, the more similar are worker's relative talents near task ρ, the larger the elasticity of substitution there.

Expressions (18) show explicitly how the efficiency-skill endowment functions $t_j(s)/\alpha(s)$ determine the empirical form of the production function. Conversely, a given production function implies endowment functions that are consistent with it. For example, what forms of $t_A(s)/\alpha(s)$ and $t_B(s)/\alpha(s)$ imply that $F(N_A, N_B)$ has a constant elasticity of substitution? The answer is easily obtained. Normalize $\alpha(s) = 1$, substitute the expression for σ in (19) into $\sigma(\rho) = \sigma$ and differentiate with respect to ρ to obtain the restrictions

$$t''_j/t'_j = \sigma(t'_j/t_j) \text{ for all } \rho, \quad j = A, B.$$

Integrating twice and obtaining boundary conditions from the fact that σ is constant for all values of ρ gives, for $\sigma > 1$,

$$t_A(s)/\alpha(s) = 1/(c_a s)^{1/\sigma - 1}$$

$$t_B(s)/\alpha(s) = 1/\{c_b(1-s)\}^{1/\sigma - 1} \tag{20}$$

where c_a and c_b are positive constants (the global CES with $\sigma \le 1$ is inadmissible because $F(0, N_B)$ or $F(N_A, 0)$ are non-zero). In (20) the relative difficulty of tasks is increasing in s for the A's, but is decreasing in s for the B's. Further, neither group has an absolute advantage in all tasks. It is interesting to note that neither restriction is consistent with a hierarchical ranking of workers along a single ability scale.

As a practical matter, this analysis suggests difficulties in using some of the official job and occupational classifications for the study of productivity and factor demand. A job is not an invariant classification, since its boundaries are endogenously determined by the economic environment itself, and price-quantity variations across observations need not be generated by a common underlying structure. For example, the apparatus is useful for clarifying the meaning of international differences in technology. It is plausible that there exist no differences in engineering technology across countries, yet the (indirect) production function may appear to be different between them. The often observed fact that a factory in one country is more productive than its identical twin in another country can arise because work assignments embodied in the design of capital are optimal for one labour force and not for another owing to differences in the distribution of worker skills and comparative advantage.

A foundation for a structural indirect production function is best built upon groupings of workers according to comparative advantage and productive capabilities, perhaps on the basis of socioeconomic characteristics rather than on job classifications. Even so, comparative advantage implies imperfect substitution between groups. For example, the fact that different skills are accumulated with work experience suggests imperfect substitution among age cohorts in the labour force, and implies that greater relative factor supplies in a large birth cohort can haunt all of its members for their lifetimes. The same phenomenon helps explain why alternative vintages of graduates in the professions fare differently when output demand conditions change. It also incorporates the common managerial practice of skill bumping by seniority associated with business cycles (see Reder, 1962): so long as layoffs are not proportional across worker types, short-run employment declines change the partition of the set of tasks optimally assigned to those remaining employed, amounting to a kind of short-run substitution effect. Finally, in so far as educational classifications index differential worker capacities, the analysis suggests how education enters production and provides a link between supply-dominated theories of human capital accumulation and less well studied demands for them. Here imperfect substitution implies that fixed weighted indexes of aggregate educational input often used for measuring total factor productivity may be subject to substantial index number bias. A more subtle difficulty arises if relative capacities indexed by school completion levels change over time. Equiproportionate increases in capacities shrink the unit isoquant uniformly towards the origin, but all other kinds of changes alter it non-homogeneously. The former appear in the measurements as neutral technical change and the latter as biased technical change, even though the engineering technology may remain unaltered.

3. Selection and Income Distribution

The other extreme case, where the number of worker types is much larger than the number of tasks, provides some interesting parallels with Section 2. It is also more convenient for studying the role of demand conditions, income distribution and the characteristics of job-worker matching in the labour market.

To begin, return to the efficient frontier of Figure 1. The presence of a third type of person, C, with comparative advantage somewhere between that of A and B adds a third facet of slope t_{2C}/t_{1C} to the frontier. Adding still more types fills in the corners and has the effect of smoothing $f(T_1, T_2)$. Its limiting behaviour is found by making use of the fact established above that free choice and competitive markets assign people efficiently. Select a person at random with some fixed capacities (t_1, t_2). The solution to (16) and (17) shows that the worker maximizes income by devoting full time to activity 2 or to activity 1 according to $t_2/t_1 \lessgtr p_1/p_2$, and is indifferent between the two if the productivity ratio equals the market price ratio. Given an arbitrary market relative price $\lambda = p_1/p_2$, all workers whose value of t_2/t_1 exceeds λ are optimally assigned to activity 2 and voluntarily choose it;

all those with comparative advantage less than λ should be assigned to activity 1 and also find it in their own interests to choose it; while those for whom $\lambda = t_2/t_1$ are arbitrarily distributed to either activity or to both of them.

Again, there is a convenient ordering by comparative advantage, but this time it refers to workers rather than to tasks. Instead of partitioning the spectrum of tasks, the efficient solution partitions the set of worker types and establishes commonality of tasks for marginal workers at its boundary. Define a continuous index u on $(0,1)$ and twice differentiable functions $t_i(u)$ and $\beta(u)$ representing productivity of worker type u on activity i and the number of workers of that type. The index u is chosen in such a way that $R(u) \equiv t_2(u)/t_1(u)$ and $R'(u) \geq 0$. Therefore the efficient frontier is defined parametrically by

$$T_1(\lambda) = \int_0^\lambda t_2(u)\beta(u)du$$

$$T_2(\lambda) = \int_\lambda^1 t_1(u)\beta(u)du$$

(21)

and its slope is determined by the productivity ratio of the marginal worker: $dT_2/dT_1 = t_2(\lambda)/t_1(\lambda)$. Furthermore, $d\ln\{-dT_2/dT_1\} = R'/R > 0$ so that $f(T_1, T_2)$ is concave. Defining the elasticity of transformation $\tau(\lambda)$ symmetrically with the elasticity of substitution yields

$$\tau = \beta(t_2/T_2 + t_1 T_1)/(R'/R)$$

(22)

where all the arguments of (22) are evaluated at λ. The curvature of $f(T_1, T_2)$ depends on both the diversity of relative productivity in the working population and the number of workers of each type. Again, the less diversity, the larger is τ. For example, the efficient frontier is a straight line if everyone is identical (apart from scale), with slope equal to the population ratio t_2^*/t_1^*. Just as in Section 2, each specification of $t_i(u)$ and $\beta(u)$ implies a specific transformation function, and vice versa.

It was tempting in Section 2 to (loosely) identify the spectrum s with the difficulty of tasks. In this case u is more closely associated with worker talents and abilities, as an equivalent derivation in terms of a distributional argument makes clear. Each worker's skills are described by a point in the (t_1,t_2) plane, and if m is very large the *potential market supply* of skills is a continuous distribution function $M\xi(t_1,t_2)$. M is the number of workers and $\xi(t_1,t_2)$ is a probability density indicating the proportion of workers in a neighbourhood of (t_1,t_2). Picture the probability contours of ξ in the (t_1,t_2) plane, cut by a ray $t_2 = \mu t_1$. Since all workers with skills below the ray devote full time to activity 1 and all persons above it devote full time to activity 2, the activity possibility frontier is defined parametrically by the conditional expectations

$$T_1 = M \int_0^\infty \int_0^{\mu t_1} t_1 \xi(t_1,t_2)\,dt_1 dt_2 = \zeta(\mu)$$

$$T_2 = M \int_0^\infty \int_{\mu t_1}^\infty t_2 \xi(t_1,t_2)\,dt_1 dt_2 = \eta(\mu). \tag{23}$$

The efficient frontier $f(T_1,T_2)$ is swept out of the distribution $M\xi(t_1,t_2)$ as μ varies from zero (everyone choosing T_2) to infinity (everyone choosing T_1). Differentiating (23),

$$dT_1/d\mu = M \int_0^\infty t_1^2 \xi(t_1,\mu t_1)\,dt_1 = \zeta'(\mu)$$

$$dT_2/d\mu = M \int_0^\infty -\mu t_1^2 \xi(t_1,\mu t_1)\,dt_1 = \eta'(\mu) \tag{24}$$

and

$$dT_1/dT_2 = \eta(u)/\xi(u) = -\mu. \tag{25}$$

The slope of the efficient frontier is the price ratio, equal to the comparative advantage ratio for the marginal worker, as in (21). Differentiating (25) shows that $f(T_1,T_2)$ is concave and that τ is related to the moments of ξ, though the precise relationships are very difficult to establish because market selection truncates the distribution of productivity in each activity. However, τ tends to be large if ξ concentrates large probability in a small area of the plane (measured, say, by the generalized variance). The limiting case of identical relative talent discussed above is equivalent to complete concentration of ξ on a ray with slope t_2^*/t_1^*.

A result analogous to the indirect production function is available here, but refers to production possibilities in the economy. Construction of the production possibility set with two goods X_1 and X_2 and technologies

$$X_1 = \min\left(T_1/\alpha_{11}, T_2\alpha_{12}\right) \qquad X_2 = \min\left(T_1/\alpha_{21}, T_2/\alpha_{22}\right)$$

is illustrated in Figure 4. The production frontier is smooth and all factors are fully employed in spite of the fact that the output technologies admit no substitution. This result is reminiscent of the surprising example in Houthakker (1975) (see also the extensive elaborations by Johansen, 1972, and Sato, 1975) of well behaved macro-structures that seem to have lives of their own, bearing little resemblance to their micro-foundations, but arising from underlying distributional phenomena. Human diversity is the crux of the matter in all these examples. In this case it implies rising supply price of production activities, which translates to rising relative supply price of outputs. Thus substitution in the micro-technology or substitution in input technologies due to population heterogeneity are seen to have very similar implications.

Figure 4 shows explicitly how final demand conditions influence the division of labour among activities and their valuations. The total activity vectors corresponding to each feasible division of output sum to a point on $f(T_1,T_2)$ and the slope of $f(T_1,T_2)$ determines both the marginal worker and the relative market price ratio p_1/p_2: any other relative price would not call forth the division of labour necessary to support that division of output. The same principle extends to any finite n. For prices so determined a worker's income prospects in the ith activity are given by $y_i = p_i t_i$, which provide a basis for transforming the density of individual productivities $\xi(t_1,...,t_n)$ into a density of *potential* income $\psi(y_1,...,y_n)$. The realized personal distribution of income is related to ψ by the fact that workers choose activities to maximize their incomes. Let $h^i(y_i)$ denote the fraction of the labour force with income y_i who choose activity i. $h^i(y_i)$ is conditioned on the fact that people actually found in the ith activity could do no better elsewhere. That is (cf. Houthakker, 1975)

$$h^i(y_i) = \Pr\{y_i | y_i = \max(y_1,...,y_n)\}$$

$$= \int_0^{y_i} \cdots \int_0^{y_i} \psi(y_1,...,y_n) \prod_{i \neq k} dy_k.$$

Therefore the fraction of people with income y or less in activity i is

$$\int_0^y h^i(y_i)dy_i$$

and the cumulative density for the observed personal distribution of income in the economy is

$$\sum_i \int_0^y h^i(y_i)dy_i \, . \tag{26}$$

The derivation of $f(T_1,T_2)$ and Figure 4 show that final demand conditions affect observed income distributions and their influence appears through the presence of market clearing prices $p_1,...,p_n$ as parameters of the potential income density ψ and hence of the functions $h^i(y_i)$ in (26).

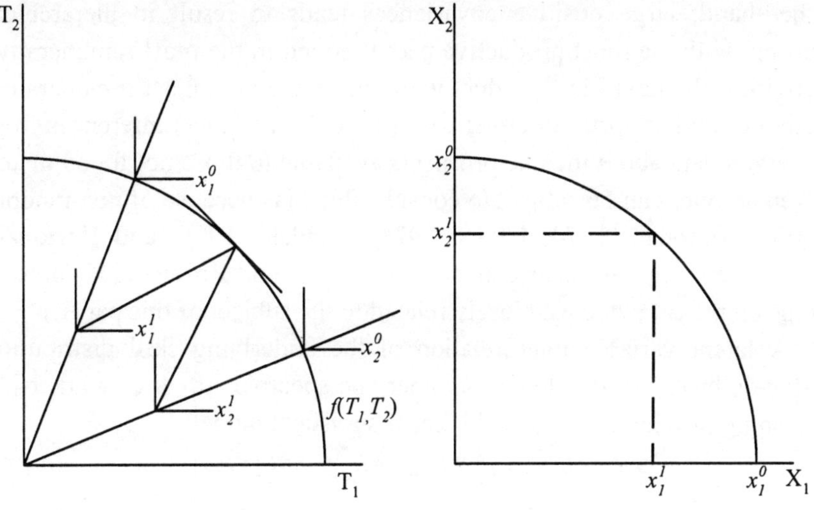

Figure 4

This kind of statistical model was first stated by Roy (1951), who elaborated the supply mechanism (see also Sattinger, 1975, and related work by Tinbergen, 1959). It has been extended to a more general demand and supply setting here. The main lesson is that observed earnings distributions are truncations of the distribution of potential earnings.

Individuals observed in each activity are selected into them by comparative advantage and therefore are not random samples of the whole population. The nature and extent of these selection effects depends on the moments of the distribution of potential earnings, which in turn are jointly determined by the moments of underlying skill distributions among various work activities embodied in members of the labour force (ξ) and by the valuations that the market places on these skills as derived from the demand for output (p). Large negative co-variances of potential earnings across activities tend to induce skewness in the overall distribution of income, because workers observed in each activity tend to be more productive in them than the population at large: there is small probability of observing someone from the lower tail of the marginal productivity distribution in any given activity since they are likely to have a much better opportunity somewhere else. On the other hand, large positive covariances tends to result in hierarchical sorting, with the most productive people found in the most remunerative activities, the next most productive found in the next most remunerative activities and so forth. In either case (not only the latter) inferences from observed data about income prospects available to those not found in any given activity can be subject to considerable bias because of non-random sorting. (Gronau, 1974; Lewis, 1974; Maddala, 1976; and Heckman, 1976 discuss this in other contexts, and Willis and Rosen, 1977, present some empirical evidence closely related to the subject of this paper.)

A latent variable interpretation of the underlying skill distribution (Man-delbrot, 1962) lends another perspective to the worker-job matching problem. Consider the linear statistical model

$$t_i = b_{0i} + b_{1i}Z_1 + b_{2i}Z_2 + \ldots + b_{vi}Z_v + \delta_i, \quad i = 1,\ldots,n \tag{27}$$

where Z is a vector of latent factors, b_i is a vector of factor loadings common to the ith activity and δ_i are independent activity-specific factors. Each worker is described by a point in the space of Z plus a random drawing from the joint distribution of δ. General equilibrium in the economy determines prices p as described above, and potential earnings in the ith activity are

$$y_i = p_i t_i = p_i b_{0i} + p_i b_{1i} z_1 + \ldots + p_i b_{vi} z_v + p_i \delta_i. \tag{28}$$

Equation (27) is similar to a "production function", with the marginal productivity (possibly non-positive) of each factor varying from activity to activity. These functions transform the joint distribution of (Z,δ) to the productivity density ξ used above, and similarly for (28) and ψ. Ignoring the specific factors for a moment, the factor space Z may be partitioned into n acceptance regions in which $y_i = \max(y_1,...,y_n)$ in region i. These regions are convex polyhedra and are completely determined by the loadings in (28). The polyhedra are cones if the constant terms $p_i b_{0i}$ in (27) or (28) are zero. (For the homogeneous case of $v = 2$, the acceptance regions would be defined by $n-1$ lines through the origin plus the coordinate axes of the (Z_1, Z_2) plane and are found in a manner very similar to the construction of Figure 2.) In any case, all individuals choosing the same activity would tend to have Z characteristics within well defined limits, with due allowance for noise from δ. The highly stratified outcome mentioned above would be likely if the relations in (28) were all positively loaded on a single factor, such as the usual interpretation of "general ability", in which case the acceptance regions are ordered partitions of a line. But that is too restrictive: most skills depend not so much on a single kind of ability as on combinations of them. Some characteristics and talents have zero or negative values for certain kinds of skills, or it may be that there are natural negative correlations among talents in human populations. Then the very notion of *hierarchical* sorting between workers and activities has little if any meaning. Nevertheless, sorting there will be, and workers in each activity will tend to have similar characteristics.

It is interesting to compare this approach to a "characteristics approach", wherein workers are considered to be fixed bundles of attributes (e.g., "strength" and "intelligence") which are themselves treated as factors of production (Welch, 1969). Then groups of workers are perfect substitutes for each other according to the fixed packages of attributes embodied in each group and a simple arbitrage argument establishes unique implicit market prices for characteristics depending on the total amounts available in the economy. A worker's income is simply the product of those prices times his embodied attributes. There is no tendency for systematic sorting of the labour force in that kind of world because any total attribute requirement can be obtained in the market by an infinite number of alternative linear combinations of worker types: there is no economic rent in earnings except the scale of a worker's characteristics. In contrast, the difference between marginal and average in this model generates economic rents that are signals for non-random assignment and sorting of workers to jobs. There is no unique market price for each attribute, but a value that varies among activities—see (29); because firms care about the amount of useful work performed, not about characteristics *per se*. Worker-job sorting and selection is too obvious and important an empirical phenomena to be ignored.

4. Conclusion

The main purpose of this essay has been to show how the division of labour inherent in the internal organization of work activities determines some observable substitution possibilities in production. Of course there is a considerable distance between what has been offered here and a complete theory; but substitution is such an important feature of economic life, that continued efforts to explain it seem worthwhile.

Engineering technologies with fixed coefficients have been used only to focus most sharply on the contribution of the division of labour to observed substitution. It is not difficult to incorporate smooth technologies of the neoclassical type into the analysis. Further, Section 3 generalizes fairly easily to multi-dimensional cases because the device of describing skill endowments by distribution functions captures the essence of the ordering property crucial to Section 2 without being quite so dependent upon it. Extending the results in Section 2 to more than two factors, beyond the mere statement of the envelope property—which always applies—is another matter. There is no counterpart to the distributional specification of Section 3. Bilateral comparisons always result in a comparative advantage ordering, but multilateral comparisons do not without further assumptions. One possibility is to order tasks by their "intrinsic difficulty", in which case it is conceivable, but still improbable, that the optimal partition of the spectrum assigns each group to occupy contiguous territories along the line as in Section 2, but with two commonalities instead of one. This is the only case where it is easy to keep track of the margins, but it is perhaps too restrictive to be of great interest.

The rules of the game that have been followed also rule out many interesting possibilities that are more difficult to analyse. First, the effect of scale on the division of labour (Stigler, 1951) plays no role here because of constant returns assumptions and the absence of indivisibilities. Second, in many labour markets there seem to be important empirical consequences of the nature of the match between different workers in the same firm that have been ignored above. The observed sorting of specific kinds of workers to specific firms in the same industry can be rationalized in many ways (see Rosen, 1974, for one possibility based on consumption aspects of the work environment); but technical task externalities and indivisibilities impose real limitations on the ability of the price system described above to achieve efficient asignments. If the price system is incomplete there is a role for entrepreneurial activity of assembling an optimal work force. Introducing such factors lead the analysis toward the economic theory of marriage (Becker, 1974) and questions of assortive matching among workers. Finally, the distribution of skills has been treated as exogenously determined. It remains to be seen how personal investments in the acquisition of skills affect the division of labour and derived factor and product substitution.

Acknowledgments

I am especially indebted to Robert Lucas, Daniel MacFadden, Michael Mussa, Kamran Noman and Robert Willis for many helpful discussions and criticism, to a referee who commented on an earlier version and to the National Science Foundation and the US Social Security Administration for financial support. Any shortcomings are my own responsibility.

                              S. Rosen

References

Becker, G. (1974). A theory of marriage. In *The Economics of the Family* (T. W. Schultz, ed.), Chicago: University Press.

Dorfman, R., Samuelson, P. and Solow, R. (1958). *Linear Programming and Economic Analysis*. New York: McGraw-Hill.

Dornbusch, R., Fischer, S. and Samuelson, P. (1977). Comparative advantage, trade, and payments in a Ricardian model with a continuum of goods. *American Economic Review*, 67, 823-839.

Gronau, R. (1974). Wage comparison—a selectivity bias. *Journal of Political Economy*, 82, 1119–11–43.

Heckman, J. (1976). *The Common Structure of Statistical Models of Truncation, Sample Selection and Limited Dependent Variables*. University of Chicago.

Houthakker, H. (1955). Pareto distributions and the Cobb-Douglas production function in demand analysis. *Review of Economic Studies*, 23, 27–31.

—, (1975). The size distribution of labor incomes derived from the distribution of aptitudes. In *Econometrics and Economic Theory: Essays in Honor of Jan Tinbergen*. (W. Sellekaerts, ed.), 177–187 New York: Macmillan.

Johansen, L. (1972). *Production Functions*. Amsterdam: North Holland.

Jones, R. (1961). Comparative advantage and the theory of tariffs: a multi-country, multi-commodity model. *Review of Economic Studies*, 28, 161–175.

Lewis, H. G. (1974). Comments on selectivity biases in wage comparisons. *Journal of Political Economy*, 82. 1145–1155.

McKenzie, L. W. (1954). Specialization and efficiency in world production. *Review of Economic Studies*, 21, 165–180.

Maddala, G. S. (1976). *Self-Selectivity Problems in Econometric Models*. University of Florida.

Mandelbrot, B. (1962). Paretian distributions and income maximization. *Quarterly Journal of Economics*, 76, 57–85.

Reder, M. (1962). Wage differentials: theory and measurement. In *Aspects of Labor Economics*. Princeton: University Press and NBER.

Rosen, S. (1974). Hedonic prices and implicit markets: product differentiation in pure competition. *Joumal of Political Economy*, 82, 34–55.

Roy, A. D. (1951). Some thoughts on the distribution of earnings. *Oxford Economic Papers* (n.s.) 3,135–146.

Sato, K. (1975). *Production Functions and Aggregation*. Amsterdam: North-Holland.

Sattinger, M. (1975). Comparative advantage and the distribution of earnings and abilities. *Econometrica*, 43, 455–468.

Stigler, G. (1951). The division of labor is limited by the extent of the market. *Journal of Political Economy*, 59, 185–193.

Tinbergen, J. (1959). On the theory of income distribution. In *Selected Papers*. Amsterdam: North-Holland.

Welch, F. (1969). A linear synthesis of skill distributions. *Journal of Human Resources*, 4, 311–327.

Whitin, T. (1953). Classical theory, Graham's theory and linear programming in international trade. *Quarterly Journal of Economics*, 67, 520–544.

Willls, R. and Rosen, S. (1977). *Education and Self Selection*. Washington: National Bureau of Economic Research.

CHAPTER 4

TRADE AND INSURANCE WITH MORAL HAZARD[*]

Avinash Dixit[+]

Princeton University

1. Introduction

It is often argued that in the absence of complete markets for risk-sharing, trade policy can have a second-best role in providing insurance. The most prominent exponents of this view are Newbery and Stiglitz (1984) and Eaton and Grossman (1985). The former construct an example where autarky is Pareto superior to free trade. The latter examine a more general model using numerical simulation methods, and find that the optimal policy usually involves some protection, i.e. has an anti-trade bias. Both pairs of authors appeal to moral hazard and adverse selection to motivate the absence of insurance markets. However, they do not include these forces explicitly in their models.

This procedure constitutes an unfair comparison between market equilibria and policy optima. First, the government's conduct of trade policy is assumed to be free from problems that would plague the market. Second, neither moral hazard nor adverse selection necessarily implies a total collapse of insurance markets or other risk-sharing arrangements.

[*] Reprinted from *Journal of International Economics*, 23, Dixit, A., "Trade and Insurance with Moral Hazard," 201-20, 1987, with permission from Elsevier.

[+] I am very grateful to the firm of (Gene M.) Grossman and (Sanford J.) Grossman for helpful advice, and the National Science Foundation for research support under grant No. SES-8509536. I also thank Norman Ireland and Kala Krishna for useful comments on an earlier draft.

To make a fair comparison, one should construct a trade model with moral hazard or adverse selection, allow markets as much play as they can have under the circumstances, and then ask if and how policy can improve upon the outcome. The purpose of this paper is to initiate this research program, for the case of moral hazard. Adverse selection will be treated in a separate forthcoming paper.

Some general issues of economic policy under moral hazard and adverse selection have been examined in this rigorous way, for example by Greenwald and Stiglitz (1986) and Arnott and Stiglitz (1986). They have identified some market failures, and examined how policy can act upon them. My aim is more specific; I shall construct a model that is closely related to those familiar in trade theory, and see which of the market failures have relevance for it.

My focus is on the role of trade and tax-transfer policies when there is uncertainty with moral hazard. To highlight the issue, I use a model where such policies would have no role in the absence of such problems: a small economy without distributive conflicts. To simplify the analysis, I keep the model small: two sectors, one being safe and the other risky, and one mobile factor of production, labor. The set-up is quite similar to Grossman's (1984) model of occupational choice, with some inessential details omitted, and moral hazard added.

Within this framework, we can have alternative assumptions about risk and insurance. Risk may be purely individual, or it may have an aggregate (systematic) component. As for insurance, if the total coverage purchased by an individual can be observed, then moral hazard is better controlled by making each insurance contract contingent upon the total coverage for that individual. The effect is just the same as requiring each person to buy all his insurance from the same (competitive) firm. This is called the exclusivity requirement; see Shavell (1979, fn. 8) and Arnott and Stiglitz (1986, pp. 3-4) for a full discussion. Thus, we have another choice: to assume exclusivity, or not to. The alternative assumptions about the nature of risk and the kind of insurance give rise to four separate cases. In the next three sections I shall examine three of these in detail; the fourth is then easy to consider by analogy.

In all the cases, some features are common, and it is convenient to state them here. The economy has N identical workers. Each has an indirect utility function $V(I, p)$ for goods' consumption with the following properties: I is disposable income in terms of the safe good (Y), p is the relative price of the good produced in the risky sector (X), and V is increasing and concave in I.

Each individual must choose the sector in which to work before any uncertainty is resolved. Let M denote the number who choose the safe sector. There is an increasing concave production function $Y = F(M)$. The wage is determined competitively:

$$w = F'(M). \tag{1}$$

The residual profits,

$$\Pi = F(M) - MF'(M), \tag{2}$$

are assumed to accrue to the government, and then enter consumers' incomes via the tax-transfer policies. It would make no difference to give each consumer a $(1/N)$th share of the profits directly. I could also stipulate a separate landlord class, and redistributive tax-transfer instruments to maximize workers' utility while holding landlords' utility constant, as in Grossman (1984). But that would give equivalent results and merely complicate the algebra.

The economy is small, and the world price of good X relative to good Y is fixed at p^*. The government's trade policy can maintain a domestic price p different from p^*. If $p > p^*$ the X-sector is favored by the policy, which is an import tariff or an export subsidy of $(p - p^*)$ depending on the direction of trade.

Other policy instruments pertaining to the risky sector will be described later. Any net revenue required by the government is raised by means of a uniform lump-sum tax t on each worker. Note that t must be determined as part of the equilibrium.

2. Individual Risk, Exclusive Insurance

There are $(N - M)$ workers in the risky sector. It is perhaps simplest to think of them as independent household farms or firms. Each of them chooses his level of effort e, measured by utility units, before the uncertainty is resolved. The probability distribution of outcomes depends on e. The expected net utility of a worker in the risky sector is thus $u_X = EV(I, p) - e$, where E is the expectation operator.

For algebraic simplicity, I shall assume that there are just two possible outcomes: low output x_L and high output x_H. The probability of the high outcome is $\pi(e)$, an increasing and concave function of e. The probabilities are independent across individuals. With a large number of workers, the per capita output is riskless.

The important assumption is that the range of possible outcomes, here the set $\{x_L, x_H\}$, does not vary with e. If they did, there would be events whose occurrence would reveal the chosen e exactly. Then contracts that mete out sufficiently severe punishments in such events could control moral hazard fully or almost fully, i.e. achieve or approximate the full-information first best. Therefore the assumption of invariance is the natural one to make in a model that sets out to examine the problems caused by moral hazard.

Otherwise, nothing hinges on the special structure. One could allow a continuum of possible outcomes X and a probability density function $f(x, e)$ at the cost only of analytical complexity; see the discussions in Hart and Holmstrom (1986). Similiarly, one could allow hired labor or material inputs, making the entrepreneur the recipient of profits, as in Grossman (1984). Since the results are unaffected, the simplest structure is the best for my purpose.

The government makes net transfers of g_L, g_H to each X-sector worker who realizes low and high output respectively. This specification can cover many policies. If $g_L > 0 > g_H$, we have some publicly provided insurance. If $g_L = g_H > 0$, we have a reward for undertaking the risky activity. If $g_L > 0 = g_H$, we have an income-support scheme.

There is private insurance, defined by each worker's net receipts z_L and z_H in the respective states. Recall that total coverage can be observed and controlled under the exclusivity assumption of this section. Therefore the individual cannot freely choose the scale of coverage at a given ratio of z_L/z_H.

The income of each X-sector worker in the two states is

$$I_L = px_L + g_L + z_L - t, \tag{3}$$

$$I_H = px_H + g_H + z_H - t. \tag{4}$$

The expected utility is

$$u_{\mathrm{x}} = \left(1 - \pi(e)\right)V\left(I_{\mathrm{L}}, p\right) + \pi(e)V\left(I_{\mathrm{H}}, p\right) - e. \tag{5}$$

Given the government policies and the insurance contract, the worker chooses e to maximize u_{x}. Assuming an interior solution ($e>0$) the first-order condition is

$$\pi'(e)\left[V\left(I_{\mathrm{H}}, p\right) - V\left(I_{\mathrm{L}}, p\right)\right] = 1. \tag{6}$$

The private insurer's zero profit condition is

$$\left(1 - \pi(e)\right)z_{\mathrm{L}} + \pi(e)z_{\mathrm{H}} = 0. \tag{7}$$

Although each person must sign up with just one insurer (exclusivity), there is competition among alternative potential insurers for clients. Therefore each insurer will choose $(z_{\mathrm{L}}, z_{\mathrm{H}})$ to maximize profit subject to providing the competitive level of expected utility u_{x}, and in equilibrium the profit will equal zero. It is equivalent and simpler to regard the choice of $(z_{\mathrm{L}}, z_{\mathrm{H}})$ as maximizing u_{x} subject to the zero profit constraint (7). The insurers are also aware of the moral hazard, i.e. the dependence of e on $(z_{\mathrm{L}}, z_{\mathrm{H}})$ via (6). Therefore we can formally regard them as choosing e as well, subject to (6) treated as a constraint on the optimization problem. The Lagrangian for the problem is

$$\begin{aligned} \ell = &\left(1 - \pi(e)\right)V\left(I_{\mathrm{L}}, p\right) + \pi(e)V\left(I_{\mathrm{H}}, p\right) - e \\ &- \lambda_{\mathrm{X}}\left[\left(1 - \pi(e)\right)z_{\mathrm{L}} + \pi(e)z_{\mathrm{H}}\right] + \mu\pi'(e)\left[V\left(I_{\mathrm{H}}, p\right) - V\left(I_{\mathrm{L}}, p\right)\right] \end{aligned} \tag{8}$$

The first-order conditions are

$$\left(1 - \pi(e)\right)\left[V_{\mathrm{I}}\left(I_{\mathrm{L}}, p\right) - \lambda_{\mathrm{X}}\right] - \mu\pi'(e)V_{\mathrm{I}}\left(I_{\mathrm{L}}, p\right) = 0, \tag{9}$$

$$\pi(e)\left[V_{\mathrm{I}}\left(I_{\mathrm{H}}, p\right) - \lambda_{\mathrm{X}}\right] + \mu\pi'(e)V_{\mathrm{I}}\left(I_{\mathrm{H}}, p\right) = 0, \tag{10}$$

$$\lambda_{\mathrm{X}}\pi'(e)\left(z_{\mathrm{L}} - z_{\mathrm{H}}\right) + \mu\pi''(e)\left[V\left(I_{\mathrm{H}}, p\right) - V\left(I_{\mathrm{L}}, p\right)\right] = 0. \tag{11}$$

The multiplier for the zero profit constraint is called λ_{X} because it is the marginal utility of a unit of sure income to an X-sector worker.

For readers unfamiliar with moral hazard problems, here is a brief characterization of the solution. First, we must have $\mu > 0$. To prove this, suppose $\mu \leq 0$. Then (9) and (10) give

$$V_I\left(I_L,p\right)=\lambda_x\Big/\left[1-\mu\pi'(e)\big/(1-\pi(e))\right]\le\lambda_x$$

$$V_I\left(I_H,p\right)=\lambda_x\Big/\left[1+\mu\pi'(e)\big/\pi(e)\right]\ge\lambda_x.$$

Then $V_I(I_H,p)\ge V_I(I_L,p)$, so $I_H\le I_L$ and $V(I_H,p)\le V(I_L,p)$. Then (6) cannot hold.

With $\mu>0$, we have $V_I(I_L,p)>\lambda_x>V_I(I_H,p)$. Then $I_L<I_H$, and insurance is incomplete. This represents the tradeoff between effort and insurance under moral hazard.

Now (11) can be written as

$$z_L-z_H=\frac{-\mu\pi''(e)}{\lambda_x\pi'(e)}[V(I_H,p)-V(I_L,p)]>0.$$

Combining this with (7), we find $z_L>0>z_H$. Thus, some insurance is offered despite moral hazard. For a detailed discussion of these issues, see Shavell (1979).

Now we can complete the description of the equilibrium. In the safe sector each worker has disposable income

$$I_Y=w-t,\tag{12}$$

and utility

$$u_Y=V\left(I_Y,p\right).\tag{13}$$

Equilibrium of occupation choice gives

$$u_X=u_Y.\tag{14}$$

It remains to ensure the consistency of the tax policy. Let the consumption of the X-good by each Y-sector worker be c_Y, and that by each X-sector worker, with respectively low and high incomes, be c_L and c_H. In fact, by Roy's Identity,

$$c_i=V_p\left(I_i,p\right)\big/V_I\left(I_i,p\right),\qquad i=\text{Y,L,H}.$$

Then total lump-sum tax receipts equal the requirements of the grant or insurance policies in the risky sector, minus the safe sector's profits, minus the trade tax revenues. So

$$Nt=-\left[F(M)-MF'(M)\right]+(N-M)\left[(1-\pi(e))g_L+\pi(e)g_H\right]$$
$$-(p-p^*)\left\{(N-M)\left[(1-\pi(e))(c_L-x_L)+\pi(e)(c_H-x_H)\right]Mc_Y\right\}.\tag{15}$$

Given the data N, x_L, x_H, and the policies p, g_L, g_H, we have to determine $M, w, z_L, z_H, I_L, I_H, I_Y, e, u_X, \mu, \lambda_X$ and t. We have the right number of equations (thirteen) in (1), (3)–(7) and (9)–(15). For my purpose, equilibrium is determinate.

In Shavell's (1979) model of moral hazard, the competitive equilibrium with exclusive insurance is constrained Pareto optimal. That is, a social planner facing the same information constraint – unobservable effort levels – cannot improve upon the market equilibrium. The simple reason is that the risky activity is the whole economy, and therefore a competitive insurer and the social planner must solve exactly the same constrained optimization problem. Here we have another sector, and labor and funds can be moved between them. The question is whether trade restrictions or public insurance policies can do so in a beneficial way. The answer is no; the competitive equilibrium with exclusive insurance remains constrained Pareto optimal.

In the text I shall develop this argument in an intuitive way; appendix A contains the formal proof. To keep the exposition simple, consider just one policy measure, namely a reward for undertaking the risky activity. Suppose each of the $(N - M)$ workers in the X sector is given a small lump sum Δg. This induces migration to that sector. As M falls, the Y sector wage rises, which eventually re-equates the utilities from working in the two sectors. But there are further effects. To finance the grant, we must raise the lump-sum tax on all workers by $\Delta g \cdot (N - M)/N$. Furthermore, as the Y sector wage rises by Δw, the profits there change downward by $\Delta \Pi < 0$, and each worker bears his $(1/N)$th share of that. Bearing in mind all these effects, we have

$$\Delta u_X = \lambda_X \left[\Delta g - \Delta g \cdot (N - M)/N + \Delta \Pi/N \right] \tag{16}$$

and

$$\Delta u_Y = \lambda_Y \left[\Delta w - \Delta g \cdot (N - M)/N + \Delta \Pi/N \right], \tag{17}$$

where λ_Y is the sure marginal utility of income in the Y sector. In the new equilibrium, we have $\Delta u_X = \Delta u_Y$. Let $K = \lambda_X/\lambda_Y$, and note that $\Delta \Pi = -M \Delta w$ by Hotelling's Lemma. Then (16) and (17) give

$$K \left[\Delta g \cdot M/N - \Delta w \cdot M/N \right] = \Delta w \cdot (1 - M/N) - \Delta g \cdot (1 - M/N).$$

This simplifies to $\Delta w = \Delta g$, and then (16) and (17) become $\Delta u_X = \Delta u_Y = 0$. Thus, the initial passive policy satisfies the first-order conditions for social optimality. Trade policy is similarly powerless.

As usual in optimal taxation theory, e.g. Diamond and Mirrlees (1971), second-order conditions are difficult to verify. However, we can be confident that we have found a maximum by observing that some special cases of the model are familiar ones where the market equilibrium is known to be Pareto optimal. Most simply, if moral hazard is vanishingly small, so $\pi(e)$ is flat at its equilibrium value, then we have a standard Arrow–Debreu model. More importantly, if the safe sector is vanishingly small, we have Shavell's (1979) model where the equilibrium is evidently constrained Pareto optimal, as we saw above.

The intuitive argument above showed how the policy favoring the risky sector was defeated by the induced migration. This bears out the general belief that if the government supports risky activities, too much risk will be taken. The principle should have wider validity than the trade context studied here.

3. Individual Risk, Unconstrained Insurance

When an individual's total insurance coverage cannot be observed, exclusivity cannot be enforced. People are tempted to expand coverage, and that in turn reduces their incentive to make effort. In this case, if a competitive equilibrium exists, it must have zero effort and complete insurance. To see this, suppose the equilibrium level of each individual's effort is e. With perfect competition, $\pi(e)/(1-\pi(e))$ units of low-state income can be purchased by giving up each unit of high-state income. If the individual purchases z such contracts,

$$I_L = px_L + g_L - t + z\,\pi(e)/(1-\pi(e)), \tag{18}$$

$$I_H = px_H + g_H - t - z. \tag{19}$$

Then z is chosen to maximize

$$(1-\pi(e))V(I_L,p) + \pi(e)V(I_H,p) - e.$$

This gives the first-order condition:

$$V_{\mathrm{I}}\left(I_{\mathrm{L}},p\right)=V_{\mathrm{I}}\left(I_{\mathrm{H}},p\right), \tag{20}$$

which implies $I_{\mathrm{L}}=I_{\mathrm{H}}$ (complete insurance) and $V(I_{\mathrm{L}},p)=V(I_{\mathrm{H}},p)$. Then the choice of effort can only be optimal if $e=0$. Arnott and Stiglitz (1986) call this the normal case in absence of exclusivity.

Suppose the economy is in such an equilibrium. What role can our policy instruments p, g_{L} and g_{H} play? None of them can alter the zero level of effort or the completeness of insurance: those properties were derived above for arbitrary p, g_{L} and g_{H}. Thus, we have in effect an economy with effort level fixed at zero, a fixed accident probability $\pi(0)$, no moral hazard, and full insurance. Standard theorems ensure that the competitive equilibrium is Pareto optimal (conditional on the effort level), and the policies can do no better. Interested readers can derive the result formally by methods similar to those of section 2.

What this situation needs is a different kind of policy – a tax at a suitably chosen rate τ on the purchase of insurance. Then giving up a unit of high-state income will get you only $(1-\tau)\pi(e)/(1-\pi(e))$ units of low-state income. People will purchase incomplete insurance, and make some effort. See Arnott and Stiglitz (1986) for a full discussion. Of course to tax insurance purchase the government must observe it, and then a simpler policy may be to enforce exclusivity.

The outcome with zero effort and full insurance may be the most natural one in the absence of exclusivity, but it is not the only one. Moral hazard contributes a non-convexity to indifference curves in a state-contingent consumption space. In section 2, exclusivity permitted the use of quantity-constrained insurance, i.e. non-linear budget sets, that overcame the problem. Now, in the absence of exclusivity, that cannot be done, and a competitive equilibrium may not exist. Some new possibilities arise. Stiglitz (1983) discusses them in detail. There may be an equilibrium involving randomized insurance contracts. There may be a non-market-clearing equilibrium with a sticky benefit-premium ratio. Finally, there may be a reactive or sophisticated conjecture equilibrium with no insurance. Each insurer is tempted to offer a contract with a small coverage that will be profitable on its own. But each realizes that when others act similarly, the resulting coverage will be much greater, the effort level will be much lower, the probability of the bad state will be much higher, and the profit on his contract will become negative.

This last possibility is not a Nash equilibrium, and therefore its intellectual foundation is shaky. But it is the only case where moral hazard is the cause of a complete cessation of private insurance, which was the staring point of the ad hoc incomplete-markets models of Newbery and Stiglitz (1984) and Eaton and Grossman (1985). Therefore I shall examine it in some detail to see how trade and tax-transfer policies by themselves can cope with moral hazard.

The model is the same as that of section 2, except of course z_L and z_H are fixed ar zero, λ_X and μ. are irrelevant, and correspondingly we drop the four equations (7) and (9)–(11).

With private markets absent, some government insurance (g_L, g_H) can be provided on an exclusive basis. If private insurance remains absent or can be prohibited, the government can trivially implement the constrained Pareto-optimal level of public insurance. More interesting is the role of trade policy. Once again, I shall offer an informal reasoning here, relegating the details to appendix B.

Suppose the domestic price is changed by Δp. Since an X-sector worker who realizes the high state produces x_H and consumes c_H, his real income rises by $(x_H - c_H)\Delta p$. Similarly, we have $(x_L - c_L)\Delta p$ for an unlucky X-sector worker. The offsetting effect on the per capita tax for everyone is a weighted average of the two, say

$$\gamma_H \left(x_H - c_H \right)\Delta p + \gamma_L \left(x_L - c_L \right)\Delta p \, .$$

where γ_H and γ_L are positive and sum to one.

The purpose of insurance is to shift some income from the high state to the low state. Therefore we want

$$\left(x_L - c_L \right)\Delta p - \left[\gamma_H \left(x_H - c_H \right)\Delta p + \gamma_L \left(x_L - c_L \right)\Delta p \right] > 0$$

and

$$\left(x_H - c_H \right)\Delta p - \left[\gamma_H \left(x_H - c_H \right)\Delta p + \gamma_L \left(x_L - c_L \right)\Delta p \right] < 0.$$

These simplify to

$$\left[\left(x_L - c_L \right) - \left(x_H - c_H \right) \right]\Delta p > 0 \, . \tag{21}$$

To see what (21) implies for trade policy, note the budget constraint for each state $i = $ L, H:

$$pc_i + d_i = px_i - t ,$$

where d_i is the consumption of the Y-good. Then $(x_i - c_i) = (d_i + t)/p$, and (21) becomes:

$$\left(d_{\mathrm{L}} - d_{\mathrm{H}}\right)\Delta p > 0 . \tag{21'}$$

If the safe sector good is normal in demand, $d_{\mathrm{L}} < d_{\mathrm{H}}$ and so (21') requires $\Delta p < 0$. The domestic price of the risky good should be kept below its world price. Therefore in this model, trade policy provides insurance by being *counter*-protective. This may sound paradoxical. The point is that the policy is in the first instance taking away more real income from those who realize high output than from those who get low output. The average is then returned to everyone by means of the lump-sum transfer. The net result is that those in the bad state are net gainers and those in the good state are net losers; this is how insurance is generated.

Other means of collecting or disbursing revenues will have different consequences. In a similar context, but without moral hazard, Grossman (1984) uses a proportional income tax and finds that free trade is the constrained optimum, provided preferences are homothetic. Now moral hazard has no first-order effect on utility because of the Envelope Theorem, and on government revenue because the initial point has $(p - p^*)$, g_{L} and g_{H} all zero. Therefore Grossman's result would continue to hold if proportional taxes were used in my model.

If the marginal shift of the tax schedule that is used for collecting or disturbing incremental revenues is progressive (a feature that can be quite independent of the progressivity of the schedule for fixed revenue requirements), then a small positive tariff will be beneficial. My conclusion from all this is that the role of tariffs as second-best insurance schemes, when risk-sharing markets shut down because of moral hazard, is ambiguous at best, and depends on an accidental conjunction between trade policy and income taxation. It is much simpler to find and implement a welfare-improving public insurance scheme.

4. Aggregate Risk, Exclusive Insurance

In this section I reimpose the exclusivity requirement on insurance, but introduce some systematic or aggregate risk. It would not make sense to remove individual risk entirely. For suppose one person's output is a function of his own effort e and an economy-wide random variable θ. Then relative outputs across people convey precise information about their relative effort levels. The full-information first best can be achieved, or closely approximated, by payments schemes based on relative performance. If moral hazard is to have some role, some individual risk is essential.

I shall therefore suppose that for each X-sector worker the probability π of high output is a function of his effort e and an economy-wide random variable θ, and that for each given θ, these events are independent across workers. Let $\phi(\theta)$ be the density function of θ. (There is a fully equivalent model with discrete values θ_i and probabilities ϕ_i. Also, a slight change of notation allows us to treat the world price p^* itself as a systematic random variable; the results below are unaffected.)

Even in this setting, relative performance schemes have some scope. In my model, it is possible to do even better by conditioning everything on θ, as we shall see in a moment. Hart (1983) constructs a model where a competitive market itself works like a relative performance scheme. That cannot happen here because the economy is small and p is fixed.

Remember that my ground-rule of fairness requires that we give the markets for risk-sharing their full role. Now the large numbers assumption ensures that, conditional on θ, the output per worker in the X-sector is riskless and is given by

$$\overline{x}(\theta) = \left(1 - \pi\left(e,\theta\right)\right)x_{\mathrm{L}} + \pi\left(e,\theta\right)x_{\mathrm{H}}. \tag{22}$$

Since the equilibrium value of e can be computed, and output can be observed *ex post*, we can infer θ *ex post*. Therefore all *ex ante* contracts and policies can be conditioned on it. So we can have a trade policy defined by a function $p(\theta)$, and transfer or insurance policies $g_{\mathrm{L}}(\theta)$, $g_{\mathrm{H}}(\theta)$, with the associated lump-sum tax $t(\theta)$. Exclusive private insurance contracts can be similar functions $z_{\mathrm{L}}(\theta)$, $z_{\mathrm{H}}(\theta)$.

People can also trade contingent claims to purchasing power, or Arrow's securities. I shall write $q(\theta)\phi(\theta)$ for the price of a claim to a unit of the numéraire if θ occurs. This is a harmless renaming that simplifies the notation by making budget constraints expectations with respect to θ. The equilibrium profile $q(\theta)$ can be found from the conditions of market-clearing I for claims for each θ; fortunately we do not need the explicit solutions.

A new feature is that with p and t dependent on θ, the Y-sector workers are also exposed to risk. They will therefore participate in the contingent claims market. Suppose their purchases are $b_Y(\theta)$. Then

$$I_Y(\theta) = w + b_Y(\theta) - t(\theta). \tag{23}$$

Suppose the wage w, although sure, is paid *ex post*. (The alternative assumption is a mere algebraic reformulation with identical results.) Then the budget constraint while trading in contingent claims is

$$\int q(\theta)\ \phi(\theta)\ b_Y(\theta)d(\theta) = 0 .$$

I shall write this more compactly as

$$E_\theta\left[q(\theta)\, b_Y(\theta)\right] = 0, \tag{24}$$

where E_θ denotes expectation with respect to θ. The maximand is

$$u_Y = E_\theta\left[V(I_Y(\theta), p(\theta))\right]. \tag{25}$$

This problem has the first-order conditions:

$$V_I(I_Y(\theta), p(\theta)) = \lambda_Y q(\theta), \tag{26}$$

for all θ. With no moral hazard in this sector, we have first-best risk allocation.

In the X-sector, we can likewise write:

$$I_L(\theta) = p(\theta)x_L + g_L(\theta) + z_L(\theta) + b_X(\theta) - t(\theta), \tag{27}$$

$$I_H(\theta) = p(\theta)x_H + g_H(\theta) + z_H(\theta) + b_X(\theta) - t(\theta), \tag{28}$$

and

$$u_X = E_\theta\left[(1 - \pi(e,\theta))V(I_L(\theta), p(\theta)) + \pi(e,\theta)V(I_H(\theta), p(\theta)) - e\right]. \tag{29}$$

Begin with the optimum choice of e, given all the other things. The first-order condition is

66

A. Dixit

$$\mathrm{E}_{\theta}\left[(\pi_{e}(e,\theta)\left[V(I_{H}(\theta),p(\theta))-V(I_{L}(\theta)p(\theta))\right]\right]=1. \tag{30}$$

Observe that $b_{X}(\theta)$ has an effect on e, that is to say a moral hazard aspect, just as do $z_{L}(\theta)$ and $z_{H}(\theta)$. Therefore we should apply exclusivity to all three, thus requiring each X-sector worker to get all his insurance for aggregate *and* individual risk from the same insurer. [An equivalent model can be had if $b_{X}(\theta)$ must be committed before $z_{L}(\theta)$ and $z_{H}(\theta)$ are determined.]

The insurer's zero-profit constraint is

$$\mathrm{E}_{\theta}\left\{\left[(1-\pi(e,\theta))z_{L}(\theta)+\pi(e,\theta)z_{H}(\theta)+b_{X}(\theta)\right]q(\theta)\right\}=0. \tag{31}$$

He chooses $z_{L}(\theta)$, $z_{H}(\theta)$ and $b_{X}(\theta)$ for all θ to maximize (29) subject to (30) and (31). The first-order conditions for $z_{L}(\theta)$ and $z_{H}(\theta)$, respectively, are

$$(1-\pi(e,\theta)-\mu\pi_{e}(e,\theta))V_{I}(I_{L}(\theta),p(\theta))-\lambda_{X}(1-\pi(e,\theta))q(\theta)=0, \tag{32}$$

$$(\pi(e,\theta)+\mu\pi_{e}(e,\theta))V_{I}(I_{H}(\theta),p(\theta))-\lambda_{X}\pi(e,\theta)q(\theta)=0. \tag{33}$$

The condition for $b_{X}(\theta)$ is just the sum of these two and therefore redundant; this is obvious since the insurer could always dispense with $b_{X}(\theta)$ as such and just add it on to each of $z_{L}(\theta)$, $z_{H}(\theta)$. The condition for e is

$$\mathrm{E}_{\theta}\left\{\mu\pi_{ee}(e,\theta)\left[V(I_{H}(\theta),p(\theta))-V(I_{L}(\theta),p(\theta))\right]\right.$$
$$\left.+\lambda_{X}\pi_{e}(e,\theta)\left[z_{L}(\theta)-z_{H}(\theta)\right]\right\}=0. \tag{34}$$

The remaining equilibrium conditions are: the requirement of indifference in occupation choice,

$$u_{X}=u_{Y}, \tag{35}$$

and the state-by-state government budget balance condition,

$$Nt(\theta)=-[F(M)-MF'(M)]$$
$$+(N-M)[(1-\pi(e,\theta))g_{L}(\theta)+\pi(e,\theta)g_{H}(\theta)]$$
$$-(p(\theta)-p^{*})[(N-M)[(1-\pi(e,\theta))(c_{L}(\theta)-x_{L})$$
$$+\pi(e,\theta)(c_{H}(\theta)-x_{H})]+Mc_{Y}(\theta)]. \tag{36}$$

Policy changes in this model consist of shifts of the whole functions $p(\theta)$, etc. Although this is an added degree of complexity, the structure of the model is very similar to the case of individual risk in section 2. Therefore it is no surprise that trade and tax-transfer policies are once again incapable of improving upon the market equilibrium. Even with systematic risk and moral hazard, competitive and exclusive insurance and state-contingent claims achieve a constrained Pareto optimum. The details are in appendix C; the intuition is similar to that developed in section 2.

I hope that cases with aggregate risk and non-exclusive insurance may now be left to the reader. If equilibrium has zero effort, full insurance for the individual risk and first-best allocation of aggregate risk, then trade and transfer policies are powerless. If the market shuts down, trade policies have the same kind of complex role, and publicly provided insurance a simpler role, as in section 3.

5.　Concluding comments

These results should not create the impression that moral hazard never matters. We know from the works of Stiglitz and his co-authors cited throughout the paper that it does. There are important externalities and non-convexities associated with moral hazard. Complicating my model will introduce some of them.

(i) If there are several risky activities with moral hazard, there can be externalities through their interaction, although such effects can be internalized by extending the exclusivity requirement.

(ii) If the economy is large, producer prices in free trade are endogenous. Changes in them affect producers' profits which become consumers' incomes; this alters the incentives to make efforts to reduce the risk. The standard monopoly optimum tariff can handle that.

(iii) If there is distorting commodity taxation for some other reason such as income redistribution or the provision of public goods, then there can be similar income effects via the tax revenue.

(iv) If an individual's probability of success is a function not only of his unobservable effort, but also of his anonymous purchase of a commodity, then welfare could be increased by subsidizing the consumption of that commodity. However, this is not a case for tariffs, i.e. for taxing domestic production and imports of the commodity differently.

(v) I have not considered non-market-clearing equilibria. These and other problems will enlarge the scope for beneficial policy interventions, although I believe the role of trade policy will remain complex and ambiguous.

All these limitations are significant, and indicate the need for more research. But I think the paper points out even more serious limitations of previous work on trade policy under uncertainty. Using models very similar or identical to those of the earlier authors, but taking explicit account of one of the causes of incomplete risk-sharing markets on which they tacitly rely, I have found that their ad hoc assumption of missing insurance markets does indeed drive their activist policy conclusions. This is yet another instance of the need for a 'level playing field' when economists compare the performance of markets and governments.

Appendix A

The model considered in this appendix is that of section 2, with individual risk and exclusive insurance. The subject is the formal analysis of the effects of the policies represented by p, g_L, and g_H on the equilibrium. Starting from an initial position where none of these policies is used, i.e. $p = p^*$ and $g_L = g_H = 0$, consider a small change $\Delta p, \Delta g_L$ and Δg_H. This will in general change all the magnitudes, e.g. M by ΔM, t by Δt, etc.

First, focus on the problem of devising the equilibrium insurance contract. This takes p, g_L, g_H and t as parametric, and chooses z_L, z_H and e to maximize u_X as given by (5), subject to the constraints (6) and (7). When the parameters change, the first order change in u_X is found using the Envelope Theorem. We calculate the *partial* effect of the parameters on the Lagrangian £ defined in (8), i.e. the effect holding the choice variables and the multipliers unchanged, and then evaluate the result at the optimum. Therefore we have

$$\Delta u_X = \left(1 - \pi(e) - \mu\pi'(e)\right)\left[V_I\left(I_L, p\right)\left(x_L\Delta p + \Delta g_L - \Delta t\right) + V_p\left(I_L, p\right)\Delta p\right]$$
$$+ \left(\pi(e) + \mu\pi'(e)\right)\left[V_I\left(I_H, p\right)\left(x_H\Delta p + \Delta g_H - \Delta t\right) + V_p\left(I_H, p\right)\Delta p\right]$$
$$= \left(1 - \pi(e) - \mu\pi'(e)\right)V_I\left(I_L, p\right)\left[\left(x_L - c_L\right)\Delta p + \Delta g_L - \Delta t\right]$$
$$+ \left(\pi(e) + \mu\pi'(e)\right)V_I\left(I_H, p\right)\left[\left(x_H - c_H\right)\Delta p + \Delta g_H - \Delta t\right]$$
$$= \lambda_X\left\{\left(1 - \pi(e)\right)\left[\left(x_L - c_L\right)\Delta p + \Delta g_L\right]\right.$$
$$\left. + \pi(e)\left[\left(x_H - c_H\right)\Delta p + \Delta g_H\right] - \Delta t\right\}. \tag{A.1}$$

The first step follows from the Envelope Theorem, the second from Roy's Identity, and the third from the first-order conditions (9) and (10). Note that if we conduct the thought-experiment of giving a sure dollar to an X-sector worker, i.e. formally set $\Delta g_H = \Delta g_L = 1$ and $\Delta p = \Delta t = 0$, we get $\Delta u_X = \lambda_X$. This proves that λ_X is the marginal utility of sure income in the X-sector.

Turning to the Y-sector, we have

$$\Delta u_Y = V_I\left(I_Y, p\right)\left(\Delta w - \Delta t\right) + V_p\left(I_Y, p\right)\Delta p$$
$$= \lambda_Y\left(F''(M)\Delta M - \Delta t - c_Y\Delta p\right). \tag{A.2}$$

Now we can set $\Delta u_X = \Delta u_Y$. Define K as λ_X/λ_Y, the ratio of marginal utilities in the two sectors. Then we find

$$F''(M)\Delta M = \Delta t + c_Y\Delta p + K\left\{\left(1 - \pi(e)\right)\left[\left(x_L - c_L\right)\Delta p + \Delta g_L\right]\right.$$
$$\left. + \pi(e)\left[\left(x_H - c_H\right)\Delta p + \Delta g_H\right] - \Delta t\right\}. \tag{A.3}$$

Finally, differentiating the government's budget constraint around the initial point of $g_L = g_H = 0$, $p = p^*$, we have

$$N\Delta t = MF''(M)\Delta M + (N - M)\left[\left(1 - \pi(e)\right)\Delta g_L + \pi(e)\Delta g_H\right]$$
$$- \Delta p\left\{(N - M)\left[\left(1 - \pi(e)\right)\left(c_L - x_L\right) + \pi(e)\left(c_H - x_H\right)\right] + Mc_Y\right\}. \tag{A.4}$$

Substituting for $F''(M)\Delta M$ from (A.3) and simplifying yields:

$$\Delta t = \left(1 - \pi(e)\right)\Delta g_{\mathrm{L}} + \pi(e)\Delta g_{\mathrm{H}}$$
$$+ \left[\left(1 - \pi(e)\right)\left(x_{\mathrm{L}} - c_{\mathrm{L}}\right) + \pi(e)\left(x_{\mathrm{H}} - c_{\mathrm{H}}\right)\right]\Delta p. \tag{A.5}$$

Then (A.1) becomes $\Delta u_{\mathrm{X}} = 0$, and so of course $\Delta u_{\mathrm{Y}} = 0$. Workers' utilities are stationary with respect to small policy changes around the initial passive position.

Appendix B

Here we have individual risk, but insurance is not constrained by exclusivity. Begin with the passive policy and consider small changes.

Differentiating the expression (5) for u_{X}, and remembering that e is chosen to maximize u_{X} (the Envelope Theorem again), we have

$$\Delta u_{\mathrm{X}} = \left(1 - \pi(e)\right)\left[V_I\left(I_{\mathrm{L}}, p\right)\left(x_{\mathrm{L}}\Delta p + \Delta g_{\mathrm{L}} - \Delta t\right) + V_p\left(I_{\mathrm{L}}, p\right)\Delta p\right]$$
$$+ \pi(e)\left[V_I\left(I_{\mathrm{H}}, p\right)\left(x_{\mathrm{H}}\Delta p + \Delta g_{\mathrm{H}} - \Delta t\right) + V_p\left(I_{\mathrm{H}}, p\right)\Delta p\right]$$
$$= \left(1 - \pi(e)\right)\lambda_{\mathrm{L}}\left[\left(x_{\mathrm{L}} - c_{\mathrm{L}}\right)\Delta p + \Delta g_{\mathrm{L}} - \Delta t\right]$$
$$+ \pi(e)\lambda_{\mathrm{H}}\left[\left(x_{\mathrm{H}} - c_{\mathrm{H}}\right)\Delta p + \Delta g_{\mathrm{H}}\right] - \Delta t, \tag{B.1}$$

where I have defined

$$\lambda_{\mathrm{L}} = V_I\left(I_{\mathrm{L}}, p\right), \quad \lambda_{\mathrm{H}} = V_I\left(I_{\mathrm{H}}, p\right).. \tag{B.2}$$

as the marginal utilities of contingent income in the two states. With $I_{\mathrm{L}} < I_{\mathrm{H}}$, we have $\lambda_{\mathrm{L}} > \lambda_{\mathrm{H}}$. The marginal utility of sure income is

$$\lambda_{\mathrm{X}} = \left(1 - \pi(e)\right)\lambda_{\mathrm{L}} + \pi(e)\lambda_{\mathrm{H}}. \tag{B.3}$$

For the Y-sector workers, we have (A.2), namely

$$\Delta u_{\mathrm{Y}} = \lambda_{\mathrm{Y}}\left(F''(M)\Delta M - \Delta t - c_{\mathrm{Y}}\Delta p\right).. \tag{B.4}$$

as before. Now we set $\Delta u_{\mathrm{X}} = \Delta u_{\mathrm{Y}}$ and simplify. Writing $K_{\mathrm{L}} = \lambda_{\mathrm{L}}/\lambda_{\mathrm{Y}}$ and $K_{\mathrm{H}} = \lambda_{\mathrm{H}}/\lambda_{\mathrm{Y}}$, we find

$$F''(M)\Delta M = \Delta t + c_Y \Delta p$$

$$+\left[K_L\left(1-\pi(e)\right)\left(x_L - c_L\right) + K_H \pi(e)\left(x_H - c_H\right)\right]\Delta p$$

$$+\left[K_L\left(1-\pi(e)\right)\Delta g_L + K_H \pi(e)\Delta g_H\right]$$

$$-\left[K_L\left(1-\pi(e)\right) + K_H \pi(e)\right]\Delta t. \tag{B.5}$$

Differentiating the government's budget constraint gives us the same equation (A.4) as before. Using (B.5) in it, and collecting terms, gives:

$$\left[N - M + MK_L\left(1-\pi(e)\right) + MK_H \pi(e)\right]\Delta t$$

$$= \Big[\left(1-\pi(e)\right)\left(N - M + MK_L\right)\left(x_L - c_L\right)$$

$$+\pi(e)\left(N - M + MK_H\right)\left(x_H - c_H\right)\Big]\Delta p$$

$$+\left(1-\pi(e)\right)\left(N - M + MK_L\right)\Delta g_L + \pi(e)\left(N - M + MK_H\right)\Delta g_H. \tag{B.6}$$

This can be written in a more transparent form as

$$\Delta t = \gamma_L\left[\left(x_L - c_L\right)\Delta p + \Delta g_L\right] + \gamma_H\left[\left(x_H - c_H\right)\Delta p + \Delta g_H\right], \tag{B.7}$$

where the weights γ_L and γ_H are readily defined by reference to (B.6), and add up to unity.

Finally, combining (B.1) and (B.6), we find that, leaving out some positive constants,

$$\Delta u_X \sim \left(\lambda_L - \lambda_H\right)\left\{\left[\left(x_L - c_L\right) - \left(x_H - c_H\right)\right]\Delta p + \Delta g_L - \Delta g_H\right\}. \tag{B.8}$$

With $\lambda_L > \lambda_H$, we see that utility *can* be increased by suitable policies that start from the passive stance of $p = p^*$ and $g_L = g_H = 0$. The general principle is that it is desirable to provide *some* insurance despite the moral hazard. Thus, tax-transfer policies that have $\Delta g_L > 0$ and/or $\Delta g_H < 0$ can increase welfare. Note that if the latter is used on its own, we have $\Delta t = \gamma_H \Delta g_H < 0$, so

$$\Delta I_L = -\gamma_H \Delta g_H > 0,$$

$$\Delta I_H = \left(1-\gamma_H\right)\Delta g_H < 0.$$

That is how income is transferred in the desirable direction by such a policy.

What about the role of tariffs as insurance? The desirable direction of change, from (B.8), is to make

$$\left[\left(x_{\mathrm{L}}-c_{\mathrm{L}}\right)-\left(x_{\mathrm{H}}-c_{\mathrm{H}}\right)\right]\Delta p > 0. \tag{B.9}$$

This can be understood in terms of the changes in the state-contingent *real* incomes, namely $(\Delta I_{\mathrm{L}}-c_{\mathrm{L}}\Delta p)$ and $(\Delta I_{\mathrm{H}}-c_{\mathrm{H}}\Delta p)$. When trade policy is on its own, using (B.7), we have

$$\Delta I_{\mathrm{L}}-c_{\mathrm{L}}\Delta p = \gamma_{\mathrm{H}}\left[\left(x_{\mathrm{L}}-c_{\mathrm{L}}\right)-\left(x_{\mathrm{H}}-c_{\mathrm{H}}\right)\right]\Delta p,$$

$$\Delta I_{\mathrm{H}}-c_{\mathrm{H}}\Delta p = -\gamma_{\mathrm{L}}\left[\left(x_{\mathrm{L}}-c_{\mathrm{L}}\right)-\left(x_{\mathrm{H}}-c_{\mathrm{H}}\right)\right]\Delta p.$$

Therefore income is shifted toward the worse state when (B.9) is satisfied.

Appendix C

Here we have some aggregate risk, but exclusive insurance. Start with passive trade and transfer policies, i.e. $p(\theta)=p^*$ and $g_L(\theta)=g_H(\theta)=0$ for all θ, and consider a small change $\Delta p(\theta)$, $\Delta g_L(\theta)$ and $\Delta g_H(\theta)$. By these I mean shifts of the whole functions $p(\theta)$, etc. and *not* movements along them such as $p'(\theta)\,\Delta\theta$.

Calculation of the effects on utilities proceeds as in appendix A, complicated only slightly by the need to take expectations with respect to θ. Thus,

$$\begin{aligned}
\Delta u_{\mathrm{Y}} &= \mathrm{E}_{\theta}\{V_I(I_{\mathrm{Y}}(\theta),p(\theta))[\Delta w-\Delta t(\theta)]+V_p(I_{\mathrm{Y}}(\theta),p(\theta))\Delta p(\theta)\} \\
&= \mathrm{E}_{\theta}\{V_I(I_{\mathrm{Y}}(\theta),p(\theta))[\Delta w-\Delta t(\theta)-c_{\mathrm{Y}}(\theta)\Delta p(\theta)]\} \\
&= \lambda_{\mathrm{Y}}\mathrm{E}_{\theta}\{q(\theta)[\Delta w-\Delta t(\theta)-c_{\mathrm{Y}}(\theta)\Delta p(\theta)]\} \\
&= \lambda_{\mathrm{Y}}\{\Delta w-\mathrm{E}_{\theta}[q(\theta)\Delta t(\theta)]-\mathrm{E}_{\theta}[c_{\mathrm{Y}}(\theta)q(\theta)\Delta p(\theta)]\}.
\end{aligned} \tag{C.1}$$

The first step uses the Envelope Theorem, the second, Roy's Identity, and the third, the first-order condition (25). The last step uses the fact that $\mathrm{E}_{\theta}q(\theta)$, being the price of a claim that pays a unit of the numéraire in every state, must equal one.

The expression for Δu_{X} gets far too lengthy. Therefore I shall omit the arguments θ, and indicate the points where V_I and V_p are evaluated simply by L and H as appropriate. Then similar steps give

$$\Delta u_X = E_\theta \Big\{ \big[(1 - \pi - \mu\pi_e) \big[V_I(L)(x_L \Delta p + \Delta g_L - \Delta t) + V_p(L)\Delta p \big]$$

$$+ (\pi + \mu\pi_e) \big[V_I(H)(x_H \Delta p + \Delta g_H - \Delta t) + V_p(H)\Delta p \big] \Big\}$$

$$= E_\theta \Big\{ (1 - \pi - \mu\pi_e) V_I(L) \big[(x_L - c_L)\Delta p + \Delta g_L - \Delta t \big]$$

$$+ (\pi + \mu\pi_e) V_I(H) \big[(x_H - c_H)\Delta p + \Delta g_H - \Delta t \big] \Big\}$$

$$= \lambda_X E_\theta \Big\{ (1 - \pi) q \big[(x_L - c_L)\Delta p + \Delta g_L - \Delta t \big]$$
(C.2)

$$+ \pi q \big[(x_L - c_L)\Delta p + \Delta g_L - \Delta t \big] \Big\}$$

$$= \lambda_X E_\theta \Big\{ q \big[(1 - \pi)(x_L - c_L) + \pi(x_H - c_H) \big] \Delta p$$

$$+ q \big[(1 - \pi)\Delta g_L + \pi\Delta g_H \big] - q\Delta t \Big\}.$$

As before, define $K = \lambda_X / \lambda_Y$, set $\Delta u_X = \Delta u_Y$, and rearrange terms. This yields:

$$F''(M)\Delta M = E_\theta[q\Delta t] - E_\theta[c_Y \Delta p]$$

$$+ K E_\theta \Big\{ q \big[(1 - \pi)(x_L - c_L) + \pi(x_H - c_H) \big] \Delta p \qquad \text{(C.3)}$$

$$+ q \big[(1 - \pi)\Delta g_L + \pi\Delta g_H \big] - q\Delta t \Big\}.$$

Differentiation of (36) for fixed θ gives

$$N\Delta t = MF''(M)\Delta M + (N - M)\big[(1 - \pi)\Delta g_L + \pi\Delta g_H \big]$$

$$- \Delta p \big[(N - M)\big[(1 - \pi)(c_L - x_L) + \pi(c_H - x_H) \big] + Mc_Y \big],$$

where once again I have omitted the arguments θ or (e, θ). On multiplying by $q(\theta)$ and taking expectations,

$$N E_\theta[q\Delta t] = MF''(M)\Delta M + (N - M) E_\theta \big[q \big[(1 - \pi)\Delta g_L + \pi\Delta g_H \big] \big]$$

$$+ (N - M) E_\theta \big[q \big[(1 - \pi)(x_L - c_L) + \pi(x_H - c_H) \big] \Delta p \big]$$

$$- M E_\theta[c_Y \Delta p]. \qquad \text{(C.4)}$$

Finally, substitute for $F''(M)\Delta M$ from (C.3) into (C.4) and simplify to get

74 *A. Dixit*

$$E_\theta \left[q\Delta t \right] = E_\theta \left[q \left[(1-\pi)(x_L - c_L) + \pi(x_H - c_H) \right] \Delta p \right]$$
$$+ E_\theta \left[q \left[(1-\pi)\Delta g_L + \pi\Delta g_H \right] \right]. \tag{C.5}$$

When we use (*C.5*) in expression (C.2) we find $\Delta u_X = 0$.

References

Arnott, Richard and Joseph Stiglitz, 1986, The welfare economics of moral hazard, Queen's University Discussion Paper no. 635.

Diamond, Peter and James Mirrlees, 1971, Optimal taxation and public production I–II, American Economic Review 61 (1) March and (2) June, 8–27, 261–278.

Eaton, Jonathan and Gene Grossman, 1985, Tariffs as insurance: Optimal commercial policy when domestic markets are incomplete, Canadian Journal of Economics 18 (2), May, 258–272.

Greenwald, Bruce and Joseph Stiglitz, 1986, Externalities in economies with imperfect information and incomplete markets, Quarterly Journal of Economics 101 (2), May, 229–264.

Grossman, Gene, 1984, International trade, foreign investment and the formation of the entrepreneurial class, American Economic Review 74 (4), Sept., 605–614.

Hart, Oliver, 1983, The market mechanism as an incentive scheme, Bell Journal of Economics 14 (2), Autumn, 366–382.

Hart, Oliver and Bengt Holstrom, 1986, The theory of contracts, in: Truman Bewley, ed., Advances in economic theory, 1985 (Cambridge University Press) forthcoming.

Newbery, David and Joseph Stiglitz, 1984, Pareto inferior trade, Review of Economic Studies 51 (1), Jan., 1–12.

Shavell, Steven, 1979, On moral hazard and insurance, Quarterly Journal of Economics 94 (4), Nov., 541–562.

Stiglitz, Joseph, 1983, Risk, incentives and insurance: The pure theory of moral hazard, Geneva Papers on Risk and Insurance 8 (26), Jan., 4–33.

<h1 style="text-align:center">CHAPTER 5</h1>

<h1 style="text-align:center">TRADE AND INSURANCE WITH IMPERFECTLY OBSERVED OUTCOMES[*]</h1>

Avinash Dixit[*]

Princeton University

1. Introduction

Interest in the use of trade restrictions to provide insurance has been stimulated by the work of Newbery and Stiglitz [1981, Ch. 23; 1984] and Eaton and Grossman [1985]. Their important contribution was to recognize that private markets for risk-bearing are often incomplete. However, they simply assumed this directly, without tracing it to underlying causes. It is important to do so, because the same causes can alter the desirability and even the feasibility of various policies. This paper is one of a series that examines different sources of the failure of risk markets from this viewpoint. Dixit [1987a] examined moral hazard, and Dixit [1987b] considered adverse selection. In this paper I examine another, and perhaps the simplest, problem—the outcomes of a risky activity may themselves be imperfectly observable to private insurers and policy makers.

After describing the general structure of the model in Section 2, I consider two cases. In Section 3 outcomes are assumed to be totally

---

[*] Reprinted from *Quarterly Journal of Economics*, 104 (1), Dixit, A., "Trade and Insurance with Imperfectly Observed Outcomes," 195-203, 1989, with permission from MIT Press Journal.

[*] I thank Mark Gertler and Gene Grossman for helpful discussions, Lars Svensson and two referees for valuable comments on earlier drafts, and the National Science Foundation for financial support under grant SES-8509536.

unobservable to anyone other than the primary risk-taker. In Section 4 outsiders can perform costly audits that yield perfect information; the scope of such auditing is endogenously determined.

In all cases, an opening for policy to improve welfare arises because the marginal utility of income of the workers in the risky sector is negatively correlated with their net sale of the risky good (output minus own consumption). A tax policy that lowers the price they face below the world price, and returns the revenues by lump sum grants, can smooth their utility across states and so raise the expected utility for each. In trade policy terms, this amounts to an export tax if the risky good is exported, and an import subsidy if it is imported.

2. The Model

To highlight the problems caused by the imperfect observability of outcomes, I use a model where trade policy has no conventional function, namely a small open economy without other distortions or distributive conflicts. To simplify the analysis, I keep the model small: two sectors (one safe and the other risky), and one mobile factor of production (labor).

The safe good Y is the numeraire. The risky good X has a constant world price p^*. There are N identical workers. Each has an indirect utility function $V(p, I)$, where I is his disposable income in units of Y, and p is the relative price of X that he faces. V is increasing and concave in I.

Each individual must choose the sector in which to work before any uncertainty is resolved. Let M denote the number who choose the safe sector. There is an increasing and concave production function $Y = G(M)$. The wage is determined competitively:

$$w = G'(M). \tag{1}$$

All N workers have an equal claim to the profits of the safe sector. Therefore, the profit income of each is given by

$$\pi = \left[G(M) - wM\right]/N. \tag{2}$$

The remaining $(N - M)$ people work in the risky X sector. The output of each is a random variable x with a cumulative distribution function

$F(x)$ and a density function $f(x)$, defined over the interval $[0, K]$. The outputs are uncorrelated across people. Each individual observes his realization of x when it occurs. However, outsiders can observe such realizations only imperfectly, or not at all. Each of the following two sections deals with a different assumption in this regard.

Equilibrium of occupational choice is attained when the utility of a Y-sector worker equals the expected utility of an X-sector worker. The expressions for these differ in the two cases, as different insurance arrangements and tax-transfer policies are compatible with different assumptions about observability.

3. Unobserved Outcomes

When the realization of an individual's x is totally unobservable to others, it is impossible to have any incentive-compatible contracts contingent on x, other than trivial constant ones. Thus, there can be no insurance, private or public. This immediately brings us to the question of tax and subsidy policies, including trade policies.

To be consistent with the information restriction, we should allow only the net market trades of the X-sector workers to be taxed or subsidized. Therefore, the prices they face in their roles as producers and consumers of good X should be equal. Let p_X denote the common value. Let p_Y be the price for consumption of good X by the Y-sector workers. Whether the government can keep p_X and p_Y distinct depends on whether it can prevent cross-sector arbitrage. I shall do the analysis with the two variables kept distinct, and derive as corollaries the policy conclusions when they must vary together. When $p_X = p_Y$, there is only one internal relative price of X, and the policy acts purely on international trade. Keeping P_X (or the common value of p_X and p_Y) above p^* means favoring the X-sector (with an import tariff if X is imported and an export subsidy if it is exported). The proceeds of any taxes are returned, or the sum for any subsidies is raised, by means of an equal lump sum transfer t for all N workers.

With this specification the utility of each Y-sector worker is

$$u_Y = V\left(p_Y, w + \pi + t\right), \tag{3}$$

and the expected utility of each X -sector worker is

$$u_X = \int_0^K V(p_X, p_X x + \pi + t)\,dF(x). \tag{4}$$

Equilibrium requires that

$$u_X = u_Y. \tag{5}$$

Using Roy's Identity, the consumption of good X by each Y-sector worker can be written as

$$c_Y = -V_P(p_Y, w + \pi + t)/V_I(p_Y, w + \pi + t). \tag{6}$$

Similarly, the consumption of good X by an X-sector worker with realized output of x is given by

$$c_X(x) = -V_P(p_X, p_X x + \pi + t)/V_I(px, p_X x + \pi + t). \tag{7}$$

The government's budget balance condition is

$$tN = (p_Y - p^*)Mc_Y + (p^* - p_X)(N - M)\int_0^K x[x - c_X(x)]\,dF(x). \tag{8}$$

As usual, this can be transformed into the trade balance condition by adding to it the budget balance conditions of all private individuals. The economy is assumed to have a large number of people. Therefore, fluctuations in the aggregate output of X are relatively small. Assuming that the resulting small imbalances in trade are financed using reserves or IMF loans, I can impose (8) in the expected value form.

Start with an equilibrium without any policy intervention, that is, $p_X = p_Y = p^*$ and $t = 0$, and perturb it. Then

$$du_Y = V_P(Y)dp_Y + V_I(Y)[dw + d\pi + dt]$$
$$= \lambda_Y[-c_Y dp_Y + dw + d\pi + dt],$$

where I have used the abbreviation $V_P(Y)$ for $V_P(p_Y, w + \pi + t)$ etc., and $\lambda_Y = V_I(Y)$.

Next, by Hotelling's Lemma applied to (2), we have $d\pi = -Mdw/N$; define $\mu = M/N$. Then

$$du_Y = \lambda_Y[-c_Y dp_Y + (1 - \mu)dw + dt]. \tag{9}$$

With similar abbreviations, we have

$$du_X = \left\{ \int_0^K \lambda_X(x)[x - c_X(x)]dF(x) \right\} dP_X + \left\{ \int_0^K \lambda_X(x)dF(x) \right\}[-\mu dw + dt]. \quad (10)$$

In the new equilibrium, $du_X = du_Y$. Therefore,

$$d\omega \left\{ \lambda_Y(1-\mu) + \mu \int_0^K \lambda_X(x)dF(x) \right\}$$

$$= \left\{ \int_0^K \lambda_X(x)dF(x) - \lambda_Y \right\} dt + \left\{ \int_0^K \lambda_X(x)[x - c_X(x)]dF(x) \right\} dP_X + \lambda_Y c_Y dp_Y. \quad (11)$$

Differentiating the budget balance equation (8) and evaluating it at the initial equilibrium, we have

$$dt = \mu c_Y dp_Y - (1-\mu) \left\{ \int_0^K [x - c_X(x)]dF(x) \right\} dp_X. \quad (12)$$

We can substitute this in (11) to find dw, and then substitute for dw and dt in (9)-or (10)-to find the change in the common value of du_X and du_Y, say du. After some tedious algebra, the result is

$$du \left\{ (1-\mu)\lambda_Y + \mu \int_0^K \lambda_X(x)dF(x) \right\} \Big/ \lambda_Y$$

$$= (1-\mu)dp_X \left\{ \int_0^K \lambda_X(x)[x - c_X(x)]dF(x) - \int_0^K \lambda_X(x)dF(x) \int_0^K [x - c_X(x)]dF(x) \right\}. \quad (13)$$

The first thing to notice is that the terms in dp_Y cancel out, so p_Y has no local effect on u. If distinct prices can be maintained in the two sectors, then the safe sector workers should go on facing the world price for their consumption of the risky sector's output.

The next point is that the bracketed expression on the right- hand side is the covariance between $\lambda_X(x)$ and $[x-c_X(x)]$. The former, being the marginal utility of income to an X-sector worker who realizes output x, is a decreasing function of x. The latter, being the net sale of good X by such a worker, is an increasing function of x provided that good Y is normal, a mild condition which I assume to be met. Now it is easy to check that if two random variables are functions, one increasing and the other decreasing, of a common third random variable, then the covariance between the two is negative.[1] Therefore, (13) says that utility can be increased by slightly lowering p_X below p^*.

---

[1] See the working paper version Dixit [1987c] for the proof.

The intuition is that such a policy has the direct effect of lowering the real incomes of the high-x people the most, and the indirect effect of raising the real incomes of all equally as the revenue is returned in a lump sum. If people with very low x become net buyers of the good X, there is an additional direct benefit to them. In any case, the policy yields some of the insurance that could not be provided in a more straightforward way.

If p_X must be kept equal to p_Y, then a slight reduction in their common value below p^* has a first-order beneficial effect on utility through the p_X aspect of the change, and only a second-order effect through the p_Y aspect. Therefore, some move in this direction is indicated. In other words, if trade policies are the only instruments available, they should be employed to disfavor the risky sector, i.e., as export taxes or import subsidies depending on the pattern of trade.

In the working paper version Dixit [1987c], I consider an extension where outcomes are partially observable. The range $[0, K]$ is divided into intervals, and it is possible to identify the interval in which the outcome lies. The same policy results emerge, because of a similar negative covariance within each interval.

4. Costly Observation

In the model of this section, an X-sector worker's output realization can be verified by an outsider using an audit that costs α units of the good Y. (A more general cost function $\alpha(p)$ makes no difference.) I assume that the results of an audit, while demonstrable to a court upon need, can be concealed from rival insurers. This avoids public-good problems in auditing. The theory of such auditing was developed by Townsend [1979], and extended by Mookherjee and Png [1987] among others. It has been applied to financial markets by many authors, most recently Bernanke and Gertler [1986].

Feasible insurance in this setting, either in competitive markets or under an actuarially fair public scheme, can be characterized using the Revelation Principle. The insurer asks each insured to report his realization of x, and commits himself to a set of rules for using this information. The auditing strategy, as well as the net payment to the insured if there is no audit, can depend only on the reported x. If audited, the net payment can depend on the actual as well as the reported x; this allows a reward for truthfulness and a penalty for lying. The scheme chosen by the insurer has to satisfy not only the breakeven constraint, but also the incentive-compatibility constraint; namely, truthful reporting should be optimal for each x.

The most general auditing strategy is a randomized one, specifying the probability of an audit as a function of the report. If the mild condition $V_I(P,0) = \infty$ is satisfied, this permits an approximation to the first-best: combine a small probability of an audit, and a dire penalty if discovered to be lying. This extreme possibility can be circumvented by using either ad hoc constraints like consumption floors, or more complex models with errors in audits. These modifications will greatly complicate my algebra without affecting the basic point, which is a simple consequence of the Envelope Theorem. Therefore, I shall allow only deterministic auditing strategies.

The results of Townsend [1979] then apply. Reports of bad outcomes will be audited, and those of good ones will not. Therefore, we have a marginal outcome ξ such that reports of x in the range $[0, \xi]$ are audited and those in $[\xi, K]$ are not. Since the insurer pools many uncorrelated risks and acts risk neutral, in the range where audits are performed there is full insurance. Therefore, the net payment to the insured in this range is $z(x) = Z - p * x$ for some constant Z. In the range with no audits, the net payment must be constant, $z(x) = \xi$, for incentive compatibility. To rule out the incentive for someone with an outcome $x < \xi$ to report falsely an $x \geq \xi$, we must have $Z - p*x \geq \xi$ for all $x < \xi$ To reduce auditing costs as far as possible, this constraint should be met with equality at $x = \xi$. Therefore, $Z = \xi + p*\xi$, and

$$z(x) = \begin{cases} \zeta + p^*(\xi - x) & \text{for } 0 \leq x < \xi \\ \zeta & \text{for } \xi \leq x < K. \end{cases} \tag{14}$$

Then the feasibility condition is

$$\int_0^\xi [\zeta + p^*(\xi - x) + \alpha] dF(x) + \int_\xi^K \zeta \, dF(x) \leq 0. \tag{15}$$

Subject to this, a competitive or socially optimal insurance contract will choose ξ and ζ to maximize the expected utility of each X-sector worker,

$$u_x = \int_0^\xi V(p^*, p^*\xi + \zeta + \pi)dF(x) + \int_\xi^K V(p^*, p^*x + \zeta + \pi)dF(x). \quad (16)$$

The first-order condition for ζ is

$$\int_0^\xi V_I(p^*, p^*\xi + \zeta + \pi)dF(x) + \int_\xi^K V_I(p^*, p^*x + \zeta + \pi)dF(x) = \gamma, \quad (17)$$

where γ is the Lagrange multiplier for the constraint (15). The condition for ξ is

$$p^* V_I(p^*, p^*\xi + \zeta + \pi)F(\xi) = \gamma[p^*F(\xi) + \alpha f(\xi)],$$

or

$$V_I(p^*, p^*\xi + \zeta + \pi) = \gamma + \gamma \alpha f(\xi)/[p^*F(\xi)]. \quad (18)$$

To interpret these, (17) defines γ as the expected marginal utility of income over all outcomes. Then (18) says that the marginal utility over the audited outcomes with full insurance is higher, so the disposable income in this range is lower, than the average over all outcomes.

Now consider the role of tax policy in such an economy. Introduce the instruments p_X, p_Y and t as in Section 3. For given tax policies, auditing and insurance will work as above, except that p^* will be replaced by p_X in (14)-(18), and t added to incomes in (16)-(18) above. On perturbing an initial laissez-faire equilibrium, we shall find that

$$du_Y = \lambda_Y[-c_Y dP_Y + (1 - \mu)d\omega + dt] \quad (19)$$

as before.

To find du_X, I use the Envelope Theorem. Since u_X is the value of a constrained maximization problem, du_X equals the differential of the Lagrangean for that problem, calculated holding the choice variables ξ, ζ and the multiplier γ constant. Therefore,

$$du_X = \int_0^\xi \lambda_x(x)\{[\xi - c_X(x)]dp_X + d\pi + dt\} dF(x)$$

$$+ \int_\xi^K \lambda_x(x)\{[x - c_X(x)]dp_X + d\pi + dt\} dF(x) - \gamma \int_0^\xi (\xi - x)dp_X dF(x).$$

Using (17), and recalling that $d\pi = -\mu d\omega$, this simplifies to

$$du_X = \left\{ \int_0^K \lambda_x(x)[\max(\xi,x) - c_X(x)]dF(x) - \gamma \int_0^\xi (\xi - x)dF(x) \right\} dp_X$$

$$+ \gamma \left[-\mu d\omega + dt \right]. \tag{20}$$

Now the argument proceeds as in Section 3. For equilibrium, set $du_X = du_Y = du$, say. Differentiate the government's budget constraint, and substitute the resulting dt. There is one new feature: the insurance contract makes an X-sector worker's disposable income $I(x)$ a nonlinear function of his output x. Using (14), we have

$$I(x) = p_X \max(\xi,x) + \pi + \zeta + t.$$

This finally yields

$$\frac{du[(1-\mu)\lambda_Y + \mu\gamma]}{\lambda_Y} = (1-\mu)dp_X \int_0^K [\lambda_x(x) - \gamma]\left[\frac{I(x)}{p_X} - c_X(x) \right]dF(x). \tag{21}$$

The integral on the right-hand side is the same kind of covariance as we met in Section 2 and is negative for the same reason. Therefore, the policy of keeping the producer price in the X-sector below the world price is again beneficial.

One would suspect that the larger the cost of auditing, the larger is the additional welfare gain from the tax policy. This may be another reason why it is more common for less developed countries to depress the prices of their agricultural sector below world prices. [2] However, the explanation based on the relative political powers of urban and rural groups is probably more pertinent here.

5. Concluding Remarks

In both the models considered above, insurance markets were incomplete because the outcomes of the individuals' risky activity were imperfectly observable. In both, the policy of keeping domestic producer prices *below* world prices by levying a tax, and returning the revenues by means of a lump sum grant, served to replace some of the missing insurance. In public policy discussions there is often a presumption that producers' incomes in a risky activity should be insured by offering them

---

[2] I thank a referee for this suggestion.

higher prices. My results here show that such conclusions are very sensitive to the way in which risk enters the economy and the underlying causes for the failure of markets for dealing with it. This leads to a general methodological point. It is important to specify such matters explicitly. Work such as Newbery and Stiglitz [1984] and Eaton and Grossman [1985], which fails to do so, may yield erroneous policy proposals

References

Bernanke, Ben, and Mark Gertler, "Agency costs, Collateral, and Business Fluctuations," working paper, Princeton University, 1986.

Dixit, Avinash, "Trade and Insurance with Moral Hazard," *Journal of International Economics*, XXIII (1987a), 201–20.

—, "Trade and Insurance with Adverse Selection," working paper, Princeton University, 1987b.

—, "Trade and Insurance with Imperfectly Observed Outcomes," working paper, Princeton University, 1987c.

Eaton, Jonathan, and Gene Grossman, "Tariffs as Insurance: Optimal Commercial Policy When Domestic Markets Are Incomplete," *Canadian Journal of Economics*, XVIII (1985), 258–72.

Mookherjee, Dilip, and Ivan Png, "Optimal Auditing, Insurance and Redistribution," working paper, Stanford University, 1987.

Newbery, David, and Joseph Stiglitz, *The Theory of Commodity Price Stabilization* (Oxford, England: Oxford University Press, 1981).

—, and —, "Pareto Inferior Trade," *Review of Economic Studies*, LI (1984), 1–12.

Townsend, Robert, "Optimal Contracts and Competitive Markets with Costly State Verification," *Journal of Economic Theory*, XXI (1979), 265–93.

Part 3

Exogenous Comparative Advantage: Corner Solutions in the Heckscher-Ohlin and Ricardian Models of Trade

CHAPTER 6

AN INFRAMARGINAL ANALYSIS OF
THE RICARDIAN MODEL[*]

Wen Li Cheng[a], Jeffrey Sachs[b] and Xiaokai Yang[c][+]

[a]*Law and Economics Consulting Group*   [b]*Harvard University* [c]*Harvard and*

Monash University

1. Introduction

Ricardo's theory of comparative advantage (Ricardo, 1817) is regarded as the foundation of modern trade theory. However, the Ricardian model has not attracted the attention it deserves. This lack of attention is attributable to the fact that the conventional marginal analysis is not applicable to the Ricardian model, and trade theorists have shown a remarkable insistence on the marginal technique[1].

There have been only a few nonmarginal analyses of the Ricardian model in the literature. Houthakker (1976) proposed a computational method to calculate the equilibrium pattern of division of labor in a two-country, many-commodity Ricardian model. Rosen (1978) applied

[*] Reprinted from *Review of International Economics*, 8 (2), Wen Li Cheng, Jeffrey Sachs, and Xiaokai Yang, "An Inframarginal Analysis of the Ricardian Model," 208-20, 2000, with permission from Blackwell.

[+] The authors are grateful to Elhanan Helpman, Lin Zhou, Monchi Lio, Meng-Chung Liu, the referee, and the participants of a seminar at Monash University for helpful comments. Financial support from Australian Research Council Large Grant A79602713 is gratefully acknowledged. We are solely responsible for the remaining errors.

[1] Dixit and Norman (1980) noted: "The Ricardo model is unsuitable for comparative statics. The phenomenon of multiple output choices with non-differentiable revenue functions makes it difficult to apply most standard techniques of analysis. For analyses which need single valued supply choices, therefore, attention has shifted to a post-Ricardian model" where "the factor(s) has diminishing returns in each use. Price change then cause a smooth shift of the factor from one use to another."(p.38)

linear programming to study the optimum work assignment in the presence of comparative advantage. He suggested that the notion of economies of division of labor is not a technical concept, but one that describes social interdependence (or "superadditivity" in Rosen's terminology): the more interactions among individuals, the greater scope for productivity improvement[2].

Rosen's work represents a significant step away from marginal analysis. However, designed to address a firm's work assignment problem, his model does not immediately relate to international trade. In this paper, we use a nonmarginal approach similar to Rosen's (1978) to study trade patterns and related issues in the Ricardian model. We intend to show that, with a nonmarginal approach, the original Ricardian model can offer numerous insights in a simple and intuitive way.

We refer to the nonmarginal approach used in this paper as "inframarginal analysis". This is, loosely speaking, a combination of marginal and total cost-benefit analysis. We shall discuss the features of inframarginal analysis later in this paper. In particular, we shall demonstrate that it is consistent with a decentralized decision-making process. We shall also show that when inframarginal analysis is applied, two types of comparative static analyses can be conducted. The first type is the conventional comparative statics which involve continuous changes in endogenous variables in response to a small change in a parameter. The second type involves discontinuous jumps of endogenous variables among different patterns of trade when changes in a parameter exceed certain threshold values.[3]

Using inframarginal analysis, we examine several issues associated with international division of labor. Firstly, we incorporate transaction costs into the simple 2x2 Ricardian model and analyze the relationship between transaction costs and the division of labor. According to Adam Smith (1776), the division of labor is limited by the extent of the market

---

[2] Rosen (1978) demonstrated that the ex post elasticities of substitution is not determined by the production technology, but by the division of labor corresponding to the optimum work assignment.

[3] A recent survey on the growing literature of inframaginal analysis and endogenous specialization can be found in Yang and Ng (1998).

(Chapter 3), and the extent of the market is determined by transportation costs (p.31-32). We shall formalize Smith's conjecture in our model.

Secondly, we examine the effect of a tariff in a 2x2 Ricardian model. We show that (1) if partial division of labor occurs in equilibrium, the country that produces both goods chooses a unilateral protection tariff, and the country producing a single good chooses a unilateral *laissez-faire* policy; and (2) if complete division of labor occurs in equilibrium, both countries would prefer tariff negotiation to tariff war. The tariff negotiation would lead to a bilateral *laissez-faire* regime. This result can be used to explain why a unilateral protection tariff and unilateral *laissez-faire* may coexist; and why tariff negotiations may sometimes be essential to achieving free trade. This result also appears to be consistent with our observation of a policy shift from unilateral protection tariffs to tariff negotiation and trade liberalization.

Finally, we introduce a third country to the Ricardian model.[4] We show that the country that has no comparative advantage over the other two countries, and/or which has the lowest transaction efficiency, may be excluded from trade despite its comparative advantage over one of the two countries. We use this result to examine the relationship between international competitiveness and the wealth of a nation.

Section 2 presents the Ricardian model with transaction costs and discusses the implications of inframarginal analysis. Section 3 examines the effects of a tariff. Section 4 considers a 3x2 model. The concluding section summarizes the findings of the paper and suggests possible extensions.

---

[4] Dornbusch, Fischer, and Samuelson (1977) developed a Ricardian model with a continuum of goods. Gomery (1994) and Houthakker (1976) have also introduced many goods to the Ricardian model. Future research can extend our model to include many goods and many countries. It should be noted that as the numbers of goods and countries increase, the numbers of configurations and structures increase more than proportionally. As a result the degree of complexity of the inframarginal analysis increases drastically.

2. A Simple 2x2 Ricardian Model and Inframarginal Analysis

2.1. The model setting

Under the usual assumptions of the Ricardian model, consider a world consisting of country 1 and country 2, each with M_i (i=1, 2) consumer-producers. The individuals within a country are assumed to be identical. The utility function for individuals in country i is

$$U_i = (x_i + kx_i^d)^\beta (y_i + ky_i^d)^{1-\beta},$$

where x_i and y_i are quantities of goods X and Y produced for self-consumption, x_i^d and y_i^d are quantities of the goods X and Y bought from the market, and k is the transaction efficiency coefficient. The transaction cost is assumed to take the iceberg form – for each unit of good bought, the buyer receives only a fraction, k, the rest being lost in transit.

The production functions for a consumer-producer in country i are

$$x_i + x_i^s = a_{ix}l_{ix},$$
$$y_i + y_i^s = a_{iy}l_{iy},$$

where x_i^s and y_i^s are quantities of goods X and Y sold; l_{ix} and l_{iy} are the proportions of labor devoted to the production of goods X and Y, and $l_{ix} + l_{iy} = 1$.

Each individual in country i needs to decide what and how much to produce for self-consumption, to sell and to buy from the market; that is, the individual has six choice variables: $x_i, x_i^s, x_i^d, y_i, y_i^s, y_i^d \geq 0$. We refer to each individual's choice on what to produce, buy and sell as a *configuration*. There are three types of configurations as explained below.

(1) *Self sufficiency.* This is configuration XY, where an individual produces both goods for self-consumption. This configuration is defined by $x_i, y_i > 0, x_i^s = x_i^d = y_i^s = y_i^d = 0$.

(2) *Partial specialization in the comparative-advantage good.* This is configuration XY/Y, where an individual produces both X and Y, and sells X in exchange for Y. This is defined by

$x_i, y_i, x_i^s, y_i^d > 0, x_i^d = y_i^s = 0$.   Configuration   XY/X,   where   an individual produces both X and Y, sells Y in exchange for X.   This configuration is defined by $x_i, y_i, x_i^d, y_i^s > 0, x_i^s = y_i^d = 0$.

(3) *Complete specialization in the comparative-advantage good.*   This is configuration X/Y, where an individual produces only X and sells X in exchange for Y; and configuration Y/X, where an individual produces only Y and sells Y in exchange for X. Configurations X/Y and   Y/X   are   defined   by $x_i, x_i^s, y_i^d > 0,$ $x_i^d = y_i = y_i^s = 0$ and $y_i, y_i^s, x_i^d > 0,$ $y_i^d = x_i = x_i^s = 0$, respectively.

The combination of all individual's configurations constitutes a *market structure*, or *structure* for short. Without loss of generality, we assume that country 1 has a comparative advantage in producing good X; i.e., $a_{1x}/a_{1y} > a_{2x}/a_{2y}$. Given this assumption, we identify four structures as illustrated in Figure 1.[5]

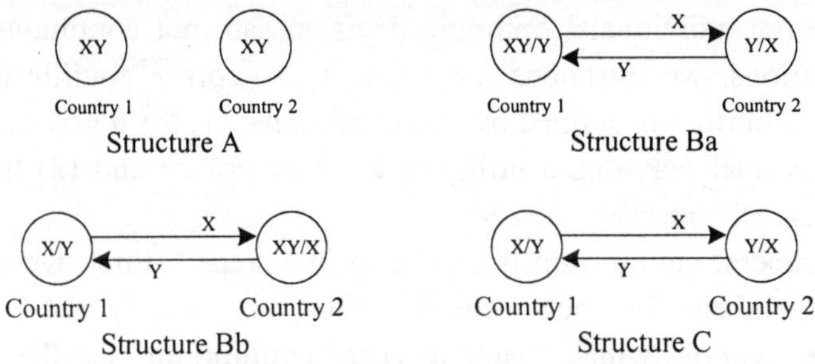

Figure 1: Configurations and Structures

Structure A is an autarky where individuals in both countries choose self-sufficiency (configuration XY).   Structures Ba and Bb are partial-division-of-labor structures where individuals in one country produce both goods X and Y and sell their comparative-advantage good in exchange for their comparative-disadvantage good. Structure C is the complete-division-of-labor structure where individuals in country 1

---

[5] It is easy to show that a country does not export its comparative disadvantage good in equilibrium.

produce X and buy Y (configuration X/Y), and individuals in country 2 produce Y and buy X (configuration Y/X).

2.2. General equilibrium and its comparative statics

The general equilibrium is defined by two conditions: (1) at a given set of prices, each individual maximizes utility with respect to configurations and quantities of production, trade, and consumption; and (2) the set of prices clears the market.

Each individual's utility-maximization decision is made using the inframarginal approach. That is, for each configuration, an individual applies marginal analysis to solve for the optimum quantities of consumption, production and trade, and then applies total cost-benefit analysis to compare his/her utility across all configurations and chooses the configuration that gives the highest utility.[6]

Since the individuals' optimum decisions are not continuous across configurations, we introduce the concept of "corner equilibrium." A corner equilibrium is defined by two conditions: (1) *for a given* structure, each individual maximizes utility at a set of prices; and (2) the set of prices clears the market.

The general equilibrium is solved in two steps. First, we solve the corner equilibria for each structure, then we identify the parameter subspace within which each corner equilibrium is the general equilibrium.

---

[6] The idea of the inframarginal approach is attributable to Coase (1946, 1960). Coase (1946) noted "a consumer does not only have to decide whether to consume additional units of a product; he has also to decide whether it is worth his while to consume the product at all rather than spend his money in some other direction" (p.173). Buchanan and Stubblebine (1962) introduced the concept of inframarginal externality which is an early application of the inframarginal analysis in welfare economics. Formally, the inframarginal analysis is associated with nonlinear or linear programming, while marginal analysis is associated with classical mathematical programming. Other applications of the inframarginal analysis can be found in Arrow, Ng, and Yang (1998), Becker (1981), Dixit (1987, 1989), Grossman and Hart (1986), Rosen (1983), and Yang and Ng (1993).

The corner equilibrium for each structure is solved by first solving the individuals' decision problems to obtain the supply and demand functions for goods X and Y, and then using the market clearing condition to find the corner equilibrium price. For instance, in structure Ba, the decision problem for individuals in country 1 is

$$\max_{x_1, x_1^s y_1, y_1^d, l_{1x}, l_{1y}} U_1 = x_1^\beta (y_1 + ky_1^d)^{1-\beta}$$

$$\text{s.t. } x_1 + x_1^s = a_{1x}l_{1x}, \quad y_1 = a_{1y}l_{1y}$$

$$y_1^d = p\, x_1^s, \quad l_{1x} + l_{1y} = 1.$$

The first-order conditions imply

$$p = a_{1y}/ka_{1x}, \quad x_1 = \beta a_{1x}, \quad x_1^s = a_{1x}(l_{1x}-\beta),$$

$$y_1 = a_{1y}(1-l_{1x}), \quad y_1^d = a_{1y}(l_{1x}-\beta)/k,$$

where $p \equiv p_x / p_y$ is the price of X in terms of Y. The decision problem for individuals in country 2 is

$$\max_{x_2^d, y_2, y_2^s} U_2 = (kx_2^d)^\beta y_2^{1-\beta}$$

$$\text{s.t. } y_2 + y_2^s = a_{2y}, \quad y_2^s = p\, x_2^d.$$

The first order conditions imply

$$x_2^d = \frac{ka_{2y}a_{1x}}{a_{1y}}\beta, \qquad y_2 = (1-\beta)a_{2y}, \qquad y_2^s = px_2^d = \beta a_{2y}.$$

From the market-clearing condition $M_1 x_1^s = M_2 x_2^d$, we obtain $l_{1x} = (ka_{2y}M_2\beta/a_{1y}M_1)+\beta$, which is less than 1 if and only if $a_{2y}/a_{1y}<M_1(1-\beta)/kM_2\beta$. That is, structure Ba is chosen only if $a_{2y}/a_{1y}<M_1(1-\beta)/kM_2\beta$.

The corner equilibria for structures A, Bb and C are solved using the same approach. The results are summarized in Table 1.

                     W. Cheng, J. Sachs, X. Yang

Table 1: Corner Equilibria

Structure	Price (p_x/p_y)	Relevant Parameter Subspace	Individual's Utility	
			Country 1	Country 2
A	NA		$U_1(A)\equiv(\beta a_{1x})^\beta$ $[(1-\beta)a_{1y}]^{1-\beta}$	$U_2(A)\equiv(\beta a_{2x})^\beta$ $[(1-\beta)a_{2y}]^{1-\beta}$
Ba	a_{1y}/ka_{1x}	$k<k_1\equiv$ $M_1a_{1y}(1-\beta)/$ $\beta M_2a_{2y}<1$	$U_1(A)$	$(k^2a_{2y}a_{1x}/a_{2x}a_{1y})^\beta$ $U_2(A)$
Bb	ka_{2y}/a_{2x}	$k<k_2\equiv$ $M_2a_{2x}\beta/$ $(1-\beta)M_1a_{1x}<1$	$(k^2a_{2y}a_{1x}/a_{2x}a_{1y})^{1-\beta}$ $U_1(A)$	$U_2(A)$
C	$\beta M_2a_{2y}/$ $M_1a_{1x}(1-\beta)$		$[\beta kM_2a_{2y}/M_1a_{1y}(1-\beta)]^{1-\beta}$ $U_1(A)$	$[(1-\beta)kM_1a_{1x}/$ $M_2a_{2x}\beta]^\beta U_2(A)$

Next, we apply the definition of general equilibrium to identify the parameter sub-spaces within which each of the structures listed in Table 1 occurs in general equilibrium. Consider structure Ba first. Structure Ba is the general equilibrium structure if the following three conditions hold.

First, under the corner equilibrium relative price in this structure $p = a_{1y}/ka_{1x}$, individuals in country 2 prefer specialization in Y (configuration Y/X) to the alternatives, namely autarky (configuration A) and specialization in X (configuration X/Y). In other words, the following conditions hold:

$$U_2(Y/X) \geq U_2(A) \quad \text{which holds iff } k \geq k_0 \equiv [(a_{2x}/a_{2y})/(a_{1x}/a_{1y})]^{0.5}; \qquad (1a)$$

$$U_2(Y/X) \geq U_2(X/Y) \quad \text{which holds iff } k \geq k_3 \equiv [(a_{2x}/a_{2y})/(a_{1x}/a_{1y})]^{0.5/\beta}. \qquad (1b)$$

Second, general equilibrium requires that all individuals in country 1 prefer configuration XY/Y to the alternatives; that is:

$$U_1(XY/Y) \geq U_1(X/Y) \quad \text{which holds iff } a_{1y}/a_{1x} \geq kp = a_{1y}/a_{1x}; \qquad (2a)$$

$$U_1(XY/Y) \geq U_1(Y/X) \quad \text{which holds iff } 1 \geq k. \qquad (2b)$$

Third, no individual in country 1 is completely specialized in X; i.e.,

$$l_{1x} < 1, \text{which holds iff } k < k_1 \equiv a_{1y}M_1(1-\beta)/a_{2y}M_2\beta. \qquad (3)$$

As $k_3 \geq k_0$, it follows that conditions (1)-(3) hold if $k \in (k_0, k_1)$. Since $k_0 < k_1$ holds iff $M_1(1-\beta)/M_2\beta > [(a_{2x}a_{2y})/(a_{1x}a_{1y})]^{0.5}$, the corner equilibrium in structure Ba is the general equilibrium if $k \in (k_0, k_1)$ and $M_1(1-\beta)/M_2\beta > [(a_{2x}a_{2y})/(a_{1x}a_{1y})]^{0.5}$, where $k_1 \equiv a_{1y}M_1(1-\beta)/a_{2y}M_2\beta$.

Similarly, we can identify the conditions for other structures to occur in general equilibrium. These conditions are summarized in Table 2

$$\text{where,} \quad k_0 \equiv (\frac{a_{1y}a_{2x}}{a_{2y}a_{1x}})^{\frac{1}{2}}, \quad k_1 \equiv \frac{M_1 a_{1y}(1-\beta)}{M_2 a_{2y}\beta}, \quad k_2 \equiv \frac{M_2 a_{2x}\beta}{M_1 a_{1x}(1-\beta)}.$$

Table 2: General Equilibrium

Parameter	$k < k_0$	$k > k_0$			
Subspaces		$\dfrac{M_1}{M_2} > (\dfrac{a_{2x}a_{2y}}{a_{1x}a_{1y}})^{\frac{1}{2}}\dfrac{\beta}{1-\beta}$		$\dfrac{M_1}{M_2} < (\dfrac{a_{2x}a_{2y}}{a_{1x}a_{1y}})^{\frac{1}{2}}\dfrac{\beta}{1-\beta}$	
		$k \in (k_0,k_1)$	$k \in (k_1,1)$	$k \in (k_0,k_2)$	$k \in (k_2,1)$
General Equilibrium Structure	A	Ba	C	Bb	C

It is clear from Table 2 that, given the parameter values, the general equilibrium is unique. Given $k < k_0$, the general equilibrium structure is autarky (structure A). Given $k > k_0$ and $M_1/M_2 > (a_{2x}a_{2y}/a_{1x}a_{1y})^{0.5}[\beta/(1-\beta)]$, the general equilibrium structure is structure Ba if $k < k_1$, and is structure

C if $k \in (k_1, 1)$. Given $k > k_0$ and $M_1/M_2 < (a_{2x}a_{2y}/a_{1x}a_{1y})^{0.5}[\beta/(1-\beta)]$, the general equilibrium is structure Bb if $k < k_2$, and is structure C if $k \in (k_2, 1)$.

It is interesting to see from Table 1 and Table 2 that, under certain conditions, only when both countries have *absolute advantage* in their comparative advantage goods can structure C be the general equilibrium structure. For instance, if $[M_1(1-\beta)]/(M_2\beta) = 1$ (which holds if, but not only if, both countries are of similar size and consumers' preference for both goods are similar), we have $k_1 = a_{1y}/a_{2y}$, and the parameter subspace $M_1/M_2 > (a_{2x}a_{2y}/a_{1x}a_{1y})^{0.5}[\beta/(1-\beta)]$ is redefined by $(a_{2x}a_{2y})/(a_{1x}/a_{1y}) < 1$. Since $k \in (0,1)$, $k > k_1$ can be satisfied only if $a_{2y} > a_{1y}$. For $k > k_1$ to hold within this parameter subspace, it is also necessary that $a_{1x} > a_{2x}$. Therefore, if $[M_1(1-\beta)]/(M_2\beta) = 1$ and $(a_{2x}a_{2y})/(a_{1x}/a_{1y}) < 1$, complete division of labor can occur in general equilibrium *only* if both countries have absolute advantage in their comparative-advantage good. A similar result can be found in Chipman (1965, 1979), although his models did not incorporate positive transaction costs.

Based on the results in Table 2, we can conduct two types of comparative static analyses of the general equilibrium. The first type is the conventional comparative static analysis for a given structure – the equilibrium price, quantities of goods and the numbers of individuals selling different goods change continuously in response to a continuous change in parameters. The second type of comparative static analysis examines how changes in parameters generate shifts of the general equilibrium across corner equilibria. It shows that the general equilibrium price, quantities, and indirect utility functions can jump discontinuously between corner equilibria as parameters reach some critical values. Suppose the general equilibrium is initially at structure A; as the transaction efficiency coefficient (k) increases from a low value to k_0, and then to k_1 or k_2, the general equilibrium jumps from autarky to partial division of labor, and then to complete division of labor. Whether the transitional structure is Ba or Bb depends on the relative size and relative productivity of the two countries, and individuals' relative preference over the two goods. As the general equilibrium pattern of division of labor changes, the equilibrium price also changes discontinuously, as do individuals' utility levels.

Note that the eight-dimension $(\beta, a_{1x}, a_{1y}, a_{2x}, a_{2y}, M_1, M_2, k)$ parameter space is completely partitioned into subspaces within each of which a particular corner equilibrium is the general equilibrium. Each parameter subspace is defined in terms of relative population size (M_1/M_2), relative tastes $(\beta/(1-\beta))$, and relative production condition $((a_{1x}/a_{2x}), (a_{1y}/a_{2y}))$. A change in any of these parameters could cause the general equilibrium to shift from one structure to another. For instance, for a given degree of comparative advantage, a sufficiently large increase in transaction efficiency can cause the general equilibrium to jump from autarky to partial division of labor. Conversely, for a given level of transaction efficiency, a sufficiently large increase in the degree of comparative advantage can shift the general equilibrium from autarky to the partial division of labor as well. In this sense, the inframarginal comparative statics reveal the degree of substitution between parameters in causing the general equilibrium to jump discontinuously.

From the above analysis, we have the following proposition.

Proposition 1: The general equilibrium structure is determined by the level of transaction efficiency, the relative productivity and relative population size of the two countries, and individuals' relative preference over the two goods. Given other parameters, improvements in transaction efficiency can make the general equilibrium structure jump from autarky to partial division of labor and then to complete division of labor.

Proposition 1 implies that transaction efficiency plays an important role in determining the size of the market, and the size of the market in turn determines the equilibrium pattern and level of the division of labor. Thus, we have formalized Smith's (1776) conjecture that the division of labor is limited by the extent of the market, and the extent of the market is determined by transportation costs.

It is interesting to note that in our model, an increase in transaction efficiency coefficient (k) can increase total transaction costs. This is because the increase in k can generate a jump of the general equilibrium from a low level of division of labor to a higher level, thus increasing the total number of transactions. This implication can be used to explain why the income share of transaction costs has increased as transaction efficiency improves (North, 1986).

3.   A 2x2 Ricardian Model with Tariff

Based on the model in section 2, suppose that country i ($i = 1, 2$) imposes an *ad valorem* tariff of rate t_i, and transfers all tariff revenue equally to all individuals in country i.   Individuals take the amount of transfer as given.   In equilibrium, the amount of transfer equals tariff revenue. We also assume that the transaction efficiency coefficient (k_i, $i=1,2$) can differ in the two counties. Using the same procedure as in section 2, we can solve for the corner equilibrium for each structure.   The corner equilibrium solutions are presented in Table 3, where

$$D_1 \equiv (1+t_1)[1+(1-\beta)t_2]/(1+\beta t_1)$$

$$D_2 \equiv (1+\beta t_1)(1+t_2)/[1+(1+\beta)t_2]$$

$$L_{1x} = \beta + (M_1/M_2)(k_1\beta a_{2y}/a_{1y})\{(1+\beta t_1)/(1+t_1)[1+t_2-\beta t_2]\} > \beta$$

$$T_1 \equiv [(1+t_1)(1+t_2-\beta t_2)]^{-1}[(1+t_2)/(1+t_2-\beta t_2)]^{(1-\beta)/\beta}$$

$$L_{2x} = \beta - (M_1/M_2)[k_2(1-\beta)a_{2x}/a_{1x}]\{(1+t_2-\beta t_2)/[(1+\beta t_1)(1+t_2)]\} < \beta$$

$$T_2 \equiv [(1+t_2)(1+\beta t_1)]^{-1}[(1+t_1)/(1+\beta t_1)]^{\beta/(1-\beta)}$$

$$T_3 \equiv (1+t_2-\beta t_2)^{-1}[(1+t_1)/(1+\beta t_1)]^{\beta/(1-\beta)}$$

$$T_4 \equiv (1+\beta t_1)^{-1}[(1+t_2)/(1+t_2-\beta t_2)]^{(1-\beta)/\beta}$$

Table 3: Corner Equilibria

Structure	Price (p_x / p_y)	Relevant Parameter Subspace	Individual Utility	
			Country 1	Country 2
A	NA		$U_1(A)$ $\equiv (\beta a_{1x})^\beta$ $[(1-\beta)a_{1y}]^{1-\beta}$	$U_2(A)$ $\equiv (\beta a_{2x})^\beta$ $[(1-\beta)a_{2y}]^{1-\beta}$
Ba	$(1+t_1)$ $a_{1y} / k_1 a_{1x}$	$k_1 < (M_1 / M_2)$ $[(1-\beta)/\beta]$ $(a_{1y}/a_{2y})D_1$	$[(1+L_{1x}t_1)/$ $(1+\beta t_1)]$ $U_1(A)$	$[k_1 k_2 (a_{1x}a_{2y})/$ $(a_{1y}a_{2x})]^\beta$ $T_1^\beta U_2(A)$
Bb	$k_2 a_{2y} /$ $[a_{2x}(1+t_2)]$	$k_2 < (M_2 / M_1)$ $[\beta/(1-\beta)]$ $(a_{2x}/a_{1x})D_2$	$[k_1 k_2 (a_{1x}a_{2y})/$ $(a_{1y}a_{2x})]^{1-\beta}$ $T_2^{1-\beta} U_1(A)$	$[(1+t_2 - t_2 L_{2x})/$ $(1+t_2 - \beta t_2)]$ $U_2(A)$
C	(M_2 / M_1) $[\beta/(1-\beta)]$ (a_{2y}/a_{1x}) $[(1+\beta t_1)/$ $(1+(1-\beta)t_2)]$		$\{(k_1 M_2 / M_1)$ $[\beta/(1-\beta)]$ $(a_{2y}/a_{1y})\}^{1-\beta}$ $T_3^{1-\beta} U_1(A)$	$\{(k_2 M_1 / M_2)$ $[(1-\beta)/\beta]$ $(a_{1x}/a_{2x})\}^\beta$ $T_4^\beta U_2(A)$

It is easy to see that if $t_1 = t_2 = 0$ and $k_1 = k_2$, Table 3 reduces to Table 1. If $t_1 = t_2 = 0$, the textbook Ricardian model predicts that the country which produces both goods does not get any gains from trade. This result can be clearly seen from Table 1 – when the general equilibrium occurs in structure Ba (or Bb), individuals in country 1 (or country 2) which produces both goods X and Y get the same level of utility as they do in autarky.

The story is different when a tariff is introduced. Refer to Table 3. If the general equilibrium occurs in structure Ba (or Bb), individuals in the country producing both goods (the "two-good" country) get a higher utility than they do in autarky. Moreover, in structure Ba, $\partial U_1/\partial t_1 > 0$ (or in structure Bb, $\partial U_2/\partial t_2 > 0$), which means that, given the tariff rate of the country producing one good (the "one-good" country), the "two-good" country can improve its own welfare by raising its tariff rate. This is because the "two-good" country determines the terms of trade, and it can improve its terms of trade by imposing a tariff. The "two-good" country's gain is at the expense of the "one-good" country as $\partial U_2/\partial t_1 < 0$ in structure Ba and $\partial U_1/\partial t_2 < 0$ in structure Bb. Although the "one-good" country may impose a tariff in retaliation, doing so would hurt itself because it has no influence on the terms of trade—as can be derived from Table 3, $\partial U_2/\partial t_2 < 0$ in structure Ba and $\partial U_1/\partial t_1 < 0$ in structure Bb. However, it is not in the interest of the "two-good" country to raise the tariff indefinitely, because there is a level where the tariff becomes prohibitive, which can drag both countries back to autarky and eliminate the gains from gain completely.

If both countries can influence the terms of trade (as in structure C), then the gains from trade are shared between the two countries. However, since $\partial U_1/\partial t_1 > 0$ and $\partial U_2/\partial t_2 > 0$ in structure C (i.e., each country can benefit from raising its own tariff given the other country's tariff rate), each country will be tempted to raise its own tariff. But if they both raise their tariff, both can be worse off as in structure C $\partial U_1/\partial t_2 < 0$ and $\partial U_2/\partial t_1 < 0$. If one country raises its tariff to a sufficiently high level, the other country may withdraw from trade and the equilibrium structure can jump discontinuously from trade to autarky. Since each country can hurt the other country by imposing a tariff, and each can benefit from a lower tariff in the other country, there are obvious ($t_1 = t_2 = 0$) gains to be had through tariff negotiations. Maximization of the Nash product $V = [U_1(C) - U_1(A)][U_2(C) - U_2(A)]$ with respect to t_1 and t_2 shows that such negotiations can lead to free trade between the two countries.

Summarizing the above analysis, we have the next proposition.

Proposition 2: (1) If partial division of labor occurs in equilibrium, the country that produces both goods can improve its welfare by imposing a tariff as long as the tariff is not prohibitive. In contrast, the country that produces a single good will be better off choosing unilateral trade liberalization.

(2) If complete division of labor occurs in equilibrium, then both countries can influence the terms of trade and have an incentive to impose a tariff. However, tariff could hurt both countries. The two countries could achieve mutual gains through tariff negotiations. These tariff negotiations could lead to free trade between the two countries.

Proposition 2 has two implications. First, in the Walrasian equilibrium with zero tariff, the country that produces both goods does not get any gains from trade. When a tariff is introduced to the model, the country that produces both goods can get most of the gains from trade through imposing a tariff. In a sense, a tariff becomes an instrument to alter the distribution of the gains of trade among trading countries.

Second, when transaction efficiency is at an intermediate level such that the general equilibrium involves partial division of labor, some countries could improve their welfare by imposing a tariff whereas other countries would be better off with a unilateral *laissez-faire* regime. As transaction efficiency improves, all countries may prefer tariff negotiations, which would lower tariffs and could lead to free trade. This result suggests that tariff and unilateral liberalization may coexist at early stages of economic development; and trade negotiation and liberalization may be preferred in later stages. This appears to be broadly consistent with the historical evolution of tariff policies. In sixteenth-century England, a unilateral tariff was advocated by mercantilists as a means of rent-seeking in international trade (Ekelund and Tollison, 1981). Tariffs gave way to trade liberalization during 1846-1860 (Kenwood and Loughleed, 1992; Bairoch, 1993). As major European countries became industrialized, protectionism came back in 1878-1913. After the Second World War, many developing countries adopted unilateral tariff protection. More recently, tariff negotiations have become increasingly prevalent.

4.   A 3x2 Ricardian Model

In this section, we extend the simple 2x2 Ricardian model to include a third country, country 3. It is assumed that transaction conditions are different from country to country such that k_1, $k_3 > k_2$, where k_i is the transaction efficiency coefficient in country i.   We intend to show that a country that does not have a comparative advantage to the other two countries and/or which has low transaction efficiency can be excluded from trade.

Assume that the production functions in country i ($i = 1, 2, 3$) are the same as in subsection 2.1.   Assume further that $(a_{3x}/a_{3y}) < (a_{2x}/a_{2y}) < (a_{1x}/a_{1y})$. That is, country 1 has a comparative advantage in good X; country 3 has a comparative advantage in good Y; country 2 has a comparative advantage over country 3 in good X, and a comparative advantage in good Y over country 1.

We consider only the case where the trading countries are completely specialized. We prove that if in equilibrium only two of the three countries trade, the two trading countries must be country 1 and country 3.   In other words, country 2, or the country that has the lowest transaction efficiency and/or has no comparative advantage to the other two countries may be excluded from trade.

Suppose only country 1 and country 2 trade.   This can occur in general equilibrium only if individuals in country 2 prefer specialization in Y (or configuration Y/X) to autarky, and individuals in country 3 prefer autarky to specialization in Y.   That is, the following inequalities hold:

$$U_2(Y/X) > U_2(A) \quad \text{which holds iff } p<(a_{2y}/a_{2x})k_2; \text{ and}$$
$$U_3(Y/X) < U_3(A) \quad \text{which holds iff } p>(a_{3y}/a_{3x})k_3;$$

where the indirect utility functions for different configurations are from Table 1. The two inequalities jointly imply $(a_{2x}/a_{2y}k_2)<(a_{3x}/a_{3y}k_3)$ which contradicts the assumption $(a_{2x}/a_{2y})>(a_{3x}/a_{3y})$ and $k_2 < k_3$.

Suppose instead only country 2 and country 3 trade.   This can occur in general equilibrium only if:

$$U_2(X/Y) > U_2(A) \quad \text{which holds iff } p>a_{2y}/a_{2x}k_2; \text{ and}$$
$$U_1(X/Y) < U_1(A) \quad \text{which holds iff } p<a_{1y}/a_{1x}k_1.$$

The two inequalities jointly imply $(a_{1y}/a_{1x}k_1)>(a_{2y}/a_{2x}k_2)$, which contradicts the assumption, $(a_{1x}/a_{1y})>(a_{2x}/a_{2y})$ and $k_2 < k_1$.

Next we examine the conditions under which the structure involving trade between only country 1 and country 3 occurs in general equilibrium. The conditions are:

$$U_1(X/Y) > U_1(Y/X) \quad \text{which holds iff } p > (a_{1y}/a_{1x})k_1^{2\beta-1};$$
$$U_1(X/Y) > U_1(A) \quad \text{which holds iff } p > a_{1y}/a_{1x}k_1;$$
$$U_2(X/Y) < U_2(A) \quad \text{which holds iff } p < a_{2y}/a_{2x}k_2;$$
$$U_2(Y/X) < U_2(A) \quad \text{which holds iff } p > (a_{2y}/a_{2x})k_2;$$
$$U_3(Y/X) > U_3(A) \quad \text{which holds iff } p < (a_{3y}/a_{3x})k_3;$$
$$U_3(Y/X) > U_3(X/Y) \quad \text{which holds iff } p < (a_{3y}/a_{3x})k_3^{2\beta-1};$$

where $p = a_{3y}M_3\beta/a_{1x}M_1(1-\beta)$ is the corner equilibrium relative price in this structure.

The six inequalities together imply $\min\{a_{2y}/a_{2x}k_2, (a_{3y}/a_{3x})k_3\} > a_{3y}M_3\beta/a_{1x}M_1(1-\beta) > \max\{a_{1y}/a_{1x}k_1, (a_{2y}/a_{2x})k_2\}$. The parameter subspace satisfying this condition is certainly not empty. For instance, if k_2 is sufficiently close to 0, and k_1 and k_3 are sufficiently close to 1, then the above condition becomes $(a_{3y}/a_{3x})k_3 > a_{3y}M_3\beta/a_{1x}M_1(1-\beta) > a_{1y}/a_{1x}k_1$, or $(a_{1x}/a_{3x})k_3 > M_3\beta/M_1(1-\beta) > a_{1y}/a_{3y}k_1$, which holds if $k_3k_1[(a_{1x}/a_{1y})/(a_{3x}/a_{3y})] > 1$. This condition can be satisfied if the relative population size is not too far away from a balance with relative tastes, the two countries' transaction conditions are sufficiently good, and the degree of comparative advantage (measured by $(a_{1x}/a_{1y})/(a_{3x}/a_{3y})$) between the two countries is great. Thus we conclude with our final proposition.

Proposition 3: In a 3x2 Ricardian model, it is possible that the country that has no comparative advantage in producing any good over both of its potential trading partners, and/or that has very low transaction efficiency will be excluded from trade.

This proposition is relevant to the recent debate on international competitiveness. Krugman (1994) says promoting free trade rather than international competitiveness should be the focus of nations. He went further to suggest that the emphasis on international competitiveness could be "a dangerous obsession". Sachs (1996a,b) and Prestowitz et. al. (1994), on the other hand, contend that international competitiveness plays an essential role in improving national welfare. Proposition 3 implies that comparative advantage is not enough for realizing gains from trade. A country can be excluded from trade even if it has comparative advantage over another country, if it is uncompetitive in the sense that it has low transaction efficiency and/or it has no comparative advantage in producing a good over both of its potential trading partners.

However, the proposition also supports Krugman's argument that a country should focus on promoting free trade and improving transaction efficiency. In our model, free trade can be promoted through reducing tariff and non-tariff barriers of trade so as to improve transaction efficiency k. Since the improvement in transaction efficiency can generate a jump of general equilibrium from a low level of division of labor to a high level of division of labor, the argument for free trade is even stronger than what conventional marginal analysis suggests. Therefore, both international competitiveness and free trade are important to a country's welfare. Krugman's emphasis on trade liberalization is particularly relevant if the pursuit of international competitiveness is used as an excuse for impeding free trade.

5. Conclusion

We have studied a general equilibrium 2x2 Ricardian model using inframarginal analysis. Departing from the neoclassical paradigm where individuals' levels of specialization are not endogenized, we explain international trade by individuals' choices of levels and patterns of specialization. In our analysis, the comparative statics involve discontinuous jumps—as transaction efficiency improves, the general equilibrium structure may jump from autarky to partial division of labor and then to complete division of labor. This result is consistent with historical evidence documented in North (1958) and North and Weingast (1989), and is supported by empirical studies by Barro (1997), Easton and Walker (1997), Frye and Shleifer (1997), Gallup and Sachs (1998), and Sachs and Warner (1995, 1997).

We have also examined the choice and effects of tariff. If the general equilibrium involves partial division of labor, the country producing both goods would impose a tariff and get most gains from trade. In contrast, the completely specialized country would be better off choosing a unilateral *laissez-faire* regime. If the complete division of labor occurs in equilibrium, then both countries can influence the terms of trade and can achieve mutual gains through trade negotiation. Tariff negotiations can lead to free trade.

Finally, we have shown that in a 3x2 model the country that does not have a comparative advantage over the other two countries, and/or that has low transaction efficiency, may be excluded from trade.

A logical extension of this paper is to incorporate fixed learning costs and other types of increasing returns to specialization to the Ricardian model. The economies of specialization will generate endogenous comparative advantage (Yang, 1994). It will be interesting to see how exogenous and endogenous comparative advantage interact, and what implications such interactions would generate. Also, more goods and countries may be introduced into our model to test the robustness of our results.

References

Arrow, Ken., Ng, Yew-Kwang, and Yang, Xiaokai eds. (1998), *Increasing Returns and Economics Analysis*, London, Macmillan.

Bairoch, Paul (1993), *Economics and World History*, Chicago, University of Chicago Press.

Barro, Robert (1997), *Determinants of Economic Growth*, Cambridge, MA, MIT Press.

Becker, Gary (1981), *A Treatise on the Family*, Cambridge, Massachusetts, Harvard University Press.

Buchanan, James M., and Stubblebine, W. Craig (1962), "Externality," *Economica*, 29, 371-84.

Chipman, John (1965), "A Survey of the Theory of International Trade, Part 1, the Classical Theory," *Econometrica*, 33(3), 477-519.

Chipman, John (1979), "Mill's 'Superstructure': How Well Does it Stand up?" *History of Political Economy*, 11(4), 477-504.

Coase, Ronald (1946), "The Marginal Cost Controversy," *Economica*, 13, 169-82.

Coase, Ronald (1960), "The Problem of Social Cost," *Journal of Law and Economics*, 3, 1-44.

Dixit, Avinish (1987), "Trade and Insurance with Moral Hazard," *Journal of International Economics*, 23, 201-20.

Dixit, Avinish (1989), "Trade and Insurance with Adverse Selection," *Review of Economic Studies*, 56, 235-48.

Dixit, Avinish and Norman, V. (1980), *Theory of International Trade,* Cambridge: Cambridge University Press.

Dornbusch, Rudiger, Fischer, Stanley, and Samuelson, Paul A. (1977), "Comparative Advantage, Trade, and Payments in a Ricardian Model with a Continuum of Goods," *American Economic Review*, 67, 823-39

Easton, Stephen and Walker, Michael (1997), "Income, Growth, and Economic Freedom", *American Economic Review, Papers and Proceedings*, 87, 328-32.

Ekelund, Robert and Tollison, Robert (1981), *Merchantilism as an Rent-seeking Society*, College Station, TX, Texas A & M University Press.

Frye, Timothy and Shleifer, Andrei (1997), "The Invisible Hand and the Grabbing Hand," *American Economic Review, Papers and Proceedings*, 87, 354-58.

Gallup, John and Sachs, Jeff (1998), "Geography and Economic Development," Working Paper, Harvard Institute for International Development.

Gomory, Ralph, E. (1994), "A Ricardo Model with Economies of Scale," *Journal of Economic Theory*, 62, 394-419.

Grossman, Saddty and Hart, Oliver (1986), "The Costs and Benefits of Ownership: A Theory of Vertical and Lateral Integration," *Journal of Political Economy*, 94, 691-719.

Houthakker, Hendrik S. (1976), "The Calculation of Bilateral Trade Patterns in a Ricardian Model with Intermediate Products and Barriers to Trade," *Journal of International Economics,* 6, 251-288.

Kenwood, A. G. and A. L. Loughleed (1992), *The Growth of the International Economy 1820-1990*, New York, Routledge.

Krugman, Paul (1994), "Competitiveness: A Dangerous Obsession," *Foreign Affairs*, 73(2), 28-44.

North, Douglas (1958), "Ocean Freight Rates and Economic Development", *Journal of Economic History*, 18, 537-55.

North, Douglas (1986), "Measuring the Transaction Sector in the American Economy", in S. Eugerman and R. Gallman, eds., *Long Term Trends in the American Economy*, Chicago, University of Chicargo Press.

North, Douglass and Weingast, Barry (1989), "Constitutions and Commitment: The Evolution of Institutions Governing Public Choice in Seventeenth-Century England," *Journal of Economic History*, 49, 803-32.

Prestowitz, Clyde V. Jr et al. (1994), "The Fight over Competitiveness," *Foreign Affairs*, 73(4), 186-197.

Ricardo, David (1817), *The Principles of Political Economy and Taxation,* London, J.M. Dent & Sons Ltd, 1965.

Rosen, Sherwin (1978), "Substitution and the Division of Labor," *Economica*, 45, 235-50.

Rosen, Sherwin (1983), "Specialization and Human Capital," *Journal of Labor Economics*, 1, 43-49.

Sachs, Jeff (1996a), "The Tankers Are Turning - Sachs on Competitiveness," *World Link*, September/October 1996.

Sachs, Jeff (1996b), "On the Tigers Trail, - Sachs on Competitiveness," *World Link*, November/December 1996.

Sachs, Jeffrey and Warner, Andrew (1997): "Fundamental Sources of Long-Run Growth." *American Economic Review, Papers and Proceedings*, 87, 184-88.

Smith, Adam (1776), *An Inquiry into the Nature and Causes of the Wealth of Nations*, reprint, Oxford, Clarendon Press, 1976.

Yang, Xiaokai (1994), "Endogenous vs. Exogenous Comparative Advantages and Economies of Specialization vs. Economies of Scale," *Journal of Economics*, 60, 29-54.

Yang, Xiaokai and Ng, Siang (1998), "Specialization and Division of Labor: A Survey," in K. Arrow, Y-K Ng and X, Yang eds., *Increasing Returns and Economics Analysis*, London, Macmillan.

Yang, Xiaokai and Ng, Yew-Kwang (1993), *Specialization and Economic Organization, a New Classical Microeconomic Framework*, Amsterdam, North-Holland.

CHAPTER 7

**A RICARDIAN MODEL WITH ENDOGENOUS
COMPARATIVE ADVANTAGE AND
ENDOGENOUS TRADE POLICY REGIMES**[*]

Wen Li Cheng[a], Meng-Chun Liu[b] and Xiaokai Yang[c][*]

*[a]Law and Economics Consulting Group   [b]Monash University   [c]Harvard and
Monash University*

1. Introduction

It is a well-accepted idea that free international trade benefits all
countries involved; it is also a well-known fact that hardly any country
has always adopeted free trade policies.   Why do countries deviate from
the free trade regime?   Traditional trade theory contends that
governments set up trade barriers because of political pressure from
interest groups – since imports competition poses a threat to some
domestic industries, these industries lobby intensely for trade protection
(Krueger 1974, Pincus 1975, Mayer 1984).   Other studies suggest that
governments are tempted to use trade bargaining to get a larger share of
the gains from trade (see, for instance, Morishima, 1989).   We can
identify three lines of research in trade bargaining.   The first line builds
on the theory of optimum tariff (Johnson 1954), and uses bargaining
games to model trade negotiations between governments (Mayer 1981,
Riezman 1982).   The second line of research belongs to the literature of

---

[*] Reprinted from *Economic Record*, 76 (233), Wen Li Cheng, Meng-Chun Liu, and Xiaokai
Yang, "A Ricardian Model with Endogenous Comparative Advantage and Endogenous
Trade Policy Regimes," 172-82, 2000, with permission from Balckwell.

[*] We are grateful for financial support from the Australian Research Council and for
comments from two referees. The remaining errors are ours.

109

the "new trade theory". It assumes an oligopolistic market structure in international trade, where governments adopt strategic trade policies to gain the economic rent associated with market power (Dixit and Kyle 1985, Krugman 1986, Grossman and Richardson 1986). The third line of research views international negotiations as a two-level game: at the first level, interest groups lobby for trade policies in their favor, which determines governments' policy preference; at the second level, the negotiation between governments determines the international equilibrium (Grossman and Helpman 1994, 1995a, 1995b).

While the existing literature provides insights as to why a particular trade regime may exist, it is silent about how it might evolve and how the equilibrium trade regime might relate to the equilibrium level of international division of labour which is affected by transaction conditions. The purpose of this paper is to study the equilibrium level of division of labour based on individuals' production and trade decisions, and to examine the general equilibrium implication of the inter-dependence between the level of division of labour and the degree of trade liberalisation.

In this paper, we develop a Ricardian model with transaction costs and endogenous comparative advantage[1]. In our model, individuals are consumer-producers, they choose first what and then how much to produce and trade. The governments make decisions on trade policies: they can choose to play a Nash tariff game, to have Nash tariff negotiations, or to have *laissez faire* policies. We show that as transaction conditions improve, the equilibrium level of division of labour increases. In the process of moving to a high level of division of labour, a country may receive more gains from trade even if its terms of trade deteriorate. This is because an expansion of the network size of division of labour can generate productivity gains that outweigh the adverse effect of the terms of trade deterioration.

---

[1] Yang and Borland (1991) and Yang (1994) draw the distinction between endogenous and exogenous comparative advantages. *Endogenous comparative advantage* results from an individual's *ex post* choice of the pattern and level of specialization in producing a certain good. *Exogenous comparative advantage* is generated by the *ex ante* differences (in tastes, in endowments, or in production functions) between individuals.

If a high level of division of labour occurs in general equilibrium, each country has some power to affect the terms of trade and has an incentive to impose a tariff. If both countries play a Nash tariff game (i.e., to choose a tariff rate taking the other country's tariff as given), there is a risk of a tariff war which can dissipate all the gains from trade.   Facing this risk, all governments would prefer trade negotiations over a trade war.   A Nash tariff negotiation would result in zero tariff rates. If a medium level of division of labour occurs in general equilibrium, i.e., one country completely specialises in producing one good while the other produces two goods, then unilateral tariff protection and unilateral *laissez faire* policies would coexist.

The result of our model suggests that the development in the level and pattern of international division of labour may be a driving force behind the evolution of the international trade regime.   This may explain the policy transformation in some European governments from Mercantilism to *laissez faire* in the 18th and 19th century and policy changes in developing countries from protection tariff to trade liberalisation and tariff negotiation.[2] The result also provides an economic rationale for trade negotiations and highlights the importance of trade negotiations in achieving stable trade liberalisation.

Two features distinguish our work from other studies on the Ricardian model. First, in our model, domestic trade and international trade may coexist due to the coexistence of endogenous and exogenous comparative advantages.   Second, we use infra-marginal analysis rather than marginal analysis.   Infra-marginal analysis is the combination of a total benefit-cost analysis between corner and interior solutions, and a marginal analysis of each corner or interior solution. The use of infra-marginal analysis allows us to study discontinuous changes of trade structures.

The rest of this paper is organised as follows.   Section 2 presents a simple Ricardian model with transaction costs and endogenous

---

[2] Mercantilism advocates the use of unilateral tariff as a means of rent seeking in international trade (Ekelund and Tollison 1981). A shift of trade policy regime from unilateral tariff to trade liberalisation is considered by some development economists as a shift from import substitution to export substitution strategy (see, for instance, Balassa 1980 and Bruton 1998).

comparative advantage, and discusses the relationship between transaction costs and the equilibrium level of division of labour. Section 3 introduces government policy choices into the model and investigates the endogeneity of trade policy regimes.

2.   A General Equilibrium Ricardian Model

2.1. The 2x2 model

Consider a world of two countries, country 1 and country 2, each with M_i (i=1, 2) individual consumer-producers.   Assume that the individuals are *ex ante* identical within each country and have the following utility function

$$U_i = (x_i + k_i x_i^d)^\beta (y_i + k_i y_i^d)^{1-\beta}$$

where x_i, y_i are quantities of goods X and Y self-provided, and x_i^d, y_i^d are quantities of the goods bought from the market. We follow the common practice in recent literature of equilibrium models with increasing returns and transaction costs (see Krugman and Venables 1995, for instance) and specify an iceberg transaction cost coefficient, avoiding formidable indices of destinations and origins of each transaction. The transaction condition coefficient is k_i ($k_i \in [0, 1]$): for each unit of good bought, only the fraction k_i is received by the buyer, $1-k_i$ is lost in transit.

The production functions for an individual in country i are

$$x_i + x_i^s = \text{Max}\{a_{ix}(l_{ix} - b), \, 0\},$$

$$y_i + y_i^s = \text{Max}\{a_{iy}(l_{iy} - b), \, 0\},$$

where l_{ix} and l_{iy} are respective amounts of labour devoted to producing good X and good Y, and $l_{ix} + l_{iy} = 1$.   Following Babbage (1832) and Houthakker (1956), we specify an individual-specific fixed learning cost in producing each good, b, which may be training costs or costs incurred in a trial-and-error learning process in production.

Country 1 is assumed to have exogenous comparative advantage in producing good X, that is, $a_{1x}/a_{1y} > a_{2x}/a_{2y}$. The existence of a fixed learning cost implies that specialising in a single good would increase utilisation rate of the fixed learning cost and improve labour productivity

(Becker 1981 and Rosen 1983). The relative productivity advantage obtained through decisions regarding specialisation is referred to as endogenous comparative advantage (Yang 1994). Endogenous comparative advantage can be the source of the gains from trade when exogenous comparative advantage is absent. When both exogenous and endogenous comparative advantage are present, they interact with each other to determine the pattern of trade[3].

The decision problem for an individual in country i involves choosing *what and how much* to produce for self consumption, to sell and to buy from the market. That is, there are six choice variables in the individual's decision problem $x_i, x_i^s, x_i^d, y_i, y_i^s, y_i^d \geq 0$. We refer to each individual's choice of *what* to produce, buy and sell as a *configuration*, and the combination of all individuals' configurations in both countries that is compatible with market clearing as a *market structure*, or *structure* for short.

There are five possible structures in our model: structures A, D, Pa, Pb, and C. Structure A is an autarkical structure where each individual produces both goods for self consumption (configuration XY), and does not trade with one another. In structure D, there is trade within each country but no trade between the two countries. In this structure, M_{ix} individuals choose to produce X (configuration X/Y), M_{iy} individuals choose to produce Y (configuration Y/X) in country i, where $M_{ix} + M_{iy} = M_i$. The two groups of individuals trade with each other, but not with individuals from another country, as a result, endogenous comparative advantage is exploited but exogenous comparative advantage is not.

In structure Pa, some individuals in country 1 choose configuration X/Y and others choose Y/X, and all individuals in country 2 choose configuration Y/X. Structure Pb is symmetrical to structure Pa. Structures Pa and Pb involve asymmetric division of labour: one country is involved in international trade but not domestic trade, while the other county has both domestic and international trade.

---

[3] Another way specifying increasing returns to scale in a Ricardian model can be found in Gomory (1994). Gomory's specification is based on the neoclassical dichotomy between consumers and firms, and his model has multiple general equilibria.

In structure C, individuals in country 1 choose configuration X/Y and individuals in country 2 choose configuration Y/X. There is no domestic trade in either country, but there is complete specialisation for each individual and for each country, and both endogenous and exogenous comparative advantages are exploited through international trade. The structures involving international trade are depicted in Figure 1.

Since the individuals' decision variables are discontinuous across structures, we introduce the concept of corner equilibrium. A corner equilibrium is defined as a set of relative prices of traded goods, numbers of individuals choosing different configurations, and the resource allocation in a *given* structure that satisfy the following conditions: (1) at the set of prices, the utility of each individual in both countries is maximised; (2) markets clear; (3) utilitities of all *ex ante* identical individuals are equalised. The general equilibrium is the corner equilibrium where each individual's utility under the corner equilibrium prices is maximised with respect to all possible configurations.

To solve for the general equilibrium, we first apply the marginal analysis to solve for the corner equilibrium for each of the five feasible structures. For instance, given structure Pa, the decision problem for individuals in country 1 who choose configuration X/Y is:

$$\max_{x_1,\,y_1,\,y_1^d} U_{1(X/Y)} = x_1^{\beta}(k_1 y_1^d)^{1-\beta}$$

$$\text{s.t.} \quad x_1 + x_1^s = a_{1x}(1-b)$$

$$p x_1^s = y_1^d.$$

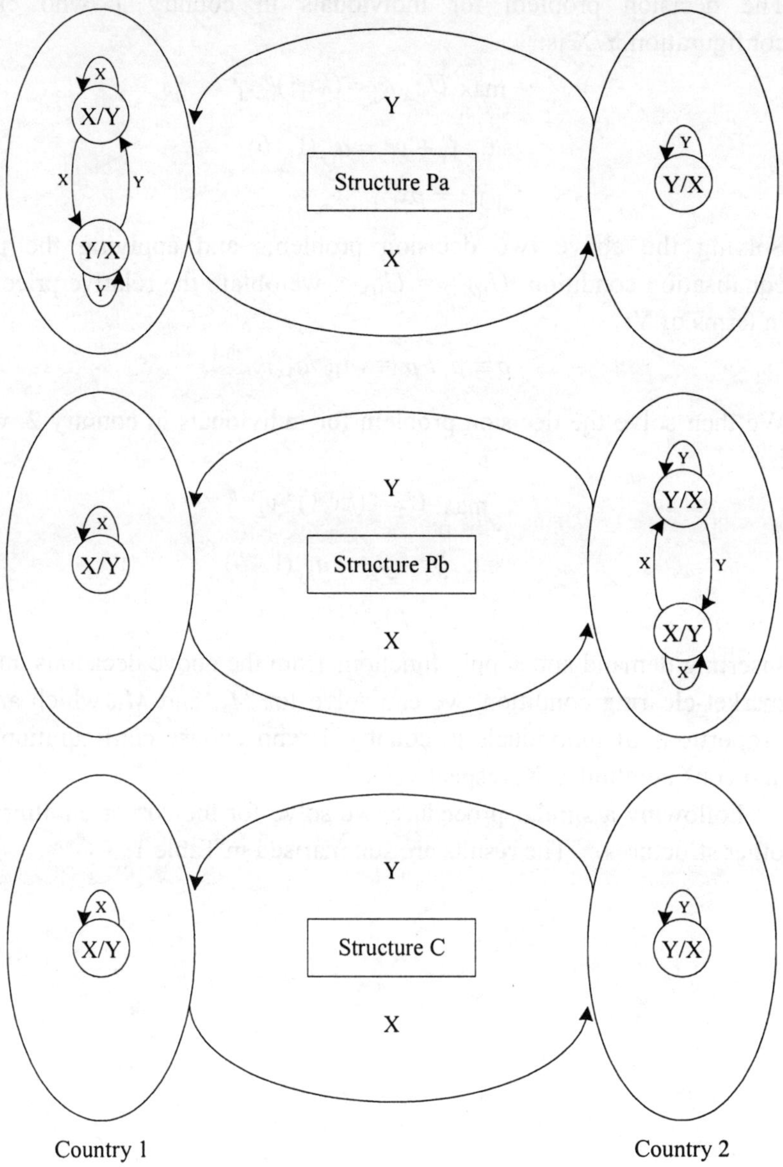

Figure 1: Configurations and Structures with International Division of Labour

The decision problem for individuals in country 1 who choose configuration Y/X is:

$$\max_{x_1^d, y_1, y_1^s} U_{1(X/Y)} = (kx_1^d)^\beta y_1^{1-\beta}$$

$$\text{s.t.} \quad y_1 + y_1^s = a_{1y}(1-b)$$

$$y_1^s = px_1^d.$$

Solving the above two decision problems and applying the utility equalisation condition, $U_{1(X/Y)} = U_{1(Y/X)}$, we obtain the relative price of X in terms of Y:

$$p \equiv p_x / p_y = (a_{1y}/a_{1x})k_1^{2\beta-1}.$$

We then solve the decision problem for individuals in country 2, which is:

$$\max_{x_2^d, y_2, y_2^s} U_2 = (kx_2^d)^\beta y_2^{1-\beta}$$

$$\text{s.t.} \quad y_2 + y_2^s = a_{2y}(1-b)$$

$$y_2^s = px_2^d.$$

Inserting demand and supply functions from the above decisions into the market-clearing condition, we can solve for M_{1x} and M_{1y} which are the proportions of individuals in country 1 who choose configuration X/Y and configuration Y/X, respectively.

Following a similar procedure, we solve for the corner equilibria for other structures. The results are summarised in Table 1.

Table 1: Five Walrasian Corner Equilibria in the Extended Ricardo Model

Structure	Relative Price	Per Capita Real Income (Utility)		Relative Price
	p_x/p_y	Country 1		Country 2
A		$Ba_{1x}{}^{\beta}a_{1y}{}^{1-\beta}(1-2b),$ $B\equiv\beta^{\beta}(1-\beta)^{1-\beta}$		$Ba_{2x}{}^{\beta}a_{2y}{}^{1-\beta}(1-2b),$ $B\equiv\beta^{\beta}(1-\beta)^{1-\beta}$
D	$(a_{iy}/a_{ix})\,k_i^{2\beta-1},$ $i=1,2$	$D_1\equiv B\,k_1^{2\beta(1-\beta)}a_{1x}^{\beta}a_{1y}^{1-\beta}(1-b)$		$D_2\equiv Bk_2^{2\beta(1-\beta)}\times$ $a_{2x}^{\beta}a_{2y}^{1-\beta}(1-b)$
P_a	$(a_{1y}/a_{1x})k_1^{2\beta-1}$	D_1		$Bk_2^{\beta}a_{2y}(1-b)\times$ $(k_1^{1-\beta}a_{1x}/a_{1y})^{\beta}$
P_b	$(a_{2y}/a_{2x})k_2^{2\beta-1}$	$Bk_1^{1-\beta}a_{1x}(1-b)(k_2^{2\beta-1}a_{2y}/a_{2x})^{1-\beta}$		D_2
C	$(M_2a_{2y}\beta)\div$ $[M_1a_{1x}(1-\beta)]$	$\beta a_{1x}{}^{\beta}a_{2y}{}^{1-\beta}(1-b)k_1^{1-\beta}\times$ $(M_2/M_1)^{1-\beta}$		$(1-\beta)a_{1x}{}^{\beta}a_{2y}{}^{1-\beta}\times$ $(1-b)k_2^{\beta}(M_1/M_2)^{\beta}$

For each corner equilibrium price, we can compare each individual's utilities associated with different configurations. An individual would choose the configuration that generates a utility level that is no lower than other alternative configurations. The condition that all individuals' utilities are maximised across all possible configurations defines a parameter subspace within which the corner equilibrium is the general equilibrium. The general equilibria and their corresponding parameter subspaces are summarised in Table 2.

Table 2: Walrasian Equilibrium and Its Inframarginal Comparative Statics

	$k_i<k^*$ $i=1,2$	$k_2>\left[\dfrac{M_1\beta a_{2x}}{M_2(1-\beta)a_{1x}}\right]^{\frac{1}{1-2\beta}}$		$k_1>\left[\dfrac{(1-\beta)M_1a_{1y}}{\beta M_2a_{2y}}\right]^{\frac{1}{1-2\beta}}$	
		$k_1\in(k^*,k^A)$	$k_1\in(k^A,1)$	$k_2\in(k^*,k^B)$	$k_2\in(k^B,1)$
Equilibrium structure	A	Pa	C	Pb	C

$$k^*\equiv\left(\frac{1-2b}{1-b}\right)^{\frac{1}{2\beta(1-\beta)}},\ k^A\equiv\left[\frac{M_1}{M_2}\frac{(1-\beta)a_{1y}}{\beta a_{2y}}\right]^{\frac{1}{1-2\beta}},\ k^B\equiv\left[\frac{M_1}{M_2}\frac{(1-\beta)a_{1x}}{\beta a_{2x}}\right]^{\frac{1}{1-2\beta}}.$$

We illustrate the results in Table 2 using structure Pa. For structure Pa to occur in equilibrium, the following conditions must hold:

$$k_2 < \left[\frac{M_1 \beta a_{2x}}{M_2 (1-\beta) a_{1x}} \right]^{\frac{1}{1-2\beta}} \quad \text{and} \quad k_1 \in (k^*, k^A).$$

These conditions imply that $M_1/M_2 \in (k_1^{1-2\beta} \beta a_{2y}/a_{1y}(1-\beta), k_2^{1-2\beta}(1-\beta)a_{2y}/\beta a_{1y})$, which implies that the relative size of the two countries is neither too great nor too small. This condition holds only if $k_2/k_1 > \{[\beta/(1-\beta)]^2 (a_{2x}a_{2y}/a_{1x}a_{1y})\}^{1/(1-2\beta)}$. In other words, structure Pa occurs in equilibrium only if the transaction efficiency in country 2 relative to country 1 is sufficiently high given other parameters.[4]

From Table 2 it is clear that when a change in k_1 or k_2 exceeds certain threshold values, the equilibrium jumps discontinuously. We refer to this analysis which investigates how equilibrium solutions change discontinuously in response to a change in parameter values as infra-marginal comparative statics. The results in Table 2 suggest that transaction efficiency determines the equilibrium level of division of labour – as transaction efficiency improves, the equilibrium level of division of labour jumps from autarky to partial division of labour (structure Pa or Pb), then to the complete division of labour (structure C). In the transitional structure (Pa or Pb), the country with lower transaction efficiency produces two goods and receives no gains from trade.

The infra-marginal analysis also allows us to study how productivity levels change as general equilibrium structure shifts. If the general equilibrium structure is autarky, the equalisation of the marginal rate of substitution and the marginal rate of transformation for each individual means that the equilibrium aggregate productivity is below the production possibility frontier (PPF). As the level of division of labour

---

[4] In addition to increasing returns, transaction costs, and endogenous decisions of specialisation, this differentiates our model from the standard Ricardo model where only the smaller country completely specialises and receives all gains from trade (see Caves, Frankel, and Jones, 1995, for instance). In our model, a small country with low transaction efficiency may produce two goods and receives no gains from trade when the larger country with better transaction condition completely specialises. Also, inframarginal comparative statics of general equilibrium in Table 2 gives exact conditions for the relationship between tastes, β, productivities, a_{ij}, transaction efficiencies, k_l, fixed learning cost, b, and population size, M_l under which a particular trade pattern occurs in equilibrium. In contrast, effects of fixed learning cost and transaction conditions on trade pattern are not addressed by the standard Ricardo model.

increases with improvement of transaction conditions, the equilibrium aggregate productivity moves closer to the PPF.

Since the general equilibrium is Pareto optimal, we can also say that if transaction efficiency coefficients are very low, the Pareto optimum is not associated with the PPF because of the trade-off between gains from (endogenous and exogenous) comparative advantages and transaction costs[5]. As transaction conditions improve, the Pareto optimum moves closer to the PPF. This result can be used to explore development implications of transaction conditions and the relationship between trade dependence and economic development -- improvements in transaction conditions lead to an expansion of the network of trade, which increases the equilibrium aggregate productivity.

It is straightforward that $dk^*/db < 0$, that is, as the fixed learning cost increases, the threshold value of transaction efficiency decreases, which means the equilibrium is more likely to involve the division of labour rather than autarky for a given value of k. But from Table 1, it can be seen that an increase in b reduces equilibrium utility. Hence, an increase in fixed learning cost has a positive effect on the equilibrium level of aggregate productivity and level of division of labour, but has a negative effect on real income.

Summarising the above discussion, we have:

Proposition 1:   If transaction efficiency is very low in both countries, the general equilibrium is autarky where no domestic or international trade takes place. As one country improves its transaction conditions, the general equilibrium jumps to partial division of labour (structure Pa or Pb) where this country completely specialises and depends on international trade, and the other country produces two goods and is dependent on domestic and international trade. All gains from trade go to the country that completely specialises. If the transaction conditions in both countries improve sufficiently, the equilibrium jumps to complete international division of labour. In this process, the equilibrium

---

[5] Zhou, Sun, and Yang (1998) prove that a general equilibrium exists for a broad class of models with consumer-producers and endogenous and exogenous comparative advantages exists if the set of individuals is a continuum. They also prove that the general equilibrium is Pareto optimal.

aggregate productivity converges to the aggregate production possibility frontier.

Another interesting result we derive from the infra-marginal analysis is that even if a country's terms of trade deteriorates, it may receive more gains from trade. For instance, suppose

$$k_1 \in (k^*, k^A), \; k_2 > k^*, \text{ and } \; k_2 > \left[\frac{M_1 \beta a_{2x}}{M_2(1-\beta)a_{1x}} \right]^{\frac{1}{1-2\beta}}.$$

Given these conditions, the general equilibrium is structure Pa and the equilibrium relative price is $p_x/p_y = (a_{1y}/a_{1x})k_1^{2\beta-1}$ (see Table 2). Now suppose that the transaction efficiency in country 1 increases, such that $k_1 \in (k^A, 1)$, the equilibrium jumps to structure C where the relative price is

$$p_x/p_y = (M_2 a_{2y}\beta)/[M_1 a_{1x}(1-\beta)]..$$

It can be shown that within the parameter subspace defined by

$$(M_2 a_{2y}\beta)/[M_1 a_{1x}(1-\beta)] < (a_{1y}/a_{1x})k_1^{2\beta-1},$$

country 1's terms of trade deteriorates as the equilibrium shifts from structure Pa to C.   Since country 1's utility in structure C is higher than in structure Pa, we conclude that a deterioration in a country's terms of trade may be associated with an increase of gains from trade received by the country. The logic behind this result is that a move towards a higher level of division of labour generates productivity gains. The productivity gains may more than compensate for the deterioration in the terms of trade.   Hence, it may be misleading to claim that a deterioration in a country's terms of trade necessarily reduces this country's gains from trade.   There has been a lot of debate about whether developing economies have suffered from worsening terms of trade (Morgan, 1970).   Our analysis suggests that the focus on the terms of trade effect may need to be shifted – a more important issue for economic development is the expansion of the network of division of labour.   In the process of the network expansion, a country's terms of trade may deteriorate, but its productivity will improve.   As long as the productivity improvement outpaces the terms of trade deterioration, the country will receive more gains from trade.

So far our focus has been on the division of labour, i.e., the source of the gains from trade. In the next section, we examine the distribution of the gains. In particular we look at what strategies governments may use in order to obtain more benefits from trade.

3. Endogenous Trade Policy Regime

It is assumed that the governments can choose from three trade policy regimes: a Nash tariff game where each government chooses its own tariff rate, taking the other country's tariff rate as given; Nash tariff bargaining, and free trade.

Since the welfare effects of tariff are different for different trade structures, we examine each structure separately, starting with structure C then moving on to structures Pa and Pb.

3.1. Structure C: Complete international division of labour

Assumed that the government in each country can impose tariff on imported goods to maximise its citizens' welfare. Tariff revenue is equally distributed among domestic residents. In structure C, the decision problems for individuals in country 1 and in country 2 are:

$$\max_{x_1 y_1^d} U_1 = x_1^{\beta}(k_1 y_1^d)^{1-\beta} \qquad\qquad \max_{x_2^d y_2} U_2 = (k_2 x_2^d)^{\beta} y_2^{1-\beta}$$

$$s.t. \quad p_x x_1^s + R_1 = p_y(1+t_1)y_1^d, \qquad\qquad s.t. \quad p_y y_2^s + R_2 = p_x(1+t_2)x_1^d,$$

$$x_1 + x_1^s = a_{1x}(1-b), \qquad\qquad\qquad y_1 + y_1^s = a_{2y}(1-b),$$

where t_i is the tariff rate in country i and R_i is the tariff revenue received by an individual in country i.

Solving the decision problems, we obtained the supply and demand functions for good X and good Y, and the average tariff revenue transferred to each individual in country 1 and country 2:

$$x_1{}^s = (1-\beta)a_{1x}(1-b)/(1+\beta t_1),$$

$$y_1{}^d = (p_x/p_y)(1-\beta)a_{1x}(1-b)/(1+\beta t_1),$$

$$R_1 = t_1 p_y y_1^d,$$

$$y_2^{\,s} = \beta a_{2y}(1-b)/[1+(1-\beta)t_2],$$

$$x_2^{\,d} = (p_y/p_x)\beta a_{2y}(1-b)/[1+(1-\beta)t_2],$$

$$R_2 = t_2 p_x x_2^d,$$

Using the market-clearing condition for good X, we can solve for the relative price of good X in terms of good Y:

$$\frac{p_x}{p_y} = \frac{M_2}{M_1}\,\frac{a_{2y}\beta}{a_{1x}(1-\beta)}\,\frac{(\beta t_1+1)}{(1-\beta)t_2+1}.$$

Substituting the demand and supply functions and the relative price into the utility functions, we get the corner equilibrium levels of utilities for individuals in the two counties:

$$u_1(t_1,t_2) = \beta(1-b)\left[\frac{(1+t_1)a_{1x}}{1+\beta t_1}\right]^{\beta}\left[\frac{a_{2y}k_1}{1+(1-\beta)t_2}\right]^{1-\beta}\left(\frac{M_2}{M_1}\right)^{1-\beta}$$

$$u_2(t_1,t_2) = (1-\beta)(1-b)\left[\frac{(1+t_2)a_{2y}}{1+(1-\beta)t_1}\right]^{1-\beta}\left[\frac{a_{1x}k_2}{1+\beta t_1}\right]^{\beta}\left(\frac{M_1}{M_2}\right)^{\beta}$$

We now look at how governments may choose from different trade policy regimes.

1. Nash tariff game

Differentiation of the two expressions with respect to t_i yields:

$$\frac{\partial u_1}{\partial t_1} = \frac{\beta(1-\beta)}{(1+t_1)(1+\beta t_1)}u_1 > 0, \qquad\qquad \frac{\partial u_1}{\partial t_2} < 0,$$

$$\frac{\partial u_2}{\partial t_2} = \frac{\beta(1-\beta)}{(1+t_2)[1+(1-\beta)t_2]}u_2 > 0, \qquad\qquad \frac{\partial u_2}{\partial t_1} < 0.$$

The above four inequalities suggest that taking the other country's tariff rate as given, each country can improve its citizens' welfare by imposing a tariff. Thus the governments could play a Nash tariff game but would not adopt *laissez faire* trade policies. However, if the governments in the two countries do play a Nash tariff game, the above four inequalities imply that in Nash equilibrium each country would impose a tariff to such a high level that individuals in the other country are just as well off participating in international trade as staying in autarky. The Nash equilibrium tariff rates are determined by equalisation conditions between utility in structure D and that in structure C. The solutions of t_1 and t_2 are implicitly given by the following two equations.

$$t_1 = \beta^{-1} k_2^{1-2(1-\beta)} \left\{ [(1-\beta)a_{1x}M_1]/\beta a_{2x}M_2 \right\}$$

$$\left\{ (1+t_2)/[1+(1-\beta)t_2] \right\}^{(1-\beta)/\beta} - \beta^{-1}$$

$$t_2 = (1-\beta)^{-1} k_2^{1-2\beta} \left\{ (\beta a_{2y}M_2)/\left[(1-\beta)a_{1y}M_1 \right] \right\}$$

$$\left[(1+t_1)/1+\beta t_1 \right]^{\beta/(1-\beta)} - 1(1-\beta)^{-1}$$

If the two governments use tariff to compete for a larger share of the gains from trade, there will be a tariff war which would exhaust all the gains from trade.   This is an example of the prisoner's dilemma.

2. Nash tariff negotiation

Alternatively, the two governments can play a Nash bargaining game; that is, they can negotiate over tariff rates. The Nash tariff negotiation maximises the Nash product which is the product of the gains from trade received by individuals in each country.   The gains from trade are measured by the difference in utility between participating in trade (structure C in this case) and staying in a structure with only domestic trade (structure D).   The Nash tariff negotiation equilibrium is given by the solution of the following problem:

$$\max_{t_1,t_2} V = [u_1(t_1,t_2) - u_1(D)][u_2(t_1,t_2) - u_2(D)]$$

The first-order conditions for this problem yield $(t_1+1)(t_2+1)=1$, which gives the equilibrium tariff rates $t_1 = t_2 = 0$.   In other words, the Nash tariff negotiation generates trade liberalisation.

The result of a tariff negotiation is in sharp contrast with the result of a Nash tariff game with the latter leading to complete dissipation of the gains from trade because of the prisoners' dilemma.   This provides an explanation as to why free trade may not be achieved through the market mechanism despite the fact that free trade benefits all countries.   It also suggests that trade negotiations may be essential for trade liberalisation and for a full exploitation of the gains from trade.

If the two governments can choose between the Nash tariff war and the Nash tariff negotiation, they will certainly choose the latter. Hence, if structure C occurs in equilibrium and the governments are allowed to choose policy regimes, the general equilibrium trade policy will be free trade resulted from a Nash tariff negotiation.

The Nash bargaining game does not explicitly spell out the bargaining process, rather, it follows the axiomatic approach. It is proven that there is a unique bargaining solution that satisfies the four basic axioms: invariance to equivalent utility representations, symmetry, independence of irrelevant alternatives, and Pareto efficiency[6]. This bargaining solution maximises the Nash product which is the product of the players' gains in utility over the disagreement outcome. Although no risk is specified in this game, the players' attitude towards risk "plays a central role" (Osborne and Rubinstein 1990, p.10). As long as some uncertainty exists about other players' behaviour, there is a chance that the negotiation would break down, thus each player intends to maximise his *expected* utility gain in the negotiation. The Nash product can be interpreted as a player's expected utility gain, with the probability of reaching an agreement being approximated by the utility gains of the other player(s). For this reason, Nash (1950) contends that the Nash bargaining solution is the outcome of a non-cooperative game despite the fact that the gains are shared fairly among players.

3.2. Structures Pa and Pb: Partial international division of labour

We now turn to the structures with partial international division of labour, structures Pa and Pb, to examine the choices of trade policies. Since the two structures are symmetrical, we only have to consider one of them, say, structure Pa.

In country 1, the decision problem for an individual specialising in good X and that for an individual specialising in good Y are, respectively

---

[6] See Osborne and Rubinstein 1990, Chapter 2.

$$\text{Max:} \quad u_1(x/y) = x_1^{\beta}(k_1 y_1^d)^{1-\beta},$$

$$\text{s.t.} \quad x_1^s + x_1 = a_{1x}(1-b), \quad p_x x_1^s + R_1 = p_y y_1^d + (1+t_1)p_y y_2^d,$$

$$\text{Max:} \quad u_1(y/x) = (k_1 x_1^d)^{\beta} y_1^{1-\beta},$$

$$\text{s.t.} \quad y_1^s + y_1 = a_{1y}(1-b), \quad p_x x_1^d = p_y y_1^s,$$

By assumption, only buyers of imported goods receive transfer from tariff revenue, the amount of transfer received by an individual specialising in good X is R_1. The solution of the decision problem is

$$x_1^s = (1-\beta)a_{1x}(1-b) - \beta\frac{R_1}{p_x},$$

$$y_1^d = (1-\beta)[a_{1x}(1-b)\frac{p_x}{p_y} + \frac{R_1}{p_y}],$$

$$y_1^s = \beta a_{1y}(1-b),$$

$$R_1 = t_1 p_y y_2^d/(1+t_1) = t_1 p_y[M_2\beta a_{2y}(1-b)]/[M_x(1+t_1)].$$

Similarly we can solve the decision problem for individuals in country 2. Applying the utility equalisation condition and the market-clearing condition for either good, we obtain the corner equilibrium in structure Pa:

$$\frac{p_x}{p_y} = \frac{a_{1y}}{a_{1x}}k_1^{2\beta-1} - \frac{t_1 a_{1y}a_{2y}M_2[\beta + (1-\beta)k_1^{2\beta-1}]}{a_{1x}(a_{1y}M_1 + M_2 a_{2y})(1+t_1)},$$

$$M_{1x} = \frac{\beta[M_2 a_{2y} + a_{1y}M_1]}{a_{1y}[(1-\beta)k_1^{2\beta-1} + \beta]},$$

$$M_{1y} = M_1 - M_{1x},$$

$$y_2^d = [M_2\beta a_{2y}(1-b)]/M_x,$$

$$u_1 = \beta^{\beta}(1-\beta)^{1-\beta}(1-b)k_1^{\beta}a_{1y}\left(\frac{p_y}{p_x}\right)^{\beta},$$

$$u_2 = \frac{(k_2\beta)^{\beta}[(1-\beta)(1+t_2)]^{1-\beta}}{1+(1-\beta)t_2}\left(\frac{p_y}{p_x}\right)^{\beta}a_{2y}(1-b)$$

From the equilibrium solution, we obtain

$$\frac{\partial u_1}{\partial t_1} = \beta^\beta (1-\beta)^{1-\beta} k_1^{2\beta(1-\beta)} (1-b) a_{1y} \left[\left(\frac{p_y}{p_x} \right)^{1+\beta} \left(-\beta \frac{\partial (p_x/p_y)}{\partial t_1} \right) \right] > 0,$$

where
$$\frac{\partial (p_x/p_y)}{\partial t_1} = -\frac{a_{1y} a_{2y} M_2 [\beta + (1-\beta) k^{2\beta-1}]}{a_{1x} (M_1 a_{1y} + M_2 a_{2y})} < 0.$$

Clearly, country 1 would not choose free trade policies. If it plays a Nash tariff game, it would want its tariff rate to be as high as possible. But since

$$\frac{\partial u_2}{\partial t_1} = -\beta^{\beta+1} (1-\beta)^{1-\beta} (1-b) k_2^\beta a_{1x}^\beta a_{2y} \left[\frac{p_y}{(1+t_1) p_x} \right]^{\beta+1}$$

$$\left[\frac{p_x}{p_y} + (1+t_1) \frac{\partial (p_x/p_y)}{\partial t_1} \right] < 0,$$

country 1 needs to ensure that its tariff rate is not so high as to drive country 2 out of international trade. Thus, the optimum tariff rate for country 1 is determined by the utility equalisation between structure Pa and structure D for individuals in country 2, which implies

$$\frac{a_{1y}}{a_{1x}} k_1^{2\beta-1} - \frac{a_{2y}}{a_{2x}} \frac{k_2^{2\beta-1}}{(1+t^*)} - \frac{t^* M_2 a_{1y} a_{2y} [\beta + (1-\beta) k_1^{2\beta-1}]}{a_{1x} (a_{1y} M_1 + a_{2y} M_2)(1+t^*)} = 0.$$

Since $\partial u_2/\partial t_2 < 0$, the optimum tariff rate for country 2 is zero.

Therefore, if structure Pa is the equilibrium structure, the result of a Nash tariff game would be the coexistence of an unilateral protection tariff imposed by country 1 (which produces both goods X and Y) and unilateral *laissez faire* policy by country 2.

In a Nash tariff game, country 1 gets most the gains from trade. Since a Nash tariff negotiation would mean sharing the gains from trade, country 1 does not have an incentive to participate in a trade negotiation. Thus even if the governments in both countries are allowed to choose between the Nash tariff game and Nash tariff negotiation, the Nash tariff negotiation would not be chosen by country 1. As a result, the equilibrium trade policy regime would feature the coexistence of unilateral protection tariff and unilateral *laissez faire*.

We may draw the distinction between the exogenous transaction cost coefficient 1-k and endogenous transaction costs caused by the deadweight loss of tariff. Exogenous transaction costs are observable before individuals have made decisions. Endogenous transaction costs are caused by conflicts between self-interested decisions.   Following the method used in section 2, we can prove that in this extended model as the exogenous transaction cost coefficient 1-k decreases, the general equilibrium jumps from autarky to the partial division of labour, where unilateral protection tariff in the less developed country and unilateral free trade in the developed economy coexist, then to the complete division of labour, where tariff negotiation generates bilateral free trade. In the transitional period with partial division of labour, endogenous transaction costs are caused by trade conflicts between the developed and less developed countries.   A less developed country can get more gains from trade in two ways. One is to improve transaction conditions so that the equilibrium jumps to the complete division of labour which ensures bilateral incentives for tariff negotiation, which leads to trade liberalisation. The other is to impose a stiff tariff to get greater gains from trade at the cost of the partner. The first approach is to get a fair share from a bigger pie and the second is to get a larger share of a smaller pie.

Summarising the above analysis, we have

Proposition 2:   As exogenous transaction conditions improve, the equilibrium jumps from autarky to the partial international division of labour where the coexistence of unilateral protection tariff and unilateral free trade generates endogenous transaction costs, then to the complete international division of labour where tariff negotiation leads to free trade and eliminates endogenous transaction costs.[7]

---

[7] In the standard Ricardo model (see, for instance, Caves *et al*, 1996), the optimum tariff for the small country is 0. But in our model, the optimum tariff for the large country with low transportation efficiency might be 0 in structure Pa or Pb.

4. Conclusion

In this paper, we have introduced transaction costs and endogenous comparative advantage into the Ricardian model. We have also examined governments' choices of different trade policy regimes. An interesting result of this paper is that the equilibrium trade policy regimes are intimately related to the level of international division of labour. At a high level of international division of labour, countries would participate in Nash tariff negotiations which would lead to free trade. If the level of division of labour is at a level such that one country produces both goods and determines the terms of trade, then at equilibrium, unilateral tariff and unilateral free trade would coexist. The model provides a plausible story about how a trade policy regime might evolve, and an explanation for the changing trade policy stances in developing countries. Given the simplicity of the model, it obviously does not tell the whole story. An obvious extension of the model is to introduce more goods and/or more countries.

In addition, the specification of the model may be varied to study other interesting issues. For instance, if we assume constant returns in production, structure D which involves only domestic division of labour may occur in equilibrium. Also, the country with poor transaction conditions may have a dual economy in which some individuals completely specialise and the others choose autarky (Zhou, Sun, and Yang 1998). This variation may be used to study under-employment in developing countries.

References

Babbage, C. (1832), *On the Economy of Machinery and Manufactures*, 4th enlarged edition of 1835, reissued in 1977, M. Kelly, New York.

Balassa, B. (1980), *The Process of Industrial Development and Alternative Development Strategies*, International Finance Section, Essays in International Finance, No. 141, Princeton University.

Becker, G. (1981), *A Treatise on the Family*, Harvard University Press, Cambridge, Massachusetts.

Bruton, Henry (1998), "A Reconsideration of Import Substitution," *Journal of Economic Literature, 36, 903-36.*

Caves, Richard, Jeffrey Frankel, and Ronald Jones (1996), *World Trade and Payments : an Introduction*, Harper Collins College Publishers, New York.

Dixit, Avinash K. and Albert S. Kyle (1985), "The Use of Protection and Subsidies for Entry Promotion and Deterrence," *American Economic Review*, 75, 139-52.

Ekelund, Robert, and Robert Tollison (1981), *Merchantilism as an Rent-seeking Society*, Texas A & M University Press, College Station, TX.

Gomory, Ralph E. (1994), "A Ricardo Model with Economies of Scale," *Journal of Economic Theory*, 62, 394-419.

Grossman, Gene M. and J. David Richardson (1986), "Strategic Trade Policy: A Survey of the Issues and Early Analysis,"   In Robert E. Baldwin and J. David Richardson, eds., *International Trade and Finance*, 3rd ed., Little, Brown, Boston, 95-113.

Grossman, Gene M. and Elhanan, Helpman (1994), "Protection For Sale," *American Economic Review*, 84, 833-50.

Grossman, Gene M. and Elhanan, Helpman (1995a), "The Politics of Free-Trade Agreements," *American Economic Review*, 85(4),667-690.

Grossman, Gene M. and Elhanan, Helpman (1995b), "Trade Wars and Trade Talks," *Journal of Political Economy*, 103(4), 675-708.

Houthakker, M. (1956), "Economics and Biology: Specialization and Speciation", *Kyklos,* 9,181-89.

Johnson, Harry G. (1954), "Optimum Tariff and Retaliation," *Review of Economic Studies*, 21(2), 142-53.

Krueger, Anne O. (1974), "The Political Economy of Rent-seeking Society," *American Economic Review*, 64, 291-303.

Krugman, Paul R., ed. (1986), *Strategic Trade Policy and the New International Economics*, MIT Press, Cambridge.

Krugman, P. and A. J. Venables (1995), "Globalization and the Inequality of Nations," *Quarterly Journal of Economics*, 110, 857-80.

Mayer, Wolfgang (1981), "Theoretical Considerations on Negotiated Tariff Adjustments." *Oxford Economic Papers*, 33, 135-53.

Mayer, Wolfgang (1984), "Endogenous Tariff Formation," *American Economic Review*, 74, 970-85.

Morishima, Michio (1989), *Ricardo's Economics: A general equilibrium theory of distribution and growth*, Cambridge University Press, Cambridge.

Nash, J. F. (1950), "The Bargaining Problem," *Econometrica*, 18, 115-62.

Osborne, Martin J., and Ariel, Rubinstein (1990), *Bargaining and Markets*, Academic Press, Inc., San Diego.

Pincus, Jonathan J. (1975), "Pressure Groups and the Pattern of Tariffs," *Journal of Political Economy*, 83, 757-78.

Riezman, Raymond (1982), "Tariff Retaliation from a Strategic Viewpoint," *Southern Economic Journal*, 48, 583-93.

Rosen, S. (1983), "Specialization and Human Capital", *Journal of Labor Economics*, 1, 43-49.

Wen, M. (1998), "An Analytical Framework of Consumer-Producers, Economies of Specialisation and Transaction Costs," in K. Arrow, Y-K. Ng, X. Yang eds., *Increasing Returns and Economic Analysis*, Macmillan, London. .

Yang, X. (1994), "Endogenous vs. Exogenous Comparative Advantages and Economies of Specialization vs. Economies of Scale", *Journal of Economics*, 60, 29-54.

Yang, X. and Borland, J. (1991), "A Microeconomic Mechanism for Economic Growth," *Journal of Political Economy*, 99, 460-82.

Zhou, Lin, Guangzhen, Sun, and Xiaokai, Yang (1998), "General Equilibria in Large Economies with Endogenous Structure of Division of Labor," Working Paper, Monash University.

CHAPTER 8

A GENERAL-EQUILIBRIUM RE-APPRAISAL OF THE STOLPER-SAMUELSON THEOREM[*]

Wen Li Cheng[a], Jeffrey Sachs[b] and Xiaokai Yang[c♣]

[a]Law and Economics Consulting Group   [b]Harvard University   [c]Harvard and

Monash University.

1. Introduction

Some of the most influential theorems in the theory of international trade are derived from the traditional 2x2x2 Heckscher-Ohlin (HO) model. These theorems include the Heckscher-Ohlin (HO) theorem, Stolper-Samuelson (1941) (SS) theorem, factor-price equalization (FPE) theorem, and Rybczynski (RY) theorem.[1]

Trade theorists often claim that these theorems are general-equilibrium comparative-static results of the traditional HO model. And partly due to the belief that the traditional HO model is able to derive unambiguous comparative-static results with very general functional forms, the HO model has dominated the field of international trade for the past few decades. The dominance of the traditional HO

---

[*] Reprinted from *Journal of Economics*, 72 (1), Wen Li Cheng, Jeffrey Sachs, and Xiaokai Yang, "A General-Equilibrium Re-Appraisal of the Stolper-Samuelson Theorem," 1-18, 2000, with permission from Springer-Verlag.

[♣] We are grateful for comments from Hugo Sonnenschein and participants of the seminar on this paper in University of Washington.

[1] The background of the SS theorem and related core trade theorems, their extensions, empirical tests, reflections about them, and a comprehensive annotated bibliography can be found in Deardorff and Stern (1994). The research to extend the HO model by introducing more goods, factors, and countries can be found from Melvin (1968) and Ethier (1974).

model did face some challenge, most notably from mathematical economists well respected in the field of general-equilibrium theory. Sonnenschein (1973), Mantel (1974) and Debreu (1974) show that without explicit model specifications, no unambiguous comparative-statics results can be derived from a general-equilibrium model except that Walras's law holds, and that the excess-demand function is homogenous of degree zero (the "everything-possible" theorem).   The "everything-possible" theorem thus questions the validity of the claim that the trade theorems mentioned above are indeed general-equilibrium comparative-static results.

The inconsistency between the "everything-possible" theorem and unambiguous predictions of the traditional HO model can be explained by the fact that the traditional HO model differs from a typical general-equilibrium model in various ways. Most importantly, in the traditional HO model, product prices (when the SS theorem and the RY theorem are proved) or factor prices (when the HO theorem is proved) are assumed to be exogenous.[2]   When prices are assumed to be exogenous, the interactions between prices and other parameters (such as endowments) are excluded from the analysis, consequently the predictions of the model become less unambiguous despite that no specific functional forms are assumed.

With exogenous product price, it is possible to describe, for instance, how factor prices would change in response to a change in product price (that is, to formulate the Stolper-Samuelson theorem). However, the response of factor price to product price is not part of comparative-statics of general-equilibrium. In a general-equilibrium model, all prices are endogenously determined. As a result, it is not appropriate to describe how factor prices would change in response of a change in product price.[3]

---

[2] Wong (1995, pp. 91-97) uses the RY theorem to prove the HO theorem with no assumption of exogenous factor prices. But he proves the RY theorem using the assumption of exogenous product prices. It is not legitimate to assume exogenous product prices in order to work out comparative-statics of general-equilibrium and to prove the RY theorem.

[3] The distinction between comparative-statics of decision and comparative-statics of equilibrium implies that comparative-statics of equilibrium should not explain changes in

It is possible however to describe how parameter changes would affect factor price and product price differently and thus describe the features of the co-movement of factor and product prices in response to parameter changes.

In this paper, we develop a general-equilibrium analysis of the HO model with endogenous prices and conduct comparative-static analysis to examine the co-movement of factor and product prices. In particular, we assess whether the general prediction of the Stolper-Samuelson theorem holds as a comparative-static result of equilibrium.

Apart from that prices are endogenous, our analysis differs from the traditional analysis of the HO model in another important aspect. When the core trade theorems are proved, comparative-statics of general-equilibrium are analyzed within the diversification cone. The shift of equilibrium across the border of the diversification cone is explained by changes in prices rather than by changes in parameters. Hence, the analysis of shift is not really part of comparative-statics of general-equilibrium, which should explain changes in trade structure by changes in parameters. Our analysis however considers all eight feasible trade structures. Which structure occurs in equilibrium is endogenously determined by values of all parameters. Since all feasible trade structures can occur in equilibrium depending on parameter values, when parameter values change, there can be two types of comparative-static responses. First, endogenous variables change continuously in response to a change in parameter values. Second, when a change in parameter values exceeds some threshold, the equilibrium structure discontinuously jumps and the values of endogenous variables jump discontinuously as well. We refer to the first type of response as marginal comparative-statics and the latter as infra-marginal comparative-statics.

We examine the Stolper-Samuelson theorem in this paper applying both the marginal and infra-marginal comparative-static analysis. The main conclusion of the paper is that the general prediction of the Stolper-Samulson theorem is not always consistent with the comparative-statics results derived from a specific general-equilibrium

---

equilibrium by changes in prices despite the legitimacy of explaining quantities demanded by prices in comparative-statics of decision.

HO model. In particular, the Stolper-Samuelson theorem's prediction does not always hold when changes in production parameters lead to changes in prices even within the diversification cone; or when the general-equilibrium jumps from one structure to another.

By rejecting the general applicability of the Stolper-Samuelson theorem, our finding confirms the "everything-possible" theorem. It also raises questions as to the general applicability of other core trade theorems derived from the same framework as the Stolper-Samuelson theorem.

The rest of the paper is organized as follows. Section 2 presents the general-equilibrium HO model. Section 3 conducts the marginal and infra-marginal comparative-statics to examine the general validity of the Stolper-Samuelson theorem. Section 4 concludes the paper.

2. The General-Equilibrium HO Model with Differences in Technology

In this section, we develop a general-equilibrium HO model of the two countries with different production technologies. The assumptions of our model are similar to those in a standard 2×2×2 HO model, namely, that perfect competition prevails in both goods and factor markets; that factors are mobile within a country but immobile between countries; that factors are fully employed; and that the production technology exhibits constant returns to scale. However, prices of goods and factors are not assumed to be exogenous, rather they are endogenously determined.

2.1. Model specification

Assume that country i ($i =1, 2$) is endowed with labor L_i and capital K_i, which can be used to produce two consumer goods X and Y. In autarky, the decision problem of a representative consumer in country i is

$$\max{}_{xi,\,yi} U_i = x_i^{\theta} y_i^{1-\theta}$$
$$s.t.\ px_i + y_i = w_i L_i + r_i K_i, \tag{1}$$

where x_i and y_i are quantities of goods X and Y, respectively; p is the price of good X in terms of good Y; w_i and r_i are wage rate and capital rental, respectively.

Assume that the production functions for X and Y in country i are:

$$x_i = a_{ix} L_{ix}{}^\alpha K_{ix}{}^{1-\alpha}, \qquad\qquad y_i = a_{iy} L_{iy}{}^\beta K_{iy}{}^{1-\beta}, \tag{2}$$

where L_{ix}, L_{iy}, K_{ix}, K_{iy} are labor and capital devoted to the production of good X and Y, repectively; a_{ij} $(i=1,2; j=x,y)$ is the total factor-productivity coefficient. Since a_{ij} is country-specific, it captures the productivity difference between the two countries. Constrained by the production technology, the representative firm producing X in country i maximizes its profit, i.e.,

$$\max_{L_{ix},K_{ix}} \pi_{ix} = px_i - w_i L_{ix} - r_i K_{ix} = pa_{ix} L_{ix}{}^\alpha K_{ix}{}^{1-\alpha} - w_i L_{ix} - r_i K_{ix}. \tag{3}$$

The decision problem for a firm producing Y is similar to (3).

From the first-order conditions of the firms' decisions problems, we obtain:

$$\frac{K_{ix}}{L_{ix}} = [p_i \frac{a_{ix}}{a_{iy}} (\frac{\alpha}{\beta})^\beta (\frac{1-\alpha}{1-\beta})^{1-\beta}]^{\frac{1}{\alpha-\beta}},$$

$$\frac{K_{iy}}{L_{iy}} = \frac{\alpha(1-\beta)}{\beta(1-\alpha)} \frac{K_{ix}}{L_{ix}}. \tag{4}$$

It is easy to see that

$$\frac{K_{ix}}{L_{ix}} > \frac{K_{iy}}{L_{iy}}$$

(that is, the X industry is capital intensive and the Y industry is labor-intensive) if and only if $\alpha < \beta$. Without loss of generality, we assume that the X industry is capital-intensive, ie., $\alpha < \beta$.

Using (4) and the market-clearing conditions for factors and goods in each country, we obtain the autarky price in country i (p_i):

$$p_i = \frac{a_{iy}}{a_{ix}} [\frac{L_i}{K_i} \frac{(1-\alpha)\theta + (1-\beta)(1-\theta)}{\alpha\theta + \beta(1-\theta)}]^{\beta-\alpha} \frac{\beta^\beta (1-\beta)^{1-\beta}}{\alpha^\alpha (1-\alpha)^{1-\alpha}}. \tag{5}$$

Given our assumption that $\alpha < \beta$, $p_1 < p_2$ if and only if

$$\left(\frac{a_{1x}}{a_{1y}}\right)^{\frac{1}{\beta-\alpha}}\frac{K_1}{L_1} > \left(\frac{a_{2x}}{a_{2y}}\right)^{\frac{1}{\beta-\alpha}}\frac{K_2}{L_2}. \tag{6}$$

In the rest of this paper, we assume that inequality (6) holds. Assumption (6) is arbitrary but does not affect the conclusions of this paper.

2.2. Trade equilibrium

There are eight possible trade structures in equilibrium as depicted in Figure 1.

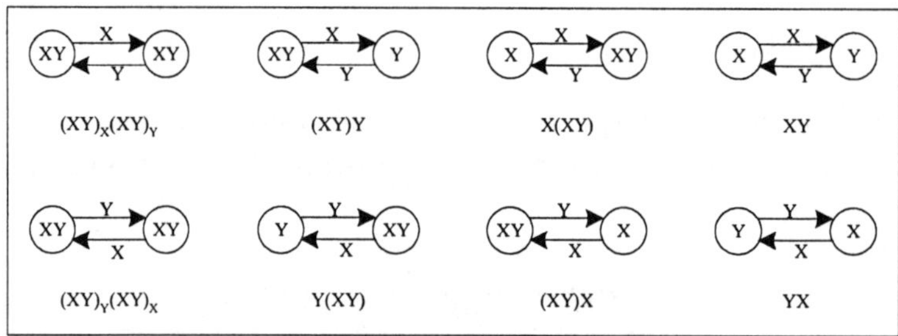

Figure 1: Possible Trade Structures

The top four structures in Figure 1 involve country 1 exporting good X, and country 2 exporting good Y but the production pattern of each country differs between structures. For instance, in structure $(XY)_x(XY)_y$ both countries produces both goods; in structure (XY)Y, country 1 produces both goods X and Y, country 2 only produces good Y, and so on. The bottom four structures in Figure 1 involve country 1 exporting good Y and country 2 exporting good X. It is easy to see that the top and bottom structures are symmetrical to each other.

With international trade, the nature of the decisions for consumers and firms is similar to that with autarky although there is only one relative price of good X in terms of Y in the world market.

From the first-order conditions of the decision problems for firms and consumers in each country, and the market-clearing conditions for factors, we can solve for factor prices and relative factor allocation as functions of product price (p).   We then use the world market-clearing condition for goods to solve for the equilibrium value of p.

The general-equilibrium is summarized as follows:

$$x_i = Aa_{ix}(a_{ix}/a_{iy})^{\alpha/(\beta-\alpha)}[\beta K_i-(1-\beta)L_i(a_{iy}/a_{ix})^{1/(\beta-\alpha)}/\gamma\mu](\gamma\mu)^{\alpha}/(\beta-\alpha), \qquad (7a)$$

$$y_i = Ba_{iy}(a_{iy}/a_{ix})^{(1-\beta)/(\beta-\alpha)}[(1-\alpha)(L_i/\gamma\mu)-\alpha K_i(a_{ix}/a_{iy})^{1/(\beta-\alpha)}](\gamma\mu)^{\beta}/(\beta-\alpha),$$

$$L_{ix} = [\alpha/(\beta-\alpha)][\beta K_i(a_{ix}/a_{iy})^{1/(\beta-\alpha)}\gamma\mu-(1-\beta)L_i], \qquad (7b)$$

$$L_{iy} = [\beta/(\beta-\alpha)][(1-\alpha)L_i-\alpha K_i(a_{ix}/a_{iy})^{1/(\beta-\alpha)}\gamma\mu],$$

$$K_{ix} = (1-\alpha)\,L_{ix}w_i/r_i\alpha, \quad K_{iy} = (1-\beta)L_{iy}w_i/r_i\beta,$$

$$p = (r_i/w_i)^{(\beta-\alpha)}Ba_{iy}/a_{ix}A, \quad r_i/w_i = \gamma\mu(a_{ix}/a_{iy})^{1/(\beta-\alpha)}, \qquad (7c)$$

where $A \equiv \alpha^{\alpha}(1-\alpha)^{1-\alpha}$, $B \equiv \beta^{\beta}(1-\beta)^{1-\beta}$, $\mu \equiv [(\beta-\alpha)\theta+1-\beta]/[\beta-\theta(\beta-\alpha)]>0$,

$$\gamma \equiv \frac{\left(\dfrac{a_{1y}^{1-\alpha}}{a_{1x}^{1-\beta}}\right)^{1/(\beta-\alpha)} L_1 + \left(\dfrac{a_{2y}^{1-\alpha}}{a_{2x}^{1-\beta}}\right)^{1/(\beta-\alpha)} L_2}{\left(\dfrac{a_{1x}^{\beta}}{a_{1y}^{\alpha}}\right)^{1/(\beta-\alpha)} K_1 + \left(\dfrac{a_{2x}^{\beta}}{a_{2y}^{\alpha}}\right)^{1/(\beta-\alpha)} K_2}.$$

x_i, and y_i are the quantities of the two goods consumed in country i, which include quantities purchased from domestic and foreign markets.

Clearly the equilibrium values of all endogenous variables are functions of 11 parameters, β, α, θ, K_i, L_i, a_{iy}, a_{ix}.   Depending on whether L_{ix} and/or L_{iy} are greater than, or smaller than or equal to zero, we can partition the 11-dimension parameter space into 8 subspaces, each corresponding to a trade structure in Figure 1. Thus which structure occurs in equilibrium would be determined by the values of the parameters. For instance, let L_{ix}, $L_{2y} > 0$ and $L_{1y} \leq 0$, we can identify the parameter subspace for structure (XY)Y to be the general-equilibrium structure.

Under assumption (6), it is easy to show that L_{ix}, $L_{1y} > 0$ and $L_{2y} \leq 0$ cannot hold simultaneously.   That is, the parameter subspace for structure (XY)X to be general-equilibrium is empty.   Similarly, we can show that the parameter subspaces for structures Y(XY) and YX to occur in general-equilibrium are empty.   In addition, we can rule out structure

$(XY)_y(XY)_x$ because under assumption (6), country 1's demand for good Y is greater than its production of good Y.

With four structures remaining, we can match each structure with a corresponding parameter subspace within which the structure is the general-equilibrium structure. The results of this match are summarized in Table 1, where γ and μ are as previously defined, $v_{1x} \equiv (1-\alpha)(a_{1y}/a_{1x})^{1/(\beta-\alpha)}L_1/\alpha K_1$, $v_{2x} \equiv (1-\alpha)(a_{2y}/a_{2x})^{1/(\beta-\alpha)}L_2/\alpha K_2$, $v_{1y} \equiv (1-\beta)(a_{1y}/a_{1x})^{1/(\beta-\alpha)}L_1/\beta K_1$, $v_{2y} \equiv (1-\beta)(a_{2y}/a_{2x})^{1/(\beta-\alpha)}L_2/\beta K_2$, under assumption (6), $v_{1y}<v_{2y}$, $v_{1x}<v_{2x}$, $v_{2x}>v_{2y}$, $v_{1y}<v_{1x}$.

Table 1: General-Equilibrium Structures and their Corresponding Parameter Subspaces

Parameter Subspace	$[(1-\alpha)\beta/\alpha(1-\beta)](a_{2x}/a_{2y})^{1/(\beta-\alpha)}K_2/L_2 > (a_{1x}/a_{1y})^{1/(\beta-\alpha)} K_1/L_1$			$[(1-\alpha)\beta/\alpha(1-\beta)](a_{2x}/a_{2y})^{1/(\beta-\alpha)}K_2/L_2 < (a_{1x}/a_{1y})^{1/(\beta-\alpha)} K_1/L_1$		
$\gamma\mu\in$	(v_{1y}, v_{2y})	(v_{2y}, v_{1x})	(v_{1x}, v_{2x})	(v_{1y}, v_{1x})	(v_{1x}, v_{2y})	(v_{2y}, v_{2x})
Equilibrium structure	$(XY)Y$	$(XY)_x$ $(XY)_y$	$X(XY)$	$(XY)Y$	XY	$X(XY)$

Table 1 indicates that given assumption (6), four different trade patterns can occur in equilibrium depending on parameter values. Table 1 also indicates the infra-marginal comparative-static results, i.e, how the general-equilibrium structure jumps discontinuously when a change in parameter values exceeds some threshold. For instance, given $[(1-\alpha)\beta/\alpha(1-\beta)](a_{2x}/a_{2y})^{1/(\beta-\alpha)}K_2/L_2 > (a_{1x}/a_{1y})^{1/(\beta-\alpha)} K_1/L_1$, if starting from $\gamma\mu\in (v_{1y}, v_{2y})$, the parameters change such that $\gamma\mu\in (v_{2y}, v_{1x})$, then the general-equilibrium structure will jump from structure $(XY)Y$ to structure $(XY)_x (XY)_y$. In the next section, we conduct both the marginal and infra-marginal comparative-statics of general-equilibrium to examine the relationship between factor prices and product prices. In particular, we assess whether the Stolper-Samuelson theorem as a general comparative-statics result of the traditional HO model where price is exogenous, holds in our specific general-equilibrium model where price is endogenously determined.

3. A Re-Appraisal of the Stolper-Samuelson Theorem

The Stolper-Samuelson theorem states that if the price of the capital-intensive (or labor-intensive) good rises, the price of capital (or labor) rises, and the price of labor falls (Stolper and Sammuelson, 1941). Since with the opening-up of international trade, the price of a country's comparative advantage good rises, a corollary of the Stolper-Samuelson theorem is that international trade benefits a country's abundant factor and hurts its scarce factor. Similarly, since a tariff reduces the relative price of the country's comparative advantage good, it benefits a country's scarce factor.

As discussed in the introduction section, the Stolper-Samuelson theorem was derived from the traditional HO model where product price is assumed to be exogenous. Since price is assumed to be exogenous, the Stolper-Samuelson theorem is formulated to describe how factor price changes in response to a change in product price. In our model, because both product price and factor prices are endogenously determined, the comparative-statics do not characterize how factor prices change in response to a change in product price. Rather both factor price and product price change in response to changes in parameters such as endowments, preferences and technology. It is still possible to describe the relative change of factor price and product price, but this relative change is a result of a change of parameters affecting product price and factor prices differently. Thus the relationship between factor price and product price is better characterized as one of correlation as far as comparative-statics are concerned, not of causation as the Stolper-Samuelson theorem seems to suggest.

In the following, we analyze the comparative-static relationship between factor price and product price. Our analysis proceeds in 3 steps: we examine whether the factor-price-product-price relationship as characterized by the Stolper-Samuelson theorem holds (1) within the diversification cone; (2) outside the diversification cone; and (3) when the general-equilibrium jumps from one structure to another.

3.1. Does the Stolper-Samuelson theorem hold within the diversification cone?

The diversification cone is defined by the following system of inequalities:

$$L_{1x} > 0; L_{1y} > 0; \qquad L_{2x} > 0; L_{2y} > 0.$$

Under assumption (6), the above inequalities imply:

$$[(1-\alpha)\beta/\alpha(1-\beta)](a_{2x}/a_{2y})^{1/(\beta-\alpha)}K_2/L_2 > (a_{1x}/a_{1y})^{1/(\beta-\alpha)} K_1/L_1, \tag{8a}$$

and

$$\gamma \in ((1-\beta)(a_{2y}/a_{2x})^{1/(\beta-\alpha)}L_2/\beta K_2, (1-\alpha)(a_{1y}/a_{1x})^{1/(\beta-\alpha)}L_1/\alpha K_1). \tag{8b}$$

Within the diversification cone, first consider an increase in total factor productivity of X in country 1 due to a neutral technological progress (i.e., an increase in a_{1x}). Differentiation of (7c) with respect to a_{1x} yields

$$dp/da_{1x} < 0 \quad \text{always holds,} \tag{9a}$$

$$d(r_1/w_1)/da_{1x} > 0 \quad \text{iff} \quad [\gamma/a_{1x}(\beta-\alpha)]+(d\gamma/ a_{1x}) > 0. \tag{9b}$$

The above results hold within the diversification cone (defined by condition (8)) if

$$\mu a_{1x}\{(a_{1y}^{1-\alpha}/a_{1x}^{1-\beta})^{1/(\beta-\alpha)}L_1K_1 + (a_{2x}^{\beta}/a_{2y}^{\alpha})^{1/(\beta-\alpha)}[(1-\beta)$$
$$(a_{1y}/a_{1x})^{1/(\beta-\alpha)}L_1K_2 + \beta(a_{2y}/a_{2x})^{1/(\beta-\alpha)}L_2K_1]\}$$
$$< (1-\alpha)(a_{1y}/a_{1x})^{1-\alpha/(\beta-\alpha)}L_1[(a_{1x}^{\beta}/a_{1y}^{\alpha})^{1/(\beta-\alpha)}K_1$$
$$+(a_{2x}^{\beta}/a_{2y}^{\alpha})^{1/(\beta-\alpha)}K_2]^2 /\alpha K_1. \tag{10}$$

It can be shown that there exists a nonempty parameter subspace where inequalities (8) and (10) hold. For instance, if α is sufficiently close to 0, the right-hand side of (10) approaches infinity while the left-hand side remains a limited positive value, thus inequality (10) holds. This means that the parameter subspace defined by (10) within the diversification cone is nonempty. Within this subspace, an increase in a_{1x} leads to an increase in the price of the capital-intensive good (X), but a decrease in the rental for capital. In other words, an increase in the price of the capital-intensive good and a decrease in the factor price for capital co-exist. This result is inconsistent with the Stolper-Samuelson theorem although it may be argued that the Stolper-Samuelson theorem is not invalidated because it is derived in a model with identical production technology between two trading countries whereas we have assumed a change in technology in only one country.

Next, we assume that the two countries have identical technologies and $a_{ij} = 1$. Consider a nonneutral technical change that raises the relative productivity of capital to labor in producing X (ie., an increase in α).

The differentiation of (7c) with respect to α yields

$$dp/d\alpha > 0 \text{ iff } -\ln[\alpha/(1-\alpha)][\beta-\theta(\beta-\alpha)][(\beta-\alpha)\theta+1-\beta]>\theta A, \qquad (11a)$$

$$d(r/w)/d\alpha < 0 \text{ always holds.} \qquad (11b)$$

It is easy to see that (11a) holds if α is sufficiently close to 0. We can also show that (11) and the condition for the general-equilibrium to occur within the diversification cone (condition 8) hold simultaneously if

$$-\ln[\alpha/(1-\alpha)][\beta-\theta(\beta-\alpha)][(\beta-\alpha)\theta+1-\beta]>\alpha[(L_1+L_2)K_1/(K_1+K_2)L_1. \qquad (12)$$

Inequality (12) holds if α is sufficiently close to 0. Hence, for a sufficiently small α, an increase in α raises the price of the capital-intensive good and at the same time reduces the rental for capital, a result that is again inconsistent with the Stolper-Samuelson theorem.

This result is rather intuitive. Refer to (7c), a change in α can be seen as having two effects: the indirect effect (a change in α affects p which in turn affects r/w) given by the first expression in (7c); and the direct effect described by the second expression in (7c). The Stolper-Samuelson theorem only accounts for the indirect effect. If the direct and indirect effect have the same sign, then the Stolper-Samuelson theorem holds. But if the two effects go opposite directions, then the Stolper-Samuelson theorem does not hold when the direct effect dominates.

We now consider a change in taste (θ) or endowments (L_i. K_i, $i=1,2$). From (7c), it is clear that a change in taste or endowment affects p and r/w in the same direction. That is, following a change in taste or endowments, the resultant relative change in product price and factor price is consistent with the Stolper-Samuelson theorem.

Summarizing the above analysis, we have

Proposition 1: Within the diversification cone, the co-movement of product price and factor price is consistent with the Stolper-Samuelson theorem if the price changes are due to changes in taste or endowment. The co-movement of product price and factor price may be inconsistent with the Stolper-Samuelson theorem if the price changes are due to changes in production parameters.

3.2. *Does the Stolper-Samuelson theorem hold outside the diversification cone?*

To determine whether the Stolper-Samuelson theorem holds outside the diversification cone, we solve for the local equilibrium in each structure outside the diversification cone.   The approach is similar to that used to solve for the local equilibrium in the interior structure (the solution presented in (7)). The equilibrium for each structure is summarized as follows:

Structure XY:

$$p = \theta a_{2y} L_2^{\beta} K_2^{1-\beta} / a_{1x} L_1^{\alpha} K_2^{1-\alpha}(1-\theta),$$
$$r_1/w_1 = (1-\alpha)L_1/\alpha K_1, \quad w_1 = \alpha\theta a_{2y} L_2^{\beta} K_2^{1-\beta}/L_1\,(1-\theta),$$
$$r_2/w_2 = (1-\beta)L_2/\beta K_2, \quad w_2 = \beta a_{2y}\,(K_2/L_2)^{1-\beta},$$
$$x_1 = a_{1x}L_1^{\alpha}K_1^{1-\alpha}, \quad y_2 = a_{2y}L_2^{\beta}K_2^{1-\beta}, \tag{13}$$

Structure (XY)Y: p is given by

$$F \equiv (a_{1y}B)^{-\alpha/(\beta-\alpha)}K_1(a_{1x}Ap)^{\beta/(\beta-\alpha)} - (1/\mu)(a_{1y}B)^{(1-\alpha)/(\beta-\alpha)}L_1(a_{1x}Ap)^{(\beta-1)/(\beta-\alpha)}$$
$$-\{\theta(\beta-\alpha)/[\beta-\theta(\beta-\alpha)]\}a_{2y}L_2^{\beta}K_2^{1-\beta} = 0, \tag{14a}$$
$$r_1/w_1 = (a_{1x}Ap/a_{1y}B)^{1/(\beta-\alpha)}, \quad w_1 = a_{1x}Ap(a_{1y}B/a_{1x}Ap)^{(1-\alpha)/(\beta-\alpha)}, \tag{14b}$$
$$r_2/w_2 = (1-\beta)L_2/K_2\beta, \quad w_2 = a_{2y}B\,[\beta K_2/L_2(1-\beta)]^{1-\beta}. \tag{14c}$$

Structure X(XY) is symmetric to structure (XY)Y.

First consider structure XY. Differentiation of prices in structure XY with respect to different parameters yields

$$d(r_i/w_i)/d\theta = 0 \quad \text{and} \quad dp/d\theta > 0;$$
$$d(r_i/w_i)/da_{ij} = 0, \quad dp/da_{2y} \neq 0, \quad \text{and} \quad dp/da_{1x} \neq 0;$$
$$d(r_1/w_1)/d\alpha < 0 \quad \text{and} \quad dp/d\alpha > 0 \text{ if } K_1 > L_1;$$
$$d(r_i/w_i)/dL_i > 0 \quad \text{and} \quad dp/dL_i < 0.$$

None of the above relationships between r/w and p is consistent with the Stolper-Samuelson theorem.

Next consider structures (XY)Y and X(XY). Because the two structures are symmetrical to each other, we can focus on structure (XY)Y only.

Consider country 1. As can be seen from (14b), the relationship between r_1/w_1 and p is independent of the taste or endowment parameter. Hence, any change in taste or endowment parameter will affect the prices of goods and the prices of factors in the same direction, that is, the Stolper-Samuelson theorem holds.

From (14a), we have

$$\partial F/\partial p > 0,\ \partial F/\partial \theta > 0,\ \partial F/\partial a_{1x} > 0,\ \partial F/\partial a_{1y} < 0,\ \partial F/\partial a_{2y} < 0.$$

And the application of the implicit-function theorem to the above yields

$$dp/d\theta = -(\partial F/\partial \theta)/(\partial F/\partial p) < 0,$$
$$dp/da_{1x} = -(\partial F/\partial a_{1x})/(\partial F/\partial p) < 0, \tag{15a}$$
$$dp/da_{1y} = -(\partial F/\partial a_{1y})/(\partial F/\partial p) > 0,$$
$$dp/da_{2y} = -(\partial F/\partial a_{2y})/(\partial F/\partial p) > 0.$$

Similarly, we can prove

$$dp/dK_i < 0,\ dp/dL_i > 0 \text{ for } i = 1, 2. \tag{15b}$$

Following the same approach as that used to prove Proposition 1, we can prove that there exist parameter subspaces such that changes in a_{1x}, a_{1y}, α, or β will generate co-movements of product and factor prices that are inconsistent with the Stolper-Samuelson theorem.

For country 2, we have

$$
\begin{aligned}
d(r_2/w_2)/d\theta &= 0, & d(r_2/w_2)/da_{1x} &= 0, \\
d(r_2/w_2)/da_{1y} &= 0, & d(r_2/w_2)/da_{2y} &= 0, \\
d(r_2/w_2)/dL_1 &= 0, & d(r_2/w_2)/dL_2 &> 0, \\
d(r_2/w_2)/dK_1 &= 0, & d(r_2/w_2)/dK_2 &< 0.
\end{aligned}
\tag{16}
$$

Conditions (15) and (16) indicate that the changes in prices caused by changes in parameters of tastes, production technology, and endowments may be inconsistent with the SS theorem.

Summarising the above analysis, we have

Proposition 2:   (i) In the structure where both countries completely specialize, the co-movements of factor and product prices are inconsistent with the Stolper-Samuelson theorem.

(ii) In the structure where only one country completely specializes, the co-movements of factor and product price are inconsistent with the SS theorem in the country that completely specializes. In the country which produces both goods, the co-movement of factor and product prices is consistent with the Stolper-Samuelson theorem if the price changes are due to taste or endowment changes; but may be inconsistent with the Stolper-Samuelson theorem if the price changes are due to production parameter changes.

The result of Proposition 2 is well-known to trade theorists. The implication of the result may deserve more attention than it has so far attracted since it is likely that the parameter subspace for the general-equilibrium to occur within the diversification cone is smaller than the subspace for the general-equilibrium to occur outside the diversification cone.

3.3. Does the Stolper-Samuelson theorem hold when the general-equilibrium jumps from one structure to another?

Let us first consider the case where two countries open up to trade with each other such that the general-equilibrium jumps from the autarky structure to structure XY where both countries completely specialize in producing a single good.

The autarky equilibrium is as follows:

$$p_i = (a_{iy}/a_{ix})(r_i/w_i)^{\beta-\alpha}B/A, \qquad r_i/w_i = L_i\mu/K_i,$$

$$x_i = a_{ix}A(\beta\mu-1+\beta)L_i^{\alpha}K_i^{1-\alpha}/(\beta-\alpha)\mu,$$

$$y_i = a_{iy}b(1-\alpha-\alpha\mu)L_i^{\beta}K_i^{1-\beta}/(\beta-\alpha)\mu, \qquad (17)$$

$$K_{ix} = (1-\alpha)(\beta\mu-1+\beta)K_i/(\beta-\alpha)\mu,$$

$$K_{iy} = (1-\beta)(1-\alpha-\alpha\mu)K_i/(\beta-\alpha)\mu,$$

$$L_{ix} = \alpha K_{ix}r_i/w_i(1-\alpha), \qquad L_{iy} = \beta K_{iy}r_i/w_i(1-\beta),$$

where $\mu \equiv [(\beta-\alpha)\theta+1-\beta]/[\beta-\theta(\beta-\alpha)]$.

Comparing the prices in autarky (given in (17)) and those in structure XY, it is easy to see that the capital rental relative to wage is higher in structure XY than in autarky, and that the price of good X is lower in XY than in autarky if

$$\mu^{(\beta-\alpha)}B/A > \theta a_{2y}(L_2/L_1)^{\beta}(K_2/K_1)^{1-\beta}/a_{1y}(1-\theta). \tag{18}$$

Condition (18) and the condition for structure XY to be the general-equilibrium (given in Table 1) hold simultaneously if

$$(1-\beta)L_2(a_{2y}/a_{2x})^{1/(\beta-\alpha)}/\beta\gamma K_2$$
$$> \theta a_{2y}(L_2/L_1)^{\beta}(K_2/K_1)^{1-\beta}/a_{1y}(1-\theta)$$

and

$$\mu^{(\beta-\alpha)}B(L_1/L_2)^{\beta}(K_1/K_2)^{1-\beta}/A$$
$$> \theta a_{2x}[(1-\alpha)\beta K_2L_1/\alpha(1-\beta)L_2K_1]^{\beta-\alpha}/a_{1x}(1-\theta).$$

The above conditions hold if θ is sufficiently close to 0, which implies the parameter subspace that satisfies both condition (18) and the condition for structure XY is nonempty. Within this parameter subspace, the co-movement of factor and product prices is inconsistent with the Stolper-Samuelson theorem.

If we compare the prices in autarky and those in structure $(XY)_x(XY)_y$, we find that when the equilibrium jumps from autarky to structure $(XY)_x(XY)_y$, both the factor price for capital and the price of the capital intensive good X increase in country 1. This is consistent with the Stolper-Samuelson theorem.

It should be noted that if transaction cost is zero, autarky would not be the general-equilibrium (i.e., the parameter subspace for autarky to be equilibrium is empty). Thus in the above analysis, we have implicitly assumed that some exogenous trade barrier existed such that autarky was the equilibrium and then the trade barrier was removed such that the general-equilibrium structure jumps from autarky to structure XY.[4]

Now consider the case when general-equilibrium jumps from structure $(XY)_x(XY)_y$ where both countries produce both goods, to structure XY where both countries completely specialize.

---

[4] If we introduce positive transaction costs to our model, the jump of equilibrium structure from autarky to trade can be endogenized.

From equations (6) and (13), it is easy to see that in country 1, the factor price for capital (relative to wage rate) is higher in structure XY than in structure $(XY)_x(XY)_y$ if and only if

$$\mu\gamma < (1-\alpha)L_1(a_{1y}/a_{1x})^{1/(\beta-\alpha)}/K_1\alpha. \tag{19}$$

Also, the price of the capital-intensive good X is lower in structure XY than in structure $(XY)_x(XY)_y$ if and only if

$$\mu\gamma > A\theta a_{2y}L_2{}^{\beta}K_2{}^{1-\beta}/L_1{}^{\alpha}K_1{}^{1-\alpha}a_{1x}(1-\theta)B. \tag{20}$$

Conditions (19) and (20) hold simultaneously if

$$(1-\alpha)a_{1y}{}^{1/(\beta-\alpha)} > \alpha a_{1x}{}^{(1-\alpha-\beta)/(\beta-\alpha)}a_{2y}L_2{}^{\beta}K_2{}^{1-\beta}K_1{}^{\alpha}/L_1{}^{1+\alpha},$$

which holds if α is sufficiently close to 0. This means that there exists a parameter subspace such that the factor price for capital (relative to wage rate) wage is higher and the price of X is lower in structure XY than in structure $(XY)_x(XY)_y$. Within this parameter subspace, the co-movement of factor price and product price in response to parameter changes that generate a jump from $(XY)_x(XY)_y$ to XY is inconsistent with the Stolper-Samuelson theorem.

The above analysis is summarized in the following proposition.

Proposition 3:   (i) The co-movement of factor and product prices is consistent with the Stolper-Samuelson theorem when the equilibrium structure jumps from autarky to the interior trade structure with partial specialization in both countries. However, the consistency may be absent when the general-equilibrium structure jumps from autarky to a trade structure with complete specialization in both countries.

(ii) The co-movement of factor and product prices may be inconsistent with the Stolper-Samuelson theorem if a change in parameters causes the general-equilibrium to jump from the structure with incomplete specialization in both countries to one with complete specialization in each country.

To summarize, our analysis in this section suggests that the general prediction of the Stolper-Samulson theorem is not always consistent with the comparative-statics results derived from a specific general-equilibrium HO model. In particular, the Stolper-Samuelson theorem's prediction does not always hold when changes in production parameters lead to changes in prices even within the diversification cone. It does not always hold outside the diversification cone; and it does not always hold when the general-equilibrium jumps from one structure to another.[5]

4. Conclusion

In this paper, we have developed a HO model with endogenous prices of goods and factors and conducted both marginal and infra-marginal comparative-statics analysis of general-equilibrium to examine the co-movement of factor and product prices.   Our analysis has invalidated the general applicability of the Stolper-Samuelson theorem, and therefore confirmed the "everything-possible" theorem of Sonnenschein (1973), Mantel (1974) and Debrew (1974).

Our analysis suggests that the traditional analysis of the core trade theorems based on the HO model is of a partial-equilibrium nature in two senses.   First, it assumes exogenous prices of goods (or factors) and investigates how factor (product) prices change in response to changes in product price   (or endowment parameters).   Such a partial-equilibrium analysis could be misleading since it ignores some interdependencies and feedback loops between prices and quantities, between consumption and production, between the markets for goods and factors, and between different agents' self-interested behaviors. Second, the traditional analysis confines itself within the interior structure and ignores corner structures.   Consequently   it   cannot   conduct   infra-marginal comparative-static analysis and thus ignores discontinuous jumps of general-equilibrium between different trade patterns.

It should be noted that the traditional analysis of the HO model improves on the classical Marshallian partial-equilibrium analysis which focuses on only one market in that it includes all markets and some (but not all) interactions between the markets. Possibly because the traditional analysis of the HO model provides a fuller picture than the Marshallian partial-equilibrium analysis, its limitations have not received much

---

[5] Note that it is enough to reject a theorem by finding a single specific counterexample.

attention although the shortcomings of the Marshallian analysis is well-known.

We are cautious about the policy implications of our results because our results are obtained from a specific model. If we change the functional forms, the results may change too. We have resisted the temptation to generalize the model because the very point the specific model makes is that comparative-statics of general-equilibrium, which are the main sources of the explaining power of economic models, are model-structure specific, functional-form specific, and parameter-value specific. Thus any attempt to generalize the model to obtain unambiguous comparative-statics predictions is likely to be ill-fated. For the same reason, it is perhaps a good rule of thumb to treat with caution any general comparative-statics results of general-equilibrium derived from models with no explicit specifications.[6]

Future research can explicitly introduce transaction costs to the model. With positive transaction costs, the jump of equilibrium from autarky to trade can be endogenized. Moreover, increasing returns can be introduced to the production process. To depart from the constant-return assumption will no doubt enrich the implications of the model, but is likely to make the model more difficult to manage.

References

Deardorff, Alan and Stern, Robert eds. (1994), *The Stolper-Samuelson Theorem*, Ann Arbor, University of Michigan Press.

Debreu, G. (1974), "Excess Demand Functions," *Journal of Mathematical Economics*, 1, 15-21.

Ethier, W. (1974), "Some of the Theorems of International Trade with Many Goods and Factors," *Journal of International Economics*, 4, 199-206.

---

[6] We examine the validity of other core trade theorems in another paper.

Mantel, R. (1974), "On the Characterization of Aggregate Excess Demand," *Journal of Economic Theory*, 7, 348-353.

Melvin, J. R. (1968), "Production and Trade with Two Factors and Three Goods," *American Economic Review*, 58, 1249-1268.

Sonnenschein, H. (1973), "Do Walras' Identity and Continuity Characterize the Class of Community Excess Demand Functions?" *Journal of Economic Theory*, 6, 345-54.

Stolper, Wolfgang and Sammuelson, Paul (1941), "Protection and Real Wages," *Review of Economic Studies*, 9, 58-73.

Wong, K-Y. (1995), International Trade in Goods and Factor Mobility, Cambridge, MA, MIT Press.

Part 4

Division of Labor in Models of Trade with Economies of Scale

CHAPTER 9

A RICARDO MODEL WITH ECONOMIES OF SCALE[*†]

Ralph E. Gomory[*]

Alfred P. Sloan Foundation

Introduction

There are significant and unavoidable technical difficulties in working with large models having scale economies, and this paper represents a direct attack on those difficulties. The techniques introduced here enable us to deal directly with two-country models having *large* numbers of traded goods and, consequently, very large numbers of equilibria. Our model is directly analogous to the classical Ricardo model but with economies of scale in place of the classical linear or diseconomies assumptions.

We show that, contrary to what one might expect, the many equilibria do not occur just anywhere. Rather they lie densely in a clearly delineated region of a graph of utility versus relative national income which we describe. This region of equilibria has a characteristic shape that persists across many different models and has significant economic consequences. We also provide algorithms that, even for large problems, select from the large array of equilibria those that tend to maximize utility for each country.

---

[*] Reprinted from *Journal of Economic Theory*, 62 (2), Gomory, Ralph E., "A Ricardo Model with Economies of Scale," 394-419, 1994, with permission from Elsevier.
[†] A summary of some of the results of this paper appeared as Gomory [2]. This paper is a revised version of C. V. Starr Economic Research Report RR 92-04 and has been greatly improved by suggestions from William J. Baumol.
[*] The author mentions with pleasure the many contributions of Herbert E. Scarf without which this paper would not have been written.

Recent work has contributed greatly to the understanding of the theoretical consequences of scale economies for trade theory. This literature has generally worked with small models, typically two countries and two goods. The results of this paper are complementary to this work. There are significant features of a scale economies world that only appear in the larger models and require the analysis of regions of equilibria. There are also features that emerge from the analysis of the individual equilibria in the smaller models which cannot be deduced from the study of equilibrium regions.

Summary of results

(i) In the presence of economies of scale of the type we specify below, the set of equilibrium solutions can be described by a *region* in which these equilibrium points lie, and which they tend to *fill up*. The equilibrium points tend to fill up the solution region in the sense that, given any arbitrarily selected point, P, in the region, then, with a sufficient number of commodities traded, an equilibrium point will appear within any pre-selected distance, however small, from P.

(ii) We give simple and rapid algorithms for obtaining from among the very large number of possible equilibria those equilibria that are very good for one country or the other. We see that the best possible equilibrium for one country is usually poor for the other. The algorithms also show that the two countries' interests are less opposed when their demand structures are similar, and more opposed when they are dissimilar.

(iii) We give a simple algorithm for calculating the boundaries of the region. This allows the location and shape of the region to be obtained rapidly even for large models.

(iv) The characteristic shape of the region of equilibria has the following implications:

(a) The region always contains a large subregion of equilibria that are advantageous and often strongly advantageous to Country 1 relative to autarky. However, the region also contains a subregion at whose equilibria Country 1 receives *less* utility than it would in autarky. This region can sometimes be substantial in size, especially for the larger trading partner.

(b) The region always contains a central subregion, often a very large one, within which the interests of the trading partners are generally opposed. At the center of this subregjon is an area of equilibria with utility above autarky for both countries as in the classical model. However, moving to the right in this subregion, which means that Country 1 captures more and more industries, generally results in significant further increases in utility for Country 1 accompanied by significant losses in utility for Country 2.

(c) As Country 1 captures an ever larger share of export industries from Country 2 there comes a point beyond which any further acquisition of industries by Country 1 is disadvantageous to *both* Country 1 and Country 2.

Statements (4a)–(4c) apply, with obvious changes, to Country 2. These results cannot be obtained from very small models because the subregions referred to will often be completely empty of equilibria. Experience indicates that with six or more industries the regions are already reasonably populated.

Assumptions of the model and of the related literature

The economic literature has employed at least three different models of the nature of scale economies. The first of these, which we use here, assumes that firms are perfectly competitive, that they operate as individual entities under constant returns to scale, and that the scale economies are produced by externalities that benefit the firms within a single industry in a given country. Under such circumstances prices are set at levels that yield zero profits. Examples of work using this approach include Kemp [8] and Ethier [1]. The assumptions of this model also match quite well the author's direct observations of industries containing small numbers of large firms which are very competitive with each other. These firms have significant internal economies at low levels of output, but at the higher levels at which they actually operate the internal economies of scale have been realized and the firms' cost structure tends to be linear.

The second widely used scale economies model assumes them to be internal to the firm, while the third model, like the first, assumes perfect competition and externalities. Externalities however are generated by the industry's output world wide.

This literature, as well as the work of Helpman and Krugman [7] and that of Grossman and Helpman [6], has greatly enlarged our understanding of scale economies. The results of this paper are consistent with and complementary to this existing work.

1.   Some Basic Properties and the Basic Graph

The outcomes from a typical model are illustrated by Figure 1 which is a type of graph we use repeatedly. Figure 1 plots Cobb-Douglas utility on the right vertical axis against normalized national income Z_1 for Country 1 on the horizontal axis. By normalized national income Z_j of Country j we mean $Z_j = Y_j/(Y_1+Y_2)$ where Y_j is the national income of Country j. Each dot in the figure represents an equilibrium point. The large dots are outcomes in which only one of the two countries is a producer for each good; these are the perfectly specialized equilibria which play a special role in this theory. The exchange rate w_1/w_2, or equivalently the ratio of the wages in the two countries corresponding to the normalized national incomes, is plotted on the top horizontal line. The utility obtained by Country 1 in a state of autarky is marked by the horizontal bar on the right. The utility of Country 2, the larger country, can be read from the left vertical axis and the normalized national income of Country 2 is $Z_2=1-Z_1$. To avoid confusion, only the outline of the region of perfectly specialized equilibria has been plotted for Country 2, not the utility for Country 2 of the individual equilibria. The utility of each country is normalized separately so that the greatest utility it attains is 1.

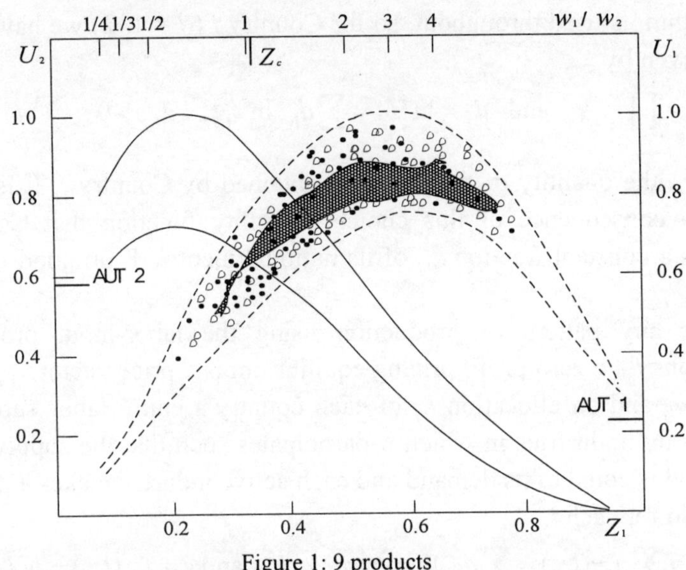

Figure 1: 9 products

There are several aspects of Figure 1 worth noting. First we see the large number of equilibria, more than 20,000, present even in this nine-industry model. Second, the equilibria form an array of points with a rather definite shape which is in fact characteristic of many models. Third, the upper edge of the array of outcomes is rather well defined. In the figure it is marked by a dotted line. The equilibria near this boundary are the ones that do relatively well for Country 1 for any given Z_1. It is this boundary line, and the equilibria near it, that we compute by simple and rapid calculations in Section 3. Fourth, there is a lower boundary as well as an upper boundary to the array of perfectly specialized equilibrium points; this lower boundary can also be computed easily.

The data tables on which Figure 1 and all other figures are based appear in Gomory [3].

2. Existence of Solutions

In this model the production functions $f_{i,j}$ for good i in Country j always have economies of scale. The Cobb-Douglas utility function, or its logarithm, is used throughout, so for Country j ($j = 1, 2$) we have utility U_j given by

$$U_j = \prod_i y_{i,j}^{d_{i,j}} \quad \text{and} \quad u_j = \ln U_j = \sum_i d_{i,j} \ln y_{i,j}, \quad d_{i,j} > 0, \quad \sum_i d_{i,j} = 1,$$

with $y_{i,j}$ the quantity of the ith good obtained by Country j. It is a well known consequence of this choice of utility function that Country j spends a constant fraction $d_{i,j}$ of its national income Y_j on good i, for all prices p_i.

For any pattern of production using the labor-input production functions $f_{i,j}$, a zero-profit pricing equilibrium is a price vector p_i, wage rates w_j, and an allocation $l_{i,j}$ of each country's entire labor supply, L_j, among the industries in which it participates such that the supply of the ith good is equal to its demand and each active industry makes a profit of zero. So for each i

$$p_i \sum_i f_{i,j}(l_{i,j}) = \sum_i d_{i,j} Y_j = \sum_i d_{i,j} w_j L_j \quad \text{and} \quad p_i f_{i,j}(l_{i,j}) = w_j l_{i,j} \quad (2.1)$$

We now make two assumptions about the production functions $f_{i,j}$:

A1. Aside from a possible initial interval in which $f_{i,j}(l_{i,j})$ is zero, average productivity $f_{i,j}(l_{i,j})/ l_{i,j}$ is continuous and strictly increasing.

A2. Each country is autarky produces a positive quantity of all goods; i.e., $f_{i,j}(d_{i,j}L_j) > 0$.

Theorem 2.1:   Under these assumptions, there is a zero-profit pricing equilibrium for any pattern of specialization in which each of the two countries is the sole producer of at least one of the goods in which it specializes. At all these equilibria each industry assigned to each country will produce positive quantities of output.

The proof of this theorem is given in Appendix 2-1 of Gomory [3]. Since the theorem allows three possibilities for each industry, two possible sole producers or both producing, we would expect something on the order of 3^n equilibria. The actual formula is $3^n - 2^{n+1} + 1$. This explains the many equilibria present in Figure 1.

To ensure stability we make a third assumption about our production functions.

A3. $$\lim f(l_{i,j})/l_{i,j} = 0 \quad \text{as} \quad l_{i,j} \to 0.$$

A3 asserts that a non-producer's unit cost for very small l_{ij} is arbitrarily large. If Country j is a non-producer of good i at some equilibrium point, A3 ensures that the non-producing industry would earn a negative profit in the immediate neighborhood of that equilibrium. Conditions A1–A3 are satisfied for all production functions of the form $f(l) = el^\alpha$ with $\alpha > 1$, as well as by any production function that satisfies the increasing average productivity condition A1, and is zero for an initial interval consistent with A2. It does not hold for the Ricardo case el^α with $\alpha = 1$, but it does hold if el is preceded by a short interval of zero output.

3. Boundaries of the Region of Equilibria

We now introduce variables $x_{i,j}$ that determine the pattern of production and play a key role in the analysis. At any equilibrium point we have the conditions (2.1). Together these imply that, for each good, expenditure equals wages, so

$$d_{i,1}Y_1 + d_{i,2}Y_2 = w_1 l_{i,1} + w_2 l_{i,2}.$$

We now define $x_{i,j}$ to be the fraction of the total expenditure on the ith product that is spent on product made in Country j. So

$$x_{i,1}\left(d_{i,1}Y_1 + d_{i,2}Y_2\right) = w_1 l_{i,1} \quad \text{and} \quad x_{i,2}\left(d_{i,1}Y_1 + d_{i,2}Y_2\right) = w_2 l_{i,2}. \quad \text{(3.la, b)}$$

By definition $0 \le x_{i,j} \le 1$ and $x_{i,1} + x_{i,2} = 1$. We sometimes refer to the collection of $x_{i,j}$ as the assignment x.

We usually use normalized national incomes $Z_j = Y_j/(Y_1 + Y_2)$. Clearly $Z_1 + Z_2 = 1$ and $0 \le Z_i \le 1$. Since there are no profits, the national incomes of the two countries are $Y_j = w_j L_j$, so $Z_1/Z_2 = Y_1/Y_2 = (w_1/w_2)(L_1/L_2)$, which shows that Z_1/Z_2 is proportional to the wage ratio. We also use Z without a subscript to denote the two-vector $Z = (Z_1, Z_2)$. In terms of these normalized national incomes, (3.1 a) and (3.1 b) become

$$x_{i,1}(d_{i,1}Z_1 + d_{i,2}Z_2) = l_{i,1}^* Z_1, \text{ and } x_{i,2}(d_{i,1}Z_1 + d_{i,2}Z_2) = l_{i,2}^* Z_2. \quad \text{(3.2a, b)}$$

Here the $l^*_{i,j}$ are normalized labor variables, $l^*_{i,1} = l_{i,j}/L_j$ representing the fraction of the labor force in Country j employed in making product i. One of the conditions for equilibrium is that the assignment of labor provided by the $x_{i,j}$ is in fact a partition of the entire labor force; i.e., that $\sum_i l^*_{i,1} = 1$. We can sum (3.2a) and (3.2b), obtaining the identities

$$\sum_i l^*_{i,1} = \sum_i \frac{1}{Z_1}\left(d_{i,1}Z_1 + d_{i,2}Z_2\right)x_{i,1} \quad \text{and}$$

$$\sum_i l^*_{i,2} = \sum_i \frac{1}{Z_2}\left(d_{i,1}Z_1 + d_{i,2}Z_2\right)x_{i,2}. \qquad (3.3a,b)$$

The n.a.s.c. for assignment x to provide a partition of the labor force is that x and the normalized national income Z make $\sum_i l^*_{i,j} = 1$.

This is equivalent to

$$\sum_i (d_{i,1}Z_1 + d_{i,2}Z_2)x_{i,1} = Z_1 \quad \text{and} \quad \sum_i (d_{i,1}Z_1 + d_{i,2}Z_2)x_{i,2} = Z_2. \qquad (3.4a, b)$$

Equations (3.4a) and (3.4b) are in fact linearly dependent and therefore we need only one of them. This dependence is a consequence of Walras Law, and can also be verified directly by adding the two equations. We refer to (3.4a) and (3.4b) as the zero excess labor condition. This condition links *any* assignment x to the Z value, $Z(x)$, required to satisfy (3.4a) and (3.4b). In economic terms $Z(x)$ gives the wage ratio w_1/w_2 at which the production pattern resulting from x exactly uses the labor of both countries.

Equilibrium conditions and integer x

We now look at the conditions that must be met for x to be an equilibrium point. For any x, whether it is an equilibrium x or not, the normalized national income $Z(x)$ required to satisfy the zero excess labor condition can be calculated from (3.4a) and (3.4b). x and $Z(x)$ then determine labor quantities $l^*_{i,j}$ from Eqs. (3.2a) and (3.2b) whose meaning is that expenditures must match wage bills. The $l^*_{i,j}$ in turn determine the amounts produced, $f_{i,j}(l_{i,j})$.

For this arbitrary x and its $Z(x)$ to determine an equilibrium point, only one more condition must hold. As in (2.1) there must be a price p_i

for the ith good at which the value of the goods produced matches the wage bill; i.e., $p_i f_{i,j} = w_j l_{i,j}$ for $j = 1, 2$. We refer to this as the price condition (3.P). When there is more than one producer both must have the same unit cost $f_{i,j}(l_{i,j})/w_j l_{i,j} = 1/p_i$. However, when there is only one producer, that producer's unit cost alone determines a p_i satisfying (3.P) since for the non-producer we always have $p_i f_{i,j} = 0 = w_j l_{i,j}$.

If any x and $Z(x)$ satisfying (3.4a) and (3.4b) meet the price condition, supply equals wage bill equals demand, the total labor force is used, and x is an equilibrium point.

While most arbitrarily chosen x and their $Z(x)$ do not satisfy (3.P), all integers x do. For integer x, i.e., $x_{i,j} = 0, 1$, there is only one producer of each good so (3.P) is always satisfied. Consequently *all integer x are equilibria.* They are of course the perfectly specialized equilibria. Condition A3 then gives these equilibria a certain degree of stability. We will also see that the perfectly specialized equilibria are the ones that largely determine the shape of the equilibrium region.

Utility and linearized utility

The logarithm of Cobb-Douglas utility is a sum of terms involving the quantity $y_{i,1}$ of the ith good Country 1 receives. The $y_{i,j}$ can be written as the product of two terms $F_{i,1}(Z)Q_i(x,Z)$, where $Q_i(x,Z)$ is the total quantity of the ith good produced in the world and $F_{i,1}(Z)$ is the fraction obtained by Country 1.

$$u_1(x,Z) = \ln U_1(x,Z) = \sum_i d_{i,1} \ln F_{i,1}(Z)Q_i(x,Z). \qquad (3.5)$$

Since the goods are all sold at a world price, the fraction going to Country 1 is its expenditure as a fraction of world expenditure and the world quantity produced is the sum of the quantities produced in each country so

$$F_{i,1}(Z) = \frac{d_{i,1}Y_1}{d_{i,1}Y_1 + d_{i,2}Y_2} + \frac{d_{i,1}Z_1}{d_{i,1}Z_1 + d_{i,2}Z_2}$$

and

$$Q_i(x,Z) = q_{i,1}(x_{i,1},Z) + q_{i,2}(x_{i,2},Z).$$

The $q_{i,j}$ are defined by $q_{i,j}(x_{i,j}Z) = f_{i,j}(l_{i,j})$ where the labor quantity $l_{i,j}$ is determined by x and Z and is found from (3.2a) and (3.2b). Substituting for $F_{i,j}$ and $Q_{i,j}$ in (3.5) gives

$$u_1(x,Z) = \sum_i d_{i,1} \ln \frac{d_{i,1}Z_1}{d_{i,1}Z_1 + d_{i,2}Z_2} \{q_{i,1}(x_{i,1},Z_1) + q_{i,2}(x_{i,2},Z_2)\}. \quad (3.6)$$

This expression is complicated both in its dependence on the assignment x and on the normalized national incomes Z. In addition, for equilibrium x, Z and x are linked to each other through (3.4a) and (3.4b). This makes it difficult to compare the many different equilibria except by fully computing each one. Although useful and suggestive experiments along that line were done as part of this work, we take a different approach in what follows. We emphasize perfectly specialized equilibria and the simplifications that are possible with them.

If x_1 and x_2 are any variables constrained to be either 0 or 1, and if $x_1 = 0$ implies $x_2 = 1$ and vice versa, then we always have for any function $g(x_1, x_2)$ the tautology $g(x_1, x_2) = x_1 g(1,0) + x_2 g(0,1)$. x_1 and x_2 act as a switch between the two possible values of g. The individual terms $x_{i,1}$ and $x_{i,2}$ of an *integer* assignment x are of course variables of this type. Letting g be successively the individual terms of the sum (3.6) and using the tautology give an expression for utility that is valid for integer x. This is the linearized utility Lu_1.

$$Lu_1(x,Z) = \sum_i \{x_{i,1}d_{i,1} \ln F_{i,1}(Z)q_{i,1}(1,Z) + x_{i,2}d_{i,1} \ln F_{i,1}(Z)q_{i,2}(1,Z)\}. \quad (3.L)$$

For integer x *only* we have $Lu_1(x,Z) = u_1(x,Z)$. The merit of $Lu_1(x,Z)$ is that for fixed Z it is linear in the variables x.

Boundary calculation preliminaries

Using the concept of boundary turns out to enormously simplify finding high utility equilibria and determining the shape of the equilibrium region in the (Z_1, U_1) plane. To find the upper boundary of the array of points (Z_1, U_1) corresponding to all perfectly specialized equilibria, we might think of defining a function $B_1(Z)$ to be the result of fixing Z and then maximizing $u_1(x,Z) = Lu_1(x,Z)$ over all perfectly specialized equilibria x having that Z value, i.e., satisfying (3.4a) and (3.4b) for that Z. This is maximizing a linear expression Lu_1 over integer x satisfying a single linear constraint, a very simple integer programming problem. The collection of values $B_1(Z)$, computed in this way for each Z, would form an upper boundary for the perfectly specialized equilibria.

The maximization problem for each fixed Z has the following economic interpretation: Once Z is fixed, the expenditure in each country for the ith good is completely determined. Therefore the fraction $F_{i,j}$ of the total production of the ith good that goes to Country j is also fixed. The only way to improve the utility that Country j gets from the ith good is to increase Q_i. This can only be done, for integer x, by assigning its production entirely to the producer who is, at that Z, the more productive one. The labor constraint (3.4a) and (3.4b) prevents this assignment from being made simultaneously for every good, and the maximization problem is to find the best assignment possible subject to the labor constraint.

While this direction and motivation are fundamentally correct, there is still one difficulty to overcome: Precisely as written, Eqs. (3.4a) and (3.4b) will not usually have *any* solution in integer x for an arbitrary Z, much less many different x to maximize over. This reflects the economic fact that there are equilibria for certain Z only. To deal with this difficulty we need one more concept, the classical level. In Gomory [2] this was referred to as the Ricardo level.

The classical level

For any Z we can define an assignment $x^C(Z)$, which we call the classical assignment. The components of $x^C(Z)$ are defined by setting $x_{i,1}=1$ if $q_{i,1}(1,Z) > q_{i,2}(1,Z)$ while otherwise $x_{i,1} = 0$. This is simply assigning the production of good i entirely to Country 1 if Country 1 is the cheaper producer at that Z, and otherwise assigning it entirely to Country 2.

For an arbitrary Z and its $x^C(Z)$, we usually do not have equality in (3.4a) and (3.4b). In fact, for Z with very small Z_1, which means a low wage in Country 1, the terms on the right in (3.3a), involving as they do

Z_2/Z_1 , will be very large, and the right side of (3.3a) will be greater than 1. In economic terms, if the wage is very low in Country 1 and production is assigned to the country that is the cheaper producer, the resulting demand for labor in Country 1 will outstrip the supply. Similarly, for any $x^C(Z)$ with large Z_1, which means a high wage in Country 1, the terms on the right in (3.4a) will be small, their total will be < 1, so demand for Country 1's labor will be less than the supply.

As wages increase, the individual terms on the right in (3.3a) only decrease, while the $x_{i,1}$ switch from 1 to 0, as Country 1 stops being the cheaper producer in industry after industry. Thus the demand for labor in Country 1 produced by $x^C(Z)$ decreases as Z_1 increases. It follows that there is a unique transition value of Z_1 which we call Z_C, the classical level. Z_C separates the Z_1 ($Z_1 < Z_C$) for which demand exceeds the labor supply from the $Z_1 (Z_1 > Z_C)$ for which the demand is less than the labor supply. More formally we define the classical level to be $Z_C = \sup Z_1$ such that if $x = x^C(Z)$, $\sum_i (d_{i,1}Z_1 + d_{i,2}Z_2)x_{i,1} > Z_1$. For Country 2 the situation is reversed. Below the classical level the demand for Country 2's labor is less than the supply, if x^C is used, and *above* Z_C the demand exceeds the supply.

Since for any Z_1 we can easily determine if it is above or below Z_C, Z_C is easily calculated iteratively. In Figures 1–3 and 5–7 the classical level is marked by a vertical bar.

The boundary $B_1(Z)$

Earlier, in outlining a boundary calculation that involved maximizing over many equilibria x for a fixed Z, we encountered the difficulty that, instead of having many specialized equilibria, there were, for most Z, no equilibria at all. To deal with this difficulty we now relax (3.4b) to an inequality, which then has many solutions for any Z, and define $B_1(Z)$ by the integer programming problem

$$B_1(Z) = \underset{x}{\text{Max}}\, u_1(x,Z) = \underset{x}{\text{Max}}\, Lu_1(x,Z) \qquad x \text{ integer,}$$

$$\text{with } \sum_i (d_{i,1}Z_1 + d_{i,2}Z_2)x_{i,2} \le Z_2. \tag{3.7}$$

The inequality assumes the direction shown if Z is above the classical level $(Z_1 > Z_C)$ and is reversed for Z below the classical level. This relaxation allows underutilization of labor in the country whose labor is scarce. Consequently maximizing utility for the given Z should push the inequality very close to equality as the attempt is made to use this valuable labor.

In (3.7) we have arbitrarily used the inequality form of (3.4b) as the constraint. Of course we could just as well have chosen (3.4a). When we need to refer to the inequality versions of (3.4a) or (3.4b) we designate them by i-(3.4a) and i-(3.4b). It is always assumed that these inequalities point in the proper directions.

Inequality i-(3.4b) only involves the variables $x_{i,2}$, but the objective function Lu_1 involves both $x_{i,1}$ and $x_{i,2}$. If we rewrite Lu_1 in terms of $x_{i,2}$ only, using $x_{i,1} + x_{i,2} = 1$ to eliminate $x_{i,1}$, we get

$$Lu_1(x,Z) = \sum_i d_{i,1} \ln F_{i,1} q_{i,1}(1,Z) + \sum_i x_{i,2} d_{i,1} \ln \frac{q_{i,2}(1,Z)}{q_{i,1}(1,Z)} \qquad (3.8)$$

so we can put the maximization problem (3.7) in a form that involves the $x_{i,2}$ only. If we use $P_1(Z)$ to denote the first sum in (3.8), which is a function of Z but not of $x_{i,2}$, and use $c_{i,2}(Z)$ to denote $d_{i,1} \ln\{q_{i,2}(1,Z)/q_{i,1}(1,Z)\}$, we obtain

$$B_1(Z) = \underset{x}{\text{Max}}\, P_1(Z) + \sum_i x_{i,2} c_{i,2}(Z)$$

$$\text{with } \sum_i (d_{i,1} Z_1 + d_{i,2} Z_2) x_{i,2} \leq Z_2 \text{ and } x_{i,2} \text{ integer.} \qquad (3.9)$$

Equation (3.9) is our basic tool in dealing with equilibrium regions. In (3.9) both the objective function and the inequality are linear in x for fixed Z. While the coefficients of the $x_{i,2}$ in the inequality are always positive, the $c_{i,2}$ in the objective function can be either positive or negative. The sign of $c_{i,2}$ is determined by the ratio $q_{i,2}(Z)/q_{i,1}(Z)$, if $q_{i,2} > q_{i,1}$. If $q_{i,2} > q_{i,1}$, Country 2 is the cheaper producer of the world supply and $c_{i,2}$ will be positive. If Country 1 is the cheaper producer $c_{i,2}$ will be negative.

            R. E. Gomory

Computation of $B_1(Z)$

The $B_1(Z)$ defined by (3.9) can be computed by any integer programming technique. For a single inequality problem such as this, ordinary dynamic programming is very effective. This calculation is spelled out in Appendix 3-2 of Gomory [3]. The dynamic program gives actual integer solutions x so that we can compute the corresponding $Z(x)$ from (3.4b) and go on to compute utility, and hence fully describes the maximizing equilibrium for each Z_1. As Section 4 shows, the equilibria so attained will be arbitrarily close to the boundary as the problem size grows. In practice we find the resulting equilibria to be extremely close to the boundary even for very moderate sized problems. We can spell out the boundary curve by computing a series of Z_1 values from $Z_1 = 0$ to $Z_1 = 1$, and we get a whole series of boundary points and nearby equilibria. This entire calculation requires only minutes on a home personal computer (see Section 5 of Gomory [3]).

The boundary $B(Z)$

There is an even easier calculation that gives a slightly weaker but extremely useful boundary curve, which we call $B(Z)$. To get $B(Z)$ we further relax the problem (3.9) by allowing *continuous* $x_{i,2}$. It is easily seen that with continuous variables the maximizing x will always satisfy the inequality in (3.9) as an equality, so in fact $B(Z)$ is given by maximizing $Lu_1(x, Z)$ subject to (3.4b); i.e.,

$$B(Z) = \max_x Lu_1(x, Z) = P_1(Z) + \sum_i x_{i,2} c_{i,2}$$

$$\text{subject to } \sum_i (d_{i,1} Z_1 + d_{i,2} Z_2) x_{i,2} = Z_2. \tag{3.9a}$$

In (3.9a) we are looking at a particularly simple linear programming problem with only one equation and upper bounds, $0 \le x_{i,2} \le 1$, on the variables $x_{i,2}$. The solution technique for such a special linear programming problem or "continuous knapsack problem" is particularly simple. Equation (3.9a) can be thought of as filling a space of length Z_2 with amounts $x_{i,2}$ (not necessarily integer) of goods. The ith good has length $d_{i,1} Z_1 + d_{i,2} Z_2$ and value $c_{i,2}$; the goal is to fill the space with the most valuable assortment of goods. The solution to such a problem is to put goods in the order of their value per unit length, which we call value density. The densest good is used first. When its turn comes the amount $x_{i,2}$ of each good is increased from zero until either the amount $x_{i,2} = 1$, or Eq. (3.4b) is satisfied; i.e., the space is used up, whichever occurs first. If the $x_{i,2}$ reaches 1, we start again with the next good in order of value density. If for the kth good (3.4b) is satisfied for some value of $x_{k,2} < 1$, the current values for all variables $x_{i,2}$ are the optimizing solution. *Note that $x_{k,2}$ is the only variable that is non-integer in this solution.* The variables that preceded it in value density are 1, and those after it are 0. This calculation is then repeated for different Z_1 to get the boundary curve. It is the results of these simple calculations that appear as the upper boundary curves in Figures 1 and 2.

This calculation too has an economic interpretation. As (3.2a) and (3.2b) show the length $d_{i,1}Z_1 + d_{i,2}Z_2$ is, for fixed Z_1, proportional to the amount of labor required to produce the ith good in Country 2 when Country 2 is the sole producer. As (3.8) shows, the expression for the value in (3.9a) represents the *change* in utility for Country 1 resulting from Country 2 becoming the producer instead of Country 1. So the algorithm selects industries in the order of value density; those which yield the greatest improvement in utility per labor hour are chosen first.

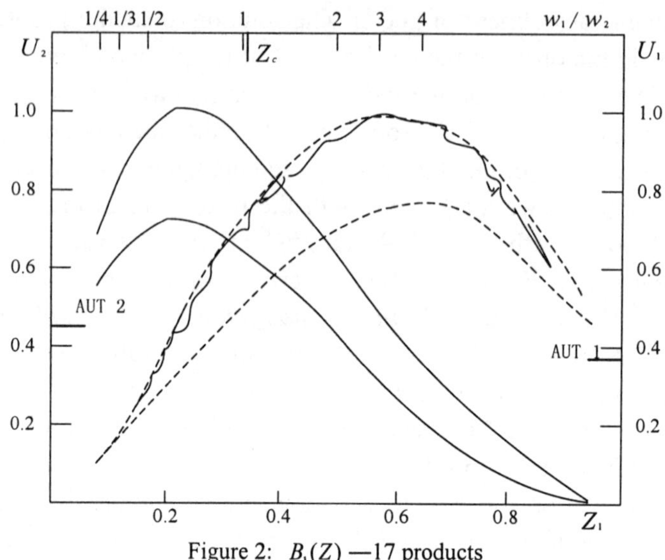

Figure 2: $B_1(Z)$ —17 products

For two countries with identical demand structure, i.e., $d_{i,1} = d_{i,2}$, the length is simply $d_{i,1}$ and the density, or change in utility per labor hour, is $c_{i,2}/d_{i,1} = \ln(q_{i,2}(1,Z)/q_{i,1}(1,Z))$. Industry i chosen in the algorithm before industry j if $\ln(q_{i,2}(1,Z)/q_{i,1}(1,Z)) > \ln(q_{j,2}(1,Z)/q_{j,1}(1,Z))$. In other words, industry i is chosen before industry j if it has greater *comparative advantage*. However, when the countries have dissimilar demand structures, the order of choice is determined by $c_{i,2}/(d_{i,1}Z_1 + d_{i,2}Z_2) = (d_{i,1}/(d_{i,1}Z_1 + d_{i,2}Z_2))\ln(q_{i,2}/q_{i,1})$ which involves q_2/q_1 but also is influenced by the term $d_{i,1}/(d_{i,1}Z_1 + d_{i,2}Z_2)$ which measures the relative importance of the ith good to Country 1.

So far we have discussed (3.9a) in terms of obtaining a boundary, not in terms of obtaining high utility equilibria. The optimizing x in (3.9a), being non-integer, is usually not itself an equilibrium point. However, equilibria can be obtained by rounding the single non-integer variable in x either up or down. This is dealing with an integer programming problem by the time-honored device of rounding.

Lower boundaries

While the goal so far has been to find the upper boundary of the array of perfectly specialized equilibria, exactly the same methods will give us the *lower* boundary. If we minimize the objective functions in problems (3.9) and (3.9a), instead of maximizing, we get lower boundaries $BL_1(Z)$ and $BL(Z)$ corresponding to the two different relaxations. The second approach produced the lower boundaries seen in Figures 1 and 2. All perfectly specialized equilibria are somewhere between these curves.

The two methods

We have described two methods of calculation, one with integer variables and the inequality i-(3.4b) and one with continuous variables and the equality (3.4b). Both generate boundary curves and also find actual equilibria near those curves.

$B_1(Z)$ is of course a tighter fit to the equilibrium points than $B(Z)$. However, for small problems, where the biggest differences exist, $B_1(Z)$ tends to be jagged. In larger models, such as the 17-industry model shown in Figure 2, we see that the two boundary curves for Country 1, the dashed $B(Z)$ and the solid $B_1(Z)$, are much more alike. Both calculations can also give us points near their respective boundaries; the integer calculation does this automatically while the continuous calculation does this by rounding the non-integer variable up or down. Figure 3 represents a problem with 27 goods. It shows the $B(Z)$ from the continuous calculation together with the integer points obtained by the integer maximization calculation. From the more than 100 million specialized equilibria in the 27-good model, the calculation has produced the 75 shown in the figure that are sitting virtually on top of $B(Z)$. If we select from these the one that maximizes the utility of Country 1, we get a utility value that is within 1/6 of 1 % of the highest point of $B(Z)$, so this equilibrium point is at least within 1/6 of 1 % of the highest utility that can be obtained by Country 1 at any specialized equilibrium. In Section 5 we show that $B(Z)$ lies above *all* the equilibria as well as above the specialized ones, so this equilibrium point is close to the best utility that can be obtained at any equilibrium. It is also worth noting that the *utility to Country 2 is low* for any of the points that are near maximal for Country 1. This is in line with statement 1 of the introduction.

Both calculations appear to have their advantages. Boundary $B(Z)$ is smoother and sometimes easier to deal with theoretically. The integer calculation is capable of producing many more actual equilibria near $B(Z)$. A very good way of combining the strengths of both methods is to use them together as a sort of coarse and fine microscope. First, using the continuous method, we obtain an entire boundary, for example $B(Z)$, the upper boundary of Country 1 in Figure 3. Then, in some narrower range of interest, for example near the maximizing hump of $B(Z)$, we compute the nearby integer points by using the integer calculation and a finer Z_1 grid. The result of doing this appears in Figure 4 which represents the Country 1 hump area of Figure 3, from $Z_1 = 0.55$ to $Z_1 = 0.75$, magnified by a factor of five. There are 119 equilibria computed in that range by the integer method while rounding the continuous method would produce 11. Using this technique it becomes possible to isolate the equilibria in a particular area, for example the equilibria between $Z_1 = 0.625$ and $Z_1 = 0.675$ at the very peak of the hump in Figure 4 and examine them for their common characteristics.

4.   Filling in

For any point $(Z_1, B(Z_1))$ on the boundary $B(Z)$ there is an x, with at most one non-integer component, that obtains the linearized utility value $B(Z_1)$ for that Z_1. This suggests that the equilibrium points obtained by rounding this x might be near the boundary in a many-industry model. Gomory [3] uses this reasoning to show that for large problems there are always equilibria near the boundary. Here we use the same basic idea to show that the entire region between the upper and lower boundaries fills in with equilibria for large problems. We now state this theorem; the proof is given in Appendix 1.

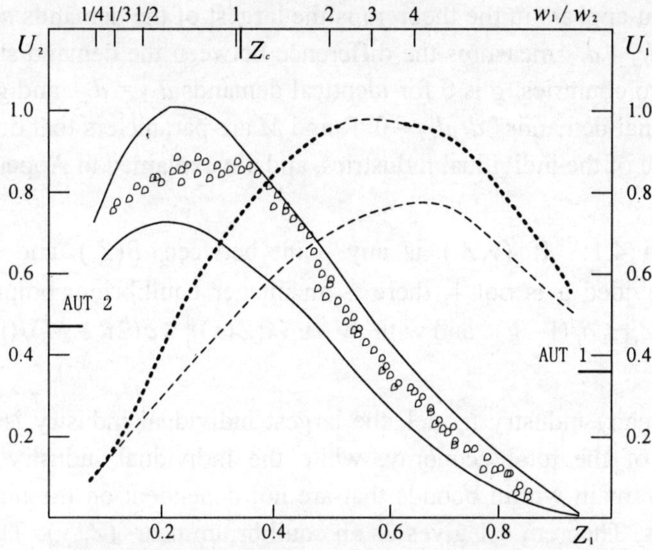

Figure 3: Near boundary equilibria—27 products

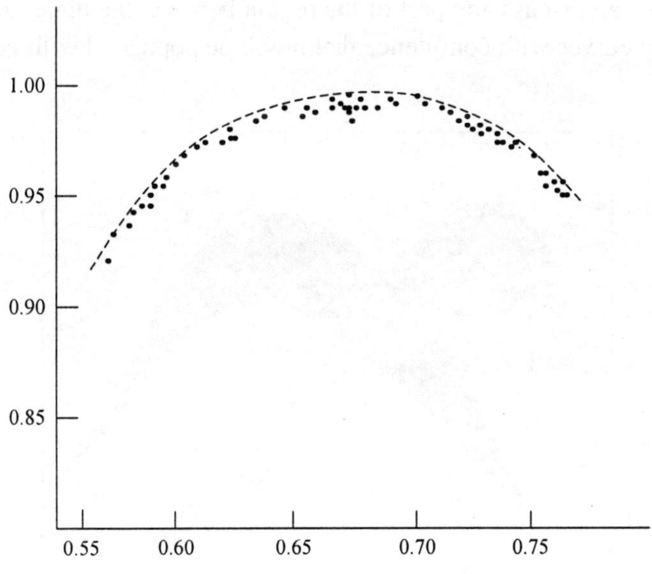

Figure 4: Hump area—27 products

The δ that appears in the theorem is the largest of the demands $d_{i,j}$, while $g = \sum_i |d_{i,1} - d_{i,2}|$ measures the difference between the demand structures of the two countries. g is 0 for identical demands $d_{i,1} = d_{i,2}$, and $g = 1$ for "orthogonal demands" $d_{i,1}d_{i,2} = 0$. R and M are parameters that depend on the nature of the individual industries, and are explained in Appendix 1.

Theorem 4.1: If (v, Z') is any point between $B(Z')$ and $B_L(Z')$, then, provided g is not 1, there is an integer equilibrium point x with $|Z_1(x) - Z_1'| \le \delta/(1-g)$ and with $|v - u_1(x, Z(x))| \le \delta(2R + M)/(1-g)$.

If, in a many industry model, the largest individual industry is a small fraction of the total economy, while the individual industry characteristics remain within bounds that are not dependent on the number of industries, Theorem 4.1 gives us an equilibrium near (Z_1, v). The fill in effect is already visible in Figure 5 which plots all the perfectly specialized equilibria from a 13-product model. Because of the fill in effect we can discuss any part of the region between the upper and lower boundary curves with confidence that it will be populated with equilibria.

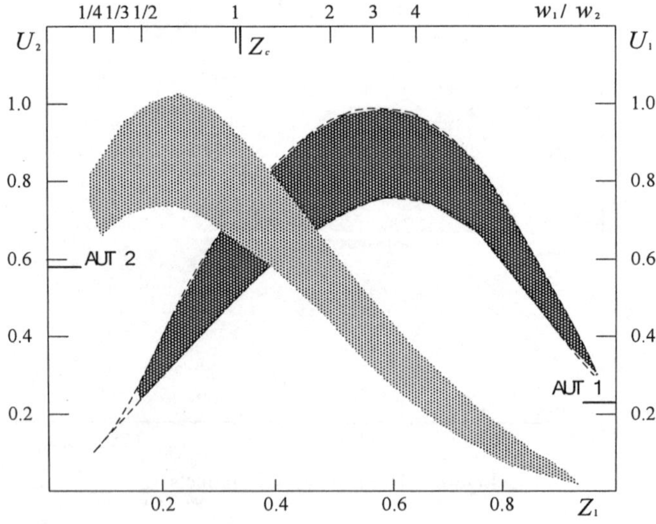

Figure 5: Filling in

5. Non-specialized Equilibria

So far we have worked entirely with integer solutions, that is to say with perfectly specialized equilibria. Considerable justification for this approach can be seen from the following theorem.

Theorem 5.1:   Let x be any equilibrium solution, whether specialized or not. Let $Z(x)$ be the corresponding Z and $u_1(x,Z)$ the utility of x to Country 1, then

$$u_1(x,Z) \le B_1(Z) \le B(Z).$$

So *all* the equilibrium points, not just the specialized ones, lie under the upper boundary curves. The proof of Theorem 5.1 is given in Appendix 2.

Non-specialized equilibria, however, can lie below the lower boundary curve as is clear from Figure 1. These equilibria are numerous and have their own interesting properties. While non-specialized equilibria in the presence of economies of scale are *usually* unstable, there are stable non-specialized equilibria as well. This is discussed in considerable detail in Gomory [3].

6. The General Shape of the Region and a Special Case

The more than 80 numerical examples that have been examined all show the same characteristic regional shape that is seen in Figures 1–3 and 5–7. These characteristics are, for Country 1, (1) a steady rise in the height of the upper and lower boundaries over the range from $Z_1 = 0$ to Z_C, (2) to the right of Z_C a height for the upper boundary that is always above the autarky level, (3) a point of maximum utility to the right of Z_C followed by a descent of the upper boundary to the autarky level, and (4) upper and lower boundaries that coincide at $Z_1 = 0$ and $Z_1 = 1$. These characteristics are not accidental but derive from the fundamental economics. We now sketch out the elements of a very rough economic rationale. A proper treatment is a key element of Gomory and Baumol [4].

At very low levels of relative national income Z_1 Country 1 is the producer of very few goods making up a small fraction of the total world demand. Since we are below the classical level Z_C, as we increase Z_1 the boundary algorithm can and will select as a new industry to add to those already in Country 1 one in which Country 1 is a cheaper producer than Country 2 is. The effects of this change are to increase Country 1's fraction $F_{i,1}$ of every good, (relative consumption) make the goods cheaper in the transferred industry, make the other goods made in Country 1 more expensive, and those made abroad less expensive. Since most goods are made abroad there is a net improvement in Country 1's utility. As more and more industries are added to Country 1, Z_1 increases and we finally reach Z_C. For $Z_1 > Z_C$ the industries added are ones in which Country 1 is the more expensive producer, and also more and more industries are in Country 1 and each addition makes their goods become still more expensive, while the goods made ever more cheaply abroad are ever fewer in number. At some point the total utility of these changes becomes negative, and the boundary turns down. Finally, as Country 1 becomes the producer of almost everything, Country 2 hardly matters to it either as a supplier or customer, and Country 1's utility approaches the autarky level. While this discussion is plausible, it remains to show that the various competing effects do play out in the way suggested. We do this in Gomory and Baumol [4].

The regional shape for identical countries

Competition among identical countries is non-trivial in this model and produces many different equilibrium outcomes. If we assume production functions of the form $e_{i,1} l^\alpha = e_{i,2} l^\alpha$ the problem simplifies. As in shown in Gomory [3] the upper and lower boundary curves coincide, and all the integer equilibria lie directly on a curve which is given exactly by the formula

$$U_1(Z) = U_1^A Z_1 \left\{ \left(\frac{1}{Z_1}\right)^{Z_1} \left(\frac{1}{(1-Z_1)}\right)^{(1-Z_1)} \right\}^\alpha$$

U_1^A = the utility in autarky of Country 1.

This result is plotted in Figure 6 for $\alpha = 1.5$.

Even in this special case, with the region collapsed to a single curve, the various regions mentioned in statements (4a)-(4c) of the Introduction are all plainly present in simple form. The subregions of (4a) that are respectively advantageous and disadvantageous relative to autarky can be read from the location of the horizontal autarky bars. Beyond the two humps are the two subregions (4c) that are relatively disadvantageous to both countries. The region of opposed interests, (4c) in the Introduction, is the curve from the point below the maximum for Country 2 up to Country 1's maximum, so the interests of the two countries are strictly opposed over that entire range, with the maximum for Country 1 being a rather poor outcome for Country 2.

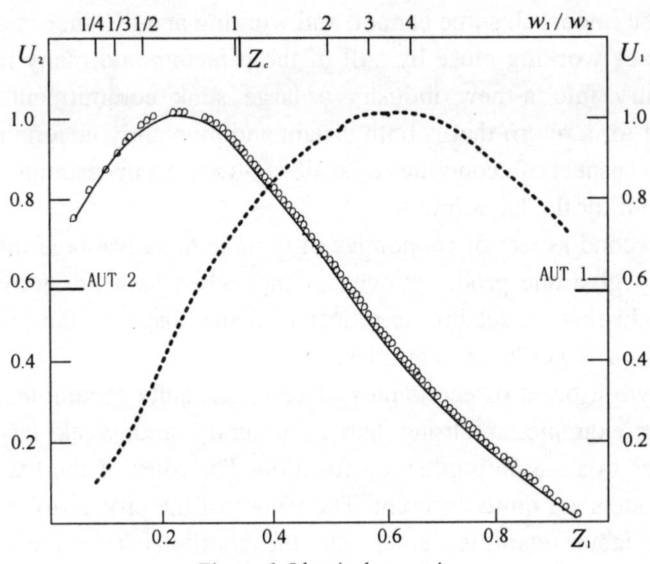

Figure 6: Identical countries

7. General Properties of the Model

Economies of scale have two distinguishable effects. The first is an "impediment to entry" effect which gives a *producing* country an advantage over a *non-producing* one. These impediments to entry come from many sources aside from the obvious possibility of economies of scale in manufacturing. Examples are knowledge and expertise in the manufacturing process, the largely experience-born ability to design a manufacturable product, knowledge of and experience with marketing channels, knowledge of customer needs, and even knowledge of and being known to particular customers. Much knowledge can only be obtained by doing, and there will be a period of doing poorly through inexperience for any new entrant. In addition, especially in the case of industries in different countries, there is the question of infrastructure. If one industry is flourishing in Country 1, and non-existent in Country 2, a large part of the difficulty in entry will be to find the people or companies who can build plants of the proper type and supply parts, specialized instruments, and specialized support services. While some of this can be imported, some cannot, and working at a distance is often not the same as working close by. All of these factors and many more can make entry into a new industry a large sunk commitment now in exchange for a return that is both distant and inherently uncertain. In our model this aspect of economies of scale shows itself in assumption A3 as little output for the labor input.

The second aspect of economies of scale is the advantage that *larger* scale may give one producer over another when *both* are active in the industry. In this model this is reflected in the shape of the production functions for larger labor quantities.

The two aspects of economies of scale are quite separable; one can have, for example, a strong barrier to entry and weak large scale economies in a single production function. The roles of the two aspects in our models are quite different. The values of the production functions for large labor quantities enter into the coefficients of the objective function in the maximization problem and thus affect the location of the boundary and of the region. The shape of the production functions for low labor levels affects the degree of stability of the individual equilibrium points. If the production functions rise sharply near 0, the impediment to entry will be feeble and the stability of the equilibrium point will be weak. On the other hand, if the production functions are zero till near the autarky level of production and then jump rapidly up, we have an extremely strong impediment to entry and a strongly stable equilibrium point. In Gomory and Baumol [5] we show the results of modifying the algorithms of Section 3 to take into account the stability of the equilibrium points.

Identical and non-identical demand structures

Any production assignment x determines a $Z(x)$, and worldwide production quantities Q_i of each good. The utilities resulting from x are $U_1 = \prod_i (F_{i,1} Q_i)^{d_{i,1}}$ and $U_2 = \prod_i (F_{i,2} Q_i)^{d_{i,2}}$. For identical demands $d_{i,1} = d_{i,2}$ we have $F_{i,1} = Z_1$ and $F_{i,2} = Z_2$ so $U_1/U_2 = Z_1/Z_2$. Since $U_1 = (Z_1/Z_2) U_2$, once Z is fixed a production pattern that is good for one country is good for the other. So the conflict between the interests of the two countries is confined to the determination of Z.

This benign property of identical demands does not carry over to the non-identical demand case. There countries will put different weights on different elements of the utility, and the production plan that is best for one is generally not best for the other, even for fixed Z. This effect is clearly illustrated in Figure 7, a 37-industry model. Using a fine grid we have computed a large number of maximizing equilibria around the hump area of Country 1 using the integer programming method. The corresponding utilities for Country 2 would be on its upper boundary in the identical demands case; here they have moved down sharply, even though the g-value of the model,

$$g = \frac{1}{2} \sum_i \left| d_{i,1} - d_{i,2} \right|,$$

is only 0.187 on a scale in which identical demands measure 0 and orthogonal demands measure 1.

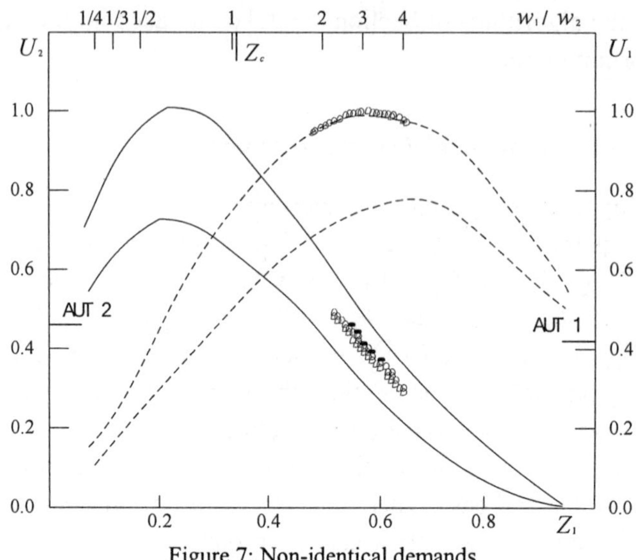

Figure 7: Non-identical demands

The effect of country size

In this model, as in those having diseconomies of scale, the relative sizes of the two trading partners matter. As is spelled out in Gomory [3], the smaller trading partner is much ore likely to benefit from trade than is the larger one. These size effects can be quite strong.

8. Summary

As promised in the Introduction we have given algorithms for the selection of good equilibria, and for obtaining the boundaries of the region of equilibria. We have shown that the equilibrium region tends to fill up with equilibrium points as the problem becomes large. It is also evident that the characteristic regional shape discussed in Section 8 and illustrated in our figures supports the conclusions (4a)–(4c) of the Introduction. The theory we have developed tells us that the various subregions we have mentioned are in fact all well populated with equilibria for large problems. The general picture that emerges from this analysis is that gains from trade are possible but not automatic, and that there is a considerable range of conflict in the interests of the two trading partners.

In Gomory and Baumol [4] we advance this work in several directions. These include a rigorous treatment of the characteristic regional shape, some strong results on gains from trade, and an analysis of the case where some industries have economies and some have diseconomies.

Appendix 1

Proof of Theorem 4.1. For any choice of Z' we define an integer equilibrium point x to be *near equality* (n.e.) at Z' if x satisfies i-(3.4b) for $Z = Z'$ while increasing some component $x_{k,2}$ of x from 0 to 1 results in a new x that does not satisfy i-(3.4b). For n.e. equilibria we have:

Lemma 4: If x is n.e. then, if δ is the largest of the individual demands $d_{i,j}$ and g is given by

$$g = \frac{1}{2}\sum_i \left| d_{i,1} - d_{i,2} \right|,$$

$$\text{then } \left| Z_1' - Z_1(x) \right| \le \delta/(1-g).$$

Proof: Using first the zero excess labor inequality i-(3.4b) involving x and Z', and then the n.e. property on the component $x_{k,2}$ gives two inequalities.

$$\sum_{i \ne k}(d_{i,1}Z_1' + d_{i,2}Z_2')x_{i,2} \le Z_2' \le \sum_{i \ne k}(d_{i,1}Z_1' + d_{i,2}Z_2')x_{i,2} + d_{k,1}Z_1' + d_{k,2}Z_2'.$$

Since x is an equilibrium point (3.4b) gives

$$\sum_i (d_{i,1}Z_1(x) + d_{i,2}Z_2(x))x_{i,2} = Z_2(x).$$

Subtracting the equality from the inequalities, rearranging terms, and using $Z_1 + Z_2 = 1$ gives

$$0 \le \left(Z_1' - Z_1(x)\right)\left\{1 - \sum_i \left(d_{i,2} - d_{i,1}\right)x_{i,2}\right\} \le Z_1'd_{k,1} + Z_2'd_{k,2} \le \delta.$$

The largest possible value of the sum is g where

$$g = \sum_i (d_{i,1} - d_{i,2}), \text{ i such that } (d_{i,1} - d_{i,2}) > 0. \text{ So } 0 \le |Z_1(x) - Z_1'| \le \frac{\delta}{1-g}.$$

We still need to convert g to the more useful form given in the lemma. If we add up all the terms $(d_{i,1} - d_{i,2})$ for which $d_{i,1} < d_{i,2}$, we get a negative sum $-g'$. But $g + g' = \sum_i d_{i,1} - \sum_i d_{i,2} = 1 - 1 = 0$. So $g = g'$. It follows that $\sum_i |d_{i,2} - d_{i,1}| = g + g = 2g$ which proves Lemma 4.1.

Since we now know that $Z(x)$ is near Z' for any n.e. equilibrium, it follows that $u_1(x, Z(x))$ is near $u_1(x, Z')$ as long as the derivative of u_1 with respect to Z_1 is bounded. It is clear that it is bounded, in Appendix 4-2 of Gomory [3] we show in a straightforward but tedious way that the bound is given explicitly by

$$M(Z') = \frac{1}{Z_m'}\left\{2 + \frac{\alpha(Z')}{Z_m'}\right\}$$

Here $Z_m' = \min(Z_1', Z_2')$, and $\alpha(Z') = \max \alpha_{i,j}(Z)$, with each $\alpha_{i,j} = f_{i,j}'(l_{i,j})l_{i,j}/f_{i,j}$, which is the ratio of marginal to average productivity evaluated at the labor level required to be sole producer. If we combine this bound with Lemma 4.1 we have

Lemma 4.2: If x is n.e. then $|u_1(x, Z') - u_1(x, Z(x))| < \delta M(Z^*)/(1-g)$, where Z^* lies between $Z(x)$ and Z'.

Linear programming enters with Lemma 4.3. As usual we assume $Z_1' > Z_C$.

Lemma 4.3: Let $B(Z')$ and $BL(Z')$ be the values of the upper and lower boundary curve for some Z'. Then for any intermediate value v,

$BL(Z') \leq v \leq B(Z')$, there is a feasible solution x' to (3.9a), with at most two non-integer components, for which the value of $Lu_1(x, Z')$ is v.

Proof: Let us add to the maximization problem (3.9a) the linear constraint $Lu_1(x, Z') \leq v$. The problem now has two constraints, so the x that attains the maximum value, which is v, will have at most *two* variables that are neither 0 or 1; this is the x' of the lemma.

x' has two non-integer components $x'_{j,2}$ and $x'_{k,2}$. x' satisfies (3.4b) as an equality, so the integer point obtained by rounding up both $x'_{j,2}$ and $x'_{k,2}$ to 1 cannot satisfy i-(3.4b), while the x obtained by rounding them both down clearly does. *It follows that either x itself or one of the two x's obtained by rounding either the jth or kth component up has the n.e. property.* Therefore Lemma 4.1 applies to that x, as does Lemma 4.2. Consequently we have for this n.e. x

$$\left| Z'_1 - Z_1(x) \right| \leq \frac{\delta}{1-g} \text{ and } \left| u_1(x, Z') - u_1(x, Z(x)) \right| \leq \frac{\delta M}{1-g}.$$

The first inequality shows that this equilibrium x is near (Z', v) in its Z-coordinate, and the second will enable us to show that it is also near in its log utility value $u_1(x, Z(x))$ if we can bound the difference between $u_1(x, Z')$ and $v = u_1(x', Z')$. To do this we observe that the change in Lu_1 produced by changing the terms $x'_{j,2}$ and $x'_{k,2}$ cannot exceed $2\delta R$ where $R(Z) = \max_i \left| \ln q_{i,2}(1, Z(x)) / q_{i,1}(1, Z(x)) \right|$. Putting together these elements we have the regional fill in theorem:

Theorem 4: If (v, Z') is any point between $B(Z')$ and $B_L(Z')$, then, provided g is not 1, there is an integer equilibrium point x with $\left| Z_1(x) - Z'_1 \right| \leq \delta/1-g$ and with $\left| v - u_1(x, Z(x)) \right| \leq \delta(2R + M)/(1-g)$.

Appendix 2

Proof of Theorem 5.1: The idea of the proof is to compare the utility at x, which for an intermediate x is not the same as the linearized utility, with the linearized utility of rounded versions of x. The key is the following lemma:

Lemma 5.1:   Let x be an intermediate equilibrium point with associated national income $Z(x)$. Let $q_{i,1}(x_{i,1},Z(x))$ and $q_{i,2}(x_{i,2},Z(x))$ be the quantities of the ith good produced in the two countries. Then
$$q_{i,1}(x_{i,1},Z(x)) + q_{i,2}(x_{i,2},Z(x)) \leq \mathrm{Min}(q_{i,1}(1,Z(x)),q_{i,2}(1,Z(x))) .$$

This lemma states that *either* country, as the sole producer of good i, *at the demand and wage levels of the equilibrium point x,* would produce more of the ith good than the two countries produce together at the equilibrium point x. The lemma does *not* assert that more would be produced if one country were actually the sole producer. For if that were to happen, we would have a normalized national income different from $Z(x)$, with different wages and therefore possibly a different outcome. It also important to realize that the lemma does not assert that for any $0 \leq x_{i,j} \leq 1$ the inequality holds, but only for those $x_{i,1}$ *that are part of an equilibrium x.* Without that restriction the result is not true.

Proof: At the equilibrium x, we have for each i prices and wages such that
$$p_1 f_{i,1} = w_i l_{i,1} \quad \text{and} \quad p_i f_{i,2} = w_i l_{i,2} .$$
If we form the ratio of these two expressions and use the relations
$$f_{i,1}(l_{i,1}) = q_{i,1}(x_{i,1},Z(x)) \text{ and}$$
$$l_{i,1} = x_{i,1}(L_1/Z_1)(d_{i,1}Z_1 + d_{i,2}Z_2) ,$$
together with similar relations for $f_{i,2}$ and $l_{i,2}$, we obtain
$$q_{i,1}(x_{i,1},Z(x))/q_{i,2}(x_{i,2},Z(x)) = x_{i,1}/x_{i,2}$$
or equivalently
$$q_{i,1}(x_{i,1},Z(x))/x_{i,1} = q_{i,2}(x_{i,2},Z(x))/x_{i,2} = C .$$
Since $x_{i,1} + x_{i,2} = 1, \quad q_{i,1}(x_{i,1},Z(x)) + q_{i,2}(x_{i,2},Z(x)) = C.$

Since the q's are the quantities produced and the $x_{i,j}$ are proportional to the amounts of labor at the fixed $Z = Z(x)$, the production economies of scale condition asserts that $q_{i,1}(x_{i,1},Z(x))/x_{i,1}$ grows with $x_{i,j}$ so

$$q_{i,1}(1,Z(x))/1 \geq q_{i,1}(x_{i,1},Z(x))/x_{i,1} = C = q_{i,1}(x_{i,1},Z(x)) + q_{i,2}(x_{i,2},Z(x)).$$

The reasoning for $q_{i,2}$ is the same, so this proves the lemma.

We now assume, as usual, that $Z_1(x)$ is above the classical level. Let x' be the integer equilibrium point obtained from x by rounding down all the non-integer $x_{i,2}$ to 0. Since all the coefficients in the inequality are non-negative and x satisfies (3,4b), x' satisfies i-(3.4b) and therefore is a feasible solution to (3.9). We compare $u_1(x',Z(x))$ with the utility of x.

Since the maxium value of the objective function in (3.9) is $B_1(Z(x))$ we already have $B_1(Z(x)) \geq u_1(x',Z(x))$. If we can show that $u_1(x',Z(x))$ is $\geq u_1(x,Z(x))$, we would have $B_1(Z(x)) \geq u_1(x',Z(x)) \geq u_1(x,Z(x))$ which would prove the theorem. To compare the values of $u_1(x,Z(x))$ and $u_1(x',Z(x))$ we look at the individual terms in the two u_1 expressions. The terms are of the form $d_{i,1} \ln F_i(Z(x))Q_i(z,Z(x))$ where z is x in $u_1(x,Z(x))$ and z is x' in $u_1(x',Z(x))$. Whenever the components of x and x' are different, because of the rounding, the x' components are always 0 while the x components come from an intermediate equilibrium point. So the conditions of Lemma 5.1 are fulfilled and we always get an equal or larger Q_i from the rounded term. This shows that $u_1(x',Z(x))$ is $\geq u_1(x,Z(x))$, which establishes the theorem.

References

W. J. Ethier. Decreasing costs in international trade and Frank Graham's argument for protection. *Econometrica* 50 (1982). 1243–1268.

R. E. Gomory. A Ricardo model with economies of scale. *Proc. Nat. Acad. Sci. U.S.A.* 88. No. 18 (1991). 8267–8271.

R. E. Gomory, "A Ricardo Model with Economies or Scale," C. V. Starr Economic Res. Rep. RR 92–29, New York University, June 1992.

R. E. Gomory and W. J. Baumol, "Scale Economies, The Regions of Multiple Trade Equilibria and Gains from Acquisition of Industries," C. V. Starr Economic Res. Rep. RR 92–10, New York University, June 1992.

R. E. Gomory and W. J. Baumol, "Toward a Theory of Industrial Policy—Retainable Industries," C. V. Starr Economic Res. Rep. RR 92–54, New York University, Dec. 1992.

G. M. Grossman and E. Helpman, "Innovation and Growth in the Global Economy," MIT Press, Cambridge, MA, 1991.

E. Helpman and P. R. KRUGMAN. "Market Structure and Foreign Trade," MIT Press, Cambridge, MA, 1985.

M. C. Kemp, "The Pure Theory of International Trade," Prentice–Hall, Englewood Cliffs, NJ, 1969.

CHAPTER 10

PATTERN OF TRADE AND ECONOMIC DEVELOPMENT IN A MODEL OF MONOPOLISTIC COMPETITION[*]

Jeffrey Sachs[a], Xiaokai Yang[b] and Dingsheng Zhang[c]

[a]Harvard University   [b]Harvard and Monash University   [c]Wuhan and Monash University

1. Introduction

The purpose of this paper is twofold. First we introduce differences in transaction and production conditions between countries into a model of monopolistic competition to investigate the trade pattern. Second, we use the model with both final and intermediate goods to investigate the interplay between trade patterns and development strategies.

In the past two decades, many general equilibrium models with economies of scale and monopolistic competition have been developed to explain some trade phenomena that conventional trade models with constant-returns-to-scale technology cannot explain. In particular, Yang (1994), Krugman and Venables (1995), and Fujita and Krugman (1995) introduce the tradeoff between global economies of scale and transaction costs into this type of models to explain productivity progress and an increase in trade dependence by improvements in transportation conditions.

In most of the models, symmetry is assumed (production and transaction conditions are the same for all agents) and therefore which

---

[*] Reprinted from *Review of Development Economics*, 6 (1), Jeffrey Sachs, Xiaokai Yang, and Dingsheng Zhang, "Pattern of Trade and Economic Development in a Model of Monopolistic Competition," 1-25, 2002, with permission from Blackwell.

185

country exports which goods is indeterminate. The current paper introduces asymmetric transaction and production conditions into the model of an endogenous number of goods and with economies of scale.[1]

This research follows a tradition in trade theory represented by Bhagwati and Dehejia (1994), who suggested that models with the CES production function and economies of scale may predict trade patterns that cannot be explained by the Heckscher-Ohlin (H-O) theorem, the Stolper-Samuelson (SS) theorem, and the factor equalization (FPE) theorem. These core trade theorems are at odds with empirical observations (Trefler, 1995; Grossman and Levinsohn, 1989). The current paper substantiates Bhagwati and Dehejia's suggestion (1994, p. 44). In the face of a sufficiently large shift in relative factor prices, goods could switch over from being intensive in one factor to being intensive in the other (factor reversal). Scale economies could generate endogenous (ex post) differences in technology and, in particular, could invalidate the SS theorem, causing both factors' real wages to rise as scale efficiencies from trade swamp the adverse effects on the scarce factor.

In addition this paper will synthesize two lines of research concerning the trade pattern. In the Ricardo model (see Cheng, Sachs, and Yang, 2000), the trade pattern is explained by exogenous comparative advantage in technologies. Here, exogenous comparative advantages come from ex ante differences between agents before they have made decisions. In the literature of endogenous specialization (see Yang and Ng, 1998 for a recent survey of this literature and references there), the trade pattern is explained by endogenous comparative advantage, which is generated by increasing returns and may exist between ex ante identical agents. As Yang (1991) shows, individuals trade those goods which have greater economies of specialization, have better transaction condition, and/or are more desirable if not all goods are traded. But who

---

[1]Helpman and Krugman (1985) explore effects of economies of scale and monopolistic competition on trade pattern. For instance, Helpman (1987) shows that when economies become more similar in size, world trade increases. However, because of symmetry in the model, it is indeterminate which country exports which goods in equilibrium. Puga and Venables (1998) introduce difference in endowment between countries into the model of monopolistic competition. But as they come to comparative statics of equilibrium, the difference is assumed away.

sells which good is indeterminate in the models of endogenous specialization because of the assumption that all individuals are ex ante identical. The present paper investigates the implications of the coexistence of endogenous and exogenous comparative advantage and transaction costs for economic development and trade. As the difference in transaction and production conditions between countries (which generates exogenous comparative advantage) is introduced into the model with economies of scale (which generate endogenous comparative advantage), marginal analysis is not enough for managing the model. We will develop inframarginal analysis (total cost-benefit analysis across different patterns of trade and development, in addition to marginal analysis of each pattern) of the model of monopolistic competition. The inframarginal analysis should generate clearer picture of patterns of trade and economic development than other models of monopolistic competition and the H-O model.

We shall show that, as relevant concepts change in response to changes in the analytical framework, relevant empirical evidence may be changed too. As Albert Einstein stated (quoted in Heisenberg, 1971, p. 31), "It is quite wrong to try founding a theory on observable magnitudes alone.... It is the theory which decides what we can observe." For instance, many economists take the notion of capital as granted. But its meaning in a model of an endogenous number of intermediate (capital) goods is totally different from that in a neoclassical H-O model. As the number of capital goods that are employed to produce a final good increases in response to improvements in transaction conditions, the equilibrium input level of capital and capital intensity increase even if production conditions, tastes, and endowment of primary resources are not changed. Hence, in a model of monopolistic competition, outsourcing trade, disintegration, and variety of goods might be better concepts than the notion of capital for capturing the essence of comparative statics of equilibrium. Hence, datasets that are designed according to the new concepts might be more appropriate for testing the new theory.

There have been many new models of monopolistic competition with transaction costs to analyze trade and development phenomena. For instance, Krugman and Venables (1995) studied industrialization and income distribution, Fujita and Krugman (1995) studied urbanization by introducing a difference in transaction conditions between industrial and agricultural sectors into the model of monopolistic competition. Puga and Venables (1998) studied import substitution and geographical concentration of industrial production.[2] As the essence of comparative statics of equilibrium in this type of model is increasingly appreciated, we can see that many conventional notions, such as import substitution, become out of date. Rethinking of the relationship between trade pattern and economic development pattern is needed.

Hence, the second purpose of the current paper is to investigate the interplay between trade and development patterns in a model of monopolistic competition. Feenstra (1998) reviews empirical evidence for the relationship between increases in trade of intermediate inputs and economic development. He points out that the distinction between effects of trade and effects of technological changes on income distribution becomes suspect if we consider equilibrium comparative statics in a model of an endogenous number of intermediate goods. As transaction conditions are improved (owing to new communication and transacting technology) the number of intermediate goods increases, final goods become more "capital-intensive," and outsourcing trade increases. Our general equilibrium comparative statics in the framework of monopolistic competition will help to clarify the discussion in which vague logic and inaccurate terms are sometimes used.

As we introduce exogenous comparative advantage in production and exogenous comparative advantage in transactions into the model with monopolistic competition and endogenous comparative advantage, we can show that a country may export goods in which it has exogenous comparative disadvantage in production if its endogenous comparative advantages in production and exogenous comparative advantage in transactions dominate its exogenous comparative disadvantage. Also, final manufactured goods may become increasingly capital-intensive, as the number of capital goods increases in response to parameter changes.

---

[2] The difference between the transaction cost coefficients of final and intermediate goods is not a distinct feature of our model, since Fujita and Krugman (1995) assume this difference too.

A country can export capital-intensive goods even if it has exogenous comparative disadvantage in producing this good.

Our model will show that a country will trade goods in which it has net comprehensive exogenous and endogenous comparative advantage in production as well as in transactions. It will exploit substitution between trades of different types of goods to avoid trade that involves high transaction costs. Various possible substitutions between endogenous and exogenous comparative advantages and between comparative advantages in production and in transactions generate a much more colorful picture of equilibrium trade and development patterns than in neoclassical trade models.

Section 2 specifies the model, identifies possible trade patterns, and solves for local equilibrium in each trade pattern. Section 3 conducts inframarginal analysis across different trade patterns and identifies parameter subspaces within each of which a local equilibrium is the general equilibrium. In section 4, our results are compared with the neoclassical theories of trade and economic development based on the models with constant-returns-to-scale technology. Final section concludes the paper.

2. The Model and Local Equilibria and Marginal Comparative Statics in Various Trade Structures

Consider two countries. The population size in country i is M_i. Migration between countries is prohibitively expensive. An agricultural good (such as food) z is produced from labor. A final (or light) manufactured good (such as car) y is produced from labor and n intermediate (or heavy manufactured) goods (such as car parts).

2.1. A consumer's decision

A representative consumer's decision problem in country i is

$$\max \quad u_i = (y_i + k_i y_{ji})^\alpha \, (z_i + k_i z_{ji})^{1-\alpha}$$

$$\text{s.t. } p_{iy} y_i + p_{jy} y_{ji} + p_{iz} z_i + p_{jz} z_{ji} = w_i \tag{1}$$

where u_i is a consumer's utility level in country i, y_i and z_i are the respective quantities of the manufactured consumption good and the agricultural good, purchased from the domestic market in country i. y_{ji} and z_{ji} are the respective quantities of the two goods imported by an individual in country i from the other country. p_{is} is the price of good s in country i. It is assumed that each individual is endowed with one unit of labor, and labor in country 1 is the *numèraire*, so that $w_1 = 1$ and $w_2 = w$. An iceberg transaction cost is assumed, so that $1\text{-}k_i \in [0, 1]$ is the transaction cost coefficient and k_i is the transaction efficiency coefficient for importing one unit of food in country i. The transaction cost coefficient is determined by the geographical conditions, transportation technology, transportation infrastructure, institutional conditions, and tariff regime.[3] We will discuss effects of a tariff on the transaction cost coefficients in section 4. Since geographical and institutional conditions and the tariff regime are country specific, the transaction cost coefficient may be different between countries. If transportation technology changes, the transaction cost coefficient may be changed uniformly.

2.2. Production of agricultural good (food) z

The production function of food in country i is

$$Z_i = \theta_i L_{iz,}$$

where Z_i is the output level of z, and L_{iz} is the amount of labor allocated to the production of food in country i. For simplicity, we assume that $\theta_2 =1$ and $\theta_1 = \theta > 1$. This implies that country 1 has exogenous absolute as well as comparative advantage in producing food, since in the next two subsections the production function of industrial goods y and x is assumed same for the two countries.

---

[3] Empirical evidence for the effects of geographical conditions on a country's transportation efficiency is provided by Gallup and Sachs (1998) and empirical evidence for the effects of institutions on a country's trading efficiency is provided by Sachs and Warner (1995), Barro (1997), and Easton and Walker (1997).

2.3. Production of final (or light) manufactured good y

The production function for a representative car manufacturer's production function in country *i* is

$$Y_i = [n_i x_i^\rho + (n-n_i)(t_i x_{ji})^\rho]^{\beta/\rho} L_{iy}^{1-\beta},$$

where Y_i is the output level of good y produced by a representative firm in country *I*; n_i and $n-n_i$ are the respective numbers of intermediate goods purchased by country *i* from the domestic market and from the other country; x_i is the amount of an intermediate good purchased by the firm in country *i* from the domestic market to produce good *y*; x_{ji} is that purchased by the firm in country *i* from the other country; and t_i is the transaction efficiency coefficient for country *i* importing the intermediate good from the other country. The elasticity of substitution $1/(1-\rho)$ is assumed to be larger than one; that is $\rho \in (0,1)$. We will use the symmetry (x_i or x_{ji} is the same for each relevant intermediate good) and omit the variety index of intermediate goods when no confusion is caused.

2.4. Production of intermediate (or heavy manufactured) goods

The production function for the monopolist producer of an intermediate good in country i is

$$X_i = (L_i - a)/b,$$

where X_i is the quantity of an intermediate good supplied by the monopolist in country *i* and L_i is the amount of labor hired by the firm to produce the intermediate good. Again, we have used the symmetry and omitted the variety index of intermediate goods when no confusion is caused.

2.5. Possible trade structures

As we introduce the ex ante differences in transaction conditions between the two countries into the model, corner solutions are possible. Hence, standard marginal analysis for interior solutions does not work. We need a little bit of innovation in the analytical method. We first apply the Kuhn-Tucker condition to identify the conditions under which a particular trade structure occurs in equilibrium. These conditions involve relative prices. Second, for a given structure, we solve for a local equilibrium using marginal analysis. We can plug the local equilibrium prices into the conditions identified in the first step. We can then partition the parameter space into subspaces within each of which a particular structure occurs in equilibrium. This is called *inframarginal analysis*.

Let us take the first step of the inframarginal analysis. The Kuhn-Tucker condition for the two representative consumers' decision problems in the two countries indicates that some trade structures never occur in equilibrium, and that each of the feasible trade structures occurs in equilibrium only if relative prices and relative transaction conditions in the two countries satisfy a certain condition. Later, we can obtain a similar result for the trade pattern of intermediate goods using the Kuhn-Tucker condition for the decision of a firm producing the final manufactured good. The two sets of Kuhn-Tucker conditions yield the following conditions for a certain trade pattern to occur in equilibrium, where x_i is the amount of an intermediate good purchased from the domestic market in country i, x_{ji} is the amount of an intermediate good imported in country *i* from country *j*, and t_i is the transaction efficiency coefficient of importing intermediate goods in country *i*.

(A) If k_1 and t_1 and/or k_2 and t_2 are sufficiently small, the optimum decision requires that $z_{ji} = x_{ji} = y_{ji} = 0$ and $x_i, y_i, z_i > 0$, which implies that no trade occurs between the countries, or the autarky structure shown in Figure 1(a) occurs in equilibrium.

(C_1) For $p_{1y}/p_{2y} < k_2$ and $p_{1z}/p_{2z} > 1/k_1$, the optimum decision requires $z_{12} = x_{12} = y_{21} = z_1 = y_2 = 0$ and $x_1, y_1, z_2, x_{21}, z_{21}, y_{12} > 0$. In this trade structure, shown in Figure 1(c), country 1 (for example, Hong Kong) exports final goods and country 2 (for example the USA) exports food and intermediate goods.

(C_2) For $p_{1y}/p_{2y} > 1/k_1$ and $p_{1z}/p_{2z} < k_2$, the optimum decision requires $z_{21} = x_{21} = y_{12} = z_2 = y_1 = 0$ and $x_2, y_2, z_1, x_{12}, z_{12}, y_{21} > 0$. This trade structure is symmetric to C_1.

(D_0) For $p_{1y}/p_{2y} \in (k_2, 1/k_1)$ and $p_{1z}/p_{2z} \in (k_2, 1/k_1)$, the optimum decision requires $z_{12} = y_{12} = z_{21} = y_{21} = 0$ and $x_1, y_1, z_1, x_2, y_2, z_2, x_{12}, x_{21} > 0$. In this trade structure, shown in Figure 1(d), the two countries have pure intraindustry trade; that is, they trade only intermediate goods.

(D$_1$) For $p_{1y}/p_{2y} \in (k_2, 1/k_1)$ and $p_{1z}/p_{2z} < k_2$, the optimum decision requires $y_{12} = z_{21} = y_{21} = z_2 = 0$ and $x_1, y_1, z_1, x_2, y_2, x_{12}, x_{21}, z_{12} > 0$. The difference between D$_0$ and D$_1$ is that there is international trade in food (z) in D$_1$, but no such trade in D$_0$.

(D$_2$) For $p_{1y}/p_{2y} \in (k_2, 1/k_1)$ and $p_{1z}/p_{2z} > 1/k_1$, the optimum decision requires $y_{21} = z_{12} = y_{12} = z_1 = 0$ and $x_2, y_2, z_2, x_1, y_1, x_{21}, x_{12}, z_{21} > 0$. This trade structure is symmetric to D$_1$.

(E$_1$) For $p_{1y}/p_{2y} < k_2$ and $p_{1z}/p_{2z} \in (k_2, 1/k_1)$, the optimum decision requires $x_{12} = z_{12} = y_{21} = z_{21} = x_2 = y_2 = 0$ and $x_1, y_1, z_1, x_{21}, y_{12}, z_2 > 0$. In this trade structure, shown in Figure 1(e), country 1 (for example, Hong Kong) exports final goods and country 2 (for example, Germany) exports intermediate goods. If the production of y is interpreted as an assembly process to transfer intermediate inputs x into the final product, country 1 can be considered as an assembly enclave.

(E$_2$) For $p_{1y}/p_{2y} > 1/k_1$ and $p_{1z}/p_{2z} \in (k_2, 1/k_1)$, the optimum decision requires $x_{21} = z_{21} = y_{12} = z_{12} = x_1 = y_1 = 0$ and $x_2, y_2, z_2, x_{12}, y_{21}, z_1 > 0$. This trade structure is symmetric to E$_1$.

(F$_1$) For $p_{1y}/p_{2y} < k_2$ and $p_{1z}/p_{2z} < k_2$, the optimum decision requires $x_{12} = y_{21} = z_{21} = x_2 = z_2 = y_2 = 0$ and $x_1, y_1, z_1, x_{21}, y_{12}, z_{12} > 0$. In this trade structure, shown in Figure 1(f), country 1 (for example, China) exports final goods and food and country 2 (for example, Japan) exports intermediate goods.

(F$_2$) For $p_{1y}/p_{2y} > 1/k_1$ and $p_{1z}/p_{2z} > 1/k_1$, the optimum decision requires $x_{21} = y_{12} = z_{12} = x_1 = z_1 = y_1 = 0$ and $x_2, y_2, z_2, x_{12}, y_{21}, z_{21} > 0$.

             J. Sachs, X. Yang, D. Zhang

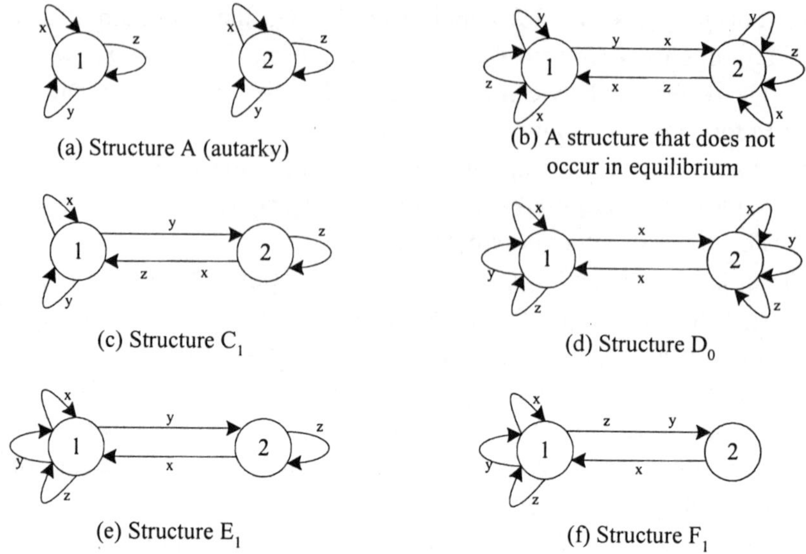

(a) Structure A (autarky)

(b) A structure that does not occur in equilibrium

(c) Structure C_1

(d) Structure D_0

(e) Structure E_1

(f) Structure F_1

Figure 1: Different Patterns of Development and Trade

Also, it can be shown that the trade pattern in Figure 1(b) and other trade structures do not occur in equilibrium except for some razor-edge cases where some of the inequalities involving relative prices in the list above become equalities.[4] The markets for goods y and z are competitive because of constant returns to scale in production. But the market for intermediate goods is monopolistically competitive.

As shown in the list above, ten market structures may occur in equilibrium in this model. We consider the local equilibrium in each of them.

---

[4] The complete partition of the parameter space when the razor edge cases are considered can be obtained from the authors upon request.

2.6. Local equilibrium in structure A (autarky)

We first consider structure A where x_i, y_i, $z_i > 0$, $x_{ij} = y_{ij} = z_{ij} = 0$. A consumer's decision yields demand functions for goods y and z. Each consumer supplies one unit of labor, and the total supply of labor in country i is M_i. The zero profit condition for the firm producing z gives the price of good z in terms of labor in country i, p_{iz}, and the symmetry implies that quantities supplied or employed are the same for n_i intermediate goods. The zero profit condition and a first order condition for the decision problem of the firm producing y yields the equilibrium relative quantity of labor and intermediate goods and an equation that determines the equilibrium p_{iy}/p_{ix}. Using the production and demand functions of y, the market clearing conditions for y and labor, and the first order conditions for the decision problem of the firm producing y, we can find the demand function for x. Using the Dixit-Stiglitz formula for own price elasticity $E = 1/(1-\rho)$, we can then work out the first order condition for the decision problem of the monopolist producer of an intermediate good. Then the zero profit condition for this firm yields the equilibrium n_i. The local equilibrium and its marginal comparative statics in this structure is summarized as follows, with $i = 1, 2$:

$$w_i = 1, \quad p_{1z} = 1/\theta, \quad p_{2z} = 1, \quad p_{ix} = b/\rho,$$

$$p_{iy} = (1-\beta)^{\beta-1}[a/(1-\rho)\beta]^{\beta/\rho}[(1-\rho)b/\rho a]^\beta (\alpha M_i)^{\beta\,(1-1/\rho)},$$

$$n_i = M_i \beta \alpha (1-\rho)/a,$$

$$u_1 = [\theta(1-\alpha)]^{(1-\alpha)}\alpha^\alpha p_{1y}^{-\alpha}, \quad u_2 = (1-\alpha)^{(1-\alpha)}\alpha^\alpha p_{2y}^{-\alpha},$$

$$dp_{iy}/dM_i < 0, \quad dn_i/dM_i > 0, \quad du_i/dM_i > 0.$$

The marginal comparative statics imply that, as the population in an integrated market increases, the equilibrium price of final manufactured good decreases and the equilibrium number of intermediate goods and per capita real income increase. Since total factor productivity of the final manufactured good is an increasing function of the number of intermediate goods, this productivity increases with population size too. Ethier (1982) uses this result to show that the opening up of international trade can increase the population size in an integrated world market. This enlarges the scope for trading off economies of scale against productivity gains from more variety of intermediate goods, and therefore generates gains from trade.

2.7. Local equilibrium in structures C

Next, we consider structure C_1 where $x_1, y_1, z_2, y_{12}, x_{21} > 0$, $x_{12} = y_{21} = z_{12} = 0$. The procedure to solve the corner equilibrium in this structure is the same as that for structure A except that the markets for x, y, z are jointly cleared for both countries. The corner equilibrium in this structure is summarized as follows.

$$w = t_1^\rho, \quad p_{1z} = 1/\theta, \quad p_{2z} = t_1^\rho, \quad p_{1x} = b/\rho, \quad p_{2x} = t_1^\rho b/\rho,$$

$$p_{1y} = (1-\beta)^{\beta-1}\beta^{\beta/\rho}(b/\rho)^\beta[(1-\rho)\alpha(M_1+k_1^\rho M_2)/a]^{\beta(1-1/\rho)},$$

$$n_1 = [(1-\rho)/a][M_1(\beta\alpha+1-\alpha)-\alpha(1-\beta)t_1^\rho M_2],$$

$$n_2 = [(1-\rho)/a][M_2\alpha-(1-\alpha)t_1^{-\rho}M_1],$$

$$u_1 = B(\theta k_1)^{1-\alpha}t_1^{-\rho(1-\alpha)}(M_1+t_1^\rho M_2)^{\alpha\beta(1-\rho)/\rho},$$

$$u_2 = Bt_1^{\rho\alpha}k_2^\alpha(M_1+t_1^\rho M_2)^{\alpha\beta(1-\rho)/\rho},$$

where

$$B \equiv (1-\alpha)^{(1-\alpha)}\alpha^\alpha[(1-\beta)^{1-\beta}\beta^{\beta/\rho}(\rho/b)^\beta]^\alpha[\alpha(1-\rho)/a]^{\alpha\beta(1-\rho)/\rho}.$$

Differentiation of the solutions yields marginal comparative statics of the local equilibrium in structure C_1:

$$dn_i/dM_i > 0, \quad dn_i/dM_j < 0, \quad dn_2/dt_1 > 0, \quad dn_1/dt_1 < 0,$$

$$dn/dt_1 > 0, \quad \text{if } (1-\alpha)M_1/\alpha(1-\beta)M_2 > t_1^{2\rho},$$

$$dn/dM_1 > 0 \text{ iff } t_1 > [(1-\alpha)/\alpha\beta+1-\alpha]^{1/\rho}, \quad dn/dM_2 > 0,$$

$$dw/dt_1 > 0, \quad du_i/dM_i > 0, \quad du_i/dk_i > 0, \quad du_2/dt_1 > 0. \tag{2}$$

where $i, j = 1, 2$ and $n = n_1 + n_2$ is the number of all intermediate goods available in the two countries. The marginal comparative statics of the local equilibrium imply that, as the transaction condition in country 1 improves, the production of intermediate goods will shift from country 1 to country 2. This relocation of industrial production increases utility levels in the two countries, while the nominal income in country 1 relative to that in country 2 increases. The improvement of the transaction condition in country 2 has no effects on industrial structure and location of industrial production, though it increases utility of each individual in country 2. An increase in the population size in country 1 will shift the production of producer goods from country 2 to country 1. But an increase in the population size in country 2 has opposite effect on location of industrial production. However, the increase in population size in either country will raise per capita real income in both countries.

As n_1 or n_2 tends to zero, the production of all intermediate goods becomes concentrated in country 2 or 1. A careful examination of the equilibrium solutions yields the following conditions for such concentration:

$$n_1 = n \quad \text{and} \quad n_2 = 0 \quad \text{if} \quad t_1 < t_a \equiv [M_1(1-\alpha)/M_2\alpha]^{1/\rho},$$

$$n_1, \ n_2 \in (0, \ n) \quad \text{if} \quad t_1 \in (t_a, \ t_b),$$

where $\quad t_b \equiv [M_1(\alpha\beta+1-\alpha)/M_2\alpha(1-\rho)]^{1/\rho},$

$$n_2 = n \quad \text{and} \quad n_1 = 0 \quad \text{if} \quad t_1 > t_b, \tag{3}$$

where $t_a < t_b$ always holds. The marginal comparative statics of the local equilibrium in structure C_1 are summarized in the following proposition.

Proposition 1: If the transaction efficiency of intermediate goods is very low in country 1, country 2 specializes in producing the agricultural good in the absence of industrialization. The production of all final and intermediate manufactured goods is located in country 1. As the transaction condition is improved in country 1, country 2 starts industrialization which relocates the production of intermediate goods from country 1 to country 2. The smaller the population size of country 1 relative to country 2, the faster is the relocation process. Per capita real incomes in both countries increase as a result of the relocation, although wage rate in country 2 increases compared to that in country 1. The wage difference between the two countries converges to 0 as transaction cost tends to 0. The per capita real income in country 1 is more likely to be higher than in country 2, the greater the income share of the final manufactured good, the greater the elasticity of substitution between intermediate goods, and/or the higher the relative transaction efficiency of country 1 to country 2. An increase in the population size of a country will move the production of intermediate goods to this country from the other country, increasing per capita real income in this country.

The local equilibrium in structure C_2 is symmetric to that in C_1. Hence, a similar proposition can be obtained from the comparative statics of that local equilibrium.

2.8. Local equilibrium in structures D

We now consider structure D_0 in which country 1 produces final goods y and z and n_1 intermediate goods. It exchanges the n_1 intermediate goods for n_2 intermediate goods produced by country 2, which self-provides goods y and z as well. Hence, for this structure we have $x_i, y_i, z_i, x_{ij} > 0$, $y_{ij} = z_{ij} = 0$. The local equilibrium in this structure is summarized as follows.

w is given by

$$f = M_1 + t_1^{\rho/(1-\rho)}[M_2 w^{-\rho/(1-\rho)} - M_1 w^{-1/(1-\rho)} - M_2 w^{-(1+\rho)/(1-\rho)} t_2^{-\rho/(1-\rho)}] = 0,$$

$$p_{1z} = 1/\theta, \quad p_{2z} = 1, \quad p_{1x} = b/\rho, \quad p_{2x} = wb/\rho,$$

$$p_{1y} = A(M_1/t_1)^\beta[(t_1^{\rho/(\rho-1)} - t_2^{\rho/(1-\rho)})/(1 - t_2^{\rho/(1-\rho)} w^{1/(1-\rho)})]^\beta [M_1 t_1^{1/(\rho-1)} + M_2 w^{\rho/(\rho-1)}]^{-\beta/\rho}$$

$$p_{2y} = wAM_2^\beta[(t_1^{\rho/(\rho-1)} - t_2^{\rho/(1-\rho)})/(t_1^{\rho/(\rho-1)} w^{1/(1-\rho)} - 1)]^\beta [M_1 t_2^{1/(1-\rho)} + M_2 w^{\rho/(\rho-1)}]^{-\beta/\rho}$$

$$n_i = \beta(1-\rho)M_i/a,$$

$$u_1 = [\theta(1-\alpha)]^{1-\alpha}(\alpha/p_{1y})^\alpha, \quad u_2 = (1-\alpha)^{1-\alpha}(\alpha w/p_{2y})^\alpha,$$

where

$$A \equiv (1-\beta)^{\beta-1}[a/(1-\rho)\beta]^{\beta/\rho}[\alpha(1-\rho)b/a\rho]^\beta.$$

The market clearing conditions for intermediate goods and the first order conditions for producers of good y in the two countries require

$$w \in (t_1^\rho, t_2^{-\rho}),$$

where $t_1^\rho < t_2^{-\rho}$ always. It is obvious that w converges to 1 as t_1 and t_2 tend to 1.

Differentiation of the solutions yields

$$dw/dt_1 = -(\partial f/\partial t_1)/(\partial f/\partial w) > 0,$$

$$dw/dt_2 = -(\partial f/\partial t_2)/(\partial f/\partial w) < 0,$$

where $\partial f/\partial t_1 > 0$, $\partial f/\partial t_2 < 0$, $\partial f/\partial w < 0$. The result implies that relative per capita nominal income of country 2 to country 1 increases as the transaction condition in country 1 improves or as the transaction condition in country 2 worsens.

Similar results can be obtained for the relationship between per capita real income in a country and the transaction conditions in the two countries. It can be shown that

$$du_1/dt_1 = (\partial u_1/\partial t_1)+(\partial u_1/\partial w)(dw/dt_1) < 0,$$

$$du_2/dt_2 = (\partial u_2/\partial t_2)+(\partial u_2/\partial w)(dw/dt_2) < 0, \qquad (4a)$$

where $dw/dt_1 > 0$, $dw/dt_2 < 0$, $\partial u_1/\partial w < 0$, $\partial u_2/\partial w > 0$, $\partial u_1/\partial t_1 < 0$, $\partial u_1/\partial t_2 < 0$, $\partial u_2/\partial t_2 < 0$.

Other marginal comparative statics in this structure are

$$du_i/dM_i > 0, \quad du_i/dM_j > 0, \quad dn_i/dM_i > 0, \quad dn_i/d\rho < 0, \quad dn_i/da < 0. \quad (4b)$$

The Kuhn-Tucker condition for a producer of good y indicates that the first order derivative of profit with respect to quantity of an imported intermediate good is always negative if the transaction efficiency coefficient is zero in this country. Hence, the equilibrium will jump to another structure if t is sufficiently close to 0 in either country.

If $1-t_i$ is interpreted as the import tariff rate in country i and all tariff revenue is exhausted by bureaucrats who collect it, then the marginal comparative statics in (4a) imply that each country has an incentive to impose a tariff which increases per capita real income in the home country.[5]

Proposition 2: As the population size or import tariff rate increases in a country, the per capita real income in this country increases. Also, the number of intermediate goods produced in a country increases with its population size. Wage difference between the two countries converges to 0 as transaction cost tends to 0.

The local equilibrium in structure D_1 is:

w is given by

$$f = \alpha\beta M_1-(1-\alpha)wM_2-\alpha\beta t_1^{\rho/(1-\rho)}w^{-1/(1-\rho)}M_1+w^{-\rho/(1-\rho)}[(1-\alpha+\alpha\beta)M_2 t_1^{\rho/(1-\rho)}$$

$$+(1-\alpha)M_2 t_2^{-\rho/(1-\rho)}-(1-\alpha+\alpha\beta)M_2 w^{-(1+\rho)/(1-\rho)}t_1^{\rho/(1-\rho)}t_2^{-\rho/(1-\rho)}] = 0,$$

$$p_{1z} = 1/\theta, \quad p_{2z} = 1, \quad p_{1x} = b/\rho, \quad p_{2x} = wb/\rho,$$

---

[5] Cheng et al. (2000) consider the tradeoff between deadweight and government revenue created by a tariff in a Ricardian model. We leave the tradeoff in the model of monopolistic competition to future research.

$$p_{1y} = A(M_1/t_1)^\beta \; [(t_1^{\rho/(\rho-1)} - k_2^{\rho/(1-\rho)})/(1 - t_2^{\rho/(1-\rho)} w^{1/(1-\rho)})]^\beta$$
$$\times [M_1 t_1^{1/(\rho-1)} + M_2 w^{\rho/(\rho-1)}]^{-\beta/\rho},$$
$$p_{2y} = wAM_2^\beta [(t_1^{\rho/(\rho-1)} - t_2^{\rho/(1-\rho)})/(t_1^{\rho/(\rho-1)} w^{1/(1-\rho)} - 1)]^\beta$$
$$\times [M_1 t_2^{1/(1-\rho)} + M_2 w^{\rho/(\rho-1)}]^{-\beta/\rho},$$
$$n_1 = [\alpha\beta M_1 - (1-\alpha)wM_2](1-\rho)/a, \quad n_2 = (1-\alpha+\alpha\beta)M_2(1-\rho)/a,$$
$$u_1 = [\theta(1-\alpha)]^{1-\alpha}\alpha^\alpha p_{1y}^{-\alpha}, \quad u_2 = (1-\alpha)^{1-\alpha}\alpha^\alpha (p_{2y}/w)^{-\alpha},$$

where

$$A \equiv (1-\beta)^{\beta-1}\alpha^\beta [a/(1-\rho)\beta]^{\beta/\rho}[(1-\rho)b/a\rho]^\beta.$$

The market clearing conditions for intermediate goods and the first order conditions for producers of good y in the two countries require

$$w \in (t_1^\rho, t_2^{-\rho}),$$

where $t_1^\rho < t_2^{-\rho}$ always.

The local equilibrium in structure D_2 is symmetric to that in D_1. Marginal comparative statics in structure D_1 or D_2 are similar to that in D_0.

2.9. *Local equilibrium in structures E*

The local equilibrium in structure E_1 is

$$w = p_{2z} = t_1^\rho, \quad p_{1z} = 1/\theta, \quad p_{1x} = b/\rho, \quad p_{2x} = wb/\rho,$$
$$p_{1y} = (1-\beta)^{\beta-1}\beta^{\beta/\rho}(b/\rho)^\beta[(1-\rho)\alpha(M_1 + M_2 t_1^\rho)/a]^{-\beta(1-\rho)/\rho},$$
$$p_{2y} = (1-\beta)^{\beta-1}\beta^\beta (b/\rho)^\beta[(1-\rho)\alpha M_2/a]^{-\beta(1-\rho)/\rho},$$
$$n_1 = [\alpha\beta M_1 - (1-\beta)\alpha \, t_1^\rho M_2](1-\rho)/a, \quad n_2 = \alpha M_2(1-\rho)/a,$$
$$u_1 = \theta^{1-\alpha}B(M_1 + t_1^\rho M_2)^{\alpha\beta(1-\rho)/\rho}, \quad u_2 = B(M_1 + t_1^\rho M_2)^{\alpha\beta(1-\rho)/\rho}k_2^\alpha t_1^{\alpha\rho},$$

where

$$B \equiv \alpha^\alpha(1-\alpha)^{1-\alpha} [(1-\beta)^{1-\beta}(\rho/b)^\beta \beta^{\beta/\rho}]^\alpha [\alpha(1-\rho)/a]^{\alpha\beta(1-\rho)/\rho}.$$

The marginal comparative statics in this structure are

$$du_i/dM_i > 0, \quad du_i/dM_j > 0, \quad du_i/dt_1 > 0, \quad du_2/dk_2 > 0,$$
$$dn_i/dM_i > 0, \quad dn_1/dM_2 < 0, \quad dn_1/dt_1 < 0. \tag{5}$$

The local equilibrium in structure E_2 is symmetric to that in E_1. The marginal comparative statics in the two structures are summarized in the following proposition.

Proposition 3:   As transaction efficiency and population size increases in either country, per capita real incomes in both countries increase. The number of intermediate goods produced in a country increases with the population size in this country. The number of intermediate goods produced by the country importing intermediate goods decreases with the population size in the other country and with the transaction efficiency coefficient in this country.

2.10. Local equilibrium in structures F

The local equilibrium in structure F_1 and its marginal comparative statics are

$$w = p_{2z} = t_1{}^{\rho}, \quad p_{1z} = 1/\theta, \quad p_{1x} = b/\rho, \quad p_{2x} = wb/\rho$$

$$p_{1y} = (1-\beta)^{\beta-1}(b/\rho)^{\beta}\beta^{\beta/\rho}[(1-\rho)\alpha(M_1+t_1{}^{\rho}M_2)/a],$$

$$p_{2y} = (1-\beta)^{\beta-1}\beta^{\beta}(b/\rho)^{\beta}[(1-\rho)M_2/a]^{-\beta(1-\rho)/\rho},$$

$$n_1 = [\alpha\beta M_1 - (1-\alpha\beta)t_1{}^{\rho}M_2](1-\rho)/a, \quad n_2 = M_2(1-\rho)/a,$$

$$u_1 = \theta^{1-\alpha}B(M_1+t_1{}^{\rho}M_2)^{\alpha\beta(1-\rho)/\rho}, \quad u_2 = B(M_1+t_1{}^{\rho}M_2)^{\alpha\beta(1-\rho)/\rho}t_1{}^{\rho}k_2,$$

$$du_i/dM_i > 0, \quad du_i/dt_1 > 0, \quad du_2/dk_2 > 0,$$

$$dn_i/dM_i > 0, \quad dn_1/dM_2 < 0, \quad dn_1/dt_1 < 0, \tag{6}$$

where

$$B \equiv \alpha^{\alpha}(1-\alpha)^{1-\alpha}[(1-\beta)^{1-\beta}(\rho/b)^{\beta}\beta^{\beta/\rho}]^{\alpha}[\alpha(1-\rho)/a]^{\alpha\beta(1-\rho)/\rho}.$$

The local equilibrium in structure F_2 is symmetric to that in F_1. The marginal comparative statics in the two structures are consistent with proposition 3.

3.   General Equilibrium and Inframarginal Comparative Statics

Inserting the local equilibrium values of prices into the ten trade structures examined in section 2, we can partition the 12-dimension parameter space $(\theta, b, a, \rho, M_1, M_2, \alpha, \beta, t_1, t_2, k_1, k_2)$ into subspaces, within each of which a local equilibrium is the general equilibrium. This analysis needs the equilibrium value of domestic price of some good in a country which does not produce this good in some structure. But we can calculate the shadow price of this good in this country from the first order condition of a firm, assuming that this firm is active in producing this good. This analysis yields the following inframarginal comparative statics of general equilibrium.

- (7a) The local equilibrium in structure A (autarky) is the general equilibrium if either k_1 and t_1 or k_2 and t_2 are sufficiently small.
- (7b) Suppose that M_1 is not too small compared to M_2 and that k_2 and t_1 are not too small.
    - –(7b-I) The local equilibrium in structure C_1 is the general equilibrium if $t_1^\rho < k_1/\theta$.
    - –(7b-II) The local equilibrium in structure E_1 is the general equilibrium if $t_1^\rho \in (k_1/\theta, 1/\theta k_2)$.
    - –(7b-III) The local equilibrium in structure F_1 is the general equilibrium if $t_1^\rho > 1/\theta k_2$.
- (7c) Suppose that M_1 is close to M_2 and t_1 is close to t_2.
    - –(7c-I) The local equilibrium in structure D_0 is the general equilibrium if $k_1 < \theta t_1^\rho$ and $k_2 < t_2^\rho/\theta$.
    - –(7c-II) The local equilibrium in structure D_1 is the general equilibrium if $k_2 > 1/\theta t_1^\rho$.
    - –(7c-III) The local equilibrium in structure D_2 is the general equilibrium if $k_1 > \theta/t_2^\rho$.
- (7d) Suppose that M_2 is not too small compared to M_1 and that t_2 and k_1 are not too small.
    - –(7d-I) The local equilibrium in structure C_2 is the general equilibrium if $t_2^\rho < \theta k_2$.
    - –(7d-II) The local equilibrium in structure E_2 is the general equilibrium if $t_2^\rho \in (\theta k_2, \theta/k_1)$.
    - –(7d-III) The local equilibrium in structure F_2 is the general equilibrium if $t_2^\rho > \theta/k_1$.

Here, we have used the upper and lower bound of the local equilibrium value of w to find sufficient conditions for D_i to occur in equilibrium since the local equilibrium value of w in D_i cannot be solved analytically. But these conditions may not be necessary. Hence, the parameter subspace (7c) is not completely partitioned.

In words, the inframarginal comparative statics state that three factors determine trade patterns: exogenous technological comparative advantage (its degree is represented by θ); endogenous comparative advantage (its degree is represented by $1/\rho$, reciprocal of elasticity of substitution); exogenous comparative advantages in transactions which relate to relative transaction efficiencies of final and intermediate goods in country 1 compared to that in country 2 (k_i/k_j, t_i/t_j, k_i/t_i, k_j/t_j) and absolute level of transaction efficiency. Here, we need more explanation about the connection between $1/\rho$ and the degree of endogenous comparative advantage. $1/\rho$ represents the effect of the number of intermediate goods on the total factor productivity of y (the smaller the elasticity of substitution, the greater the positive effect of the number of intermediate goods on the total factor productivity). Hence, a larger $1/\rho$ implies that the endogenous change in the total factor productivity is more sensitive to changes in the number of intermediate goods. Since an increase in total factor productivity generates endogenous difference in productivity between different specialist firms, $1/\rho$ represents the degree of endogenous comparative advantage between different specialists.

If the absolute level of transaction efficiency is low for all goods, autarky is equilibrium. As transaction efficiency is improved, the general equilibrium jumps from autarky to a structure with trade. It is the interplay between exogenous and endogenous comparative advantage in production and transactions that determines to which structure the equilibrium will jump.

In order to understand the complicated comparative statics, we adopt take a three-step analysis. We first consider inframarginal analysis between structures, then marginal analysis for each structure. For inframarginal analysis, we first compare between cases (7b), (7c), and (7d), then compare between different structures in each case. The comparison between the cases indicates that, when transaction conditions of intermediate goods are similar in the two countries, each country exports and imports intermediate goods. That is, a structure D occurs in equilibrium. Otherwise, the country with the better transaction condition of intermediate goods imports such goods. This is case (7b) or (7d). Case (7b), in which only country 1 imports intermediate goods, is more likely to occur in equilibrium than case (7d) in which country 2 imports intermediate goods, if the transaction efficiency of intermediate goods relative to that of final goods is higher in country 1 than in country 2 and/or if the population size in country 1 is larger.

We now take the second step. We consider case (7b) first. Suppose that the transaction condition and exogenous comparative advantage change in the following way. k_1 decreases and/or k_2 increases, and/or θ (degree of exogenous comparative advantage) increases, and t_1 increases over three periods of time. Hence, in period 1, $k_1 > t_1^p \theta$, which implies that country 1's transaction efficiency of final goods is high, its transaction efficiency of intermediate goods is low, and exogenous comparative advantage is not significant. Hence, the local equilibrium in structure C_1 is the general equilibrium (see (7b-I)). In this structure, country 1 imports z and x and country 2 imports y. Then, these parameters change: k_1 decreases, θ increases, and/or t_1^p increases, such that, in period 2, $t_1^p k_2 \theta < 1 < t_1^p \theta / k_1$. Hence, the equilibrium jumps to structure E_1 where country 1 no longer imports the final good z (see (7b-II)). In period 3, k_2 increases, and/or t_1^p, θ further increase, such that $k_2 \theta t_1^p > 1$. Then the equilibrium jumps to structure F_1 where country 2 imports one more final good z (see (7b-III)). This implies that, as the degree of exogenous comparative advantage increases and as country 2's relative transaction efficiency of importing final and intermediate goods increases compared to that for country 1, the equilibrium trade pattern shifts as to increase country 2's imported final goods compared to country 1. Also, the equilibrium trade pattern shifts from exporting goods with exogenous comparative disadvantage in production to exporting goods with exogenous comparative advantage.

Repeating this analysis for other cases, we can obtain similar results. In summary, if exogenous and endogenous comparative advantages in production and transactions go in the same direction, then a country exports its comparative advantage goods. If it has endogenous comparative advantage in production and exogenous comparative advantage in transactions, but exogenous comparative disadvantage in production for exporting a good, then it will export this good if the advantage dominates the disadvantage. Otherwise, it imports this good. In other words, a country exports a good with net comprehensive endogenous and exogenous comparative advantage in production and transactions. It will use substitution between trades of different types of goods to avoid trade with low transaction efficiency.

Inframarginal comparative statics of general equilibrium are summarized in Table 1. Here, A is autarky, C is a structure in which a country is an assembly enclave and the other exports food and intermediate goods, E is a structure in which a country is an assembly enclave and the other exports intermediate goods, F is a structure in which a country is an assembly enclave exporting food and the other exports intermediate goods, and D is a structure of intra-industry trade.

Table 1: Inframarginal Comparative Statics of General Equilibrium

Trading efficiency	small k_1, t_2, k_2, t_2	large k_i, t_2, small t_1, large M_1/M_2	large k_i, t_1, small t_2, small M_1/M_2	large t_i, small k_i, M_1/M_2 close to 1	large t_i, k_2, small k_1, M_1/M_2 close to 1	large t_i, k_1, small k_2, M_1/M_2 close to 1
Equilibrium structure	A	C_1	C_2	D_0	D_1	D_2

Trading efficiency	k_2, t_1 not too small, k_1, t_2 very small, M_1/M_2 large		k_1, t_2 not too small, k_2, t_1 very small, M_1/M_2 small	
	$t_1^\rho < 1/k_2\theta$	$t_1^\rho > 1/k_2\theta$	$t_2^\rho < \theta/k_1$	$t_2^\rho > \theta/k_1$
Equilibrium structure	E_1	F_1	E_2	F_2

The CES production function is essential for endogenizing the number of intermediate goods, which represents the degree of industrialization. Without the CES function, we cannot figure out the relationship between the trade pattern and the industrialization pattern. The assumption of $\theta \neq 1$ is essential for predicting a trade pattern where a country exports a good in which it has exogenous comparative disadvantage. This assumption generates exogenous comparative technology advantage in addition to exogenous comparative endowment advantage, which is based on the difference in population size between the countries. The assumption of global economies of scale, which

          J. Sachs, X. Yang, D. Zhang

generates endogenous comparative advantage, is essential for the tradeoff between economies of scale and transaction costs. The trade-off yields positive effects of an increase in the trading efficiency coefficient on industrialization and trade dependence.

Marginal comparative statics of each local equilibrium are summarized in Table 2. Since marginal comparative statics in structures D_1 and D_2 are similar to that in structure D_0, structure C_2 is symmetric to C_1, E_2 is symmetric to E_1, and F_2 is symmetric to F_1, we omit these structures in Table 2.

Putting marginal comparative statics for structure C given in (2), and inframarginal comparative statics, given in (7), together, we can see that if the local equilibrium in structure C_1 is the general equilibrium, then the conditions for $dn/dt_1 > 0$ and $dn/dM_1 > 0$, given in (2), are satisfied.

Table 2: Marginal Comparative Statics of Local Equilibria

Structure	A						C_1					
Variable Parameter	n_1	n_2	p_{1y}	p_{2y}	u_1	u_2	n_1	n_2	w	n	u_1	u_2
M_1	+	0	-	0	+	0	+	-	0	+		+
M_2	0	+	0	-	0	+	-	+	0	+	+	+
t_1	0	0	0	0	0	0	-	+	+	+		+
t_2	0	0	0	0	0	0	0	0	0	0	0	0
k_1	0	0	0	0	0	0	0	0	0	0	+	0
k_2	0	0	0	0	0	0	0	0	0	0	0	+

Structure	D_0					E_1			
Variable Parameter	n_1	n_2	w	u_1	u_2	n_1	n_2	u_1	u_2
M_1	+	0		+	+	+	0	+	+
M_2	0	+		+	+	-	+	+	+
t_1	0	0	+	-		-	0	+	+
t_2	0	0	-		-	0	0	0	0
k_1	0	0	0	0	0	0	0	0	0
k_2	0	0	0	0	0	0	0	0	+

Table 2 (*continued*): Marginal Comparative Statics of Local Equilibria

Structure	F_1					
Variable Parameter	n_1	n_2	p_{1y}	p_{2y}	u_1	u_2
M_1	+	0	-	0	+	+
M_2	-	+	0	-	+	+
t_1	0	0	+	0	+	+
t_2	0	0	0	0	0	0
k_1	0	0	0	0	0	0
k_2	0	0	0	0	0	+

Sign + (- or 0) in this table represents a positive (negative or zero) derivative of an endogenous variable with respect a parameter. For instance, "+" in column 8 and row 3 in Table 2 implies that $dn_1/dM_1 > 0$ in structure C_1.

Hence, $dn/dt_1 > 0$ and $dn/dM_1 > 0$ if structure C_1 occurs in equilibrium. All marginal and inframarginal comparative statics are summarized in the following proposition.

Proposition 4:

(1) If transaction efficiencies for all goods are low, then autarky structure is equilibrium in which no international trade occurs though the number of intermediate goods, productivity, and per capita real income in each country increases with its population size. As transaction efficiency is improved, the equilibrium jumps to a structure with trade. In an equilibrium trade pattern, a country exports goods with net endogenous and exogenous comparative advantages in production and transactions. It exports a good if its endogenous comparative advantage in production and exogenous comparative advantage in transactions dominate its exogenous comparative disadvantage in producing this good. Otherwise, it imports this good. Each country will exploit the substitution

between trades of different types of goods to avoid trading goods that are associated with low transaction efficiency.[6]

(2) If a country exports the agricultural good and imports the final manufactured good (structure C), as the transaction efficiency of intermediate goods in the other country increases from a very low to a high level, this country shifts from specialization in producing the agricultural good to exporting increasingly more intermediate goods. Changes in relative population size will shift the production of producer goods to the country with increased relative population size. Improvements in transaction conditions of final goods benefit both countries too. Improvements in transaction conditions and increases in population size raise per capita real incomes in both countries and the total number of producer goods in the whole economy.

(3) If a country specializes in producing producer goods (structure E or F occurring in equilibrium), an increase in population size and/or in transaction efficiency in either country raises per capita real income. But an increase in a country's transaction efficiency or in the population size in the other country will relocate the production of producer goods from the former country to the latter.

(4) If the two countries trade producer goods (structure D occurring in equilibrium), then an increase in the transaction efficiency in a country may reduce its per capita real income, although increases in population sizes may have positive effects on industrialization and per capita real income. This implies that the government in each country may have an incentive to impose a tariff (reduces transaction efficiency for importing goods) to improve terms of trade and raise home residents' per capita real income.

In many models of endogenous network size of division of labor—see a survey of this literature by Yang and Ng (1998)—the two following results in Proposition 4 hold. The equilibrium network size of

---

[6] The effects of transaction conditions on economic development are verified by historical evidence documented in North (1958) and by empirical evidence provided in Barro (1997), Easton and Walker (1997), Frye and Shleifer (1997), Gallup and Sachs (1998), and Sachs and Warner (1995, 1997).

division of labor, the number of traded goods, and aggregate productivity increase as the trading efficiency coefficient increases. Individuals will exploit the substitution between trades of different types of goods to avoid trading goods that are associated with low transaction efficiency, meanwhile getting them involved in the division of labor. Also, Sachs et al. (2000) and Cheng et al. (2000) show that a country may export a good with exogenous comparative disadvantage if endogenous comparative advantage dominates this disadvantage. Hence, these three results in Proposition 4 are not sensitive to those changes of model specification that have been already explored in the existing literature of endogenous network size of division of labor. Other results are model specific. They may not be robust to changes in model specification.

4. Comparison with the Models with CRS

In this section, we compare our analysis of patterns of trade and economic development with the conventional theories. We first show that our theory may make the core theorems of neoclassical trade theory irrelevant and then compare it with neoclassical development economics based on the models with constant returns to scale.

4.1. The H-O theorem

We first show that our theory may make the H-O theorem irrelevant. It is interesting to see that our comparative statics may generate a prediction that is empirically equivalent to rejecting the H-O theorem. If we interpret intermediate goods as capital or producer goods, then empirically, the aggregate output level of intermediate goods in our model can be considered to be total value of capital. With this interpretation, good y is capital-intensive and z is labor intensive (which needs no capital goods for production). Hence, as the number of intermediate goods endogenously increases in response to improvements in the transaction condition or to population growth, capital intensity of good y increases. There is no reason that the country producing a lot of capital goods must export good y in our model. Hence, it is perfectly reasonable that, from empirical observation, a country producing a lot of capital goods exports labor intensive goods z and imports capital-intensive goods y. This analysis is consistent with the proposition made by Bhagwati and Dehejia (1994) that, as increasing returns and intermediate goods are introduced, the neoclassical core trade theorems may become irrelevant.

4.2. The S-S theorem

Next, we compare our results with the S-S theorem. Using the results in (2)-(6), it can be shown that, if structure C, E, or F occurs in equilibrium, we have

$$d(p_{ix}/w_i)/dt_i = 0 \text{ and } d(p_{iy}/p_{iz})/dt_i < 0,$$
$$d(p_{ix}/w_i)/dM_i = 0 \text{ and } d(p_{iy}/p_{iz})/dM_i < 0,$$
$$d(p_{ix}/w_i)/dM_j = 0 \text{ and } d(p_{iy}/p_{iz})/dM_j < 0.$$

Also, if structure D occurs in equilibrium, we have

$$d(p_{ix}/w_i)/dt_j = 0 \text{ and } d(p_{iy}/p_{iz})/dt_j < 0,$$
$$d(p_{ix}/w_i)/dM_i = 0 \text{ and } d(p_{iy}/p_{iz})/dM_i < 0,$$
$$d(p_{ix}/w_i)/dM_j = 0 \text{ and } d(p_{iy}/p_{iz})/dM_j < 0.$$

All of these marginal comparative statics imply that, as relative prices of goods and inputs change in response to changes in parameters, the direction of the changes of relative prices are inconsistent with the S-S theorem. In other words, the final manufactured good y is capital-intensive and the agricultural good is labor intensive. As the relative price of the two final goods decreases in response to changes in transaction conditions, the relative price of capital goods to labor does not change.

The S-S theorem has been used to show that a tariff can be used to redistribute income toward the scarce factor. But common sense is inconsistent with the logic of the S-S theorem. Common sense says that, as the tariff increases in a country that exports capital-intensive goods and imports labor intensive goods, labor will marginally benefit. But this tariff foregoes the opportunity to increase productivity by expanding the trade network. Hence, it is the net effect that determines if labor can benefit from the increased tariff.

Our model substantiates this common sense. From (7b), we can see that if k_2 and t_1 are large, structure C_1 occurs in equilibrium. Assume that country 1 is the US and country 2 is Taiwan. Now the government in the US increases its import tariff rate, so that t_1 decreases. Its inframarginal effect is to make the equilibrium jump to autarky. From the ten trade structures listed in section 2, and the local equilibrium in autarky, we can see that the relative wage rate of the US to Taiwan is $1/t_1^p > 1$ in C_1, and is 1 in autarky. Hence, the inframarginal effect of the tariff increase is to reduce the relative wage of the US. But the marginal effect of a decrease in t_1 is to raise the relative wage rate in the US since $d(1/w)/dt_1 = d(1/t_1^p)/dt_1 < 0$. Also, the terms of trade of the US, p_{1y}/p_{2z}, marginally increases as t_1 decreases (or as the tariff rate in the US increases). These are positive marginal effects of this tariff increase on the terms of trade and wage rate in the US. But it generates a negative marginal effect by reducing trade and productivity gains that can be exploited. The net marginal effect of this tariff increase is represented by resulting changes in per capita real incomes (equilibrium utility). From (2), it is obvious that this net marginal effect is negative since per capita real income decreases as a result of the tariff increase in the US (du_1/dt_1, $du_2/dt_1 > 0$). If we take into account the negative inframarginal effect of the tariff increase which reduces the relative wage rate of the US, the total net effect of the tariff increase is to hurt labor in the US. We have conducted similar analysis for other structures C, E, F and obtained similar results.

It is interesting to see that, in this example, labor in the US benefits from a decrease in tariff rate, even if this reduction marginally deteriorates the US's terms of trade. This is because productivity gains from an expanded trade network (an increase in the number of traded intermediate goods n) may outweigh the negative effect of deteriorated terms of trade.[7]

But the analysis of structure D indicates that the net marginal effect of a tariff increase in the US is positive (u_1 increases as t_1 decreases), though it marginally deteriorates terms of trade p_{1x}/p_{2x} and relative wage

---

[7] Empirical evidence to support this prediction can be found from Sen (1998). In the literature of development strategy, a decrease in k (associated with an increase in tariff on imported final goods) in structure D_0 is considered as first-stage import substitution. A decrease in t is considered as second-stage import substitution.

$1/w$. But total net marginal and inframarginal effect could be still negative.

It is straightforward, from the local equilibria in C, D, E, and F, that the factor price equalization does not hold in general since the equilibrium value of w is not 1 in general, though it tends to 1 as the transaction cost goes to 0. Hence, transaction costs explain the difference in factor prices between the countries. As transaction conditions are improved, the factor price tends to be equal for a given structure. But inframarginal comparative statics (jumps of equilibrium between structures) will invalidate the generalized FPE theorem. For instance, as k_2 increases, the equilibrium may jump from D_0 to C_1, which may cause an increase in the difference in wage rates between the two countries.

4.3. Further comparisons

It is not appropriate to directly compare our comparative statics with the core trade theorems in the H-O model because of different specifications of model structures. Hence, we should pay more attention to the distinct features of comparative statics of our model which are summarized in Propositions 1-4 and Tables 1 and 2. The effects of changes in transaction conditions on the number of traded goods and intermediate goods (degree of industrialization), productivity, and per capita real income and on discontinuous jumps of trade patterns are much more important than their effects on structure of relative prices. No such regularity of comparative statics that relate to changes of structure of relative prices stands out in general in our model. Anything is possible even if a specific model is explicitly specified. The regularity of comparative statics that relates to price structure is not only model specific, but also trade structure specific (or parameter subspace specific). Hence, it is inconsequential to try finding the counterparts of the S-S theorem.

We now attempt a comparison between our comparative statics and conventional development economic theories. We first consider the development trap; then the relationship between industrialization, income distribution, and evolution of a dual structure; and finally development strategy.

4.4. The development trap

Assume that food z is a necessity and its minimum per capita consumption must not be smaller than 1 for subsistence. Suppose all labor is allocated to the production of z. Then per capita output and therefore per capita consumption of z is θ_i, which is not greater than 1 if and only if $\theta_i \leq 1$. Hence, for a value of θ_i that is small enough to be close to 1, the equilibrium number of intermediate goods must be at its minimum value 1. In other words, each intermediate good is not a necessity individually for the production of the final manufactured good y, and therefore labor must be concentrated in the production of food rather than dispersed in producing many intermediate goods if productivity of food is very low. If transaction efficiency for international trade is very low too, then importing food is not an optimum choice. Therefore, a country with very low transaction efficiency and low productivity of agricultural goods will be locked in the development—trap where the number of available producer goods is very small, productivity of final manufactured goods is low, and trade dependence and per capita income are low.

4.5. Industrialization, income, and structure

It is not difficult to show that, as transaction conditions are improved, the relative output of industrial goods x and y to the agricultural good z increases, though the income share of industrial goods is always a constant regardless of the degree of industrialization (an increase in the number of intermediate goods and a decrease of price of final manufactured goods). As industrialization continues, changes in the difference in per capita real income between countries have no such general regularity.

Suppose structure C_1 occurs in equilibrium; then from (2), we can see that per capita real income in country 1 is higher than in country 2 if and only if $(\theta k_1)^{1-\alpha} t_1^{1-\rho-\alpha} > (k_2 t_2)^{\alpha}$. If this inequality holds, the difference in per capita real income between the two countries increases with θ and k_1, and decreases with k_2 and a. Its relationship with t_1 is ambiguous. Hence, there are many determinants of the relationship between trade and inequality of income distribution between countries.

Suppose industrialization and increases in trade are driven by improvements in transaction conditions. The relative speed of change of transaction conditions in the two countries affects changes in the difference in per capita real income between them. There is no monotonic correlation, nor simple inverted-U curve between the difference and trade, which increases with transaction efficiency and with industrialization. If marginal comparative statics in other structures and inframarginal comparative statics are considered, our conclusion will be strengthened: no general regularity of the relationship between inequality and economic development and related trade exists. This prediction is supported by recent empirical evidence in Ram (1997), which rejects the inverted-U curve for the relationship between inequality and per capita income; and in Jones (1998, p. 65) which shows that the ratio of GDP per worker in the fifth-richest country to that in the fifth-poorest country fluctuated from 1960 to 1990. This result differentiates our model from that in Krugman and Venables (1995), which predicts an inverted-U curve.

4.6. Development strategies

We now consider the implications of our comparative statics for development strategies. Again, we may take country 1 as the US and country 2 as Taiwan. Suppose that transaction efficiency for international trade in the initial period of time is very low in both countries, then autarky occurs in equilibrium. Assume further that the US has a quite large autarky-equilibrium number of intermediate goods (quite a high degree of industrialization), owing to the relatively large population and Taiwan being in the development trap. We consider two cases. In case (a), Taiwan is in the development trap owing to low relative productivity of the agricultural sector (bad climate condition and limited arable land). In case (b), Taiwan's relative productivity of the agricultural sector is high, but its population size is too small.

Assume that in period 2, transaction efficiency for international trade is slightly improved.   The equilibrium will jump to structure F_1 for case (a)—since (7a) and (7b-III) indicate that, for a large θ (country 2's relative productivity of the agricultural good is low), as transaction conditions are slightly improved, the equilibrium jumps from autarky to F_1. For case (b), as transaction conditions are improved, the equilibrium jumps from autarky to structure C_1—since (7b-I) indicates that, for a small θ (country 2's relative productivity of the agricultural good is high), structure C_1 is more likely to occur in equilibrium. Suppose that the slight improvement in the transaction condition is not enough to ensure $t_1 > t_a$, so that $n_2 = 0$ as shown in (3). This implies that Taiwan specializes completely in producing and exporting the agricultural good (without industrialization), though it can gain from exogenous comparative advantage in production.

In period 3, Taiwan has several options, dependent on the transaction cost coefficient or tariff rate in the US, $1\text{-}t_1$. Suppose $1\text{-}t_1$ decreases over time through liberalization reforms or a preferential tariff rate for Taiwan in the US. Then Taiwan starts industrialization. Production of some intermediate goods relocates from the US to Taiwan, increasing per capita real income in both countries and the relative wage rate in Taiwan (see (2) and (3)). This increase of n_2 in C_1 looks like an export oriented development pattern, pursued by Taiwan in the 1960s, 1970s, and 1980s. The driving forces of this industrialization are the open door policy of the US (an increase in t_1 and k_1, see (2) and (7b-I)) and Taiwan's liberalization and internalization policy (a large k_2, see (7b)). In the literature of development economics, structure C_1 with a small n_2 is sometimes called a "development pattern of dependence" (e.g., Myrdal, 1957; Nelson, 1956; Palma, 1978).

But if k_2 is small compared to t_1 and t_2 because of a high tariff for imported final goods and a low tariff for imported producer goods in Taiwan, then the equilibrium will jump from C_1 with a small n_2 to D_0 as Taiwan lows its import tariff of producer goods. This policy regime is just like the import substitution strategy carried out in Taiwan in the 1950s (e.g., Balassa, 1989; Chenery, Robinson and Syrquin, 1986; Meier, 1989, pp.297-306; Bruton, 1998). The jump from C_1 with a small n_2 to D_0 is just like an import substitution process. The difference between export oriented and import substitution development patterns lies in the fact, shown in Propositions 1-4, that all countries have incentives to raise import tariff rates in structure D_0 which will reduce per capita real incomes in both countries; while in structure C, E, or F, both countries have incentives to reduce tariff rates.

In other words, if a government distorts a tariff structure to pursue structure D (import substitution), D itself will justify a more distorted tariff structure which impends economic development. Hence, this distorted tariff policy could generate a particular type of development trap. In the absence of such distorted tariff, structure D may occur naturally in equilibrium as a consequence of a certain pattern of endogenous and exogenous comparative advantages in production and transactions. Since utilities of both countries increase with transaction efficiencies in structures C, E, and F, liberalization and internationalization policy is easier to carry out in these structures. This explains why an export oriented development pattern is more successful than the pattern of import substitution. But the notion of import substitution is inaccurate, since this pattern of trade and development relies on increases in imported intermediate goods, though it promotes domestic production of final manufactured goods.

Another interesting difference in development patterns is between structure E_1 or F_1 and structure E_2. F_1 is like that the less developed country (country 2) imports final goods and exports parts and components of the final manufactured goods. Taiwan does not export automobiles but exports a lot of parts and components of automobiles and computers. In structure E_2, the less developed country imports intermediate goods and exports final manufacture goods, similar to Hong Kong's development pattern in the 1970s and 1980s. However, if E_1 or F_2 occurs in equilibrium in the absence of government intervention, which of them takes place is determined by natural endogenous and exogenous comparative advantage in production and transactions. It is counter-productive to pursue a particular one of them by using tariff policy. Any improvements in transaction efficiencies will promote productivity progress and increase per capita real income, regardless which of E and F occurs in equilibrium.

5. Concluding Remarks

We have developed a model of monopolistic competition to provide a unified framework for the analysis of patterns of trade and economic development. The coexistence of exogenous and endogenous comparative advantages in production and differences in transaction conditions between countries distinguishes our model from other models of monopolistic competition. Inframarginal comparative statics distinguishes our results from marginal analyses of other models of monopolistic competition. Our model shows that a country exports goods with net endogenous and exogenous comparative advantage in production and transactions. It may export a good with exogenous comparative disadvantage in production, if its endogenous comparative advantage in producing this good and its comparative advantage in transactions dominate this disadvantage. Decision makers will use substitution between trades of different types of goods to avoid trade with high transaction costs.

Improvements in transaction conditions or increases in population sizes will promote industrialization, increase productivity, per capita real incomes, and trade dependence. But an increase in the population size in a country may relocate the production of intermediate goods to this country from the other country. In an asymmetric trade pattern which looks like an export oriented development pattern, improvements in transaction conditions in a country has positive effects on per capita real incomes in all countries. But in a symmetric trade pattern which looks like a development pattern of import substitution, a decrease in transaction efficiency in a country may increase per capita real income in this country. This creates incentives for manipulating terms of trade by imposing an import tariff. This tariff war will impede economic development in all countries.

No general regularity exists for the relationship between inequality of income distribution between countries and economic development and related trade, nor for the relationship between relative prices of goods and relative prices of inputs.

One shortcoming of this model is that it predicts two types of scale effects. Type I scale effect implies that industrialization, economic development, and trade will be promoted by an increase in population size in the whole economy. The scale effect is rejected by empirical evidence surveyed in National Research Council (1986) and Dasgupta (1995). Also, our model generates Type II scale effect which implies that productivity of manufactured goods goes up if and only if the average size of the manufacturing firms increases. The scale effect is rejected by empirical evidence provided by Liu and Yang (2000).

There are two ways to avoid the scale effects. One is to specify local economies of scale. This makes the algebra very complicated owing to feedback loops between positive profit and consumers' demand functions. The other way is to develop the models with endogenous levels of specialization for individuals (Sun, 2000; Yang and Ng, 1995; Shi and Yang, 1995; Liu and Yang, 2000). These models of endogenous specialization formalize the concept of the irrelevance of firm size, proposed by Coase (1937), Cheung (1983), Stigler (1951), and Young (1928). According to this argument, if a division of labor develops between firms, productivity increases while the average size of firms declines (outsourcing, downsizing, contracting out, disintegration, focusing on core competence). If a division of labor develops within each firm, then the average size of firms and productivity increase simultaneously.

References

Balassa, Bela (1989), "Outward Orientation," in H. Chenery and T.N. Srinivasan (eds.), *Handbook of Development Economics,* Amsterdam, North-Holland, vol. II, pp. 1645-90.

Barro, R. (1997), *Determinants of Economic Growth,* Cambridge, MA, MIT Press.

Bhagwati, J. and V. Dehejia (1994), "Freer Trade and Wages of the Unskilled: Is Marx Striking Again?" in J. Bhagwati and M. Kosters (eds.), *Trade and Wages: Leveling Wages Down?*, Washington, American Enterprise Institute.

Bruton, Henry (1998), "A Reconsideration of Import Substitution," *Journal of Economic Literature,* 36, 903-36.

Chenery, Hollis B., Sherman Robinson and Moshe Syrquin, eds. (1986), *Industrialization and Growth: A Comparative Study*, New York, Oxford University Press.

Cheng, Wenli, Meng-Chun Liu and Xiaokai Yang (2000), "A Ricardian Model with Exogenous and Endogenous Comparative Advantages," *Economic Record*, 76, 172-82.

Cheng, Wenli, Jeffrey Sachs and Xiaokai Yang (2000), "An Inframarginal Analysis of the Ricardo Model," *Review of International Economics*, 8, 208-20.

Cheung, S. (1983), "The Contractual Nature of the Firm," *Journal of Law & Economics*, 26, 1-21.

Coase, R. (1937), "The Nature of the Firm," *Economica*, 4, 386-405.

Dasgupta, Partha (1995), "The Population Problem: Theory and Evidence," *Journal of Economic Literature*, 33, 1879-1902.

Easton, Stephen and Michael, Walker (1997), "Income, Growth, and Economic Freedom," *American Economic Review Papers and Proceedings*, 87, 328-32.

Ethier, W. (1982), "National and International Returns to Scale in the Modern Theory of International Trade," *American Economic Review*, 72, 389-405.

Feenstra Robert C. (1998), "Integration of Trade and Disintegration of Production in the Global Economy," *Journal of Economic Perspectives*, 12, 31-50.

Frye, Timothy and Andrei Shleifer (1997), "The Invisible Hand and the Grabbing Hand," *American Economic Review Papers and Proceedings*, 87, 354-58.

Fujita, Masahisa and Paul Krugman (1995), "When is the Economy Monocentric: von Thünen and Chamberlin Unified," *Regional Science & Urban Economics*, 25, 505-28.

Gallup, John and Jeffrey Sachs (1998), "Geography and Economic Development," Working Paper, Harvard Institute for International Development.

Grossman, G. M. and J. Levinsohn (1989), "Import Competition and the Stock Market Return to Capital," *American Economic Review*, 79, 1065-87.

Heisenberg, Werner (1971), *Physics and Beyond: Encounters and Conversations*. Trans. Arnold Pomerans, New York, Harper & Row.

Helpman, Elhanan (1987), "Imperfect Competition and International Trade: Evidence from Fourteen Industrial Countries," *Journal of Japanese and International Economics*, 1, 62-81.

Helpman, Elhanan and Paul Krugman (1985), *Market Structure and Foreign Trade*, Cambridge, MA, MIT Press.

Jones, Charles I. (1998), *Introduction to Economic Growth*, New York, W. W. Norton.

Krugman, Paul and A. J. Venables (1995), "Globalization and the Inequality of Nations," *Quarterly Journal of Economics*, 110, 857-80.

Liu, Pak-Wai and Xiaokai Yang (2000), "Division of Labor, Transaction Cost, Evolution of the Firm and Firm Size," *Journal of Economic Behavior and Organization*, 42, 145-65.

Meier, G. (1989), *Leading Issues in Economic Development*, New York, Oxford University Press.

Myrdal, G. (1957), Economic Theory and the Underdeveloped Regions, London, Duckworth.

National Research Council (1986), *Population Growth and Economic Development: Policy Questions*, Washington, DC, National Academy of Sciences Press.

Nelson, R. (1956), "A Theory of the Low Level of Equilibrium Trap in Under-developed Economies," *American Economic Review*, 46, 894-908.

North, D. (1958), "Ocean Freight Rates and Economic Development," *Journal of Economic History*, 18, 537-55.

Palma, Babriel (1978), "Dependency: A Formal Theory of Underdevelopment or a Methodology for the Analysis of Concrete Situations of Underdevelopment?" *World Development*, 6, 899-902.

Puga, Diego and Anthony Venables (1998), "Agglomeration and Economic Development: Import Substitution vs. Trade Liberalisation," Centre for Economic Performance Discussion Paper No. 377.

Ram, Rati (1997), "Level of Economic Development and Income Inequality: Evidence from the Postwar Developed World," *Southern Economic Journal*, 64, 576-583.

Sachs, Jeffrey and Andrew Warner (1995), "Economic Reform and the Process of Global Integration," *Brookings Papers on Economic Activity,* 1, 1-95.

Sachs, Jeffrey and Andrew Warner (1997), "Fundamental Sources of Long-Run Growth," *American Economic Review Papers and Proceedings*, 87, 184-88.

Sachs, Jeffrey, Xiaokai Yang, and Dingsheng Zhang (2000), "Globalization, Dual Structure, and Economic Development," *China Economic Review*, 11, 189-209.

Sen, Partha (1998), "Terms of Trade and Welfare for a Developing Economy with an Imperfectly Competitive Sector," *Review of Development Economics*, 2, 87-93.

Shi, Heling and Xiaokai Yang (1995), "A New Theory of Industrialization," *Journal of Comparative Economics*, 20, 171-89.

Stigler, G. (1951), "The Division of Labor is Limited by the Extent of the Market," *Journal of Political Economy*, 59, 185-93.

Sun, Guangzhen (2000), "The Size of the Firm and Social Division of Labor," *Australian Economic Papers*, 39, 263-77.

Trefler, Daniel (1995), "The Case of the Missing Trading and Other Mysteries," *American Economic Review*, 85(5), 1029-1046.

Yang, Xiaokai (1991), "Development, Structure Change, and Urbanization," *Journal of Development Economics*, 34, 199-222.

Yang, Xiaokai (1994), "Endogenous vs. Exogenous Comparative Advantages and Economies of Specialization vs. Economies of Scale," *Journal of Economics*, 60, 29-54.

Yang, Xiaokai and Siang, Ng (1998), "Specialization and Division of Labor: A Survey," in K. Arrow, Y-K Ng and X. Yang (eds.), *Increasing Rreturns and Economics Analysis*, London, Macmillan.

Yang, Xiaokai and Yew-Kwang Ng (1995), "Theory of the Firm and Structure of Residual Rights," *Journal of Economic Behavior and Organization*, 26, 107-28.

Young, Allyn (1928), "Increasing Returns and Economic Progress," *The Economic Journal*, 38, 527-42.

CHAPTER 11

MARKET LED INDUSTRIALIZATION AND GLOBALIZATION[*]

Jeffrey Sachs[a] and Xiaokai Yang[b][♣]

[a]*Harvard University*   [b]*Harvard and Monash University*

1. Introduction

The purpose of the paper is threefold. First, it formalizes one branch of high development economics which describes industrialization as a market led gradual spreading process. Second, it investigates effects of transaction conditions, which are affected by geography, institutions, and transportation and communication technology, on gradual spread of industrialization. Finally, this paper devises a new method to handle the Murphy-Shleifer-Vishny (MSV) model (1989). This new method will extend applicability of this model to the analysis of many trade and development phenomena. Let us motivate the three tasks one by one.

Since the end of the 1980s, many general equilibrium models with increasing returns have been developed to formalize what is called by Krugman (1995) "high development economics." There are two different views in high development economics. One is referred to as the theory of big push and balanced industrialization, represented by Rosenstein-Rodan (1943) and Nurkse (1952). The other is referred to as the theory of unbalanced industrialization, represented by Fleming (1954)

[*] Reprinted from *Journal of Economic Integration*, 17 (2), Jeffrey Sachs and Xiaokai Yang, "Market Led Industrialization and Globalization," 223-242, 2002, with permission from Sejong University.

[♣] We are grateful to Francisco Rodriguez for stimulating discussion and to the participants of the seminar at the Harvard Center for International Development and of 1999 Conference of Development Economics for comments. Also, comments from an anonymous referee are appreciated. We are solely responsible for the remaining errors.

and Hirschman (1958). When economists were not familiar with technical substance of general equilibrium models, they can only use vague words to address general equilibrium phenomena, such as circular causation, interdependent decisions in different industries, pecuniary externality of industrial linkages, and so on.

In essence, Rosenstein-Rodan's idea (1943) about big push industrialization is to advocate for state led industrialization because of coordination failure in exploiting network effects of industrial linkages in a decentralized market. This idea is formalized by the MSV model with the feedback loop between the extent of the market and economies of scale that can be exploited. Hirschman's idea (1958) about pecuniary externality of industrial linkages relates more or less to market led industrialization since the network effects of industrial linkages are pecuniary (which can be exploited by the price system). Term "balanced vs. unbalanced industrialization" may be misleading. Unbalanced industrialization strategy may be associated with specialization of a country in a particular sector and international division of labor between countries. Hence, from a view of the world market, such a strategy is a balanced industrialization strategy, although it is not balanced within a single country (Sheahan, 1958). We shall extend the MSV model to formalize Hirschman's idea on market led spread of industrialization.

Casual observation indicates that industrialization was gradually spread from the UK to Netherlands and France, then to Germany and other Central and Northern European countries, and finally reached Southern Europe and the rest of the world. In Asia, industrialization started in Japan in the end of 19th century, then gradually spread to Hong Kong, Singapore, Taiwan, South Korea, and other Asian countries.

The observed spread of industrialization is affected by transaction conditions. There are three major determinants of transaction conditions: institutions, geography, and technology. Industrialization started in the island countries, then spread to coastal regions of the continent, then to hinterland countries. It was so in Europe in the 18th and 19th century (the UK is an island country, Netherlands and France are in coastal region, and Germany and other central European countries are hinterland countries) and in Asia in the 19th and 20th century (Japan and Taiwan are island countries, Singapore, Hong Kong, and South Korea are in coastal region, China and India are continental countries with vast hinterland areas).

Effects of institutions on transaction conditions and thereby on economic development have been investigated by North (1981), North and Weingast (1989), Mokyr (1990, 1993), and others. Gallup and Sachs (1998) provide empirical evidence for effects of geography on transportation conditions and thereby on economic development. They use cross country data to show that the population share of coast region and distance from the major international market have very significant impact on per capital income.

Institutions and geography are not independent of each other. Baechler (1976, pp. 78-80) notes that geographical conditions of Europe created a variety of polity and rivalry between hostile sovereignties within the same cultural whole in Europe, which encouraged many different institutional experiments. A particular geographical condition ensured that Britain could avoid war with other countries at low defense expenses and had transportation advantage for trade. Pursuit of riches was legitimated under the prevailing ideology, so that talents were diverted from military, religious, and bureaucratic careers to business activities prior to and during the Industrial Revolution.

In the paper, we will introduce asymmetric production conditions between firms and asymmetric transaction conditions between countries into the MSV model of industrialization (1989). In the MSV model market prices are determined by the zero profit condition in the traditional sector with constant returns to scale technology and therefore its algebra is easy to manage. The feedback loops between the extent of the market, dividend earnings, economies of scale that can be exploited, and quantities demanded nicely formalize a general equilibrium mechanism that can talk to circular causation, network effects of industrial linkages, and interdependence between production and market conditions and decisions in different sectors, which concerned high development economists.

There is some technical difficulty of this kind of models that restricts its broad application. The price of the goods produced by the active modern sectors is a constant, determined by the zero profit condition of cottage firms. This paralyzes the functioning of the price system to transmit information of the production condition of the modern firms to consumers. Hence, the number of modern sectors cannot be endogenized by using the zero profit condition. Kelly (1997) introduces the trade off between economies of scale and transaction costs into the MSV model to endogenize the number of modern sectors. Because of zero profit condition, consumers' utility does not go up as the number of modern sectors increases in that model. If the assumption of positive profit is maintained to keep the flavor of feedback loop between the extent of the market and economies of scale that can be exploited, the model is short of one equation to endogenize the number of modern sectors.

In this paper, we develop an analytical approach to specifying a zero profit condition for a marginal modern firm, while keeping positive profit for other active modern firms. Following Kelly, we specify the trade off between economies of scale and transaction costs to endogenize the numbers of active modern and traditional firms. This approach keeps the original flavor of the MSV model: interdependence between the extent of the market and economies of scale, and compatibility between price taking and global economies of scale. A key ingredient that makes this approach work is asymmetry of production conditions between different modern firms and asymmetry of transaction conditions between countries. This new approach to handling the MSV model will make this model more applicable to the analysis of many problems in economic development, trade, urbanization, and industrial organization.

The introduction of the trade off between economies of scale that can be exploited and transaction costs can accommodate empirical evidence that is at odds with the MSV model. The MSV model predicts that a large population size has a positive effect on industrialization. But the first country that was industrialized (UK) was not the most populous country (which was China). Empirical evidence provided in National Research Council (1986) and Dasgupta (1995) rejects this type of scale effect. Murphy, Shleifer, and Vishny (1989) suggest introducing transaction costs to counteract the scale effect. Our model will substantiate their idea and show that there exists substitution between population size and trading efficiency in promoting industrialization and economic development and that a large country can be locked in the development trap if its transaction efficiency is low.

In section 2, equilibrium and comparative statics of the extended MSV model are solved. We then extend the model to the case with many countries to endogenize a dual structure between integrated developed world and autarkic less developed world in section 3. In addition, a dynamic version of the model is considered. The final section concludes the paper.

2. An Extended Murphy-Shleifer-Vishny Model of Industrialization

Consumers' decisions

Following MSV, we assume that the set of consumption goods produced by the industrial sector is a continuum with mass m. Each consumer-worker-owner has a Cobb-Douglas-CES utility function. Her decision problem is:

$$\text{Max: } U = [\textstyle\int_0^m x(j)^\rho dj]^{\alpha/\rho} z^{1-\alpha}, \text{ s.t. } \int_0^m p(j)x(j)d_j + p_z z = I = (\pi + w). \quad (1)$$

where $j \in [0, m]$ is an index of industrial goods, $x(j)$ is the quantity of good j consumed, $p(j)$ is the price of good j, z is the quantity of agricultural good consumed, p_z is the price of the agricultural good. Each consumer endowed with one unit of labor has income I which consists of dividend earning π and wage income w. Labor is assumed to be the numeraire, so that $w = 1$. Ownership of all firms is equally shared by all consumers. Later, we shall show that in equilibrium $p(j) = 1$ for all j. Hence, the optimum quantity demanded of good j is the same for all j. Using the symmetry, the solution to the problem (1) can be found as follows.

$$x = \alpha I/m, \quad z = (1-\alpha)I/p_z$$

The total market demand is:

$$X^d = \alpha IL/m = \alpha(\Pi + L)/m, \quad Z^d = (1-\alpha)(\Pi + L)/p_z, \quad \Pi = \pi L. \quad (2)$$

where Π is total dividend earning which is equal to total profit. We now consider the production of z. The production function of z is

$$Z = \theta L_z \quad (3)$$

where θ is an agricultural productivity parameter, L_z is the amount of labor allocated to the production of z. The equilibrium price of good z is thus $p_z = 1/\theta$ and the equilibrium quantity of good z consumed and produced is then $Z = (1-\alpha)\theta(\Pi+L)$.

Production of industrial goods

For each industrial good, there are two available technologies. The modern one exhibits economies of scale and the traditional one is $x_h = L_{hx}$, x_h is the output of a traditional (cottage or handcraft) sector and L_{hx} is the amount of labor allocated to this sector. Because of the existence of the traditional technology, the labor prices of all industrial goods are always 1, so that the quantity demanded is the same for all industrial goods. The production function of the modern sector producing good j is

$$x_j = (L_j\text{-}F_j)/b \, , \quad F_0 = \delta, \quad F_j = \gamma j > \delta \text{ for } j \in (0, m]. \tag{4}$$

where x_j is the quantity supplied, L_j is the amount of labor allocated to the production of the industrial good, and F_j is the fixed production cost of good j. We assume that the fixed cost differs across modern sectors and that the industrial goods are indexed according to their fixed costs. Industrial good 0 has the smallest fixed cost δ, which is a very small positive number, industrial good m has the largest fixed cost γm, and for $j \in (0, m]$, $F_j = \gamma j \in (\delta, \gamma m]$. Here, γ can be considered as a general production condition parameter. As γ decreases, the fixed cost for any modern sector j decreases. Also, F_j can be interpreted as the degree of capital intensity. A large value of F_j implies that the modern sector j needs a high investment in fixed cost before a positive output can be produced. Hence, index j can be considered as an index of capital intensity of the modern sectors. Here, we assume that there is only one active or potential traditional firm for each sector since the number of traditional firms is not essential for our results. This assumption implies that subscript j can represent an industrial sector, an active traditional firm, or an active modern firm when no confusion is caused. For each sector, either a traditional firm or a modern firm is active. Without lose of generality, we use the symmetry to assume that the continuum set of modern firms is $[0, n]$ and that of traditional firms is $[n, m]$, where the equilibrium value of $n \in [0, m]$ is endogenously determined.

We assume further that there is a variable transaction cost for each modern firm. The transaction condition differs across countries. The transaction cost incurred to a modern firm in country i is

$$C_i = c_i x_j, \quad c_0 = s, \quad c_i = \mu i > s \quad \text{for } i \in (0, M). \tag{5}$$

where $i \in [0, M]$ is an index of countries, s, a very small positive number, is the transaction cost coefficient for country 0, and x_j is the output level of modern sector j which is the same in any country and in any sector as we have shown. The set of countries is a continuum. The specification implies that two factors determine the transaction cost coefficient: a general transaction condition μ and country specific transaction condition represented by index i. for a larger i, the transaction cost coefficient c_i is larger.[1] A country's geographical condition and institutional and cultural tradition determines its ranking index i. For any given i, the transaction cost coefficient c_i decreases as μ decreases. A decrease in μ can be caused by worldwide changes in transportation technology or institutions. For instance, innovation of automobile manufacturing technology reduces transportation cost worldwide. Institution of World Trade Organization reduces trade barriers and related transaction costs.

We may consider country 0 as the country with the best transaction condition and country M as the country with the worst transaction condition. The country specific transaction cost is affected by country specific geographical and institutional conditions. For instance, Britain as an island country has very favorable transportation condition for international trade via seas. Its common law tradition and constitutional order established in 1688 are conducive to reduction of transaction costs.

The transaction cost is an iceberg transaction cost, which implies that for each unit of output, the seller can receive only revenue $1-c$. You may consider that each unit of good sold melts on the way from the seller to

---

[1] We take the transaction cost coefficient as a black box. The literature of endogenous transaction cost has opened the black box and shown that moral hazard, adverse selection, and other opportunism may generate endogenous transaction costs. See Milgrom and Roberts (1992), Hart (1995), and Holmstrom and Roberts (1998).

the buyer, so that the seller can only make revenue of 1-*c* from the sale. Hence, the total revenue received by the seller is $(1-c)x_j$ instead of x_j. The coefficient *c* can be considered as a tax rate when all tax revenue is wasted. The iceberg transaction cost is specified in many recent models with the trade off between economies of scale and transaction costs (see Krugman and Venebles, 1995 for instance) since it can ensure tractability of comparative statics of general equilibrium by avoiding notoriously formidable index set of origins and destinations of trade flows. Trade of goods produced by cottage firms involves no transaction costs except that international trade of the goods may involve infinitesimally positive transaction cost, compared to domestic trade. The assumption is justified by the following facts. Productivity and prices of goods produced by cottage firms are independent of the size of the firm and thereby independent of the extent of the market. Hence, each cottage firm can avoid transaction cost by locating next to the buyer. But international trade involves visa cost and other costs that are absent in domestic trade. It will be clear later that with the assumptions a country never participate in international trade if all modern firms are inactive in equilibrium.

The profit of firm *j* in country *i* is

$$\pi_{ij} = x_j - L_j - c_i x_j = (1-\mu i-b)x_j - \gamma j \tag{6}$$

where $x_j = X^d/(1-c_i)$ is determined by the market clearing condition and demand function given in (2). Total dividend earning is equal to total profit of *n* active modern firms.

$$\Pi = \int_0^n \pi_{ij} dj \tag{7}$$

where $n \in [0, m]$ is endogenously determined. Plugging this expression for total dividend earning into (2), total market demand for the good produced by firm *j* and this firm's output are, respectively:

$$X^d = \alpha(\Pi+L)/m \quad \text{and} \quad x_j = X^d/(1-c_i) \tag{8}$$

where the number of all industrial goods is *m*, the number of active traditional sectors is *m–n*. (6)-(8) nicely captures the feedback loop between income, demand, and production conditions. It also captures the idea of big push industrialization. If the transaction cost is 0, as more modern firms operate (*n* increases), dividend earning and income increases, demand increases, which makes more modern firms profitable.

Hence, as the population size reaches a threshold level, the equilibrium number of modern sectors, n, jumps from 0 to its upper bound m (see Murphy, Shleifer, and Vishny, 1989). But in our model, transaction costs counteract the positive feedback between the extent of the market and economies of scale that can be exploited, so that industrialization may occur gradually as the transaction conditions are improved.

Inserting (8) into (6), then inserting the resulting expression into (7), we can conduct integration and then express total income $\Pi+L$ as a function of n.

$$\Pi+L = (L-0.5\gamma n^2)m/\{m-\alpha n[1-b/(1-\mu i)]\} \tag{9}$$

where $L-0.5\gamma n^2 > 0$ and $m-\alpha n[1-b/(1-\mu i)] > 0$ are required by positive income. We now consider the zero profit condition for the most capital intensive active modern sector n. Letting j equal n in (6) and $\pi_n = 0$, we get the zero profit condition, $\pi_n = (1-b-\mu i)x_j-\gamma n = 0$. Inserting the demand function, given in (8), into the zero profit condition for the marginal active modern firm generates another expression of $\Pi+L$.

$$\Pi+L = \gamma mn(1-\mu i)/(1-b-\mu i)\alpha. \tag{10}$$

where $1-b-\mu i > 0$ is required by positive income. (9) and (10) together give the equilibrium number of active modern firms n as a function of parameters γ, μ, L, b, i, α.[2]

$$f(n, \gamma, \mu, L, b, i, \alpha) = An^2-Bn+D = 0 \tag{11}$$

where $A \equiv 0.5\alpha\gamma[1-b/(1-\mu i)]$, $B \equiv m\gamma$, $D \equiv \alpha L[1-b/(1-\mu i)]$ are positive. The graph of this quadratic equation of n in the first and forth quadrants of the n-f coordinates is a convex curve cutting the vertical axis above the horizontal axis since $f(0) = D > 0$, $f'(0) = -B < 0$, $f''(n) = 2A > 0$. The unique minimum point $n = B/2A > 0$ of this curve is given by $f'(n) = 0$. Hence, this curve may have two cutting points of the right half horizontal axis, which means two equilibria, given by $f(n^*) = 0$. Call the two solutions of $f(n) = 0$　n_1 and n_2, respectively, and assume $n_2 > n_1$. Hence, we can see that $f'(n_1) < 0$ and $f'(n_2) > 0$ for a convex curve with

---

[2] The market clearing condition for labor is not independent of (9) and (10) according to Walras' law. Hence, it can be used to check if the algebra is correct. Indeed, inserting the equilibrium values of the endogenous variables and transaction costs in terms of labor into this market clearing condition for labor confirms that it is the same as (9).

the unique minimum point that is below the horizontal axis. But we can show that for a positive income, $\partial f/\partial n = (\alpha/n)[1-b/(1-\mu i)](0.5\gamma n^2-L) < 0$ must hold when the first order condition (11) holds since positive income in (9) requires $1- b/(1-\mu i) > 0$ and $0.5\gamma n^2-L < 0$. This implies that n_2 cannot be an equilibrium. We have then established the claim that there is only one equilibrium in this model.[3]

Differentiating (11) and using the implicit function theorem, we can identify the comparative statics of the equilibrium number of active modern firms.

$$dn/dL = -(\partial f/\partial L)/(\partial f/\partial n) > 0, \quad dn/d\mu = -(\partial f/\partial\mu)/(\partial f/\partial n) < 0,$$

$$dn/db = -(\partial f/\partial b)/(\partial f/\partial n) < 0, \quad dn/di = -(\partial f/\partial i)/(\partial f/\partial n) < 0. \tag{12}$$

where $\partial f/\partial n = (\alpha/n)[1-b/(1-\mu i)](0.5\gamma n^2-L) < 0$ if (11) holds and $\partial f/\partial\gamma < 0$ if (11) holds, $\partial f/\partial b, \partial f/\partial i, \partial f/\partial\mu < 0, \partial f/\partial L > 0$. (12) implies that there is substitution between trading efficiency and population size in promoting industrialization. For a given μ, a larger population size generates a higher degree of industrialization. For a given L, better general transaction conditions generate a higher degree of industrialization. $dn/di < 0$ implies that the degree of industrialization is lower for a country with the larger transaction cost coefficient which implies a larger i. This implies that a large country may have low degree of industrialization if its transaction conditions are very bad.

General equilibrium and comparative statics

The general equilibrium in country i is summarized as follows.

$$p_x = 1, \quad p_z = 1/\theta \quad L_z = (1-\alpha)(\Pi+L),$$

$$X^d = \alpha(\Pi+L)/m, \quad Z = (1-\alpha)\theta(\Pi+L) \tag{13}$$

$$L_x = \int_0^n\{[b\alpha(\Pi+L)/(1-c)m]+\gamma j\}dj = [b\alpha(\Pi+L)n/(1-c)m]+0.5\gamma n^2$$

$$R \equiv L_x/L, \quad U = m^{\alpha(1-\rho)/\rho}\alpha^\alpha[\theta(1-\alpha)]^{1-\alpha}[(\Pi/L)+1]$$

$$(\Pi/L)+1 = \gamma mn(1-\mu i)/\alpha(1-b-\mu i)L, \text{ and}$$

n is given by (11),

---

[3] Multiplicity of equilibria is discussed in Murphy, Shleifer, and Vishny (1989).

where U is per capita real income (equilibrium utility level), $(\Pi/L)+1$ is per capita income in terms of labor, L_x is the amount of labor allocated to all active modern firms, and $R \equiv L_x/L$ represents the relative work force in the modern and traditional sectors. Differentiating U in (13) and using (11) and (12), it can be shown that

$$dU/dL > 0, \quad \text{and} \quad dU/d\mu < 0, \quad dR/dL > 0, \quad dR/d\mu < 0, \quad (14)$$
$$dn/dL < 0, \quad dn/d\mu < 0, \quad dn/db < 0,$$
$$d(m\text{-}n)/dL = -dn/dL < 0, \quad d(m\text{-}n)/d\mu = -dn/d\mu > 0.$$

It is straightforward that the number of active traditional sectors $m\text{-}n$ decreases as the population size increases and/or as transaction conditions are improved. Hence, duality of economic structure is endogenized.

The comparative statics can be summarized in the following proposition.

Proposition 1: As population size increases and/or as general transaction conditions are improved, the equilibrium number of active modern sectors, relative population size of modern and traditional sectors, degree of capital intensity of active modern firms, productivity, and per capita real income increase. For a given general transaction condition and population size, the country with more favorable country specific transportation conditions has higher degree of industrialization than in other countries.

Suppose general transaction conditions are very bad in the initial time. Then no modern firm operates in any country. As time goes by, general transaction conditions are improved, so that some modern firms operate in the country with the smallest transaction cost coefficient $c_0 = s$. But other countries are not industrialized. As general transaction conditions are further improved, those countries with slightly larger transaction cost coefficient start industrializing and the number of active modern firms in each of the industrializing countries increases. As general transaction conditions are further improved, those countries with the largest transaction cost coefficients are eventually industrialized. This process goes on until all countries and all sectors in each country are industrialized.

3. Extension and Applications

In the industrialization process described in the preceding section, each less developed country gradually duplicates the industrialization in the relatively more developed country in the absence of international trade. This looks like that each less developed country carries out import substitution strategy and relies on domestic market for industrialization. Because of positive effect of population size on industrialization, as shown in (14), we can extend our model to the analysis of international trade and export oriented industrialization. The opening up of international trade will increase the population size in the integrated world market, thereby promoting industrialization and economic development. But in our model transaction costs counteract unlimited expansion of international trade. Hence, the degree of market integration can be endogenized using the trade off between economies of scale and transaction costs.

Suppose a continuum of countries with mass M are divided between the set of developed countries with mass N and the set of underdeveloped countries with mass $M-N$. We now interpret L in (13) and (14) as the total population size in the N developed countries. In each of the N countries, some modern sectors operate and sell their produce to domestic as well as the world market. The dividing line between the developed world and the underdeveloped world is endogenously determined by the condition that in a marginal country between the two worlds the least capital-intensive modern sector has non-positive profit. This implies that in this country all modern sectors which cannot have more profit than the least capital-intensive sector, will not operate in equilibrium. Recall that countries are indexed according to their country specific trading efficiencies. Country 0 has the smallest country specific transaction cost coefficient $c_0 = s$ and country M has the largest transaction cost coefficient $c_M = \mu M$. The transaction cost coefficient for the marginal country N, $c_N = \mu N$ is in between the two extremes. This implies that for all countries $i > N$, profit for each modern sector is negative. Hence, in each of the M-N less-developed countries with low trading efficiencies, only traditional firms operate. Since productivity and therefore price of goods produced by the traditional sectors are independent of the size of the firm, the productivity and prices in the traditional sectors are independent of the extent of the market. We assume that international trade of cottage firms' produce involves infinitesimally transaction cost although domestic trade of their produce involves no transaction cost. Then, when no modern firm operates, firms and consumers have no incentive to participate in international trade. But if some modern firms operate, then international trade can increase the extent of the market and more economies of scale can be exploited at the cost of transportation of goods. This assumption will ensure that each less developed country will endogenously choose autarky, where all goods are self-provided by local cottage firms, in equilibrium.[4]

The dividing line between the developed countries and the underdeveloped countries is given by the zero profit condition for the active modern sector with the smallest fixed cost in the marginal N-th country. This implies that profit in all other modern sectors with larger fixed cost in this country are negative. Also profit in all modern sectors in M-N less developed countries which have larger transaction cost coefficients than the marginal country are negative. This zero profit condition is

$$\pi_{N0} = (1-\mu N\text{-}b)x_j-\delta = 0 \tag{15}$$

where δ is the smallest fixed cost in the modern sector producing good 0 and x_j is the total output of this good in the integrated world market consisting of N developed countries.

Now, the zero profit condition for the marginal firm in the integrated developed world can be obtained by assuming the profit in n-th modern sector in country 0, which has the smallest transaction cost coefficient c_0

---

[4] We need the assumption that migration from the less developed countries to the developed ones is prohibitively expensive. Otherwise, all individuals in the less developed countries will migrate to the developed countries which have better transaction condition. Also, we need the assumption that all individuals in the developed countries can freely migrate between countries and they equally share ownership of all active modern firms. The two assumptions are quite ad hoc. But they are essential for keeping the extended model tractable.

$= s$, to be zero. If this firm cannot break even in the marginal sector which has the largest fixed cost among all active modern sectors, the other countries with larger transaction cost coefficients than country 0 cannot possibly break even in this sector. This zero profit condition is

$$\pi_{0n} = (1-s-b)x_j - \gamma n = 0. \tag{16}$$

The number of active modern sectors n in the integrated developed world is endogenously determined by this equation.

The general equilibrium in the extended model consists of several components. The first of them is a local equilibrium in the integrated developed world with N countries. Interpreting L in (9) as the population size in the integrated market with N developed countries, (9), (15), and (16) determine the equilibrium n in the developed world in the extended model. Using (15) and (16) to eliminate the total market demand x_j, which must be the same for all industrial goods, we can identify the connection between the network size of international trade N and the number of active modern sectors in the integrated developed world, n.

$$N = [(1-b)(1-s)n - \delta(1-b-s)]/[(1-s)n - \delta(1-b-s)]\mu, \tag{17}$$

$$dN/d\mu = (\partial N/\partial \mu) + (\partial N/\partial n)(dn/d\mu) < 0.$$

where $\partial N/\partial \mu < 0$, $\partial N/\partial n > 0$, and $dn/d\mu < 0$ due to (12). Beside (17), the rest of comparative statics of the local equilibrium is the same as in (14).

The local autarky equilibrium in each of the M-N less developed countries is a component of the general equilibrium. In each of the countries all industrial goods are supplied by traditional (or cottage, handcraft) sectors. Because of the assumption that domestic trade of goods produced by cottage firms involve no transaction costs, the difference in transaction cost coefficient for trade of goods produced by modern sectors between countries will not generate difference in per capita real income between less developed countries. Therefore, per capita income is the same in all less developed countries, lower than in the developed countries. The autarky equilibrium for each of those countries is

$$p_z = 1/\theta, \quad p_x = 1, \quad X = \alpha L_i/m, \quad Z = (1-\alpha)\theta L_i$$

$$U = m^{\alpha(1-\rho)/\rho}\alpha^\alpha[\theta(1-\alpha)]^{1-\alpha}$$

where L_i is the population size of country $i \in (N, M]$. We now assume that in the initial period μ is so large that $c_i = \mu i$ is too large for any modern firm to break even in all countries $i > 0$. Hence, only country 0 (the UK) has modern sectors. As time goes by, μ decreases, the scope for trading off economies of scale against transaction costs is enlarged, so that the modern sectors with low fixed cost (low capital intensity) become profitable, this increases income and thereby demand, which makes more modern firms become profitable. This higher degree of industrialization in the developed world makes more of less developed countries be willing to use international trade to exploit economies of scale, which extends overseas market for domestic produce in the developed countries, which in turns attracts more participants of the network of trade. But increased transaction costs counteract the positive feedback between the extent of the market and economies of scale that can be exploited and between the number of countries involved in international trade and gains from trade. A new equilibrium is established that balances the trade off between economies of scale and transaction costs. Those countries with larger transaction cost coefficients and those modern sectors that are more capital intensive are not involved in international trade in the early stage of world development.

As general transaction conditions are further improved, the equilibrium number (measure) of modern sectors n and the number (measure) of countries involved in industrialization and international trade, N, increase. The newly industrializing countries produce and export goods of low capital intensity and those old industrialized countries produce and export capital intensive goods. This process continues until the most capital intensive sectors are produced by the modern sector and all countries are involved in the integrated world market. This is what happened in the Western Europe in the 18th and 19th century. Figure 1 gives an intuitive illustration of this spread of market led industrialization.

                    J. Sachs, X. Yang

Two types of dual structure

Our model endogenizes not only duality between modern and traditional sectors, but also duality between the developed and underdeveloped worlds. As worldwide transaction conditions are improved (μ decreases) or population size increases, the comparative statics indicate that per capita income increases for the developed countries involved in international trade, but per capita income in the less developed countries which are still left out of the world market does not change. Hence, inequality of per capita income between the developed and less developed countries increases. This inequality decreases as the last less developed country jumps into the world market.

Figure 1, together with (13) and (17), captures a general equilibrium mechanism that entails circular causation: each modern firm's profit and thereby its decision of being active is determined by the network size of industrial linkages and trade flows (or the thickness of the market), while the network size is determined by all firms' decisions on whether they participate in this industrialization process. Each country's decision of being involved in the world market is dependent not only on the size of the world market, N, but also on the degree of industrialization, n, in the developed world, while the degree of industrialization and the network size of international trade is determined by all countries' decisions on whether they participate in this networking process. Our model shows that the notion of general equilibrium (fixed point) is a powerful vehicle for figuring out the networking mechanism in a decentralized market.

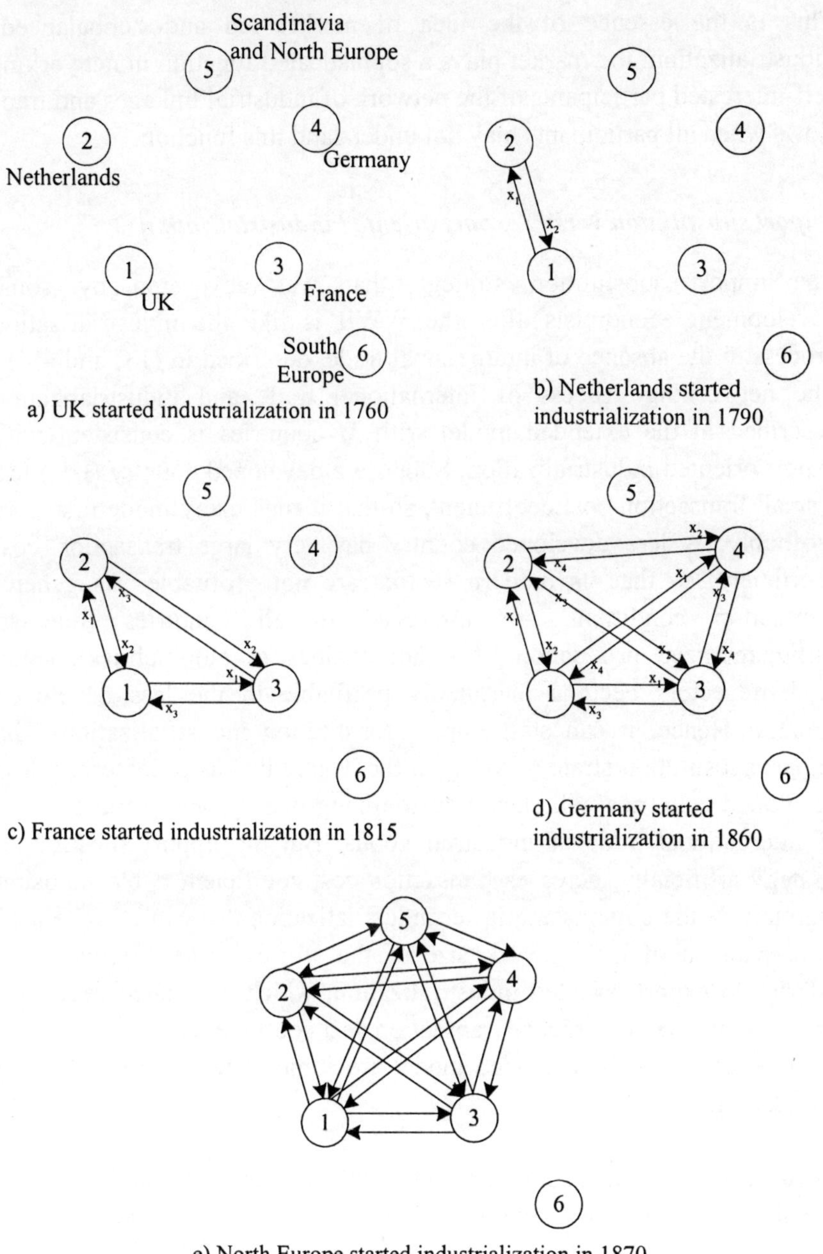

Figure 1: Map of Industrialization in Europe in 18th and 19th Centuries

This is the essence of the idea of market led and "unbalanced" industrialization: the market plays a sophisticated function in networking self-interested participants of the network of industrial linkages and trade flows when all participants may not understand this function.

Import substitution versus export oriented industrialization

The import substitution strategy that was advocated by some development economists after the WWII is like the industrialization process in the absence of international trade, described in (13) and (14).[5] The networking process of international trade and industrialization described in the extended model with M countries is consistent with export oriented industrialization. Suppose a developed country (UK) has a small transaction cost coefficient, so that it runs many modern sectors profitably. A less developed country has very large transaction cost coefficient, so that its modern sectors are not profitable. As general transaction conditions are improved in all countries (due to commercialized production of steam engines or automobiles), some modern sectors become marginally profitable in the less developed country. Hence, it can start import substitution industrialization. The import substitution strategy works to the degree that as μ decreases, less developed countries will start industrializing one by one in the absence of international trade of industrial goods. But the import substitution strategy artificially increases transaction cost coefficient c_i by imposing high tariffs, thereby missing faster industrialization that can be generated by expansion of the network size of the world market. Hence, it is inferior to export oriented industrialization, which uses tariff reduction and free trade zone to reduce transaction cost coefficient c.

The results of the extended model are summarized in the following proposition.

Proposition 2:   As transaction conditions are improved, and/or as the population size increases, the following development phenomena concur.

---

[5] See, for instance, Balassa (1980), Chenery, Robinson, and Syrquin (1986), Meier (1989, pp.297-306), and Bruton (1998) for discussion of development strategies.

The equilibrium dividing line between the developed world and less developed world moves in the direction that more less-developed and self-sufficient countries are involved in the integrated developed world. In the developed world, the number of operating modern firms, per capita income, and trade dependence increase. In this process inequality of income distribution increases as dual structure emerges from the transitional stage and then declines as the dual structure disappears. The countries with better transaction conditions are involved in international trade before other countries are.

If we use the zero profit conditions in all active modern sectors to determine the prices of their produce, we can then express the representative consumer's utility as a function of the degree of industrialization, n. Maximizing the utility with respect to n yields the Pareto optimum degree of industrialization which is higher than the equilibrium one. This is because the price mechanism fails to transmit information of the production and transaction conditions of the modern firms to consumers. In other words, consumers receive benefit of industrialization via dividend earnings, but they allocate the same share of dividend earnings to buy a good produced by a modern or a cottage firm because of the misinformation of price signals. In the Pareto optimum, each consumer consumes more of produce of each modern sector than that of each cottage sector. Slight differentiation between a good produced by the cottage firm and that by the modern firm will eliminate the distortions. But we will go to the regime of monopolistic competition which causes another type of distortion.

4. Concluding Remarks

This paper introduces the trade off between economies of scale and transaction costs into the MSV model to endogenize the number of modern sectors. We have developed an approach to analyzing the MSV model by specifying the zero profit condition for a marginal modern firm and keeping the original flavor of the MSV model which is the feedback loop between positive dividend earning, the extent of the market, and economies of scale that can be exploited. However, as transaction costs are introduced, big push industrialization will not occur unless transaction conditions have a sudden big improvement. Our model predicts a gradual spread of industrialization from the countries with better transaction conditions to other less developed countries, as general transaction conditions are improved. In this process inequality of income between the developed and less developed countries increases as a dual structure emerges and finally decreases as the dual structure disappears eventually. Also, the number of modern sectors increases, the degree of trade dependence increases, productivity of the industrial sector increases, per capita income increases, the degree of market integration increases, and the number of traditional sectors decreases.

This model formalizes the idea of unbalanced and market led industrialization. Our model suggests that the feedback loop between dividend earning (based on private property rights to residual returns of firms), the extent of the market, and economies of scale that can be exploited is essential for successful industrialization though the networking function of the market is not perfect.

References

Balassa, Bela (1989), "Outward Orientation," in H. Chenery and T.N. Srinivasan (eds), *Handbook of Development Economics,* Amsterdam: North-Holland, vol. II, pp. 1645-90.

Barro, R. (1997), *Determinants of Economic Growth*, Cambridge, MA, MIT Press.

Baechler, Jean (1976), *The Origins of Capitalism*, Translated by Barr Cooper, Oxford, Blackwell.

Bruton, Henry (1998), "A Reconsideration of Import Substitution," *Journal of Economic Literature*, 36, 903-36.

Chenery, Hollis, Robinson, Sherman, and Syrquin, Moshe (1986) (eds.), *Industrialization and Growth: A Comparative Studies*, New York, Oxford University Press.

Dasgupta, Partha (1995), "The Population Problem: Theory and Evidence," *Journal of Economic Literature*, 33, 1879-1902.

Easton, Stephen and Walker, Michael (1997), "Income, Growth, and Economic Freedom," *American Economic Review, Papers and Proceedings*, 87, 328-32.

Fleming, Marcus (1955), "External Economies and the Doctrine of Balanced Growth," *Economic Journal*, 65, 241-56.

Frye, Timothy and Shleifer, Andrei (1997), "The Invisible Hand and the Grabbing Hand," *American Economic Review, Papers and Proceedings*, 87, 354-58.

Gallup, John and Sachs, Jeff (1998), "Geography and Economic Development," Working Paper, Harvard Institute for International Development.

Hart, O. (1995), *Firms, Contracts, and Financial Structure*, Oxford, Clarendon Press.

Hirschman, Albert (1958), *The Strategy of Economic Development*, New Haven, Yale University Press.

Holmstrom, Bengt and Roberts, John (1998), "The Boundaries of the Firm Revisited," *Journal of Economic Perspectives*, 12, 73-94.

Kelly, Morgan (1997), "The Dynamics of Smithian Growth," *Quarterly Journal of Economics*, 112, 939-64.

Krugman, Paul (1995), *Development, Geography, and Economic Theory*, Cambridge, MIT Press.

Krugman, P. and Venables, A.J. (1995), "Globalization and the Inequality of Nations," *Quarterly Journal of Economics*, 110, 857-80.

Meier, G. (1989), *Leading Issues in Economic Development*, New York, Oxford University Press.

Milgrom, P. and Roberts, J. (1992), *Economics, Organization and Management*, Englewood Cliffs, Prentice-Hall.

Mises, L. (1922), *Socialism: An Economic and Sociological Analysis*, Indianapolis: Liberty Classics, reprinted in 1981.

Mokyr, Joel (1990), *The Lever of Richs: Technological Creativity and Economic Progress*, New York, Oxford University Press.

Mokyr, Joel (1993) (ed.), *The British Industrial Revolution, An Economic Perspective*, Boulder, Westview Press.

Murphy, K., Shleifer, A., and Vishny, R. (1989), "Industrialization and the Big Push," *Journal of Political Economy*, 97: 1003-26.

National Research Council (1986), *Population Growth and Economic Development: Policy Questions,* Washington, DC, National Academy of Sciences Press.

North, Douglas (1981), *Structure and Change in Economic History*, New York, Norton.

North, Douglass and Weingast, Barry (1989), "Consititutions and Commitment: The Evolution of Institutions Governing Public Choice in Seventeenth-Century England," *Journal of Economic History*, XLIX, pp 803-32.

Nurske, R. (1953), *Problems of Capital Formation in Underdeveloped Countries*, New York, Oxford University Press.

Rosen, S. (1983), "Specialization and Human Capital," *Journal of Labor Economics*, 1, 43-49.

Rosenstein-Rodam, P. (1943), "Problems of industrialization in Eastern and Southeastern Europe," *Economic Journal*, June-September issue.

Sachs, Jeffrey (1996), "Notes on the Life Cycle of State-led Industrialization," *Japan and the World Economy*, 8, 153-74.

Sachs, J. and Woo (1993), "Structural Factors in the Economic Reforms of China, Eastern Europe and the Former Soviet Union." Working Paper, Harvard University, Department of Economics.

Sachs, Jeffrey and Warner, Andrew. (1995), "Economic Reform and the Process of Global Integration," *Brookings Papers on Economic Activity,* 1.

Sachs, Jeffrey and Warner, Andrew (1997), "Fundamental Sources of Long-Run Growth," *American Economic Review, Papers and Proceedings*, 87, 184-88.

Sheahan, J. (1958), "International Specialization and the Concept of Balanced Growth," *Quarterly Journal of Economics*, 52, 183-97.

Shi, H. and Yang, X. (1995), "A New Theory of Industrialization," *Journal of Comparative Economics*, 20, 171-89.

Shi, H. and Yang, X. (1998), "Centralised Hierarchy within a Firm vs. Decentralised Hierarchy in the Market ," in K. Arrow, Y-K. Ng, and X. Yang eds. *Increasing Returns and Economic Analysis*, London, Macmillan.

Stigler, G. (1951), "The Division of Labor is Limited by the Extent of the Market," *Journal of Political Economy*, 59, 185-93.

Sun, G. and Lio, M. (1997), "A General Equilibrium Model Endogenizing the Level of Division of Labor and Variety of Producer Goods", Working Paper, Department of Economics, Monash University.

Yang, X. and Ng, S. (1998), "Specialization and Division of Labor: a Survey," K. Arrow et al (ed.), *Increasing Returns and Economic Analysis,* London, Macmillan.

Young, Allyn (1928), "Increasing Returns and Economic Progress," *The Economic Journal*, 38, 527-42.

Part 5

Economies of Specialization and Endogenous Comparative Advantage

CHAPTER 12

SPECIALIZATION AND PRODUCT DIVERSITY[*]

Xiaokai Yang[a] and He-Ling Shi[b][*]

[a]Harvard and Monash University   [b]Monash University

Casual observation indicates a positive correlation between the level of specialization and the variety of available goods in an economy. The variety of available goods is small in a less developed and autarkical economy in which the level of division of labor and specialization is extremely low and everyone self-provides all goods he needs. In contrast, the variety of available goods is great in a developed economy in which the level of division of labor and specialization is extremely high. This positive correlation may relate to some important mechanism that is essential for trade and growth theory. Two research lines are related to two aspects of the mechanism in isolation.

The first line has been developed by Avinash K. Dixit and Joseph E. Stiglitz (1977), Paul R. Krugman (1981), Wilfred J. Ethier (1982), Paul Romer (1988), and Gene M. Grossman and Elhanan Helpman (1989). Their models have endogenized the variety of goods by formalizing a trade-off between the distortions arising from economies of scale and preferences for diverse consumption or economies of complementarity in production. The crucial element of the models is the constant-elasticity-of-substitution (CES) utility or production function in which all goods are not necessities individually, so that the number of

---

[*] Reprinted from *American Economic Review*, 82 (2), Xiaokai Yang and Heling Shi, "Specialization and Product Diversity," 392-98, 1992, with permission from American Economic Association.

[*] The authors are grateful to Sherwin Rosen, Jeff Borland, Yew-Kwang Ng, Richard Snape, Richard Arnott, and Gene Grossman for discussions and criticism. Any remaining errors are our own responsibility.

goods can be endogenized. However, their models cannot endogenize the level of specialization for each individual. To endogenize the level of specialization, the degree of self-sufficiency of consumers and the range of production of each individual must be endogenized.

On the other hand, Sherwin Rosen (1978), James R. Baumgardner (1988), Sunwoong Kim (1989), Luis Locay *(1990),* Yang (1990), Yang and Ian Wills *(1990)* and Yang and Jeff Borland (1991) have endogenized the level of specialization, leaving the number of goods exogenously fixed. The static and dynamic equilibrium models of Yang (1990), Yang and Wills (1990), and Yang and Borland (1991) have endogenized the level of specialization by formalizing a trade-off between economies of specialization and transaction costs. However, the variety of available goods is not endogenized in their models because the Cobb-Douglas utility function (a special case of the CES function) assumed in their models entails an exogenously fixed number of goods.

A natural conjecture is that a synthesis of the thinking along the two lines may enable us to decipher the mechanism behind the concurrent increases in specialization and consumption variety. This idea motivates the paper. In the model to be considered, each individual is a consumer/producer, and an increase in the division of labor is therefore interpreted as an increase in the proportion of an individual's consumption that is purchased from other people. Each individual is assumed to have a CES utility function with the number of goods consumed as a decision variable, so that there is a preference for consumption variety. However, a fraction of utility that is proportional to the number of goods consumed is lost because of management costs associated with the variety of consumption. In the model, consumption goods can be either self-produced or purchased, but if they are purchased there is a transaction cost incurred. Each consumer / producer's production function displays a positive relationship between labor productivity and his level of specialization in producing any good.

Since all individuals are *ex ante* identical and the parameters of production, preference, and transaction costs are the same for every good, the problem of resource allocation is too trivial to be interesting. The most important decision for an individual in our model is choosing his level of specialization and consumption variety. The aggregate outcome of such individual decisions is an endogenously determined division of labor and the variety of available goods for the economy.

We will show that, if the elasticity of substitution is positive and economies of specialization do not dominate economies of complementarity, the number of traded goods and the number of all goods may take on interior solutions in a competitive equilibrium that balances a trade-off between economies of specialization and transaction costs. For a sufficiently low efficiency in transactions, each person has to self-provide all goods that he needs, since transaction costs outweigh economies of specialization when transaction efficiency is small. A trade-off between economies of specialization and economies of complementarity may force each person to produce a few goods to capture economies of specialization at the cost of economies of complementarity in autarky. An improvement in transaction efficiency will create more scope for a balance of the trade-off between economies of specialization and economies of complementarity such that people can increase the variety of available goods and the level of specialization at the same time via the division of labor among many specialists producing different goods. As transaction efficiency is improved, the number of traded goods and the number of all goods increase with the first number rising more rapidly than the second. Hence, all goods produced will be traded if transaction efficiency is sufficiently large. In this process, domestic and international trade dependence, the extent of the market, the number of markets, the level of specialization, the degree of diversification of economic structure, the degree of integration of the market, the extent of endogenous comparative advantages,[1] per capita real income, and labor productivity of each traded good increase simultaneously.

---

[1] Endogenous or *ex post* comparative advantage is defined in Yang and Borland (1991) as the difference in productivity between a buyer and a seller of a good when all individuals are *ex ante* identical in all aspects. In that paper, the conventional concept of comparative advantage is called exogenous (or *ex ante*) comparative advantage.

1. A Model of Consumers/Producers

Let us consider an economy with M consumers / producers and m consumer goods. M is a given large constant and m is a decision variable for each consumer/producer. The amount self-provided of good i is x_i. The amount sold of good i is x_i^s. The amount purchased of good i is x_i^d.

An "iceberg" type of transaction technology is characterized by the coefficient K. A fraction $1-K$ of any shipment disappears in transit because of transaction costs. Thus, $K x_i^d$ is the amount a person receives from the purchase of good i. The amount consumed of good i is $x_i + K x_i^d$.

We assume further that the more goods are consumed, the greater is the cost in calculating the optimum pattern of consumption, production, and trade, in terms of utility loss. Suppose that c is a cost coefficient for an individual to manage one good and cm is therefore the proportion of utility that is lost because of the management costs when m goods are consumed. The utility function is assumed to be identical for all individuals, given by

(1) $U = (1 - cm)V$

$$V = \left[\sum_{i=1}^{m} (x_i + K x_i^d)^\rho \right]^{1/\rho} \quad c, \rho \in (0,1)$$

where V represents a preference for diverse consumption. V monotonically increases with the number of consumer goods, m. The elasticity of substitution between any pair of goods in the CES utility function is $1/(1 - \rho)$. Since the substitution elasticity increases with ρ and preference for diverse consumption decreases with the substitution elasticity, $1/\rho$ can be interpreted as the degree of economies of complementarity in consumption. Suppose, further, that the coefficient K depends on the number of a person's trade partners and that a person sells one good and buys $n - 1$ goods. If all people are located at the vertices of a grid of triangles with equal sides, the distance between each pair of neighbors will be an equal constant, and the average distance between a person and his trade partners will be an increasing function of the number of his trade partners and of the distance between a pair of neighbors (under assumption that trade occurs first with those closest). Assume that the transaction-cost co-efficient $1 - K$ increases with the average distance between a person and his trade partners (i.e., the coefficient K decreases with this distance). Suppose that this relationship is given by

$$(2) \qquad K = [k/(n-1)]^{a-1} \quad k \in (0,1) \quad a > 1$$

where k is a constant that characterizes transaction efficiency, $n-1$ is the number of goods purchased, and $a-1$ is a parameter characterizing the degree of increasing returns, which is consistent with the degree of economies of specialization that will be specified in the production functions.[2]

A system of production functions and time constraint for each consumer/producer is

$$(3) \qquad x_i + x_i^s = L_i^a \quad a > 1$$

$$\sum_{i=1}^{m} L_i = 1 \quad L_i \in [0,1] \quad i = 1,...,m$$

where $x_i + x_i^s$ is the output level of good i and L_i is the labor spent producing good i. We assume that the total available hours for an individual is 1. Here L_i is the labor share spent producing good i as well. It represents the level of specialization that differs from the scale of labor if the total available hours are not 1. This system of production functions exhibits increasing returns to specialization. Labor productivity $(x_i + x_i^s)/L_i$ of a good increases with the level of specialization in producing this good L_i. Economy of specialization is a sort of "diseconomy of scope," different from an economy of scale.

However, specialization will incur transaction costs because each consumer/producer has a preference for diverse consumption. This preference counteracts the gains from specialization, leading to a trade-off between economies of specialization and transaction costs.

---

[2] The second-order condition for an interior equilibrium n will not be satisfied if K is independent of n. In other words, equilibrium will be at a corner, either autarky or extreme specialization; that is, no interior n will occur if the transaction cost coefficient $1 - K$ does not increase with n.

2. Individual Decisions and Equilibrium

Since all consumers / producers are *ex ante* identical in all aspects, there are many potential producers of each good. Hence, competition for the rights to produce a good occurs between identical peers, rather than between "experts" and "novices." No individual will possess monopoly powers, because economies of specialization are specific to each consumer / producer and to each activity. This justifies a Walrasian regime with price-taking behavior.

Following the approach to proving lemma 1 in Yang and Borland (1991), we can prove that, according to the Kuhn-Tucker theorem, an individual does not buy and sell the same goods, does not self-provide and buy the same goods, and sells one good at most. Taking this into account, the decision problem for a person selling good i is as follows:

$$(4) \qquad \max\left\{U_i = (1 - cm)\left[x_i^p + \sum_{r \in R}(Kx_r^d)^\rho + \sum_{j \in J}x_j^\rho\right]^{1/\rho}\right\}$$

subject to

$$x_i + x_i^s = L_i^a \qquad x_j = L_i^a \quad j \in J \qquad \text{(production function)}$$

$$L_i + \sum_{j \in J}L_j = 1 \qquad\qquad \text{(endowment constraint)}$$

$$K = \left[k/(n-1)\right]^{a-1} \qquad\qquad \text{(transaction technology)}$$

$$p_i x_i^s = \sum_{r \in R}p_r x_r^d \qquad\qquad \text{(budget constraint)}$$

where the set of goods bought R consists of $n - 1$ elements and the set of nontraded goods J consists of $m - n$ elements; P_y is the price of good $y(y = i, r, r \in R)$; and $L_y, x_y (y = i, j, j \in J), x_i^s, x_r^d (r \in R), n \in [1, m]$, and $m \in [1, \infty]$ are decision variables. The first-order conditions for the problem yield the optimum n, m, L_y, x_y, x_i^s, and x_r^d as functions of relative prices of all traded goods. The optimum x_i^s and x_r^d are individual demand and supply. Inserting the optimum decisions into U_i gives an indirect utility function for a person Son selling good i.

Equilibrium is characterized by the market-clearing conditions based on individual demand and supply and utility-equalization conditions based on the indirect utility functions. Assume that the number of persons selling good i is M_i; we need to solve only for the relative numbers of persons selling different goods, because the population size $M = \sum_i M_i$ is given. The market-clearing conditions are

$$(5) \qquad M_r x_r^s = \sum_i M_i x_{ir}^d \qquad r = 1,...,n$$

where $M_r x_r^s$ is the aggregate supply of good $r, \sum_i M_i x_{ir}^d$ is the aggregate demand for good r, x_{ir}^d is the demand of a person selling good i for good r, and x_{ir}^d, is the same as x_r^d in (4) due to symmetry. Expression (5) consists of $n - 1$ independent equations due to Walras's law.

The utility-equalization conditions are

$$(6) \qquad U_1 = U_2 = \ldots = U_n.$$

Expression (6) consists of $n - 1$ equations. Together, (5) and (6) determine the $n - 1$ equilibrium relative prices and $n - 1$ relative numbers of persons selling different goods which define equilibrium. Because of symmetry, the equilibrium values of all prices and numbers of different specialists are equal across goods. Inserting the equilibrium relative prices into (4) and (5), the first-order conditions for the problem in (4) yield equilibrium values of all variables, given by

$$
\begin{aligned}
(7) \quad & x_i = (1-k)L_i^a & & \forall i = 1,...,n \\
& x_r^d = (n-1)x_i^s & & \forall r \in R \text{ and } i = 1,...,n \\
& x_i^s = kL_i^a & & \forall i = 1,...,n \\
& L_i = (n-1)/[n-1+k(m-n)] & & \forall i = 1,...,n \\
& x_j = L_j^a & & \forall j \in J \\
& L_j = k/[(n-1)+k(m-n)] & & \forall j \in J \\
& n-1 = k(1-k)^{(\rho-1)/(1-a\rho)} & &
\end{aligned}
$$

for all individuals

$$m = \frac{\left[1+(1-a\rho)/\rho c\right]-(1-k)^{(\rho-1)/(1-a\rho)}}{1+(1-a\rho)/\rho}$$

for all persons.

The second-order conditions for an equilibrium with $n \in (1, m)$ and $m \in (1, \infty)$ are that substitution elasticity is positive ($\rho < 1$); economies of specialization do not dominate economies of complementarity ($a < 1/\rho$); and transaction efficiency (k) and management efficiency of a variety of goods ($1/c$) are neither too large nor too small. Assume that these conditions for interior n and m are satisfied. The comparative statics are then given by

$$(8a) \quad dn/dk > 0 \qquad dn/da > 0 \qquad dn/dc = 0$$

$$(8b) \quad dm/dk > 0 \qquad dm/dc < 0 \qquad dm/da \text{ is ambiguous}$$

$$(8c) \quad d(m-n)/dk < 0 \qquad d[(m-n)/m]/dk < 0$$

$$(8d) \quad dx_i^s/dk > 0$$

$$(8e) \quad dL_i/dk > 0 \qquad dL_i/da > 0$$

$$(8f) \quad dL_i^{a-1}/dk > 0 \qquad dL_i^{a-1}/da > 0$$

$$(8g) \quad dU^*/dk = \partial U/\partial k > 0 \qquad dU^*/dc = \partial U/\partial c < 0$$

where n is the number of traded goods that can be taken to be the level of division of labor, m is the number of all goods that can be taken to be the degree of diversity of goods, and $m - n$ is the number of self-provided goods (note that an interior solution of n is greater than 1 and no goods are traded at the corner with $n = 1$); $(m - n)/m$ can be interpreted as the degree of self-sufficiency; k is the transaction efficiency; c is the variety management cost coefficient (or, $1/c$ is the efficiency in managing a variety of goods); a is the degree of economies of specialization; and x_i^s is the per capita production value sold in the market, which is equal to per capita total demand for all traded goods. This demand can be taken to be the extent of the market. Mx_i^s can be taken to be the equilibrium aggregate demand and supply. Our model has endogenized equilibrium aggregate demand and supply that cannot be taken care of by neoclassical microeconomics. Here x_i^s is identical across i, and it increases with k. L_i is the labor share spent producing traded goods, or the value share of traded goods in terms of labor. This share can be taken to be domestic and international trade-dependence. Also, this share can be interpreted as the level of specialization for an individual, as well as the degree of commercialization. L_i^{a-1} is the labor productivity of a good sold. Since each individual does not spend labor producing goods purchased, his labor productivity of goods purchased is $L_r^{a-1} = 0$ for $r \in R$, the set of goods bought. Therefore, the difference in labor productivity between a seller and a buyer of goods is $(L_i^{a-1} - L_r^{a-1}) = L_i^{a-1}$, where i and r are the same good, sold by one person and bought by the other. We define the extent of endogenous comparative advantage as this difference. U^* is the equilibrium level of utility, or per capita real income. We have employed the envelope theorem in deriving (8g). The inequalities in (8c) imply that n converges to m as k increases. This implies that equilibrium n increases more rapidly than equilibrium m as k increases. We refer to the state with $m = n$ as complete division of labor.

Taking the location problem into account, people will trade first with those closest. Moreover, complete symmetry implies that each individual buys any one good from only one seller, and each individual sells only one good to the market. Therefore, n individuals will establish a local business community or the local markets for n goods in order to reduce transaction costs. Each member of such a community sells one good to the other $n - 1$ members and buys one good from each of them. The complete symmetry leads to the same size of all such local markets. The number of local communities and the number of producers of each traded good is M/n, where M is the population size and n is the number of traded goods as well as the number of individuals in a local community. The degree of integration and the degree of production concentration can be defined as n/M. The degree of market integration and production concentration increases as the level of division labor increases with transaction efficiency. Expression (8) leads us to

Proposition 1: If the elasticity of substitution is positive and economies of complementarity are not dominated by economies of specialization, all of the following increase as transaction efficiency is improved: the number of traded goods, the variety of goods, domestic and international trade dependence, the extent of the market, the level of specialization, the degree of commercialization, the extent of endogenous comparative advantage, the degree of market integration and production concentration, the population size of a local business community, labor productivity, and per capita real income. The number of traded goods increases more rapidly than the number of all goods. The degree of self-sufficiency and the number of producers of each traded good decrease with transaction efficiency. The economy will be in autarky if transaction efficiency is sufficiently small and will be in complete division of labor if transaction efficiency is sufficiently large. The degree of economies of specialization has positive effects on the number of traded goods, trade dependence, and labor productivity of traded goods. Efficiency in managing a variety of goods has a positive effect on consumption variety and per capita real income.

3.   Concluding Remarks

Our model can predict concurrent increases in specialization and consumption variety. It is interesting to see that the implications for international trade differentiate our model from the model of Dixit and Stiglitz (1977). For their model, the total factor productivity increases with the size of an economy. Hence, international trade is always superior to autarky, since the size of the pooling economy in the world market is always larger than the size of individual economies. However, our model predicts that a local business community is enough for exploiting economies of specialization net of transaction costs, and a domestic national market and international trade are not needed if transaction efficiency is small. As transaction efficiency is improved, the national market will emerge from a higher level of division of labor. If transaction efficiency is extremely large, then international trade will emerge from domestic trade.

References

Baumgardner, James R., "The Division of Labor, Local Markets, and Worker Organization," *Journal of Political Economy,* June 1988, 96, 509–27.

Dixit, Avinash K. and Stiglitz, Joseph E., "Monopolistic Competition and Optimum Product Diversity," *American Economic Review,* June 1977, 67, 297–308.

Ethier, Wilfred J., "National and International Returns to Scale in the Modern Theory of International Trade," *American Economic Review,* June 1982, 72, 389–405.

Grossman, Gene M. and Helpman, Elhanan, "Product Development and International Trade," *Journal of Political Economy,* December 1989, 97, 1261–83.

Kim, Sunwoong, "Labor Specialization and the Extent of the Market," *Journal of Political Economy,* June 1989, 97, 692–709.

Krugman, Paul R., "Intraindustry Specialization and the Gains from Trade," *Journal of Political Economy,* October 1981, 89, 959–73.

Locay, Luis, "Economic Development and the Division of Production Between Households and Markets," *Journal of Political Economy,* October 1990, 98, 965–82.

Romer, Paul, "Endogenous Technological Change," *Journal of Political Economy,* October 1990, 98, S71–S102.

Rosen, Sherwin, "Substitution and the Division of Labor," *Economica,* August 1978, 45, 235-50.

Yang, Xiaokai, "Development, Structural Changes, and Urbanization," *Journal of Development Economics,* November 1990, 34, 199–222.

Yang, Xiaokai and Borland, Jeff, "A Microeconomic Mechanism for Economic Growth," *Journal of Political Economy,* June 1991, 99, 460–82.

Yang, Xiaokai and Wills, Ian, "A Model Formalizing the Theory of Property Rights," *Journal of Comparative Economics,* June 1990, 14, 177–98.

ENDOGENOUS VS. EXOGENOUS COMPARATIVE ADVANTAGE AND ECONOMIES OF SPECIALIZATION VS. ECONOMIES OF SCALE[*]

Xiaokai Yang

Monash and Harvard University

1. Introduction

Casual observation indicates that technical progress, higher productivity, increases in trade dependence, increases in the degree of comparative advantage and in the extent of the market, increases in the degree of specialization for individuals and in the degree of diversity of professions for society as a whole, are all associated with the development of division of labor. An extremely exciting story, similar in its aesthetic beauty to the one occurring within an atom or within, the molecular structure of DNA, must be behind the concurrence of so many interesting phenomena, some of them seemingly contradictory to each other. Deciphering the exciting story should be the focus of 1 economists' curiosity because economists are deeply concerned with the interrelationships among the phenomena. Yet, what we are told by neoclassical microeconomics cannot predict the concurrence of these interesting phenomena.

It seems to us that the shift of focus in economic analysis from Adam Smith's (1976) concept of economies of division of labor from 1776 to David Ricardo's (1973) concept of comparative advantage from 1817

---

[*] Reprinted from *Journal of Economics*, 60 (1), Xiaokai Yang, "Endogenous vs. Exogenous Comparative Advantage and Economies of Specialization vs. Economies of Scale," 29-54, 1994, with permission from Springer-Verlag.

was critical for the incapability of neoclassical microeconomics in predicting the concurrence of the above phenomena. The concept of comparative advantage substantially differs from the concept of economies of the division of labor. Many economists hold that Ricardo's concept of comparative advantage is a progress of economic theory compared to Smith's theory of economies of the division of labor based on increasing returns. Smith's economies of the division of labor exist only if an individual is more productive than another individual in at least one activity, that is, only if there exist absolute advantages. According to Ricardo's theory gains to trade may exist in the absence of any absolute advantage if comparative advantages exist.

However, it can be shown that Smith's absolute advantage may exist in the absence of Ricardo's comparative advantage.[1] As Yang (1990), Yang and Borland (1991), and Yang and Wills (1990) have shown, endogenous absolute and comparative advantages may emerge between ex ante identical individuals if they choose different levels of specialization in producing goods and if there exist increasing returns to specialization. That is, absolute and comparative advantages in terms of Smith's definition may exist in the absence of comparative advantages in terms of Ricardo's definition which cannot exist if all individuals are ex ante identical. The former comparative advantage does not exist if all ex ante identical individuals choose the same level of specialization in producing a good. In other words, the existence of such comparative advantages depends upon people's decision of level of specialization. Hence, Yang and Borland (1991) refer to such comparative advantage as endogenous comparative advantage and refer to Ricardo's notion of comparative advantage as exogenous comparative advantage which is based on exogenously given differences in technology and endowments between individuals. Grossman and Helpman (1989) refer to gains to trade based on increasing returns to scale as acquired comparative advantage and refer to Ricardo's notion of comparative advantage as

---

[1] To our knowledge, Houthakker (1956) is the first economist who has shown with the aid of a graph that Smith's notion of economies of division of labor may be more general than Ricardo's notion of comparative advantage.

natural comparative advantage.[2] In this paper, we will discuss the difference and connection between the concept of economies of specialization, used by Rosen (1978, 1983) and Yang and Borland, and the concept of economies of scale, used by Grossman and Helpman.

Many economists have noted that the inherited differences in productivity in producing different goods between individuals are much less important than the differences in productivity between individuals that are generated by the division of labor.[3] Yang and Borland (1991) have shown that endogenous comparative advantages may evolve as division of labor evolves over time and that the evolution of endogenous comparative advantage is the driving force that speeds up accumulation of knowledge and endogenous progress in productivity. Certainly, exogenous comparative advantages cannot endogenously evolve and hence they have no implications for the evolution of division of labor, progress in productivity, and the speeding up of knowledge accumulation.

When Alfred Marshall (1920) adopted an analytical framework featured with a dichotomy between pure consumers and firms in order to formalize classical economic thinking within an internally consistent mathematical framework in the late 19th century, he replaced Smith's concept of economies of division of labor with the concept of economies of scale. According to Smith and Young (1928), economies of the division of labor are based on economies of specialization. Economies of specialization can be well defined only in a model that endogenizes a range of outputs produced by an individual. The division of labor is based on specialization, but differs from specialization. There is no division of labor if all individuals are specialized in the same activity. The division of labor is an organizational pattern where individuals are

---

[2] The Grossman and Helpman model (1989) is the first model that generates endogenous evolution of the number of goods based on internal economies of scale and a monopolistically competitive regime. Romer's model (1986) is the first model that generates endogenous evolution of the number of goods based on external economies of scale.

[3] Smith (1976: Chap. 1) argued that "The difference in natural talents in different men is, in reality, much less than we are aware of, and the very genius which appears to distinguish men of different professions, when grown up to maturity, is not on many occasions so much the cause, as the effect of the division of labor."

specialized in different activities. Hence, specialization and diversity between different professions are two aspects of the division of labor.[4] Smith's and Young's concept of economies of division of labor are related to, but different from, the concept of economies of scale.

The concept of economies of division of labor intimately relates to the endogenization of the range of output produced by an individual. The concept of economies of scale for a firm may be irrelevant to the level of specialization of an individual. The scale of a firm may be large and its level of specialization may be low at the same time. The endogenization of the level of specialization inevitably involves corner solutions. The Marshallian framework avoids corner solutions by using the dichotomy between pure consumers and firms in order to make marginalism based on interior solutions work. Therefore, it cannot endogenize the level of specialization of an individual. In most neoclassical microeconomic models the range of output is not explicitly specified as a decision variable of a firm, so that the endogenization of level of specialization cannot be explicitly considered in these models. Therefore, the concept of economies of scale differs from the concept of economies of division of labor based on specialization.[5]

The purpose of this paper is to use a simple equilibrium model within Yang's framework of consumer-producers, economies of specialization, and transaction costs to investigate the general equilibrium implications of the distinctions between endogenous and exogenous comparative advantages and between economies of specialization and economies of scale. The implications are particularly important for trade theory because exogenous comparative advantage and economies of scale are two central concepts in neoclassical theory on gains to trade. We first specify an equilibrium model to draw the distinctions between

---

[4] Durkheim (1964) indicated in 1933 that the division of labor increases not only specialization and solidarity, but also individuality and the differentiation between individuals.

[5] In comparison to the replacement of the concept of economies of division of labor with the concept of economies of scale, the debate, as Stigler (1951) noted, between Marshall's line that treats economies of scale as external to firms and the research line that treats economies of scale as internal to firms has less serious implications for the shift of economists' attention from the economic organization problem to the resource allocation problem.

exogenous and endogenous comparative advantages and between economies of specialization and economies of scale. Then, a multiple step approach to solving for the Walrasian equilibrium based on corner solutions is devised in Sect. 3. Finally, the model is compared with a neoclassical trade model based on exogenous comparative advantage and with a new trade model based on a tradeoff between economies of scale and transaction costs in order to explore the equilibrium implications of the distinctions between exogenous and endogenous comparative advantages and between economies of scale and economies of specialization.

2. A System of Production for a Consumer-producer and Transaction Costs

In the paper, economies of specialization can be defined on the basis of the following system of production functions and time constraint, specified for each consumer-producer:

$$x_i + x_i^s = l_{xi}^a, \quad y_i + y_i^s = l_{yi}^a, \quad l_{xi} + l_{yi} = L, \tag{1}$$

where subscript i denotes consumer-producer, $i = 1, 2, ..., M$. M is the population size which is assumed large. x_i is the quantity of a consumer good self-provided and y_i is that of the other consumer good self-provided by person i. By self-provided we shall mean that quantity of a good produced by an individual for his own consumption. x_i^s is the quantity of x sold and y_i^s is that of y sold by person i. $x_i + x_i^s$ is the output level of x and $y_i + y_i^s$ is that of y for person i. l_{ji} is time spent producing good $j = x, y$ by person i. The total available quantity of time for an individual is L. Here we assume L is time for production and abstract from the tradeoff between work and leisure. This implies that time is equivalent to labor. We call (1) a *system of production* which is comprised of several production functions and a time endowment constraint for a consumer-producer.

We define the *level of specialization* of a consumer-producer in producing a good as his time share spent producing this good when his labor can be spent producing more than one good. It is not difficult to see the distinction between this concept and the concept of *operation scale*.

If we specify a production function that allows a firm to produce only one good, then the level of specialization is fixed exogenously, but the scale of operation is still variable and defined by the output level of the firm. The level of specialization of a firm is a function of the levels of specialization of individuals in this firm. Therefore, we cannot measure the level of specialization of a firm in the absence of measurement of levels of specialization of individuals and the internal organization within the firm. On the other hand, the measurement of the operation scale of a firm may be independent of the levels of specialization of individuals and the internal organization within the firm. The concept of the level of specialization relates more closely to the concept of operation scope than to the concept of scale. The level of specialization of an individual increases as his operation scope decreases.

Let $X_i \equiv (x_i + x_i^s)/l_{xi}$ denote person i's labor productivity of x and $Y_i \equiv (y_i + y_i^s)/l_{yi}$ denote that of y. Let $L_{ji} \equiv l_{ji}/L$ denote person i's level of specialization in producing good j. Using these notations and rearranging (1), we may express labor productivity of a good as a function of a person's level of specialization in producing this good.

$$X_i = L^{a-1}L_{xi}^{a-1}, \quad Y_i = L^{a-1}L_{yi}^{a-1}, \quad L_{xi} + L_{yi} = 1, \tag{2}$$

where X_i is person i's labor productivity of x and Y_i is that of y, and L_{ji} is person i's level of specialization in producing good j. X_i increases (or decreases) with L_{xi} and Y_i with L_{yi} if $a > 1$ (or $a < 1$). This implies that a person's labor productivity of a good increases with his level of specialization in producing this good, that is, the system of production exhibits economies of specialization if $a > 1$. The system of production exhibits diseconomies of specialization if $a < 1$ and exhibits constant returns to specialization if $a = 1$. Parameter $a - 1$ characterizes the degree of economies of specialization. Here, the system of production is identical for all individuals and the production function is identical for all goods. This means that no difference in the endowment constraint or technology exists between individuals. We define gains to trade that are based on this difference as exogenous comparative advantage. Hence, for this system of production, there is no exogenous comparative advantage.

It is not difficult to see the distinction and connection between economies of specialization and economies of scale. This distinction is given by the distinction between the concept of specialization and the concept of scale. For production function (1), there are economies of scale for each person in producing each good if $a > 1$. However, such economies of scale are limited. They are specific to each consumer-producer as well as to each activity. The concept of economies of specialization relates more closely to the concept of diseconomies of scope than to the concept of economies of scale. We will discuss the relationship and distinctions between economies of specialization and scope after we have defined the concept of economies of division of labor.

Roughly speaking, an economic organizational pattern is called division of labor, if it divides individuals' labor among different activities. Hence, the levels of specialization for individuals and the number of professional activities are two sides of the level of division of labor. It is extremely difficult to well define the notions of division of labor and level of division of labor because the level of division of labor is determined by many individuals' levels of specialization and the number of different professions. If the population size, M, equals two in the model of this paper, we can define division of labor as a pattern of economic organization in which at least one person specializes producing a single good. However, this definition is relevant only to the model with two goods and two persons. For the model with many goods and persons, the definition of division of labor will be much more complicated. Moreover, a pattern of economic organization is said to have a higher level of division of labor than the other pattern if (a) all individuals' levels of specialization in the former pattern are not lower than in the latter and (b) at least one person's level of specialization in the former pattern is higher than one person's in the latter or (a), and (c) the number of traded goods is larger in the former than in the latter. A pattern of economic organization in this paper is said to be autarky if every individual produces his own consumption. In our framework the transformation curve is organization dependent. If the division of labor generates a higher transformation curve than autarky, or a higher level of division of labor generates a higher transformation curve, then the related system of production is said to exhibit economies of division of labor.

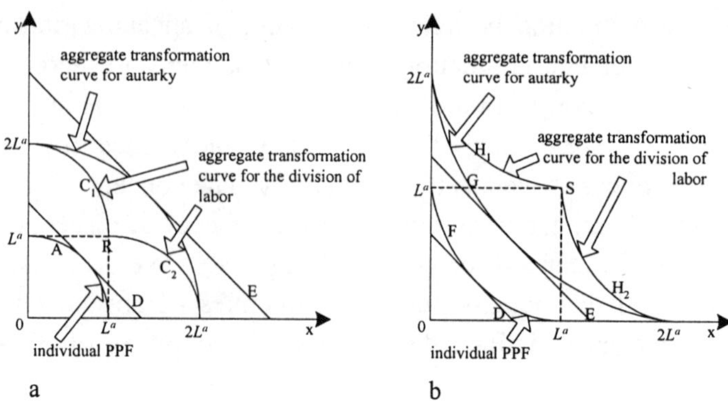

Figure 1: Individual and aggregate transformation curves.
a, PPF for a < 1.   b, PPF for a > 1.

Suppose $L > 1$ in (1); then curve A of Figure 1a is an individual transformation curve for $a < 1$. This curve exhibits a diminishing marginal rate of transformation. Assume $M = 2$, that is, there are only two individuals in our model; then curve B in this panel is a simple addition of two persons' individual transformation curves. This is one of the aggregate transformation curves in autarky for $a < 1$. Curve B can be drawn as follows. First rays are drawn from the origin. For each ray we plot the end point of a segment line which is as double lengthy as the segment determined by the origin and the intersection between the individual production possibility frontier (PPF) and the ray. A smooth curve connecting the end points of all such segments is the aggregate transformation curve for autarky. Assume that a person specializes producing y and the other produces one or two goods. The first person's output level of y is L^a, represented by the horizontal dashed line that cuts point R. The second person's PPF is the same as curve A. The aggregate transformation curve for the two persons can be obtained by shifting individual transformation curve A up by L^a. The aggregate transformation curve is curve C_1. Similarly, if a person specializes producing x and the other produces one or two goods, we can obtain the aggregate transformation curve by shifting individual transformation curve A to the right by L^a. The aggregate transformation curve is curve C_2. C_1 and C_2 constitute the aggregate transformation curve for the division of labor when $a < 1$. This aggregate transformation curve is lower than the aggregate transformation curve for autarky that is curve B. According to the definition of economies (or diseconomies) of division of labor, the system of production (1) exhibits diseconomies of division of labor if $a < 1$. Here diseconomies of specialization are equivalent to diseconomies of division of labor because a is the same across goods. If $a > 1$ for a good and $a < 1$ for the other, then the equivalence may not hold. At the point of intersection R between C_1 and C_2, each person completely specializes producing one good. We call this point *complete division of labor*. A consumer-producer completely specializing in producing one good is referred to as a *specialist* of this good. A sector consisting of specialists of the same good is referred to as a *professional sector*. From Figure la, we can see that the difference between the transformation curve for autarky and one for the division of labor is maximized at this point. This implies that if there is the same degree of diseconomies of specialization in producing two goods, diseconomies of division of labor are maximized by the complete division of labor.

If $a = 1$, then the individual transformation curve is D and the aggregate transformation curve is E in Figure la. The aggregate transformation curve is organization independent because of constant returns to specialization. Curve F in Figure 1b is the individual transformation curve for $a > 1$ and curve G is a simple addition of the two individual transformation curves for $a > 1$. The two transformation curves have increasing marginal rates of transformation. Curve G represents the production possibilities in autarky. For $a > 1$, the aggregate transformation curve for the division of labor which is H_1 and H_2 in Figure 1b can be drawn following the same procedure in drawing C_1 and C_2. The aggregate transformation curve for the division of labor is higher than that for autarky for $a > 1$. This implies the equivalence between economies of division of labor and economies of specialization.

The analysis above implies that economies of division of labor may exist in the absence of exogenous comparative advantage. At point S in Figure 1b, person 1 specializes producing x and person 2 specializes producing y. Person 1's labor productivity of x is L^{a-1} and person 2's is zero. Person 2's labor productivity of y is L^{a-1} and person 1's is zero. Comparative advantages, which are also absolute advantages here, emerge between ex ante identical individuals. The emergence of such comparative advantages depends upon people's choice of pattern of economic organization. If all individuals choose autarky and spend the same time for an activity, there is no difference in productivity. Differences exist between ex ante identical individuals only if people choose different levels of specialization in producing a good. Hence, we call such differences in productivity that depends on individuals' decisions on level of specialization *endogenous comparative advantages*. In contrast, the differences in productivity that generate exogenous comparative advantages are independent of people's decision of organizational pattern. Essentially, the concept of endogenous comparative advantage relates to Smith's emphasis on productivity implications of the division of labor, and differs from Ricardo's concept of exogenous comparative advantage.

Our concept of endogenous comparative advantage differs from Grossman and Helpman's (1989) concept of acquired comparative advantage because our concept is based on the concept of economies of specialization and their concept is based on economies of scale. However, our concept of exogenous comparative advantage is equivalent to their concept of natural comparative advantage.[6]

---

[6] In addition, our concepts of economies of division of labor and specialization can be used to clarify some confusion generated by probably misleading concept of economies of scope. On the one hand, a person's economies of specialization in producing a good are inversely related to economies of his scope of activities. On the other, a firm's operation scope and its members' levels of specialization can increase at the same time if all individuals' levels of specialization, the number of different specialists, and the number of different specialties within the firm increase simultaneously. The second example seemingly indicates a positive correlation between economies of specialization and economies of scope. The two examples which contradict with each other indicate that the recent research on economies of scope has not addressed the subtle distinction between economies of specialization and diseconomies of scope. If the term "economies of scope" is replaced by the terms economies of specialization and economies of division of labor, then the contradiction between the above two examples can be avoided. Since specialization and diversity of professional activities are two sides of the division of labor, simultaneous increases in levels of specialization of all individuals and in the number of different professional jobs within a firm can be seen as an increase in the level of division of labor within the firm. Hence, if a higher productivity of a firm is generated by a higher level of division of labor which is associated with higher levels of specialization of all members (a narrow scope of each individual's activities) and a greater variety of professional jobs within the firm (a broader scope of the firm's

Suppose that $a > 1$; then there is a tradeoff between economies of specialization and transaction costs. This tradeoff is based on two critical assumptions: (i) a framework of consumer-producer and (ii) preferences for diverse consumption.

Suppose that the quantities of the two goods purchased are x^d and y^d respectively and that the fraction $1 - k$ of the quantities purchased disappears in transit because of transaction costs. Then a person receives kx^d or ky^d when he buys x^d or y^d. Here, it is assumed $k \in [0,1]$. The transaction cost coefficient $1 - k$ represents transportation costs and other costs necessary for executing a transaction. Such costs depend on transaction technology, institutional arrangements, and urbanization.

In this paper we assume that preferences are identical for all consumer-producers and are represented by the utility function

$$u_i = (x_i + kx_i^d)(y_i + ky_i^d),\qquad(3)$$

where x_i and y_i are self-provided amounts of the two goods respectively, kx_i^d and ky_i^d are the amounts of the two goods, respectively, received by person i from purchases. $x_i + kx_i^d$ and $y_i + ky_i^d$ are amounts of the two goods, respectively, consumed by person i. We define a preference for diverse consumption as one that can be represented by a quasi-concave utility function. (3) is a specific Cobb-Douglas utility function for which the two goods are necessities. Later we will specify a CES utility function to represent a preference for diverse consumption in which goods are not necessities individually. We need explicit specification of utility functions because corner solutions make the model intractable in the absence of explicit specification of functional forms. We shall discuss the difficulty arising from corner solutions in the next section.

3. Equilibrium and Its Comparative Statics

This section characterizes the equilibrium and its comparative statics for the economy described in the previous section. Each individual makes a decision about which goods to produce and on his demand for and supply of any traded good. A given pattern of production and trade activities for

---

activities), then it can be said that there exist economies of division of labor as defined in the paper.

any individual is defined as a *configuration*. There are $2^6 = 64$ combinations of zero and nonzero values of x, x^s, x^d, y, y^s, y^d and therefore 64 possible configurations. Lemma 1 establishes that an optimal configuration for any individual must be a corner solution with the properties that the individual sells at most one good and does not buy and self-provide the same good. The combination of configurations of the M individuals in the economy is defined as a *market structure*, or simply a structure. A feasible market structure consists of a set of choices of configurations by individuals such that for any traded good, demand for the good is matched by supply of the good. For each structure there exists a corner equilibrium which is defined as a set of relative prices and relative numbers of individuals choosing different configurations such that (i) for any traded good market supply equals market demand (i.e., market clearing); and (ii) each individual maximizes utility for the given prices and for a given structure. With the assumption of free entry, (ii) implies that the utility of all individuals is equalized in any corner equilibrium. As proven in Yang (1988, 1990), the general equilibrium is the corner equilibrium that generates the highest per capita real income, and other corner equilibria cannot be general equilibria since some individuals have an incentive to deviate from those corner equilibria.

In Yang (1990) it is proven that an optimal configuration for any individual is such that

Lemma 1:   An individual sells at most one good and does not simultaneously buy and self-provide or simultaneously buy and sell the same good if $a > 1$.

Without loss of generality, in this section we assume that $L = 1$ which implies $L_{ji} = l_{ji}$. For notational simplicity, we omit subscript i when no confusion is caused. Lemma 1, together with the budget constraint and positive utility constraint, rules out 60 corner solutions and the interior solution from the list of candidates for the optimum decision, We can thus focus our attention on the three configurations.

Taking into account Lemma 1, there are three configurations. This section solves for the corner solutions for the three configurations.

(1) Configuration autarky. Denoting autarky by A, configuration A is the profile of zero and nonzero variables given by $x^s = y^s = x^d = y^d = 0$ and $x, y, l_x, l_y > 0$. A person choosing configuration A self-provides all goods he needs.

(2) Denoting a configuration in which an individual sells good x and buys good y by $(x \, / \, y)$, this configuration is a profile of zero and nonzero variables given by $x, x^s, y^d > 0, l_x = 1, x^d = y = y^s = l_y = 0$.

(3) Denoting a configuration in which an individual sells good y and buys good x by $(y \, / \, x)$, this configuration is a profile of zero and nonzero variables given by $y, y^s, x^d > 0, l_y = 1, y^d = x = x^s = l_x = 0$.

A corner solution can be solved for each configuration. For autarky, the corner solution is a corner equilibrium. A combination of configurations (x/y) and (y/x) constitutes another market structure. We call this structure D (division of labor).

Applying the two-step approach to solving equilibrium model based on corner solutions, developed in Yang (1990), the equilibrium can be solved and summarized as in the following proposition.

Proposition 1:   The equilibrium is the division of labor where $x^s = 1/2$ and $y^d = 1/(2p)$ for configuration (x/y) and $y^s = 1/2$ and $x^d = p/2$ for configuration (y/x), $u = k/4$, and $M_x/M_y = p = 1$ if $k > k_0 \equiv 2^{2-2a}$. The equilibrium is autarky where $x = y = 0.5^a$ and $u = 0.5^{2a}$ for all individuals if $k < k_0$.

In this Proposition, M_x is the number of individuals choosing configuration (x/y), M_y is the number of individuals choosing configuration (y/x), and p is the price of good y in terms of good x. The algebra for establishing Proposition 1 is provided in Appendix A.

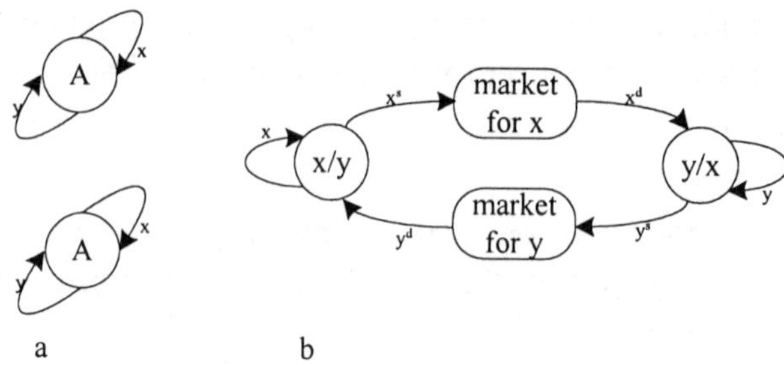

Figure 2: Autarky and division of labor. a, Autarky. b, The division of labor

Figure 2 illustrates this proposition. Two individuals in Figure 2a are used to illustrate autarky. In fact there are more individuals than shown in Figure 2. Circles represent configurations. The lines represent flows of goods self-provided. In autarky there is no market demand and supply. Productivity is low because of a low level of specialization. However, transaction costs do not exist because people do not do business with each other. Figure 2b represents the division of labor (structure *D)*. The lines represent the flows of goods. For structure *D,* there is a local business community comprised of two persons. There are two markets, one for *x* and the other for *y*. There are two distinctive professional sectors. The per capita output of each good is higher than in autarky because of a higher level of specialization for each person. But transaction costs are higher than in autarky because each person has to undertake two transactions to obtain the necessary consumption.

Proposition 1 states that the general equilibrium is the division of labor if transaction efficiency and the degree of economies of specialization are sufficiently great and is autarky if transaction efficiency and/or the degree of economies of specialization are sufficiently low. Suppose $a = 1$ (that is, constant returns to specialization and $k_o \equiv 2^{2-2a} = 1$) and $k < 1$ (that is, $1 - k > 0$ or transaction cost is nonzero), then $k < k_0 = 1$, so that the equilibrium is autarky. If $a > 1$ (that is, economies of specialization exist and $k_o < 1$) and $k = 1$ (that is, $1 - k = 0$ or transaction cost is zero), then $k > k_0$, so that the equilibrium is always the division of labor. If $a > 1$ that is, economies of division of labor exist and if $k_o \in (0, 1)$, and $k = 0$ (that is, all traded goods disappear on the way from a seller to a buyer due to a large transaction cost), then $k < k_0$, so that the equilibrium is autarky. If $a > 1$, which means $k_0 \in (0, 1)$, and $k \in (0, 1)$, then which structure is the equilibrium depends on whether economies of specialization outweigh transaction costs, that is whether $k > k_0$.

Suppose we start with an extremely small $k < k_0$, then the equilibrium is autarky. As transaction efficiency is sufficiently improved, the equilibrium shifts from autarky to the division of labor. For the division of labor, a specialist's labor productivity of each good is one and per capita output of each good is 0.5. In autarky, labor productivity of each good is $0.5^{a-1} < 1$ and the per capita output of each good is $0.5^a < 0.5$ for $a > 1$. As the number of traded goods increases, the number of producers of each good decreases. The number of producers of each good equals the population size in autarky. As transaction efficiency is sufficiently improved, the equilibrium shifts from autarky to the division of labor and the number of producers for each good turns to be half of the population size. That is, the degree of production concentration increases with transaction efficiency. Also, the level of specialization for each individual and the number of distinctive professional sectors increases as the level of division of labor is increased. It is straightforward that the extent of the market, defined by aggregate market demand, the degree of integration of the economy, defined by the number of trade partners of each person, and the degree of commercialization, defined by per capita commercialized income divided by his total income increase, and the degree of self-sufficiency decreases as the division of labor evolves. This analysis leads us to

Proposition 2: A sufficient improvement in transaction efficiency generates the following concurrent phenomena: progress in labor productivity, the increases in the level of specialization, in the level of division of labor, in the number of professional sectors, in the degrees of production concentration and integration of the economy, in the extent of the market, and in the degree of commercialization, and the decrease in self-sufficiency of each person.

If the utility function takes a general Cobb–Douglas form, $u = (x + kx^d)^\alpha (y + ky^d)^{1-\alpha}$, where $\alpha \in (0, 1)$, and the respective elasticity parameters for the production functions of goods x and y are a and b, then Proposition 1 becomes: The equilibrium is the division of labor if

$$k > k_1 \equiv \left(\frac{(a\alpha)^{a\alpha} \left[b(1-\alpha)\right]^{b(1-\alpha)}}{\left[a\alpha + b(1-\alpha)\right]^{a\alpha + b(1-\alpha)} \alpha^\alpha (1-\alpha)^{1-\alpha}} \right)^{1/[2\alpha(1-\alpha)]}$$

and is autarky if $k < k_1$. The corner equilibrium for the division of labor is $p = k^{1-2\alpha}$ and $M_x/M_y = \alpha k^{1-2\alpha}/(1-\alpha)$. Hence, the essence of Propositions 1 and 2 will not be changed if we specify more general forms of utility and production functions. This extended version of our model can be used to show that the existence of economies of division of labor may be compatible with the existence of diseconomies of specialization in a sector provided economies of specialization which exist in the other sector dominate the diseconomies. The above proposition implies that the equilibrium will be the division of labor if b is close to and smaller than one (that is, there exist diseconomies of specialization in producing good y), a is sufficiently large, and k is close to one.

A specialist's supply function is still a constant for the more general model because the elasticity of substitution between consumer goods for the Cobb–Douglas utility function is unitary. It can be shown that a specialist's supply function is not independent of price if the elasticity of substitution is not unitary. Suppose the utility function is of the CES (constant elasticity of substitution) type, given by $u = [(x + kx^d)^\rho + (y + ky^d)^\rho]^{1/\rho}$, where $\rho \in (0, 1)$, and the system of production is the same as in (1). Then supply and demand functions for the two configurations and the per capita real income for autarky and the division of labor are

$$x^s = \frac{1}{1 + (k/p)^{\rho/(\rho-1)}}, y^d = \frac{x^s}{p}, u_A = 2^{(1-a\rho)/\rho};$$

$$y^s = \frac{1}{1 + (kp)^{\rho/(\rho-1)}}, x^d = py^s, u_D = k[1 + k^{\rho/(\rho-1)}]^{(1-\rho)/\rho}.$$

The supply and demand functions are consistent with the neoclassical demand law for a normal good and with the neoclassical supply law based on the tradeoff between leisure and consumption or based on decreasing returns to scale despite economies of specialization in our framework. It can be shown that the equilibrium is the division of labor for the model with the CES utility function iff

$$k > k_3 \equiv (2^{(1-a\rho)/(1-\rho)} - 1)^{(1-\rho)/\rho},$$

where $k_3 \in (0,1)$ if $a > 1$ and $\rho \in (0, 1)$.[7]

4. A Comparison Between Our Model and a Neoclassical Trade Model

In order to identify the distinction between our model with endogenous comparative advantage and a neoclassical trade model with exogenous comparative advantage, and the different implications generated by the two types of models, we specify a neoclassical trade model with two goods, two countries, and transaction costs. There is a representative pure consumer in each country. Each consumer has the same utility function specified in (4) and is endowed with one unit of labor. The transaction efficiency coefficient is k. Because of the dichotomy between pure consumers and pure producers, (domestic or international) trade is necessary for the pure consumers to receive positive utility, so that autarky in the sense of each individual's self-sufficiency is infeasible. This, together with constant returns to scale technology, implies that no tradeoff exists between increasing returns and transaction costs. Each pure consumer's decision problem and its solutions are

$$\max \ u = (kx)^\alpha (ky)^{1-\alpha}, \ \text{s.t.} \ p_x x + p_y y = 1,$$

$$x^* = \frac{\alpha}{p_x}, \quad y^* = \frac{1-\alpha}{p_y}, \tag{4}$$

---

[7] Yang and Ng (1994) have shown that within the framework of consumer-producers and economies of specialization, the firm is not needed in the absence of producer goods. Hence, firms will not emerge from our model without producer goods here. Also, it is shown that the institution of the firm will emerge from the division of labor between production of final goods and production of intermediate goods if transaction efficiency of an intermediate good is lower than transaction efficiency for labor hired to produce the intermediate good.

where the quantities x and y of the two goods consumed are decision variables and $k \in (0, 1)$ is the transaction efficiency coefficient. The price of good i in terms of labor p_i is a given parameter. Labor is the numeraire. Let subscript $j = 1, 2$ represent country j. The production functions of the two goods and the endowment constraints for the two countries are

$$x_1 = aL_{1x}, y_1 = L_{1y}, L_{1x} + L_{1y} = 1, a > 1,$$
$$x_2 = L_{2x}, y_2 = L_{2y}, L_{2x} + L_{2y} = 1, \tag{5}$$

where i_j is the quantity of good $i(=x,y)$ produced by a representative firm in country $j(=1,2)$ and L_{ji} is the quantity of labor of country $j(=1,2)$ employed to produce good $i(=x,y)$. (5) implies that country 2 has no absolute advantage in producing any good but has a comparative advantage in producing good y. The separate equilibria for the two countries in the absence of international trade are

$$p_{1x} = 1/a, p_{1y} = 1, \; x_1 = \alpha a, \; y_1 = 1 - \alpha, \; u_1 = (\alpha a)^\alpha (1-\alpha)^{1-\alpha} k,$$
$$p_{2x} = 1, \quad p_{2y} = 1, \; x_2 = \alpha, \; y_2 = 1 - \alpha, \; u_2 = (\alpha)^\alpha (1-\alpha)^{1-\alpha} k, \tag{6}$$

where p_{ji} is the price of good i in terms of labor in country j. The pooling equilibrium in the integrated world market is

$$p_x = 1/a, \; p_y = 1, \; x_1 = x_2 = \alpha a,$$
$$y_1 = y_2 = 1 - \alpha, u_1 = u_2 = (\alpha a)^\alpha (1-\alpha)^{1-\alpha} k. \tag{7}$$

Gains to trade exist because u_2 is larger and u_1 is not smaller in the pooling equilibrium than in the separate equilibria. It is interesting to see that the equilibrium always involves international trade regardless of what is the transaction efficiency coefficient k as long as $k \in (0, 1)$. This is because there is no tradeoff between increasing returns and transaction costs. This is in turn based on the dichotomy between pure consumers and pure producers and constant returns technology. Therefore, the number of transactions cannot be endogenized. Compared to our model, the neoclassical trade model cannot explore the productivity implications of transaction efficiency and cannot explain simultaneous increases in productivity, in each individual's level of specialization, and in trade dependence. For the neoclassical model, each firm is completely specialized in an activity and each consumer is completely "specialized" in consumption. Autarky in the sense of each person's self-sufficiency is infeasible. In other words, trade dependence, level of specialization, productivity are not endogenized in the neoclassical trade model.

If we assume that $a = 1$ and introduce parameters representing exogenous comparative advantages into the production functions in (2), then the Walrasian equilibrium for the division of labor in a model with consumer-producers does not exist despite the existence of exogenous comparative advantages and a large transaction efficiency coefficient. A Nash bargaining equilibrium for the division of labor may exist, but the algebra is too complicated to manage. In other words, a model with exogenous comparative advantage but with neither endogenous comparative advantage nor the dichotomy between pure consumers and pure producers is extremely difficult to handle. This might be the reason why neoclassical trade theory needs the dichotomy between pure consumers and pure producers to secure tractability of the models.

5. A Comparison Between Our Model and an Extended Dixit-Stiglitz Model

The Dixit-Stiglitz (D-S) model (1977) formalizes a tradeoff between economies of scale and consumption diversity. Since an increase in the size of an economy in their model enlarges agents' scope for trading off economies of scale against consumption diversity, per capita real income, the number of goods, and productivity increase with the size of the economy. This implies that international trade will increase per capita real income and productivity because the size of the pooling economy in the integrated world market is larger than that of any individual country. Many works use this basic idea to explore the implications of the tradeoff for growth theory (see, for instance, Romer, 1986; Grossman and Helpman, 1989), for trade theory (see, for instance, Ethier, 1979; Krugman, 1979), and for macroeconomics (see, for instance, Blanchard and Kiyotaki, 1987; Rotemberg, 1987). Since transaction costs are not specified in the D-S model and in its variants, the productivity implications of transaction efficiency cannot be explored by the models. However, if we introduce transaction costs into the D-S model, a tradeoff between economies of scale and transaction costs may be used to explore the productivity implications of transaction efficiency. There are many ways to specify transaction costs in the D-S model. According to our experience, many of the specifications render intractable the comparative statics that may generate the productivity implications of transaction efficiency. In this section, we first present a version of the D-S model with transaction costs and show how it generates the productivity implications of transaction efficiency. Then we will examine the differences between the new version of the D-S model and our model.

A representative consumer's decision problem is

$$\max u = \left(\sum_{i\in I} x_i^\rho\right)^{1/\rho}, \quad \text{s.t.} \quad \sum_{i\in I}(1+t)\,p_i x_i = 1, \tag{8}$$

where u is a consumer's utility level, x_i is his quantity of good i consumed, I is the set of n goods, and t is a coefficient of transaction costs that is incurred to a consumer, which can be interpreted as an ad valorem tax. Each pure consumer is endowed with one unit of labor which is the numeraire. The size of labor force (which is the population size as well) is L and the price of good i in terms of labor is p_i. The elasticity of substitution $1/(1-\rho)$ is assumed to be larger than one, that is $\rho \in (0, 1)$. All production sectors have the same homogeneous production function

$$X_i = L_{ix}^a, \quad a > 1, \tag{9}$$

where X_i is the quantity of good i supplied by a monopolist and $X_i = Lx_i$, where x_i is each consumer's quantity of consumption good i. L_{ix} is the amount of labor hired by the firm producing good i. Due to the complete symmetry of the model, we will skip subscript i when no confusion is caused. This production function displays global economies of scale.

Since Dixit–Stiglitz's approach to solving this model generates the incorrect result that implies nonexistence of equilibrium, we will apply the Yang–Heijdra approach (1993) to solve this model. The solution of general equilibrium is summarized as follows.

$$n^* = \frac{(a-1)\rho}{a\rho-1}, \quad p^* = \left[\frac{(1+t)(a-1)\rho}{(a\rho-1)L}\right]^{a-1}$$

$$x^* = \left[\frac{a\rho-1}{(1+t)(a-1)\rho}\right]^{a} L^{a-1}, \quad X^* = Lx^*, \tag{10}$$

$$u^* = \left[\frac{(a-1)\rho}{a\rho-1}\right]^{(1/\rho)-a} \frac{L^{a-1}}{(1+t)^{a-1}}, \quad LP^* = \frac{1}{p^*},$$

where LP^* is the equilibrium labor productivity of a good. The equilibrium exists if $a\rho > 1$ and it does not exist for $a\rho \leq 1$. It is straight-forward that the labor prices of all goods decrease with the size of the economy, L, (or with the opening up of international trade) and increase with the transaction cost coefficient, t, while the labor productivity, per capita consumption, total output level of each good, and per capita real income (utility) increase with the size of the economy and decrease with the transaction cost coefficient.

Nevertheless, the equilibrium number of goods, n^*, is independent of the size of the economy and the transaction cost coefficient in the model with homogeneous production functions. If we specify production functions as linear functions with a fixed cost, then Appendix B shows that the number of goods and per capita real income increase as the transaction cost coefficient decreases and/or as the size of the economy increases.

The extended version of the D–S model is featured with both trade-off between economies of scale and diverse consumption and tradeoff between economies of scale and transaction costs, so that it can generate a richer story than the one generated by D–S's original model and its variants. It explains prices and quantities of goods, productivity, and per capita real income not only by the size of an economy (due to the first tradeoff), but also by the transaction cost coefficient (due to the second tradeoff). For instance, if a country, such as China prior to the economic reform, has a very large size of its economy, but the transaction cost coefficient is very large due to a deficient legal system, then D–S's original model unrealistically predicts a very high productivity and per capita real income, while the extended D–S model predicts a very low productivity and per capita real income. The extended D–S model predicts high productivity, per capita real income, and trade dependence when the size of an economy is large (or many local economies merge into the integrated world market) *and* the transaction cost coefficient is sufficiently small (or transaction efficiency is sufficiently high). If the tradeoff between economies of scale and transaction costs is introduced into Grossman–Helpman's dynamic model (1989), an even more interesting story may be generated.

An extended version of our model in this paper with many goods and CES utility function (see Yang and Shi, 1992) can generate a richer story than the one generated by the extended version of the D–S model. It endogenizes the number of all goods, productivity, the degree of market integration, the number and size of separate local markets, and trade dependence which are endogenized by the extended D–S model, plus the level of specialization of each individual which is not endogenized by the extended D–S model. The method of explaining productivity and trade dependence by transaction efficiency in the Yang–Shi model differs from that in the extended D–S model. According to the Yang–Shi model, a large size economy such as the Indian economy will be divided into many separate local business communities and has a low productivity and trade dependence, if the transaction cost coefficient is extremely large (or transaction efficiency is low). It will be integrated into a unifying market such that productivity and the degree of commercialization are very high if the transaction cost coefficient is sufficiently small. This is because the Yang-Shi model endogenizes the level of specialization and the number of each person's traded goods which may be different from his number of all consumption goods, so that the size of separate local markets can be endogenized. If transaction efficiency is low and individuals trade first with those closest, then the number of each person's traded goods is smaller than his number of all consumption goods and therefore his number of trade partners is smaller than the population size. Thus, an economy will be divided into several separate local markets. As transaction efficiency is improved, the local markets will merge into an integrated market. In contrast, for the extended D–S model, each consumer's number of traded goods equals his number of consumption goods, so that the economy is always an integrated market. In other words, the degree of market integration, the size and number of local markets, and the level of self-sufficiency are not endogenized in the extended D–S model. However, because of the similar assumption of increasing returns, both the extended D–S model and the model in Sect. 2 can explain the Linder-type trading pattern (trade is concentrated among the similar industrialized countries).

There are two methods of endogenizing trade dependence and aggregate demand. One is to endogenize the number of goods using the CES function as in Krugman's and Grossman and Helpman's new trade, models and the other is to endogenize the level of specialization of consumer-producers as in the model in Sect. 2. The Yang–Shi model (1992) is a blend of the two methods, which introduces the CES function into Yang's framework with consumer-producers, economies of specialization, and transaction costs. Their model is featured with both tradeoff between economies of specialization and consumption variety and tradeoff between economies of specialization and transaction costs. If their model is extended to include producer goods and the time dimension, much higher explaining power can be achieved.

As in a neoclassical trade model, the driving force of domestic trade is the dichotomy between pure consumers and pure producers in the D–S model, but the driving force of international trade is exogenous comparative advantage in a neoclassical trade model and is economies of scale in the new trade models. In the new trade models, the dichotomy between pure consumers and pure producers is equivalent to absolute advantages between the two types of agents. Pure consumers' absolute advantage is to consume and they cannot produce and pure producers absolute advantage is to produce and they cannot consume. The exogenous absolute advantages generate domestic trade because autarky in the sense of each person's self-sufficiency is infeasible. But in our model, no such exogenous advantages exist, the driving force of domestic and international trade is the same: endogenous (or ex post) comparative advantages between ex ante identical consumer-producers.

We speculate that there are many possible applications of the extended D–S model and the Yang–Shi model in the theories of international trade, economic growth, and micro- and macroeconomics.

6. Concluding Remarks

There are several features of equilibrium that distinguish our framework from the neoclassical framework. The first is that aggregate demand and supply can be endogenized in this framework even though Say's law holds. Say's law holds in our model. That is, demand is the reciprocal of supply, and demand always equals supply. For the division of labor, demand equals supply in. the market place. From Proposition 1, we see that demand is the reciprocal of supply. In autarky, self-demand always equals self-supply because they are the two sides of self-provided quantity of goods. However, there is no market demand and supply in autarky and such demand and supply exist only if the division of labor emerges. In Young's words (1928), demand and supply are the two sides of the division of labor and the level of division of labor and the extent of the market are two sides of the same coin. For our framework, the economic story consists of two parts. One is the problem of resource allocation for a given pattern of economic organization which is solved by a corner equilibrium. The other is the problem of economic organization which is solved by the general equilibrium. The general equilibrium endogenizes aggregate demand and aggregate supply when it endogenizes the level of division of labor.

The second feature of our framework is a possible disparity between the production possibility frontier (PPF) and the Pareto optimum. The PPF in our model is associated with the complete division of labor because of economies of specialization. However, the Pareto optimum or the utility frontier may be associated with autarky if transaction costs outweigh economies of division of labor. As transaction efficiency is improved, equilibrium as well as the Pareto optimum will become closer to the PPF due to the tradeoff between economies of division of labor and transaction costs. In contrast, the Pareto optimum always coincides with the PPF in neoclassical microeconomics. This feature generates productivity implications of transaction efficiency. Such implications become extremely important in the view of the effects of institutional arrangements, urbanization, and policies on transaction efficiency.

Related to the second feature, our model formalizes the concept of endogenous comparative advantages. If transaction efficiency is extremely low, autarky is equilibrium. Labor productivity for two goods is the same for all individuals. No comparative advantages exist. If transaction efficiency is sufficiently large, then division of labor is the equilibrium where the labor productivity of the seller of a good is higher than that of the buyer of the good because the level of specialization of the former in producing the good is higher than that of the latter. That is, ex post comparative advantages between ex ante identical individuals endogenously emerge from the division of labor and specialization.

Finally, our model can be used to explore the equilibrium implications of the distinctions between the concept of economies of specialization and the concept of economies of scale and between the concepts of endogenous and exogenous comparative advantages. Compared to a neoclassical trade model which is based on the concept of exogenous comparative advantage, our model can explain simultaneous increases in productivity and trade dependence which cannot be explained by a neoclassical trade model. Compared to the new trade models which are based on the concept of economies of scale, our model can explain the level of specialization and simultaneous increases in the level of specialization, productivity, trade dependence, and production concentration which cannot be predicted by the new trade models.

Appendix

A) *Proof of Proposition 1*

The appendix provides the algebra for the solution of the equilibrium of the model in Sect. 3. We first solve for three corner solutions, then for two corner equilibria, and finally identify the general equilibrium and its comparative statics.

(1) Configuration autarky. Let $x^s = y^s = x^d = y^d = 0$ in (1) and (3) and insert (1) into (3); the decision problem in configuration A is given by

$$\max_{l_x} u = l_x^a (1 - l_x)^a \,,$$

where we have used (1) and (3) to obtain

$$u = xy = l_x^a l_y^a = l_x^a (1 - l_x)^a \,.$$

The first order condition $du/dl_x = 0$ yields the corner solution for configuration A, given by

$$l_x^* = l_y^* = 0.5, \quad x^* = y^* = 0.5^a, \quad u_A = 0.5^{2a}, \tag{A.1}$$

where u_A is the per capita real income in configuration A.

(2) Configuration (x/y) is given by $x, x^s, y^d > 0$, $l_x = 1$, $x^d = y = y^s = l_y = 0$. The decision problem for this configuration is

$$\max_{x, x^s, y^d} u = xky^d$$

$$\text{s.t.} \ \ x + x^s = l_x^a, l_x = 1 \qquad \text{(system of production)}, \tag{A.2a}$$

$$py^d = x^s \qquad\qquad\qquad \text{(budget constraint)},$$

where p is the price of good y in terms of good x. Replacing x in u with its equivalent in the production function and y^d with its equivalent in the budget constraint yields $u = (1-x^s)kx^s / p$. The first order condition $du/dx^s = 0$ yields the optimum decisions as

$$x^s = 0.5, \quad y^d = \frac{1}{2p}, \quad u_x = \frac{k}{4p}, \tag{A.2b}$$

where $u_x(p)$ is the indirect utility function for configuration (x/y).

(3) Configuration (y/x) is given by $x, y^s, x^d > 0$, $l_y = 1$, $y^d = x = x^s = l_x = 0$. The optimum decision for this configuration is symmetric to the problem (A.2) given by:

$$y^s = 0.5, \quad x^d = \frac{p}{2}, \quad u_y = \frac{kp}{4}, \tag{A.3}$$

where $u_y(p)$ is the indirect utility function for configuration (y/x).

There are two structures. Autarky itself is a structure. Hence, the corner solution for autarky is a corner equilibrium. A combination of configurations (x/y) and (y/x) constitutes structure D (division of labor).

Let M_x be the number of individuals selling good x and M_y selling good y. Multiplying M_i ($i = x, y$) with individual demand or supply gives market demand or supply. Equalizing market demand to market supply establishes the market clearing conditions. The assumption of free entry together with utility-maximization ensures a utility equalization condition. From the utility equalization condition and market clearing condition, we can solve for the corner equilibrium relative number of individuals choosing the two configurations, $M_{xy} \equiv M_x/M_y$, and relative price p. The values of M_x and M_y are determined by M_{xy} and the population size $M = M_x + M_y$.

The utility equalization condition for this structure is

$$u_x(p) \equiv \frac{k}{4p} = \frac{kp}{4} \equiv u_y(p). \qquad (A.4a)$$

Equation (A.4a) gives the corner equilibrium relative price p and the per capita real income in structure D:

$$p = 1, \quad u_{\mathrm{D}} = \frac{k}{4}, \qquad (A.4b)$$

where u_{D} is the per capita real income in structure D. The market clearing condition for x gives the equilibrium relative number of individuals choosing the two configurations:

$$M_x x^s = M_y x^d, \quad \text{or} \quad M_{xy} = 1, \qquad (A.4c)$$

where $x^s = 0.5$ and $x^d = 0.5/p$ are given in (A.2b) and (A.3) and $p = 1$ is given in (A.4b). The market clearing condition for good y is not independent of (A.4c) due to Walras' law.

A comparison between u_{D}, given in (A.4b), and u_{A}, given in (A.1), together with (A.2)–(A.4), yields Proposition 1.

B) An extended D–S model with a linear production function

A linear production function, $L_x = \alpha X + a$, is introduced into the extended D-S model developed in the paper. Following the Yang–Heijdra approach to solving the D-S model, the equilibrium is

 X. Yang

$$n^* = \frac{(1-\rho)L}{a(1+t)} + \rho, \qquad p^* = \frac{\alpha L}{\rho[L - a(1+t)]},$$

$$x^* = \frac{a\rho[L - a(1+t)]}{\alpha L[(1-\rho)L + \rho a(1+t)]}, \qquad X^* = Lx^*,$$

$$LP^* = \frac{\rho[L - a(1+t)]}{\alpha L}, \qquad u^* = \frac{(n^*)^{(1-\rho)/\rho}}{p^*}. \qquad \text{(B.1)}$$

where LP^* is equilibrium labor productivity of a good. It is straight-forward that

$$\frac{dn^*}{dt} < 0, \ \frac{dn^*}{dL} > 0, \ \frac{dp^*}{dt} > 0, \frac{dp^*}{dL} < 0,$$

$$\frac{dx^*}{dt} < 0, \frac{dX^*}{dL} > 0, \frac{dLP^*}{dt} < 0, \frac{dLP^*}{dL} > 0, \qquad \text{(B.2)}$$

$$\frac{du^*}{dt} < 0, \frac{du^*}{dL} > 0.$$

Acknowledgements

The author is grateful to Jeff Borland, Gene Grossman, John Freebairn, Yew–Kwang Ng, Sherwin Rosen, and two referees for comments and criticism on an early version of this paper. I am responsible for any remaining errors.

References

Blanchard, O., and Kiyotaki, N. (1987): "Monopolistic Competition and the Effects of Aggregate Demand." *American Economic Review* 77: 647–666.

Durkheim, E. (1964): *The Division of Labor in Society,* transl. with an introduction by *G.* Simpson. New York: Free Press.

Ethier, W. (1979): "Internationally Decreasing Costs and World Trade." *Journal of International Economics* 9: 1–24.

Grossman, *G.,* and Helpman, E. (1989): "Product Development and International Trade." *Journal of Political Economy* 97: 1261–1283.

Houthakker, M. (1956): "Economics and Biology: Specialization and Speciation." *Kyklos* 9 (2): 181–189.

Krugman, P. (1979): "Increasing Returns, Monopolistic Competition, and International Trade." *Journal of International Economics* 9: 469–479.

Marshall, A. (1920): *Principles of Economics.* London: Macmillan.

Ricardo, D. (1973): *The Principle of Political Economy and Taxation.* London: Gaernsey Press.

Romer, P. (1986): "Increasing Returns, Specialization, and External Economies: Growth as Described by Allyn Young." Working Paper No. 64, Center for Economic Research, University of Rochester.

Rotemberg, J. (1987): "The New Keynesian Microfoundations." In *NBER Macroeconomics Annual* 1987, edited by S. Fischer. Cambridge, MA: MIT Press.

Rosen, S. (1978): "Substitution and the Division of Labor." *Economica* 45: 235–250.

— (1983): "Specialization and Human Capital." *Journal of Labor Economics* 1: 43–49.

Smith, A. (1976): *An Inquiry into the Nature and Causes of the Wealth of Nations,* edited by E. Cannan. Chicago: University of Chicago Press.

Stigler, *G.* (1951): "The Division of Labor is Limited by the Extent of the Market." *Journal of Political Economy* 59: 185–193.

Yang, X. (1988): *An Approach to Modeling the Division of Labor Based on Increasing Returns to Specialization.* Ph.D. Dissertation, Department of Economics, Princeton University, Princeton, NJ.

— (1990): "Development, Structural Changes, and Urbanization." *Journal of Development Economics* 34: 199–222.

Yang, X., and Borland, J. (1991): "A Microeconomic Mechanism for Economic Growth." *Journal of Political Economy* 99: 460–482.

Yang, X., and Heijdra, B. (1993): "Monopolistic Competition and Optimum Product Diversity: Comment." *American Economic Review* 83: 295–301.

Yang, X., and Ng, Y. (1994): "Theory of the Firm and Structure of Property Rights." *Journal of Economic Behaviour* and *Organization* (forthcoming).

Yang, X., and Shi, H. (1992): "Specialization and Product Diversity." *American Economic Review* 82: 392–398.

Yang, X., and Wills, I. (1990): "A Model Formalizing the Theory of Property Rights." *Journal of Comparative Economics* 14: 177–198.

Young, A. (1928): "Increasing Returns and Economic Progress." *Economic Journal* 152: 527–542.

CHAPTER 14

A NEW THEORY OF DEMAND AND SUPPLY AND EMERGENCE OF INTERNATIONAL TRADE FROM DOMESTIC TRADE[*]

Xiaokai Yang[*]

Monash and Harvard University

1. Introduction

The purpose of this paper is threefold. First, a new theory of demand and supply is developed on the basis of the endogenization of individuals' levels of specialization. This new theory explains demand and supply as two sides of the division of labor. This inquiry is motivated by economists' curiosity about the intrinsic relationship between productivity progress and the division of labor (Adam Smith, 1776, chs 1-3; Karl Marx, 1867, vol. 1; Amasa Walker, 1874; Alfred Marshall, 1890, chs 8-12; Allyn Young, 1928; and many others).

Not only has economic thinking been stimulated by the intimate relationship between productivity, learning by doing, accumulation of knowledge, and the division of labor; but we are also puzzled why so many things increase concurrently as the division of labor evolves: the

---

[*] Reprinted from *Pacific Economic Review*, 1 (3), Xiaokai Yang, "A New Theory of Demand and Supply and Emergence of International Trade from Domestic Trade," 215-37, 1996, with permission from Blackwell.

[*] The author is grateful for comments of the participants of seminars at Harvard University , University of Pennsylvania, the World Bank, Michigan State University, University of Minnesota, and the National Bureau of Economic Research. Special thanks are due to Bill Ethier, Jeff Sachs, T. N. Srinivasan, Fisher Black, Lok Sang Ho, and two anonymous referees for helpful discussions and comments. I am responsible for any remaining errors.

291

extent of the market, aggregate demand, productivity, trade dependence, the degree of market integration, the degree of production concentration, diversity of economic structure, variety of different professions, each person's level of specialization, and the extent of endogenous comparative advantage (the difference in productivity of a good between its sellers and buyers). Why does the evolution of the division of labor increase the learning ability of society as a whole while decreasing a single individual's ability to survive independently of society? An extremely exciting story must be behind the concurrence of so many interesting phenomena, some of them seemingly contradictory. Deciphering the exciting story should be the focus of economists' curiosity.

One of the questions above distinguishes between the learning and knowledge accumulation that are associated with the division of labor and learning by doing which does not depend on the division of labor. The first category of learning is associated with increases in the degree of organization and in the degree of interdependence between individuals, while the second category of learning is independent of organization. Learning by doing without the division of labor has been studied by Arrow (1962), Alwyn Young (1991), and others. Learning by doing based on the division of labor has been studied by Yang and Borland (1991). The current paper takes an approach to specifying learning through the division of labor that is different from the one in Yang and Borland. The latter incorporated Arrow's specification of learning by doing into a dynamic equilibrium model based on comer solutions to endogenize the evolution of division of labor. That specification of learning by doing implies that productivity is an increasing function of accumulated quantities of inputs or outputs. In the current paper I follow Rosen (1983) and Barzel and Yu (1984) to specify a fixed-cost component of investment in learning or training which yields a rate of return on the investment which is increasing in its rate of utilization. This characteristic of learning generates gains arising from specialized learning and from social learning through the division of labor. However, the fixed learning cost is individual-specific and activity-specific. As Rosen (1978) conjectures, these types of economy of specialization are compatible with perfect competition and with the efficiency of the invisible hand.

I adopt an analytical framework, developed in Yang and Borland (1991) and Yang and Ng (1993), with consumer-producers, economies of specialization, and transaction costs. In the framework, the extent of the market is an aspect of the division of labor. As Allyn Young (1928, p. 539) indicated, not only does the division of labor depend on the extent of the market, "but the extent of the market also depends on the division of labor". According to him, demand and supply are two sides of the division of labor. This view of demand and supply differs substantially from Marshall's analysis of demand and supply which is separated from the endogenization of individuals' levels of specialization. In a Marshallian framework with dichotomy between pure consumers and pure producers, demand for goods is determined by consumers' tastes and endowment while supply is determined by pure producers' production functions. The equilibrium level of total demand or supply is determined by tastes, technology, endowment, and market structure. The essence of the story of demand and supply is the tradeoff between quantities of different consumer goods in raising utility level and quantities of different factors in raising output.

In the current paper, I shall tell a different story of demand and supply. In the story, all individuals are consumer-producers with preference for diverse consumption and equipped with production functions that involve a fixed learning cost in each production activity. The division of labor and specialization can save on the learning cost by avoiding duplicated learning and thereby generate economies of specialization. [1] Each consumer-producer can choose his level of specialization in production. He can either self-provide all goods he needs, or sell one good and buy all of other goods, or choose any level of specialization in between the two polar extremes. A tension between diverse consumption and specialized production for consumer-producers generates the tradeoff between economies of specialization and transaction costs. If a transaction cost coefficient for trading a unit of goods is large, then economies of specialization generated by a high level

---

[1] Charles Babbage (1835, pp. 170-4) was the first author to propose this.

of division of labor are outweighed by transaction costs. Hence, each individual will choose autarky (self-sufficiency) where there is no demand and supply in the market place and the extent of the market is zero. If the transaction cost coefficient is very small, economies of specialization generated by a high level of division of labor outweigh related transaction costs, so that individuals will choose the extreme specialization and division of labor where each individual produces only one good and sells the good in exchange for all other goods that he does not produce. Hence, the extremely high level of division of labor generates enormous demand and supply in the marketplace and a great extent of the market. As the transaction cost coefficient falls from a high to a low level as a result of a better transaction technology, urbanization, or government liberalization policy, the level of division of labor and extent of the market (aggregate demand and supply) increase simultaneously. Also, as the division of labor develops, many other things develop: productivity, trade dependence, the degree of market integration, the degree of production concentration, diversity of economic structure, variety of different professions, each person's level of specialization, and the extent of endogenous comparative advantage.

The new model will show that the demand law may not hold even if all goods are normal because of complicated interdependencies between demand and individuals' levels of specialization and between the level of specialization and relative prices of traded goods.

On the basis of the endogenization of *ex ante* identical individuals' levels of specialization, an endogenous trade theory may be developed. As shown by Wong and Yang (1996), the degree of involvement of countries in international trade cannot be endogenized by neoclassical trade theory based on constant returns to scale or by the new trade theory based on increasing returns to scale (Dixit-Stiglitz, 1977; Krugman, 1979; Grosman and Helpman, 1989) even if a transaction cost coefficient between 0 and 1 is introduced into the models. Autarky never takes place in equilibrium if any of the following elements is there: differences in tastes and endowment, comparative advantages, and economies of scale. Differing degrees of involvement of countries in international trade and the emergence of international trade from domestic trade cannot be explained by the neoclassical and new trade models. This is because the models do not explain international trade by endogenizing individuals' levels of specialization and the rationale for international trade differs from the rationale for domestic trade. The dichotomy between pure consumers and firms is the rationale for domestic trade. This implies that domestic trade must take place in equilibrium even in the absence of differences in tastes and endowments and comparative advantage between individuals and of economies of scale. But international trade cannot take place in the absence of these elements. This dichotomy makes the theories incapable of endogenizing individuals' levels of specialization, although the pattern of specialization between countries is studied. If a general equilibrium model can be developed to endogenize individuals' levels of specialization, then an endogenous trade theory that endogenizes the degree of involvement of countries in international trade and the emergence of international trade from domestic trade can be developed.

A function with constant elasticity of substitution (CES) will be specified to endogenize the number of all goods in addition to the endogenization of individuals' levels of specialization. This is motivated by the need to explain concurrent increases in specialization and consumption variety and the emergence of new goods.

Casual observations indicate that in an autarkic society with much division of labor, the variety of available goods is small, whereas in a developed economy with a high level of division of labor and specialization, the variety of available goods is great. An extended model is motivated to explain the correlation between specialization and variety of available goods.

The paper is organized as follows. The model is specified in section 2, its equilibrium and the comparative statics are solved in section 3. The model is extended in Section 4 to endogenize the level of division of labor and variety of consumption simultaneously. The implications of the results for microeconomics, trade theory and development economics are discussed in Section 5.

2. The Model

Let us consider an economy with M consumer-producers and m consumer goods. The self-provided amount of good i is x_i. The amount sold in the market of good i is x_i^s. The amount purchased in the market of good i is x_i^d. The transaction cost is assumed to be proportional to the quantity purchased, so that the transaction cost coefficient for a unit of goods bought is $1 - k$. Thus, kx_i^d is the amount an individual obtains when he purchases x_i^d.

The amount consumed of good i is $x_i + kx_i^d$. The utility function is identical for all individuals:

$$u = \prod_{i=1}^{m} \left(x_i + kx_i^d \right)^{\alpha} \tag{1}$$

where $\alpha = 1/m$. This Cobb-Douglas utility function represents a preference for diverse consumption. The amount consumed of any good cannot be zero if utility is positive. A tension between diverse consumption and specialized production will generate a tradeoff between economies of specialization and transaction costs.

Each consumer-producer has a system of production functions and endowment constraint of labor, given by

$$x_i + x_i^s = \mathrm{Max}\left\{ \alpha\left(L_i - A \right), 0 \right\}, \qquad i = 1, \ldots, m$$

$$\sum_{i=1}^{m} L_i = 1, \quad L_i \in [0,1] \tag{2}$$

where $x_i + x_i^s$ is the output level of good i and A is a fixed learning or training cost in producing good i.[2] Parameter a is a productivity parameter or $1/a$ is a variable cost coefficient. L_i is the amount of labor allocated to production of good i as well as labor share in producing good i. We define the labor share as a person's *level of specialization* in producing good i. It is easy to see from (2) that labor productivity of

---

[2] Marshall (1890, pp. 250-1) described the nature of the fixed learning cost in acquiring knowledge and skill. The fixed cost is caused by a difficult learning process which needs intensive exertion of the central nerve system in coordinating local nerve centers. As the learning process has reached a threshold level, reflex action becomes routes which do not need much exertion of the central nerve system.

good i, $(x_i + x_i^s)/L_i = a(1 - A/L_i)$, increases with a person's level of specialization in producing good i. A system of production functions and endowment constraint that has this property is said to exhibit *economies of specialization*.

As Rosen (1978, 1983) indicates, the division of labor can avoid duplicated learning cost and yields a rate of return on the investment which is increasing in its rate of utilization. Suppose there are two consumer-producers and $m = 2$. In autarky two persons repeat learning in producing goods 1 and 2, so total learning cost is $4A$. For the division of labor, person 1 spends A for learning about production of good 1 and he does not spend time learning about production of good 2 despite the fact that he can consume good 2 through selling good 1 in exchange for good 2. The story for person 2 is symmetrical: he can save on learning cost in producing good 1 and raise the return rate to his investment in learning about production of good 2 through producing good 2 for two persons rather than for himself only. Hence, total learning cost for the division of labor is $2A$ instead of $4A$.

The system of production functions and endowment constraints (2) is identical for all individuals and the production function is identical for all goods. This means that no difference in the endowment constraint or technology exists between individuals. We define gains to trade that are based on this difference as *exogenous comparative advantage*. Hence, for this system of production functions and endowment constraint, there is no exogenous comparative advantage. Assume that in the model there are two persons, $m = 2$; person 1 specializes in producing good 1, and person 2 specializes in producing good 2. Person 1's labor productivity of good 1 is $a(1 - A)$ and person 2's labor productivity of good 1 is Max $\{ a(1 - (A/L_1)), 0\} = $ Max $\{ -\infty, 0\} = 0$ if $L_1 = 0$ for person 2. Person 2's labor productivity of good 2 is $a(1 - A)$ and person 1's is 0. Comparative advantages, which are also absolute advantages here, emerge between *ex ante* identical individuals. The emergence of such comparative advantages depends upon individuals' choices of pattern of economic organization. If all individuals choose autarky and spend the same time for an activity, there is no difference in productivity. The differences exist between *ex ante* identical individuals only if individuals choose different levels of specialization in producing a good. Hence, we call such differences in productivity that depends on individuals' decisions of the level of specialization *endogenous comparative advantages*.[3] In contrast, the differences in productivity that generate exogenous comparative advantages are independent of individuals' decisions of organizational pattern. Essentially, the notion of endogenous comparative advantage relates to Smith's emphasis on productivity implications of the division of labor, and differs from Ricardo's notion of exogenous comparative advantage.

Equations (1) and (2) specify physical conditions for our model. If population size M is assumed to be very large, a Walrasian regime prevails in this model because economies of specialization are individual-specific and increasing returns are localized. The Walrasian equilibrium and its comparative statics are treated in the next section.

3. The Equilibrium Level of Division of Labor

3.1. An individual's optimal decision of level of specialization

Because of the distinction between quantities self-provided, produced and traded in the model, there are a myriad of corner solutions plus the interior solution that we have to consider in order to solve for individuals' decisions. Yang (1990) has proven the following lemma which can be used to rule out the interior solution and many corner solutions from consideration.

Lemma 1:   A person sells at most one good and does not simultaneously buy and sell or simultaneously buy and self-provide the same good.

This lemma implies that for a person trading n goods, he sells a good, self-provides this good, buys $n - 1$ goods, and self-provides $m - n$ non-traded goods. Here $n \in (1, m)$ is the number of traded goods if $n >$

---

[3] To my knowledge, Houthakker (1956) was the first economist to show with the aid of a graph that Smith's concept of economies of division of labor may be more general than Ricardo's concept of comparative advantage.

1. Autarky is associated with $n = 1$ or $n - 1 = 0$ (the number of goods purchased is zero). Because of symmetry, there is indeterminacy of trade composition. Only the number of traded goods n matters. Without loss of generality, assume that goods 1, 2, ..., i, ..., n are traded by individuals selling good i and goods $n + 1$, $n + 2$, ..., m are not traded ($n \in (1, m)$). Let R be a set of $n - 1$ goods purchased; set R contains all traded goods except good i. Let J be a set of $m - n$ nontraded goods. Then for a person selling good i,

$$x_i > 0, x_i^s > 0, x_i^d = 0, L_i > 0$$
$$x_r = x_r^s = L_r = 0, \ x_r^d > 0 \forall r \in R \qquad (3)$$
$$x_j, L_j > 0, x_j^s = x_j^d = 0, \forall j \in J.$$

Hence, the forms of the utility function and the system of production functions differ across persons selling different goods, although the original functional forms are identical for all individuals. If a person who sells good i is signified by subscript i, then u, $x_j, x_i, x_i^s, L_i, L_j, x_r^d$, and n should have subscript i. Later, I will show that the optimum values of decision variables are the same for all individuals. To simplify the notation, subscript i of n, $x_j, x_i, x_i^s, L_i, L_j$ and x_r^d is omitted when no confusion is caused. Subscript i of u is kept to avoid confusion. Having considered the budget constraint, the decision problem for an individual selling good i becomes

$$\text{Max: } u_i = x_i \prod_{r \in R} k x_r^d \prod_{j \in J} x_j \qquad (4)$$

$$\text{s.t.} x_i + x_i^s = \text{Max}\left\{a\left(L_i - A\right), 0\right\}$$

$$x_j = \text{Max}\left\{a\left(L_j - A\right), 0\right\}, \forall j \in J \qquad \text{(production function)}$$

$$L_i + \sum_{j \in J} L_j = 1 \qquad \text{(endowment constraint)}$$

$$p_i x_i^s = \sum_{r \in R} p_r x_r^d \qquad \text{(budget constraint)}$$

where p_i is the price of good i, $x_i, x_i^s, x_r^d, L_i, x_j, L_j$ and n are decision variables. Since a is the same for all goods and has no effect on the optimum decisions, I have omitted a in u_i.

Using all constraints, u_i can be expressed as a function of L_i, x_i^s, x_r^d, and n. Maximizing u_i with respect to L_i, x_i^s, and x_r^d yields the optimum values of the decision variables as functions of n:

$$L_i = A + n\left[1 - (m - n + 1)A\right]/m, \; x_i^s = (n-1)a\left[1 - (m - n + 1)A\right]/m$$

$$x_i = x_j = a\left[1 - (m - n + 1)A\right]/m, \; L_j = \left[1 - (m - n + 1)A\right]/m \tag{5}$$

$$x_r^d = p_{ir}x_i^s/(n-1) = p_{ir}a\left[1 - (m - n - 1)A\right]/m, \forall r \in R$$

where $p_{ir} \equiv p_i / p_r$. Inserting (5) into u_i yields

$$u_i = x_i^n (kp_i)^{n-1} \left(\prod_{r \in R} p_r^{-1}\right) x_j^{m-n} = u_i(n, a, A, k, p_{ir}) \tag{6}$$

where $r \in R$ and x_i and x_j are given in (5). Maximizing u_i with respect to n yields the optimal number of traded goods for a specialist selling good i. The optimal value, n^{**}, is the integer in the neighborhood of n^* which is given by the first-order condition

$$\partial u_i(n^*, a, A, k, p_{ir})/\partial n = 0 \tag{7}$$

where $r \in R$. There are two integers next to n^* if n^* is not an integer. One of them is greater and the other is smaller than n^*. Inserting the two integers into u, we can identify n^{**} that generates the greater value of u. However, we can use n^* as a good proxy of n^{**} because later we can see from (11) that u_i is concave in n. From (7), n^* can be derived to be a function of p_{ir}:

$$n = n(p_{i1}, p_{i2}, ..., p_{in}, a, c, k) . \tag{8}$$

n is the same for all individuals selling the same good because the form $n(.)$ and p_{ir} are exactly the same for all individuals selling good i. Since (8) is exactly the same for all individuals (even if they sell different goods) except p_{ir} differ, n will be the same for all individuals if $p_{ir} = 1$ for all i and r.

The system of x_r^d (p_{ir}, n) in (5) is a demand system. The relationship between demand and supply and the dependence of demand and supply on the level of specialization differ from the conventional demand system.

3.2. Equilibrium and its comparative statics

The previous subsection solved the optimal resource allocation and optimal level of specialization for individuals, which are functions of relative prices of traded goods. Using these individual optimal decisions, this subsection solves for equilibrium. The definition of equilibrium is neoclassical: all markets for goods are cleared and each person allocates his resources and chooses his level of specialization and a professional job to maximize his utility for price parameters which are determined by the numbers of persons selling different goods. An equilibrium is characterized by the relative prices of traded goods, the relative numbers of persons selling different goods, and the level of specialization for individuals.

The equilibrium is determined by market clearing conditions, utility equalization conditions, and the condition that the real return to labor is maximized with respect to the level of specialization by each person. Let us establish these conditions one by one.

Let the number of individuals selling good i be M_i. We need to solve only for the relative numbers of individuals selling different goods because the total number of all individuals in the whole economy, M, is given. That is, M_i can be solved from $M_i + \sum_{r \in R} M_r = M$ if all $M_r (r \neq i)$ are known. The market clearing conditions are

$$M_i x_i^s = \sum_{r \in R} M_r x_{ri}^d \quad \text{for } i = 1, \ldots, n \tag{9}$$

where x_{ri}^d is the demand for good i by individuals selling good r. x_{ri}^d is a function of p_{rq} and n. n is a function of p_{rq} (q, $r \in R$) due to (8). Only $n-1$ equations in (9) are independent of one another owing to Walras' law.

With free entry, individual utility maximizer's behavior will lead to the equalization of utilities of individuals selling different goods in equilibrium. Hence, we have the conditions of utility equalization in equilibrium. Inserting (5) and (8) into u_i, the indirect utility function u_i (p_{ir}) can be solved, where $r \in R$. Note, (8) implies that all individuals selling the same good have identical n, so that all individuals selling good i have identical indirect utility functions u_i (p_{ir}). Let these indirect utility functions be equal for all indexes i; we have

$$u_1(p_{1r}, r=2,...,n) = u_2(p_{2r}, r=1,3,...,n) = ... = u_n(p_{nr}, r=1,...,n-1) \quad (10)$$

where u_i is the indirect utility function of individuals selling good i. Since individual optimal decisions in (6) and (8) and the market clearing conditions in (9) are completely symmetric, and the form of the indirect utility functions are completely symmetric for all individuals selling different goods, the $n-1$ equations in (10) determine the equilibrium relative prices of $n-1$ traded goods which are $p_{ir}=1$ for all i and r. Inserting the equilibrium price system into (8) yields that the optimum n is identical for all individuals selling different goods. Inserting the equilibrium price system and n into demand and supply functions in (9) yields equal M_i for all i. Therefore, the general equilibrium is

for goods $i = 1, ..., n$,

$$L_i = \left[1 - (\ln k)^{-1} + (A-1)/m\right] mA/(-\ln k)$$
$$x_i^s = aA\left[m - (1/A) - (m/\ln k)\right]/(-\ln k)$$
$$x_i = x_r^d = x_j = -aA/\ln k, \forall r \in R, \forall j \in J$$

$$p_{ir} = 1, M_{ir} = 1, \text{ for } r = 1,...,n$$
$$u_i = k^{n-1}a[1 - (m - n + 1)A]/m \text{ for } i = 1,...,n \quad (11)$$
$$n = m + 1 - \left(1/A\right) - \left(m/\ln k\right)$$

where $M_{ir} \equiv M_i/M_r$ and $\sum_{i=1}^{n} M_i = M$. $M_{ir} = 1$ for all i and r implies that in equilibrium there are M/n local business communities, if we assume that individuals trade first with the nearest partners. In each community n individuals trade n goods. Each of the individuals in a community sells one good to $n-1$ other individuals and buys one traded good from each of them.[4] There is no trade between communities.

---

[4] Because of symmetry, it is indeterminate which goods are traded. By n combinations of m goods there are $m!/(m-n)!n!$ equilibria. Possible equilibria are more than these because the number of traded goods for the whole economy may be larger than that for an individual. For example, if person 1 sells good 1 to person 2 who sells good 2 to person 3 who sells good 3 to person 1, then each person trades two goods but three persons trade three goods. All equilibria generate the same *per capita* real income. We restrict attention to those equilibria where all people trade the same bundle of goods since their comparative statics are easier to analyze. A slight difference in the preference and technology parameters across goods will rule out the indeterminacy. But multiple equilibria may also be caused by indeterminacy of who specializes in producing which

It is trivial to prove that the Walrasian equilibrium is Pareto optimal because economies of specialization are individual-specific (increasing returns are localized) and no monopoly power exists (see Yang and Ng, 1993, chs 2 and 6).

Because of the symmetry of this model, the optimum number of traded goods, *n,* is the same for all individuals and equals the number of traded goods for the economy. By Lemma 1, a person sells at most one good. This means that with a larger number of traded goods, more goods are purchased and a larger share of labor has to be allocated producing the good sold in exchange for more goods purchased. Consequently, the level of specialization for each person and the level of division of labor for the economy is higher. Hence, for the symmetric model, the equilibrium number of traded goods for the economy, which equals the optimum number of traded goods for each person, characterizes the *level of division of labor.*

A careful examination of (11) indicates that the equilibrium entails a corner $n=m$ if $A \geq \ln k / (\ln k - m)$ which implies that $L_i^* \geq 1$ or $n^* \geq m$. Also, the equilibrium value of n is one (autarky) if $A \leq \ln k / (\ln k - 1)$, which implies $n^* \leq 1$. Hence, the following comparative statics for $n^* \in (1, m)$ are relevant only if $A \in (\ln k / (\ln k - 1), \ln k / \ln(k - m))$. Differentiating n with respect to k and A yields the comparative statics of equilibrium level of division of labor as follows:

$$dn^* / dk > 0 \text{ and } dn^* / dA > 0. \tag{12}$$

The comparative statics imply that if transaction efficiency k is exogenously and continuously improved due to a better transaction technology, urbanization, government liberalization policies, and/or a better legal system, division of labor will evolve. I refer to such evolution of division of labor generated by comparative statics of a static general equilibrium model as *exogenous evolution of the division of labor,* which is different from endogenous evolution of the division of labor in Yang and Borland (1991). Since the comparative statics of the general equilibrium model based on corner solutions are much easier to manage than the dynamics of the Yang and Borland model, the model in this

---

goods. An infinitesimally small *ex ante* differential in productivity between individuals will rule out that indeterminacy.

paper can predict more concurrent economic phenomena than does the Yang and Borland model.

Applying the envelope theorem to utility function yields

$$du\left(n^{*},A,k,a\right)/dk = \partial u\left(n^{*},A,k,a\right)/\partial k$$
$$du\left(n^{*},A,k,a\right)/dA = \partial u\left(n^{*},A,k,a\right)/\partial A. \tag{13}$$

Equations (13) imply that the equilibrium real return to labor (real labor productivity or *per capita* real income) is an increasing function of transaction efficiency and a decreasing function of the fixed learning cost.

From (11) it can be seen that the equilibrium values of all other variables – such as quantities consumed, produced, and traded and level of specialization – all depend on the equilibrium level of division of labor n. Hence, (12) can be used to predict concurrent economic phenomena discussed in the introductory section as different aspects of exogenous evolution of the division of labor. The rest of the section is devoted to an analysis of the relationship between the comparative statics and the concurrent phenomena.

A.   Level of specialization, degree of commercialization, degree of trade dependence, and degree of self-sufficiency

A person's equilibrium level of specialization is given by L_i in (11). In order to identify the relationship between the level of specialization and n, we first show that

$$1 - (m - n + 1)A > 0. \tag{14}$$

The inequality can be established by replacing n in the inequality with its equilibrium value, given in (11). It is straightforward that the equilibrium level of specialization increases with the level of division of labor n since

$$dL_i/dn = (1 - (m - 2n + 1)A)/m > (1 - (m - n + 1)A)/m > 0 \tag{15a}$$

where the first inequality is obvious and the final inequality comes from (14). Hence

$$dL_i/dk = (dL_i/dn)\,(dn/dk) > 0 \tag{15b}$$

where $dn/dk > 0$ is given in (12).

In the model, the quantity of labor allocated to production of a good can be considered as the labor value of the good. Hence, L_i represents the labor value of the good sold by an individual, which equals the labor value of all traded goods consumed by him. The labor value of all goods including traded and nontraded goods is 1 because each person is endowed with 1 unit of labor. The ratio of value of traded goods to value of all goods including nontraded ones is $L_i/1 = L_i$. The ratio is defined as the degree of commercialization. Hence, (15) implies that the degree of commercialization increases as the division of labor evolves. This also implies that trade volume increases more rapidly than total real income as division of labor evolves, because an increase in the degree of commercialization is equivalent to an increase in the ratio of trade volume to total income, defined as the degree of trade dependence. The degree equals to 2 times the degree of commercialization in the model. Since $1 - L_i = (m - n)L_j$ is the ratio of the value of nontraded goods to value of all goods, $1 - L_i$ is the degree of self-sufficiency, which decreases as the division of labor evolves.

B.   *The extent of the market*

Let E denote the equilibrium extent of the market. E is defined by the product of the population size M and *per capita* aggregate demand for traded goods. Here, the distinction is drawn between *aggregate demand* and *total market demand*. The former is the sum of total market demands for all goods and the latter is the quantity of one good demanded by all individuals. Since the equilibrium prices of all goods are the same for the symmetric model, *per capita* aggregate demand can be represented by the quantity of goods sold by each person, x_i^s, given in (11), which equals the volume of goods bought by each person:

$$E = Mx_i^s = a(n-1)\big[1-(m-n+1)A\big]M/m,$$
$$dE/dk = (dE/dn)(dn/dk) > 0. \tag{16}$$

where $dn/dk > 0$ is due to (12) and $dE/dn > 0$ is obvious.[5]

C.   *Labor productivity of traded goods*

Let P denote equilibrium labor productivity of each traded good. P is given by the ratio $(x_i + x_i^s)/L_i$. Using (11), the equilibrium level of labor productivity of each traded good is therefore

$$P = (x_i + x_i^s)/L_i$$

$$= a(n/m)\left[1-(m-n+1)A\right]/\left\{A+(n/m)\left[1-(m-n+1)A\right]\right\} \quad (17a)$$

$$dP/dk = (dP/dn)(dn/dk) > 0 \quad (17b)$$

where (14) and $1-(m-n+1)A > 1-(m+1)A$ are used to establish $dP/dn > 0$.

D.   *The extent of endogenous comparative advantage*

The extent of endogenous comparative advantage is defined by the difference in labor productivity of a traded good between its sellers and buyers. A seller's productivity of a traded good is given by (17a). A buyer's labor productivity is zero since he does not produce the good. Hence, P in (17a) can be interpreted as the extent of endogenous comparative advantage, which increases as the level of division of labor n increases.

E.   *The degree of diversification of economic structure and variety of different professions*

When transaction efficiency k is extremely low, then the equilibrium is autarky where all individuals engage in a broad range of the same activities. Hence, economic structure is homogeneous. As the level of

---

[5] Becker and Murphy (1992) explain the extent of the market by the efficient level of division of labor using an aggregate model with the tradeoff between economies of division of labor and coordination costs. Yang and Wills (1990) explain the equilibrium degree of reliability by formalizing the tradeoffs among economies of specialization, coordination reliability, transaction costs in specifying and enforcing property rights, and a risk of losing property rights in a general equilibrium model.

division of labor n increases due to improvements in transaction efficiency, the number of professional sectors that are distinctive from each other and the number of markets for different goods, which is n, increase. As n increases, the difference in structure of consumption, production and trade between different specialists increases too. This implies that specialization for individuals and diversity of different professions for society as a whole are two sides of the division of labor. Hence, the Herfindahl index of specialization cannot reflect the level of division of labor and thereby may be misleading because it does not reflect another side of the division of labor: diversity of different professions. According to the index, the level of specialization of Los Angeles, Chicago, San Francisco and New York City are lower than Albany, Gary and Norfolk. But from casual observation, we can perceive that the four large cities have certainly a much higher level of division of labor than the three small cities because of a higher degree of diversity of different professions in the four large cities than in the three small cities.[6] Chandler (1990) has documented that full exploitation of economies of scale and scope was a precondition for rapid economic growth in the US at the end of the nineteenth century and early in the twentieth century. In essence, the economies of scale and scope are two sides of economies of division of labor which can be fully exploited only if transaction efficiency is sufficiently great.

F.   The degree of production concentration

In the symmetric model the equilibrium number of producers of a traded good is $N=M/n$, where M is the population size and n is the equilibrium number of traded goods. The degree of production concentration is defined as the reciprocal of the number of producers for each traded goods, N. Hence, the degree is

$$1/N=n/M, \quad d(1/N)/dn>0, \quad d(1/N)/dk= (d(1/N)/dn) \, (dn/dk) >0. \quad (18)$$

---

[6] As estimated by Diamond and Simon (1990, pp. 180-3), the Herfindahl index of specialization of Los Angeles, Chicago, San Francisco, New York City, Albany, Gary, and Norfolk are 0.1201,0.1180,0.1442,0.1466,0.1482,0.1692 and 0.1608 respectively. According to this index, a city is said to be perfectly specialized when employment is concentrated in a single industry.

This implies that the degree of production concentration increases as the division of labor evolves.

G.   *The degree of market integration*

In the equilibrium of the symmetric model, the economy is divided into N local business communities. In each of them, there are n different specialists. Each of them sells one good to $n - 1$ other members of the community and buys one good from each of them. Hence, population size of each local community is n and the number of such local communities is $N = M / n$. The degree of market integration can be defined as the reciprocal of the number of local communities. Hence $1/N$ can be interpreted as the degree of market integration, which increases as division of labor evolves.

The comparative statics of the equilibrium identified in the section are summarized in the following proposition.

Proposition 1:   A continuous increasing transaction efficiency will generate exogenous evolution of the division of labor. Labor productivity, per capita real income, each person's level of specialization, the degree of commercialization, the degree of trade dependence, the extent of the market, the extent of endogenous comparative advantage, the degree of production concentration, the degree of diversity of economic structure, and the degree of market integration simultaneously increase as different aspects of the evolution of the division of labor. Trade volume increases more rapidly than per capita real income does in the evolutionary process. The comparative statics which generate exogenous evolution of the division of labor are illustrated in figure 1 where it is assumed that $M = m = 4$.

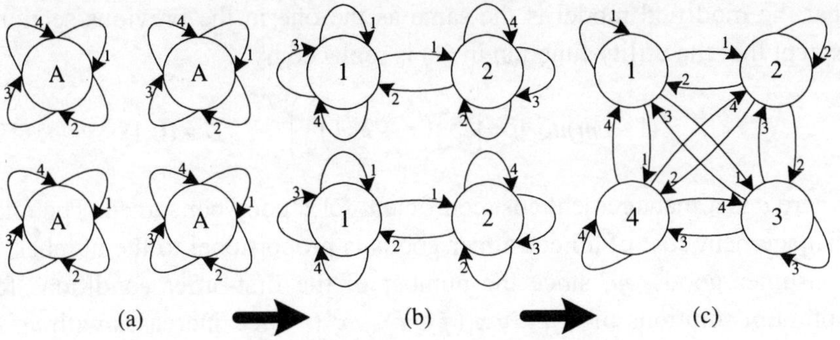

(a) (b) (c)

Figure 1: Exogenous evolution of the division of labor: (a) autarky, n = 1, four communities => (b) partial specialization, n = 2, two communities => (c) complete specialization, n = 4, the integrated market

The lines in figure 1 signify goods flows. The small arrows indicate the direction of goods flows. The numbers beside the lines signify the goods involved. A circle with number i signifies a person selling good i. Panel (a) denotes autarky where each person self-provides four goods, i.e. $n - 1 = 0$, because of small transaction efficiency. Panel (b) denotes partial specialization where each person sells one good, buys one good, trades two goods, and self-provides three goods, i.e. $n = 2$, because of a larger transaction efficiency. Panel (c) denotes extreme specialization where each person sells and self-provides one good, buys three goods, and trades four goods, i.e. $n = 4$, because of a very large transaction efficiency.

4. A Modified Version with the CES Utility Function

In order to check the sensitivity of the comparative statics to the specification of functional forms, I shall in this section replace the Cobb-Douglas utility function with the CES utility function. Suppose

310   *X. Yang*

that the modified model is the same as the one in the previous sections
except that the utility function in (1) is replaced by

$$V = (1 - cm)u, \quad u = \left(\sum_i (x_i + kx_i^d)^\rho\right)^{1/\rho}, \quad \rho \in (0,1) \tag{19}$$

where c is a management cost coefficient for a good consumed. The total
management cost of all consumer goods is proportional to the number of
consumer goods, m, since the number of the first-order conditions for
optimum solutions of x_i, x_i^s, $x_j (j \in J)$, $x_r^d (r \in R)$ increases with m. A
fraction $(1 - cm)$ of utility u cannot be enjoyed by the individual owing
to the management cost. The management cost can be interpreted as all
kinds of cost caused by calculation of the optimum decision. Utility V
involves a tradeoff between economies of complementarity between
consumer goods in raising utility (or economies of consumption variety)
and the management cost of a variety of consumption. This tradeoff in
addition to the tradeoff between economies of specialization and
transaction costs can be used to endogenize the number of all consumer
goods m (or variety of consumption) as well as the number of traded
goods.

Following the approach developed in the previous sections, we can
stake the equilibrium and its comparative statics for the modified model:

for goods $i = 1, ..., n$,

$$L_i = \{(n-1)[1 - A(m-n)] + K\} / [n - 1 + K(m - n + 1)]$$

$$x_i^s = a(n-1)[1 - A(m-n+1)] / [n - 1 + K(m - n + 1)]$$

$$x_i = x_r^d = x_j = aK[1 - A(m-n+1)] / [n - 1 + K(m-n+1)], \forall r \in R, \forall j \in J$$

$$p_{ir} = 1, M_{ir} = 1, \text{ for } r = 1, ..., n$$

$$u_i = ak[1 - A(m-n+1)][n - 1 + K(m-n+1)]^{(1-\rho)/\rho} \text{ for } i = 1, ..., n \tag{20a}$$

$$n^* = 1 + \left[(A-c)(1-K) + \rho\left(A - (1-K)^2\right)\right] / cA(1+\rho)(1-K), \tag{20b}$$
$$dn^*/dk > 0, dn^*/dc < 0$$

$$m^* = [A + c\rho(1-K)] / c(1+\rho), \tag{20c}$$
$$dm^*/dk > 0, dm^*/dc < 0, dm/d\rho < 0$$

$$m^* - n^* = \left[1/A(1+\rho)\right] - 1 + \left[\rho/c(1+\rho)(1-K)\right]$$

$$d(m^* - n^*)/dk < 0, d(m^* - n^*)/dc > 0,^7 \quad (20d)$$

where we have used the fact that

$$K \equiv k^{\rho/(\rho-1)}, \ dK/d\rho > 0, \ \partial m^*/\partial K < 0,$$

$$\partial m^*/\partial \rho < 0, \text{ and } dK/dk < 0.$$

Equations (20d) imply that the number of traded goods n will eventually reach the number of all goods m since n increases more quickly than m as transaction efficiency is improved. As soon as n has reached m, then the comparative statics of n and m in (23) are no longer relevant. Letting $m = n$ in (19) and differentiating V with respect to m yields

$$m^* = n^* = \left[(1-\rho)/c\right] + \rho(1-K), dm^*/dk > 0, dm^*/dc < 0. \quad (21)$$

The second-order condition for the interior maximum points of n and m requires a negative definite Hessian determinant of V. It can be shown that $\partial^2 V/\partial n^2$ and $\partial^2 V/\partial m^2$ are negative when the first-order conditions, $\partial V/\partial n = \partial V/\partial m = 0$, are satisfied. The condition that $(\partial^2 V/\partial n^2)(\partial^2 V/\partial m^2) - (\partial^2 V/\partial n\partial m) > 0$ requires

$$k > k_0 \equiv [\rho/(1+\rho-\rho^2)]^{(1+\rho)/2\rho} \quad (22)$$

where $dk_0/d\rho > 0$. Parameter ρ is positively related to the elasticity of substitution $1/(1 - \rho)$. Since the elasticity of substitution is inversely related to the degree of economies of complementarity, $1/\rho$ can be interpreted as the degree of economies of complementarity (or of economies of consumption variety). Equation (22) requires a value of ρ that is sufficiently small compared with k. Or it requires a great degree of economies of complementarity compared with transaction efficiency. This implies that the second-order condition for interior m and n requires that the degree of economies of complementarity is not too small compared with transaction efficiency. Otherwise, the equilibrium m would be at a corner, either $m = n$ or $m = \infty$. Since the corner $m = \infty$ is incompatible with the endowment constraint, the equilibrium entails $m = n$ if the second-order condition (22) is not satisfied. Therefore, the

---

[7] Strictly speaking, the equilibrium n^{**} is a step function of parameters. But as far as n^* is a good proxy of n^{**}, the comparative statics of n^* is a good proxy of that of n^{**}.

X. Yang

equilibrium m and n are given by (21) instead of (20) if the degree of economies of complementarity is sufficiently small compared with transaction efficiency. The second-order condition for the interior maximum points of n and m is always satisfied if $m = n$. Also, the formulae for m^* and n^* indicate that they will be at a corner if c, k and/or A are too large or too small.

It is interesting to note that the demand and supply functions depend not only on relative prices of traded goods, but also on the optimum number of traded goods, n, and the optimum number of all consumption goods, m, which are in turn dependent on the relative prices. The supply function of good i and demand function for goods r, by a person selling good i and buying goods r, are

$$x_i^s = a[1 - A(m - n + 1)](n - 1)/[(m - n + 1)(kp_i / p_r)^{\rho/(\rho-1)} + n - 1]$$

$$x_r^d = p_i x_i^s / p_r (n - 1), \qquad \forall r \in R \tag{23}$$

where $r \in R$ is a good purchased. The symmetry of the model, which implies p_r is the same $\forall r \in R$, is used for an individual to derive his supply function. It can be shown that the supply law holds, but the demand law for normal goods in this model may not hold. Differentiating x_i^s and x_r^d yields

$$dx_i^s / dp_i = [\partial x_i^s / \partial(m - n)][d(m - n)/dp_i]$$
$$+ (\partial x_i^s / \partial n')(dn'/dp_i) + (\partial x_i^s / \partial p_i) > 0 \tag{24a}$$

$$dx_r^d / dp_r = (\partial x_r^d / \partial x_i^{s'})(dx_i^s / dp_r) + (\partial x_r^d / \partial n)(dn/dp_r) + (\partial x_r^d / \partial p_r) < 0$$
$$\text{iff} \left| (\partial x_r^d / \partial x_i^s)(dx_i^s / dp_r) + (\partial x_r^d / \partial p_r) \right| > (\partial x_r^d / \partial n)(dn/dp_r) \tag{24b}$$

where n' is used to draw the distinction between the n that is not in $m - n$ and the n that is in $m - n$.

Expressions

$$m - n = \left[1/A(1+\rho) \right] - 1 + \left\{ \rho \big/ c(1+\rho) \left[1 - (p_i k / p_r)^{\rho/(\rho-1)} \right] \right\} \text{ and}$$

$$n = 1 + \left\{ (A - c)(1 - K) + \rho \left[A - \left(1 - (p_i k / p_r)^{\rho/(\rho-1)} \right)^2 \right] \right\} \Big/$$
$$cA(1+\rho) \left[1 - (p_i k / p_r)^{\rho/(\rho-1)} \right]$$

give the optimum number of self-provided goods and the optimum number of traded goods, respectively. They may not be the equilibrium values of the respective numbers. It can be shown that $d(m-n)/dp_i < 0$, $d(m-n)/dp_r > 0$, $dn/dp_i > 0$, $dn/dp_r < 0$, $\partial x_i^s / \partial(m-n) < 0$, $\partial x_i^s / \partial n' > 0$, $\partial x_i^s / \partial p_i > 0$, $\partial x_r^d / \partial x_i^s > 0$, $dx_i^s / dp_r < 0$, $\partial x_r^d / \partial p_r < 0$, $\partial x_r^d / \partial n < 0$ and $dn/dp_r < 0$. It is surprising that the demand law may not hold even for normal goods that are substitutes for one another. This is because a decrease in prices of goods demanded will cause an increase in the optimum number of traded goods, that will decrease the quantity demanded. The demand law no longer holds if this effect dominates the direct effect of a decrease in own price on the quantity demanded. Also, it is interesting to note that even if the supply function does not directly depend on the price of goods sold when the elasticity of substitution is 1 or $\rho = 0$ (the case of the Cobb-Douglas utility function), the supply curve is upward sloping. This is because of the indirect interdependencies between the number of traded goods and the quantity supplied and between the number of traded goods and the price of goods sold.

The analysis in this section yields the following proposition.

Proposition 2: In addition to concurrent economic phenomena predicted by the previous model, exogenous evolution of the division of labor which is driven by continuous improvements in transaction efficiency will increase the number of all goods consumed. In the evolutionary process, the number of traded goods increases more quickly than the number of all goods consumed if the degree of economies of complementarity is not too small compared with transaction efficiency. The number of traded goods and the number of all goods are always the same except for autarky if the degree of economies of complementarity is sufficiently small compared with transaction efficiency. Supply law holds, but demand law may not hold even if all goods are normal.

Figure 2 provides an intuitive illustration of the comparative statics for the model with a variable number of all goods m. The circles, the lines and the numbers beside the lines have the same meanings as in Figure 1. Panel (a) denotes autarky where each person self-provides two goods, because of low transaction efficiency. Panel (b) denotes partial specialization where each person sells one good, buys one good, trades two goods, and self-provides two goods, i.e. $n = 2$ and $m = 3$, because of a slightly larger transaction efficiency. Panel (c) denotes extreme specialization where each person sells and self-provides one good, buys two goods, and trades three goods, i.e. $n = m = 3$, because of a large transaction efficiency. Panel (d) denotes extreme specialization with $n = m = 4$, because of an extremely large transaction efficiency.

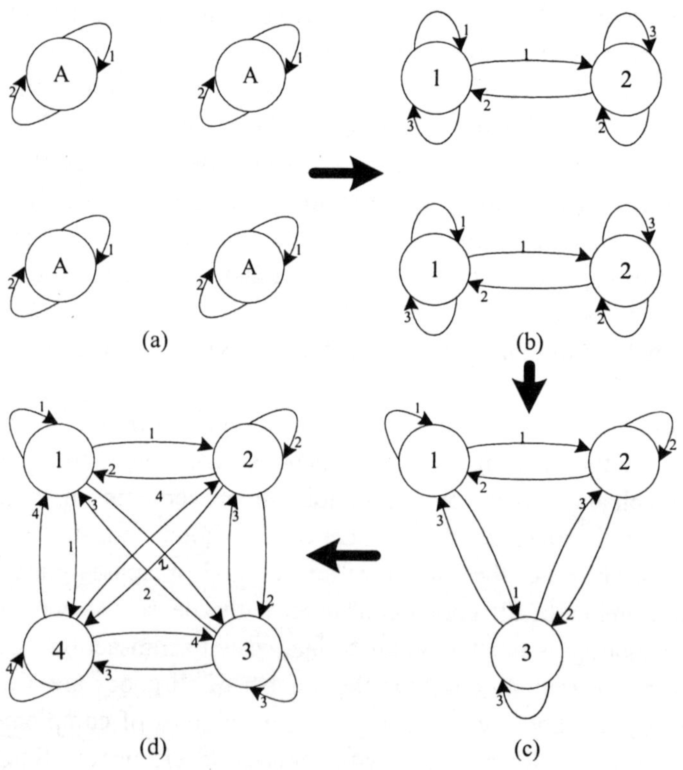

Figure 2: Evolution of specialization and product diversity: (a) autarky, n=1,m=2 => (b) partial division of labor, n=2, m=3=> (c) n=m=3=> (d)n=m=4

5.   Implications for Microeconomics, Trade Theory and Development Economics

5.1. Organizational efficiency versus allocative efficiency

In this model there are two functions of a free market system. The first is to allocate resources for a given level of division of labor (a given *n*). This function is the major concern of traditional microeconomics. The second is to search for the efficient level of the division of labor which determines the efficient extent of the market. This function of the free market has not received enough attention from traditional microeconomics in comparison with its importance in economic analysis. Accordingly, there are two kinds of inefficiencies (distortions). The first is *allocative inefficiency* and the second is *organizational inefficiency*. Here allocative inefficiency is defined as a departure of relative prices from the efficient ones and organizational inefficiency is defined as a departure of *n* from the efficient one. Our concept of organizational inefficiency resembles X-inefficiency which is defined as a departure of equilibrium from the PPF in neoclassical microeconomics.

If a government places a tax on trade volume that reduces the transaction efficiency coefficient *k*, relative prices will not be affected as long as such a tax rate is identical for all goods. Hence, there is no allocative inefficiency caused by the tax. But the tax will affect the real returns to labor (the absolute price of labor), decrease the equilibrium level of division of labor and productivity, and thereby result in a distortion and organizational inefficiency.

In the model here, a story about resource allocation seems too trivial to be interesting. Our symmetric model cannot generate any interesting story if a dichotomy between pure consumers and pure producers or constant returns are assumed. But with economies of specialization arising from a fixed learning cost, transaction costs, and consumer-producers, our model here can generate so many interesting stories about organizational efficiency. In this sense, our framework is organization-orientated whereas conventional microeconomics is orientated to resource allocation.[8]

5.2. Emergence of international trade from domestic trade

Now I use the model to address the question: Why and how does international trade emerge from domestic trade and what is the distinctive contribution of this framework to trade theory?

Suppose there are 100 countries in the world and the population size of a country is 10 million, the same for all countries. Assume further that the number of goods m and the population size over the world is one billion and that transaction efficiency is slightly greater for trade within the same country than across countries. Then our theory tells a story of trade as follows.

If transaction efficiency is extremely low, then autarky for each person is equilibrium and therefore domestic and international trade are not needed. If transaction efficiency is improved such that equilibrium n = 1000, then 10000 local markets emerge from the division of labor in each country. The equilibrium number of business communities is M/n, where M is the population size of the economy and n is the number of traded goods as well as the population size of a local business community. Each member of a local business community sells one traded good to the other 999 individuals and buys one traded good from each of them. Under the assumption that trade occurs first with those closest, there is no trade between the local communities and therefore the national market does not exist. Suppose that transaction efficiency is further improved such that $n^* = 10\ 000\ 000$. Then the national market

---

[8] For a model of the kind in this paper, Yang and Ng (1995) have shown that the institution of the firm is not needed in the absence of producer goods and that the division of labor in producing final goods and intermediate goods is necessary but not sufficient for the emergence of firms. They have shown that the institution of the firm will emerge from the division of labor in producing intermediate goods and final goods if trading of intermediate goods is more expensive than trading of labor employed to produce the intermediate goods. According to Yang and Ng's theory of indirect pricing, the institution of the firm can get the activity with the lowest transaction efficiency involved in the division of labor while avoiding direct pricing of the activity, thereby saving on transaction costs and promoting the division of labor.

emerges from the higher level of division of labor, but international trade does not exist. If $n*$ turns out to be 100 million owing to an improvement in transaction efficiency, such as that caused by the invention of the steam engine, the world will be divided into ten common markets. In each of these common markets, ten countries have an integrated market and international trade emerges from domestic trade but no trade occurs between the ten common markets. If transaction efficiency is extremely large, then an integrated world market will emerge from the complete division of labor.

The difference between this story and that from neoclassical theory is obvious. For a neoclassical model with constant returns to scale, international trade instead of autarky is the equilibrium in the absence of government intervention if exogenous comparative advantages exist. For the Dixit-Stiglitz model with economies of scale, international trade instead of autarky is always the equilibrium in the absence of government intervention. But for the present model autarky for each individual or for each country may be the equilibrium in the absence of government intervention. In other words gains to international trade are exogenously given either by exogenous comparative advantages or by economies of scale in neoclassical theory whereas gains to international trade and the degree of involvement in international trade are endogenized by this model.

5.3. Trade policy: laissez-faire versus protectionism

The policy implications of this model may highlight its distinctive feature. According to the literature of strategic trade policy (Krugman, 1986), any unilateral tax exemption over all imported goods will put the country that implements such exemption in an inferior position. According to the present theory such an exemption will however benefit all countries via its effects on the equilibrium level of division of labor and productivity. Suppose there are two countries 1 and 2 with identical production functions, utility functions, transaction technology, and endowment constraints for all individuals. The population size M is the same for the two countries. For simplicity, we assume that no difference in transaction efficiency exists between international trade and domestic trade when taxation is absent. Country 1 does not tax on trade and country 2 places a tax on imported goods. Hence, the transaction efficiency coefficient for country 1, k_1, is larger than that for country 2, k_2. Thus each individual in country 1 trades n_1 goods which exceeds the number for country 2, n_2. Assume that k_1 and k_2 are so large that $n_1 > n_2 > M$. Therefore country 1 domestically trades M goods and imports $n_1 - M$ goods in the symmetric model. Country 2 domestically trades M goods and imports $n_2 - M$ goods from country 1. If the number of all consumer goods m is larger than n_1 and n_2, this pattern of trade is possible because each country can domestically trade the goods such that part of those goods differ from the goods domestically traded by the other country, so that each country can import the goods not domestically produced. According to Proposition 1, this pattern of trade implies that country 1 has higher *per capita* real income than country 2. That is, the country pursuing the *laissez-faire* policy receives more gains from trade than the country pursuing the protectionist policy in an asymmetric policy scenario. This theory is supported by policy practice of the Hong Kong government.

5.4. Growth implications of policy to birth control

The other policy implication that distinguishes the present model from traditional theory relates to the effects of population size on productivity. According to Solow's growth model (1956), a larger growth rate of population has a negative effect on the growth rate of *per capita* consumption. On the other hand, the Dixit-Stiglitz model (1977) predicts a positive relationship between total factor productivity and the population size of an economy. However, we can find empirical evidence such as experience in Hong Kong after the Second World War and in nineteenth-century New Zealand (where the rapid growth of population contributes to economic growth) that is incompatible with Solow's theory. On the other hand, it is easy to find empirical evidence from many African countries (where the rapid growth of population has a negative effect on economic growth) that is against Dixit and Stiglitz's theory.

The present model solves this puzzle. According to the theory, the population size *per se* does not explain productivity. If transaction efficiency is large such as in Hong Kong, a high population density and a large growth rate of population may create more scope for the division of labor, thereby generating a higher productivity. If transaction efficiency is small such as in the pre-reform mainland China, a huge population will be fragmented into many separate local business communities, so that the potential contribution of a high density or growth rate of population to the division of labor cannot be realized. Hence an improvement in transaction efficiency generated by liberalization policies or by changes in the legal system has much more important growth implications than a policy for birth control.

5.5. *Explaining the Linder-type trading pattern*

Because of the common feature of increasing returns, both the present model and the Dixit-Stiglitz model are more powerful than traditional trade models in predicting the Linder-type trading pattern (trade is concentrated among the industrialized countries) and in explaining why international trade dependence for a large country is lower than that for a small country. Markusen (1986) constructs a factor-endowments cum scale-economies model with non-homothetic preferences in order to explain the Linder pattern. The present model can explain the Linder trading pattern by the impacts of the level of division of labor and transaction efficiency on trade volume even if preferences are homothetic. Indeed, if we assume that transaction efficiency is much larger in industrialized countries than in less-developed countries, then this model can be used to show that the equilibrium level of division of labor in industrialized countries is much greater than in less-developed countries. Hence, the former are more likely to have gains from international trade. Krugman (1979) uses a specific version of the Dixit-Stiglitz model to explain the Linder trading pattern by the degree of similarity between industrialized economies. According to the present model, transaction efficiency rather than similarity is the crucial determinant of the Linder pattern.

6.   Concluding Remarks

There are several features of equilibrium that distinguish the present model from other equilibrium models. The first is that aggregate demand and supply (the extent of the market) can be endogenized in the model even though Say's law (1803), which states that demand is the reciprocal of supply and demand always equals supply, holds. For the division of labor, market demand equals market supply. From (5), we see that demand is the reciprocal of supply. In autarky, self-demand always equals self-supply because they are two sides of self-provided quantity of goods. However, there is no market demand and supply in autarky and such demand and supply evolves as the division of labor evolves. In Young's words (1928), demand and supply are the two sides of the division of labor. For our model, the economic story consists of two parts. One is the problem of resource allocation for a given level of division of labor (or a given extent of the market). The other is the problem of economic organization which is solved by the equilibrium level of the division of labor (or equilibrium extent of the market). The general equilibrium endogenizes aggregate demand and aggregate supply when it endogenizes the level of the division of labor.

The second feature of this new framework is a possible disparity between the production possibility frontier (PPF) and the Pareto optimum. The PPF in the present model is associated with the complete division of labor because of economies of specialization. However, the Pareto optimum or the utility frontier may be associated with autarky if transaction costs outweigh economies of specialization for the division of labor. As transaction efficiency is improved, equilibrium as well as the Pareto optimum will become closer to the PPF. In contrast, the Pareto optimum always coincides with the PPF in neoclassical microeconomics. This feature generates productivity implications of transaction efficiency. Such implications become extremely important in view of the effects of institutional arrangements, organizational patterns, urbanization, the use of money, and policies on transaction efficiency.

Related to the second feature, the present model formalizes the notion of endogenous comparative advantages. If transaction efficiency is extremely low, autarky is the general equilibrium. Labor productivity of each good is the same for all individuals. No comparative advantages exist. If transaction efficiency is sufficiently large, then the general equilibrium is the division of labor where the labor productivity of the seller of a good is higher than that of the buyer of the good because the level of specialization of the former in producing the good is higher than that of the latter. That is, *ex post* comparative advantages between *ex ante* identical individuals endogenously evolve as the division of labor evolves.

The features of the present model have been used to develop a new theory of demand and supply which explains demand and supply as two sides of the division of labor. In addition an endogenous trade theory is developed to explain the emergence of international trade from domestic trade and to endogenize the degree of involvement of countries in international trade.

References

Arrow, K. J. (1962) "The Economic Implications of Learning by Doing," *Review of Economic Studies* 29, 155-73.

Babbage, C. (1835) *On the Economy of Machinery and Manufactures,* New York: Kelly, 1977.

Barzel, Y. and B. T. Yu (1984) "The Effect of the Utilization Rate on the Division of Labor," *Economic Inquiry* 22, 18-27.

Becker, C. and K. Murphy (1992) "The Division of Labor, Coordination Costs, and Knowledge," *Quarterly Journal of Economics* 107, 1137-60.

Chandler, A. (1990) *Scale and Scope the Dynamics of Industrial Capitalism,* Cambridge, MA: Belknap Press of Harvard University Press.

Diamond, C. and C. Simon (1990) "Industrial Specialization and the Returns to Labor," *Journal of Labor Economics* 8, 175-201.

Dixit, A. and J. Stiglitz (1977) "Monopolistic Competition and Optimum Product Diversity," *American Economic Review* 67, 297-308.

Grossman, G. and E. Helpman (1989) "Product Development and International Trade," *Journal of Political Economy* 97, 1261-83.

Houthakker, M. (1956) "Economics and Biology: Specialization and Speciation," *Kyklos* 9, 181-9.

Krugman, P. (1979) "Increasing Returns, Monopolistic Competition, and International Trade," *Journal of International Economics* 9, 469-79.

— (ed.) (1986) *Strategic Trade Policy and the New International Economics*, Cambridge, MA: MIT Press.

Markusen, J. R. (1986) "Explaining the Volume of Trade: an Eclectic Approach," *American Economic Review* 5, 1002-11.

Marshall, A. (1890) *Principles of Economics,* New York: Macmillan, 8th edn, 1948.

Marx, K. (1867) *Capital, a Critique of Political Economy Vols I-III,* New York: International Publishers, 1967.

Rosen, S. (1978) "Substitution and the Division of Labor ," *Economica* 45, 235-50.

— (1983) "Specialization and Human Capital," *Journal of Labor Economics* 1, 43-9.

Say, J. (1803) *A Treatise on Political Economy.*

Smith, A. (1776) *An Inquiry into the Nature and Causes of the Wealth of Nations.* Chicago: University of Chicago Press, 1976, reprint edited by E. Cannan.

Solow, R. M. (1956) "A Contribution to the Theory of Economic Growth," *Quarterly Journal of Economics* 70, 65-94.

Walker, A. (1874) *Science of Wealth: A Manual of Political Economy,* Boston: Little Brown, and New York: Kraus, reprint 1969.

Wong, K-Y. and X. Yang (1996) "An Extended Ethier Model Model with the Tradeoff Between Economies of Scale and Transaction Costs," in K. Arrow, Y.-K. Ng and X. Yang (eds), *Increasing Returns and Economic Analysis,* London: Macmillan, forthcoming.

Yang, X. (1990) "Development, Strucural Changes, and Urbanization," *Journal of Development Economics* 34, 199-222.

— and J. Borland (1991) "A Microeconomic Mechanism for Economic Growth," *Journal of Political Economy* 99, 460-482.

— and Y.-K. Ng (1993) *Specialization and Economic Organization: A New Classical Microeconomic Framework*, Amsterdam: North-Holland.

— and Y.-K. Ng (1995) "Theory of the Firm and Structure of Residual Rights," *Journal of Economic Behavior and Organization* 26, 107-28.

— and I. Wills (1990) "A Model Formalizing the Theory of Property Rights," *Journal of Comparative Economics* 14, 177-98.

Young, Allyn (1928) "Increasing Returns and Economic Progress," *The Economic Journal* 38, 527-42.

Young, Alwyn (1991) "Learning by Doing and the Effects of International Trade," *Quarterly Journal of Economics* 106, 369-406.

CHAPTER 15

**WALRASIAN EQUILIBRIUM COMPUTATION,
NETWORK FORMATION, AND THE WEN THEOREM**[*]

Shuntian Yao[♣]

Nanyang Technological University

1. Introduction

Economic growth and development are two of the most challenging issues facing all developed and developing countries. All countries require a good international economic environment, and each country itself needs to improve its domestic economic infrastructure. Both these issues can be related to so-called "economic networking theory," which studies how economic agents should choose their activities, how they should choose their trading partners, and how they could improve transaction efficiency; and in general, how they can maximize their utility with their given resources. As is well known, given some economic resource, different economic infrastructures or different economic networking decisions can lead to totally different economic outcomes. China can serve as a convincing example. Following the introduction of economic reforms, China has developed a more efficient economic network for its domestic market and for its international affairs. The per capita GNP of the Chinese economy has more than tripled over the past 20 years or so. Most recently, because of the rapid development

---

[*] Reprinted from *Review of Development Economics* 6(3), Shuntian Yao, "Walrasian Equilibrium Computation, Network Formation, and the Wen Theorem," 415–427, 2002, with permission from Blackwell.

[♣] I wish to thank Mei Wen for helpful discussion.

325

of the computer industry and Internet communication, all economic agents are potentially linked to a worldwide e-commerce network.

This, on the one hand, gives more freedom to any economic agent (including any developing country) to make decisions. However, the decision process becomes more complicated because the agent has to deal with more variables than before. In this sense, the study of economic networking theory has become more important for development economists. The topics addressed by this paper are some of the basic analytical issues in the general-equilibrium theory of economic networks. As will be seen later, the results presented here provide a systematic approach for computation of general equilibria and for identification of equilibrium network structures.

As pioneers in applying inframarginal analysis to increasing-returns -to-scale economic models, Xiaokai Yang and Yew Kwang Ng, together with many of their colleagues, have made a series of helpful contributions to the general-equilibrium theory of division of labor and economic networking theory (e.g., Yang and Ng, 1998; Wen, 1998a, b; Ng, 2001). They have investigated many typical examples, with interesting results. For example, they have shown that, as the transaction costs in an economy became sufficiently low, a higher level of division of labor should lead to a higher-efficiency general equilibrium.

To concentrate on the relationship between economic efficiency and specialization, in most of their examples Yang and his colleagues consider simple models with a population of identical individuals and with a limited number of goods. The most interesting feature of the general equilibria of these examples is that, when the transaction costs are low, the ex-ante identical individuals, aiming at utility maximization, divide themselves into several groups, each group choosing a different "configuration" and trading with the other groups of individuals. Such a configuration is characterized by the subset of goods to be produced, the subset of goods to be sold, and the subset of goods to be bought.

In the Yang–Ng framework, determining the different basic configurations is the most important step in both the equilibrium existence proof and the equilibrium computation (Sun et al., 2000). In this respect, the following result—referred to as the "Wen theorem" by Yang and his colleagues (Yang, 2001), plays a very important role: *In any Walrasian market with any price vector given, any rational agent with convex production technique will never sell more than one of her produces, and will never simultaneously produce and buy the same good.* With the help of this, they can divide the population of ex-ante identical agents into several groups, each consisting of those selling one single good. They can then compute an equilibrium at which all agents in the same group choose the same optimal decision, and a trading network is formed.

However, as I will show in the next section, what Mei Wen proved (1998a, p. 170-85; and 1998b) does not have the general implications mentioned above. Moreover, some of her claims appear to be false.

2. Wen's Result and a Counter Example

What is referred to as the Wen theorem is her following result in Wen (1998a):

Consider an economy E with a population of individuals and a finite number of goods and with the presence of transaction costs. Assume that the following assumptions hold. (1) Every individual in E has a strictly quasi-concave and twice continuously differentiable utility function. (2) The production function f_i of every individual i satisfies either (2i) $f_i'(\cdot) > 0$, $f_i''(\cdot) > 0$, and f_i'' is continuous for $l_i > 0$; or (2ii) $f_i(l_i) = a_i l_i - b_i$, where a_i, $b_i > 0$. (3) Every transaction function has positive first derivative and nonnegative second derivative in the whole domain. Then given any price vector p for the goods, the optimal decision of any individual does not involve buying and selling the same good, does not involve selling more than one good, and does not involve self-providing and buying the same good.

In Wen's proof, her arguments under assumption (2i) are correct, but the requirements in (2i) are too strong. Actually, in order to derive the consequences we need only assume the strict convexity of the production functions (see later). It is well known that production functions with positive second derivative in the whole domain just form an extremely tiny subset of the set of strictly convex production functions. In most of the examples studied by Yang, Ng, and their colleagues, the conditions in (2i) were not satisfied, and Wen's result was inappropriately applied.

With regard to Wen's assumption (2ii), what Wen should have used is the following functional form:

$$f_i(l_i) = \max\{0, a_i l_i - b_i\};$$

otherwise the meaning of negative quantities of the produce needs to be explained. The main reason for Wen to choose the functional form in (2ii) seems to be that the inverse of the production function is required in her arguments for not involving buying and selling the same good (Wen, 1998a, p. 174). But under her assumption that the transaction efficiency k' is below 1, claim 1 in her analysis could be easily established without using the existence of the inverse production function.

Wen's claim 2 (selling one good at most) is not correct under assumption (2ii). In her arguments for claim 2, she did pay attention to (2ii). However, in discussing the sign of $p_j a_j - p_k a_k$ she ignored the case of $p_j a_j - p_k a_k = 0$, and it is then that claim 2 is false!

Let us turn to Wen's claim 3 (not self-providing and buying the same good). On the one hand her argument relies on the conclusion of claim 2, which is false under assumption (2ii). On the other hand, to establish the consequence, she requires the strict inequality:

$$X_j''(l) = f_j''(l) + \left(\frac{p_{i0}}{p_j} f_{i0}'(\overline{l} - l)\right)^2 k_j'' + \frac{p_{i0}}{p_j} k_j' f_{i0}''(\overline{l} - l) > 0.$$

The inequality could be false for a weakly convex transaction function k_j under assumption (2ii) (where all the $f_j'' = 0$), because $k_j'' = 0$ will lead to $X_j''(l) = 0$. Thus Wen's arguments in claim 3 are only good for the case under assumption (2i).

A counter example

To see that Wen's claim 2 is false under her assumption (2ii), let us consider an economy E with four goods $\{1, 2, 3, 4\}$ and a set of agents I. Assume that one of the agents has an initial endowment of 1 unit of labor, and has the same utility function given by $u(w, x, y, z) = wxyz$, where w, x, y, and z are, respectively, the quantities of good 1, good 2, good 3, and good 4 she consumes. Assume that this agent has a set of production functions $q_j = \max\{0, L_j - 0.1\}$, $j = 1, 2$ and $q_j = \max\{0, L_k - 0.6\}$, $k = 3$, 4. Here L_j is the amount of labor allocated for good j's production, and L_k is the amount of labor for good k's production. Finally assume that, because of the presence of the transaction costs, when this agent buys y_j units of any good j, the amount she actually receives is $0.6y_j$. Let us imagine that a price vector $p = (2, 2, 1, 1)$ is announced by the referee. We look at the optimal decision of this agent. If she chooses autarky, because of the fixed learning costs, she can never produce these four goods simultaneously all in positive amounts. As a result her maximal utility in an autarky is 0. On the other hand, if she wants to trade, in view of her production technology and the market prices she should never produce good 3 or good 4; instead she should produce good 1 or good 2 or both, selling part of her produces in exchange for the other two goods.

We first consider the case in which she produces good 1 only. We may assume that she allocates all her labor towards good 1 production, producing 0.9 units of good 1, then selling x units of good 1 for buying good 2, selling y units of good 1 again for buying good 3, and selling y units of good 1 again for buying good 4. Because of the transaction costs, she will consume $0.9 - x - 2y$ units of good 1, $0.6x$ units of good 2, and $0.6(2y)$ units of each of the other two goods. As a result she gets a utility of $u = (0.9 - x - 2y)(0.6x)(1.2y)^2$. By elementary calculus it is easy to verify that her utility is maximized at $x = 9/40$ and $y = 9/40$. The maximal utility in this case is $4(0.6)^3(9/40)^4 = 0.00221$.

The second case is that she produces good 2 only. By symmetry it is easy to see that her maximal utility in this case is also $4(0.6)^3(9/40)^4$.

Now consider the third case in which this agent produces both good 1 and good 2. In view of her production technique and the transaction costs, when these two goods are produced she will no longer buy one of them by selling the other; i.e., her consumption of these two goods will be all self-provided. On the other hand, she will sell part of her produce for buying good 3 and good 4. By symmetry, she does not care which good she sells as long as she has sufficient of it left for self-consumption. Let us assume that she self-consumes x units of each of good 1 and good 2. Since she can produce 0.8 units of these two goods as a whole, she will sell $0.8 - 2x$ units of them in the market, which is sufficient for buying

0.8 − 2x of each of the other two goods. (Note that the price of good 1 or good 2 is twice as high as that of good 3 or good 4.) Because of the transaction costs, her utility will be $u = x^2[0.6(0.8-2x)]^2$, which is maximized at $x = 0.2$. The maximal utility is $(0.2)^2(0.24)^2 = 0.00230$. Compared with the first two cases, this case gives the highest utility she can achieve.

To sum up, with the price vector $p = (2, 2, 1, 1)$ given, this agent has a continuum of different optimal decisions: allocating l units of labor for good 1's production and $1 - l$ units of labor for good 2's production ($0.3 \leq l \leq 0.7$), keeping 0.2 units of good 1 and 0.2 units of good 2 for self-consumption, selling all the remainder of them for buying 0.4 units of each of good 3 and good 4. In particular, when $l = 0.5$, she sells 0.2 units of each of good 1 and good 2. Thus Wen theorem does not hold in this example.

3.   Revised Theorems

Although most readers may be familiar with the definitions and properties of weakly convex functions and strictly convex functions, for convenience I present a brief review here. For more details refer to Stromberg (1981), for example.

Definition 1:   A function f: $[0, 1] \rightarrow \mathbf{R}$ is said to be *weakly convex*[1] if, for any x, $x' \in [0,1]$, $x < x'$ and any $\lambda \in (0, 1)$:

$$f\left(\lambda x + (1-\lambda)x'\right) \leq \lambda f(x) + (1-\lambda)f(x').\tag{1}$$

Moreover, f is said to be *strictly convex* if in the above inequality the sign "$\leq$" is replaced with "$<$".

Proposition 1:   *Assume that f: $[0, 1] \rightarrow \mathbf{R}$ is weakly convex. Then for any $x \in [0, 1]$, $\Delta x > 0$, and $a > 0$ such that $x + a + \Delta x \leq 1$, it holds that*

$$\frac{f(x+a+\Delta x) - f(x+a)}{\Delta x} \geq \frac{f(x+a) - f(x)}{a}.\tag{2}$$

---

[1] Note that linear functions are included in the class of weakly convex functions.

Moreover, if f is strictly convex, then the above inequality holds with "$\geq$" replaced by "$>$".

Proof: Choose $\lambda = \Delta x / (a + \Delta x)$ and $x' = x + a + \Delta x$ in (1). It is easy to verify that $1 - \lambda = a / (a + \Delta x)$ and that $\lambda x + (1 - \lambda) x' = x + a$. As a result we have

$$f(x+a) \leq \frac{\Delta x}{a + \Delta x} f(x) + \frac{a}{a + \Delta x} f(x + a + \Delta x). \qquad (3)$$

On multiplying both sides of (3) by $(a + \Delta x)$ and re-arranging terms, we obtain

$$a\left[f(x + a + \Delta x) - f(x + a) \right] \geq \Delta x \left[f(x + a) - f(x) \right]. \qquad (4)$$

On dividing both sides of (4) by $a\Delta x$, (2) thus follows.

We now consider a Walrasian market with m goods. Assume that a price vector $p \gg 0$ for all these goods is given. Assume that an agent is endowed with 1 unit of labor. A decision by her consists of $3m$ nonnegative variables: L_j, Δx_j, Δy_j, $j = 1, ..., m$, where L_j is the amount of labor she allocates for good j's production, Δx_j is the amount of good j she sells, and Δy_j is the amount of good j she buys. We will denote by f_j her production function for good j, and by g_j her transaction function for good j. Assume that this agent has a continuous utility function given by $u = u(z_1, ..., z_m)$, where z_j is the amount of good j she consumes.

Statement of Theorem 1

Consider a Walrasian market with m goods with or without transaction costs; i.e., $g_j(y_j) < y_j$ or $g_j(y_j) = y_j$, respectively. Assume that the utility function U is continuous and is nondecreasing in each of the variables. Assume that the production functions f_j are all defined and weakly convex on $[0,1]$. Then for any given price vector $p \gg 0$, the maximal utility $U(p)$ for this agent *can always be achieved* by a decision to sell no more than one good. Moreover, if u is strictly increasing in each of the variables and all the f_j are strictly convex on $[0,1]$, then any utility-maximization decision made by her *must* involve no more than one good being sold.

Proof of Theorem 1

First consider the case that u is nondecreasing and the f_j are weakly convex. Assume that u is maximized by a decision in which there are two or more goods being sold. It suffices to show that this agent can reduce the number of goods sold and still achieve the same maximal utility.

Assume that originally good 1 and good 2 are sold by her. Let L_1 and L_2, respectively, be the amounts of labor she allocates for the production of these two goods. Let x_1 and x_2, respectively, be the quantities of these two goods produced. Let Δx_1 and Δx_2, respectively, be the amounts of them being sold. Let l_j be the amount of labor satisfying

$$f_j\left(l_j\right) = x_j - \Delta x_j, \quad j = 1,2 \,. \text{ Let } \Delta l_j = L_j - l_j \,.$$

We then have

$$\Delta x_j = f_j\left(l_j + \Delta l_j\right) - f_j\left(l_j\right), \quad j = 1,2 \,. \tag{5}$$

Let p_j be the price of good j. Then the contribution to the budget by selling these two goods is

$$\sum_{j=1}^{2} p_j \left[f_j\left(l_j + \Delta l_j\right) - f_j\left(l_j\right) \right] = k_1 \Delta l_1 + k_2 \Delta l_2 \,, \tag{6}$$

where

$$k_j = \frac{p_j \left[f_j\left(l_j + \Delta l_j\right) - f_j\left(l_j\right) \right]}{\Delta l_j} \,. \tag{7}$$

Proof of the first part of the theorem: It suffices to show that this agent can achieve a looser (or at least not tighter) budget for buying through reallocating labor on the production of these two goods, selling just one of them but not changing the self-consumed amounts of each, and not changing the *other part* of her decision on production and selling of the other goods (if any). We need to consider two different cases.

Case (i): $k_1 \le k_2$

In this case we will consider her decision to sell good 2 only. Imagine that she now allocates just l_1 units of labor for good 1's production, producing $x_1 - \Delta x_1$ units of good 1 all for self-consumption; and she allocates $l_2 + \Delta l_2 + \Delta l_1$ units of labor on good 2's production, consuming the same amount $x_2 - \Delta x_2 = f_2(l_2)$ as before. By selling the other part of good 2, she receives an amount of money

$$p_2\left[f_2\left(l_2 + \Delta l_2 + \Delta l_1\right) - f_2\left(l_2\right)\right]$$

$$= p_2\left[f_2\left(l_2 + \Delta l_2 + \Delta l_1\right) - f_2\left(l_2 + \Delta l_2\right)\right] + p_2\left[f_2\left(l_2 + \Delta l_2\right) - f_2\left(l_2\right)\right]$$

$$= \Delta l_1 \frac{p_2\left[f_2\left(l_2 + \Delta l_2 + \Delta l_1\right) - f_2\left(l_2 + \Delta l_2\right)\right]}{\Delta l_1}$$

$$+ \Delta l_2 \frac{p_2\left[f_2\left(l_2 + \Delta l_2\right) - f_2\left(l_2\right)\right]}{\Delta l_2}$$

$$\ge \left(\Delta l_2 + \Delta l_1\right) \frac{p_2\left[f_2\left(l_2 + \Delta l_2\right) - f_2\left(l_2\right)\right]}{\Delta l_2} = \left(\Delta l_2 + \Delta l_1\right) k_2$$

$$\ge k_1 \Delta l_1 + k_2 \Delta l_2.$$

Thus we can see by selling good 2 only, she can really guarantee a budget at least as good as before, and, as a result, she can achieve a utility either greater than or at least equal to the original one. Note that, in deriving the above inequality, Proposition 1 was applied to obtain

$$\frac{p_2\left[f_2\left(l_2 + \Delta l_2 + \Delta l_1\right) - f_2\left(l_2 + \Delta l_2\right)\right]}{\Delta l_1} \ge \frac{p_2\left[f_2\left(l_2 + \Delta l_2\right) - f_2\left(l_2\right)\right]}{\Delta l_2} = k_2 . (8)$$

Case (ii): $k_1 > k_2$

In this case we consider her decision to sell good 1 only. Assume that she allocates $l_1 + \Delta l_1 + \Delta l_2$ units of labor for good 1's production, and l_2 units of labor for good 2's production. Using a very similar argument to that for case (i), we can conclude that by selling good 1 only, she can guarantee a *looser* budget and can achieve a *higher* utility.[2]

---

[2] Note that, unlike in case (i), here we have a strict inequality $k_1 > k_2$.

334   S. Yao

On combining cases (i) and (ii), the first part of the theorem is proved.

Proof of the second part of the theorem: Simply note that when strict convexity is assumed, the expression (8) becomes a strict inequality. As a result, this agent can always achieve a higher budget by reducing the number of goods sold. She can thus buy more and consumes more. In view of the strictly increasing property of her utility function, she can thus achieve a higher utility.

Statement of Theorem 2

Consider a Walrasian market with m goods as described in Theorem 1. Assume that all the transaction functions g_j are weakly convex (including the linear case). If all the f_j of the agent are weakly convex and her utility function u is nondecreasing in each of the variables, then for any given price vector $p \gg 0$ her maximal utility $U(p)$ *can be always achieved* by a decision to not buy and produce the same good simultaneously. Moreover, if the f_j are strictly convex and u is strictly increasing in each variable, then any utility-maximization decision by her *must not* allow any good being simultaneously produced and purchased.

Proof of Theorem 2

Proof of the first part of the theorem: Assume that p is given, and that in her utility-maximization decision the agent produces and purchases good 1 simultaneously. According to Theorem 1, we may assume she sells just one good, say good 2. (Obviously in any case there is no need for her to sell and buy the same good.) Let p_j be the market price of good j. Let $x_1 = f_1(l_1)$ be the amount of good 1 she produces for herself. Let y_1 be the amount of good 1 she buys. Let $x_2 = f_2(l_2 + \Delta l_2)$ be the amount of good 2 she produces, and $x_2 - \Delta x_2 = f(l_2)$ be the amount of good 2 she would just require if she had no need to buy y_1 units of good 1. Thus Δl_2 is the amount of labor she can save if she does not buy good 1. We then have

$$y_1 = (p_2/p_1)\left[f_2\left(l_2 + \Delta l_2\right) - f_2\left(l_2\right)\right]. \tag{9}$$

Because of the presence of the transaction costs, the actual amount of good 1 she receives from the market is

$$\Delta x_1 = g_1\left(\frac{p_2}{p_1}\left[f_2\left(l_2 + \Delta l_2\right) - f_2\left(l_2\right)\right]\right). \tag{10}$$

Let us fix l_2 and define $h(x) = g_1((p_2/p_1)[f_2(l_2 + x) - f_2(l_2)])$. Note that h is a weakly convex function; this is because $f_2(l_2 + x)$ is weakly convex and increasing in x, and $(p_2/p_1)[f_2(l_2 + x) - f_2(l_2)]$ is linear in $f_2(l_2 + x)$ and hence weakly convex and increasing in x. As a composite function of two weakly convex increasing functions, h is also weakly convex.

With our new notation we can write

$$\Delta x_1 = h\left(\Delta l_2\right), \tag{11}$$

and consider the following two new decision options of the agent.

In option (i), she saves Δl_2 units of labor from the production of good 2, not selling Δx_2 units of good 2 to exchange for good 1 but adding the saved amount of labor Δl_2 to l_1 for good 1's production. As a result she will consume $f_1(l_1 + \Delta l_2)$ units of good 1 and the same amounts of good 2 and all the other goods as before.

In option (ii), she does not produce good 1 at all, adding l_1 units of labor saved to $l_2 + \Delta l_2$ for good 2 production, selling $f_2(l_2 + \Delta l_2 + l_1) - f_2(l_2)$ units of good 2 to exchange for good 1. As a result she will consume $h(\Delta l_2 + l_1)$ units of good 1 and the same amounts of good 2 and all the other goods as before.

The first part of the theorem will be proved if we can show that at least one of $f_1(l_1 + \Delta l_2)$ and $h(\Delta l_2 + l_1)$ is not less than $f_1(l_1) + h(\Delta l_2)$, which is the original amount of good 1 she consumes. Define k_1 and k_2 by

$$k_1 = \frac{f_1(l_1)}{l_1}, \qquad k_2 = \frac{h(\Delta l_2)}{\Delta l_2} = \frac{h(\Delta l_2) - h(0)}{\Delta l_2}, \tag{12}$$

where we have used the fact that $h(0) = 0$.

We first consider the case $k_1 \geq k_2$. With the help of Proposition 1 we have

$$f_1(l_1 + \Delta l_2) = \frac{f_1(L_1 + \Delta l_2) - f_1(l_1)}{\Delta l_2} \Delta l_2 + \frac{f_1(l_1)}{l_1} l_1$$

$$\geq k_1(\Delta l_2 + l_1) \geq k_1 l_1 + k_2 \Delta l_2 = f_1(l_1) + h(\Delta l_2),$$

which implies that the new option (i) is better than (or at least not worse than) her old decision.

We now consider the case $k_2 > k_1$. We have

$$h(\Delta l_2 + l_1) = \frac{h(\Delta l_2 + l_1) - h(\Delta l_2)}{l_1} l_1 + h(\Delta l_2)$$

$$\geq \frac{h(\Delta l_2) - h(0)}{\Delta l_2} l_1 + h(\Delta l_2)$$

$$= k_2 l_1 + h(\Delta l_2) > k_1 l_1 + h(\Delta l_2) = f_1(l_1) + h(\Delta l_2),$$

which implies that option (ii) is better than her old decision. As a result, the first part of Theorem 2 is proved.

Proof of the second part of the theorem: Simply note that the strict convexity of the production functions implies the strict convexity of h. As a result either option (i) or (ii) will lead to a higher amount of good 1 being consumed than in her original decision.

4.   Equilibrium Computation and Network Formation

In most published computed examples of general-equilibrium models of a pure exchange economy, the convexity of the consumption sets is assumed and the agents' preferences are assumed to be strictly quasiconcave. With such assumptions, given any price vector, each individual has but a unique optimal decision. To compute the optimal decision of every individual in terms of the prices, an equilibrium price vector can be then determined by the market-clearing conditions. In all these examples, net trade occurs only between ex-ante different agents, either because they have different utility functions, or because they have different initial endowments. In Walrasian models where the convexity of the consumption sets or the convexity of the production sets is lacking, although equilibrium existence can still be established for large economies with the *convexification* idea, no systematic computation method has been proposed. The difficulty is that, given any price vector, an agent usually has quite a few different optimal decisions, all leading to the same maximal utility, but any convex combination of these decisions is no longer feasible to her. On the other hand, if all ex-ante identical agents in the population choose the same optimal decision, the market would not be cleared. As a result, a general equilibrium can be achieved only when the mass of ex-ante identical agents divide into several groups, each group with a suitable measure, and when agents in different groups choose different optimal decisions. An important feature of these economic models is that net trades may occur between ex-ante identical agents.

The importance of the Wen theorem is that it provides a systematic approach for the equilibrium computation where convexity is lacking and convexification is required. To explain the application of the two new theorems established in the last section, I next consider a large economy E with m goods and a continuum set $I = [0, 1]$ of ex-ante identical consumer–producers, each being endowed with 1 unit of labor. I will use the same notations as before, f_j for the production functions, g_j for the transaction functions, and u for the utility function. Denote by L^i_j the labor units that i allocates for good j's production, by x^i_j the amount of good j that i sells, and by y^i_j the amount of good j that i buys. We will assume weak convexity of the production functions, linearity of the transaction functions, and a continuous and nondecreasing utility function. In addition we also assume the following property of u: for any given j and any given $z_1 > 0, \ldots, z_{j-1} > 0, z_{j+1} > 0, \ldots, z_m > 0$, it holds that

$$\lim_{z_j \to \infty} u\left(z_1, \ldots, z_{j-1}, z_j, z_{j+1}, \ldots, z_m\right) = \infty . \tag{13}$$

It is easy to see that, as a special example, the Cobb-Douglas utility functions satisfy all the requirements mentioned here.

Definition 2: Given a large economy E as described above, a price vector $p \gg 0$ together with a decision

$$d^i = (L^i_j, x^i_j, y^i_j : j = 1, \ldots, m)$$

for each and every agent i $\in$ I is said to be a Walrasian equilibrium of E if (i) the decision of every consumer–producer is a utility-maximizing decision under p, and (ii) the market for every good is cleared under p and the abovementioned individuals' decisions.

While the existence of a Walrasian equilibrium is an easy consequence following the idea of the classical equilibrium theory for large economies with the convexification trick (Zhou et al., 1999; Hildenbrand, 1974), the computation problem, as mentioned above, has never been systematically addressed before. The existence proof itself does not provide any computational approach. On the other hand, the *revised* Wen theorems do provide a systematic approach for equilibrium computation. The general algorithm consists of three steps:

(i) Divide the population of agents into m groups with the measure of the mass w_j in group j to be determined later. Assume that every agent in group j is allowed to sell good j only if she does want to sell anything. (She is allowed, however, to produce any good and buy any good.) Assume that all the agents in the same group choose the same optimal decision, and compute a *constrained* optimal decision $d_j(p)$ and the constrained maximal utility $U_j(p)$ for every member in each group j in terms of the prices $(p_1, \ldots, p_m)$. Here we use the word "constrained" because each agent in group j is allowed to sell good j only.

(ii) Compute a price vector p^* which equates the maximal utilities of the agents across all different groups:

$$U_1(p^*) = \ldots = U_m(p^*) = U(p^*).$$

(iii) Determine the measure of the mass $w^*_j \geq 0$ of each group by the market-clearing conditions under the price vector p^*. (Note that $w^*_j = 0$ means that no agents are in group j, and good j is not sold in the market although it may still be produced.)

Proposition 2:   Assume that the price vector p^* and the weights w^*_j have been computed in the above algorithm. Then p^* together with the

$d^*_j \equiv d_j(p^*)$ (chosen by every agent in group j) is a Walrasian equilibrium.[3]

Proof: The maximal utility $U(p^*)$ that every agent receives in the above algorithm is under the constraint that she is allowed to sell only one specific good. We need to show that this is actually the maximal utility she can achieve under p^* even if such a constraint is removed. In fact, according to Theorem 1, given p^*, it is always possible for her to achieve the (unconstrained) maximal utility $\bar{U}$ by choosing a decision to sell no more than one good. Let this be good j; then $\bar{U} = U_j(p^*) = U(p^*)$. The result of Proposition 3 thus follows.

The trade network of this Walrasian equilibrium can be constructed in the following procedure:

(a) *Vertices.* Assume that at the abovementioned equilibrium, I is divided into m groups: $I = G_1 \cup ... \cup G_m$, but only the first n groups are of positive measure, which means that at the equilibrium only the first n goods are traded. To construct the network, we first draw n vertices $v_1,...,v_n$, each denoted by a small circle, with v_j representing group j. Inside the small circle of each vertex we put w^*_j, which is the measure of the mass of agents in group j ($j = 1, \ldots, n$).

(b) *Reflexive arcs.* If each of the members in group j produces amount x^j_h of good h for self-consumption, then an arc jj labeled with h is constructed, starting from and ending at the same vertex v_j.

(c) *Nonreflexive arcs.* If each of the members in group j buys an amount y^j_k of good k, then an arc kh labeled with k is constructed, starting from vertex v_k and ending at vertex v_j.

---

[3] For the general existence proof *of* the p^* and the w^*_j, refer to Sun et al. (1999).

Thus the equilibrium network structure constructed above is a weighted digraph. I explain all the details of equilibrium computation and network construction with a simple example in the next section.

5. A Simple Example

Consider a large economy E with three goods $\{1, 2, 3\}$ and a continuum of ex-ante identical agents $I = [0, 1]$. Each agent is endowed with 1 unit of labor. The production functions of each agent are given by $f_j(L_j) = L_j$, $j = 1, 2$, and $f_3(L_3) = \max\{0, L_3 - 0.5\}$. The transaction functions are given by $g_j(y_j) = ky_j$, $j = 1, 2, 3$, $k \in [0,1]$. The utility function for every agent is given by $u(z_1, z_2, z_3) = z_1 z_2 z_3$. With the symmetry in good 1 and good 2, one can expect that the equilibrium price vector has the form of $(1, 1, p)$. According to the revised Wen theorems, we can divide the population into three groups: G_1, G_2, and G_3, with agents in each G_j selling only good j (if they sell anything at all) and not simultaneously producing and buying the same good. Assume that the measures of masses in group j is w_j. By symmetry we may assume $w_1 = w_2 = w$, and $w_3 = 1 - 2w$. The value of w will be determined in the final stage.

Under the price vector $(1, 1, p)$, consider the decision of any agent in group G_1. She may choose autarky, allocating l units of labor for the production of each of good 1 and good 2, and $1 - 2l$ units of labor for the production of good 3, achieving a utility of $u = l^2(0.5 - 2l)$. By elementary calculus it is easy to verify that the best she can do in an autarky structure is to choose $l = 1/6$, so $1 - 2l = 4/6$, yielding a utility of $1/216$.

The second option for the agent is to produce and sell part of good 1, to self-provide good 2, and to buy good 3 from the market. Assume that she allocates l units of labor for good 1's production and $1 - l$ units of labor for good 2's production, selling x units of good 1 in order to buy x/p units of good 3. Her utility is then $u = (l - x)(1 - l)(kx/p)$, which is maximized at $l = 2/3$ and $x = 1/3$. The maximal utility is $k/27p$.

The third option for the agent is to produce and sell part of good 1, to self-provide good 3, and to buy good 2. Assume that she allocates l units of labor for good 1's production and $1 - l$ units of labor for good 3's production, selling x units of good 1 in order to buy x units of good 2.

Her utility is then $u = (l - x)(kx)(0.5 - l)$, which is maximized at $l = 1/3$ and $x = 1/6$. The maximal utility is $k/216$, which is not greater than the maximal utility in autarky no matter what value k assumes.

The last option is to produce and sell part of good 1, and to buy both good 2 and good 3. Assuming she sells x units of good 1, buying y_2 units of good 2 and y_3 units of good 3. The budget constraint is $x = y_2 + py_3$. If we write $y = y_2$, then $y_3 = (x - y)/p$. Her utility is $u = (1 - x)(ky)[k(x - y)/p]$, which is maximized at $x = 2/3$ and $y = 1/3$. The maximal utility is $k^2/27p$, which is not greater than the maximal utility in the second option no matter what value k assumes.

To sum up, we have:

(a) Any agent in group 1 will choose autarky if $k/p < 1/8$, and choose the second option if $k/p > 1/8$.

  (By symmetry)

(b) Any agent in group 2 will choose autarky if $k/p < 1/8$, and choose self-providing good 1 and buying good 3 if $k/p > 1/8$.

Now consider the decision of any agent in group 3. If she chooses autarky, her maximal utility is $1/216$. If she produces and sells part of good 3, self-provides good 1, and buys good 2, she has a utility of $u = (1 - l)(kpx)(l - 0.5 - x)$, where l is the amount of labor allocated for good 3's production, $1 - l$ is the amount of labor allocated for good 1's production, and x is the amount of good 3 she sells in order to buy px units of good 2. The maximal utility is $kp/216$, achieved at $l = 5/6$ and $x = 1/6$. If she produces and sells part of good 3, self-provides good 2, and buys good 1, she ends up with the same maximal utility.

Finally she may produce good 3 only and buy both good 1 and good 2. Let x be the amount of good 3 she sells, y the amount of good 1 she buys; then $(px - y)$ is the amount of good 2 she buys. Her utility is then $u = ky[k(px - y)](0.5 - x)$, which is maximized at $x = 1/3$ and $y = p/6$. The maximal utility is $(kp)^2/216$.

To sum up, we have:

(c) Any agent in group 3 will choose the autarky if $kp < 1$, and choose the last option (buying both good 1 and good 2) if $kp > 1$.

342   *S. Yao*

If trade does occur among the three groups, at any equilibrium, individuals across all groups must have the same maximal utility, otherwise there is an incentive for individuals of some group to switch to another group. Thus, comparing (a) and (b) with (c), any equilibrium price vector for an active trade market must equate $k/27p$ with $(kp)^2/216$, from which one can solve $p = 2/k^{1/3}$, which is the equilibrium price for good 3.

Now it is not difficult to verify that, with the equilibrium price vector $(1, 1, 2/k^{1/3})$:

1. If $k < 1/\sqrt{8}$, we have both $k/p < 1/8$ and $kp < 1$, and the only Walrasian equilibrium network is the autarky structure.

2. If $k > 1/\sqrt{8}$, we have both $k/p > 1/8$ and $kp > 1$, and one Walrasian equilibrium network is with three vertices v_1, v_2, and v_3. In v_1, every agent produces $2/3$ units of good 1 and $1/3$ units of good 2, selling $1/3$ units of good 1 in order to buy $k^{1/3}/6$ units of good 3. In v_2, each agent produces $1/3$ units of good 1 and $2/3$ units of good 2, selling $1/3$ units of good 2 in order to buy $k^{1/3}/6$ units of good 3. In v_3 each agent allocates all her labor for good 3's production, producing 0.5 units of good 3, selling $1/3$ units of it in order to buy $p/6$ units of each of good 1 and good 2. Finally to determine the measure of the mass of each group, we use the market-clearing condition, say for good 3: $(1 - 2w)(1/3) = 2 \times w \ (k^{1/3}/6)$. We thus obtain $w = 1/(2 + k^{1/3})$.

3. In particular, when the transaction costs for good 3 is zero ($k = 1$), the equilibrium price vector is (1, 1, 2), the measures of the masses in the three groups are all equal to 1/3, and the equilibrium utility for every agent is 1/54—four times as large as the maximal utility from autarky!

The equilibrium structures are depicted in Figure 1.

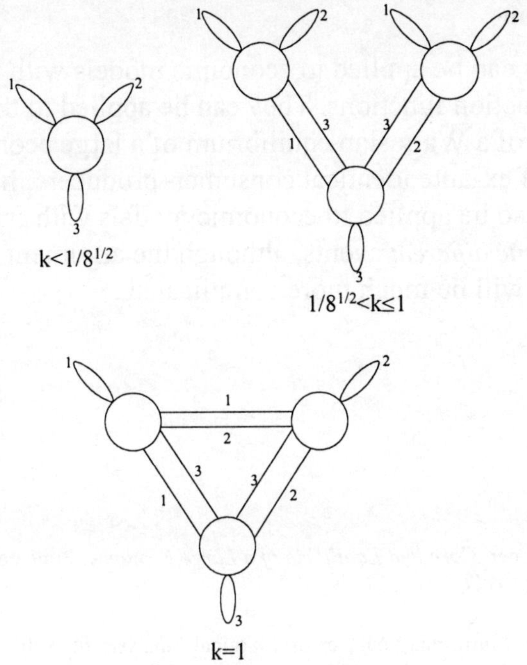

Figure 1: The Equilibrium Network Structures

It is interesting to note that, in the final two equilibrium structures, the costs of high production technology (or high fixed learning costs) paid by the good 3 producers are compensated by the high equilibrium price they receive for their produce.

Remarks. (i) In this example we do not have an equilibrium structure with complete division of labor for any $k < 1$, which results from the linearity of the production functions for good 1 and good 2. In fact it is not rational to sell one of them to buy another, unless the transaction cost is 0. (ii) In most of situations there is no unique equilibrium structure.

6. Conclusion

These results can be applied to economic models with weakly convex production functions. They can be applied to the computation of a Walrasian equilibrium of a large economy with a continuum of ex-ante identical consumer–producers. In fact the results can also be applied to economic models with finitely many types of *ex-ante different* agents, although the argument and the computation will be much more complicated.

References

Hildenbrand, Werner, *Core and Equilibria of a Large Economy,* Princeton, NJ: Princeton University Press (1974).

Ng, Yew-Kwang, "Infra-marginal versus Marginal Analysis of Networking Decisions and E-Commerce," a speech at the International Symposium of E-Commerce and Networking Decisions, Monash University (2001).

Stromberg, Karl R., *An Introduction to Classical Real Analysis,* Dordrecht: Kluwer (1981).

Sun, Yang, and Yao, "Theoretical Foundation of Economic Development Based on Networking Decisions in the Competitive Market," Harvard Center for International Development working paper 17 (1999).

Wen, Mei, "An Analytical Framework of Consumer-Producers, Economies of Specialization and Transaction Costs," in Arrow, Ng, and Yang (eds), *Increasing Returns and Economic Analysis,* London: Macmillan (1998a):170-85.

—, "The Dichotomy between Production and Consumption Decisions and Economic Efficiency," University *of* Melbourne Economics Department working paper (1998b).

Yang, Xiaokai and Siang Ng, "Specialization and Division of Labor: A Survey," in Arrow, Ng, and Yang (eds), *Increasing Returns and Economic Analysis,* London: Macmillan (1998):3-63.

Yang, Xiaokai and Yimin Zhao, "Endogenous Transaction Costs and Evolution of Division of Labor," Monash University Economics Department working paper (1998).

Zhou, Sun, and Yang, "General Equilibrium in Large Economies with Endogenous Structure of Division of Labor", Monash University Economics Department working paper (1998).

Part 6

Inframarginal Analysis of Trade Policy, Dual Structures, and Globalization

CHAPTER 16

GLOBALIZATION, DUAL ECONOMY, AND ECONOMIC DEVELOPMENT[*]

Jeffrey Sachs[a], Xiaokai Yang[b] and Dingsheng Zhang[c]

[a]*Harvard University*   [b]*Harvard and Monash University*   [c]*Wuhan and Monash University*

1. Introduction

The purpose of this paper is threefold. First we introduce endogenous comparative advantage into the Ricardo model with exogenous comparative advantage to show that a dual structure with underemployment in a less developed economy can occur as a general equilibrium phenomenon in the transitional stage of economic development. Here, dual economy implies not only unequal distribution of gains from trade between the developed and less developed economies, but also a dual structure of commercialized sector and self-sufficient sector in the less developed economy. Those self-sufficient individuals look like in underemployment. They have low productivity and cannot find jobs to work for the market. We will show that China's WTO membership might not benefit China if China's trading efficiency is low due to the absence of further institutional reforms and that China can gain a lot if WTO membership promotes further reforms to increase its trading efficiency.

Second, we use inframarginal analysis, which is total cost-benefit analysis across corner solutions in addition to marginal analysis of each

---

[*] Reprinted from *China Economic Review*, 11(2), Jeffrey Sachs, Xiaokai Yang, and Dingsheng Zhang, "Globalization, Dual Economy, and Economic Development," 189-209, 2000, with permission from Elsevier.

corner solution, to show that deteriorated terms of trade for a country may be associated with increasing gains that this country receives from trade if productivity gains generated by expanding network of division of labor more than compensate the deteriorated terms of trade.[1]

Finally, we will examine implications of the coexistence of exogenous and endogenous comparative advantages for China's pattern of trade. Let us motivate the three tasks one by one.

Yang (1994) and Yang and Borland (1991) have drawn the distinction between David Ricardo's exogenous comparative advantage (Ricardo, 1817) and Adam Smith's endogenous comparative advantage (Smith, 1776).[2] There is an extensive literature on exogenous comparative advantage in trade theory (see, for instance, Dixit & Norman, 1980). Separately, there are many models of endogenous comparative advantage in the growing literature on endogenous specialization (see Yang & Ng, 1998 for a recent survey on this literature and references there). The current paper develops a general equilibrium model with both endogenous and exogenous comparative advantages. The coexistence of endogenous and exogenous comparative advantage may provide a general equilibrium mechanism for explaining phenomena of underdevelopment and dual structure with underemployment in a transitional stage of economic development.

Lewis (1955) noted development implications of dual structure of commercialized versus noncommercialized sectors and evolution of

---

[1] The essence of the inframarginal approach can be found in Coase (1946, 1960). Coase (1946) noted "a consumer does not only have to decide whether to consume additional units of a product; he has also to decide whether it is worth his while to consume the product at all rather than spend his money in some other direction" (p.173). Hence, marginal cost pricing is not applicable to a good with increasing returns in production. Buchanan and Stubblebine (1962) introduced the concept of inframarginal externality, which is an early application of the inframarginal analysis in welfare economics. Formally, the inframarginal analysis is associated with nonlinear or linear programming, while marginal analysis is associated with classical mathematical programming. Other applications of the inframarginal analysis can be found in Becker (1981), Dixit (1987, 1989), Grossman and Hart (1986), Rosen (1977, 1983), and Yang and Ng (1998).

[2] Endogenous comparative advantage is associated with economies of specialization and referred to by Grossman and Helpman (1990) as acquired comparative advantage, whereas exogenous comparative advantage is associated with constant returns to scale in production, referred to by them as natural comparative advantage.

commercialization. Therefore, Ranis (1988, p. 80) emphasizes that the real guiding principle of organizational dualism is "commercialized" versus "noncommercialized" rather than "agricultural" versus "nonagricultural." But Lewis was unable to appropriately model evolution of the division of labor which is associated with the reallocation of resources from the noncommercialized, self-sufficient sector to the commercialized modern sector. He did not have access to models of general equilibrium with increasing returns to scale to describe the evolution of a dual structure, nor did he have access to the method of inframarginal analysis, which is associated with corner solutions. Hence, he used neoclassical marginal analysis of a model with constant returns to scale and disequilibrium in labor market to investigate development implications of evolution in division of labor. Chenery (1979) used market disequilibrium to explain structural changes to avoid a general equilibrium analysis of structural changes. Recently, general equilibrium models were used to study dual structure. In some of these models, such as in Khandker & Rashid's (1995) equilibrium model, dual structure is exogenously assumed. [3] They cannot predict the emergence and evolution of dual structure. In a recent literature of formal equilibrium models of high development economics, evolution of dual structure between the manufacturing sector with economies of scale in production and the agricultural sector with constant returns to scale can be predicted (see Fujita & Krugman, 1995; Krugman & Venables, 1995, 1996). The equilibrium models with endogenous geographical location of economic activities of Baldwin and Venables (1995) and Krugman and Venables (1995) attribute the emergence of dual structure to the geographical concentration of economic activities in economic development that marginalizes peripheral areas. Kelly (1997), based on Murphy, Shleifer, and Vishny (1989), develops a dynamic general equilibrium model that predicts spontaneous evolution of a dual structure between the modern sector with economies of scale and the traditional sector with constant returns technology. As transaction conditions are sufficiently improved, the level of division of labor increases and dual structure disappears. Our

---

[3] Also, in Dixit's (1968) dynamic planning model, the existence of labor surplus is exogenously assumed.

model in this paper is complementary to these general equilibrium models that predict the emergence and evolution of dual structure. We pay more attention to the effects of evolution of individuals' levels of specialization and the coexistence of exogenous and endogenous comparative advantages on the emergence and evolution of dual structure.[4]

In our model endogenous and exogenous comparative advantages generate pecuniary positive network effects of division of labor on aggregate productivity. The tradeoff between the network effects and transaction costs implies that if a transaction cost coefficient for a unit of goods traded is large, total transaction cost outweighs economies of division of labor, so that autarky, where aggregate productivity is lower than the PPF, is equilibrium. As transaction conditions are improved, the equilibrium network of trade expands. In the transitional stage from a low to a high level of domestic and international division of labor, the country with lower transaction efficiency is partly involved in the division of labor. Some residents trade with foreign country and the rest of the population are in autarky. This underemployed labor looks like labor surplus that forces down the terms of trade of this country, so that all gains from international trade go to the developed country that has a better transaction condition and is completely involved in the division of labor. As the transaction condition in the less developed country is further improved, the equilibrium network of division of labor expands further, the equilibrium aggregate productivity reaches the PPF, and gains from trade are shared by all individuals, so that dual structure disappears.[5]

---

[4] Mokyr (1993, pp. 65-66) documents evolution of individuals' level of specialization during the Industrial Revolution in Britain. This evolution is sometimes referred to as "industrious revolution," which implies that self-provided home production is replaced with commercialized production. Yang, Wang, and Wills (1992) find empirical evidence for this evolution from China's data. A difference in empirical implications generated by the Krugman and Venables model and our model is that the former yields scale effects (productivity of the manufacturing firm increases if and only if its size increases), but the latter does not.

[5] The effects of transaction conditions on economic development are verified by historical evidences documented in North (1958) and by empirical evidences provided in Barro (1997), Easton and Walker (1997), Frye and Shleifer (1997), Gallup and Sachs (1998), and Sachs and Warner (1995, 1997).

We shall show that in the process of moving to a high level of division of labor, a country may receive more gains from trade even if its terms of trade deteriorate.   This is because an expansion of the network of division of labor can generate productivity gains that outweigh the adverse effect of the terms of trade deterioration. Many economists try to find empirical evidence for or against the claim that terms of trade are worsening for developing economies or to measure adverse effects of worsening terms of trade on economic development (see, for instance, Kohli & Werner, 1998; Morgan, 1970). Recent empirical evidence provided by Sen (1998) shows that economic development and deteriorated terms of trade may concur. Sen uses a partial equilibrium model with monopolistic competition, where prices in the world market are exogenously given, to predict this phenomenon. Hence, his model cannot explore feedback loops between the network size of international division of labor, the extent of the market, aggregate productivity, and terms of trade.[6]

There are two separate literatures on the patterns of trade. Standard trade theory, in the Ricardo and Heckscher-Ohlin models with constant returns to scale in production, explains trade patterns by exogenous technological and endowment advantages. The literature of trade models with economies of scale are silent about which country exports which good since this makes no difference due to the symmetry assumed in these models (see Ethier 1982; Krugman, 1980). In the literature of endogenous specialization, trade patterns are explained by endogenous comparative advantage. Individuals trade those goods that have greater economies of specialization, better transaction condition, and/or are more desirable if not all goods are traded (see Yang, 1991). But who sells which good is indeterminate in the models too because of the assumption that all individuals are ex ante identical.

In the current paper, individuals' characteristics might be ex ante different, while endogenous comparative advantage can be acquired via the decisions in choosing a pattern of specialization and a network of

---

[6] Cypher and Dietz (1998) develop a dynamic model to investigate effects of declining terms of trade on economic development in the presence of dynamic comparative advantage.

trade patterns. Both increasing returns and constant returns are allowed.[7] We then show that if a country has endogenous comparative advantage and exogenous comparative disadvantage in producing a good, it may export the good with exogenous comparative disadvantage if the endogenous comparative advantage dominates exogenous comparative disadvantage.

Our findings have the following implications for China's policy debate on WTO access. In the debate, some argue that China's access to the WTO will generate a dual structure in which capitalist core exploits peripheral China. Others contend that China's WTO membership will initiate a new round of reforms and China can gain from globalization. Our model shows that if China's transaction efficiency is very low, then China cannot gain from globalization in a dual structure where some Chinese are involved in international trade and others are in autarky since low income in autarchic part forces terms of trade against China, bring all gains from trade to the developed country with a higher transaction efficiency. If China's further reforms can significantly raise transaction efficiency, China can then gain from globalization from a high level of international and domestic division of labor and a fairer division of gains from the division of labor.

Many Chinese economists argue that China's trade policy should utilize its exogenous comparative advantages. Our findings in this paper show that China should push further institutional reforms to increase trading efficiency rather than promoting export of goods in which China has exogenous comparative advantages. For instance, China has exogenous comparative advantage in labor intensive sector. However, China may export capital intensive satellite launching if China's endogenous comparative advantages outweigh its exogenous comparative disadvantages in satellite launching.

---

[7] Panagariya (1983) develops a model with variable returns to scale to reestablish core trade theorems on trade pattern. Kemp (1991), Young (1991), and others examine implications of variable returns to scale for trade too. In these papers, dual structure and underemployment are not considered. Gomory (1994) introduces economies of scale into the Ricardian model. Since he adopts neoclassical dichotomy between consumers' decisions and firms' decisions, there are multiple equilibria and equilibrium trade pattern is indeterminate.

The rest of this paper is organized as follows.   Section 2 presents the 2x2 Ricardian model with transaction costs and endogenous and exogenous comparative advantages.   Section 3 solves for general equilibrium and its inframarginal comparative statics. Section 4 extends the analysis to different combinations of endogenous and exogenous comparative advantages for the two countries and two goods.   The concluding section summarizes the findings of the paper and suggests possible extensions.

2.   A Ricardian Model with Endogenous and Exogenous Comparative Advantages

Consider a world consisting of two countries, each with a continuum of consumer-producers of mass M_i ($i=1$, 2).[8] The individuals within a country are assumed to be identical.   The utility function for an individual in country i is

$$U_i = (x_i + k_i x_i^{d})^{\beta} (y_i + k_i y_i^{d})^{1-\beta} \tag{1}$$

where x_i, y_i are quantities of goods x and y produced for self-consumption, x_i^{d} and y_i^{d} are quantities of the two goods bought from the market, and k_i is the transaction efficiency coefficient in country i. The transaction cost is assumed to take the iceberg form: for each unit of good bought, a fraction $1\text{-}k_i$ is lost in transit, the remaining fraction k_i is received by the buyer.

The production functions for a consumer-producer in country i are

$$x_1 + x_1^{s} = L_{1x}^{b}, \qquad\qquad y_1 + y_1^{s} = L_{1y}, \tag{2a}$$

$$x_2 + x_2^{s} = aL_{2x}, \qquad\qquad y_2 + y_2^{s} = L_{2y}^{c}, \tag{2b}$$

where x_i^{s}, y_i^{s} are respective quantities of the two goods sold by a person in country i; L_{ij} is the amount of labor allocated to the production of good j by an individual in country i, and $L_{ix} + L_{iy} = B > 1$. For simplicity, we assume that $B = 2$. It is assumed that a, b, $c > 1$. In Section 4, the sensitivity of our results to the special form of production function is

---

[8] Zhou, Sun, and Yang (1998) have shown that if the set of individuals is finite, it is easy to find examples of nonexistence of Walrasian equilibrium in a general class of models of which the models in this paper are special cases.

                 J. Sachs, X. Yang, D. Zhang

analyzed by extending the model to the cases with different production functions. This system of production functions and endowment constraint displays economies of specialization in producing good x for an individual in Country 1 and in producing good y for an individual in Country 2. It exhibits constant returns to specialization for an individual in Country 1 to produce good y and for an individual in Country 2 to produce good x. But an individual in Country 2 has a higher productivity in producing good x than an individual in Country 1 in producing good y. Economies of specialization are individual specific and activity specific, that is they are localized increasing returns, which are compatible with the Walrasian regime.

Suppose that $b = c = 2$. If all individuals allocate the same amount of labor to the production of each goods, then an individual in Country 1 has the same average labor productivity of goods x and y as an individual in Country 2 in producing good y. But the average labor productivity of good x for an individual in Country 2 is higher. This is similar to the situation in a Ricardian model with exogenous comparative advantage. Country 1's productivities are not higher than Country 2 in producing all goods, but may have exogenous comparative advantage in producing good y. But if an individual in Country 1 allocates much more labor to the production of x than an individual in Country 2, her productivity is higher than that of the latter. Similarly, if an individual in Country 2 allocates more labor to the production of good y than an individual in Country 1, her productivity of good y will be higher. This is referred to as endogenous comparative advantage, since individuals' decisions on labor allocation determine difference in productivity between them. But an individual in Country 1 has no endogenous comparative advantage in producing good y and an individual in Country 2 has no endogenous comparative advantage in producing good x since respective productivities never change, independent of their labor allocation.

The decision problem for an individual in country i involves deciding on what and how much to produce for self-consumption, to sell and to buy from the market. In other words, the individual chooses six variables $x_i, x_i^s, x_i^d, y_i, y_i^s, y_i^d \geq 0$. Hence, there are $2^6 = 64$ possible corner and interior solutions. As shown by Wen (1998), for such a model, an individual never simultaneously sells and buys the same good, never simultaneously produces and buys the same good, and never sells more than one good. We refer to each individual's choice of what to produce, buy and sell that is consistent with the Wen theorem as a *configuration*.

There are three configurations from which the individuals can choose:

(1) self-sufficiency.   Configuration A, where an individual produces both goods for self-consumption.   This configuration is defined by

$$x_i, y_i > 0, x_i^{\,s} = x_i^{\,d} = y_i^{\,s} = y_i^{\,d} = 0, i = 1, 2.$$

(2) specialization in producing good x.   Configuration (x/y), where an individual produces only x, sells x in exchange for y, is defined by

$$x_i, x_i^{\,s}, y_i^{\,d} > 0, x_i^{\,d} = y_i = y_i^{\,s} = 0.$$

(3) specialization in producing good y.   Configuration (y/x), where an individual produces only y, sells y in exchange for x, is defined by

$$y_i, y_i^{\,s}, x_i^{\,d} > 0, y_i^{\,d} = x_i = x_i^{\,s} = 0.$$

The combination of all individual's configurations constitutes a *market structure*, or *structure* for short.   Given the configurations listed above, there are 13 feasible structures that may satisfy market clearing and other conditions for a general equilibrium.

Structure AA, as shown in of panel (1) of Figure 1, is an autarky structure where individuals in both countries choose self-sufficiency (configuration A).   Structure AD, shown in of panel (2) of Figure 1, is asymmetric between the two countries: all individuals in Country 1 choose autarky configuration A, while some individuals in Country 2 choose configuration (x/y) and others choose configuration (y/x). Hence, there is domestic division of labor and related domestic trade in Country 2, but no international division of labor and related international trade. Structure DA is symmetric to structure AD: Country 1 has domestic division of labor and Country 2 is in autarky. This structure involves a type I dual structure between countries.

Structure PC$_+$, shown in of panel (4) of Figure 1, involves a type II dual structure between the two countries as well as in Country 1. Some individuals in Country 1 choose configuration (x/y), the rest of the population choose autarky, and all individuals in Country 2 choose configuration (y/x). There is a dual structure between professional individuals choosing (x/y) and self-sufficient individuals in Country 1 despite their ex identical characteristics. The professional individuals in Country 1 are involved in international trade with Country 2. Structure CP_+ is symmetric to structure PC_+.

Structure PC_-, shown in panel (6) of Figure 1, is the same as structure PC_+ except that professional individuals in Country 1 choose configuration (y/x) instead of (x/y) and individuals in Country 2 choose configuration (x/y) instead of (y/x). Structure CP_- is the same as structure CP_+ except that individuals in country 1 choose configuration (y/x) instead of (x/y) and professional individuals in Country 2 choose configuration (x/y) instead of (y/x).

Structure DC_+, shown in panel (9) of Figure 1, is the same as structure PC_+ except that those individuals choosing autarky in Country 1 in structure PC_+ choose configuration (y/x) instead in structure DC_+. Hence, in structure DC_+ all individuals completely specialize, but Country 1 is involved in both domestic and international trade, whereas Country 2 is involved only in international trade. Also, Country 1 exports good x and Country 2 exports good y. Structure DC_- is the same as structure DC_+ except that Country 1 exports good y instead of good x and Country 2 exports good x instead of good y.

Structure CD_+, shown in panel (8) of Figure 1, is symmetric to structure DC_+: Country 1 has only international trade whereas Country 2 has both international and domestic trade, and Country 1 exports good x and Country 2 exports good y. Structure CD_- is the same as CD_+ except that Country 1 exports good y instead of x; Country 2 exports good x instead of y.

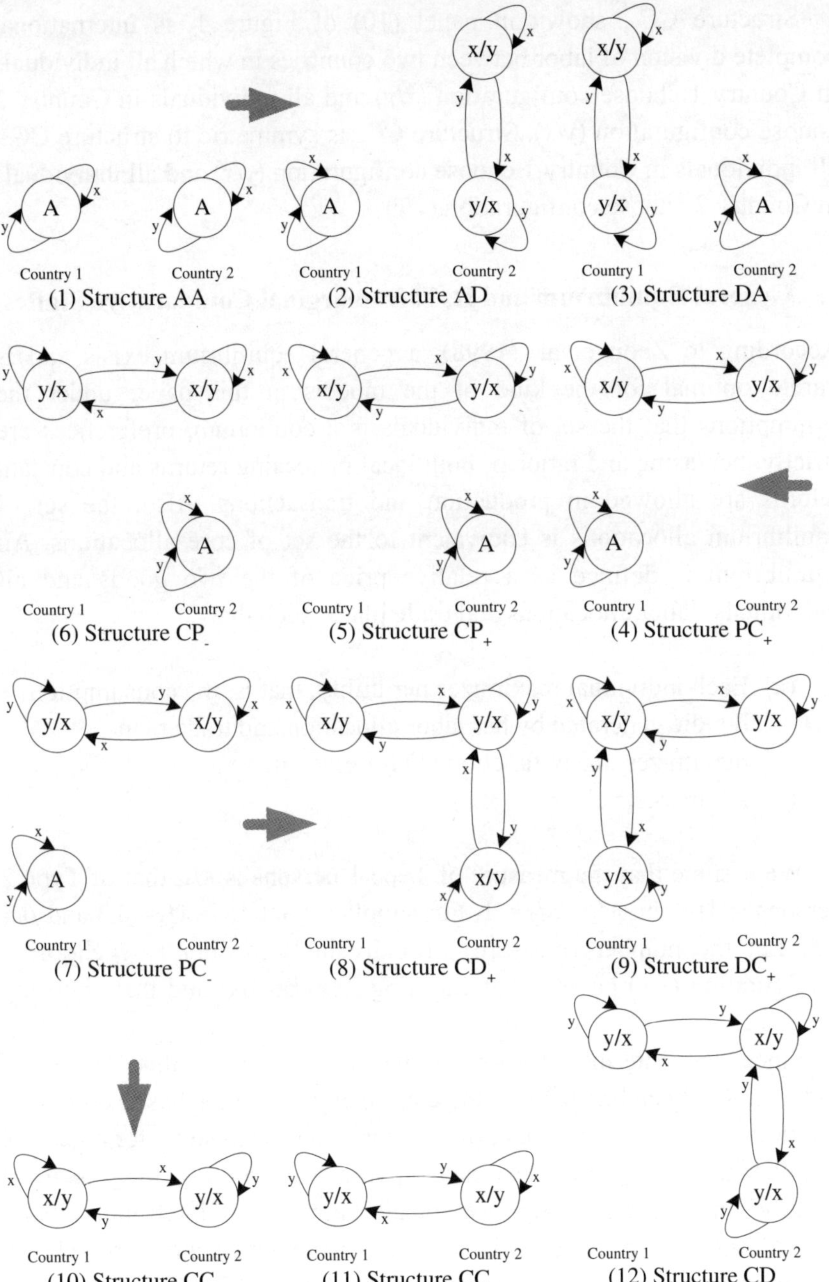

Figure 1: Configurations and Structures

Structure CC$_+$, shown in panel (10) of Figure 1, is international complete division of labor between two countries in which all individuals in Country 1 choose configuration (x/y) and all individuals in Country 2 choose configuration (y/x). Structure CC$_-$ is symmetric to structure CC$_+$: all individuals in Country 1 choose configuration (y/x) and all individuals in Country 2 choose configuration (x/y).

3.   General Equilibrium and Its Inframarginal Comparative Statics

According to Zhou et al. (1998), a general equilibrium exists and is Pareto optimal for the kind of the models in this paper under the assumptions that the set of individuals is a continuum, preferences are strictly increasing and rational; both local increasing returns and constant returns are allowed in production and transactions. Also, the set of equilibrium allocations is equivalent to the set of core allocations. An equilibrium is defined as a relative price of the two goods and all individuals' labor allocations and trade plans, such that

(a)   Each individual maximizes her utility, that is, the consumption bundle generated by her labor allocation and trade plan maximizes utility function (1) for given p.

(b)   All markets clear.

We assume that the measure of Type 1 persons is M_1, that of Type 2 persons is M_2, and $M_1 + M_2 = 1$. For simplicity, let $M_1 = M_2 = 0.5$ and $\beta = 0.5$. Let the number (measure) of individuals in country i choosing configuration (x/y) be M_{ix}, that choosing (y/x) be M_{iy}, and that choosing A be M_{iA}.

Since the interior solution is never optimal in this model of endogenous specialization and there are many structures based on corner solutions, we cannot use standard marginal analysis to solve for a general equilibrium. We adopt a two-step approach to solving for a general equilibrium. In the first step, we consider a structure. Each individual's utility maximizing decision is solved for the given structure. Utility equalization condition between individuals choosing different configurations in the same country and market clearing condition are used to solve the relative price of traded goods and numbers (measure) of individuals choosing different configurations. The relative price and numbers, and associated resource allocation are referred to as a corner equilibrium for this structure.

According to the definition, a general equilibrium is a corner equilibrium in which all individuals have no incentive to deviate, under the corner equilibrium relative price, from their chosen configurations. Hence, in the second step, we can plug the corner equilibrium relative price into the indirect utility function for each constituent configuration in this structure, then compare corner equilibrium values of utility across those configurations and the configurations in other structures. The comparisons are called total cost-benefit analysis which yields the conditions under which the corner equilibrium utility in each constituent configuration of this structure is not smaller than in any alternative configuration. This system of inequalities can thus be used to identify a subspace of parameter space within which this corner equilibrium is a general equilibrium.

With the existence theorem of general equilibrium proved by Zhou et al. (1998), we can completely partition the parameter space into subspaces, within each of which the corner equilibrium in a structure is a general equilibrium. As parameter values shift between the subspaces, the general equilibrium will discontinuously jump between structures. The discontinuous jumps of structure and all endogenous variables are called inframarginal comparative statics of general equilibrium.

We now take the first step of the inframarginal analysis. As an example, we consider structure CP_+. Assume that in this structure M_{2y} individuals choose configuration (y/x) and M_{2A} individuals choose autarky in country 2, where $M_{2y} + M_{2A} = M_2 = 0.5$. $M_1 = 0.5$ individuals in Country 1 choose configuration (x/y). Since all individuals in the same Country are ex ante identical in all aspects (the same utility and production functions, the same transaction condition, and the same endowment), the maximum utilities in configurations A and (y/x) must be the same in Country 2 in equilibrium. Marginal analysis of the decision problem for an individual in Country 2 choosing autarky yields the maximum utility in configuration A: $U_{2A} = (a2^{c+1}\gamma)^{0.5}$, where $\gamma \equiv c^c/(c+1)^{c+1}$. Marginal analysis of the decision problem for an individual in

Country 2 choosing configuration (y/x) yields the demand function $x_2^d = 2^{c-1}/p$, the supply function $y_2^s = 2^{c-1}$, and indirect utility function: $U_{2y} = 2^{c-1}(k_2/p)^{0.5}$. The utility equalization condition $U_{2y} = U_{2A}$ yields $p \equiv p_x/p_y = k_2 2^{c-3}/a\gamma$. Similarly, the marginal analysis of the decision problem of an individual choosing configuration (x/y) in Country 1 yields the demand function, $y_1^d = 2^{b-1}/p$, the supply function $x_1^s = 2^{b-1}$, and indirect utility function: $U_{1x} = 2^{b-1}(k_1 p)^{0.5}$. Inserting the corner equilibrium relative price into the market clearing condition for good x, $M_1 x_1 = M_{2y} x_2^d$, yields the number of individuals selling good y, $M_{2y} = 0.5\, k_2/2^{3-c} a\gamma$, where $M_1 = 0.5$ by assumption. Indirect utility functions for individuals choosing various configurations in the two countries are listed in Table 1.

Table 1: Indirect Utility Functions

	Indirect Utility Functions		
Configurations	(x/y)	(y/x)	A
Country 1	$U_{1x} = 2^{b-1}(k_1 p)^{0.5}$	$U_{1y} = (k_1/p)^{0.5}$	$U_{1A} = \left(2^{b+1}\gamma\right)^{0.5}$
Country 2	$U_{2x} = a(k_2 p)^{0.5}$	$U_{2y} = 2^{c-1}(k_2/p)^{0.5}$	$U_{2A} = \left(2^{c+1}a\gamma\right)^{0.5}$

Following this procedure, we can solve for corner equilibrium in each structure. The solutions of all corner equilibria are summarized in Table 2. Then we can take the second step to carry out total cost-benefit analysis for each corner equilibrium and to identify the parameter subspace within which the corner equilibrium is a general equilibrium. Consider the corner equilibrium in structure CP$_+$ as an example again.

Table 2: Corner Equilibria

Structure	Relative price of x to y	Numbers of individuals choosing various configurations
AA		$M_{1A} = M_{2A} = 0.5$
AD	$2^{c-1}/a$	$M_{1A} = 0.5,\ M_{2x} = M_{2y} = 1/4$
DA	2^{1-b}	$M_{2A} = 0.5,\ M_{1x} = M_{1y} = 1/4$
PC+	$2^{3-b}\alpha/k_1$	$M_{2y} = 0.5,\ M_{1A} = 0.5(1 - k_1 2^{c-3}/\alpha),\ M_{1x} = 0.5k_1 2^{c-3}/\alpha$
CP+	$2^{c-3}k_2/\gamma a$	$M_{1x} = 0.5,\ M_{2A} = 0.5(1 - k_2 2^{b-3}/\gamma\alpha),\ M_{2y} = 0.5k_2 2^{b-3}/\gamma\alpha$
CP_	$2^{c+1}\gamma/ak_2$	$M_{1y} = 0.5,\ M_{2x} = 0.5k_2 2^{-c-1}/\gamma,\ M_{2A} = 0.5(1 - k_2 2^{-c-1}/\gamma)$
CC+	2^{c-b}	$M_{1x} = M_{2y} = 1/2$
CD+	$2^{c-1}/a$	$M_{1x} = 0.5,\ M_{2y} = (1 + 2^{b-1}/a)/4,\ M_{2x} = (1 - 2^{b-1}/a)/4$
CD_	$2^{c-1}/a$	$M_{1y} = 0.5,\ M_{2x} = 0.25 + 2^{-c-1},\ M_{2y} = 0.25 - 2^{-c-1}$

In this structure M_1 individuals choose configuration (x/y) in Country 1, and M_{2y} individuals choose configuration (y/x) and M_{2A} individuals choose autarky in Country 2. For an individual in Country 1, equilibrium requires that her utility in configuration (x/y) is not smaller than in configurations (y/x) and A under the corner equilibrium relative price in structure CP$_+$. Also equilibrium requires that all individuals in Country 2 are indifferent between configurations (y/x) and A and receive a utility level that is not lower than in configuration (x/y). In addition, this structure occurs in equilibrium only if $M_{2y}\in(0, 0.5)$. All the conditions imply

$$U_{1x} \geq U_{1y}, \quad U_{1x} \geq U_{1A}, \quad U_{2A} = U_{2y} \geq U_{2x}, \quad M_{2y}\in(0, 0.5),$$

where indirect utility functions in different configurations and corner equilibrium relative price are given in Tables 1 and 2. The conditions define a parameter subspace:

$$k_1 k_2 \geq 2^{6-b-c}a\alpha\gamma, \quad k_2 \in (2^{4-b-c}a\gamma, \min\{4\gamma, a\gamma 2^{3-b}\}), \quad a < 2^{4-b-c},$$
$$k_1 > \max\{2^{4-b-c}a\alpha, \alpha 2^{3-c}\},$$

where $\alpha \equiv b^b/(1+b)^{b+1}$ and $\gamma \equiv c^c/(c+1)^{c+1}$. Within this parameter subspace, the corner equilibrium in structure CP$_+$ is the general equilibrium. Following this procedure, we can do total cost-benefit analysis for each structure. The total cost-benefit analysis in the second step and marginal analysis of each corner equilibrium in the first step yields inframarginal comparative statics of general equilibrium, summarized in Table 3. From this Table, we can see that the parameter subspace for structure DC_+, DC_-, or CC_- to occur in general equilibrium is empty.

C stands for complete specialization in a country, D stands for the domestic division of labor in a country, A stands for autarky in a country, P stands for the partial division of labor where the population is divided between autarky and specialization in a country, subscript + stands for a pattern of trade in which Country 1 exports good x and imports good y, and subscript stands for a trade pattern in which Country 1 exports good y and imports good x. Hence, structure AA involves autarky in both countries, structures AD and DA involve autarky in one country and division of labor in the other, structures PC and CP involve complete specialization in one country and coexistence of autarky and complete specialization in the other. The country with the lower transaction efficiency in this structure looks like underdeveloped in the sense that it receives none of the gains from trade and income differential between it and the other country with higher transaction efficiency increases as a result of a shift of equilibrium from autarky to this structure. Also, ex ante identical individuals in the less developed country in this structure are divided between a professional occupation that trades with the foreign country and those who are self-sufficient and not involved in commercialized production. These self-sufficient individuals look like in underemployment since they cannot find a job to work for the market. All individuals completely specialize in structures CD and CC. But CC involves complete specialization of both countries in the absence of domestic trade, whereas CD involves complete specialization in Country 1 and domestic division of labor in Country 2. Figure 1 illustrates the

Table 3: General Equilibrium Structure: Inframarginal Comparative Statics   [where $\alpha \equiv b^b/(1+b)^{b+1},\ \gamma \equiv c^c/(1+c)^{c+1}$]

<table>
<tr>
<td></td>
<td colspan="6">$k_2 \in (0,4\gamma)$</td>
<td colspan="6">$k_2 \in (4\gamma,1)$</td>
</tr>
<tr>
<td rowspan="6">$k_1 \in (0,4\alpha)$</td>
<td colspan="5">$a < 2^{b+c-2}$</td>
<td colspan="1">$a > 2^{b+c-2}$</td>
<td colspan="4">$a < 2^{b+c-2}$</td>
<td colspan="2">$a > 2^{b+c-2}$</td>
</tr>
<tr>
<td colspan="2">$k_1 k_2 < a\alpha\gamma 2^{6-b-c}$</td>
<td colspan="3">$k_1 k_2 > a\alpha\gamma 2^{6-b-c}$</td>
<td colspan="1">$k_1 k_2 < \alpha\gamma 2^{b+c+2}/a$</td>
<td colspan="2">$a < 2^{b-1}$</td>
<td colspan="2">$a > 2^{b-1}$</td>
<td colspan="2">$k_1 < \alpha 2^{b+c}/a$</td>
</tr>
<tr>
<td colspan="2" rowspan="4">AA</td>
<td colspan="2">$a < 2^{b-1}$</td>
<td colspan="1">$a > 2^{b-1}$</td>
<td colspan="1">AA</td>
<td colspan="4">$k_1 < a\alpha 2^{4-b-c}$
AD</td>
<td colspan="2">AD</td>
</tr>
<tr>
<td colspan="2">$k_1 < \alpha 2^{3-c}$
PC$_+$</td>
<td colspan="1" rowspan="3">CP$_+$</td>
<td colspan="1">$k_1 k_2 > \alpha\gamma 2^{b+c+2}/a$</td>
<td colspan="2" rowspan="2">$k_1 \in (a\alpha 2^{4-b-c},\ \alpha 2^{3-c})$
PC$_+$</td>
<td colspan="2" rowspan="3">$k_1 > a\alpha 2^{4-b-c}$
CD$_+$</td>
<td colspan="2" rowspan="3">$k_1 \in (\alpha 2^{b+c}/a,\ 4\alpha)$
CD$_-$</td>
</tr>
<tr>
<td colspan="2">$k_2 < a\gamma 2^{3-b}$
CP$_+$</td>
<td colspan="1" rowspan="2">CP$_-$</td>
</tr>
<tr>
<td colspan="2">$k_1 > \alpha 2^{3-c},\ k_2 > a\gamma 2^{3-b}$
CC$_+$</td>
<td colspan="2">$k_1 > \alpha 2^{3-c}$
CC$_+$</td>
</tr>
<tr>
<td rowspan="4">$k_1 \in (4\alpha,1)$</td>
<td colspan="3">$a < 2^{b-1}$</td>
<td colspan="3">$a > 2^{b-1}$</td>
<td colspan="2">$k_2 < \gamma 2^{b+c}/a$</td>
<td colspan="2">$a < 2^{b-1}$</td>
<td colspan="1">$a > 2^{b-1}$</td>
<td colspan="1" rowspan="4">CD$_-$</td>
</tr>
<tr>
<td colspan="6">$k_2 < a\gamma 2^{4-b-c}$
DA</td>
<td colspan="2">DA</td>
<td colspan="2" rowspan="3">CC$_+$</td>
<td colspan="1" rowspan="3">CD$_+$</td>
</tr>
<tr>
<td colspan="3">$k_2 \in (a\gamma 2^{4-b-c},\ a\gamma 2^{3-b})$
CP$_+$</td>
<td colspan="3" rowspan="2">$k_2 > a\gamma 2^{4-b-c}$
CP$_+$</td>
<td colspan="2">$k_2 > \gamma 2^{b+c}/a$</td>
</tr>
<tr>
<td colspan="3">$k_2 > a\gamma 2^{3-b}$
CC$_+$</td>
<td colspan="2">CD$_-$</td>
</tr>
</table>

equilibrium structures.[9] We say the level of division of labor increases if occurrence of letter A or P decreases or the occurrence of letter D or C increases in a structure.

In order to accurately describe the inframarginal comparative statics, we define endogenous comparative advantage as productivity difference between individuals that is caused by individuals' labor allocations and define exogenous comparative advantage as productivity difference between individuals that is independent of labor allocation. Since marginal and average productivity never changes as labor allocation alters for a production function with constant returns to scale, these definitions imply that endogenous comparative advantages come from economies of specialization and exogenous comparative advantages come from exogenous difference of production conditions with constant returns. Parameter b represents the degree of endogenous comparative advantage for a person in Country 1 producing good x since as b increases, increases in productivity become more responsive to an increase in the amount of labor allocated to its production. Similarly, c represents the degree of endogenous comparative advantage for a person in Country 2 producing good y.

If $b=c=1$, then Country 2 has exogenous absolute and comparative advantage in producing good x and Country 1 has exogenous comparative advantage in producing good y since $a > 1$ in Eqs. (2a-b). This implies that a represents the degree of exogenous comparative advantage.

With the definitions, we can now have a close examination of Table 3 that consists of four blocks. The northwest block is associated with low transaction efficiencies in both countries. The northeast block is associated with low transaction efficiency in Country 1 and high transaction efficiency in Country 2. The southwest block is associated with low transaction efficiency in Country 2 and high transaction efficiency in Country 1. The southeast block is associated with high transaction efficiencies in both countries. As parameter values move from the northwest toward the southeast, the occurrence of letter A

---

[9] It can be shown that there are multiple equilibria in some razor edge cases. For instance, if $2^{b-1} > a$, $0 < k_1 < 4\alpha$, $k_1 < a\alpha 2^{4-b-c}$, $k_2 = 4\gamma$, multiple equilibria occur.

representing autarky and letter P representing partial division of labor decreases and the occurrence of letters D and C representing complete division of labor increases. Hence, as transaction conditions are improved, the level of domestic and international division of labor increases because of the tradeoff between economies of division of labor generated by endogenous and exogenous comparative advantages and transaction costs. If the transaction efficiency is low in one country and high in the other (northeast or southwest block), the country with the lower transaction efficiency has a dual structure (P) or in autarky (A) in a structure with asymmetric division of labor between countries (AD, DA, PC, or CP). If the transaction efficiencies are high in both countries, then complete division of labor occurs and dual structure disappears in equilibrium.

Each block consists of several sections. If the degree of exogenous comparative advantage a is small compared to the degree of endogenous comparative advantage (b, c), each country exports the good with economies of specialization in production. This is denoted by subscript +. Otherwise, a country exports the good with constant returns and exogenous comparative advantage.

All the results on evolution of division of labor, dual structure, and trade pattern are summarized in the following proposition, illustrated in Figure 1 where large arrows indicate the direction of the evolution in division of labor.

Proposition 1: As transaction efficiency increases from a very low to a very high level, the equilibrium level of domestic and international division of labor increases from complete autarky in both countries to the complete division of labor in both countries. In the transitional stage, two types of dual structure may occur. In a type I dual structure the country with the lower transaction efficiency is in autarky and the other has domestic division of labor and higher productivity and per capital real income. In a Type II dual structure, the country with higher transaction efficiency completely specializes and obtains all of gains from trade, the other country has a domestic dual structure between commercialized sector and self-sufficient sector (autarky) that looks like in underemployment. The dual structures of two types disappear as individuals in all countries are involved in international and domestic division of labor. Each country exports goods of exogenous comparative advantage if exogenous comparative advantage dominates endogenous comparative advantage in producing this good. Otherwise, each country exports goods with endogenous comparative advantage and economies of specialization in production.

The inframarginal comparative statics of general equilibrium can be used to establish two corollaries. The first is that evolution in division of labor generated by improvements in transaction conditions will raise equilibrium aggregate productivity. In order to establish the above statement, we consider the aggregate PPF for Individual 1 (from Country 1) and Individual 2 (from Country 2). As shown in Figure 2 where $b = c = 2$, the PPF for Individual 1 is curve AB, that for Individual 2 is curve CD. In autarky, the two persons' optimum decisions for taste parameter $\beta \in (0, 1)$ are $x_1 = [4\beta/(1+\beta)]^2$, $x_2 = 2a\beta/(2-\beta)$, $y_1 = 2(1-\beta)/(1+\beta)$, $y_2 = [4(1-\beta)/(2-\beta)]^2$. Let β change from 0 to 1; we can calculate values of $Y = y_1+y_2$ and $X = x_1+x_2$ as functions of β. The values of X and Y for different values of β constitute curve EGH in Figure 2. The equilibrium aggregate production schedule in structure AA is a point on the curve, dependent on value of β. But the aggregate PPF for the two individuals is the curve EFH. Since in structure CC, CD, or DC the equilibrium production schedule is point F which is on the aggregate PPF, the aggregate productivity in a structure with the complete division of labor is higher than in structure AA. The difference between EFH and EGH can be considered as economies of division of labor.

Following the same reasoning, we can prove that the equilibrium aggregate productivity in structure AD, DA, PC, or CP is lower than the PPF. Hence, Proposition 1 implies that as transaction efficiencies are improved, the equilibrium level of division of labor and equilibrium aggregate productivity increase side by side.

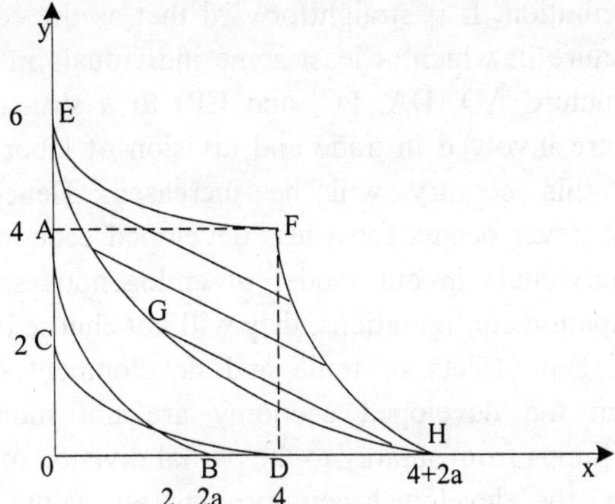

Figure 2: Economies of Division of Labor Based on Endogenous and Exogenous
Comparative Advantage

The second corollary is that deterioration of a country's terms of trade
and increase of gains received by this country from trade may concur.
Suppose that the initial values of parameters satisfy $k_1 \in (0, 4\alpha)$, $k_2 \in (0, 4\gamma)$, and $k_1 k_2 > a\gamma\alpha 2^{6-b-c}$, which implies, from Table 3, that we are
considering the northwest block. Suppose that the initial value of k_2
satisfies $k_2' < a\gamma 2^{3-c}$, so that the equilibrium structure is CP$_+$ in which
Country 2 exports y and imports x and its terms of trade, from Table 2, is
$1/p = 2^{c-3} a\gamma/k_2'$. Now, the value of k_2 increases to $k_2'' > a\gamma 2^{3-c}$, which
implies, from Table 3, the general equilibrium jumps from CP$_+$ to
structure CC$_+$ in which Country 2's terms of trade, from Table 2, is 2^{b-c}.
It can then be shown that Country 2's terms of trade deteriorate as a
result of the change in k_2. But this shift of the equilibrium from CP$_+$ to
CC$_+$ increases utility of each individual in Country 2 from autarky level.
This has established the claim that the deterioration of a country's terms
of trade and an increase of gains that this country receives from trade
may concur. There are other parameter subspaces within which changes
in parameters may generate concurrence of the deterioration of one
country's terms of trade and an increase in its gains from trade.

Although an equilibrium in this model is always Pareto optimal, it
generates interesting implications of economic development and trade for

income distribution. It is straightforward that as the equilibrium jumps from a structure in which at least some individuals in a country are in autarky (structure AD, DA, PC, and CP) to a structure in which all individuals are involved in trade and division of labor, all individuals' utilities in this country will be increased. Hence, immiserizing development never occurs for a less developed economy in our model since all individuals in our model of endogenous specialization can choose occupation configurations, they will not choose trade if autarky is better off.[10] But effects of trade and development on utility of an individual in the developed economy are not monotonic. As the equilibrium jumps from autarky to the partial division of labor (AD, DA, PC, or CP), the developed country gets all gains from trade and development. But as the equilibrium jumps, say from PC_+ to CC_+, it is possible that utility of a person in the developed country may decline. It can be shown that this takes place within the parameter subspace in the southwest block in Table 3. This prediction is consistent with the fact, documented in Krugman and Venables (1995, pp. 857-58), that in the 1970s the general view was that integration of world markets produced a rise in the living standards of rich nations at the expense of the poor, but in the 1990s, it is believed that the rise of Third World manufacturing nations had serious adverse impacts on developed economies. But according to our model, this reverse of tide is just compensation to the less developed economies that did not receive gains from trade in the early development stage. Also, in our model there exists some parameter subspace within which such immiserizing development never occurs. This is the case when the improvements in the transaction efficiency of the developed country keep the pace of the improvements of the transaction efficiency of the less developed country (for instance in the northeast block of Table 3).

This corollary generates the following policy implications. In the transitional stage of economic development and globalization, the terms of trade are against the less developed country that has relatively low transaction efficiency: the less developed country receives autarky utility

---

[10] This differentiates our model from Krugman and Venables (1995) which predicts a decline of real income in the less developed economy in the early development stage.

and all gains from trade go to the developed country. There are two policies to change this inferior position. One is to impose tariff to improve terms of trade and the other is to improve transaction condition to expand the network of trade. The former is to increase share of gains received by the less developed country from a shrunk pie because of the deadweight caused by tariff. The latter is to get greater share of gains from trade by enlarging the pie. The expanded network of division of labor can generate productivity gains. As long as productivity improvements outpace the deterioration of terms of trade, the less developed country can receive more gains from trade not only because of productivity gains, but also because of more equal division of gains from trade between the countries as all individuals are involved in the international and domestic division of labor. We can apply this theory to the analysis of China's WTO membership. If China's trading efficiency were not significantly improved, China might not be able to benefit from the membership and globalization. All gains from globalization may go the developed countries. If China's WTO membership promoted further reforms, thereby improving China's trading efficiency, China would benefit from this membership.

Many Chinese economists argue that China's trade policy should promote exports of goods in which it has exogenous comparative advantages. Our model shows that China should push further institutional reforms to increase its trading efficiency and that it might be efficient to export a good in which China has exogenous comparative disadvantage if China's endogenous comparative advantage dominates its exogenous comparative disadvantage in producing this good.

The inframarginal comparative statics in Table 3 can be used to address a recent debate on competitiveness between Krugman (1994a, 1994b), on the one hand, and Sachs (1996a, 1996b) and Prestowitz et al. (1994) on the other. Krugman argued that a nation should focus on promoting free trade and that the emphasis on international competitiveness can be "a dangerous obsession". Sachs and Prestowitz et al. contended that international competitiveness plays an essential role in improving national welfare. Our results show that absolute level of transaction efficiency affects a country's performance of development and trade. A country with low transaction efficiency cannot receive gains from trade in the transitional stage of economic development. From the northwest block of Table 3, we can also see that if the degree of economies of specialization in Country 1, b which negatively relates to α, is small, relative to c which negatively relates to γ, or $k_1 < \alpha 2^{3-c}$, structure PC is the equilibrium where this country is in an inferior position in the transitional stage. If c is small relative to b, or $k_2 < \alpha\gamma 2^{3-b}$, structure CP occurs in equilibrium where Country 2 is in an inferior position in the transitional stage. If we interpret absolute level of transaction efficiency and degree of economies of specialization for a country in producing a good as degree of competitiveness, our results support the view of Sachs and Prestowitz et al. that competitiveness matters. However, the proposition also supports Krugman's (1995) argument that a country should focus on promoting free trade and improving transaction efficiency. In our model, the promotion of free trade can be done through reducing tariff and nontariff barriers of trade so as to improve transaction efficiency k. And Krugman's emphasis on trade liberalization is particularly relevant if the pursuit of international competitiveness is used as an excuse for impeding free trade. Recently, some Chinese economists argue that China should enhance its competitiveness and others argue that China should utilize its exogenous comparative advantage, instead. Our model provides a sophisticated way to reconciliate two sides of the debate.

4. Other Combinations of Endogenous and Exogenous Comparative Advantages

Since the inframarginal comparative statics change with the specification of the system of production functions, we report the sensitivity analysis of our result. The system of production functions in Eqs. (2a-b) displays economies of specialization in producing good x by a person in Country 1 and in producing good y by a person in Country 2. We now assume that there are economies of specialization for all individuals in producing x, but constant returns prevail in the production of good y. Hence, the system of production functions in Eqs. (2a-b) is replaced by

$$x_1 + x_1^s = L_{1x}^b, \qquad\qquad y_1 + y_1^s = L_{1y},$$

$$x_2 + x_2^s = L_{2x}^c, \qquad\qquad y_2 + y_2^s = aL_{2y},$$

Then the inframarginal comparative statics of general equilibrium are summarized in Table 4.

Table 4: Equilibrium Structure (economies of specialization
in producing one good for all countries)

	$k_2 \in (0,4\gamma)$		
	$a > 2^{c-b}$		$a < 2^{c-b}$
$k_1 \in$ $(0,4\alpha)$	$k_1 k_2 < \alpha\gamma 2^{c-b+4}/a$ AA	$k_1 k_2 > \alpha\gamma 2^{c-b+4}/a$ CP$_+$	$k_1 k_2 < a\alpha\gamma 2^{4+b-c}$ AA $k_1 k_2 > a\alpha\gamma 2^{4+b-c}$ CP$_-$
$k_1 \in$ $(4\alpha,1)$	$k_2 < \gamma 2^{2+b-c}/a$ DA $k_2 > \gamma 2^{2+b-c}/a$ CP$_+$		$k_2 < a\gamma 2^{2+b-c}$ DA $k_2 > a\gamma 2^{2+b-c}$ CP$_-$

	$k_2 \in (4\gamma,1)$		
	$a > 2^{c-b}$		$a < 2^{c-b}$
$k_1 \in$ $(0,4\alpha)$	$2^{c-b} > 1$ $k_1 < \alpha 2^{2+c-b}/a$ AD	$2^{c-b} < 1$	$k_1 < a\alpha 2^{2+b-c}$ AD
	$k_1 > \alpha 2^{2+c-b}/a$ CD$_+$	$k_1 > \alpha 2^{2+c-b}/a$ CC$_+$	$k_1 > a\alpha 2^{2+b-c}$ CD$_-$
$k_1 \in$ $(4\alpha,1)$	$2^{c-b} > 1$ CD$_+$	$2^{c-b} < 1$ CC$_+$	CD$_-$

where $\quad \alpha \equiv b^b/(1+b)^{b+1}, \gamma \equiv c^c/(1+c)^{c+1}$

The result yields the following proposition.

Proposition 2:   As transaction efficiency is improved, the equilibrium level of division of labor and aggregate productivity increase. The country with lower transaction efficiency and/or insignificant economies of specialization has a dual structure with underemployment in the transitional stage of the economic development. If a country has endogenous comparative advantage and exogenous comparative disadvantage in producing a good, it exports this good if the former dominates the latter. Otherwise it imports this good.

This proposition can provide a theoretical explanation for recent empirical evidence that shows significant effects of geographical conditions on a country's performance of development and trade. Gallup and Sachs (1998) use cross-country and cross-region data to show that the countries with favorable geographical conditions for transportation have better development performance. They have also shown that the countries in the temperate regions outperform those in the tropic regions. According to them, this is because the geographical conditions in the tropic regions adversely affect health and production conditions. This is equivalent to a small value of productivity parameter a, b, or c. Our theory shows that this will put the countries in the tropic regions in an inferior position in economic development and trade. This analysis is different from Fujita and Krugman (1995), Krugman (1980), and Yang (1991) who explain economic development, structural changes, and trade pattern by economic changes in the absence of ex ante differences between decision-makers. It is different from conventional trade theory and development economics concerning only exogenous comparative advantages. We explain complicated development and trade phenomena by the coexistence of endogenous and exogenous comparative advantages.

If we assume that there are economies of specialization only for individuals in Country 1 in producing two goods, whereas constant returns prevail in Country 2 in producing the two goods, the system of production functions is then:

$$x_1 + x_1^s = L_{1x}^b, \qquad\qquad y_1 + y_1^s = L_{1y}^c,$$
$$x_2 + x_2^s = aL_{2x}, \qquad\qquad y_2 + y_2^s = L_{2y}.$$

The inframarginal comparative statics of general equilibrium are summarized in Table 5. The result is consistent with Propositions 1 and 2 except that the evolution of division of labor is more sensitive to the transaction efficiency in the country that has economies of specialization in producing all goods than to that in the country with constant returns technologies. Also, structures DC_+ and CC_-, which never occur in equilibrium in Tables 3 and 4, may now occur in equilibrium.

Table 5: Equilibrium Structure (economies of specialization for Country 1 to produce all goods)

<table>
<tr><td></td><td colspan="4">$k_2<1$</td></tr>
<tr><td rowspan="6">$k_1\in$
$(0,4\theta)$</td><td colspan="3">$a>2^{b-c}$</td><td>$a<2^{b-c}$</td></tr>
<tr><td>$k_1k_2<\theta2^{b-c+2}/a$</td><td colspan="2">$k_1k_2>\theta2^{b-c+2}/a$</td><td>$k_1k_2<a\theta2^{c-b+2}$</td></tr>
<tr><td rowspan="4">AA</td><td>$a>2^{b-1}$</td><td>$a<2^{b-1}$</td><td>AA</td></tr>
<tr><td>$k_1<\theta2^{b+1}/a$
PC_-</td><td rowspan="3">CP_+</td><td rowspan="3">$k_1k_2>$
$a\theta2^{c-b+2}$

PC_+</td></tr>
<tr><td>$k_2<2^{1-c}$
CP_-</td></tr>
<tr><td>$k_1>\theta2^{b+1}/a$
$k_2>2^{1-c}$
CC_-</td></tr>
<tr><td rowspan="4">$k_1\in$
$(4\theta,1)$</td><td>$a>2^{b-1}$</td><td colspan="2">$a<2^{b-1}$</td><td rowspan="2">$k_2<a2^{c-b}$

DA</td></tr>
<tr><td>$k_2<2^{b-c}/a$</td><td colspan="2">DA</td></tr>
<tr><td>$k_2\in\left(2^{b-c}/a,2^{1-c}\right)$
CD_-</td><td colspan="2" rowspan="2">$k_2>2^{b-c}/a$

DC_-</td><td rowspan="2">$k_2>a2^{c-b}$

DC_+</td></tr>
<tr><td>$k_2>2^{1-c}$
CC_-</td></tr>
</table>

where $\theta\equiv b^b c^c/(b+c)^{b+c}$

376

J. Sachs, X. Yang, D. Zhang

Table 5 *(continued)*: Equilibrium Structure (economies of specialization for Country 1 to produce all goods)

<table>
<tr><td></td><td colspan="3">$k_2 = 1$</td></tr>
<tr>
<td rowspan="5">$k_1 \in$
$(0, 4\theta)$</td>
<td colspan="2">$a > 2^{b-c}$</td>
<td>$a < 2^{b-c}$</td>
</tr>
<tr>
<td>$a > 2^{b-1}$</td>
<td>$a < 2^{b-1}$</td>
<td>$k_1 < a\theta 2^{c-b+2}$</td>
</tr>
<tr>
<td colspan="2">$k_1 < \theta 2^{c-b+2}/a$

AD</td>
<td>AD</td>
</tr>
<tr>
<td>$k_1 \in (\theta 2^{c-b+2}/a, \theta 2^{b+1}/a)$

PC_</td>
<td rowspan="2">$k_1 > \theta 2^{c-b+2}/a$

PC_</td>
<td rowspan="2">$k_1 > a\theta 2^{c-b+2}$

PC_+</td>
</tr>
<tr>
<td>$k_1 > \theta 2^{b+1}/a$

CC_</td>
</tr>
<tr>
<td rowspan="2">$k_1 \in$
$(4\theta, 1)$</td>
<td>$a > 2^{b-1}$</td>
<td>$a < 2^{b-1}$</td>
<td rowspan="2">DC_+</td>
</tr>
<tr>
<td>CC_</td>
<td>DC_</td>
</tr>
</table>

where $\theta \equiv b^b c^c / (b+c)^{b+c}$

5. Conclusion

In this paper, we have conducted inframarginal analysis of a 2x2 Ricardian model. Departing from the neoclassical paradigm where individuals' levels of specialization are not endogenized, we explain international and domestic trade by individuals' choices of their levels and patterns of specialization. We provide a general equilibrium mechanism for the phenomena of underdevelopment and dual structure with underemployment in the less developed economy in the transitional stage of economic development. If transaction efficiencies in all countries are low, domestic and international autarky occurs in equilibrium. As the transaction efficiency in the developed country is improved, the equilibrium shifts to Type I dual structure where there is domestic division of labor in the developed economy and the less developed economy stays in autarky. As the transaction efficiencies are further improved, Type II dual structure occurs in equilibrium where each individual in the developed country completely relies on international trade and some individuals in the less developed country are involved in international trade and the rest of the population are in autarky. All gains from international trade go to the developed country. This dual structure is generated by the difference in transaction conditions between the developed and less developed countries. The relatively low transaction efficiency in the less developed country implies that not all home residents can be involved in the division of labor, so that their low productivity and per capita real income forces down average per capita real income and generates inferior terms of trade. As the transaction efficiency in the less developed country is sufficiently improved, the equilibrium network of domestic and international division of labor expands, so that aggregate productivity increases and more gains from trade are created and shared by all individuals. Hence, the less developed country will receive more gains from trade even if terms of trade deteriorate. Two types of dual structure disappear as the transitional stage is over due to further improvements in transaction conditions. For China, this model implies that if China did not use WTO membership to push further institutional reforms, its access into the WTO might not generate much benefit to China in a dual structure in which developed countries get all gains from trade. If China's trading efficiency is significantly increased by such institutional reforms, WTO membership will generate great benefit to China.

Finally, we have shown that China may benefit from exporting a good in producing which it has exogenous comparative disadvantage, if endogenous comparative advantage dominates the exogenous comparative disadvatage.

This model cannot analyze political economics of dual structure. Cheng, Sachs, and Yang (2000) have shown that if government tariff is introduced, a similar model with endogenous specialization can show that in a dual structure, the less developed country that has a low transaction efficiency and is not completely specialized has an incentive to impose an unilateral protection tariff to get more gains from trade, while the developed country has an incentive to implement an unilateral free trade regime. As transaction efficiency is improved, equilibrium jumps to the complete division of labor where all countries have incentive to have a Nash bargaining game (like WTO tariff negotiation), which generates a multilateral free trade regime. Also, the model in this paper is too simple for formalizing political economics of constitutional transition and dual track approach to economic reforms, which generates a more complicated dual structure with inefficiently unequal income distribution. Sachs, Woo, and Yang (2000) have reviewed research on political economics of that kind of dual structure in China.

References

Baldwin, Richard E. and Venables, Anthony J. (1995), "Regional Economic Integration," in Grossman, Gene M. and Rogoff, Kenneth, eds., *Hanbook of International Economics. Volume 3*, Amsterdam; New York and Oxford, Elsevier, North-Holland.

Barro, R. (1997), *Determinants of Economic Growth*, Cambridge, MA, MIT Press.

Becker, Gary (1981), *A Treatise on the Family*, Cambridge, Massachusetts, Harvard University Press.

Buchanan, James M. and Stubblebine, W. Craig (1962), "Externality," *Economica*, 29, 371-84.

Chenery, M. (1979), *Structural Change and Development Policy*, New York, Oxford University Press.

Cheng, W., Sachs, J., and Yang, X. (2000), "An Inframarginal Analysis of the Ricardian Model," *Review of International Economics*, 8, 208-20.

Coase, Ronald (1946), "The Marginal Cost Controversy," *Economica*, 13, 169-82.

Coase, Ronald (1960), "The Problem of Social Cost," *Journal of Law and Economics*, 3, 1-44.

Cypher, James and Dietz, James (1998), "Static and Dynamic Comparative Advantage: A Multi-period Analysis with Declining Terms of Trade," *Journal of Economic Issues*, 32, 305-14.

Dixit, A. (1968), "The Optimal Development in the Labour Surplus Economy," *Review of Economic Studies*, 35, 23-34.

Dixit, A. (1987), "Trade and Insurance with Moral Hazard," *Journal of International Economics*, 23, 201-20.

Dixit, A. (1989), "Trade and Insurance with Adverse Selection," *Review of Economic Studies*, 56, 235-48.

Dixit, A. and Norman, V. (1980), *Theory of International Trade*, Cambridge, Cambridge University Press.

Easton, Stephen and Walker, Michael (1997), "Income, Growth, and Economic Freedom," *American Economic Review, Papers and Proceedings*, 87, 328-32.

Ethier, W. (1982), "National and International Returns to Scale in the Modern Theory of International Trade," *American Economic Review*, 72, 389-405.

Frye, Timothy and Shleifer, Andrei (1997), "The Invisible Hand and the Grabbing Hand," *American Economic Review, Papers and Proceedings*, 87, 354-58.

Fujita, Masahisa and Krugman, Paul (1995), "When is the Economy Monocentric: von Thünen and Chamberlin Unified," *Regional Science & Urban Economics*, 25, 505-28.

Gallup, John and Sachs Jeff (1998), "Geography and Economic Development," Working Paper, Harvard Institute for International Development.

Gomory, Ralph E. (1994), "A Ricardo Model with Economies of Scale," *Journal of Economic Theory*, 62, 394-419.

Grossman, S. and Hart, O. (1986), "The Costs and Benefits of Ownership: A Theory of Vertical and Lateral Integration," *Journal of Political Economy*, 94, 691-719.

Grossman, G. and Helpman, E. (1990), "Comparative Advantage and Long-Run Growth," *American Economic Review*, 80, 796-815.

Kelly, Morgan (1997), "The Dynamics of Smithian Growth," *Quarterly Journal of Economics*, 112, 939-64.

Kemp, Murray (1991), "Variable Returns to Scale, Non-uniqueness of Equilibrium and the Gains from International Trade," *Review of Economic Studies*, 58, 807-16.

Khandker, A. and Rashid S. (1995), "Wage Subsidy and Full Employment in a Dual Economy with Open Unemployment and Surplus Labor," *Journal of Development Economics*, 48, 205-23.

Kohli, Ulrich and Werner, Augustin (1998), "Accounting for South Korean GDP Growth: Index-Number and Econometric Estimates," *Pacific Economic Review*, 3, 133-52.

Krugman, P. (1980), "Scale Economies, Product Differentiation, and the Pattern of Trade," *American Economic Review*, 70, 950-59.

Krugman, Paul (1994a), "Europe Jobless, America Penniless?" *Foreign Policy*, 95, 19-34.

Krugman, Paul (1994b), "Competitiveness: A Dangerous Obsession," *Foreign Affairs*, 73(2), 28-44.

Krugman, Paul (1995), "Technology, Trade, and Factor Prices." NBER Working Paper No. 5355, National Bureau of Economic Research.

Krugman,P. and Venables, A. J. (1995), "Globalization and the Inequality of Nations," *Quarterly Journal of Economics*, 110, 857-80.

Krugman,P. and Venables, A. J. (1996), "Integration, specialization, and adjustment," *European Economic Review*, 40, 959-67.

Lewis, W. (1955), *The Theory of Economic Growth*, London, Allen and Unwin.

Mokyr, Joel (1993), "The New Economic History and the Industrial Revolution," in Mokyr, J., ed., *The British Industrial Revolution: An Economic Perspective*, Boulder and Oxford, Westview Press.

Morgan, T. (1970), "Trends in Terms of Trade, and their Repercussion on Primary Products," in Morgan, T. and Betz G., eds., *Economic Development Readings in Theory and Practice*, Belmont, Wadsworth.

Murphy, K., Schleifer, A., and Vishny, R. (1989), "Income Distribution, Market Size and Industrialization," *Quarterly Journal of Economics*, 104, 537-64.

North, D. (1958), "Ocean Freight Rates and Economic Development," *Journal of Economic History*, 18, 537-55.

Panagariya, Arvind (1983), "Variable Returns to Scale and the Heckscher-Ohlin and Factor-Price-Equalization Theorems," *World Economics*, 119, 259-80.

Prestowitz, Clyde V. Jr., Thurow, L. C., Scharping, R., Cohen, S. S., Steil, B., and Krugman, P. (1994), "The Fight over Competitiveness," *Foreign Affairs*, 73(4), 186-197.

Ranis, G. (1988), "Analytics of Development: Dualism," in Chenery, H. and Srinivasan, T., eds., *Handbook of Development Economics, Vol. 1*, Amsterdam, North Holland, pp. 74-92.

Ricardo, David (1817), *The Principles of Political Economy and Taxation*, reprint, London, J.M. Dent & Sons Ltd, 1965.

Rosen, S. (1978), "Substitution and the Division of Labor," *Economica*, 45, 235-50.

Rosen, S. (1983), "Specialization and Human Capital," *Journal of Labor Economics*, 1, 43-49.

Sachs, Jeff (1996a), "The Tankers Are Turning - Sachs on Competitiveness," *World Link*, September/October.

Sachs, Jeff (1996b), "On the Tigers Trail - Sachs on Competitiveness," *World Link*, November/December.

Sachs, J. and Warner, A. (1995) "Economic Reform and the Process of Global Integration," Brookings Papers on Economic Activity, *Macroeconomics*, 1, 1-95.

Sachs, Jeffrey and Warner, Andrew (1997), "Fundamental Sources of Long-Run Growth," *American Economic Review, Papers and Proceedings*, 87, 184-88.

Sachs, Jeffrey, Woo, Wing Thye, and Yang, Xiaokai (2000), "Economic Reforms and Constitutional Transition," *Annals of Economics and Finance*, 1, 260-274.

Sen, Partha (1998), "Terms of Trade and Welfare for a Developing Economy with an Imperfectly Competitive Sector," *Review of Development Economics*, 2, 87-93.

Smith, Adam (1776), *An Inquiry into the Nature and Causes of the Wealth of Nations*, reprint, Oxford, Clarendon Press, 1976.

Wen, M. (1998), "An Analytical Framework of Consumer-Producers, Economies of Specialisation and Transaction Costs," in Arrow, K., Ng, Y-K., and Yang, X., eds., *Increasing Returns and Economic Analysis*, London, Macmillan.

Yang, X. (1991), "Development, Structure Change and Urbanization," *Journal of Development Economics*, 34, 199-222.

Yang, Xiaokai (1994), "Endogenous vs. Exogenous Comparative Advantages and Economies of Specialization vs. Economies of Scale," *Journal of Economics*, 60, 29-54.

Yang, X. and Borland, J. (1991), "A Microeconomic Mechanism for Economic Growth," *Journal of Political Economy*, 99, 460-82.

Yang, Xiaokai and Ng, Siang (1998), "Specialization and Division of Labor: A Survey," in Arrow, K., Ng, Y-K, and Yang, X., eds., *Increasing returns and Economic Analysis*, London, Macmillan.

Yang, X., Wang, J., and Wills, I. (1992), "Economic Growth, Commercialization and Institutional Changes in Rural China, 1979-1987," *China Economic Review*, 3, 1-37.

Young, Leslie (1991), "Heckscher-Ohlin Trade Theory with Variable Returns to Scale," *Journal of International Economics*, 31, 183-90.

Zhou, Lin, Sun, Guangzhen, and Yang, Xiaokai (1998), "General Equilibria in Large Economies with Endogenous Structure of Division of Labor," Working Paper, Department of Economics, Monash University.

CHAPTER 17

ENDOGENOUS STRUCTURE OF THE DIVISION OF LABOR, ENDOGENOUS TRADE POLICY REGIME, AND A DUAL STRUCTURE IN ECONOMIC DEVELOPMENT[*]

Xiaokai Yang[a] and Dingsheng Zhang[b]

[a]*Harvard and Monash University* [b]*Wuhan and Monash University*

1. Introduction

It is a well-accepted idea that free international trade benefits all countries involved; it is also a well-known fact that hardly any country has always been practicing free trade policies. Why do countries deviate from the free trade regime? Traditional trade theory contends that governments set up trade barriers because of political pressure from interest groups. Since imports competition poses a threat to some domestic industries, these industries lobby intensely for trade protection (Krueger, 1974, Pincus, 1975, Mayer, 1984). Other studies suggest that governments are tempted to use trade bargaining to get a larger share of the gains from trade (see, for instance, Morishima, 1989). We can identify three lines of research in trade bargaining. The first line builds on the theory of optimum tariff (Johnson, 1954), and uses bargaining games to model trade negotiations between governments (Mayer, 1981, Riezman, 1982). The second line of research is associated with the literature of the "new trade theory". It assumes an oligopolistic market structure in international trade, where governments adopt strategic trade

---

[*] Reprinted from *Annals of Economics and Finance*, 1, Xiaokai Yang and Dingsheng Zhang, "Endogenous Structure of the Division of Labor, Endogenous Trade Policy Regime, and a Dual Structure in Economic Development," 211-230, 2000, with permission from Annals of Economics and Finance.

policies to gain the economic rent generated by market power (Dixit and Kyle, 1985, Krugman, 1986). The third line of research views international negotiations as a two-level game: at the first level, interest groups lobby for trade policies in their favor, which determines governments' policy preference; at the second level, the negotiation between governments determines the international equilibrium (Grossman and Helpman, 1994, 1995a, 1995b).

While the existing literature provides insights as to why a particular trade regime may exist, it is silent about how it might evolve and how the equilibrium trade regime might relate to the equilibrium level of the division of labor between trading countries which is affected by transaction conditions. The purpose of this paper is to study the equilibrium level of the division of labor based on individuals' production and trade decisions, and to examine the general equilibrium implication of the inter-dependence between the level of the division of labor and the degree of trade liberation.

In this paper, we develop a Ricardian model with transaction costs and endogenous comparative advantage. In our model, individuals are consumer-producers, they choose first between self-sufficiency and trade, and then what and how much to produce and trade. The governments make decisions on trade policies: they can choose to play a Nash tariff game, to have Nash tariff negotiations, or to have *laissez faire* policies. We shall show that as transaction conditions improve, the equilibrium level of the division of labor increases. If a high level of the division of labor occurs in general equilibrium, each country has some power to affect the terms of trade and has an incentive to impose a tariff. If both countries play a Nash tariff game (i.e., to choose a tariff rate taking another country's tariff as given), there is a risk of a tariff war that can dissipate all the gains from trade. Facing this risk, all governments would prefer trade negotiations to a tariff war. A Nash tariff negotiation would result in zero tariff rates. If a medium level of the division of labor occurs in general equilibrium, i.e., one country is completely specialized in producing one good while the other produces two goods, then unilateral tariff protection and unilateral *laissez faire* policies would coexist.

The results of the model suggest that the development in the level and pattern of international division of labor may be a driving force behind the evolution of the international trade regime. This may explain the policy transition in some European governments from mercantilism to *laissez faire* in the 18th and 19th century and policy changes in developing countries from protection tariff to trade liberalization and tariff negotiation. The results also provide an economic rationale for trade negotiations and highlight the importance of trade negotiations in achieving stable trade liberalization.

Our paper is distinguished from Cheng, Sachs, and Yang (2000), in which technology displays constant returns to scale, and from Cheng, Liu, and Yang (2000), which cannot predict a dual structure with *ex ante* identical individuals choosing different levels of specialization (or different degrees of commercialization) and different levels of productivity.

The rest of this paper is organized as follows. Section 2 presents a simple Ricardian model with transaction costs and endogenous comparative advantage, and discusses the relationship between the transaction cost and the equilibrium level of the division of labor. Section 3 introduces government policy choices into the model and investigates the endogeneity of trade policy regimes.

2. A General Equilibrium Ricardian Model

2.1. The 2x2 model

Consider a world consisting of two countries, country 1 and country 2, each with a continuum set of individual consumer-producers of mass M_i ($i = 1, 2$). Assume that the individuals are *ex ante* identical within each country and have the following utility function:

$$U_i = (x_i + k_i x_i^d)^\beta (y_i + k_i y_i^d)^{1-\beta},$$

where x_i, y_i are quantities of goods x and y self-provided, and x_i^d, y_i^d are quantities of the goods x and y bought from the market. k_i ($k_i \in [0,1]$) is the transaction condition coefficient, which relates to an iceberg type transaction costs, for each unit of good bought, only the fraction k_i is received by the buyer, $1-k_i$ is lost in transit.

The production functions for an individual in country 1 and country 2 are:

$$x_1 + x_1^s = \max \{0, c(L_{1x}-b)\}, \quad y_1 + y_1^s = L_{1y},$$

$$x_2 + x_2^s = \max \{0, c(L_{2x}-b)\}, \quad y_2 + y_2^s = aL_{2y},$$

where L_{ix} and L_{iy} are respectively amounts of labor devoted to producing good x and good y, and $L_{ix}+L_{iy}=2$. x_i^s and y_i^s are respectively amounts of good x and good y sold in the market. We follow Charles Babbage (1832) and Houthakker (1956) to specify an individual specific fixed learning cost in producing good x, b, which is caused by a trial-error learning process in production or in a training process. The production technology of good y exhibits constant returns to scale. Country 2 is assumed to have exogenous comparative advantage in producing good y, or $a > 1$.

The existence of a fixed learning cost implies that specializing in a single good would increase utilization rate of the fixed training cost and improve labor productivity (Becker, 1981, and Rosen, 1983). The relative productivity advantage obtained through decisions regarding specification is referred to as endogenous comparative advantage (Yang, 1994). Endogenous comparative advantage can be the source of the gains from trade when exogenous comparative advantage is absent. When both exogenous and endogenous comparative advantage are present, they interact with each other to determine the pattern of trade.

The decision problem for an individual in country i involves deciding on what and how much to produce for self-consumption, to sell and to buy from the market. In other words, the individual chooses six variables $x_i, x_i^s, x_i^d, y_i, y_i^s, y_i^d \geq 0$. Hence, there are $2^6 = 64$ possible corner and interior solutions. As shown by Wen (1998), for such a model, an individual never simultaneously sells and buys the same good, never simultaneously produces and buys the same good, and never sells more than one good. We refer to each individual's choice of what to produce, buy and sell that is consistent with the Wen theorem as a *configuration*.

There are three configurations from which the individuals can choose:

(1) self sufficiency.   Configuration A, where an individual produces both goods for self-consumption.   This configuration is defined by

$$x_i, y_i > 0, x_i^s = x_i^d = y_i^s = y_i^d = 0, i = 1, 2 \, .$$

(2) specialization in producing good x.   Configuration (x/y), where an individual produces only x, sells x in exchange for y, is defined by

$$x_i, x_i^s, y_i^d > 0, x_i^d = y_i = y_i^s = 0 \, .$$

(3) specialization in producing good y.   Configuration (y/x), where an individual produces only y, sells y in exchange for x, is defined by

$$y_i, y_i^s, x_i^d > 0, y_i^d = x_i = x_i^s = 0$$

The combination of all individual's configurations constitutes a *market structure*, or *structure* for short.   Given the configurations listed above, there are eight feasible structures that may satisfy market clearing and other conditions for a general equilibrium.

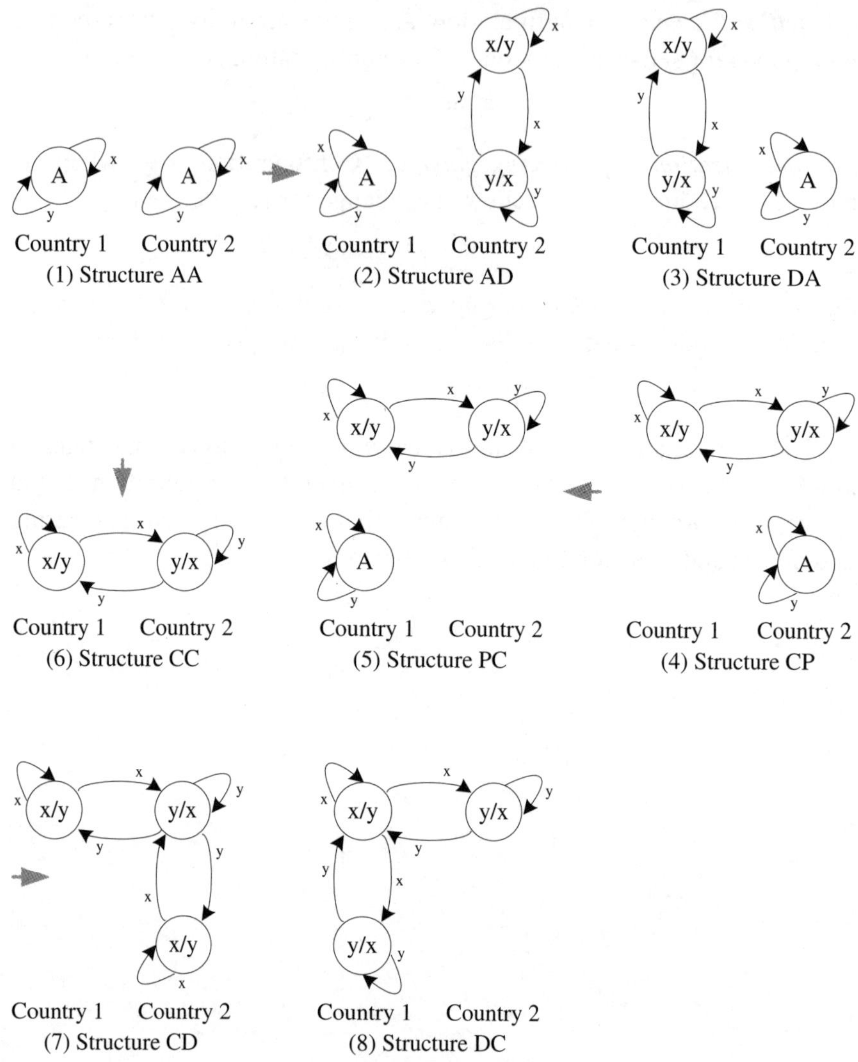

Figure 1: Configuration and Structures

Structure AA, as shown in panel (1) of Figure 1, is an autarky structure where individuals in both countries choose self-sufficiency (configuration A). Structure AD, shown in panel (2) of Figure 1, is asymmetric between the two countries: all individuals in country 1 choose autarky configuration A, while some individuals in country 2 choose configuration (x/y) and others choose configuration (y/x). Hence, there is domestic division of labor and related domestic trade in country 2, but without international division of labor and related international trade. Structure DA is symmetric to structure AD: country 1 has domestic division of labor and country 2 is in autarky. This structure involves a type I dual structure between countries.

Structure CP, shown in panel (4) of Figure 1, involves a type II dual structure between the two countries as well as in country 2. Some individuals in country 2 choose configuration (y/x), the rest of the population choose autarky, and all individuals in country 1 choose configuration (x/y). There is a dual structure between professional individuals choosing (y/x) and self-sufficient individuals in country 2 despite their *ex ante* identical characteristics. The professional individuals in country 2 are involved in international trade with country 1. Structure PC is symmetric to structure CP.

Structure CC, shown in panel (6) of Figure 1, is international complete division of labor between two countries in which all individuals in country 1 choose configuration (x/y) and all individuals in country 2 choose configuration (y/x).

In Structure CD, shown in panel (7) of Figure 1, country 1 has only international trade whereas country 2 has both international and domestic trade, and country 1 exports good x and country 2 exports good y.

Structure DC, shown in panel (8), is the same as structure PC except that those individuals choosing autarky in country 1 in structure PC choose configuration (y/x) instead in structure DC. Hence, in structure DC all individuals completely specialize, but country 1 is involved in both domestic and international trade, whereas country 2 is involved only in international trade. Also, country 1 exports good x and country 2 exports good y.

Since the optimal values of individuals' decision variables are discontinuous across structures, we introduce the concept of corner equilibrium. A corner equilibrium is defined as a set of relative prices of traded goods, numbers of individuals choosing different configurations, and the resource allocation in a given structure that satisfies the following conditions: (1) at the set of prices, the utility of each individual in both countries is maximized; (2) markets clear; (3) utilities of all individuals in the same country are equalized. The general equilibrium is the corner equilibrium where each individual's utility is maximized with respect of all possible configurations under the corner equilibrium prices.

To solve for the general equilibrium, we first apply the marginal analysis to solve for the corner equilibrium for each of the eight feasible structures. For instance, given structure PC, Some individuals in country 1 choose configuration (x/y), the rest of the population choose autarky, the number of choosing (x/y) and choosing autarky are M_{1x} and M_{1A}, respectively, $M_{1x} + M_{1A} = M_1$, and all individuals in country 2 choose configuration (y/x), that is, $M_{2y} = M_2$. For simplicity, we assume $\beta = 0.5$. The decision problems for individuals in country 1 who choose configuration (x/y) and autarky are respectively:

$$\max_{x_1, y_1^d} U_{1(x/y)} = x_1^{1/2} (k_1 y_1^d)^{1/2},$$

$$s.t. \quad x_1 + x_1^s = c(2-b),$$

$$px_1^s = y_1^d.$$

$$\max_{x_1, y_1} U_{1(A)} = x_1^{1/2} (y_1)^{1/2},$$

$$s.t. \quad x_1 = c(L_{1x} - b),$$

$$y_1 = L_{1y},$$

$$L_{1x} + L_{1y} = 2.$$

Since all individuals in country 1 are *ex ante* identical, utilities of individuals choosing different configurations should be equalized in equilibrium. This condition can determine the price of good x in terms of good y, p. Solving above two decision problems and applying $U_{1(x/y)} = U_{1(A)}$, we can derive relative price $p = 1/k_1 c$. Then we solve for the decision problem of an individual in country 2. Since all individuals in country 2 choose specialization in producing good y, their decision problem is :

$$\max_{x_2^d, y_2} U_{2(y/x)} = (k_2 x_2^d)^{1/2} (y_2)^{1/2},$$

$$s.t. \quad y_2 + y_2^s = 2a,$$

$$y_2^s = px_2^d.$$

We can solve M_{1x} and M_{1A} from the market clearing condition. The corner equilibrium in structure PC can then be solved, as shown in Table 1.

Following a similar procedure, we have solved the corner equilibria in other structures. The results are summarized in Table 1.

Table 1: Corner Equilibrium

Structure	Relative price of x to y	Numbers of individuals choosing various configurations
AA		$M_{1A} = M_1, M_{2A} = M_2$
CP	$4k_2 a / c(2-b)^2$	$M_{1x} = M_1, M_{2y} = 2M_1 k_2 /(2-b),$ $M_{2A} = M_2 - 2M_1 k_2 /(2-b)$
PC	$1/k_1 c$	$M_{1x} = M_1, M_{2y} = 2M_1 k_2 /(2-b),$ $M_{2A} = M_2 - 2M_1 k_2 /(2-b)$
AD	$2a / c(2-b)$	$M_{1A} = M_1, M_{2x} = M_{2y} = M_2 /2$
DA	$2 / c(2-b)$	$M_{1x} = M_{1y} = M_1 /2, M_{2A} = M_2$
CC	$2aM_2 / c(2-b)M_1$	$M_{1x} = M_1, M_{2y} = M_2$
DC	$2 / c(2-b)$	$M_{1x} = (M_1 + aM_2)/2, M_{2y} = M_2$ $M_{1y} = (M_1 - aM_2)/2$
CD	$2a / c(2-b)$	$M_{1x} = M_1, M_{2x} = (M_2 - M_1)/2$ $M_{2y} = (M_1 + M_2)/2$

For the given corner equilibrium price in a structure, we can compare each individual's utilities across different configurations. An individual would choose the configuration that generates a utility level that is not lower than other alternative configurations.

This condition that all individuals' utilities are maximized across all possible configurations defines a parameter subspace within which the corner equilibrium is the general equilibrium. The general equilibrium and their corresponding parameter subspaces are summarized in Table 2.

The results in Table 2 suggest that transaction efficiency determines the equilibrium level of the division of labor – as transaction efficiency improves, the equilibrium level of the division of labor jumps from autarky to partial division of labor (structure CP or PC), then to the complete division of labor (structure CC, DC,CD). In the transitional structure (CP or PC), the country with the lower transaction efficiency produces two goods and receives no gains from trade.

In table 2, C stands for complete specialization in a country, D stands for the domestic division of labor in a country, A stands for autarky in a country, P stands for the partial division of labor where the population is divided between autarky and specialization in a country. Hence, structure AA involves autarky in both countries, structures AD and DA involve autarky in one country and the division of labor in the other, structures PC and CP involve complete specialization in one country and coexistence of autarky and complete specialization in the other. The country with the lower transaction efficiency in this structure looks like underdeveloped in the sense that it receives none of gains from trade and income differential between it and the other country with higher transaction efficiency increases as a result of a shift of equilibrium from autarky to this structure. Also, *ex ante* identical individuals in the less developed country in this structure are divided between a professional occupation that trades with the foreign country and those who are self-sufficient and not involved in commercialized production. These self-sufficient individuals look like in underemployment since they cannot find a job to work for the market. All individuals completely specialize in structures CD and CC. But CC involves complete specialization of both countries in the absence of domestic trade, whereas CD involves complete specialization in country 1 and domestic division of labor in country 2. Figure 1 illustrates the equilibrium structures. We say the level of the division of labor increases if occurrence of letter A or P decreases or the occurrence of letter D or C increases in a structure.

Hence, the inframarginal comparative statics of general equilibrium can be summarized as follows.

Table 2: Walrasian Equilibrium and its Inframarginal Comparative Statics

<table>
<tr>
<td></td>
<td colspan="4">$0<k_2<\frac{2-b}{2}$</td>
<td colspan="4">$\frac{2-b}{2}<k_2<1$</td>
</tr>
<tr>
<td rowspan="3">$0<k_1<\frac{2-b}{2}$</td>
<td>$k_1k_2<\frac{(2-b)^2}{4a}$</td>
<td colspan="3">$k_1k_2>\frac{(2-b)^2}{4a}$</td>
<td>$k_1<\frac{2-b}{2a}$</td>
<td colspan="3">$k_1>\frac{2-b}{2a}$</td>
</tr>
<tr>
<td rowspan="2">AA</td>
<td>$\frac{M_1}{M_2}\le1$</td>
<td>$1<\frac{M_1}{M_2}<a$</td>
<td>$\frac{M_1}{M_2}>a$</td>
<td rowspan="2">AD</td>
<td>$\frac{M_1}{M_2}\le1$</td>
<td>$1<\frac{M_1}{M_2}<a$</td>
<td>$\frac{M_1}{M_2}>a$</td>
</tr>
<tr>
<td>CP</td>
<td>$k_1<\frac{M_1(2-b)}{2aM_2}$: PC
$k_2<\frac{M_2(2-b)}{2M_1}$: CP
$k_1>\frac{M_1(2-b)}{2aM_2}$, $k_2>\frac{M_2(2-b)}{2M_1}$: CC</td>
<td>PC</td>
<td>AD</td>
<td>$k_1<\frac{M_1(2-b)}{2aM_2}$: PC
$k_1>\frac{M_1(2-b)}{2aM_2}$: CC</td>
<td>CC</td>
</tr>
<tr>
<td rowspan="3">$\frac{2-b}{2}<k_1<1$</td>
<td>$k_2<\frac{2-b}{2a}$</td>
<td colspan="3">$k_2>\frac{2-b}{2a}$</td>
<td colspan="2">$\frac{M_1}{M_2}\le1$</td>
<td>$1<\frac{M_1}{M_2}<a$</td>
<td>$\frac{M_1}{M_2}>a$</td>
</tr>
<tr>
<td rowspan="2">DA</td>
<td>$\frac{M_1}{M_2}\le1$</td>
<td>$1<\frac{M_1}{M_2}<a$</td>
<td>$\frac{M_1}{M_2}>a$</td>
<td colspan="2" rowspan="2">CD</td>
<td rowspan="2">CC</td>
<td rowspan="2">DC</td>
</tr>
<tr>
<td>DA</td>
<td>$k_2<\frac{M_2(2-b)}{2M_1}$: CP
$k_2>\frac{M_2(2-b)}{2M_1}$: CC</td>
<td>DC</td>
</tr>
</table>

                              X. Yang, D. Zhang

Proposition 1: If transaction efficiencies are very low in the two countries, the general equilibrium is autarky where no domestic and international trade takes place. As the transaction conditions in one country improve, a type I dual structure emerges from the coexistence of domestic division of labor in one country and autarky in the other (structure AD or DA). As trading efficiencies further improve, a type II dual structure emerges (structure CP or PC) where all gains from trade go to the country that completely specializes and the population in the country with a lower trading efficiency is divided between the commercialized sector and autarky. If the transaction efficiencies in both countries sufficiently improve, the equilibrium jumps to the complete international division of labor. In this process, the equilibrium aggregate productivity converges to the aggregate production possibility frontier.

Since marginal rate of substitution and marginal rate of transformation must be equalized for each individual in autarky, the equilibrium aggregate productivity occurs under the production possibility frontier if autarky is the general equilibrium. As transaction conditions are improved, the equilibrium aggregate productivity becomes closer to the PPF. Zhou, Sun, and Yang (1998) prove that a general equilibrium for a general class of models with consumer-producers and endogenous and exogenous comparative advantages exists if the set of individuals is a continuum and that the general equilibrium is Pareto optimal. Hence, our inframarginal comparative statics imply that if transaction efficiencies are very low, the Pareto optimum is not associated with the PPF because of the trade off between (endogenous and exogenous) comparative advantages and transaction costs. As transaction conditions are improved, the equilibrium as well as Pareto optimal become closer to the PPF. This result can be used to explore development implications of transaction conditions and intimate relationship between trade dependence and economic development. Improvements in transaction conditions generate expansion of the network of trade, which increases the equilibrium aggregate productivity.

Also, our results can be used to explain "underdevelopment phenomenon" in the transitional period of economic development. As an economy develops from autarky to high level of international trade, real income differential between developed countries, which have better transaction conditions, and less developed countries may increase due to the unequal distribution of gains from international trade. This generates trade conflict between developed and less developed countries, which may motivate rent seeking via tariff policy. We turn to this issue in the next section.

3. Endogenous Trade Policy Regime

This section introduces governments' decisions on trade policies into the model. The governments can choose from three trade policy regimes: a Nash tariff game where each government chooses its own tariff rate, taking the other country's tariff rate as given; Nash tariff bargaining; and *laissez faire*.

Since the welfare effects of tariff are different for different trade structures, we examine structures separately, starting with CC, then moving on to structures DC and CD, finally to structure PC and CP. Because of the symmetry between DC and CD, and between CP and PC, we only need to consider structures CC, CD, and CP.

3.1. Structure CC: Complete international division of labor

Assumed that the government in each country can impose tariff on imported goods to maximize its citizen's welfare. Tariff revenue is equally distributed among the domestic buyers of the imported goods. In structure CC, the decision problems for individuals in country 1 and country 2 are:

$$\max_{x_1, y_1^d} U_1 = x_1^{1/2}(k_1 y_1^d)^{1/2}, \qquad \max_{x_2^d, y_2} U_2 = (k_2 x_2^d)^{1/2}(y_2)^{1/2},$$

$$s.t. \quad x_1 + x_1^s = c(2-b), \qquad s.t. \quad y_2 + y_2^s = 2a,$$

$$p_x x_1^s + R_1 = p_y(1+t_1)y_1^d, \qquad p_y y_2^s + R_2 = p_x(1+t_2)x_2^d,$$

where t_i is the tariff rate in country i and R_i is the tariff revenue received by an individual in country i, $R_1 = t_1 p_y y_1^d$, $R_2 = t_2 p_x x_2^d$ in equilibrium.

Solving the decision problems, we obtain the supply and demand functions for good x and good y:

$$x_1 = \frac{c(2-b)}{2}\frac{2(1+t_1)}{2+t_1}, \quad x_1^s = \frac{c(2-b)}{2}\frac{2}{2+t_1}, \quad y_1^d = \frac{c(2-b)}{2}\frac{2}{2+t_1}\frac{p_x}{p_y},$$

$$y_2 = a\frac{2(1+t_1)}{2+t_1}, \quad y_2^s = a\frac{2}{2+t_1}, \quad y_2^d = a\frac{2}{2+t_1}\frac{p_y}{p_x}.$$

Using the market clearing condition for good x, we can solve for the price of good x in terms of good y:

$$\frac{p_y}{p_x} = \frac{M_1}{M_2}\frac{c(2-b)}{2a}\frac{2+t_2}{2+t_1}.$$

Substituting the demand and supply functions and the relative price into the utility functions, we get the corner equilibrium levels of utilities for individuals in the two countries:

$$u_1(t_1,t_2) = [k_1\frac{M_2}{M_1}\frac{ac(2-b)}{2}\frac{4(1+t_1)}{(2+t_1)(2+t_2)}]^{1/2},$$

$$u_2(t_1,t_2) = [k_2a^2\frac{M_1}{M_2}\frac{c(2-b)}{2a}\frac{4(1+t_2)}{(2+t_1)(2+t_2)}]^{1/2}$$

We now look at how governments may choose different trade policy regimes.

3.1.1. Nash tariff game

Differentiation of the two expressions with respect to t_i yields:

$$\frac{\partial u_1}{\partial t_1} > 0, \quad \frac{\partial u_1}{\partial t_2} < 0, \quad \frac{\partial u_2}{\partial t_2} > 0, \quad \frac{\partial u_2}{\partial t_1} < 0.$$

The above four inequalities suggest that, taking the other country's tariff rate as given, each country can improve its citizens' welfare by imposing a tariff. Thus the governments could play a Nash tariff game rather than adopting *laissez faire* trade policies. However, if the governments in the two countries do play a Nash tariff game, the above four inequalities imply that in the Nash equilibrium each country would impose a tariff to such a high level that individuals in the other country is just indifferent between participating in international trade and autarky. The Nash equilibrium tariff rates (t_1^*, t_2^*) are determined by equalization conditions between utility in structure AA and in structure CC:

$$u_1(t_1^*, t_2^*) = u_1(A), \quad u_2(t_1^*, t_2^*) = u_2(A),$$

$$t_1^* = \frac{1}{8k_1} \frac{M_1}{M_2} (2-b)(2+t_1^*)(2+t_2^*) - 1,$$

$$t_2^* = \frac{1}{8k_2} \frac{M_2}{M_1} (2-b)(2+t_1^*)(2+t_2^*) - 1,$$

and the solution (t_1^*, t_2^*) are implicitly given by the two equations above.

In other words, if the two governments use tariff to compete for a larger share of the gains from trade, there will be a tariff war which would exhaust all the gains from trade. This is an example of the prisoner's dilemma.

3.1.2. Nash tariff negotiation

Alternatively, the two governments can play a Nash bargaining game, that is, they can negotiate over tariff rates. The Nash tariff negotiation maximizes the Nash product, which is the product of the gains from trade received by individuals in each country. The gains from trade are measured by the difference in the utility between participating in trade (structure CC in this case) and staying in structure AA, AD, or DA. The Nash tariff negotiation equilibrium is given by the solution of the following problem:

$$\max_{t_1, t_2} V \equiv [u_1(t_1, t_2) - u_1(A)][u_2(t_1, t_2) - u_2(A)],$$

where $u_i(A)$ denotes the utility of a person in country i in an alternative structure with autarky or domestic division of labor. The first order conditions for this problem yield $(1+t_1)(1+t_2) = 1$, which gives the equilibrium tariff $t_1^* = t_2^* = 0$. In other words, the Nash tariff negotiation generates trade liberation.

The result of a tariff negotiation is in sharp contrast with the result of a Nash tariff game with the latter leading to complete dissipation of the gains from trade because of the prisoners' dilemma. This provides an explanation as to why trade negotiations may be essential for trade liberalization and for the full exploitation of the gains from trade.

If the two governments can choose between the Nash tariff war and Nash tariff negotiation, they will certainly choose the latter. Hence, if structure CC occurs in equilibrium and if the governments are allowed to choose policy regimes, the general equilibrium trade policy will be free trade resulted from a Nash tariff negotiation.

3.2. Structures CD: Partial international division of labor

We now turn to the structures with partial international division of labor, structure CD, to examine the choices of trade policies.

In country 1, the decision problem for an individual specializing in good x is:

$$\max_{x_1,y_1^d} U_1 = x_1^{1/2}(k_1 y_1^d)^{1/2},$$

$$s.t. \quad x_1 + x_1^s = c(2-b),$$

$$p_x x_1^s + R_1 = p_y(1+t_1)y_1^d.$$

the solution of this problem is:

$$x_1 = \frac{c(2-b)}{2}\frac{2(1+t_1)}{2+t_1}, \quad x_1^s = \frac{c(2-b)}{2}\frac{2}{2+t_1}, \quad y_1^d = \frac{c(2-b)}{2}\frac{2}{2+t_1}\frac{p_x}{p_y}.$$

In country 2, the decision problem for an individual specializing in good x and that for an individual specializing in good y are, respectively

$$\max_{x_2,y_2^d} U_2(x/y) = x_2^{1/2}(k_2 y_2^d)^{1/2},$$

$$s.t. \quad x_2 + x_2^s = c(2-b),$$

$$p_x^D x_2^s = p_y y_2^d.$$

$$\max_{x_2^d,y_2} U_2(y/x) = (k_2 x_2^d)^{1/2}(y_2)^{1/2},$$

$$s.t. \quad y_2 + y_2^s = 2a,$$

$$p_y y_2^s + R_2 = p_x^D x_{22}^d + p_x(1+t_2)x_{12}^d.$$

where p_x^D is price of good x in country 2, $p_x^D = p_x(1+t_2)$, x_{12}^d and x_{22}^d are foreign demand and domestic demand of good x by individuals choosing configuration (y/x) in country 2, respectively, t_i is the tariff rate in country i, R_i is the tariff revenue received by an individual purchasing foreign good in country i, and $R_1 = t_1 p_y y_1^d$, $R_2 = t_2 p_x x_{12}^d$, $x_2^d = x_{12}^d + x_{22}^d$.

Solving above two problems yields:

$$x_2 = \frac{c(2-b)}{2}, \quad x_2^s = \frac{c(2-b)}{2}, \quad y_2^d = (1+t_2)\frac{p_x}{p_y}\frac{c(2-b)}{2},$$

$$y_2 = a + t_2 \frac{p_x}{p_y}\frac{M_1}{M_{2y}}\frac{c(2-b)}{4}\frac{2}{2+t_1}, \quad y_2^s = a - t_2 \frac{p_x}{p_y}\frac{M_1}{M_{2y}}\frac{c(2-b)}{4}\frac{2}{2+t_1},$$

$$x_2^d = \frac{1}{1+t_2}\frac{p_y}{p_x}\left[a + t_2\frac{p_x}{p_y}\frac{M_1}{M_{2y}}\frac{c(2-b)}{4}\frac{2}{2+t_1}\right].$$

Using the utility equalization condition and the market clearing condition for either good, we obtain the corner equilibrium in structure CD:

$$\frac{p_x}{p_y} = \frac{2a}{c(2-b)}\frac{[2M_1 + M_2(2+t_1)]}{[2M_1 + M_2(2+t_1)(1+t_2)]},$$

$$M_{2y} = \frac{2M_1(1+t_2) + M_2(1+t_2)(2+t_1)}{2(1+t_2)(2+t_1)},$$

$$u_1(t_1,t_2) = k_1\frac{ac(2-b)}{2}\frac{4(1+t_1)[2M_1 + M_2(2+t_1)]}{(2+t_1)^2[2M_1 + M_2(2+t_1)(1+t_2)]},$$

$$u_2(t_1,t_2) = k_2\frac{ac(2-b)}{2}\frac{(1+t_2)[2M_1 + M_2(2+t_1)]}{[2M_1 + M_2(2+t_1)(1+t_2)]}.$$

From the corner equilibrium solution, we obtain

$$\frac{\partial u_1}{\partial t_1} < 0, \quad \frac{\partial u_1}{\partial t_2} < 0, \quad \frac{\partial u_2}{\partial t_1} < 0, \quad \frac{\partial u_2}{\partial t_2} > 0.$$

Clearly, country 2 would not choose free trade policies. If it plays a Nash game, it would want its tariff rate to be as high as possible. But since

$$\frac{\partial u_1}{\partial t_2} < 0 \,,$$

country 2 needs to ensure that its tariff rate is not so high as to drive country 1 out of international trade. Thus, the optimum tariff rate for country 2 is determined by the utility equalization between structure CD and structure AA for individuals in country 1, which (after some algebraic simplification) is

$$u_1(0,t_2^*) = u_1(A) \quad \text{or} \quad t_2^* = \frac{2M_1(2a-2+b)+4aM_2}{(2-b)M_2} - 1 \,.$$

Since $\dfrac{\partial u_1}{\partial t_1} < 0$, the optimum tariff rate for country 1 is zero, therefore, if structure CD occurs in equilibrium, the result of a Nash tariff game would be the coexistence of an unilateral *laissez faire* policy by country 1 and unilateral protection tariff by country 2.

In a Nash tariff game, country 2 gets most the gains from trade. Since a Nash tariff negotiation would mean sharing the gains from trade, country 2 does not have an incentive to participate in a tariff negotiation. Thus even if the governments in both countries are allowed to choose between the Nash tariff game and Nash tariff negotiation, the Nash tariff negotiation would not be chosen by country 2. As a result, the equilibrium trade policy regime would feature the coexistence of unilateral protection tariff and unilateral *laissez faire*.

3.3. Structures CP: Dual economy

In structure CP, all individuals in country 1 choose configuration (x/y), so $M_{1x} = M_1$. Some individuals in country 2 choose configuration (y/x), other individuals choose autarky. Numbers choosing (y/x) and choosing autarky are M_{2y} and M_{2A}, respectively, $M_{2y} + M_{2A} = M_2$. The decision problem of individuals in country 1 is the same as in structure CC. For individuals in country 2, we assume tariff revenue is equally distributed to each individual, so the decision problems of individuals choosing (y/x) and choosing autarky in country 2 are respectively:

$$\max_{x_2^d, y_2} U_2(y/x) = (k_2 x_2^{d})^{1/2}(y_2)^{1/2},$$

$$s.t \quad y_2 + y_2^{s} = 2a,$$

$$p_y y_2^{s} + R_2 = p_x(1+t_2)x_{12}^{d}.$$

$$\max_{x_2, y_2, x_{2A}^d, y_{2A}^d} u_2(TA) = (x_2 + k_2 x_{2A}^d)^{1/2}(y_2 + k_2 y_{2A}^d)^{1/2},$$

$$s.t. \quad x_2 = c(L_{2x} - b),$$

$$y_2 = aL_{2y},$$

$$L_{2x} + L_{2y} = 2,$$

$$p_x(1+t_2)x_{2A}^d + p_y y_{2A}^d = R_2,$$

where TA denotes the decision problem in autarky with government tariff, x_{2A}^d and y_{2A}^d are the demand for good x and y, respectively,

$$R_2 = \frac{M_{2y} t_2 p_x + M_{2A} t_2 x_{2A}^d}{M_2}$$

is the per capita tariff revenue. For simplicity, we assume $x_{2A}^d = 0$, that is to say, individuals who choose autarky do not buy imported good.

Solving above problems yields the demand function. Using utility equalization condition and market clearing conditions yields the relative price, numbers of individuals choosing different configurations, and the corner equilibrium utility level:

$$\frac{p_x}{p_y} = \frac{a}{c(1+t_2)},$$

$$M_{2y} = \frac{2M_2(1+t_2)(2\sqrt{k_2} - 2 + b)}{t_2(2k_2 - 2 + b)},$$

$$u_1(t_1, t_2) = [k_1 ac(2-b)^2 \frac{(1+t_1)}{(1+t_2)(2+t_1)^2}]^{1/2},$$

$$u_2(y/x) = u_2(TA) = [\frac{ac(2-b-2k_2)^2}{4(1-\sqrt{k_2})^2}]^{1/2}$$

If $k_2 < \dfrac{(2-b)^2}{4}$, we have $M_{2y} < M_2$. Hence, $k_2 < \dfrac{(2-b)^2}{4}$ is a necessary condition that structure CP occurs in equilibrium. It is easy to show $u_2(y/x) = u_2(TA) > u_2(A)$,this implies the government in country 2 prefers a tariff on imported goods. But $\dfrac{\partial u_1}{\partial t_1} < 0$ and $\dfrac{\partial u_1}{\partial t_2} < 0$, thus, the optimum tariff rate for country 1 is zero. The equilibrium trade policy regime would feature the coexistence of unilateral protection tariff and unilateral *laissez faire*.

We may draw the distinction between the exogenous transaction costs coefficient and the endogenous transaction costs caused by the deadweight of tariff. Exogenous transaction costs can be seen before individuals have made their decisions. Endogenous transaction costs are caused by conflicts between self-interested decisions that generate distortions. Following the method used in section 2, we can prove that in this extended model, the general equilibrium jumps from autarky to the partial division of labor, where unilateral protection tariff in the less developed country and unilateral *laissez faire* in the developed economy coexist, then to the complete division of labor, where tariff negotiation generates bilateral free trade, as the exogenous transaction costs coefficient decreases. In the transitional period with partial division of labor, endogenous transaction costs are caused by trade conflicts between the developed and less developed countries. There are two ways for a less developed country to get more gains from trade in the transitional period. One is to improve transaction conditions in the less developed country, so that the equilibrium jumps to the complete division of labor that ensures bilateral incentives for tariff negotiation, which leads to trade liberalization. The other is that the less developed country imposes a stiff tariff to get greater gains from trade at the cost of the partner. The first way is to get a larger share by enlarging the pie and the second way is to get a larger share of a shrinking pie.

The results are summarized as follows.

Proposition 2:　As exogenous transaction conditions are improved, the equilibrium jumps from autarky to the partial international division of labor where coexistence of unilateral protection tariff and unilateral *laissez faire* generates endogenous transaction costs, then to the complete international division of labor where tariff negotiation leads to free trade and eliminates endogenous transaction costs.

Proposition 2 may be used to explain two phenomena.　First, despite the distortions caused by tariff, tariff may be used by the government in a less developed economy with low transaction efficiency to get a larger share of gains from trade, since the Walrasian equilibrium terms of trade with no tariff may be very unfavorable to the less developed country. Second, when transaction condition is inadequate and when the equilibrium is associated with an intermediate level of the division of labor, a country that has low transaction efficiency and does not completely specialize may prefer a unilateral tariff, whereas the other country that has higher transaction efficiency and completely specializes may prefer a unilateral *laissez faire* regime. But as transaction conditions improve further, all countries may prefer tariff negotiations to a unilateral tariff.

In the 16th century, unilateral tariff was advocated by Mercantilists as a means of rent seeking in international trade.　It gave way to trade liberalization in the 18th and 19th centuries in some European countries. However, even after the World War II, many governments in developing countries have still adopted unilateral tariff protection. More recently, tariff negotiations have become increasingly prevalent.　Some economists use the Walrasian model to explain the emergence of the *laissez faire* regime, but the model cannot explain why other trade regimes persisted in many countries for a long period of time.　Other economists use the theory of import substitution and export substitution to explain the transition from unilateral tariff to trade liberalization (see, for instance, Balassa, 1980), but the theory cannot explain why the *laissez faire* regime was unstable even between developed countries; why unilateral protection tariff and *laissez faire* regime may coexist; or why tariff negotiations may be necessary for free trade and for the exploitation of the gains from trade.　Proposition 2 in this paper seems to offer a more plausible explanation as to why unilateral tariff prevailed in the early stage of economic development; why trade liberalization is preferred in later stages of economic development; and other associated questions.

4. Conclusion

In this paper, we have introduced transaction costs and endogenous comparative advantage into the Ricardian model. We have also examined governments' choices of different trade policy regimes. An interesting result of this paper is that the equilibrium trade policy regimes are intimately related to the level of international division of labor. At a high level of international division of labor, countries would participate in Nash tariff negotiations that would lead to free trade. If the level of the division of labor is at a level such that one country produces both goods (some of residents in this country completely specialize and the rest of them choose autarky) and determines the terms of trade, then at equilibrium, unilateral tariff and unilateral free trade would coexist. The model provides a plausible story about how a trade policy regime might evolve, and an explanation for the changing tides of trade policy stances in developing countries.

References

Babbage, C. (1832), *On the Economy of Machinery and Manufactures,* 4th enlarged edition of 1835, reissued in 1977, New York, M. Kelly.

Balassa, B. (1980), "The Process of Industrial Development and Alternative Development Strategies," Princeton University, International Finance Section, *Essays in International Finance,* No. 141.

Cheng, W., Sachs, J. and Yang, X. (2000), "An Inframarginal Analysis of the Ricardian Model," *Review of International Economics*, 8, 208-20.

Cheng, W., Liu, M. and Yang, X. (2000), "A Ricardo Model with Endogenous Comparative Advantage and Endogenous Trade Policy Regime," *Economic Record*, 76, 172-82.

Dixit, Avinash K. and Kyle, Albert S. (1985), "The Use of Protection and Subsidies for Entry Promotion and Deterrence," *American Economic Review*, 75, 139-52.

Ekelund, Robert and Tollison, Robert (1981), *Merchantilism as an Rent-Seeking Society*, College Station, Texas A & M University Press.

Gomory, Ralph E. (1994), "A Ricardo Model with Economies of Scale," *Journal of Economic Theory,* 62, 394-419.

Grossman, Gene M. and Richardson, J. (1986), "Strategic Trade Policy: A Survey of the Issues and Early Analysis," In Robert E. Baldwin and J. David Richardson, eds., *International Trade and Finance,* 3rd ed., 95-113, Boston, Little Brown.

Grossman, Gene M. and Helpman, Elhanan (1994), "Protection for Sale," *American Economic Review*, 84, 833-50.

Grossman, Gene M. and Helpman, Elhanan (1995a), "The Politics of Free-Trade Agreements," *American Economic Review,* 85(4), 668-690.

Grossman, Gene M. and Helpman, Elhanan (1995b), "Trade Wars and Trade Talks," *Journal of Political Economy*, 103(4), 675-708.

Houthakker, M. (1956), "Economics and Biology: Specialization and Speciation," *Kyklos,* 9, 181-89.

Johnson, Harry G. (1954), "Optimum Tariff and Retaliation," *Review of Economic Studies*, 21(2), 142-53.

Krueger, Anne O. (1974), "The Political Economy of Rent-Seeking Society," *American Economic Review*, 64, 291-303.

Krugman, Paul R., ed., (1986), *Strategic Trade Policy and the New International Economics*, Cambridge, MIT Press.

Mayer, Wolfgang (1981), "Theoretical Considerations on Negotiated Tariff Adjustments," *Oxford Economic Papers*, 33, 135-53.

Mayer, Wolfgang (1984), "Endogenous Tariff Formation," *American Economic Review*, 74, 970-85.

Morishima, Michio (1989), *Ricardo's Economics: A General Equilibrium Theory of Distribution and Growth*, Cambridge, Cambridge University Press.

Nash, J. F. (1950), "The Bargaining Problem," *Econometrica*, 18, 115-62.

Osborne, Martin J. and Rubinstein, Ariel (1990), *Bargaining and Markets,* San Diego, Academic Press, Inc.

Pincus, Jonathan J. (1975), "Pressure Groups and the Pattern of Tariffs," *Journal of Political Economy*, 83, 757-78.

Pomfret, Richard (1992), "Internal Trade Policy with Imperfect Competition," *Special Papers in International Economics*, 17, August.

Riezman, Raymond (1982), ""Tariff Retaliation from a Strategic Viewpoint," *Southern Economic Journal*, 48, 583-93.

Rosen, S.(1983), "Specialization and Human Capital," *Journal of Labor Economics*, 1, 43-49.

Wen, M. (1998), "An Analytical Framework of Consumer-Producers, Economies of Specialization and Transaction Costs," In K. Arrow, Y-K. Ng, X. Yang, eds., *Increasing Returns and Economic Analysis*, London, Macmillan.

Yang, X. (1994), "Endogenous Comparative Advantages and Economies of Specialization vs. Economies of Scale," *Journal of Economics*, 60, 29-54.

Zhou, Lin, Sun, Guangzhen and Yang, Xiaokai (1998), "General Equilibria in Large Economies with Endogenous Structure of the Division of Labor," *Working Paper*, Monash University.

Part 7

Dynamic Inframarginal Analysis of Trade Models with Endogenous Comparative Advantage

CHAPTER 18

A MICROECONOMIC MECHANISM FOR ECONOMIC GROWTH[*]

Xiaokai Yang[a] and Jeff Borland[b*]

[a]Monash and Harvard University   [b]University of Melbourne

1. Introduction

There are two basic approaches to explaining economic growth. The first approach, represented in the work of Solow (1956) and Swan (1956), has exogenous technical change as the source of economic growth. The second approach, which has received much attention recently, allows the sources of economic growth to be endogenously determined. By formalizing a trade-off between the allocation of resources to current consumption (production of final goods), the production of knowledge, and investment in physical capital, a number of studies have established a role for endogenous accumulation in generating economic growth. For example, in Romer *(1986a, 1989a),* Lucas (1988), and Aghion and Howitt (1990), the rate of growth depends on the endogenous accumulation of human capital and technical change; in Romer *(1986b)* and Grossman and Helpman (1989), endogenous increases in the number of intermediate inputs (which raise productivity in the production of final goods) explain economic growth.

---

[*] Reprinted from *Journal of Political Economy*, 99 (3), Xiaokai Yang and Jeff Borland, "A Microeconomic Mechanism for Economic Growth," 460-82, 1991, with permission from University of Chicago Press.

[*] We are grateful to Gene Grossman, Edwin Mills, Barry Nalebuff, Sherwin Rosen, James Schmitz, Jr., T. N. Srinivasan, and two referees for their comments on an earlier version of this paper. Thanks also go to Yew-Kwang Ng for helpful discussions. We are responsible for any remaining errors.

By interpreting an expanding range of intermediate inputs to represent a greater division of labor, these latter studies have initiated a formal analysis of Adam Smith's (1776) and Allyn Young's (1928) proposition that increases in the division of labor will create economic growth. However, division of labor is based not only on an expanding range of intermediate inputs but also on increases in the level of specialization of individual agents. In this paper we investigate this second aspect of the division of labor and take up the issue of the relationship between the evolution of the level of specialization and economic growth.

In the model to be considered, each individual is a consumer-producer, and growth in the division of labor is therefore interpreted as an increase in the proportion of an individual's production that is sold to other people and the proportion of an individual's consumption that is purchased from other people. Each individual is assumed to have a Cobb-Douglas utility function with a positive discount rate so that there is a preference for both diverse and current consumption. Consumption goods can be either self-produced or purchased, but if they are purchased there is a transaction cost incurred. Each individual's production function, which is nontransferable, displays increasing returns to specialization and learning by doing.

Because all individuals are ex ante identical and the parameters of production, preference, and transaction cost are the same for every good, the problem of resource allocation is resolved in a straightforward manner with the relative numbers of persons selling the different goods playing the role of relative prices in a conventional Walrasian regime. The most important decision for an individual in our model is choosing his or her level of specialization. The aggregate outcome of such individual decisions is an endogenously determined division of labor for the economy.

With the market structure and level of specialization endogenous, the number of producers of each good will vary over time. By contrast, in models in which the degree of division of labor is associated with the number of intermediate goods, there is always a single producer of any good. These models, which exogenously fix the level of specialization of an individual agent, are unable to explain why an economy evolves from autarky (each person self-provides all the goods he wants) to a state in which there is a highly developed division of labor between individuals in a firm, between firms, and between countries.

At any time there is a trade-off involved in an individual's decision on the optimum level of specialization. Choosing to specialize more in the current period has the benefit of generating higher productive capacity in future periods (because of learning by doing and increasing returns). However, because of the preference for diverse consumption, greater specialization must be accompanied by a greater number and higher quantity of goods purchased from other individuals. This higher level of trade will incur greater transaction costs, which is undesirable because of the individual's preference for current consumption. The existence of this trade-off, combined with the assumption that economies of specialization are specific to each person and activity, secures the existence of a dynamic competitive equilibrium and a Pareto optimum over an infinite horizon even if increasing returns prevail in all activities.[1]

One dynamic equilibrium of this model involves evolution of the economy from autarky to a state in which there is a high degree of division of labor. This equilibrium will occur if in early periods the discounted value of the benefits from specialization is not significant compared to the associated utility losses that arise because of transaction costs. Later, the effects of learning by doing will increase an individual's scope for trading off the dynamic gains from specialization against the costs of forgone consumption, and a higher level of specialization will be adopted. The evolution of the division of labor will enlarge the extent of the market, speed up the accumulation of human capital, and raise trade dependence and endogenous comparative advantage. As long as the division of labor has evolved to a sufficient degree and the potential for further division of labor remains, the rate of growth of per capita income will increase over time.

---

[1] By contrast, in the models of Arrow (1962), Romer (1986a), Lucas (1988), and Grossman and Helpman (1989), neither a competitive equilibrium nor a Pareto optimum over an infinite horizon may exist if increasing returns prevail in all activities.

In the dynamic equilibrium just described, as the division of labor evolves, monopoly power will accrue to producers (since learning by doing and increasing returns create entry barriers). This monopoly power, however, will be nullified by the assumption that all trade is mediated through a futures market that operates at time $t = 0$ (and that establishes contracts that cannot be renegotiated at a later date). Since all decisions are therefore made at $t = 0$ and all individuals are ex ante identical, at the time at which equilibrium prices of traded goods are determined there is no monopoly power. Hence a Walrasian regime prevails despite the fact that in equilibrium for a sufficiently great t there may be a single producer of a good.

Earlier studies have dealt with the issue of increasing returns either by assuming that such returns are "external" so that returns at the level of the firm are nonincreasing and a price-taking equilibrium is supported (the Marshallian line), or by departing from price-taking behavior and assuming that firms operate in a monopolistically competitive market.[2] The distinguishing feature of our model in this respect is therefore the compatibility between the existence of an internal economy and a competitive market.[3]

The issue of specialization, which is at the center of this paper, has previously been examined in a range of contexts. In a partial equilibrium framework, Rosen (1978) has shown how specialization can occur because of comparative advantage and the different endowments of economic agents, and Stigler (1951), Rosen (1983), Barzel and Yu (1984), and Edwards and Starr (1987) have examined the incentive for specialization that arises because of increasing returns. Other studies, most notably Baumgardner (1988), Kim (1989), and Yang (1990), have endogenized the level of specialization in a static general equilibrium economy. However, the level of specialization in a dynamic general equilibrium model thus far has not been considered.[4]

---

[2] Romer (1989*b*) provides an excellent survey of this literature.

[3] Rosen (1978) has previously conjectured about the compatibility between the existence of internal economies and a competitive market.

[4] It is worth noting that the concept of specialization differs from the concept of scale. In those models discussed above that involve internal economies of scale, the number of

The role of learning by doing in generating economic growth was first considered by Arrow (1962). In that work, knowledge is assumed to be a by-product from the production of capital so that increasing returns are external to the individual firm. By contrast, in this paper learning by doing gives rise to an internal economy and evolution of the level of specialization.

The rest of the paper is organized as follows. Section 2 presents the model. Section 3 investigates the individual's decision on an optimum level of specialization and establishes the nature of the dynamic equilibrium. In Section 4, the paper's conclusions are summarized and the relationship between these results and some earlier literature is discussed.

2.   A Dynamic Model

We consider an economy with m consumers-producers and m consumer goods.[5] The self-provided amount of a good i at time t is x_{it}. The amounts sold and purchased of the good at that time are, respectively, x_{it}^{s} and x_{it}^{d}. It is assumed that a fraction $1 - K_t$ of any shipment disappears in transit so that $K_t x_{it}^{d}$ is the amount available for consumption after purchasing x_{it}^{d} of good i. The total amount of good i consumed is therefore $x_{it} + K_t x_{it}^{d}$. The utility function at time t for any individual is

$$u_t = \prod_{i=1}^{m} \left(x_{it} + K_t x_{it}^{d} \right). \tag{1}$$

The coefficient K_t is assumed to depend on the number of a person's trade partners; this number is $n_t - 1$ if he sells one good and buys $n_t - 1$ goods, where n_t is then the total number of traded goods. If all people are located at the vertices of a grid of triangles with equal sides, the average distance between a person and his trade partners will be an increasing function of the number of his trade partners and of the distance between

---

goods produced by an agent is exogenously given, whereas the number must be endogenously determined in a model with economies of specialization.

[5] The assumption that the number of goods equals the population size is made to simplify the analysis. It implies that the division of labor is limited by population size.

a pair of neighbors (under the assumption that trade occurs first with those closest). If the transaction cost $1 - K_t$ increases with the average distance between a person and his trade partners, then K_t is a decreasing function of n_t. More specifically, it is assumed that

$$K_t = \frac{k}{n_t}, \quad 0 < k < 1, \tag{2}$$

where k is a constant that characterizes transaction efficiency. Equation (2) implies that the fraction of any purchase available for consumption decreases less than proportionally with n_t.[6]

It is assumed that all trade in this economy is mediated through contracts signed in futures and spot markets that operate at time $t = 0$. These contracts cannot be renegotiated at some later date. Assume that the futures market horizon and an individual's decision horizon are infinity.[7] The objective functional for the individual's decision problem is therefore

$$U = \int_0^\infty u_t e^{-rt} dt, \tag{3}$$

where r is a subjective discount rate. This objective functional represents a preference for diverse consumption and for current over future consumption.

The production technology available to an individual is assumed to exhibit learning by doing and increasing returns:

$$x_{it} + x_{it}^s = (L_{it})^a, \quad L_{it} = \int_0^t l_{i\tau} d\tau, \quad a > 1,$$

$$\sum_{i=1}^m l_{it} = 1, \quad 0 \le l_{it} \le 1, \quad i = 1,...,m, \tag{4}$$

---

[6] The second-order conditions for an interior dynamic equilibrium will not be satisfied if K_t is independent of n_t. In other words, the dynamic equilibrium will be at a corner, either autarky or extreme specialization forever, so that no evolution of the division of labor will occur.

[7] Obviously, the assumption is not quite realistic. If a more realistic assumption is imposed that the horizon of the futures market or individuals' decision making is limited, then monopoly powers will arise from learning by doing. However, the dynamic equilibrium of such a model is intractable.

where $x_{it} + x_{it}^s$ is the output level of good i at time t, $l_{i\tau}$ is the labor spent producing good i at time τ, and L_{it} is the labor accumulated in activity i up to time t.[8] Hence L_{it} represents the level of experience, knowledge, or human capital accumulated in producing good i up to t, and l_{it} is the labor input to production of good i at t.[9] It is assumed that the total of available hours for an individual at any time t is one, and these hours are nontransferable to other individuals' production technologies.

3. Individual Decisions and Dynamic Equilibrium

In this section we begin by arguing that the assumption that all trade is determined in a futures market that operates at time $t = 0$ is sufficient to ensure price-taking behavior by individual agents. Hence any dynamic equilibrium will be characterized by a set of market-clearing conditions and a set of utility equalization conditions. Lemma 1 establishes the optimal structure of consumption, production, and trade for any individual. This result allows the individual's utility-maximization problem and associated indirect utility functional to be simplified. Lemma 2 characterizes the optimal structure of trade for the economy; it is used to establish that all individuals' decision problems are symmetric. Together with the symmetry of the market-clearing and utility-equalization conditions, this implies that the equilibrium number of traded goods is identical for all individuals (lemma 3). When this symmetry is taken into account, the first-order conditions that characterize a dynamic equilibrium are presented and the properties of the equilibrium division of labor are studied. The main results of the paper concerning the evolution of the division of labor are presented in proposition 1.

---

[8] A more realistic specification is $x_{it} + x_{it}^s = (L_{it})^b (l_{it})^a$, where L_{it} is accumulated labor input to good i and l_{it} is current labor input to good i. In this case, production of a good at t is impossible in the absence of some labor input to the production of that good at t. Unfortunately, this specification renders intractable the system of differential equations that characterize the evolution of the division of labor.

[9] Later we shall show that both learning by doing and increasing returns are necessary for the evolution of the division of labor.

At time $t = 0$, all individuals are ex ante identical, and hence there are many potential producers of each good. That is, no individual has experience in any production activity at $t = 0$ so that competition for the rights to produce a good in the future occurs between identical peers rather than between "experts" and "novices". Since all trade is entirely determined in a futures market that operates at $t = 0$, although over time producers will gain monopoly power from learning by doing, at the time at which contracts are signed, no such monopoly power exists. Combined with the perfect foresight of all individuals, this justifies a Walrasian regime with price-taking behavior at time $t = 0$.

In the model described in the previous section, the number of producers of each traded good and therefore the market structure are endogenously determined. Since the quantity of a good that is self-provided is distinguished from the quantity traded of the same good, individuals' optimal decisions are always corner solutions. Although there are 2^{3m} possible combinations of zero and nonzero variables and thereby 2^{3m} possible corner solutions, with the Kuhn-Tucker theorem it is possible to rule out myriad corner solutions from the list of candidates for the optimum decision. In Appendix A, we prove that the optimal pattern of consumption, production, and trade for any individual is as described in the following lemma.

Lemma 1: An individual does not buy and produce the same good. He self-provides a good that is sold and does not sell more than one good (if any).

This lemma implies that for an individual who sells good i and trades n_t goods at t ($n_t \leq m$),

$$x_{it}, \quad x_{it}^s, \quad l_{it} > 0, \quad x_{it}^d = 0,$$

$$x_{rt} = x_{rt}^s = l_{rt} = 0, \quad x_{rt}^d > 0, \quad \text{for } n_t - 1 \text{ other traded goods,} \qquad (5)$$

$$x_{jt}, l_{jt} > 0, \quad x_{jt}^s = x_{jt}^d = 0, \quad \text{for } m - n_t \text{ nontraded goods,}$$

where $r \in R$, the set of goods bought, and $j \in J$, the set of nontraded goods. The set R consists of $n_t - 1$ elements, and the set J consists of $m - n_t$ elements. Note that $n_t = 1$ or $n_t - 1 = 0$ implies that the number of goods purchased is zero (i.e., the economy is in autarky).

The intuition for lemma 1 is straightforward: x_{rt}, x_{rt}^s and x_{rt}^d are quantities of the same good but x_{rt}^d will incur transaction costs. Hence, $x_{it}^s > 0$ implies $x_{it} > 0$ and $x_{it}^d = 0$ because if a person sells a good, then he has to produce it; therefore, it is not worth buying the good because of the transactions cost involved in such a purchase. If the optimum $x_{rt}^d > 0$, then $x_{rt} = x_{rt}^s = 0$ because the consumer-producer can concentrate his labor in producing the good he sells and capture greater economies of specialization in exchange for more x_{rt}^d. Similarly, selling two goods is not efficient because of increasing returns. The set of conditions in (5) means that this person sells and self-provides good i, buys $n_t - 1$ other traded goods, and self-provides $m - n_t$ nontraded goods. Let u_{it} and U_t denote, respectively, the utility of a person who sells good i and his objective functional. Then the decision problem for such an individual is

$$\max U_i = \int_0^\infty u_{it} e^{-rt} dt \tag{6}$$

subject to

$$u_{it} = x_{it} \left[\prod_{r \in R} (K_t x_{rt}^d) \right] \left(\prod_{j \in J} x_{jt} \right) \quad \text{(utility function at } t\text{)},$$

$$x_{it} + x_{it}^s = (L_{it})^a, \quad x_{jt} = (L_{jt})^a, \quad j \in J \quad \text{(production function)},$$

$$l_{it} + \sum_{j \in J} l_{jt} = 1 \quad \text{(endowment constraint)},$$

$$K_t = \frac{k}{n_t} \quad \text{(transaction technology)},$$

$$p_{it} x_{it}^s = \sum_{r \in R} p_{rt} x_{rt}^d \quad \text{(budget constraint)},$$

$$n_t \big|_{t=0} = 1, \quad L_{yt} \big|_{t=0} = 0, \, y = i, j, j \in J \quad \text{(boundary condition)},$$

and

$$l_{yt} = \frac{dL_{yt}}{dt}, \quad 0 \le l_{yt} \le 1 \quad \text{(state equation)},$$

where p_{yt} is the price of good y at time t ($y = i, r$, where $r \in R$). It is implicitly assumed that an individual does not save or borrow, although all trading decisions are made at $t = 0$. Hence, there is an instantaneous budget constraint. Replacing x_{it} and x_{jt} in U_i with their equivalents in the production functions and one of x_{rt}^d $(r \in R)$ with its equivalent in the budget constraint, we can construct a Hamiltonian function

$$H_i = u_{it} + \lambda_t \left(1 - l_{it} - \sum_{j \in J} l_{jt} \right) + \sum_{j \in J} \gamma_{jt} l_{jt} + \gamma_{it} l_{it} , \qquad (7)$$

where λ_t is the discounted dynamic shadow price of the labor endowment at time t, and γ_{yt} $(y = i, j,$ where $j \in J)$ is the discounted shadow price of the labor input to good y at time t. The Hamiltonian H_i is a function of state variables L_{yt}, x_{it}^s and x_{rt}^d $(r \in R)$; costate variables λ_t and γ_{yt}; and control variables l_{yt}. Only $n_t - 2$ of the x_{rt}^d are in u_{it} because the other is canceled using the budget constraint.

The first-order conditions for the control problem are given by the maximum principle. It is interesting to note that calculus of variations cannot be used to solve this model because the optimum labor input for a good will jump to a corner solution from an interior solution as the number of traded goods increases. That is, we are solving a "bang-bang control problem" in which l_{it} will jump to one from an interior solution and l_{jt} will jump to zero from an interior solution as n_t tends to m. The optimum n_t, L_{jt}, L_{it} x_{it}^s, and x_{rt}^d depend on the dynamic prices of all traded goods and on t. Inserting these optimal x_{it}^s and x_{rt}^d into U_i, we can therefore express total utility as a functional of the prices of traded goods. This is a dynamic indirect utility functional.

A dynamic equilibrium is characterized by a set of market-clearing conditions and a set of utility-equalization conditions. The market-clearing conditions are based on the individual dynamic demands and supplies derived from individuals' decision problems, and the utility-equalization conditions are based on the dynamic indirect utility functionals.

Let M_i represent the number of persons selling good i; since the population size $m = \sum_i M_i$ is given, we need to solve only for the relative numbers of persons selling the different goods. If no stocks of goods exist, the market-clearing conditions at time t are:

$$M_r x_{rt}^s = \sum_{i \neq r} M_i x_{irt}^d, \quad r = 1,\dots, m, \qquad (8)$$

where $M_r x_{rt}^s$ is the aggregate supply of good r, x_{irt}^d is the demand of a person selling good i for good r at time t, and hence $\sum_i M_i \, x_{irt}^d$ is the aggregate demand for good r. Later we shall show that x_{irt}^d is identical for all $i = 1, \ldots, m$ except r. Hence x_{irt}^d is the same as x_{rt}^d in equation (7). Condition (8) consists of m equations; however, by Walras's law, only $m - 1$ are independent.

Utility-maximizing behavior by individual agents will ensure that the indirect utility functional is equalized across persons who sell different goods. This gives the utility-equalization condition

$$U_1 = U_2 = \ldots = U_m. \tag{9}$$

Condition (9) consists of $m - 1$ equations. Together, (8) and (9) determine the relative prices and the $m - 1$ relative numbers of persons selling different goods that define the dynamic equilibrium.

At this stage, we turn to a discussion of the optimal structure of trade in the market.[10] In one possible equilibrium, each person trades few goods in early periods but trades a progressively larger range of goods as time continues. In the early period there are many possible market structures. One of them, which we shall signify as A, is that all people trade the same bundle of goods. As the number of a person's traded goods increases over time, the number of sellers of each good previously involved in trade decreases, and some people change their "professions" to produce the new traded goods. Another market structure, signified by P, is that there is a single seller of each good. People trade different bundles of goods but with the same number of traded goods for each person. As the number of a person's traded goods increases over time, he buys more goods and sells more of a good to a larger set of persons, but he will not change his profession.

To illustrate this point, consider the example of $m = 4$ depicted in figure 1. For $m = 4$, market structure A is shown in figure 1a and market structure P in figure 1b. The heavy lines signify the flow of trade, and the light lines represent the flow of self-provided goods. The arrows indicate the direction of flows of goods. The numbers beside the lines signify the goods involved. A circle with number i signifies a person selling good i.

---

[10] This discussion of the market structure is relevant only in those cases in which trade will occur (i.e., obviously in an autarky market structure P could not arise).

In market A, each person trades goods 1 and 2 and self-provides goods 3 and 4. The number of traded goods for each person as well as for the economy is two. In market P, person 1 sells good 1 to person 2, who sells good 2 to person 3, who sells good 3 to person 4, who sells good 4 to person 1. Each person trades two goods, but four goods are traded in the economy.

It is not difficult to see that if all goods will eventually be traded, market P is Pareto superior to market A. There are two reasons: (1) Because of the complete symmetry of the model, the composition of trade has no effect on welfare in the early periods; only the number of each person's traded goods matters. Thus individuals' welfare in the early period is the same for the two market structures. (2) However, individuals' welfare is greater in later periods in market P than in market A because more experience in producing goods 3 and 4 has been accumulated in market P. In market P, experience in producing goods 3 and 4 is accumulated from the outset, and hence the productivity of labor input to these goods is raised in the future. In market A, however, such experience is not accumulated in the early periods.

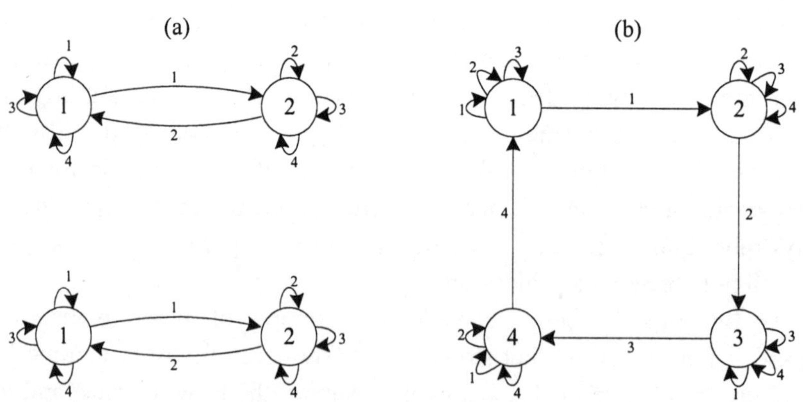

Figure 1: Different market structures. (a), market A: two traded goods; (b), market P: four traded goods.

It is also possible to demonstrate that market A is not an equilibrium market structure. The reason is that there exist unexploited gains to trade in market A that can be captured through the Walrasian regime that prevails at $t = 0$, and hence some individual will always have an incentive to deviate from this market structure. Suppose that there is a dynamic "quasi equilibrium" of market A in which the market-clearing conditions are satisfied. In this quasi equilibrium, in the early period some individual sells good 1 and others sell good 2; at a later period, all goods are traded. Consider the following deviation from market structure A: in the early period, some individual switches to selling good 3 at a price equivalent to those of goods 1 and 2 (this is feasible by the symmetry properties of the model) and at a later stage sells good 3 at a marginally lower price than in market A (feasible because of learning by doing and increasing returns). With this deviation, both the seller and buyers of good 3 will have higher total utility than in market A. Therefore, each individual in market A would have an incentive to switch to selling good 3 from selling good 1 or 2 in the early period. By this argument, market A cannot constitute a dynamic equilibrium market structure.

With similar reasoning it can be established that all other market structures are less efficient than market P and that a dynamic equilibrium does not exist for any market structure apart from P. Therefore, we have the following lemma.

Lemma 2: For $n_t \geq 2$, the equilibrium market structure is P, in which there is a unique seller of every good; m goods are traded in the economy although the number of any individual's purchased goods, $n_t - 1$, increases from zero to $m - 1$.[11]

In the equilibrium market structure described in lemma 2, the individual's decision problems are exactly symmetric. Combined with

---

[11] If the returns to specialization, preference, and transaction cost parameters differ across goods, then the equilibrium market structure in the early stages may be A rather than P. The reason is that trading only those goods with a greater degree of increasing returns, lower transaction costs, or more desirability in the early periods is more efficient than trading other goods. However, introducing ex ante differences in these parameters across goods removes the symmetry between decision problems so that the dynamic model becomes intractable.

the symmetry of the market-clearing conditions in (8) and the utility-equalization conditions in (9), this implies that when trade occurs,

$$\frac{p_{it}}{p_{yt}} = 1 \quad \text{for all } i, y = 1,..., m,$$

$$M_i = 1 \quad \text{for all } i = 1,..., m. \tag{10}$$

When we insert the equilibrium relative prices given by (10) into (6) and (7), the first-order condition with respect to x_{rt}^d for the control problem implies that

$$x_{rt}^d \text{ is identical for all } r \in R. \tag{11a}$$

With this information, the first-order condition with respect to x_{it}^s gives

$$x_{it}^s = \frac{(n_t - 1)(L_{it})^a}{n_t},$$

$$x_{rt}^d = \frac{(L_{it})^a}{n_t} \quad \text{for all } r \in R, \text{ for } i = 1,..., m. \tag{11b}$$

Here we have used the budget constraint to derive x_{rt}^d. When (10), (11a), and (11b) are inserted into (6) and (7), the complete symmetry of the necessary conditions for utility maximization of individuals selling different goods, the market-clearing conditions, and utility-equalization conditions imply the following lemma.

Lemma 3: x_{it}^s is identical for $i = 1,..., m$; L_{it} and l_{it} are identical for $i = 1,..., m$; L_{jt} and l_{jt} are identical for all people; n_t is identical for all people;

$$u_{it} = u_t = (k)^{n_t - 1}(n_t)^{1 - 2n_t}(L_{it})^{an_t} \prod_{j \in J}(L_{jt})^a, \quad \text{for } i = 1,..., m;$$

$$U_i = U = \int_0^\infty u_t e^{-\gamma t} dt, \quad \text{for } i = 1,..., m;$$

and

$$H_i = H = u_t + \lambda_t \left(1 - l_{it} - \sum_{j \in J} l_{jt}\right) + \sum_{j \in J} \gamma_{jt} l_{jt} + \gamma_{it} l_{it}, \quad \text{for } i = 1,..., m.$$

The equilibrium n_t, L_{it}, and L_{jt} are therefore determined by the first-order conditions[12]

$$\frac{\partial H}{\partial \gamma_{yt}} = \frac{dL_{yt}}{dt}, \quad y = i, j, \; j \in J, \tag{12a}$$

$$\frac{\partial H}{\partial L_{yt}} = r\gamma_{yt} - \frac{d\gamma_{yt}}{dt}, \quad y = i, j, \; j \in J, \tag{12b}$$

$$\max H \text{ with respect to integer } n_t, \tag{12c}$$

$$\max H \text{ with respect to } l_{yt}, \quad y = i, j, \; j \in J, \tag{12d}$$

$$l_{it} + \sum_{j \in J} l_{jt} = 1. \tag{12e}$$

Condition (12c) is equivalent to an instantaneous problem, $\max u_t$ with respect to integer n_t, since the rate of change of n_t does not appear in H. The time path of n_t that is given by

$$\frac{\partial u_t}{\partial n_t} = 0 \tag{12f}$$

is a good approximation of the optimum time path of n_t if m is very large because u_t is strictly concave in n_t if n_t takes on a continuous interior value. Hence, we can approximate the optimum time path of n_t, which is solved from a dynamic integer programming problem by the time path of n_t given by equation (12f). In what follows, the n_t analyzed is the approximation of the optimum n_t. Equation (12d) determines a "bang-bang control problem" given by (B1c) in Appendix B. From equations (12a)–(12f) and the second-order condition, the following results are derived in Appendix B:

$$\rho_n \equiv \dot{n}_t / n_t = a\rho_i \left[2 + (1/n_t) \right] > 0 \quad \text{for } m > n_t$$

$$\text{if } k \text{ and } a \text{ are neither too large nor too small,} \tag{13a}$$

where $\rho_i \equiv l_{it}/L_{it}$;

$\partial H / \partial n_t < 0$ for any n_t if k and a are sufficiently small and

$$\partial H / \partial n_t > 0 \text{ for any } n_t \text{ if } k \text{ and } a \text{ are sufficiently large;} \tag{13b}$$

---

[12] The explicit forms of (12a)-(12e) are given in App. B.

$$dn_t/dt \quad \text{increases with k if} \, n_t < \text{m.} \tag{14}$$

Expressions (13a) and (13b) imply that $n_t = 1$ forever from $t = 0$ if k and a are sufficiently small, n_t jumps to m at $t = 0$ and stays there forever if k and a are sufficiently large, and n, increases over time until $n_t = m$ if k and a are neither too large nor too small. Expressions (13a) and (14) imply that the increase in n_t is faster if k is larger (i.e., the larger the transaction efficiency, the faster the evolution of the division of labor).

Consider the case in which a is close to one and k is close to zero. Then since there is little benefit to specialization and almost all of any good will be lost in transit, the equilibrium will be autarky forever. At the other extreme, suppose that a is large and k is close to one. In this case the equilibrium will involve individuals completely specializing from time $t = 0$ since the benefits from the consequently higher volume of output outweigh any transaction costs incurred in purchasing the other necessary consumption goods.

For intermediate values of a and k, the equilibrium may involve evolution of the division of labor. If in early periods the discounted value of the benefits from specialization is outweighed by the current utility losses caused by such specialization due to transaction costs, then the level of specialization will be low. However, over time, learning by doing in production will raise the benefits from specializing relative to the costs of forgone consumption and a greater degree of specialization will occur. In order for the benefits from specialization to increase over time, both learning by doing and increasing returns are necessary. Without learning by doing, although specialization may occur, the optimal level of specialization is invariant over time. On the other hand, in the absence of increasing returns and given a positive transaction cost, specialization will never be optimal. The results from expressions (13)–(14) are summarized in the following proposition.

Proposition 1: Dynamic equilibrium is autarky forever from the outset if transaction efficiency and the degree of increasing returns are sufficiently small, and is extreme specialization forever from the outset if transaction efficiency and the degree of increasing returns are sufficiently large. The division of labor will evolve gradually until n_t

reaches m if transaction efficiency and the degree of increasing returns are neither too large nor too small. For such intermediate values of k and a, the larger the transaction efficiency, the faster the evolution of the division of labor.

Note that the source of economic growth is not growth in population size or exogenous changes in the transaction, production, or preference parameters. Rather, growth is generated by the evolution of the division of labor. An example of such an evolution is illustrated in figure 2 for the case of $m = 4$. In panel a, each person self-provides all goods he needs. In panel b, each person sells a good, buys a good, and self-provides three goods ($n_t = 2$). In panel c, each person sells a good, buys two goods, and self-provides two goods ($n_t = 3$). In panel d, each person sells and self-provides a good, buys three goods, and trades four goods ($n_t = 4$). The circles, lines, and numbers in Figure 2 have the same interpretation as in Figure 1. The dynamic equilibrium depicted in figure 2 is also Pareto optimal because of the Walrasian regime.[13]

It is also possible to examine the nature of economic growth in equilibrium. From differentiation of u_t with respect to t and from (12a)–(12f), it follows that (see App. B)

$$\rho_u \equiv \frac{\dot{u}_t}{u_t} = a\left(n_t\rho_i + \sum_{j\in J}\rho_j\right) = \frac{a\alpha n_t^{1-(2/a)}k^{1/a}e^{(1/an_t)-(2/a)}}{\beta} > 0 \qquad (15)$$

and $d\rho_u/dt > 0$ if m is sufficiently large and n_t is sufficiently close to m, where $\rho_i = l_{it}/L_{it}$, $\rho_j = l_{jt}/L_{jt}$, $\alpha = n_t^2(2n_t+1) + m - n_t$, and $\beta = m(2n_t+1) - an_t(m-n_t)$. Condition (15) implies that if the potential for

---

[13] In the models of Romer (1986a), Lucas (1988), and Grossman and Helpman (1989), the dynamic equilibrium is not Pareto optimal either because increasing returns are external to agents or because of the existence of monopoly power.

                    X. Yang, J. Borland

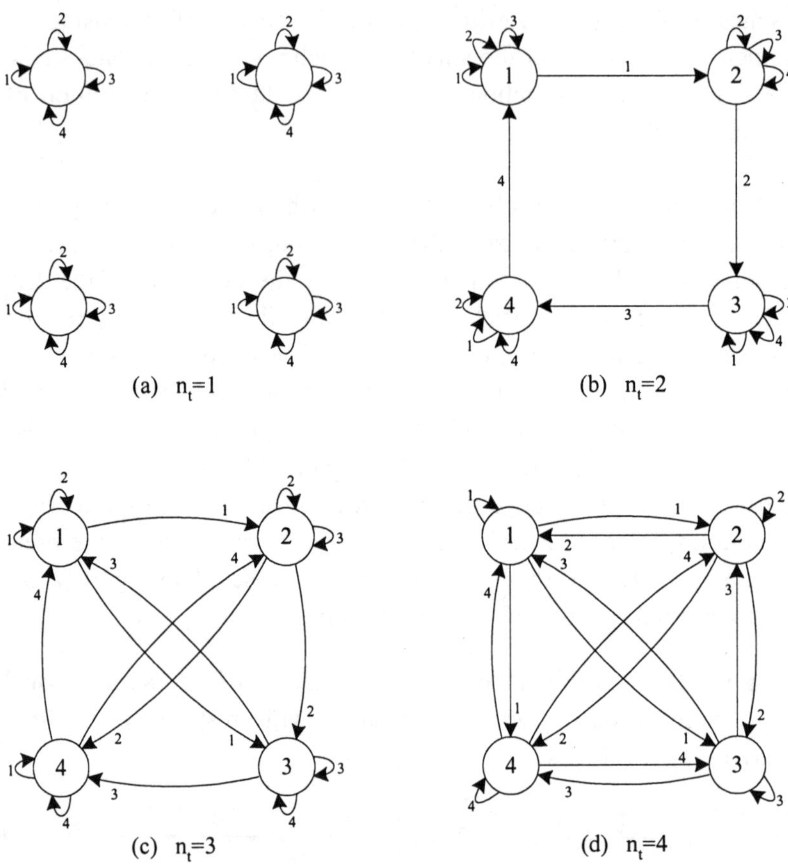

(a) $n_t=1$

(b) $n_t=2$

(c) $n_t=3$

(d) $n_t=4$

Figure 2: Evolution of the Division of Labor

the evolution of the division of labor is significant (large m) and if the division of labor is sufficiently advanced (n_t close to m), the rate of economic growth will increase over time. The growth rate will decline over time after n_t reaches m because the set J becomes empty, l_{it} equals one, and L_{it} is increasing in t.

The result that the growth rate will increase only when the division of labor reaches some critical level is suggestive of the distinction drawn by

Rostow (1960) between the "transition" and "takeoff" stages of economic growth. Furthermore, it has been argued that important tests of any model of economic growth should be its ability to predict increasing growth rates over time (see Romer [1986*a*] for empirical evidence that across those countries estimated to have had the highest level of productivity growth in each of four different epochs since 1700, growth rates have consistently increased) and its ability to predict sustainable disparities in growth rates between countries.

It has been demonstrated above that as long as the division of labor has evolved to a sufficient degree and the potential for further division remains, the model in this paper does predict increasing rates of economic growth. In addition, if transaction efficiency differs across countries because of, for example, differences in institutional arrangements, the evolution of the division of labor will start earlier in those countries with higher transaction efficiency. Countries in which evolution of the division of labor begins earlier will also enter the takeoff stage earlier. More generally, since the speed of evolution of the division of labor depends on the initial conditions, any disparity in growth rates across countries will be sustainable.[14]

A special case of economic growth arises when the dynamic equilibrium is autarky forever. In such a dynamic equilibrium, an individual evenly distributes his labor between the m activities because of the symmetry property. His utility at t is therefore

---

[14] It is worth noting that this model also provides the basis for a special category of gains to international trade. Assume that international futures markets are not available and the population size of the world, which consists of several countries, is m (equals the number of goods). In the absence of an international futures market, people will make myopic decisions at $t = 0$. For example, all people in different countries domestically trade the same bundle of goods in an early period. Later, international trade arises as the number of traded goods per head increases to be larger than the population size of an individual country. At this time, some people will have to change professions as goods not previously traded domestically become involved in international trade. As shown previously, such a dynamic equilibrium based on myopic decisions because of the absence of an international futures market will significantly reduce economic growth. Hence the emergence of an international futures market would create gains to international trade.

$$u_t = \left(\frac{t}{m}\right)^{am} \tag{16a}$$

and hence

$$\rho_u \equiv \frac{\dot{u}_t}{u_t} = \frac{am}{t}. \tag{16b}$$

Therefore, the economy will grow slowly in autarky because of learning by doing despite the absence of division of labor; however, the growth rate of per capita real income declines monotonically. From (15) and (16) we have the following proposition.

Proposition 2:   The evolution of the division of labor generates growth in per capita real income. The rate of growth of income increases if the division of labor has evolved to a sufficiently high degree. It declines in autarky or if the potential for the evolution of the division of labor has been exhausted.

In the remainder of this section we consider some further implications of equilibria that involve evolution of the division of labor. Let E denote the extent of the market and define this to be equal to trade volume per head, $2(n_t - 1)(L_{it})^a/n_t$, where $(L_{it})^a$ is the output level of the good an individual produces for sale, and $(n_t - 1)/n_t$ is the portion of the good that is sold. Differentiating E with respect to t yields

$$\rho_E \equiv \frac{\dot{E}}{E} > 0 \quad \text{if} \quad \frac{\rho_n}{n_t - 1} + a\rho_i > 0. \tag{17}$$

Here, $\rho_n/(n_t - 1)$ is the contribution of the evolution of the division of labor to the expansion of the market, and $a\rho_i$ is the contribution of learning by doing. If the potential for further evolution of the division of labor has been exhausted ($n_t = m$), the first term tends to zero and thereby the rate of growth of the extent of the market depends on the second term alone.

Trade dependence, R, is assumed to be represented by the ratio of traded goods to consumption goods for an individual, n_t/m. The rate of growth of trade dependence is therefore

$$\rho_R \equiv \frac{\dot{R}}{R} = \rho_n. \tag{18}$$

This growth rate is positive for $n_t < m$ and tends to zero as the potential for further evolution of the division of labor falls.

The endogenous comparative advantage of a producer is characterized by the difference between a seller's per capita output of a good and a buyer's per capita output of that good. Denoting this difference by D, we have $D = [(L_{it})^a / n_t] - G$, where G is the buyer's per capita output and is a constant since the buyer's accumulation of experience in producing the good has ceased. If we differentiate this difference, it is immediate that

$$\rho_D \equiv \frac{\dot{D}}{D} > 0 \quad \text{if} \quad a\rho_i > \rho_n. \tag{19}$$

By (13), $a\rho_i > \rho_n$ if k and a are neither too large nor too small. In these circumstances, the comparative advantage of an expert over a novice increases endogenously as the division of labor evolves (even though there is initially no comparative advantage).

The income share of the transaction cost, S, is equal to the ratio of the cost of bought goods lost in transit to nominal income. Since $p_{rt}x_{rt}^d$ is the same for all $r \in R$, therefore, $(1 - K_t)(n_t - 1)\, p_{rt}x_{rt}^d$ is the transaction cost and $(n_t - 1)\, p_{rt}x_{rt}^d = p_{rt}x_{rt}^s$ is per capita nominal income at time t. Hence

$$S \equiv \frac{(1 - K_t)(n_t - 1)p_{rt}x_{rt}^d}{(n_t - 1)p_{rt}x_{rt}^d} = 1 - \frac{k}{n_t} \tag{20a}$$

is the income share of the transaction cost. From (20a),

$$\frac{\partial S}{\partial n_t} > 0, \quad \frac{dS}{dk} = \frac{(kdn_t/n_t dk) - 1}{n_t} \quad \text{if} \quad n_t < m. \tag{20b}$$

Condition (20b) implies that the income share of the transaction cost increases as the division of labor evolves and as transaction efficiency is improved (the latter result holds provided that the level of the division of labor is elastic with respect to transaction efficiency). Since transaction costs can be viewed as nonproductive costs or roundabout productive costs, condition (20b) implies that the income share of the roundabout sector rises as the division of labor evolves. The results from (17)–(20) are summarized in the following proposition.

Proposition 3: The extent of the market, trade dependence, the endogenous comparative advantage of an expert relative to a novice, and the income share of transaction costs increase as the division of labor evolves over time.

It is evident that transaction efficiency has an important effect on the evolution of the division of labor and thereby on economic growth, changes in the extent of the market, trade dependence, endogenous comparative advantage, and the speed of human capital accumulation. Since government policies, institutional arrangements, [15] and urbanization all affect transaction efficiency in important ways, their effects on the evolution of the division of labor and thereby on economic growth are also critical.[16]

4. Conclusion

This paper has developed a formal model in order to describe a microeconomic mechanism for economic growth. It has been shown that interactions among the effects of accumulated experience and specialization on productivity, the effects of transaction costs, and preferences for current and diverse consumption can generate economic growth based on the evolution of the division of labor.

With its emphasis on the role of learning by doing and specialization, our model is clearly part of the rapidly growing literature that associates economic growth with endogenous accumulation. What differentiates this study from previous work is that it makes endogenous the level of specialization of individual agents. This feature allows us to capture

---

[15] Yang (1988) introduces producer goods, a professional transaction activity, and firms into a model similar to that in this paper in order to explore the relationship between the evolution of the division of labor and development of the institution of the firm.

[16] This model can be used in support of the argument of Ng (1985) that a cardinal theory of utility is necessary in economic analysis since a monotonic increasing transformation of (I) will change the pattern of the evolution of division of labor and hence welfare.

Young's (1928, p. 539) insight that "the securing of increasing returns depends on the progressive division of labor." It also establishes a formal basis for his extension of Smith's famous proposition: that not only does the division of labor depend on the extent of the market "but the extent of the market also depends on the division of labor." In proposition 2 it was shown that as the division of labor evolves, the extent of the market (per capita trade volume) will increase. Exploitation of the economies of specialization yields a per capita income effect that will generate a higher level of specialization in the future since it enhances an individual's scope for trading off the future gains from specialization against the costs of forgone consumption.

Our model can also provide a common foundation for theories of international and domestic trade. If the population sizes of individual countries are smaller than the number of goods, then international trade is a natural extension of domestic trade. The gains to both domestic and international trade are based on the evolution of endogenous comparative advantage rather than on exogenous comparative advantage, and hence the rationale for domestic trade is the same as that for international trade. By contrast, in traditional neoclassical theory the rationale for international trade differs from that for domestic trade. According to the neoclassical theory, domestic trade may be based on the artificial separation of pure producers (firms) from pure consumers, so that there exist gains to domestic trade even if no exogenous comparative advantage or increasing returns exist. However, in the absence of exogenous comparative advantage and scale economies, gains to international trade do not exist in the neo-classical model.

Appendix A

Proof of Lemma 1

Since time derivatives of x_{it}, x_{it}^s, and x_{it}^d do not appear in the model, optimization with respect to these variables is time independent. Assume that x_{it}^s and x_{it}^d are both positive. Then we can replace x_{it}^d with its equivalent in the budget constraint ($\sum_r p_{rt} x_{rt}^d = \sum_r p_{rt} x_{rt}^s$) and x_{it}^s with its equivalent from the production function of good i. Then from (1) the first derivative of u_t with respect to x_{it} is

$$\frac{\partial u_t}{\partial x_{it}} > 0 \quad \text{for any } x_{it} \text{ if } k < 1 \text{ and if } x_{it}^s, x_{it}^d > 0. \tag{A1}$$

This implies that the optimum x_{it} is as large as possible. But this contradicts $x_{it}^s > 0$ because $x_{it} + x_{it}^s = (L_{it})^a$ is limited at any time $t < \infty$. Hence x_{it}^s and x_{it}^d cannot be positive at the same time, or

$$x_{it}^s = 0 \text{ if } x_{it}^d > 0; \quad x_{it}^d = 0 \text{ if } x_{it}^s > 0. \tag{A2}$$

Condition (A2) implies that the quantity bought and sold of the same good cannot simultaneously be positive. Since the utility level at t will be zero if $x_{it} = x_{it}^d = 0$, (A2) and the positive utility constraint imply

$$x_{it} > 0, \quad x_{it}^d = 0 \quad \text{if } x_{it}^s > 0. \tag{A3}$$

Now without loss of generality we assume $x_{1t}^s, x_{2t}^s > 0$ and $x_{it}^s = 0$ for all $i \neq 1,2$. We shall show that this violates the second-order condition for an interior maximum. According to (A2) and (A3), $x_{1t}^d = x_{2t}^d = 0$ if $x_{1t}^s, x_{2t}^s > 0$. Using this information and replacing x_{it} with $(L_{it})^a - x_{it}^s$ for $i = 1, 2$, we can show that

$$\frac{\partial^2 u_t}{\partial (x_{it}^s)^2} = 0 \quad \text{if} \quad \frac{\partial u_t}{\partial x_{it}^s} = 0, \; i = 1, 2, \tag{A4}$$

and therefore the Hessian of u_t with respect to x_{1t}^s and x_{2t}^s is negative (i.e., the second-order condition indicates that the interior extreme is a minimum). Hence it is not possible for the solutions of x_{1t}^s and x_{2t}^s to be interior at the same time. This implies that if one of the variables takes on an interior value, the other must be at a corner, either zero or as large as possible. Similarly, it is possible to show that any pair of x_{it}^s and x_{rt}^s cannot be positive at the same time. Therefore,

$$x_{it}^s \text{ and } x_{rt}^s \text{ cannot be positive at the same time at an optimum}$$

$$\text{(for } i, r = 1, \ldots, m \text{ and } i \neq r). \tag{A5}$$

Together, (A2), (A3), and (A5) give lemma 1. Q.E.D.

Appendix B

First- and second-order conditions

This Appendix investigates the first- and second-order conditions for a dynamic equilibrium and derives expressions (13)–(14) using these conditions. The actual forms of the first-order conditions in (12a)–(12e) are

$$\frac{an_t u_t}{L_{it}} = r\gamma_{it} - \dot{\gamma}_{it}, \frac{au_t}{L_{jt}} = r\gamma_{jt} - \dot{\gamma}_{jt}$$

$$l_{yt} = \frac{dL_{yt}}{dt}, y = i, j, j \in J ,$$

$$l_{it} + \sum_{j\in J} l_{jt} = 1; \tag{B1a}$$

$$\frac{\partial H}{\partial n_t} = u_t B_t = 0 \quad \text{if (B1a) holds;} \tag{B1b}$$

$$l_{yt} = 1 \qquad \text{if } \gamma_{yt} > \lambda_t ,$$

$$l_{yt} \in [0,1] \qquad \text{if } \gamma_{yt} = \lambda_t ,$$

$$l_{yt} = 0 \qquad \text{if } \gamma_{yt} < \lambda_t , y = i, j, j \in J , \tag{B1c}$$

where $B_t \equiv \log(k) - 2[\log(n_t) + 1] + (1/n_t) + a \log(L_{it})$. Here, B_t tends to negative infinity as k converges to zero and a converges to one for any n_t if L_{it} is limited. Hence, $\partial H/\partial n_t$ is negative for any n_t if k and a are too small. This implies that the equilibrium is $n_t = 1$ for all t. If a and k are sufficiently large that $B_t > 0$, then $\partial H/\partial n_t > 0$ for any positive $n_t \leq m$. Therefore, the equilibrium n_t is the maximum, m, for all t. This gives (13b). If k and a are neither too large nor too small, then n_t must be between one and m for at least some t. From lemma 1 and (B1c), this implies that l_{it} and l_{jt} (for $j \in J$) are between zero and one when $0 < n_t < m$. Hence, $\gamma_{it} = \gamma_{jt} = \lambda_t$ (for $j \in J$). Differentiating this equality with respect to t and using (B1a), we can derive expression (13a).

We can derive a differential equation on n_t for $1 < n_t < m$ and $0 < l_{jt} < 1$ ($j \in J$) from (B1):

$$\frac{dn_t}{dt} = \frac{an_t^{3-(2/a)}k^{1/a}e^{[(1/n_t)-2]/a}}{(2n_t+1)m - an_t(m-n_t)}. \tag{B2}$$

The equilibrium time path for an interior n_t is determined by this equation and the boundary conditions $n_t\big|_{t=0} = 1$ and $dn_t/dt\big|_{n_t=m} = 0$. Since dn_t/dt in (B2) increases with k for $n_t < m$, expression (14) holds. The equilibrium time path of L_{yt} for interior l_{yt} can be derived from (B1a), which depends on n_t, according to

$$L_{it} = k^{-1/a}n_t^{2/a}e^{-1/an_t}, \qquad L_{jt} = \frac{L_{it}}{n_t}. \tag{B3}$$

According to the bang-bang control problem in (B1c), the value of some l_{jt} must jump to zero as n_t increases (i.e., an individual must cease self-providing those goods that he starts to buy over time).

Differentiating L_{it} and L_{jt} with respect to t and making use of (B2), we obtain

$$\rho_u = a\left(\frac{n_t l_{it}}{L_{it}} + \sum_{j\in J}\frac{l_{jt}}{L_{jt}}\right) = a\left(\frac{2n_t+1}{a} + \frac{m-n_t}{an_t^2}\right)n_t = \frac{a\alpha n_t^{1-(2/a)}k^{1/a}e^{(1/an_t)-(2/a)}}{\beta},$$

$$\tag{B4}$$

where α and β are defined in (15). Differentiating ρ_u in (B4) and n_t in (B2), we get

$$\frac{d\rho_u}{dt} > 0 \text{ if } a(3a-2)n_t^3 + [2(a-1)(2-a)m - a]n_t^2 + 4(a-1)mn_t - m > 0 \tag{B5a}$$

or if m is sufficiently large and n_t is sufficiently close to m. Actually, as n_t tends to m, we have

$$\lim_{n_t\to m}\frac{d\rho_u}{dt} > 0 \text{ if } (a^2+4a-4)m^2 + (3a-4)m - 1 > 0. \tag{B5b}$$

From (B5b), it is straightforward to see that $\lim_{n_t\to m} d\rho_u/dt > 0$ if m is sufficiently large. Expressions (B4) and (B5) yield condition (15).

References

Aghion, Philippe, and Howitt, Peter. "A Model of Growth through Creative Destruction." Working Paper no. 3223. Cambridge, Mass.: NBER, January 1990.

Arrow, Kenneth J. "The Economic Implications of Learning by Doing." *Rev. Econ. Studies* 29 (June 1962): 155–73.

Barzel, Yoram, and Yu, Ben T. "The Effect of the Utilization Rate on the Division of Labor." *Econ. Inquiry* 22 (January 1984): 18–27.

Baumgardner, James R. "The Division of Labor, Local Markets, and Worker Organization." *J.P.E.* 96 (June 1988): 509–27.

Edwards, Brian K., and Starr, Ross M. "A Note on Indivisibilities, Specialization, and Economies of Scale." *A.E.R.* 77 (March 1987): 192–94.

Grossman, Gene M., and Helpman, Elhanan. "Comparative Advantage and Long-Run Growth." Working Paper no. 2809. Cambridge, Mass.: NBER, January 1989.

Kim, Sunwoong. "Labor Specialization and the Extent of the Market." *J.P.E.* 97 (June 1989): 692–705.

Lucas, Robert E.,Jr. "On the Mechanics of Economic Development." *J. Monetary Econ.* 22 (July 1988): 3–42.

Ng, Yew-Kwang. "Some Fundamental Issues in Social Welfare." In *Issues in Contemporary Microeconomics and Welfare,* edited by George R. Feiwel. London: Macmillan, 1985.

Romer, Paul M. "Increasing Returns and Long-Run Growth." *J.P.E.* 94 (October 1986): 1002–37. (*a*)

———. "Increasing Returns, Specialization, and External Economies: Growth as Described by Allyn Young." Working Paper no. 64. Rochester, N.Y.: Univ. Rochester, Center Econ. Res., 1986. (*b*)

———. "Endogenous Technological Change." Working Paper no. 3210. Cambridge, Mass.: NBER, December 1989. (*a*)

———. "Increasing Returns and New Developments in the Theory of Growth." Working Paper no. 3098. Cambridge, Mass.: NBER, September 1989. (*b*)

Rosen, Sherwin. "Substitution and the Division of Labour." *Economica* 45 (August 1978): 235–50.

—. "Specialization and Human Capital." *J. Labor Econ.* 1 (January 1983): 43–49.

Rostow, Walt W. *The Stages of Economic Growth: A Non-Communist Manifesto.* Cambridge: Cambridge Univ. Press, 1960.

Smith, Adam. *An Inquiry into the Nature and Causes of the Wealth of Nations.* 1776. Reprint. Edited by Edwin Cannan. Chicago: Univ. Chicago Press, 1976.

Solow, Robert M. "A Contribution to the Theory of Economic Growth." *Q.J.E.* 70 (February 1956): 65–94.

Stigler, George J. "The Division of Labor Is Limited by the Extent of the Market." *J.P.E.* 59 (June 1951): 185–93.

Swan, Trevor W. "Economic Growth and Capital Accumulation." *Econ. Record* 32 (November 1956): 334–61.

Yang, Xiaokai. "A Microeconomic Approach to Modelling the Division of Labor Based on Increasing Returns to Specialization." Ph.D. dissertation, Princeton Univ., 1988.

—. "Development, Structural Changes and Urbanization." *Development Econ.* 34 (November 1990): 199–222.

Young, Allyn A. "Increasing Returns and Economic Progress." *Econ. J.* 38 (December 1928): 527–42.

CHAPTER 19

**SPECIALIZATION AND A NEW APPROACH TO ECONOMIC
ORGANIZATION AND GROWTH[*]**

Jeff Borland[a] and Xiaokai Yang[b,♣]

[a]University of Melbourne   [b]Monash and Harvard University

Although Adam Smith's story of the pin factory would seem to have enshrined in the minds of economists the relation between the degree of specialization and the level of welfare of individuals in an economy, almost two centuries later, Henrick S. Houthakker (1956 p. 182) expressed the belief that:

> Most economists have probably regarded the division of labor, in Schumpeter's words, as an "external commonplace," yet there is hardly any part of economics that would not be advanced by a further analysis of specialization.

While this exhortation does not seem to have effected any immediate upsurge in work on the topic, nevertheless in the past decade the role of specialization in economic activity has begun to attract greater attention. In this paper an overview is provided of several recent studies which involve the application of a new framework for formally modeling specialization, developed in Yang (1988), to issues relating to the organization of production and exchange.

---

[*] Reprinted from *American Economic Review*, 82, Jeff Borland and Xiaokai Yang, "Specialization and a New Approach to Economic Organization and Growth," 386-91, 1992, with permission from American Economic Association.

[♣] We are grateful to Jürgen Eichberger and Simon Grant for helpful discussions.

437

In what has been referred to as the Ricardian approach to modeling specialization, the benefits of specialization are due to the utilization of exogenous comparative advantages (see e.g., Sherwin Rosen, 1978). In the alternative Smithian approach, individuals are assumed to be identical;[1] incentives for specialization may nevertheless exist due to, for example, the existence of a fixed set-up cost incurred when labor switches between production activities (Brian K. Edwards and Ross M. Starr, 1987), or from a fixed-cost component of an investment in training which yields a rate of return on the investment which is increasing in its rate of utilization (Rosen, 1983). In each of these situations, the indivisibility of labor gives rise to increasing returns to specialization. However, as Houthakker (1956 p. 184) has emphasized:

> Although specialization will lead to the avoidance of individual coordination costs, it may in turn call for coordination between ... individuals.

It is the existence of a trade-off of the type suggested by Houthakker, between the transactions cost incurred through trade which becomes necessary when individuals specialize in production and the increasing returns to specialization, which is developed formally in the next section. In Sections 2 and 3 this framework is applied to explaining economic growth and the role of money in an economy.[2]

1.   Model

The economy is assumed to consist of m individuals (where m is large). Each individual is an *ex ante* identical consumer /producer who derives utility from consumption goods and is endowed with a set of individual-specific production functions which allow production of each

---

[1] Adam Smith (1776 p. 19) argued that "The difference in natural talents in different men is, in reality, much less than we are aware of; and the very genius which appears to distinguish men of different professions, when grown up to maturity, is not on many occasions so much the cause, as the effect of the division of labor."

[2] Other applications of this framework are to explaining the nature of institutions which exist for organizing production (Borland and Yang, 1990) and the relation between the specification of property rights and division of labor (Yang and Ian Wills, 1990).

good. All goods require labor as an input, and each individual is assumed to have a fixed endowment of labor to allocate across production activities in each period; this endowment of labor cannot be transferred to other individuals' production functions. The labor input to each production activity can be interpreted as the level of specialization in that production activity. Increasing returns to specialization are assumed to exist in each production activity.

Trade of goods between individuals is assumed to incur an "iceberg"-type transaction cost; for example, if an individual purchases z units of a consumption good, there is a transactions cost of $(1-k)z$ so that the individual receives kz from the purchase. Hence, k can be interpreted as the transaction efficiency coefficient. It is assumed that all trade is mediated through contracts for bilateral exchange which are negotiated prior to any production taking place; the restriction to bilateral exchange is imposed to prevent the moral hazard problem which might arise in the absence of this constraint.[3]

Figure 1 depicts two stylized models of production which will be used to illustrate applications of this framework. In model A, there are three consumption goods, each of which is produced using labor. In model B, a single consumption good is produced using an intermediate good and labor; that intermediate good is produced using labor and a further intermediate good, which is itself produced using labor. For example, in model B, Y might be taken to represent a car, and X and Y might be taken to represent steel and iron ore.

An important point regarding this model is that, despite the existence of increasing returns and monopoly power which may accrue to individuals due to specialization in production, individual agents will adopt price-taking behavior. Usually, an assumption of increasing returns to an input would be incompatible with price-taking behavior since it implies that individuals would want to purchase an infinite amount of

---

[3] As Joseph Ostroy and Starr (1990 p. 31) have noted, without this "quid pro quo" restriction "... there might be no effective means to prevent violation of the budget constraint and a resultant shortage of some good at the completion of trade."

     J. Borland, X. Yang

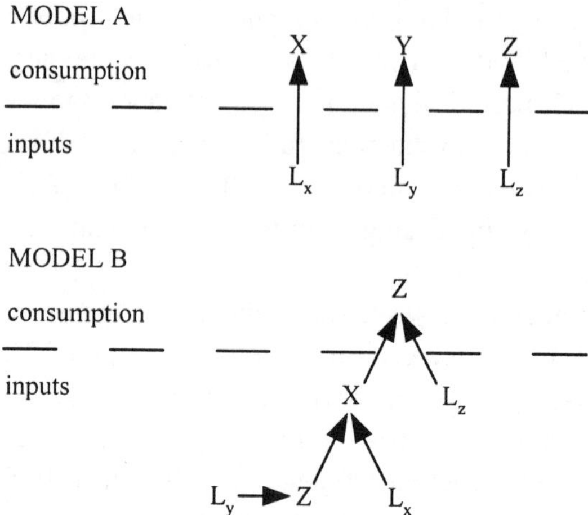

Figure 1: Two stylized models of production: A) Three consumption goods produced using labor; B) A single production good produced using labor and an intermediate good.

that input. However, since the labor input in any production function is assumed to be individual-specific and each individual has a finite labor endowment, this problem does not arise. Furthermore, although the equilibrium number of producers of a traded good may be small, since there is free entry to any production activity and since at the time of deciding on production activities all individuals are *ex ante* identical, no individual will possess monopoly power.

In each period, individuals make decisions on allocation of labor between production activities and on demands for, and supplies of, any traded good. A set of production activities and trade decisions for an individual in a given period is defined as a *configuration*. Although for each model of production there are myriad feasible interior and corner solutions of choices of labor allocation and trade for an individual, it can be shown that (except for cases in which a good is purchased for resale as commodity money) an optimal configuration must satisfy the following conditions:

Lemma 1: An individual (i) does not buy and sell, or self-provide the same good; (ii) does not sell more than one good; and (iii) does not self-provide an intermediate good unless used in production of a good.

The intuition for this result is that, if an individual sells a good, then it is not worth buying that good due to the transactions costs involved in such a purchase; on the other hand, if an individual buys a good, then she should not also self-provide the good but should instead concentrate her labor in production of the good that is sold. Similarly, selling two goods is not efficient due to the presence of increasing returns. An individual who does not produce a good will not self-provide the intermediate input for that good since this would make no contribution to utility.

The combination of choices of configurations of the m individuals in the economy is defined as a *market structure;* a feasible market structure consists of choices of configurations by individuals such that, if there is a positive supply of a traded good, there is also a positive demand for that good. The *general-equilibrium* market structure is a set of relative prices and allocation of resources such that: (i) for any traded good, aggregate demand equals aggregate supply; and (ii) each individual maximizes utility at the given prices. With the assumption of free entry, condition (ii) implies that the utilities of all individuals are equalized in equilibrium. It has been shown (Yang, 1988) that for any non-Pareto-optimal market structure, at a set of relative prices that is market-clearing, some individual will not be maximizing utility with respect to choice of configuration; hence, only for the Pareto-optimal market structure which maximizes per capita utility does there exist a set of relative prices that satisfies both conditions for general equilibrium.

2. Economic Growth

Recent studies of endogenous-growth models have established formally a relation between economic growth and the division of labor which occurs through product development (for a survey see Paul Romer [1989]). An alternative aspect of the division of labor is the level of specialization of individual agents; and the role of this factor in explaining economic growth may be examined through an application of the model described in the previous section.

Consider production-structure A from Figure 1 and assume that all individuals have identical Cobb-Douglas utility functions. Then, from Lemma 1 the set of feasible market structures is as depicted in Figure 2. For example, in autarky each individual self-provides all goods; by contrast, with the complete division of labor each individual self-provides a single consumption good and trades that good in exchange for each of the other necessary consumption goods.

Yang (1990) examines a static version of this model and shows that choosing a higher level of specialization will increase production, but because of the preference for diverse consumption this must be accompanied by more extensive trade, which will incur higher transactions costs; therefore the general-equilibrium market structure will depend on the relative size of transaction efficiency and increasing returns to specialization. The general-equilibrium market structure will involve the complete division of labor if transaction efficiency and returns to specialization are sufficiently high, the partial division of labor if transaction efficiency and returns to specialization are at an intermediate level, and autarky if transaction efficiency and returns to specialization are sufficiently low.

In any multiperiod version of the model described above, a dynamic equilibrium will involve repetition of the static equilibrium in each period. However, if learning-by-doing is introduced, then for intermediate values of transaction efficiency and returns to specialization, the dynamic equilibrium may involve evolution of the division of labor (Yang and Borland, 1991a). This will occur if in early periods, due to the discounted value of the benefits from specialization being outweighed by current utility losses, the optimal level of specialization is low, but over time, as learning-by-doing in production raises the benefits from specialization relative to the costs of foregone consumption, a greater degree of specialization occurs. Unless scope for further expansion in the division of labor is exhausted, the evolution in the division of labor will be associated with growth in per capita income, an increase in the extent of trade and market size, and the development of endogenous comparative advantage. In this equilibrium, the rate of evolution in the division of labor will increase with the degree of transaction efficiency so that differences in transaction efficiency can explain sustainable disparities in growth rates across countries.

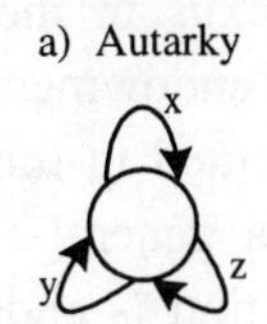

a) Autarky

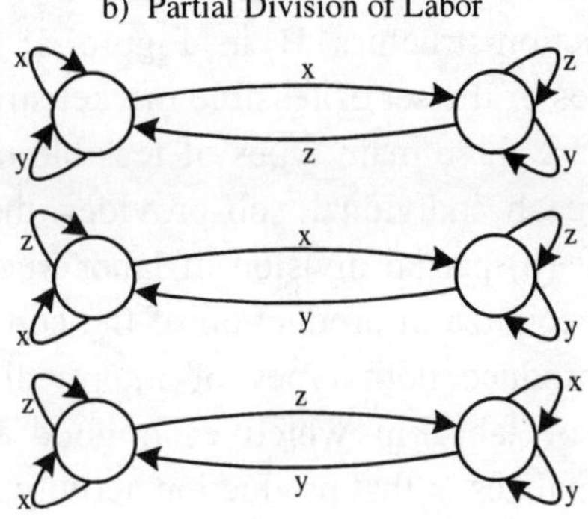

b) Partial Division of Labor

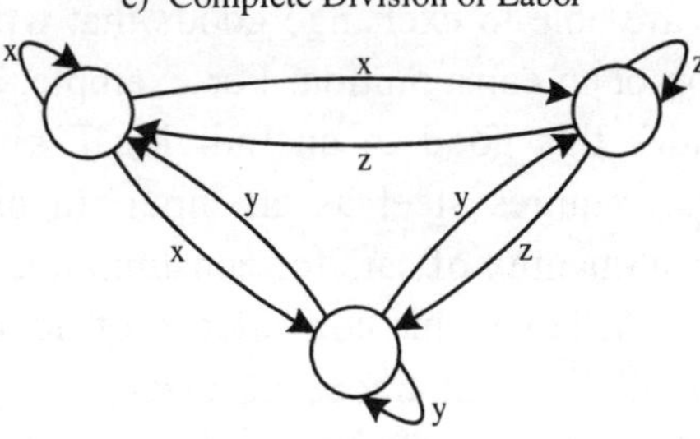

c) Complete Division of Labor

Figure 2:   The set of feasible market structures for production-structure A in Figure 1

3. Money

The role of money as a medium of exchange has often been identified with the existence of specialization in production activities. Some recent studies have examined this nexus in the context of a pure exchange economy with specialization in endowments (for a survey see Ostroy and Starr [1990]). The model presented in this paper allows analysis of the role and nature of money in a general-equilibrium economy when an individual's level of specialization is endogenously determined. In this framework, a role for money arises from the failure of bilateral exchange to implement adequately all desired transactions.

Consider production-structure B in Figure 1; for this model of production, examples of the set of feasible market structures are depicted in Figure 3. There are three main types of feasible market structure: (a) autarky in which each individual self-provides the intermediate and consumption goods; (b) partial division of labor in which, for example, some individuals specialize in production of the consumption good, and other individuals produce both types of intermediate goods; and (c) complete division of labor in which each good is produced by an individual who specializes in that production activity.

Those market structures with division of labor will also necessarily involve the introduction of trade. Where the partial division of labor exists, individuals are able to exchange goods that will be used directly either in production or in consumption. For example, an individual who produces steel trades this good to an individual who, specializing in production of cars, requires steel as an input. In exchange, the first individual receives a quantity of cars for consumption. However, if there is complete division of labor, this coincidence of demands and supplies does not exist for all bilateral trades necessary for production of the consumption good. For example, an individual who specializes in production of iron ore wishes to purchase cars; however, an individual who specializes in production of cars has a zero demand for iron ore.

Therefore, to implement through bilateral trade those exchanges necessary for production of the consumption good, some medium of exchange must be introduced. One possibility is that *commodity money* will act as a medium of exchange; this occurs when a commodity is accepted in trade, not to be consumed or to be used as an input in production, but to facilitate trade. For ex ample, Figure 3c(i) depicts the case in which good Z acts as commodity money. Alternatively, an object with no intrinsic value, referred to as *inside money* may be introduced as a medium of exchange; this is depicted in Figure 3c(ii). It is assumed that trade in any commodity money incurs an iceberg-type transactions cost but that trade in inside money incurs no transactions cost.

It is shown in Yang and Borland (1991b) that, given a sufficiently high degree of returns to specialization and transaction efficiency, the general-equilibrium market structure will involve the complete division of labor; if returns to specialization and transaction efficiency are at intermediate levels, the general equilibrium will involve the partial division of labor; and if returns to specialization and transaction efficiency are low, individuals will remain in autarky. For the market structure with complete division of labor, if an enforceable credit system exists, the medium of exchange will be inside money, as this minimizes transactions costs. If inside money is unavailable, the medium of exchange will be that commodity with the highest transaction efficiency; if transaction efficiency is the same for all goods, the intermediate good at the mid-point of the roundabout production process for the consumption good will act as commodity money.

References

Borland, Jeff and Yang, Xiaokai, "The Organization of Production and Exchange," mimeo, University of Melbourne, 1990.

Edwards, Brian K. and Starr, Ross M., "A Note on Indivisibilities, Specialization, and Economies of Scale," *American Economic Review,* March 1987, 77, 192-94.

Houthakker, Henrick S., "Economics and Biology: Specialization and Speciation," *Kyklos,* 1956, 9, (2), 181-87.

Ostroy, Joseph and Starr, Ross M., "The Transactions Role of Money," in Benjamin Friedman and Frank Hahn, eds., *Handbook of Monetary Economics,* Vol.1, Amsterdam: North-Holland, 1990, pp. 3-62.

Romer, Paul, "Increasing Returns and New Developments in the Theory of Growth," National Bureau of Economic Research (Cambridge, MA) Working Paper No. 3098, September 1989.

Rosen, Sherwin, "Substitution and the Division of Labor," *Economica,* August 1978, 45, 235-50.

___,"Specialization and Human Capital," *Journal of Labor Economics,* Janaury 1983, 1, 43-9.

Smith, Adam, *An Inquiry into the Nature and Causes of the Wealth of Nations,* London: W. Strahan and T. Cadell, 1776; reprint, Chicago: University of Chicago Press, 1976.

Yang, Xiaokai, "A Microeconomic Approach to Modelling the Division of Labor Based on Increasing Returns to Specialization," Ph.D. dissertation, Princeton University, 1988.

___,"Development, Structural Changes and Urbanization," *Journal of Development Economics,* November 1990, 34, 199-222.

___and Borland, Jeff, (1991a) "A Microeconomic Mechanism for Economic Growth," *Journal of Political Economy,* June 1991, 99, 460-82.

___and ___, (1991b) "Specialization and Money as a Medium of Exchange," mimeo, Monash University, 1991.

___and Wills, Ian, "A Model Formalizing the Theory of Property Rights," *Journal of Comparative Economics,* June 1990, 14, 177-98.

CHAPTER 20

SPECIALIZATION, INFORMATION, AND GROWTH: A SEQUENTIAL EQUILIBRIUM ANALYSIS[*]

Yew-Kwang Ng[a] and Xiaokai Yang[b+]

[a]*Monash University*   [b]*Monash and Harvard University*

1. Introduction

The purpose of this paper is twofold. First, we explore the implications for economic growth of interactions between evolution of the division of labor and evolution in information about the efficient pattern of the division of labor that is acquired by society through the price system. Second, we develop the notion of Walrasian sequential equilibrium to model concurrent evolution of the division of labor and of information concerning economic organization acquired by society.

Recent endogenous growth models, represented by Judd (1985), Romer (1990), Grossman and Helpman (1989), and Yang and Borland (1991), explain economic growth not only by endogenous accumulation, but also by evolution in division of labor which generates increases in the number of goods and in individuals' levels of specialization as two aspects of economic development. Spontaneous evolution of the division of labor in these models generates not only growth phenomena (growth in per capita real income, in productivity, and in per capita consumption)

[*] Reprinted from *Review of Development Economics,* 1 (3), Yew-Kwang Ng and Xiaokai Yang, "Specialization, Information, and Growth: A Sequential Equilibrium Analysis," 257-74, 1997, with permission from Blackwell.

[+] We are grateful to a referee, Jeff Borland, Bob Rice, and participants of an AEA session on development economics and of an international symposium on Dynamic Modeling for helpful comments. Financial support from the Australian Research Council is gratefully acknowledged. We are responsible for any remaining errors.

in the absence of exogenous changes in parameters, but also development phenomena, such as increases in individuals' levels of specialization, in the number of traded goods, in the degree of market integration, in the degree of diversification of economic structure, in the number of markets, in income share of transaction costs, and so on. In contrast, neoclassical growth models, represented by Ramsey (1928), can generate evolution in per capita real income or in per capita consumption, although they may generate endogenous growth in the absence of exogenous changes in parameters, as shown by Barro and Sala-i-Martin (1995).

However, evolution of the division of labor in the literature of endogenous growth is generated by a deterministic mechanism based on individuals' dynamic decisions with an infinite horizon. This evolutionary process involves no uncertainties. As Nelson (1995) points out, real economic growth is an evolutionary process that is characterized by uncertainties in the direction of the evolution and by a certain trend of the evolution. The first aim of the present paper is to develop an endogenous growth model that generates evolution of division of labor, characterized by the two features.

Since productivity depends on the level and pattern of the division of labor chosen by individuals, while information about the efficient level and pattern of division of labor acquired by society determines which level and pattern will be chosen, the dynamic nature of the information acquisition is essential for us to understand economic development. As shown by Yang and Ng (1993), an individual's decision on his level and pattern of specialization is always a corner solution. As he changes his level of specialization, he discontinuously jumps from a corner solution to another corner solution. Hence, a person can only use total benefit-cost analysis to identify the optimum corner solution after he has conducted marginal analysis of each corner solution. The discontinuity of decision variables across corner solutions generates two kinds of complexities. Suppose it takes a period of time for a person to try a corner solution; then for a given set of prices, a person can sort out the optimum corner solution only after a sufficiently large number of periods. However, market prices are determined by each and every individuals' decisions to choose certain corner solutions. For instance, no market prices will be available if all individuals choose an autarkic corner solution that involves no trade (that is, quantities of traded goods are 0). Hence, individuals' decisions to choose corner solutions determine what information on prices is available, while the information determines individuals' decisions in choosing their levels and patterns of specialization (or in choosing corner solutions). When the time dimension is spelt out, the interactions between information and dynamic decisions will generate a concurrent evolution in information about the efficient pattern of organization acquired by society, and evolution in the level of division of labor that is chosen by individuals.

An example may illustrate the nature of the information acquisition process. The founding of McDonald's restaurant network can be considered as an experiment with a pattern of high level of division of labor between specialized production of management and planning and specialized production of direct services within the franchise and between specialized production of food and specialized production of other goods. Since all variables and demand and supply functions are discontinuous from corner solution to corner solution, a marginal analysis based on interior solutions could not provide the founder of this franchise with information for the right decision. The founder of McDonald's restaurant network decided to use the market to experiment with his new pattern of business organization, which involves a higher level of division of labor within the franchise and between the franchise and the rest of the economy. Instead of adjusting prices at the margin, he tried to price restaurant services much lower than the prevailing price. According to his calculation, the higher level of division of labor would generate productivity gains, on the one hand, and more transaction costs, on the other. However, his franchise arrangements might reduce transaction costs to the extent that the benefit of the higher level of division of labor outweighed them, so that the substantially lower price of services could stand the test of the social experiment. This idea was substantiated later, as has been seen in the real world. However, the founder might have gone on to bankruptcy if the business had been proved by the social experiment to be inefficient compared with the prevailing pattern of organization. Social experiments through the price system are necessary for society to acquire information about the efficient pattern of the division of labor, even if this leads to business failures because of the interdependency between decisions in choosing a pattern of organization and available information of prices and because of discontinuity of decision variables between different patterns of division of labor.

Kreps and Wilson's concept of sequential equilibrium might be a vehicle for analyzing the interactions between dynamic strategies and information. However, it is a formidable task to endogenize the evolution of the division of labor in addition to endogenizing the interactions between dynamic decisions and information using their concept. Usually, even without the endogenization of evolution of the division of labor, only extremely simple models of sequential equilibrium can be solved. Hence, the second purpose of the paper is to develop the concept of Walrasian sequential equilibrium that simplifies modeling of the endogenous evolution of the division of labor and evolution in information of economic organization. Concurrent evolution is based on adaptive behavior and on a limited horizon, so that it is closer to a real economic development process than that predicted by Romer (1990) and Yang and Borland (1991), who assume perfect information and an infinite decision horizon. In some repects the present paper bridges the literature of endogenous growth and the literature of bounded rationality.[1]

In the model to be considered, there are many *ex ante* identical consumer-producers with preferences for diverse consumption and production functions displaying economies of specialization. Complicated interactions between economies of specialization and transaction costs in the market generate uncertainties about real income for different patterns of the division of labor. Each person's optimal decision is a corner solution. Combinations of different corner solutions generate many possible candidates (corner equilibria) for general equilibrium. Individuals may experiment with each possible pattern of division of labor via a Walrasian auction mechanism at a point in time and thereby eliminate uncertainties and acquire information about

---

[1] Conlisk (1996) provides an updated survey on the latter literature.

the efficient pattern of division of labor over time. However, the costs of discovering prices generate a tradeoff between information gains and experimentation costs in the information acquisition process. A decentralized market will trade off gains from information acquisition against experimentation costs to determine the equilibrium pattern of experiments with patterns of division of labor over time. In the process, individuals use Bayes' rule and dynamic programming to adjust their beliefs and behavior according to updated information. Hence, we refer to the solution to the model as Walras sequential equilibrium. The determinants of the dynamics of the Walras sequential equilibrium are: a transportation cost coefficient for trading one unit of goods; the degree of economies of specialization; the discount rate; and a pricing cost coefficient.

Suppose the transportation cost coefficient and the degree of economies of specialization are fixed. If pricing costs are high, then the market will not experiment with any sophisticated pattern of division of labor. If pricing costs are sufficiently low, all possible patterns of division of labor will be tried. In this process, simple patterns of division of labor are tried before the more complicated ones, so that a gradual evolution of the division of labor may occur. If pricing costs are at an intermediate level, then only simple patterns of division of labor will be tried, so that society cannot acquire complete information about the efficient economic organization. For a fixed pricing cost coefficient, more patterns of division of labor will be experimented with as the transportation cost coefficient decreases and/or as the degree of economies of specialization increases.

Our concept of Walras sequential equilibrium is an analogue to Kreps and Wilson's concept of sequential equilibrium. In the game model of Kreps and Wilson (1982), players use dynamic programming to choose strategies for a given sequence of their beliefs of their opponents' types, and the sequence of beliefs is updated according to Bayes' rule and the observed strategies. In our model, individuals use dynamic programming to solve for their experimentation sequence with different patterns of division of labor for given information of the ranking of each person's incomes generated by various patterns of specialization. The information is updated according to Bayes' rule and observed prices.

The difference between our concept of Walras sequential equilibrium and Kreps and Wilson's concept of sequential equilibrium will be discussed in a later section.

The result in this paper is more limited to a specific model than that of Aghion et al. (1991), because the discontinuity of payoff functions in a general equilibrium model based on corner solutions makes their general model intractable. Because of corner solutions and discontinuity of payoff functions across corner solutions, we assume the absence of information in this paper, while incomplete information is assumed by Aghion et al. An experimentation cost in addition to the discount rate is specified to be generated by the process of discovering prices. By contrast, Aghion et al.'s experiment cost is generated only by the discount rate. Finally, our model is a general equilibrium model while their model is a partial equilibrium model. This makes our model more difficult to manage, so that we confine attention to a specific model where all individuals' decisions on learning-by-experimenting with the patterns of economic organization are symmetric. The symmetry avoids the problem of coordination and mismatch in experimentation with various patterns of the division of labor, thereby keeping the model tractable at the cost of realism. We leave for future research the analysis of a more realistic model with the coordination problem caused by information asymmetry, which may generate interesting implications of the role of entrepreneurship in experiments with economic organization.

This paper is organized as follows. First we specify an equilibrium model that endogenizes the determination of the efficient pattern of the division of labor in a Walrasian regime. We then introduce a pricing cost and the information problem into the model to generate a story about learning-by-experimenting with various patterns of the division of labor. We then solve for the dynamic equilibrium and discuss the implications of the results.

2. Efficient Division of Labor in a Walrasian Regime

The model in this section is the same as in Yang (1990). In the next section, the time dimension and a fixed pricing cost for possible transactions will be introduced. There are *M ex ante* identical consumer-producers. and *M* is assumed to be large. The respective quantities of the three consumer goods self-provided are denoted by x, y, and z. The respective quantities of the three goods sold are denoted by x^s, y^s, and z^s. The respective quantities of the three goods bought are denoted by x^d, y^d, and z^d. The transaction cost of a unit of goods purchased is 1-k, so that kx^d, ky^d, or kz^d is the amount available for consumption from the purchase of a good. Utility for all consumer-producers is a Cobb-Douglas function of quantities consumed:

$$u = (x+kx^d)(y+ky^d)(z+kz^d). \tag{1}$$

Each consumer-producer's system of production is:

$$x+x^s = l_x^{\alpha}, \quad y+y^s = l_y^{\beta}, \quad z+z^s = l_z^{\gamma}, \quad \alpha>\beta>\gamma>1, \tag{2a}$$

$$l_x +l_y +l_z = 1, \quad l_i \in [0,1], \tag{2b}$$

where l_i is a person's labor share in producing good i which is defined as his level of specialization in producing good i. This system of production function and endowment constraint displays economies of specialization since labor productivity of good i increases with a person's level of specialization in producing good i.

A Walrasian regime is assumed. Proposition 1 in Yang (1990), which states that a person sells at most one good and does not buy and produce the same goods, can be used to rule out the interior solution and most of corner solutions from consideration. A combination of zero and nonzero variables that is compatible with this proposition is called a *configuration*. There are three *classes* of ten configurations. The first class is *autarky*, denoted by A and shown in Figure 1(a) where circles represent configurations and lines with arrows represent flows of goods. The configurations from the second class are denoted by (i/j). An individual choosing (i/j) sells and self-provides good i and buys good j. He does not buy good i and does not produce good j. He self-provides good $r \neq i, j$. That is, i, i^s, j^d, r, l_i, $l_r > 0$ and $i^d = j^s = j = r^s = r^d = l_j = 0$. There are six configurations from this class: (x/y), (y/x), (x/z), (z/x), (y/z), (z/y). Configurations (x/y) and (y/x) are shown in Figure 1(b). The configurations from the third class are denoted by (i/jr) and shown in Figure 1(c). An individual choosing (i/jr) self-provides and sells good i

and buys goods j and r, that is, i, i^s, j^d, r^d, $l_i > 0$ and $i^d=j=j^s=r=r^s=l_j=l_r=0$. There are three configurations from this class: (x/yz), (y/xz), (z/xy).

A combination of configurations that is compatible with the market-clearing conditions is called a *market structure* or simply a *structure*. There are five structures derived from feasible combinations of the ten configurations. Autarky itself is a structure. Hence, a corner solution for A is a corner equilibrium. Three market structures are referred to as *partial division of labor* with goods i and j traded and denoted by P(ij). P(ij) consists of configurations (i/j) and (j/i). P(xy) is shown in Figure 1(b). Finally, market structure C, the complete division of labor shown in Figure 1(c), consists of configurations (x/yz), (y/xz), and (z/xy). The market-clearing and utility-equalization conditions determine a corner equilibrium for each market structure with trade.

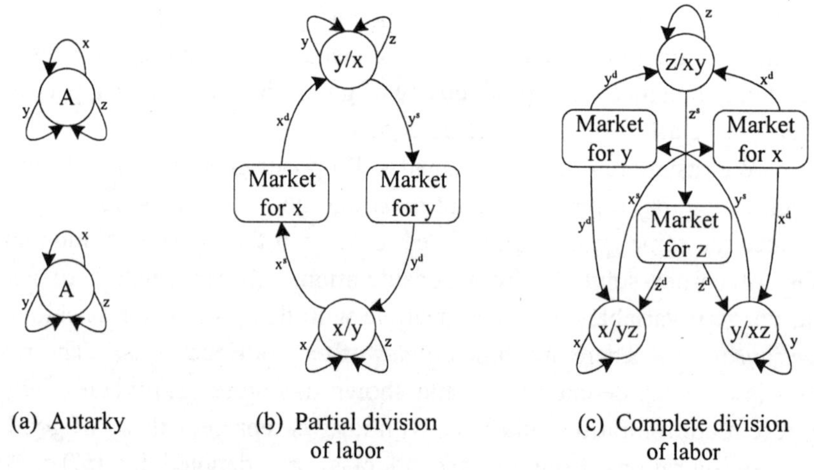

(a) Autarky   (b) Partial division   (c) Complete division
                                 of labor   of labor

Figure 1: Endogenous Evolution in Division of Labor based on Experiments with Patterns of Division of Labor

Following Yang and Ng (1993, chapter 6), it can be shown that the Walrasian equilibrium is the corner equilibrium that generates the highest per capita real income. Following the two-step approach to solving for equilibrium based on corner solutions, developed in Yang (1990), the following lemma has been established in Appendix A, which is available from the second author upon request. It is shown in Yang (1990) that only market structure P(xy) out of the three market structures with the partial division of labor is the equilibrium, and P(xz) and P(yz) cannot be the equilibrium when two goods are traded if $\alpha>\beta>\gamma$. We will denote P(xy) by P when no confusion is caused. In Lemma 1,

$$k_1\equiv[(2\alpha+\gamma)^{2\alpha+\gamma}(2\beta+\gamma)^{2\beta+\gamma}]^{0.5}/2^{\alpha+\beta-2}(\alpha+\beta+\gamma)^{\alpha+\beta+\gamma},$$

$$k_2\equiv3^32^{\alpha+\beta-2}\alpha^\alpha\beta^\beta\gamma^\gamma/[(2\alpha+\gamma)^{2\alpha+\gamma}(2\beta+\gamma)^{2\beta+\gamma}]^{0.5},$$

$$k_3\equiv[3^3\alpha^\alpha\beta^\beta\gamma^\gamma/(\alpha+\beta+\gamma)^{\alpha+\beta+\gamma}]^{0.5}.$$

Lemma 1

(1) When $k_2>k_1$, the equilibrium is autarky (structure A), where per capita real income is $\alpha^\alpha\beta^\beta\gamma^\gamma/(a+\beta+\gamma)^{\alpha+\beta+\gamma}$, if transaction efficiency $k<k_1$. The equilibrium is the partial division of labor (structure P), where the relative price of the traded goods is $p_y/p_x=(2\alpha)^\alpha(2\beta+\gamma)^{\beta+0.5\gamma}/(2\beta)^\beta(2\alpha+\gamma)^{\alpha+0.5\gamma}$, the relative number of different specialists is $M_y/M_x=(2\alpha+\gamma)/(2\alpha+\gamma)]^{0.5\gamma}$, and per capita real income is $2^{\alpha+\beta-2}k\alpha^\alpha\beta^\beta\gamma^\gamma/(2\alpha+\gamma)^{\alpha+0.5c}(2\beta+\gamma)^{\beta+0.5c}$, if $k\in(k_1,k_2)$. The equilibrium is the complete division of labor (structure C), where $p_x=p_y=p_z$, $M_x=M_y=M_z$, and per capita real income is $k^2/3^3$, if $k>k_2$.

(2) When $k_2<k_1$, the equilibrium is autarky if transaction efficiency $k<k_3$. The equilibrium is the complete division of labor if $k>k_3$. The partial division of labor can never be an equilibrium. The partial division of labor generates a greater value of per capita real income than autarky iff $k>k_1$.

3. Costs of Acquiring Information about Efficient Division of Labor

A time dimension is now introduced into the model. The decision horizon of an individual is assumed to be limited and discrete. There are three periods for an individual's decision problem. It is assumed that in period 0, M individuals are in autarky. They must decide which market structure, among autarky, partial division of labor, and complete division of labor, to experiment with in each of periods 1, 2, 3. For this dynamic model, it is possible that individuals experiment with one of several corner equilibria via a Walrasian auction mechanism in each period.

Individuals may find the corner equilibrium that maximizes their real income if they have experimented with all market structures through such a Walrasian pricing mechanism. In this section we will specify the dynamic model. The next section solves for the dynamic equilibrium which determines the experimentation pattern as a function of the parameters of pricing efficiency, transportation efficiency, the degree of economies of specialization, and the discount factor.

Suppose that the utility function and the system of production for each consumer-producer are the same as in the preceding section, independent of time. It is further assumed that a fraction, $1-s$, of an individual's expected utility disappears because of pricing costs in the experiment with the transactions in one corner equilibrium in a period, but no pricing costs are incurred for the similar transactions in subsequent periods. In a Walrasian regime, a Walrasian pricing mechanism sorts out relative prices of traded goods through communications between the Walrasian auctioneer and each individual in a tatonnement process. The pricing cost is incurred in the communication process. Note that an exchange of good x for good y in structure P is considered to be different from an exchange of good x for good y in structure C since the relative price of the goods may differ between the two market structures. Assume further that a person can choose at most one configuration involving trade in any period, and thereby society can experiment at most with one market structure in each period. Also, as soon as individuals have found the relative prices in a corner equilibrium, they can instantly choose between this structure and those which had been previously tried. For instance, if individuals have experimented with structure P in period 1, then they can immediately choose whichever is better between structures A and P at the end of period 1. Suppose that the pricing cost coefficient, which is equivalent to an experimentation cost coefficient of a structure, is slightly smaller for structure P than that for structure C because each person must find the relative prices of three traded goods in C, but only the relative price of two traded goods in P.

In period 0, each individual has information on autarky, but has no information about other individuals' parameters of preference, production function, and endowments and about relative prices in market structure P or C. Therefore, they cannot obtain complete information about economic organization unless they have experimented with the other two market structures. The assumption that all individuals have no information of the relative prices in market structures P and C implies that they have no information about their real incomes in the two market structures. This assumption of the absence of information differs from the assumption of incomplete information. For the assumption of incomplete information, a person knows the distribution function of his real income in market structure P or C. For the assumption of the absence of information, a person does not know such a distribution function. What he knows is that the ranking of real income in structures A, P, and C is subject to a certain distribution.

An individual's information set in period 0 is specified as follows. He knows that three types of configurations may generate three levels of real income. Let the per capita real income in autarky be u_A, that in the partial division of labor be u_P, and that in the complete division of labor be u_C. Each individual knows the real value of u_A, but does not know the real values of u_P and u_C. Nor does he know the distribution functions of u_P and u_C. Signifying the ranking of real income by the order of letters, there are six possible rankings of per capita real income: $u_A u_P u_C$, $u_A u_C u_P$, $u_P u_A u_C$, $u_P u_C u_A$, $u_C u_A u_P$, $u_C u_P u_A$. For instance, $u_P u_A u_C$ implies that structure P generates the highest per capita real income, structure C generates the lowest per capita real income, and structure A generates an intermediate level of per capita real income. Suppose that in period 0 each individual knows that the difference between the two consecutive levels of per capita real income generated by the three structures is b. Each individual's subjective distribution density is that each state occurs with probability 1/6. Since the real value of b depends on the degree of economies of specialization, he estimates b according to the following rule. Let parameter of the degree be a, then $a=(\alpha,\beta,\gamma)$. Assume a person's prior knowledge of the relationship between b and a

is $b=f_i(a)$. This function depends on the ranking of real incomes generated by the three structures. Suppose $b=f_1(a)$ for ranking $u_A u_P u_C$. For this ranking, a lower level of division of labor generates a higher level of per capita real income. But an increase in the degree of economies of specialization, a, will increase per capita real income in a structure with a higher level of division of labor, thereby reducing the difference between consecutive levels of real incomes, b. Hence, $df_1/da < 0$. Suppose $b=f_2(a)$ for ranking $u_A u_C u_P$, $b=f_3(a)$ for ranking $u_P u_A u_C$, $b=f_4(a)$ for ranking $u_P u_C u_A$, $b=f_5(a)$ for ranking $u_C u_A u_P$, and $b=f_6(a)$ for ranking $u_C u_P u_A$. Following the same logic for proving $df_1/da < 0$, it can be shown that $df_2/da < 0$ between structures A and C and $df_2/da > 0$ between structure C and P; $df_3/da > 0$ between structures P and A and $df_3/da < 0$ between structure A and C; $df_4/da < 0$ between structures P and C and $df_4/da > 0$ between structures C and A; $df_5/da > 0$ between structures C and A and $df_5/da < 0$ between structures A and P; and $df_6/da > 0$. Since each of the six rankings takes place with equal probability, the estimate of b at $t=0$ is

$$(1/6)\Sigma_i f_i(a). \tag{3a}$$

We define this "information set" to be characterized by an *absence of information* because the expected value of u_P (or u_C) equals u_A, which implies that a person does not know more than the real value of u_A, and the entropy of the system with the six states is at its maximum, which implies that the information that a person has is at its minimum. The expected value of u_P (or u_C) is $(1/3)[(u_A+b)+(u_A-b)]+(1/6)[(u_A+2b)+(u_A-2b)] = u_A$. The entropy of the system with six states is $-6(1/6)log_2(1/6) = 2.5850$ bits, which is the maximum level of entropy for a system with six states.[2]

As soon as any one of structures P and C is experimented with, a person's knowledge of b is updated according to Bayes' law and the observed difference $|u_A-u_P|$ or $|u_A-u_C|$ which is dependent on the parameters of production, transactions, and tastes. For instance, suppose a person decides to try structure P in period 1 and he finds $u_A>u_P$ after he has seen prices in structure P and has calculated his utility according to

---

[2] Entropy is maximized when each and every state occurs with equal probability. Maximum entropy implies minimum information.

the prices. Then at the end of period 1, $u_P u_A u_C$, $u_P u_C u_A$, and $u_C u_P u_A$ are ruled out according to Bayes' rule since the three rankings are incompatible with $u_A > u_P$. Suppose the observed difference between u_A and u_P is $\bar{b}$ and each individual still believes that true b is the same between consecutive real income levels. Then $\bar{b}$ equals b with conditional probability 2/3 since $u_A u_P u_C$ takes place with probability 1/3 and $u_C u_A u_P$ takes place with probability 1/3 after a person has seen $\bar{b}$ $=u_A - u_P > 0$, while $u_A - u_P = b$ for the two rankings. Also, $\bar{b}$ equals $2b$ with conditional probability 1/3 since $u_A u_C u_P$ takes place with probability 1/3 after a person has seen $\bar{b}$ $= u_A - u_P$ > 0, while $u_A - u_C = u_C - u_P = b = (1/2)(u_A - u_P) = (1/2)\bar{b}$ for this ranking. Therefore, the expected value of b is $(2/3)\bar{b} + (1/3)2\bar{b} = 5\bar{b}/6$ after a person has seen $\bar{b}$ $= u_A - u_P > 0$.

With the knowledge about b and rankings of per capita real incomes in different structures, each individual can calculate his expected real income in order to make a decision on the optimal pattern of experiments with market structures. He has chosen an experimentation pattern even if he stays with autarky forever. This special pattern of experimentation with organization can be denoted AAAA; that is, the initial state is structure A and A is chosen in periods 1, 2, and 3. If an individual chooses configuration (i/j) in period 1 and (i/jr) in period 2 and stays with the one that generates the highest real income among the three configurations, then structure P will be tried in period 1 and structure C will be tried in period 2. Here there is no difficulty for individuals to match each other's choices of configurations for two reasons. First, each person's objective function, specified in (4) below, is affected only by the difference in the number of traded goods. The difference between (i/j) and (j/i) or between (i/jr) and (j/ir), or (r/ij) has no effect on each person's real income because of the utility equalization condition. Owing to the same discount rate, the same information, and the same pricing cost coefficient for all individuals, players will choose the same number of traded goods and they have no difficulty in coordinating the choice of the same number of traded goods. This implies that if a person chooses configuration (i/j) in period 1, then nobody will choose (i/jr) in the same period.

Second, players will not have difficulties in matching each other's choice of different occupations (configurations) as soon as they participate in the Walrasian auction mechanism in a certain period after they have chosen the pattern of experimentation sequence.   Appendix A, available upon request, shows that the indirect utility function of a specialist producer of good i increases with the price of good i in terms of other goods.   The market-clearing condition implies that the price of good i in terms of good j is inversely related to the number of specialist producers of good i relative to those of good j.   Hence, when the number of specialists of a good is small, the price of this good will be high, so that the utility level of the specialists will be high.   Thus, individuals have incentives to choose this profession.   This implies that a person has an incentive to choose configuration (i/j) if other individuals choose (j/i).

In the absence of mismatch, market structure P will be chosen if an individual chooses configuration (i/j) and market structure C will be chosen if an individual chooses configuration (i/jr).   If structure P is experimented with in period 1, then the Walrasian relative prices in structure P will be ascertained via a Walrasian auction mechanism. As soon as the corner equilibrium relative price in structure P is ascertained in period 1, each individual can calculate his real income in structure P. He will choose autarky if $u_A > u_P$.   Otherwise he will choose structure P. Denoting an expectation formed in period t by E_t, the utility level in period τ expected in period t for option $i(\tau)$ can be expressed as $E_t[u_\tau(i)]$, where $i =$ A, P, C.[3]   In period 0 a person expects that he will receive utility $E_0[u_1(P)]$ in period 1 if he chooses P in period 1.   If the pricing cost, the discount factor, and what a person knows in period 0 are taken into account, in period 0 he expects his discounted real income for period 1 to be

---

[3] It can be assumed that in a period individuals have to choose the structure tried in that period even if they have found out it to be inferior to the structure previously chosen, and that they can return to the better previous structure only in the next period. This assumption would substantially complicate the algebra, but contribute little to the explanatory power of the model.

$$E_0[ru_1(P)] = sr[(1/2)u_A + (1/3)(u_A + b) + (1/6)(u_A + 2b)]$$
$$= sr(u_A + 2b/3),\tag{3b}$$

where he decides to choose configuration (i/j) in period 1. Here s is the fraction of expected real income that has been received. The fraction $1-s$ is assumed to disappear because of pricing cost. $1-s$ is a person's fixed communication cost with the Walrasian auctioneer. The cost is necessary for sorting out the relative prices in the structure concerned and is independent of quantities to trade. The discount factor r is between 0 and 1. The probability for u_A to be $\max\{u_A, u_P\}$ is 0.5 because $u_A u_P u_C$ occurs with probability 1/6 and so does $u_A u_C u_P$ or $u_C u_A u_P$. Hence, if a person chooses the structure that generates the highest real income to him after the experiment with structure P, he receives u_A with probability 0.5. He receives $u_A + b$ with probability 1/3 because $u_P u_A u_C$ occurs with probability 1/6 and so does $u_C u_P u_A$ and because the difference between two consecutive levels of real income is b. He receives $u_A + 2b$ with probability 1/6 because $u_P u_C u_A$ occurs with probability 1/6 and the maximum difference between two levels of real income is $2b$. Note that a person knows u_A but does not know the values of u_P and u_C in period 0. He uses (3a) to estimate b at $t=0$.

From (3b) a tradeoff exists between potential gains arising from information, generated by experiments, and pricing costs, incurred in such experiments. Without the experiment with structure P in period 1, a person receives ru_A in period 1. He expects to receive a higher discounted real income $r(u_A + 2b/3)$ if he experiments with structure P at the cost $(1-s)r(u_A + 2b/3)$. However, such experimentation costs are incurred only once. If he does not experiment with structure C in periods 2 and 3, he can receive expected discounted real income $r^2(u_A + 2b/3)$ in period 2 and $r^3(u_A + 2b/3)$ in period 3 without experimentation costs. The pricing cost coefficient $1-s$ can be interpreted as an investment in acquisition of information regarding organization. It generates perpetual benefits at the cost of current consumption. Current real income decreases because of the experimentation costs but the discounted future real income increases because of the perpetual benefits generated by the experiments. Hence, this tradeoff between preferences for current real income over future income, represented by the discount factor, and gains to information acquisition, is similar to the conventional tradeoff between the preference for current consumption and the productivity gains to investment.

If a structure with trade is experimented with in period 1, then individuals will sort out the relative prices of traded goods and relative numbers of individuals choosing different configurations through a Walrasian auction mechanism. Using the updated information, each individual can calculate his real income in the structure and decide if he implements the transactions. Since the values of the relative prices and relative numbers of different specialists in the corner equilibria are the same for all individuals, the updated information is the same for all individuals. Using Bayes' rule, each individual updates his beliefs of ranking of utilities in different structures and adjusts his dynamic decision of further experimentation with the structures that have not been tried. The utility equalization condition in each corner equilibrium implies that all individuals' adjustment of dynamic decisions based on the updated beliefs are consistent with one another. Hence, no coordination problem exists.

4. Information Costs and Endogenous Evolution of the Division of Labor

In this section, the concept of Walras sequential equilibrium is defined and an individual's dynamic programming problem in period 0 is specified and solved. Then an individual's dynamic programming problems in other periods are solved using Bayes' rule. Finally, the Walras sequential equilibrium is solved.

4.1. Pattern of experiment with organization in period 0

Sequential equilibrium is defined as a fixed point which satisfies the following conditions. (1) In each period each individual maximizes his total discounted utility with respect to the sequence of configurations and quantities of goods produced, consumed, and traded for a given history of the system and his information in this period. (2) Each individual's information is updated on the basis of observed prices, using Bayes' rule.

(3) A sequence of relative number of individuals who choose different configurations and a sequence of relative prices of all traded goods clear the markets for goods and equalize utilities across individuals in each period. The difference between the concept of Walras sequential equilibrium and Kreps and Wilson's concept of sequential equilibrium is that (i) our sequential equilibrium consists of several Walrasian static equilibria over periods, and (ii) in each period, each individual has a dynamic programming problem over subsequent periods which might be different from his dynamic programming problem in the next period because of adaptive decisions to updated information. The difference (i) implies that in Kreps and Wilson's sequential equilibrium, there are direct interactions between individuals' strategies and information; while in our sequential equilibrium, interactions between information and individuals' decisions take place indirectly through a sequence of Walrasian equilibria which are fixed points determined by the interactions between prices and quantities over several periods. If information asymmetry is introduced into our model, a coordination problem will generate a story which is more like the story based on Kreps and Wilson's concept of sequential equilibrium.

An individual's dynamic decision problem in period 0 can be represented by a dynamic programming problem that is illustrated in Figure 2. Nodes in Figure 2 denote the options available to an individual. An option can be either a structure that an individual can choose to experiment with or a pattern of experiment. In period 1, an individual can choose one out of A (staying with autarky), P (experimenting with structure P and choosing the best among all structures that have been tried), and C (experimenting with structure C and choosing the best between all structures that have been tried). The payoff generated by an option is denoted by the letters above the line that leads to the option in the next period. For instance, option A in period 1 generates utility $u \equiv u_A$, option P in period 2 generates discounted utility $srv \equiv sr(u_A + 2b/3)$.

This system remembers whatever happened before. Thus, the options available in period 2 are more numerous than in period 1. Options A, P, and C in period 2 are the same as in period 1. Node PO denotes the option that a person experiments with structure P in period 1 and no new experiment in period 2 when he stays with the best between A and P. Node CO denotes the option that a person experiments with structure C in period 1 and no new experiment in period 2 when he stays with the best between A and C. A sequence of option P in period 1 and C in period 2 implies that a person is informed about relative prices in all corner equilibria. Following the procedure for calculating $E_0[u_1(P)]$, given by equation (3b), the expected discounted real income for option C in period 2 following P in period 1 is $sr^2 (u_A +b)$. The two further options PO and CO in period 2 that are distinctive from any options available in period 1, underline the fact that payoffs depend not only upon current options, but also upon the time path of decisions in the past. Such an option generates discounted expected real income in period 2, $r^2 (u_A +2b/3)$, which differs from that generated by option C in period 2, $sr^2 (u_A +b)$. A person will not experiment with a structure that has been experimented with previously owing to the perpetual value of information on organization.

Options A, P, C, PO, and CO in period 3 are the same as in period 2. However, there is one more option PCO available in period 3 because payoffs depend on the decision path. Option PCO denotes that a person has experimented with structures P and C and stays in period 3 with the best among A, P, and C. Therefore, there are six terminal points in period 3. Payoffs associated with a certain option are indicated above the line leading to the corresponding node in Figure 2.

The objective function for the dynamic programming problem at $t{=}0$ is

$$\max_{i(t)}: \Sigma_{t=1}\, E_0\, [r^{\,t} u_t(i)], \tag{4a}$$

where $i(1){=}$A,P,C, $i(2){=}$A,P,C,PO,CO, $i(3){=}$A,P,C,PO,CO,PCO, and

$$E_0[ru_1(A)]{=}ru_A,\; E_0[ru_1(P)]{=}E_0[ru_1(C)]{=}sr(u_A{+}2b/3); \tag{4b}$$

$$E_0[r^2u_2(A)]{=}r^2u_A;$$

$E_0[r^2u_2(P)]{=}E_0[r^2u_2(C)]{=}sr^2(u_A{+}2b/3)$ if A is tried in period 1;

$E_0[r^2u_2(P)]{=}E_0[r^2u_2(C)]{=}sr^2(u_A{+}b)$ if C or P is tried in period 1;

$E_0[r^2u_2(PO)]{=}E_0[r^2u_2(CO)]{=}r^2(u_A{+}2b/3);$

$E_0[r^3u_3(A)]{=}r^3u_A;$

$E_0[r^3u_3(P)]{=}E_0[r^3u_3(C)]{=}sr^3(u_A{+}2b/3)$ if only A is previously tried;

$E_0[r^3u_3(P)]=E_0[r^3u_3(C)]=sr^3(u_A+b)$ if C or P is previously tried;

$E_0[r^3u_3(PO)]=E_0[r^3u_3(CO)]=r^3(u_A+2b/3)$;

$E_0[r^3u_3(PCO)]=E_0[r^3u_3(CPO)]=r^3(u_A+b)$;

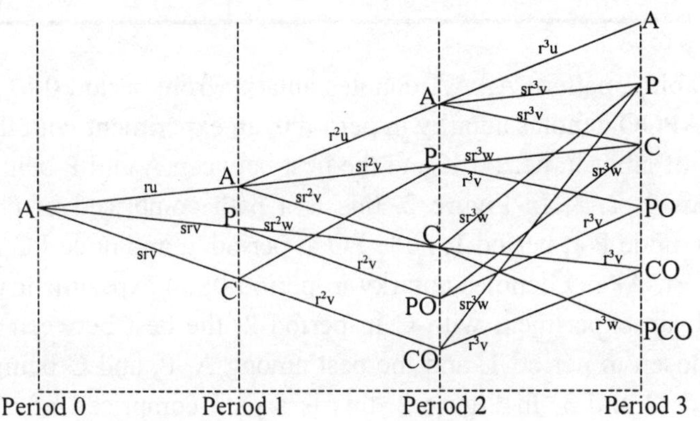

Figure 2: Dynamic Programming Problem in Period 0

$u \equiv u_A$, $v \equiv u_A + 2b/3$, $w \equiv u_A + b$.

Figure 2 provides an intuitive illustration of the payoffs for different options in the three periods.

Applying the Bellman optimality principle, a backward decision rule yields the solution to the dynamic programming problem in period 0. This solution is summarized in Table 1, where $s_0 \equiv [u_A+2br(1+r)/3]/(u_A+2b/3)$, $s_1 \equiv [u_A+b(2-r)/3]/(u_A+b)$, and $s_1 > s_0$. The technical detail of the derivation of the solution is in Appendix B, available upon request. Owing to the same information, same discount rate, and same pricing cost coefficient, which is slightly larger for structure C than for structure P, for all individuals, individual's dynamic decisions on optimal patterns of experiments with organization are symmetric. Hence, all individuals will experiment with the same market structure in each period.

Table 1: Solution of the Dynamic Programming Problem in Period 0

$s<s_0$	$s\in(s_0,s_1)$	$s>s_1$
AAAA	APOO	APCO

In Table 1 pattern AAAA denotes autarky from period 0 to period 3. Pattern APOO denotes autarky in period 0, an experiment with the partial division of labor in period 1, and the best between A and P being chosen in periods 1, 2, 3. In Figure 2, this is a path comprised of node A at period 0, node P at period 1, node PO at period 2, and node PO at period 3. Pattern APCO denotes autarky in period 0; an experiment with P in period 1, an experiment with C in period 2, the best between A and P being chosen in period 1, and the best among A, P, and C being chosen in periods 2 and 3. In Figure 2, this is a path comprised of node A at period 0, node P at period 1, node C at period 2, and node PCO at period 3. Table 1 shows that individuals will stay with autarky forever and undertake no experiments with structure P or C if pricing efficiency $s<s_0$. One structure involving trade will be experimented with and the best between A and that structure will be chosen in period 1 if $s\in(s_0,s_1)$. Two structures involving trade will be tried over periods 1 and 2 and the best among A and them will be chosen if $s>s_1$.

4.2. Walras sequential equilibrium

Now suppose $s>s_0$. Then structure P will be tried in period 1. Hence, uncertainties about the value of u_P and about the ranking of u_A and u_P are solved after the relative price p_x/p_y and relative number M_x/M_y are sorted out by the Walrasian auction mechanism. With the updated information, each individual knows $u_P>u_A$ iff $k>k_1$. Assume $k>k_1$, then each person's updated information based on Bayes' rule in period 1 is: $u_P>u_A$ for certain; ranking $u_Pu_Au_C$, $u_Pu_Cu_A$, or $u_Cu_Pu_A$ occurs with probability 1/3. Also, an updated estimate of b can be calculated according to observed u_P-u_A and Bayes' rule. On the basis of the updated information, each person can specify a dynamic programming problem from period 1 to period 3, which is analogous to the one in (4). For $k<k_1$ or other values

of k, similar but different problems can be specified. Following an analogous backward decision rule, the dynamic programming problems can be solved. The solution to each individual's all dynamic programming problems in periods 0, 1, and 2, together with the corner equilibrium relative prices of traded goods and relative numbers of different specialists in relevant structures, determine the Walras sequential equilibrium. Which sequence of structure is associated with the sequential equilibrium depends upon the values of the parameters of transportation efficiency, pricing efficiency, degree of economies of specialization, and discount factor. The sequential equilibrium and its comparative dynamics are summarized in Figure 3, where the capitalized letters in brackets represent the structures that have been tried in a certain period and those without brackets represent the structures that have been ultimately chosen after the experiments. Definitions are as follows:

$$s_0 \equiv [u_A + 2br(1+r)/3]/(u_A + 2b/3), \quad s_2 \equiv (u_A - br/3)/(u_A + b/3) > s_0,$$

$$s_3 \equiv (u_P - br/3)/(u_P + b/3),$$

$$k_1 \equiv [(2\alpha + \gamma)^{2\alpha + \gamma}(2\beta + \gamma)^{2\beta + \gamma}]^{0.5}/2^{\alpha + \beta - 2}(\alpha + \beta + \gamma)^{\alpha + \beta + \gamma},$$

$$k_2 \equiv 3^3 2^{\alpha + \beta - 2}\alpha^\alpha \beta^\beta \gamma^\gamma/[(2\alpha + \gamma)^{2\alpha + \gamma}(2\beta + \gamma)^{2\beta + \gamma}]^{0.5},$$

$$k_3 \equiv [3^3 \alpha^\alpha \beta^\beta \gamma^\gamma/(\alpha + \beta + \gamma)^{\alpha + \beta + \gamma}]^{0.5}.$$

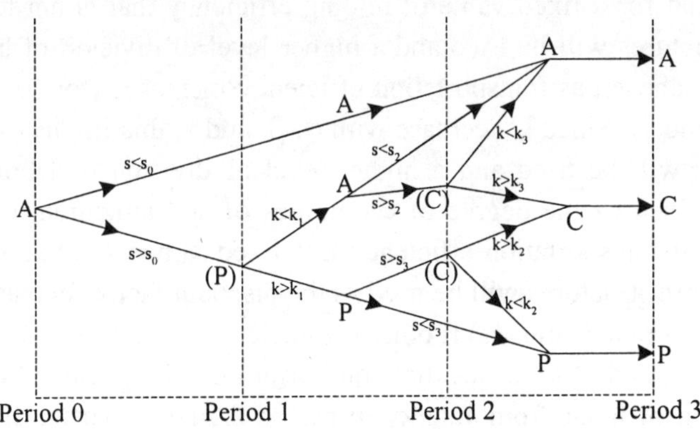

Figure 3: The Sequential Equilibrium

Also,

$$s_3 > s_2 \text{ iff } k > k_1. \tag{5}$$

The corresponding sequential equilibrium relative prices and relative numbers of different specialists can be found from Lemma 1.

From Figure 3 we can see that if k is fixed such that $k < k_3$, then no structure with trade will be tried and no information will be acquired by society for $s < s_0$. Structure P will be experimented with in period 1 but autarky will be finally chosen over all periods if $s \in (s_0, s_2)$. Hence, partial information will be acquired by society. Structure P will be tried in period 1 and structure C will be tried in period 2, but autarky will be finally chosen over all periods if $s > s_2$. All information of relative price, relative numbers of different specialists, and real incomes for structures P and C which are given in Lemma 1 are learned by individuals over three periods despite the fact that P and C are not finally chosen. This implies that more structures will be tried as pricing efficiency s increases for a fixed transportation efficiency k.

Fig. 3 indicates also that if s is fixed such that $s \in (s_3, s_2)$ for $k < k_1$ or $s > s_3$ for $k > k_1$, then only structure P is experimented with in period 1 and autarky is finally chosen over all periods if $k < k_1$; structure P will be tried in period 1 and C will be tried in period 2, and P will be finally chosen over period 1 and C will be chosen over periods 2 and 3 if $k > k_1$.[4] This implies that for a fixed value of pricing efficiency that is not too small, more structures will be tried and a higher level of division of labor will be finally chosen as transportation efficiency increases (for fixed values of α, β, and γ). Since k_i decrease with α, β, and γ, this implies that more structures will be tried and a higher level of division of labor will be finally chosen as the degree of economies of specialization, α, β, or γ increases if transportation efficiency k is fixed. Since s_2 and s_3 decrease with r, more structures will be tried as the discount factor increases (or as the discount rate decreases) if other parameters are fixed.

For $s > s_3$ and $k > k_1$, sequential equilibrium involves gradual evolution of division of labor from autarky in period 0 first to partial division of labor in period 1, finally ending up with complete division of labor in

---

[4] Here we have used the facts, based on (5), that $s_2 < s_3$ and thereby $s \in (s_3, s_2)$ is impossible if $k > k_1$ and that $s_2 > s_3$ and thereby $s \in (s_3, s_2)$ is possible if $k < k_1$.

periods 2 and 3. All individuals have gradually learnt and implemented all prices and real incomes generated by various patterns of division of labor. The concurrent evolution of division of labor and information will generate progress in productivity as well as many other structural changes. The concurrent evolution of productivity and the division of labor may occur due to the information gains from learning by experimentation with different patterns of the division of labor even in the absence of learning by producing goods that was specified in Yang and Borland (1991). It is interesting to note the following feature of the concurrent evolution. Individuals do not know where the system heads for at $t=0$. They gradually learn the direction of the evolution as they use adaptive decision rules to resolve uncertainties. Despite the uncertainties of the direction of the evolution, it displays a trend from simple to complex patterns of division of labor. The adaptive behavior, uncertainties of the direction of evolution, and a certain trend of the evolution distinguish our endogenous growth model from deterministic endogenous growth models of Judd, Romer, Grossman and Helpman, and Yang and Borland.

The algebra for establishing the results in Figure 3 is in Appendix B, available upon request. The results yield the following proposition.

Proposition 1: Autarky is chosen over all periods and no experiments with organizational patterns will take place and therefore no information about economic organization can be acquired by society if pricing efficiency s is too low and/or the discount rate is too large. All market structures will be experimented with and society will acquire complete information about economic organization via the price system if pricing efficiency, transportation efficiency, the degree of economies of specialization and the discount factor are sufficiently large. More market structures will be experimented with, more information of organization will be acquired, and a higher level of division of labor will be finally chosen as pricing efficiency, transportation efficiency, the degree of economies of specialization, and/or discount factor increase. If pricing efficiency, transportation efficiency, and the degree of economies of specialization are sufficiently large, a gradual evolution of the division of labor and productivity will take place.

In terms of the terminology in Aghion et al. (1991), this proposition identifies the conditions under which adequate learning will or will not occur.   However, the difference is that the condition for adequate *social* learning to occur in our model is a sufficiently high pricing efficiency and a sufficiently low discount rate, while in Aghion et al. it is that the payoff function is analytical or is smooth and quasi-concave or the discount rate is zero.

Figure 1 gives an intuitive illustration of the evolution of the division of labor.   In period 0, individuals are in autarky, as shown in panel (a), where there are no markets or trade, and productivity is low because economies of specialization cannot be exploited.   For sufficiently great pricing efficiency, transportation efficiency, and degree of economies of specialization, the partial division of labor illustrated in panel (b) will be experimented with and chosen in period 1.   There are two markets, and hence each person must undertake two transactions to obtain all necessary goods.   Each individual sells one good, self-provides two goods, and trades two goods.   The degree of production concentration is higher than in autarky.   Each individual's level of specialization is higher than in autarky. The number of distinct professional sectors (configurations) is two.

Finally, the complete division of labor will be experimented with and will be chosen in period 2.   Trade dependence, productivity, the number of traded goods, the number of markets, the diversity of the economic structure, production concentration, and the level of specialization for each person are all higher than in the partial division of labor.   In particular, the size of the market network and the   degree of integration of the market increase as the division of labor evolves over time.

For the model presented in this paper a gradual evolution of the division of labor will not occur in the absence of experimentation costs of economic organization if $k_2 < k_1$.   Individuals will either jump to the complete division of labor and stay there forever (if $k > k_2$) or remain in autarky forever (if $k < k_2$).   The experimentation costs of economic organization restrain individuals from obtaining complete information about economic organization within a single period, and therefore it takes time for people to experiment with all possible patterns of the division of labor and to obtain complete information regarding economic organization. In this process, a gradual evolution of the division of labor will be observed even if the complete division of labor given perfect information is most efficient.

The essence of the model presented in this paper is that knowledge of economic organization determines productivity and technical conditions. Suppose $k > k_2$, then the production possibility frontier and the welfare frontier are associated with the complete division of labor. However, owing to pricing costs and the lack of information about organization, an economy may remain in autarky forever if pricing efficiency (i.e. experimentation efficiency) and/or the discount factor are sufficiently small. This point becomes even more evident if many goods are introduced into the model such that the number of patterns of the division of labor and the number of experimentation patterns are increased. In this case the number of periods that is necessary for experimenting with all possible patterns of the division of labor will increase more than proportionally. For a completely symmetric model, the number of possible distinct patterns of the division of labor is m-1 if there are m goods. Suppose m=10,000 and it takes one year for an economy to experiment with one pattern of the division of labor. It will take ten thousand years to have experimented with all patterns of the division of labor. This indicates the significant implications of the information costs of organization for economic growth.

This theory can be used to tell the following story. Several thousand years ago, if people had had a very developed division of labor and a right pattern of the division of labor, they could have developed modern technology by employing gains arising from the sophisticated division of labor within a relatively short period of time. However, they failed to achieve this not just because of a technical constraint, but also because of the lack of information about the efficient pattern of the division of labor that may generate advanced technology. If this story makes sense, then we can see how substantial is the information cost of organization. This cost constrained people to a low level of productivity for several thousand years. That is, it took such a long time for people to experiment with sufficiently many patterns of the division of labor that they were not able to find the efficient one until the Industrial Revolution in Britain during the eighteenth century.

5. Concluding Remarks

This paper has shown that the price system is a way to coordinate experiments with economic organization. The price system does not convey complete information about efficient organization if all possible patterns of organization have not been tried. As long as pricing costs are not trivial and people are short of information about the efficient pattern of the division of labor, the most efficient pattern of organization may not be experimented with and therefore may not be discovered in a dynamic equilibrium based on bounded rationality due to the lack of information. A certain irrational behavior based on limited information may increase the chance for experiments with all possible patterns of organization including efficient as well as inefficient ones. Seemingly irrational experiments with inefficient patterns of organization are necessary for distinguishing the efficient pattern from inefficient ones.

An increase in pricing efficiency s or transportation efficiency k may increase the chance of more patterns of organization being tried. Institutional arrangements, urbanization, the legal system, government policies, and technical conditions for transactions, all affect pricing efficiency in experiments with patterns of economic organization, and thereby determine productivity and welfare. The angle from which we approach the informational role of prices differs from that of Grossman (1989). He asserted the price system works in such a way that it seems to convey all information to everybody. We have shown that the price system may not carry all information about economic organization if experiments have not exhausted all possible patterns of organization. The price system is only a vehicle for individuals to coordinate experiments with organization that are necessary for acquiring information about the efficient pattern of the division of labor.

Another implication of our model for development economics is that it can be used to explain a big jump (rather than a big push) in the industrialization process in a less developed country.[5]   A less developed country as a newcomer in the industrialization process can always obtain free information on efficient division of labor: it can mimic the organizational pattern that has been verified to be efficient by experiments in developed countries. Hence, a gradual evolution of its division of labor is no longer efficient for a newcomer: a big-jump industrialization to a very high level of division of labor from autarky is possible.   In terms of our model, if $k>k_2$ a newcomer can jump, over structure P, to structure C from autarky, if other countries have already experimented with P and C.[6]

Our story here is consistent with Young's idea (1928) that savings and investments are not a matter of available resources and technology, but rather they are a matter of the evolution of the division of labor.   In our model, the experimentation cost is a type of investment in acquiring information about the efficient pattern of division of labor that determines productivity and technical progress.

References

Aghion, Philippe, Bolton, P., and Jullien, B., "Optimal Learning by Experimentation", *Review of Economic Studies*, 58 (1991): 621-54.

Barro, Robert and Sala-i-Martin, Xavier, *Economic Growth*, New York, McGraw-Hill, 1995.

---

[5] Murphy, Shleifer, and Vishny (1989) have developed some formal models to explain big push industrialization by some factors other than low information costs for a newcomer.

[6] It is unrealistic to attribute all obstacles to economic growth to the experimentation cost of organization because we can find many less developed countries which cannot exploit information provided by organizational experiments in developed economies. If learning-by-doing specified in Yang and Borland (1991) is introduced into the current model with learning-by-experimenting with organization, then a blend of the two kinds of learning may yield a more realistic story.

Conlisk, John, "Why Bounded Rationality?", *The Journal of Economic Literature*, 34 (1996): 669-700.

Grossman, Gene and Helpman, Elhanan, "Product Development and International Trade", *Journal of Political Economy*, 97 (1989): 1261-83.

Grossman, Saddy, *The Informational Role of Prices*, Cambridge, MA, MIT Press, 1989.

Judd, K., "On the Performance of Patents", *Econometrica*, 53 (1985): 579-85.

Kreps, David and Wilson, R., "Sequential Equilibria", *Econometrica*, 50 (1982): 863-94.

Murphy, Kervin, Shleifer, A., and Vishny, R., "Industrialization and the Big Push", *Journal of Political Economy*, 97 (1989): 1003-26.

Nelson, Richard, "Recent Evolutionary Theorizing About Economic Change", *Journal of Economics Literature*, 33 (1995): 48-90.

Ramsey, Frank, "A Mathematical Theory of Saving", *Economic Journal*, 38 (1928): 543-59.

Romer, Paul, "Endogenous Technological Change", *Journal of Political Economy*, 98 (1990): S71-S102.

Yang, Xiaokai, "Development, Structural Changes, and Urbanization", *Journal of Development Economics*, 34 (1990): 199-222.

Yang, Xiaokai and Borland, Jeff, "A Microeconomic Mechanism for Economic Growth", *Journal of Political Economy*, 99 (1991): 460-82.

Yang, Xiaokai and Ng, Yew-Kwang, *Specialization and Economic Organization: A New Classical Microeconomic Framework*, Amsterdam, North-Holland, 1993.

Yang, Xiaokai and Ng, Siang, "Specialization and Division of Labor: A Survey", in K. Arrow, Y-K. Ng, and X. Yang eds. *Increasing Returns and Economic Analysis*, London, Mcmillian, 1997.

Young, Allyn, "Increasing Returns and Economic Progress", *The Economic Journal*, 152 (1928): 527-542.

CHAPTER 21

**EVOLUTION IN DIVISION OF LABOR AND
MACROECONOMIC POLICIES***

Junxi Zhang*

University of Hong Kong

1. Introduction

In the public finance/macroeconomics literature, a central question is
whether the mode of financing a given path of real government
purchases—by taxes, nonmonetary debt issue, or money creation—has
real effects, in particular real effects of macroeconomic consequences. It
is widely agreed by now that different government financing methods
may have different level effects on an aggregate economy (Haliassos and
Tobin, 1990).

There have been some attempts to answer this question within a wider
class of general equilibrium models, including an endogenous growth
paradigm. The latter becomes even more interesting, because various
government financing policies could also have different growth-rate
effects. In a Ramsey–Cass economy, Turnovsky (1992) assesses the
relative merits of three modes of expenditure financing: an increase in
lump-sum taxes, an increase in tax rate on income from labor, and an
increase in tax rate on income from capital. Ploeg and Alogoskoufis
(1994), on the other hand, examine the impact of different government
consumption financing—taxes, nonmonetary debt issue, or money

---

* Reprinted from *Review of Development Economics*, 1(2), Junxi Zhang, "Evolution in
Division of Labor and Macroeconomic Policies," 236-45, 1997, with permission from
Blackwell.
* I wish to thank Xiaokai Yang and Mei Wen for helpful comments.

475

creation—in an endogenous growth model. Finally, Palivos and Yip (1996) develop a generalized cash-in-advance model of endogenous growth to study the effects of income-tax-financed and money-financed increases in government expenditure. They find that money financing (seigniorage) leads to higher growth and inflation rates, pointing to a tradeoff between growth and inflation.

This paper is devoted to a more fundamental investigation of the relative merits of alternative methods of government finance. It attempts to answer the following questions: Does the mode of financing affect the course of a country's development, or its evolution in division of labor? Do different methods invoke different impacts? Do they also affect the set of available goods in the economy? The answer to the latter question is vital from a policy perspective, since Romer (1994) argues that relaxation of this implicit assumption in most economic theory—public policies do not affect the number of available goods—can result in some important positive and normative consequences.

These questions are investigated in a monetary version of the dynamic learning-by-doing model with endogenous specialization developed by Yang and Borland (1991). In this model, each individual is a consumer-producer who either self-provides or purchases goods for her consumption, but if she purchases goods there is a transaction cost incurred and money is used for such transactions. Each individual chooses optimally to produce only a subset of the goods she consumes so as to take advantage of gains from specialization. By this virtue, the present model endogenizes market structure, level of specialization, and the set of goods for which money is required.

I first derive some results regarding the real effects under two alternative financing schemes: an increase in the income tax rate and an increase in the nominal money growth rate (seigniorage or inflation tax). It is shown that, not surprisingly, different financing methods generate different real effects. Then, I compare the equilibrium solutions of the two regimes. Interestingly, it is found that various consumption levels achieved under money financing are higher than those achieved under income-tax financing when the level of specialization is exogenous; however, these results are reversed when the level of specialization is endogenous. This suggests that ignoring the level of specialization can lead to very misleading results. It is also found that both the speed of the evolution of the division of labor and the rate of economic growth under money financing are higher, implying that introducing fiat money into a direct barter economy aids the evolution of division of labor. Given the way that the rate of growth is defined, the latter effect amounts to the welfare effect.

2. The Model

The economic environment

The basic model differs from Yang and Borland's only in that I introduce policy variables—both fiscal and monetary. Every other aspect of their model is preserved so that the idea can be made transparent by being presented in a familiar framework.

Time is continuous and extends from zero to infinity. In the economy there are N consumers-producers and N consumer goods. All individuals are *ex ante* identical in tastes and opportunities; they differ by their names and the types of goods they produce. At every period of time each individual produces and consumes some traded goods that are also sold to the market, self-provides nontraded goods, and purchases other traded goods from the market. It is assumed that a fraction $1 - K_t$ of any good shipment acquired from the market disappears in transit, where $K_t = k/n_t$, k is a constant parameter and n_t is the total number of traded goods.

Let individuals be indexed by $i \in [0, N]$ and vectors $(x_{it}^s, \{x_{it}^s\}, \{x_{it}^d\}) \in \mathbb{R}^N$ be the levels of self-provision, sales and purchases of each of the N goods. The ith individual seeks to maximize

$$U_i = \int_0^\infty e^{-\beta t} u_{it} dt, \tag{1}$$

where $\beta > 0$ is the constant discount rate, and the instantaneous utility function is given by

$$u_{it} = x_{it} \left[\prod_{r \in R} (K_t x_{rt}^d) \right] \left[\prod_{j \in J} x_{jt} \right]. \tag{2}$$

478   *J. Zhang*

As demonstrated by Yang and Borland (1991), in equilibrium every individual sells only one good, purchases $n_t - 1$ goods, where the set is denoted as R, and self-provides the rest, $N - n_t$, nontraded goods, where the set is denoted as J. Given the fact that the number of goods traded is endogenously determined, the market structure is also endogenous.

At each instant of time, individual i faces two constraints. The first is a modified Sidrauski-type budget constraint[1]

$$x_{it} + \sum_{r \in R} x_{rt}^d + \dot{m}_{it} = \left(L_{it} \right)^a + T_{it} - \tau x_{it}^s - \pi_t m_{it}, \tag{3}$$

where m_{it}, L_{it}, T_{it}, τ, and π_t denote real money balances, the amount of labor accumulated in activity i up to time t, a lump-sum transfer from the government, a propositional tax rate on sales income, and the inflation rate, respectively, and $\dot{m} \equiv dm/dt$. Note that L_{it} represents the level of experience, knowledge, or human capital accumulated in the past; $(L_{it})^a$, where $a > 1$, is output produced for good i.

The second constraint is a cash-in-advance constraint. Following Lucas and Stokey's (1983, 1987) distinction of two types of goods, "cash goods" and "credit goods," I interpret home-produced goods as credit goods and goods purchased on the market as cash goods where only the latter require money for purchases. Formally,

$$\sum_{r \in R} x_{rt}^d \le m_{it} + T_{it}. \tag{4}$$

The production technology exhibits learning-by-doing and increasing returns:

$$x_{it} + x_{it}^s = \left(L_{it} \right)^a, \quad L_{it} = \int_0^t \ell_{iv} dv, \quad a > 1, \tag{5a}$$

$$x_{jt} = \left(L_{jt} \right)^a, \quad L_{jt} = \int_0^t \ell_{jv} dv, \quad j \in J, \tag{5b}$$

$$\ell_{it} + \sum_{j \in J} \ell_{jt} = 1, \tag{5c}$$

---

[1] Since preferences and opportunities are symmetric with respect to all goods, symmetry guarantees a unitary value of relative price between different traded goods (sold or acquired).

where ℓ_{it} is the amount of labor spent on producing good i at time t. Equation (5c) normalizes the total hours available for an individual at each period to unity.

The government operates in the following way. It raises revenue by imposing a proportional income (or sales) tax and/or by printing money. All revenue is used to finance government expenditures, including government purchases and lump-sum transfers. Thus, the government budget constraint is

$$E_t \equiv G_t + T_t = \tau \sum_i x_{it}^s + \mu \sum_i m_{it}, \tag{6}$$

where E_t, G_t, T_t ($= \sum T_{it}$), and μ denote government (aggregate) expenditures, purchases, lump-sum transfers, and the (constant) money growth rate.

Finally, I specify the market-clearing conditions. Money market equilibrium requires that $T_t = \mu \sum m_{it}$, and

$$\sum_i \dot{m}_{it} = (\mu - \pi_t) \sum_i m_{it}. \tag{7}$$

By Walras' law, the goods market also clears.

Equilibrium path

Consider the ith individual's optimization problem. As in Yang and Borland (1991), it is assumed that all trade is mediated through a futures market that operates at time $t = 0$, which is sufficient to ensure price-taking behavior by individual agents. Given policy variables, the agent selects $(x_{it}, x_{rt}^d, x_{it}^s)$ so as to maximize (1) subject to (2)–(7) and the nonnegativity constraints.

It can be easily shown that the solution to this maximization is described by the following first-order conditions:[2]

$$x_{it} = \frac{1+\mu}{n_t + \mu} (L_{it})^a, \tag{8a}$$

---

[2] Since the focus is on the effects on the goods market, I implicitly assume that a 1 % increase in the growth rate of money is translated into a 1 % increase in the rate of inflation.

$$x_{rt}^d = \frac{1-\tau}{n_t + \mu}\left(L_{it}\right)^a, \quad \forall r \in R, \tag{8b}$$

$$x_{it}^s = \frac{n_t - 1}{n_t + \mu}\left(L_{it}\right)^a. \tag{8c}$$

Note that x_{rt}^d is identical for all $r \in R$. Evidently, both fiscal and monetary policies invoke real effects here.

Next, I solve for the time paths of the amounts of labor spent on producing goods i and j, ℓ_{it} and ℓ_{jt}, and hence the amounts of accumulated time in activities i and j, L_{it} and L_{jt}. In equilibrium, the utility function (2) can be rewritten as

$$u_{it} = \left(k\right)^{n_t-1}\left(1-\tau\right)^{n_t-1}\left(n_t\right)^{1-n_t}\left(1+\mu\right)\left(n_t+\mu\right)^{-n_t}\left(L_{it}\right)^{an_t}\prod_{j \in J}\left(L_{jt}\right)^a. \tag{9}$$

The time paths of L_{it} and L_{jt} can be obtained from the maximization of (1) with u_{it} replaced by (9) subject to (5c) and the nonnegativity constraints of ℓ_{it} and ℓ_{jt}, given by

$$L_{it} = \left(k\right)^{-1/a}\left(1-\tau\right)^{-1/a}\left(n_t\right)^{1/a}\left(n_t+\mu\right)^{1/a}e^{[2-1/n_t-\mu/(n_t+\mu)]/a}, \tag{10a}$$

$$L_{jt} = \frac{L_{it}}{n_t}, \quad \forall j \in J. \tag{10b}$$

Direct differentiations of (10a) and (10b) also yield the time paths for the optimal levels of specialization ℓ_{it} and ℓ_{jt}, respectively.

3. Alternative Methods of Financing Government Expenditure

This section examines the effects of the aforementioned two modes of expenditure financing.

Income-tax financing

Under income-tax financing, $T = 0$, $\mu = 0$, and (6) becomes $E_t = \tau \sum x_{it}^s$. Since $\sum x_{it}^s$ represents the aggregate income level in the economy, τ is simply the government size. Denoting $\gamma (\equiv E_t / \sum x_{it}^s)$ as the government size, the equilibrium set (8) is given by

$$x_{it} = \frac{1}{n_t}\left(L_{it}\right)^a, \quad x_{rt}^d = \frac{1-\gamma}{n_t}\left(L_{it}\right)^a, \quad x_{it}^s = \frac{n_t-1}{n_t}\left(L_{it}\right)^a. \tag{11}$$

Clearly, when L_{it} is exogenous, $dx_{it}/d\gamma = dx_{it}^s/d\gamma = 0$, and $dx_{rt}^d/d\gamma < 0$. When L_{it} is endogenous, however, these results can be shown to be substantially different, to which attention now turns.

The time spent on producing good i, ℓ_{it}, and the accmulated time, L_{it}, under this scheme are given by

$$\ell_{it} = \frac{n_t\left(2n_t+1\right)}{N\left(2n_t+1\right)-an_t\left(N-n_t\right)}, \tag{12a}$$

$$L_{it} = \left(k\right)^{-1/a}\left(1-\gamma\right)^{-1/a}\left(n_t\right)^{2/a} e^{(2-1/n_t)/a}. \tag{12b}$$

Combining (12b) with (11), one can easily verify that $dx_{it}/d\gamma > 0$, $dx_{it}^s/d\gamma > 0$, and $dx_{rt}^d/d\gamma = 0$. To grasp the intuition of these different results, note that with an increase in government purchases there must be a corresponding increase in the tax rate to satisfy the government budget constraint. This increase in the individual's tax rate then affects her production input through a "supply-side" mechanism, since $(L_{it})^a$ is the total output produced by her. When this positive supply-side factor is taken into account (i.e. $dL_{it}/d\gamma > 0$), the total effects on various consumption levels will consist of two effects: the direct income effect and the indirect tax incentive (supply-side) effect.

For $1 < n_t < N$, we can obtain a differential equation of n_t by differentiating (10a) and (10b) and substituting them into the endowment constraint (5c):

$$\rho_n \equiv \frac{\dot{n}_t}{n_t} = \frac{an_t^{2-2/a}k^{1/a}\left(1-\gamma\right)^{1/a} e^{(1/n_t-2)/a}}{N\left(2n_t+1\right)-an_t\left(N-n_t\right)}. \tag{13}$$

Thus, the solution of (13) gives the equilibrium time path for an interior n_t subject to the boundary conditions $n_t\big|_{t=0} = 1$ and $dn_t/dt\big|_{n=N} = 0$. In this model, ρ_n is referred to as *the speed of the evolution of the*

482   *J. Zhang*

division of labor. It is straightforward to show that $d\rho_n/d\gamma < 0$. Finally, it is also possible to derive the rate of economic growth in this model:[3]

$$\rho_u \equiv \dot{u}_t/u_t = ak^{1/a}n_t^{1-2/a}(1-\gamma)^{1/a}\,e^{(1/n_t-2)/a}. \tag{14}$$

Thus, $d\rho_u/d\gamma < 0$. This suggests that an increase in the government size through income tax is growth-depressing. These results are conveniently summarized in the following proposition.

Proposition 1: In the case of income-tax financing, an increase in the government size, ceteris paribus:

(i)   *increases the fraction of labor each consumer-producer devotes to the good she produces, home-consumes, and sells to the market;*
(ii) *does not affect the fraction of that good which is home-consumed and sold to the market, but decreases the amount of all goods each consumer-producer buys in the market, if the level of specification is exogenous;*
(iii) *increases the fraction of that good which is home-consumed and sold to the market, but does not affect the amount of all goods each consumer-producer buys in the market, if the level of specification is endogenous;*
(iv) *reduces the speed of the evolution of the division of labor;*
(v)   *lowers the growth rate of the economy.*

Money financing

Now consider the case where public expenditure is financed by an inflation tax (seigniorage); hence $G = 0$, $\tau = 0$, and (6) becomes $E_t = \mu\sum m_{it}$. Using the cash-in-advance constraint (4), I can obtain the following expression for the endogenously determined money growth rate: $\mu = \gamma/(1-\gamma)$. Substituting μ into the equilibrium set (8), I have

$$x_{it} = \frac{1}{n_t(1-\gamma)+\gamma}(L_{it})^a, \quad x_{rt}^d = \frac{1-\gamma}{n_t(1-\gamma)+\gamma}(L_{it})^a,$$

---

[3] Equation (14) is obtained by differentiating (9) with respect to t and making use of (10) and (13).

$$x_{it}^s = \frac{(n_t - 1)(1 - \gamma)}{n_t(1 - \gamma) + \gamma}(L_{it})^a.$$ (15)

It is obvious that in the case of $1 < n_t < N$, $dx_{it}/d\gamma > 0$, $dx_{rt}^d/d\gamma < 0$, and $dx_{it}^s/d\gamma < 0$, if L_{it} is exogenous.[4] It should be noted that these results are broadly different from their counterparts in the case of income-tax financing.

The time spent on producing good i, ℓ_{it}, and the accumulated time, L_{it}, under this scheme are given by

$$\ell_{it} = n_t \left\{ n_t + 1 + n_t^2 \left[\frac{1}{n_t + \mu} + \frac{\mu}{(n_t + \mu)^2} \right] \right\} \Big/ B,$$ (16a)

$$L_{it} = (k)^{-1/a}(n_t)^{1/a}(n_t + \mu)^{1/a} e^{[2 - 1/n_t - \mu/(n_t + \mu)]/a},$$ (16b)

where

$$B = N(n_t + 1) - a(N - n_t)n_t + N(n_t)^2 \left[1/(n_t + \mu) + \mu/(n_t + \mu)^2 \right] > 0$$

and

$$\mu = y/(1 - \gamma).$$

When L_{it} is endogenous, the effects of a rise in y on various consumption levels remain the same, although the supply-side effect is present now. Moreover, $dL_{it}/d\gamma > 0$.

Similarly, ρ_n and ρ_u are given by

$$\rho_n = \dot{n}_t/n_t = an_t^{(2 - 1/a)}(n_t + \mu)^{(-1/a)} k^{1/a} e^{(1/n_t + \mu/(n_t + \mu) - 2)/a} \Big/ B,$$ (17)

$$\rho_u = \dot{u}_t/u_t = ak^{1/a} n_t^{1 - 1/a}(n_t + \mu)^{-1/a} e^{(1/n_t + \mu/(n_t + \mu) - 2)/a}.$$ (18)

Therefore, it can be shown that $d\rho_u/d\gamma < 0$; but $d\rho_n/d\gamma$ is ambiguous, depending on parameter values of a and k.[5] The next proposition documents these results.

---

[4] The reader is reminded that the following effects apply only to small and moderate rates of money growth but not to hyperinflation.

[5] The expression for $d\rho_n/d\gamma$ is given by $d\rho_n/d\gamma = -\mu/\left[a(n_t + \mu)^2 \right] + 2\mu N(n_t)^2 /\left[B(n_t + \mu)^3 \right]$. Since the two terms are in opposite sign, it is ambiguous.

Proposition 2: In the case of money financing, an increase in the government size, ceteris paribus:

(i)   increases the fraction of labor each consumer-producer devotes to the good she produces, home-consumes, and sells to the market;
(ii)   increases the fraction of that good which is home-consumed, but decreases the fraction which is sold to the market and the amount of all goods each consumer- producer buys in the market;
(iii) affects the composition of traded and nontraded goods;
(iv)   lowers the growth rate of the economy; and finally
(v)   these effects become less important with the level of specialization.

Result (v) in Proposition 2 has an important implication, since it suggests that the effectiveness of monetary policies may vary with the extent of the division of labor. It can be easily demonstrated that when the economy is in autarky ($n_t = 1$), or when it is evolved to a state with a high degree of division of labor (n_t is sufficiently close to N), money is neutral. For intermediate values of n_t, money invokes various real effects, but these effects decline with n_t. The fact that monetary policies may affect the course of a country's division of labor deserves further theoretical and empirical studies. Some preliminary evidence on cross-country data reported in Zhang (1996) appear to support the above story, at least for developing countries.

4.   Comparison of the Two Regimes

This section compares the equilibrium paths of the two financing methods on model variables, including the various consumption levels, the level and speed of the evolution of specialization, and the rate of economic growth. To yield a meaningful comparison, I restrict the analysis to a case where the number of traded goods, n_t, is the same under the two regimes. Let a variable with subscripts "*T*" and "*M*" denote it under an income tax and an inflation tax, respectively. Consider first the accumulated time in producing good i, L_{it}. From equations (12b) and (16b), I can immediately prove the following proposition.

Proposition 3: For $1 < n_t < N$, the accumulated time under income-tax financing is higher than that under money financing; i.e. $(L_{it})_T > (L_{it})_M$. Moreover, it is more elastic with respect to a change in the government size under income-tax financing.

Proof: By contradiction. Suppose that $(L_{it})_T < (L_{it})_M$. Equations (12b) and (16b) imply that $(1-\gamma)^{-1/a}(n_t)^{1/a} < \exp\{[-\mu/(n_t+\mu)]/a\}$. Or equivalently, I can rewrite it as $(1-\gamma)^{-1} n_t/(n_t+\mu) < \exp[-\mu/(n_t+\mu)]$. By making use of the relation $\mu = \gamma/(1-\gamma)$, the left-hand side is equal to $n_t/[n_t(1-\gamma)+\gamma]$, which is greater than one. However, the right-hand side is always smaller than one, a contradiction. Thus, $(L_{it})_T > (L_{it})_M$.

For the second part, define an elasticity measure $\varepsilon_{it} \equiv (\gamma/L_{it}) dL_{it}/d\gamma$. It can be easily shown that under the two methods they are given by

$$(\varepsilon_{it})_T = \frac{\gamma}{a(1-\gamma)}, \quad (\varepsilon_{it})_M = \frac{\gamma}{a(1-\gamma)}\frac{\gamma}{[n_t(1-\gamma)+\gamma]^2}.$$

Since $n_t > 1$, the result follows immediately.

Recall that $(L_{it})^a$ is simply the total output produced for good i. Proposition 3 implies that output under income-tax financing is higher than its counterpart under money financing. Moreover, people react more strongly to changes in γ when the government's budget is financed by an income tax. These results seem to have good intuition. Since income taxation directly affects individuals' earnings while an inflation tax has an indirect effect, they tend to adjust their behavior more quickly to the direct channel. A rise in the tax rate induces them to work harder and produce more.

Next, an important result of this paper is established on the comparison of various consumption levels.

Proposition 4:   When the level of specialization is exogenous, money financing yields higher consumption levels than income-tax financing; i.e. $(x_{it})_M > (x_{it})_T$, $(x_{rt}^d)_M > (x_{rt}^d)_T$, and $(x_{it}^s)_M > (x_{it}^s)_T$. When the level of specialization is endogenous, however, the above relations are reversed.

Proof: When L_{it} is exogenous, the first part is obvious from (11) and (15). When L_{it} is endogenous, I only prove the relation that $(x_{it})_T > (x_{it})_M$. Suppose otherwise. Substituting (12b) into (11) and (16b) into (15) and rearranging terms, it follows that $1 < \exp\left\{-\gamma/\left[n_t(1-\gamma)+\gamma\right]\right\}$, which is impossible. Hence the result that $(x_{it})_T > (x_{it})_M$ must hold. Similar arguments can be made for the other two consumption levels.

It is evident that the results with exogenous and endogenous specialization are substantially different, where it is the indirect incentive effect that drives the wedge. This suggests that endogenizing specialization in the model economy can be quite essential in a sense that failing to do so can lead to very misleading conclusions.

Then, when (13) is compared with (17), the speed of the evolution of the division of labor under the two regimes can be examined.

Proposition 5:   For a given starting value of the number of traded goods, n_t, division of labor under money financing evolves faster than that under income-tax financing; i.e. $(\rho_n)_M > (\rho_n)_T$.

Proof: By contradiction. Suppose that $(\rho_n)_T > (\rho_n)_M$. Equations (13) and (17) imply that the following inequality must hold:

$$\left[\frac{(n_t+\mu)(1-\gamma)}{n_t}\right]^{1/a} \frac{B}{N(2n_t+1)-an_t(N-n_t)} > e^{[\mu/(n_t+\mu)]/a}.$$

Using $\mu = \gamma/(1-\gamma)$, the first term in the left-hand side is smaller than one. Rewrite B as

$$B = N(2n_t+1) - an_t(N-n_t) - N(n_t)^2$$

$$\mu^2/(n_t+\mu)^2 < N(2n_t+1) - an_t(N-n_t),$$

which indicates that the second term in the left-hand side is also smaller than one. Therefore, the product is smaller than one. But, the right-hand side is greater than one, a contradiction.

It is easy to grasp the intuition by rewriting ρ_n as:

Income-tax financing: $\rho_n = a\rho_i / \left(2 + 1/n_t\right),$

Money financing: $\rho_n = a\rho_i / \left[1 + 1/n_t + n_t/\left(n_t + \mu\right) + n_t\mu/\left(n_t + \mu\right)^2\right],$ (19)

where $\rho_i \equiv \ell_{it}/L_{it}$. It can readily be shown that the denominator in the second equation is smaller than that in the first equation; furthermore, $(\rho_i)_M > (\rho_i)_T$. Or, roughly speaking, ρ_n is proportional to the reciprocal of L_{it}. From Proposition 1, it is learned that income-tax financing generates higher L_{it}, and therefore the result follows. This suggests that in the model economy with a sufficiently large number of roundabout activities, introducing money is crucial in that it can fully exploit economies of division of labor. By contrast, since direct barter cannot ensure bilateral and "quid pro quo" trade when the level of division of labor in roundabout activities is exogenous, it hinders the evolution process.[6]

Finally, the rate of growth in the two schemes is compared.

Proposition 6: The rate of economic growth under money financing is higher than that under income-tax financing; i.e. $(\rho_u)_M > (\rho_u)_T$

Proof: The proof is similar to that of Proposition 5. Suppose the opposite is true. One can simplify terms to yield the following:

$\left[n_t\left(1 - \gamma\right) + \gamma\right]/n_t > \exp\left\{\gamma/\left[n_t\left(1 - \gamma\right) + \gamma\right]\right\}$, which is impossible.

Similarly, in both cases, we can rewrite ρ_u as

$$\rho_u = a\left[n_t\rho_i + \sum_{j \in J}\rho_j\right],$$ (20)

---

[6] "Quid pro quo" means that any good A bought by a person who sells good B is sold by a buyer *of* good B.

where $\rho_i \equiv \ell_{jt} / L_{jt}$. Since $(\rho_i)_M > (\rho_i)_T$ and $(\rho_j)_M > (\rho_j)_T$, the above result is highly intuitive.[7] Interestingly, Palivos and Yip (1996) develop a generalized cash-in-advance model of endogenous growth and report that money financing leads to higher growth. My result with endogenous specialization reinforces it, pointing out that this is also true along a transitional path.

5. Conclusion

The relative merits of income-tax and seigniorage financing of government expenditure in the course of economic development have been analyzed. Many new and different results have been produced. In particular, it is found that some of the results in this model with endogenous market structure, level of specialization and a set of traded goods are markedly different from those in conventional models without the aforementioned characteristics. From a growth and welfare perspective, this suggests that seigniorage should be preferred.

The analysis represents a crude attempt to study macroeconomic policies in the early stages of economic development and calls for further research. It is true that any government considering existing or new spending programs must decide on how to raise the necessary revenue, but it is unlikely that the government will rely solely on one source. Since the government has access to various sources of finance, it is interesting to study the best mix of these policies. In addition, another source—nonmonetary debt issue—should be considered, which is presently absent in this paper. In doing so, it is conceivable that one must explicitly model individuals' saving behavior. These extensions will enable us to understand better the effects of government policies in the development process.

---

[7] It is observed that this model also points out to a tradeoff between growth and inflation, since the inflation rate is higher under seigniorage financing than that under income-tax financing.

References

Haliassos, Michael and James Tobin, "The Macroeconomics of Government Finance," in Benjamin M. Friedman and Frank Hahn (eds), *Handbook of Monetary Economics,* New York: Elsevier Science Publishers, 1990.

Lucas, Robert E. and Nancy L. Stokey, "Optimal Fiscal and Monetary Policy in an Economy without Capital," *Journal of Monetary Economics* 12 (1983):55–93.

——, "Money and Interest in a Cash-in-Advance Economy," *Econometrica* 55 (1987):491–513.

Palivos, Theodore and Chong K. Yip, "Government Expenditure Financing in an Endogenous Growth Model: A Comparison," *Journal of Money, Credit, and Banking* (1996, forthcoming).

Ploeg, Frederick van der and George S. Alogoskoufis, "Money and Endogenous Growth," *Journal of Money, Credit, and Banking* 26 (1994):771–91.

Romer, Paul M., "New Goods, Old Theory, and the Welfare Costs of Trade Restrictions," *Journal of Development Economics* 43 (1994):5–38.

Turnovsky, Stephen J., "Alternative Forms of Government Expenditure Financing: A Comparative Welfare Analysis," *Economica* 59 (1992):235–52.

Yang, Xiaokai and Jeff Borland, "A Microeconomic Mechanism for Economic Growth," *Journal of Political Economy* 99 (1991):460–82.

Zhang, Junxi, "Specialization and the Real Effects of Anticipated Inflation: Theory and Cross-Country Evidence," manuscript, 1996.

CHAPTER 22

DIVISION OF LABOR, MONEY AND ECONOMIC PROGRESS[*]

Wen Li Cheng

Law and Economics Consulting Group

1. Introduction

More than two hundred years ago, Adam Smith (1776, Chapter 1-5) expounds the relationship between the division of labor, the use of money and economic development. According to Smith, the division of labor is one of the most important sources of productivity improvement and economic progress; the division of labor is not a result of human wisdom, but a gradual consequence of a human propensity, namely, "the propensity to truck, barter, and exchange one thing for another". The certainty of being able to exchange encourages people to specialize. However, when the division of labor first began, exchange must have been frequently frustrated by situations where one party did not have the commodity the other party wanted. To avoid such inconvenience, prudent men started to carry a certain commodity (or commodities) which they thought would most likely be accepted by other people, and such a commodity (or commodities) became money.

Smith's insight is well known to economists, and there have been some recent studies that reflect Smith's idea. For instance, Kiyotaki and Wright (1989, 1991, 1993) took a "search theoretic" approach to model money as a medium of exchange. In their model, money facilitates

---

[*] Reprinted from *Review of Development Economics*, 3(3), Wen Li Cheng, "Division of Labor, Money, and Economic Progress," 354-68, 1999, with permission from Blackwell.

exchange by reducing search costs in the exchange process. Yang and Ng (1993, Chapter 17) took a different approach by explicitly linking the division of labor and the emergence of money. Their model shows that the division of labor is a necessary but not sufficient condition for the emergence of money, and that the role of money is to facilitate a higher level of division of labor in roundabout production. Cheng (1996) followed Yang and Ng's approach and developed a model to endogenize the emergence and the value of money.

Built on these studies, and especially on Cheng (1996), this paper formalizes Smith's insight into the relationship between the division of labor, the emergence of money and economic development. Specifically, this paper incorporates into its assumptions Smith's idea that the division of labor is a driving force of productivity improvement, and develops a general equilibrium model which demonstrates that as the division of labor develops, a certain commodity would become money to mediate exchange and the commodity chosen as money would be the one that involved the least transaction costs. The paper also shows that the use of money substitutes enhances welfare. The model setup in this paper is the same as Cheng (1996), but the emphasis of the model is different. This paper also differs from Cheng (1996) technically in two important aspects: this paper solves the general equilibrium analytically, whereas Cheng (1996) only illustrates the equilibrium properties using computer simulations; and this paper establishes the uniqueness of the general equilibrium.

2. The Model Setting

The economy is assumed to consist of M *ex ante* identical consumer-producers, two consumption goods, food (F) and clothing (C), and an intermediate good silk (S). We use f, c, and s to denote the quantities of food, clothing and silk produced for self use. A superscript d denotes quantities purchased from the market; a superscript R denotes quantities received from the market, and a superscript m denotes quantities of goods used as commodity-money.

An individual consumes both F and C which can be either self-provided or purchased from the market if the market exists. His utility function is

$$U = (f + f^R)(c + c^R)$$

The production of all goods F, C and S requires labor. We use l_i ($i = C, F, S$) to denote an individual's labor devoted to the production of good i. Each individual is assumed to be endowed with one unit of labor such that $l_F + l_C + l_S = 1$. He incurs a fixed learning cost for each production activity. The learning cost is assumed to be the same for all production activities and is denoted as α. Because of the fixed learning cost, the production exhibits economies of specialization which means that there is a positive correlation between an individual's labor productivity in producing good i and his level of specialization in that good. This captures Smith's idea that the division of labor is an important source of productivity improvement. An individual's level of specialization in good i is measured by the proportion of his labor devoted to producing good i. A larger α implies a higher level of economies of specialization.

The production function of F and S are as follows:

$$f + f^S = \max(l_F - \alpha, 0),$$

$$s + s^S = \max(l_S - \alpha, 0).$$

Clothing is assumed to be produced with labor and the intermediate good silk (S) using the Leontief production technology:

$$c + c^S = \min\{\beta s, \max(l_C - \alpha, 0)\},$$

where β is the input ratio in clothing production, and s is the quantity of the input silk. A larger β indicates that more economies of specialization in the silk industry can be utilized by the clothing industry.

There are costs in market transactions, assumed to be proportional to the quantity purchased. Thus for any amount x_i of good i purchased, $(1-k_i)x_i$ is lost in the transaction, only $k_i x_i$ is received by the buyer. We refer to k_i ($0 < k_i < 1$) as the transaction efficiency coefficient. In market transactions, goods purchased by an individual are used either as consumption/production goods or as commodity-money. Thus we have

$$k_F f^d = f^R + f^m,$$

$$k_C c^d = c^R + c^m,$$

$$k_S s^d = s^R + s^m.$$

In the economy, each individual chooses his own structure of production and trade activities (i.e., what to produce and how much, whether or not to trade, etc.). He can choose to produce all three goods and be self-sufficient; partially specialize in producing any two goods and trade; or completely specialize in producing a single good and trade.[1] But his choice must satisfy Lemma 1 below.

Lemma 1: When economies of specialization and transaction costs are present, a utility maximizing individual does not buy and sell the same good unless the good is commodity-money; he does not buy and self-provide the same good, and he sells at most one good not including commodity-money.

This lemma was formally proved for the case not involving money (Wen, 1994), but its generalization to include money is intuitively straightforward: buying and selling the same good involves unnecessary transactions costs; and selling more than one good forgoes the benefit of economies of specialization from concentrating on selling one good.

An individual's choice profile of consumption, production and trade activities is referred to as a *configuration*. In making his choices, an individual applies the infra-marginal analysis. That is, he first uses marginal analysis to choose the quantities of production, consumption and trade for each configuration, and then uses total benefit-cost analysis

---

[1] To make the exchange between *S* and *C* possible without including inventories in the model, I assume that production is instantaneous once the required factors of production are available. Thus a clothing producer can buy silk from a silk producer, produce clothing, and pay the silk producer with some of the clothing produced. I also assume that trade is strictly bilateral and that an individual cannot trade with two different (groups of) individuals simultaneously. This rules out the possible existence of a central clearing house and makes sequential exchanges necessary.

to find the configuration that gives the highest utility. The aggregate of all individuals' choices is referred to as a *market structure*, or *structure* for short. Given Lemma 1, each individual's budget constraint and the nonzero utility constraint, seven feasible market structures can be identified as depicted in Figure 1.

In Figure 1, each circle represents a different configuration. The letters before a slash represent goods self-provided; the letters after the slash represent goods bought from the market.

In autarky (structure A), each individual self-provides all the production and consumption goods he needs; thus no market exists.

There are three structures involving partial division of labor: Ba, Bb and Bc. In structure Ba, a group of individuals specialize in producing F, while another group partially specialize in producing C and S. The two groups trade F and C in the market. In structure Bb, F and S are traded; and in structure Bc, C and S are traded. Since bilateral trade can take the form of direct barter, money is not needed in these structures.

There are four structures involving complete division of labor: Ca, Cb, Cc and D. In these structures, there are three groups of specialists: farmers who specialize in producing food, tailors who specialize in producing clothing, and weavers who specialize in producing silk. Since silk is not needed by farmers, yet weavers need food, a medium of exchange is needed to facilitate trade between them. Clothing, silk and food serve as media of exchange in structures Ca, Cb and Cc respectively. A money substitute, which is defined as a token that replaces the physical circulation of commodity-money at zero transaction cost, is used as a medium of exchange in structure D.

In structure Ca, weavers exchange silk with tailors for clothing; and of the clothing received, they keep a proportion for their self-consumption, and use the remaining as commodity-money to buy food from farmers. Farmers exchange food with tailors for clothing.

1. Autarky

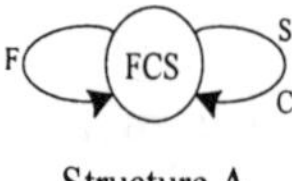

Structure A

2. Partial Division of Labor

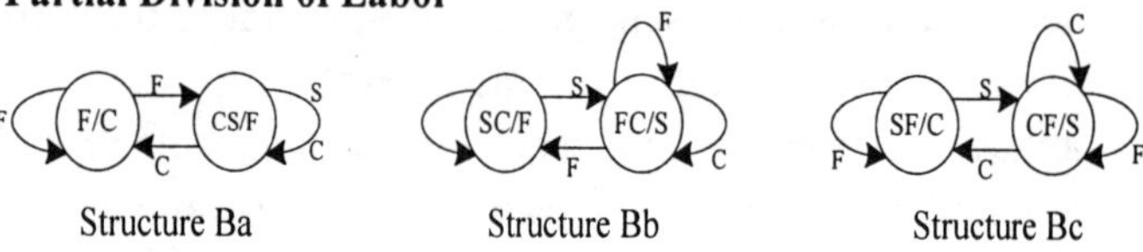

Structure Ba   Structure Bb   Structure Bc

3. Complete Division of Labor

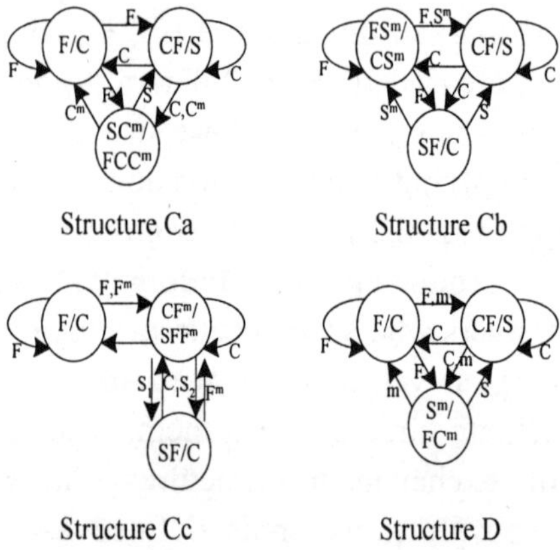

Structure Ca   Structure Cb

Structure Cc   Structure D

Figure 1: Feasible Economic Structures

In structure Cb, weavers exchange silk with tailors for clothing, and with farmers for food. Since farmers do not need silk in production, the silk they receive is to be used as commodity-money to buy part of the clothing they need from tailors. However, by accepting silk as commodity-money farmers incur unnecessary transaction costs. Weavers, on the other hand, could gain from exchanging silk for food instead of getting food some other way (e.g. exchanging clothing for food as in structure Ca) if the transaction efficiency of silk is higher than that of the other two goods. To encourage farmers to accept silk as commodity-money, weavers compensate for the additional transaction costs imposed on farmers by offering them a discounted price of silk. The equilibrium rate of discount equals the transaction cost coefficient for silk $(1- k_s)$.

In structure Cc, tailors buy some silk from weavers, and then buy food from farmers. They consume part of the food and use the rest as commodity-money to buy more silk from weavers. Using food as commodity-money benefits weavers if the transaction efficiency of food is higher than that of the other two goods, but imposes additional transaction costs on tailors. To induce tailors to use food as commodity-money, weavers offer a discounted price of silk when silk is exchanged with food. The equilibrium discount rate is $(1- k_F)$.

3. The General Equilibrium

In the economy described above, individuals are *ex ante* identical, and are free to enter each production and trade activity. Hence, monopoly power does not exist, and each individual is a price-taker. Market prices are assumed to be determined by a Walrasian auctioneer. The general equilibrium of the economy is defined as a fixed point that satisfies (1) each individual uses infra-marginal analysis to maximize his utility at given relative prices; and (2) the relative prices clear all markets and equalize all individuals' utility levels. The utility equalization condition flows from the assumption that *ex ante* identical individuals are free to choose their production and trade activities.

To solve for the equilibrium, we first solve for the corner equilibrium for each structure, and then compare corner equilibria across all structures and identify the one that generates the highest utility for each individual. A corner equilibrium is defined as the fixed point such that *given the market structure*, each individual maximizes his utility at given prices; all markets clear and all individuals' utility levels are equalized. The corner equilibrium for structure Ca is solved in the following.

In structure Ca, each specialist makes decisions to maximize his own utility.

(1) For the weaver:

$$\max\, U = f^R c^R$$

$$\text{subject to } s^S = \max(1-\alpha,\, 0)$$

$$P_S s^S = P_C c^d \quad \text{(trade with tailor)}$$

$$k_C c^d = c^R + c^m$$

$$P_C c^m = P_F f^d \quad \text{(trade with farmer)}$$

$$k_F f^d = f^R.$$

The decision variables are f^d, f^R, c^d, c^m, and s^S.

(2) For the farmer

$$\max\, U = f c^R$$

$$\text{subject to } f + f_C{}^S + f_S{}^S = \max(1-\alpha,0)$$

$$P_F f_C{}^S = P_C c_C{}^d \qquad \text{(trade with tailor)}$$

$$P_F f_S{}^S = P_C c_S{}^d \qquad \text{(trade with weaver)}$$

$$k_C(c_C{}^d + c_F{}^d) = c^R$$

where f_C^S, f_S^S denote F sold to the tailor and the weaver respectively, and $c_C{}^d$ and $c_S{}^d$ denote C bought from the tailor and the weaver respectively.

The decision variables are $f, f_C{}^S, f_S{}^S, c, c_C{}^d$ and $c_S{}^d$

(3) For the tailor

$$\max\, U = f^R c$$

$$\text{subject to } c + c_F{}^S + c_S{}^S = \min\{\beta s^R,\ \max(1-\alpha,\,0)\}$$

$$P_C c_S{}^S = P_S s^d \quad \text{(trade with weaver)}$$

$$P_C c_F{}^S = P_F f^d \quad \text{(trade with farmer)}$$

$$k_F f^d = f^R$$

$$k_S s^d = s^R,$$

where c_F^S, c_S^S denote C sold to the farmer and the weaver respectively. The decision variables are f^R, f^d, c, c_F^S, c_S^S, s^d and s^R.

Solving each specialist's decision problem, we obtain their indirect utility functions:

$$U_{SC^m/FCC^m} = [(1-\alpha)^2/4]k_C^2 k_F[P_S^2/P_C P_F] \quad \text{for the weaver;}$$

$$U_{F/C} = [(1-\alpha)^2/4]k_C(P_F/P_C) \quad \text{for the farmer;}$$

$$U_{C/FS} = [(1-\alpha)^2/4]k_F(P_C/P_F)[1-(1/k_S\beta)(P_S/P_C)]^2$$

for the tailor.

We then use the utility equalisation condition

$$U_{SC^m/FCC^m} = U_{F/C} = U_{C/FS}$$

to obtain the relative prices:

$$P_C/P_F = (1+k_C k_S\beta)/[k_S\beta(k_C k_F)^{\frac{1}{2}}],$$

$$\frac{P_C}{P_S} = (1+k_C k_S\beta)/(k_S\beta).$$

On substituting the prices into any of the three indirect utility functions, we have the per capita real income for this structure:

$$U_{Ca} = [(1-\alpha)^2/4][k_F^{\frac{1}{2}} k_C^{\frac{3}{2}} k_S\beta/(1+k_C k_S\beta)].$$

On substituting the prices into the optimum quantity of clothing used as commodity-money (which is obtained from solving the weaver's decision problem), we get a weaver's equilibrium demand (net of the transaction cost of using money) for money:

$$C^m = [(1-\alpha)/2][k_S\beta/(1+k_C k_S\beta)].$$

As all markets clear at the corner equilibrium, we also have

$$M_S s^S = M_C s^d,$$

$$M_F f^S = M_C(f^d)_C + M_S(f^d)_S,$$

where M_i ($i=S,F,C$) is the number of individuals specializing in producing good i; $(f^d)_C$ and $(f^d)_S$ represent the demand of food by a tailor and that by a weaver respectively.

Solving the market clearing conditions gives the relative number of individuals in each profession, we obtain

$$M_C / M_F = [k_S\beta / (1+k_S\beta)](k_F / k_C)^{\frac{1}{2}},$$

$$M_C / M_S = k_S\beta.$$

Given population size $M = M_c + M_F + M_S$, we can then solve for the absolute number of individuals in each profession, and hence the aggregate demand for money:

Money Demand =

$$[M(1-\alpha)k_F^{\frac{1}{2}}k_S\beta][2(1+k_S\beta)(1+k_Ck_S\beta)(k_C^{\frac{1}{2}} + k_F^{\frac{1}{2}})].$$

Using the same approach, we can also solve for the corner equilibria for other structures. The solutions are presented in Table 1.

Obviously, the corner equilibrium associated with the highest per capita utility satisfies the two conditions in our definition of general equilibrium. To demonstrate that the economy does not have multiple equilibria, we prove that other corner equilibria cannot be the general equilibrium.

Theorem 1: The corner equilibria that do not generate the highest per capital real income are not general equilibria.

Table 1: Corner Equilibrium Structures

Structures	Configurations	Relative Numbers of Individuals for Each Configuration	Relative Prices
A	FCS	NA	NA
Ba	CS/F F/C	$\dfrac{M_C}{M_F}=\left(\dfrac{k_F}{k_C}\right)^{\frac{1}{2}}$	$\dfrac{P_C}{P_F}=\dfrac{(1-\alpha)(1+\beta)}{(1-2\alpha)\beta}\left(\dfrac{k_C}{k_F}\right)^{\frac{1}{2}}$
Bb	SC/F FC/S	$\dfrac{M_F}{M_S}=\dfrac{\left[\beta^2 k_F^{\,2}k_S^{\,2}+4k_F k_S(1+\beta)\right]^{\frac{1}{2}}}{2k_F}+\dfrac{\beta k_F k_S}{2k_F}$	$\dfrac{P_S}{P_F}=\dfrac{\left[\beta^2 k_F^{\,2}k_S^{\,2}+4k_F k_S(1+\beta)\right]^{\frac{1}{2}}}{2k_F}-\dfrac{\beta k_F k_S}{2k_F}$
Bc	SF/C CF/S	$\dfrac{M_S}{M_C}=\dfrac{1}{\beta k_s}$	$\dfrac{P_S}{P_C}=\dfrac{\beta k_S}{1+\beta k_S k_C}$
Ca	C/FS F/C SC^m/FCC^m	$\dfrac{M_C}{M_F}=\dfrac{k_S\beta}{1+k_S\beta}\left(\dfrac{k_F}{k_C}\right)^{\frac{1}{2}}$ $\dfrac{M_C}{M_S}=k_S\beta$	$\dfrac{P_C}{P_F}=\dfrac{1+k_C k_S\beta}{k_S\beta}(k_C k_F)^{-\frac{1}{2}}$ $\dfrac{P_C}{P_S}=\dfrac{1+k_C k_S\beta}{k_S\beta}$
Cb	FS^m/CS^m C/FS S/FC	$\dfrac{M_S}{M_F}=\dfrac{2k_F^{\frac{1}{2}}}{2k_F^{\frac{1}{2}}+(1+k_S)k_C^{\frac{1}{2}}k_S\beta}$ $\dfrac{M_C}{M_F}=\dfrac{k_F^{\frac{1}{2}}(1+k_S)k_S\beta}{2k_F^{\frac{1}{2}}+(1+k_S)k_C^{\frac{1}{2}}k_S\beta}$	$\dfrac{P_S}{P_F}=\left(k_F k_C\right)^{\frac{1}{2}},\quad \lambda=k_S$ $\dfrac{P_S}{P_C}=\dfrac{k_S\beta}{1+k_C^{\frac{1}{2}}k_S^{\frac{3}{2}}\beta}$
Cc	F/C CF^m/FSF^m S/FC	$\dfrac{M_S}{M_C}=\dfrac{1}{k_S\beta}$ $\dfrac{M_F}{M_C}=\dfrac{1+k_C^{\frac{1}{2}}k_F^{\frac{1}{2}}k_S\beta}{k_F k_S\beta}$	$\dfrac{P_F}{P_C}=\dfrac{k_F k_S\beta}{1+k_C^{\frac{1}{2}}k_F^{\frac{1}{2}}k_S\beta}$ $\dfrac{P_F}{P_S}=k_F,\quad \lambda=k_F$
D	Fm/Cm Cm/SFm Sm/FCm	$\dfrac{M_F}{M_C}=\dfrac{1+k_C^{\frac{1}{2}}k_S\beta}{k_F^{\frac{1}{2}}k_S\beta}$ $\dfrac{M_S}{M_C}=\dfrac{1}{k_S\beta}$	$\dfrac{P_C}{P_F}=\dfrac{1+k_C^{\frac{1}{2}}k_S\beta}{k_F^{\frac{1}{2}}k_S\beta}$ $\dfrac{P_S}{P_C}=\dfrac{k_S\beta}{1+k_C^{\frac{1}{2}}k_S\beta}$ $\dfrac{P_F}{P_S}=k_F^{\frac{1}{2}}$

Table 1 (*continued*): Corner Equilibrium Structures

Struc-tures	Configur-ations	Real Income	Demand for Money
A	FCS	$\dfrac{(1-2\alpha)(1-4\alpha)\beta}{4(1+\beta)}$	0
Ba	CS/F F/C	$\dfrac{(1-\alpha)(1-2\alpha)\beta}{4(1+\beta)}k_C^{\frac{1}{2}}k_F^{\frac{1}{2}}$	0
Bb	SC/F FC/S	$\dfrac{(1-2\alpha)^2\beta}{4(1+\beta)}\left\{\dfrac{-\beta k_F k_S}{2}+\dfrac{\left[\beta^2 k_F^{\,2}k_S^{\,2}+4k_F k_S(1+\beta)\right]^{\frac{1}{2}}}{2}\right\}$	0
Bc	SF/C CF/S	$\dfrac{(1-2\alpha)^2\beta k_S k_C}{4(1+\beta k_S k_C)}$	0
Ca	C/FS F/C SC^m/FCC^m	$\dfrac{(1-\alpha)^2 k_F^{\frac{1}{2}}k_C^{\frac{3}{2}}k_S\beta}{4(1+k_C k_S\beta)}$	$\dfrac{M(1-\alpha)k_F^{\frac{1}{2}}k_S\beta}{2(1+k_S\beta)(1+k_C k_S\beta)(k_C^{\frac{1}{2}}+k_F^{\frac{1}{2}})}$

Table 1 (*continued*): Corner Equilibrium Structures

Struc-tures	Configur-ations	Real Income	Demand for Money
Cb	FS^m/CS^m C/FS S/FC	$\dfrac{(1-\alpha)^2}{4}\times\dfrac{k_F^{\frac{1}{2}}k_C k_S^{\frac{3}{2}}\beta}{1+k_C^{\frac{1}{2}}k_S^{\frac{3}{2}}\beta}$	$\dfrac{M(1-\alpha)k_F^{\frac{1}{2}}\left[4k_F^{\frac{1}{2}}+(1+k_S)k_S\beta(k_C^{\frac{1}{2}}+k_F^{\frac{1}{2}})\right]}{\left[2k_F^{\frac{1}{2}}+(1+k_S)k_S k_C^{\frac{1}{2}}\beta\right]^2}$
Cc	F/C CF^m/FSF^m S/FC	$\dfrac{(1-\alpha)^2}{4}\times\dfrac{k_F k_C k_S\beta}{1+k_C^{\frac{1}{2}}k_F^{\frac{1}{2}}k_S\beta}$	$\dfrac{M(1-\alpha)}{2\left[1+k_F+k_S\beta(k_F+k_C^{\frac{1}{2}}k_S^{\frac{1}{2}})\right]}$
D	Fm/Cm Cm/SFm Sm/FCm	$\dfrac{(1-\alpha)^2}{4}\times\dfrac{k_F^{\frac{1}{2}}k_C k_S\beta}{1+k_C^{\frac{1}{2}}k_S\beta}$	$\dfrac{M(1-\alpha)k_F^{\frac{1}{2}}k_S\beta}{2(1+k_C^{\frac{1}{2}}k_S\beta\left[1+k_F^{\frac{1}{2}}+k_S\beta(k_C^{\frac{1}{2}}+k_F^{\frac{1}{2}})\right])}$

Proof: Assume that structure Ca generates the highest per capita real income, but individuals are at the corner equilibrium structure Ba.

In structure Ca, there are three configurations involving selling F, C and S, respectively. The indirect utility functions for the three configurations are $U^{Ca}{}_F(q_{FC}, q_{FS})$, $U^{Ca}{}_C(q_{CF}, q_{CS})$, and $U^{Ca}{}_S(q_{SF}, q_{SC})$ respectively, where $q_{ij} \equiv q_i / q_j$ is the corner equilibrium prices in structure Ca. The utility equalization condition implies $U^{Ca}{}_F = U^{Ca}{}_C = U^{Ca}{}_S = U^{Ca}$.

In structure Ba, each individual's utility level is U^{Bb} and the corner equilibrium relative prices are p_{FC}, p_{FS} and p_{CS}, where $p_{ij} \equiv p_i / p_j$. Because good S is not traded in structure Ba, p_{FS} and p_{CS} are shadow prices which are equal to the equilibrium marginal rates of transformation.

Since each individual is free to choose any configurations, he can compare his current utility level (U^{Ba}) with the utility level they can get if they switch to a configuration in structure Ca *at the relative prices they are facing*, that is, at the corner equilibrium relative prices of structure Ba. If the latter is larger, then the individuals have an incentive to move away from their current configuration in structure Ba,, thus breaking the corner equilibrium. In other words, structure Ba cannot be a general equilibrium if any of the following inequalities holds:

$$U^{Ca}{}_F(p_{FC}, p_{FS}) > U^{Ba}, \tag{1a}$$

$$U^{Ca}{}_C(p_{CF}, p_{CS}) > U^{Ba}, \tag{1b}$$

$$U^{Ca}{}_S(p_{SF}, p_{SC}) > U^{Ba}. \tag{1c}$$

The assumption that structure Ba generates the highest per capita real income implies

$$U^{Ca}{}_F(q_{FC}, q_{FS}) > U^{Ba}, \tag{2a}$$

$$U^{Ca}{}_C(q_{CF}, q_{CS}) > U^{Ba}, \tag{2b}$$

$$U^{Ca}_{\;S}(q_{SF},q_{SC}) > U^{Ba} . \tag{2c}$$

On joining inequalities (1) with (2), we see that if any of the following holds, then one of the inequalities (1a), (1b) or (1c) must hold:

$$U^{Ca}_{\;F}(p_{FC},p_{FS}) \geq U^{Ca}_{\;F}(q_{FC},q_{FS}), \tag{3a}$$

$$U^{Ca}_{\;C}(p_{CF},p_{CS}) \geq U^{Ca}_{\;C}(q_{CF},q_{CS}), \tag{3b}$$

$$U^{Ca}_{\;S}(p_{SF},p_{SC}) \geq U^{Ca}_{\;S}(q_{SF},q_{SC}) . \tag{3c}$$

Since an individual's indirect utility function is an increasing function of the price of the good sold in terms of the good bought by him, to establish one of inequalities (3a), (3b) or (3c) we only need to establish one of the following:

$$P_{FC} \equiv p_{FC}/q_{FC} \geq 1 \quad \text{and} \quad P_{FS} \equiv p_{FS}/q_{FS} \geq 1, \tag{4a}$$

$$P_{CF} \equiv p_{CF}/q_{CF} \geq 1 \quad \text{and} \quad P_{CS} \equiv p_{CS}/q_{CS} \geq 1, \tag{4b}$$

$$P_{SF} \equiv p_{SF}/q_{SF} \geq 1 \quad \text{and} \quad P_{SC} \equiv p_{SC}/q_{SC} \geq 1. \tag{4c}$$

We first show that it is logically impossible to violate only one inequality in each pair of the above inequalities. A case of such a violation is as follows:

$$P_{FC} < 1 \text{ and } P_{FS} \geq 1, \tag{5a}$$

$$P_{CF} \geq 1 \text{ and } P_{CS} < 1, \tag{5b}$$

$$P_{SF} < 1 \text{ and } P_{SC} \geq 1. \tag{5c}$$

It is easy to show that the three pairs of inequalities cannot hold simultaneously. Suppose (5a) and (5b) hold, then we have $P_{FS} > P_{FC}$ and $P_{CF} > P_{CS}$. This implies that $P_{FS}P_{CF} > P_{FC}P_{CS}$ or $P_{SC} > P_{SF}$, which contradicts (5c). Similarly we can show that other cases involve contradictions too. Hence we conclude that at least one pair of inequalities in (4) has to hold simultaneously or be violated simultaneously.

We next show that if one pair of the inequalities in (4) is violated simultaneously, then at leat one of the remaining two pairs must hold. Suppose both inequalities in (4a) are violated; we have $P_{FC} < 1$ and

$P_{FS} < 1$. If (4b) does not hold—that is, $P_{CF} > 1$ and $P_{CS} < 1$ (the first inequality in (5b) cannot be violated otherwise it will contradict our assumption of $P_{FC} < 1$)—it follows that $P_{SF} > 1$ and $P_{SC} > 1$, which means (4c) holds.

Therefore we have shown that at least one pair of the inequalities (4a), (4b) and (4c) must hold for any p_{ij} and q_{ij}. This means an individual has an incentive to break away from structure Ba, so structure Ba cannot be a general equilibrium.

Following the same procedure as above, we can show that any other corner equilibria that do not generate the highest per capita real income are not general equilibria.

Using Theorem 1, we can identify the structure that generates the highest per capita utility as the unique general equilibrium structure. Based on the general equilibrium solutions, we conclude the following.

Proposition 1: (1) If the levels of transaction efficiency (the magnitude of k_i, $i=F, C, S$) and economies of specialization (the magnitude of α) are sufficiently high, the general equilibrium is associated with complete division of labor (structure C); if they are at intermediate/low levels, the general equilibrium is associated with partial division of labor/autarky. (2) If the general equilibrium involves complete division of labor, in the absence of an enforceable credit system or a central clearing house, commodity-money has to be used to facilitate trade.

Proposition 1(2) is straightforward because with complete division of labor, "double coincidence of wants" does not occur among all individuals; money is needed to mediate trade. Proposition 1(1) is proved in the Appendix.

Proposition 1 implies that money would emerge as a medium of exchange as the division of labor progressed to a certain level. It shows that the division of labor is a necessary but not sufficient condition for the emergence of money—should the general equilibrium involve autarky or partial division of labor, money is not needed.

In this model, the general equilibrium is reached through individual utility-maximizing choices. Individuals' choices about their own production and trade activities constitute a network of division of labor. The power of this model is that it focuses on the interactions of individuals within the network to work out the mechanism which simultaneously determines the values of all endogenous variables. In the model, money demand is one of the endogenous variables which is simultaneously determined with other variables such as the quantities of goods produced, goods traded, relative prices, etc., and interacts with on these other variables.

Next we look at which commodity would be chosen as money. On comparing the real income levels of structures Ca, Cb and Cc, we obtain

$$U_{Ca} > U_{Cb} \text{ iff } k_C > k_S,$$
$$U_{Ca} > U_{Cc} \text{ iff } k_C > k_F,$$
$$U_{Cb} > U_{Cc} \text{ iff } k_S > k_F.$$

These inequalities mean that structure Ca (or Cb or Cc) is the general equilibrium structure if the transaction efficiency of C (or S or F) is the highest of the three goods. Since commodity-money C (or S or F) is used in structure Ca (or Cb or Cc), the above inequalities impliy that good C (or S or F) would chosen as commodity-money if the transaction efficiency of C (or S or F) is the highest. Hence we have the following

Proposition 2: The choice of the commodity money depends on the transaction costs associated with the commodities; the commodity with the lowest transaction cost would be chosen as commodity-money.

Proposition 2 reflects Smith's idea that the commodity which is least likely to be refused by others, (i.e., the most marketable commodity) would be chosen as commodity-money. However, in the present model, transaction efficiency coefficients (and economies of specialization) determine the level of specialization, and specialization in turn gives rise to the use of money. Thus the connection between commodity-money and specialization through transaction efficiency is more fundamental than the marketability of commodities. In the present model, all three goods can be used as commodity-money depending on their transaction efficiency coefficients. In particular, silk, which is not demanded by many people for production or consumption use, is perhaps most likely to be used as money because of its high transaction efficiency.

Proposition 2 seems to be consistent with historical evidence: in the ancient nomadic economy, cattle was used as commodity-money as their transaction efficiency is relatively high. With further division of labor, the handicraft industry flourished, which made metal more efficient in transaction than cattle. Consequently, cattle-money was gradually replaced by metal (Menger, 1950, pp.263-67). Later in history, precious metals (especially gold) were widely used as commodity-money because of their high transaction efficiency.

4. The Use of Money Substitutes

I now consider the implications of using money substitutes in the model. A money substitute is defined as a token that replaces commodity-money in physical circulation, and the issue and the circulation of money substitutes are assumed to be costless. Suppose these exists an effective legal system which makes money substitutes credible; then the use of money substitutes avoids the high transaction costs associated with physical circulation of commodity-money, an thus should normally enhance welfare.

The market structure with the use of a money substitute is depicted in Figure 1, structure D. Table 1 presents the corner equilibrium solution for this structure.[2] Comparing the real income level of structure D with the real income levels of structure C, we see that the former is higher than the latter. Applying Theorem 1, we have the following

---

[2] As a money substitute can represent three different kinds of commodity-money, structure D has three variants. A different backing commodity only changes the sequence of trade, and does not alter the equilibrium solution.

Proposition 3: If a money substitute is generally acceptable, it will be used in the general equilibrium with complete division of labor, and its use is welfare-improving.

In addition, it is possible to find cases where partial division of labor marginally dominates complete division of labor. The introduction of a money substitute at the equilibrium would then lead to complete division of labor (examples of such cases from computer simulation can be obtained from the author). That is, the use of money promotes further specialization.

The use of money (or money substitutes) is often regarded as transaction saving methods. In fact, total transaction costs may increase with the use of money because while the use of money reduces unit transaction cost, it also stimulates the division of labor and increases the number of transactions. An increase in total transaction costs is not necessarily "bad" since the benefits from the division of labor often more than compensate for the increase in total transaction costs.

5. Conclusion

This paper has developed a general equilibrium model that formalises Smith's insights that the division of labor is an important driving force of productivity improvement; that the division of labor gave rise to the use of money; and that the use of money in turn stimulates further division of labor. The model has also demonstrated that the use of money substitutes can be welfare-improving.

Moreover, the paper has derived two interesting results. First, the use of money may increase total transaction costs as it increases in the number of transactions. Second, the choice of commodity-money depends on the transaction efficiencies of the commodities. The good that is not demanded for production or consumption use by many individuals may be chosen as a medium of exchange.

A technical feature of this model is that it uses the infra-marginal analysis, which allows economic agents to choose *what* to produce and *whether or not to trade*, and the quantities of consumption, production and trade. The choices of individuals form an equilibrium network of division of labor, and their interactions within this network simultaneously determine the equilibrium values of the endogenous variables and also the equilibrium structure. While many different production and trade structures can occur in equilibrium, the paper proves that for a given set of parameters, the equilibrium is unique—the structure that gives all individuals the highest real income will be the general equilibrium.

Appendix   Proof for Proposition 1 (1)

First we need to establish the relationship between the determination of the general equilibrium structure and the level of economies of specialization.   If we compare any structure with a lower level of division of labor with one with higher level of division of labor, it is easy to see that when economies of specialization (α) increases, the structure with higher level of division of labor is more likely to generate a higher real income and thus more likely to be the general equilibrium structure. For example, compare structure A and structure Ba.

$$U_A > U_{Ba} \ \textit{iff} \ (1-4\alpha)/(1-\alpha) > k_C^{0.5} k_F^{0.5}.$$

Since the left-hand-side term decreases as α increases, structure Ba is more likely to produce higher real income than structure A when α is large. Similar results can be obtained if we compare structures A and Bb, A and Bc, Ba and Ca, etc.

Next we establish the relationship between the determination of the general equilibrium structure and the transaction efficiency coefficients. We start by finding the complete division-of-labor structure that generates the highest per capita real income (call it structure C*). From the penultimate column in Table 1, we derive

$$U_{Ca} > U_{Cb}, U_{Cc} \ \textit{iff} k_C > k_S, k_F,$$
$$U_{Cb} > U_{Cc}, U_{Ca} \ \textit{iff} k_S > k_F, k_C,$$
$$U_{Cc} > U_{Cb}, U_{Ca} \ \textit{iff} k_F > k_S, k_C.$$

These inequalities imply that structure C* is structure Ca (or Cb or Cc) if k_C (or k_S or k_F) is the highest among k_i ($i=C$, S, F). We then find the partial division-of-labor structure that generates the highest per capita real income (call it structure B*). Now $U_{Ba} > U_{Bb}$ iff

$$F_1 \equiv \{[\sqrt{\beta^2 k_F^2 k_S^2 + 4k_F k_s(1+\beta)} - \beta k_F k_S]/$$
$$(2k_C^{0.5} k_F^{0.5})\}(1-2\alpha)/(1-\alpha) < 1,$$

and $U_{Ba} > U_{Bc}$ iff

$$F_2 \equiv \{[(1+\beta)k_S k_C^{0.5}]/[(1+\beta k_S k_C)k_F^{0.5}]\}(1-2\alpha)/(1-\alpha) < 1.$$

Thus, $U_{Ba} > U_{Bb}$, U_{Bc} iff max $(F_1, F_2) < 1$; that is, structure B* is structure Ba iff max $(F_1, F_2) < 1$. Similarly, we derive that structure B* is structure Bb iff $\max(F_1^{-1}, F_3) < 1$ where F_1^{-1} is the inverse of F_1, and

$$F_3 \equiv [2k_S k_C(1+\beta)]/[(1+\beta k_S k_C)$$
$$(\sqrt{\beta^2 k_F^2 k_S^2 + 4k_F k_s(1+\beta)} - \beta k_F k_S)].$$

Further, we derive that structure B* is structure Bc iff $\max(F_2^{-1}, F_3^{-1}) < 1$, where F_2^{-1} and F_3^{-1} are the inverses of F^2 and F^3, respectively.

To find out the general equilibrium structure, we compare structures A, B*, and C*. Since B* can be Ba, Bb, or Bc under different conditions, and C* can be Ca, Cb, or Cc under different conditions, we need to do nine comparisons.

(1) if $k_C > k_S, k_F$ and max $(F_1, F_2) < 1$, C* is Ca, and B* is Ba, so we compare A, Ba and Ca. Similarly,

(2) if $k_C > k_S, k_F$, and $\max(F_1^{-1}, F_3) < 1$, we compare A, Bb, and Ca.

(3) if $k_C > k_S, k_F$, and $\max(F_2^{-1}, F_3^{-1}) < 1$, we compare A, Bc, and Ca.

(4) if $k_S > k_C, k_F$, and max $(F_1, F_2) < 1$, we compare A, Ba, and Cb.

(5) if $k_S > k_C, k_F$, and $\max(F_1^{-1}, F_3) < 1$, we compare A, Bb, and Cb.

(6) if $k_S > k_C, k_F$, and $\max(F_2^{-1}, F_3^{-1}) < 1$, we compare A, Bc, and Cb.

(7) if $k_F > k_C, k_S$, and $\max(F_1, F_2) < 1$, we compare A, Ba, and Cc.

(8) if $k_F > k_C, k_S$, and $\max(F_1^{-1}, F_3) < 1$, we compare A, Bb, and Cc.

(9) if $k_F > k_C, k_S$, and $\max(F_2^{-1}, F_3^{-1}) < 1$, we compare A, Bc, and Cc.

Table 2: General Equilibrium Structure when $k_C > k_S, k_F$ and $\max(F_1, F_2) < 1$

Genreal equilibrium Structure if $k_0 < k_1$	$K_C < k_0$	$K_C \in (k_0, k_1)$	$K_C < k_1$
	A	Ba	Ca
General equilibrium Structure if $k_0 > k_1$	$K_F < k_2$		$K_F > k_2$
	A		Ca
$k_0 \equiv \dfrac{(1-4\alpha)^2}{k_F(1-\alpha)^2}, k_1 \equiv \dfrac{1-2\alpha}{ks(1-\alpha+\beta\alpha)}, k_2 \equiv \dfrac{(1-2\alpha)^2(1-4\alpha)^2(1+kcks\beta)^2}{k_S^2 k_C^3(1-A)^4(1+\beta)^2}$			

We now conduct comparison (1), which is $k_C > k_S, k_F$ and $\max(F_1, F_2) < 1$:

(i) $U_A > U_{Ba}$ *iff* $k_C < (1-4\alpha)^2 / [k_F(1-\alpha)^2] \equiv k_0$.

(ii) $U_{Ba} > U_{Ca}$ *iff* $k_C < (1-2\alpha) / [k_S(1-\alpha+\beta\alpha)] \equiv k_1$.

(iii)   *if* $k_0 < k_1$, then we know that

(a) when $k_C < k_0$, the general equilibrium occurs in structure A;

(b) when $k_C \in (k_0, k_1)$, the general equilibrium occurs in structure Ba;

(c) when $k_C > k_1$, the general equilibrium occurs in structure C.

If $k_0 > k_1$, U_{Ba} is either smaller than U_A or smaller than U_{Ca}; thus the general equilibrium cannot occur in structure Ba. Thus we need to consider *only* structure A and structure Ca:

$$U_A > U_{Ca} \text{ iff } \quad k_F < [(1-2\alpha)^2(1-4\alpha)^2(1+k_C k_S\beta)^2] / [k_S^2 k_C^3(1-A)^4(1+\beta)^2] \equiv k_2.$$

That is, structure A is the general equilibrium structure if $k_F < k_2$; and structure Ca is the general equilibrium structure if $k_F > k_2$.

I have summarized the above results in Table 2. Consider the case where $k_0 < k_1$. Since k_0 decreases in k_F, k_1 decreases in k_S, structure A is likely to be the general equilibrium if k_C and k_F are small (i.e., $k_C < k_0$ is likely to hold). Structure Ba is likely to be the general equilibrium if k_C, k_F are at intermediate level; and structure Ca is likely to be the general equilibrium if k_C and k_F are large. Now consider the case where $k_0 > k_1$. Since k_2 decreases in k_S and k_C, structure A is likely to be the general equilibrium if k_F, k_S and k_C are small, and structure Ca is likely to be the general equilibrium if k_F, k_S and k_C are large. Thus I have established Proposition 1(1) within comparison 1. The same approach can be used to establish Proposition 1(1) in the other eight comparisons.

References

Cheng, Wen Li, "Specialization and the Emergence and the Value of Money," in Kenneth Arrow, Yew-Kwang Ng and Xiaokai Yang eds. *Increasing Returns and Economic Analysis*, London: Macmillan, 1996.

Kiyotaki, Nobuhiro and Randall Wright, "On Money as a Medium of Exchange," *Journal of Political Economy*, 97 (1989): 927-54.

__, "A contribution to the Pure Theory of Money," *Journal of Economic Theory*, 53 (1991): 215-35.

__, "A Search-Theoretic Approach to Monetary Economics," *American Economic Review*, 83 (1993): 63-77.

Menger, Carl, *Principle of Economics,* second edition, Glencoe: Free Press, 1950.

Smith, Adam, *An Inquiry into the Nature and Causes of the Wealth of Nations*, reprint, Oxford: Clarendon Press, 1976.

Wen, Mei, "The Framework of Consumer-Producers, Economies of Specialization, and Transaction Costs," Working Paper, Monash University, 1994.

Yang, Xiaokai and Yew-Kwang Ng, *Specialization and Economic Organisation: A New Classical Microeconomic Framework*, Amsterdam: North-Holland, 1993.

Index